**St. Louis Community
College**

Forest Park
Florissant Valley
Meramec

Instructional Resources
St. Louis, Missouri

"Suicide, assisted or otherwise, will replace abortion in the headlines as the ethical issue of the next decade. In an era when individuals are prone to put conditions on their living, this book is an excellent resource for understanding that terror, despair, and wish to die faced by those who contemplate suicide, and how to deal with it."

C. Everett Koop, M.D.
former Surgeon General of the United States

"It is a truly amazing fact that at this point in history, when the world has never been richer and when the world at least claims never to have been happier, the emerging great moral debate should focus on whether we should overturn many hundreds of years of moral vision and allow/encourage people to kill themselves. What is more, the focus of the debate is in medicine: which finally, at least where there are resources, is in a good position to ensure that very few people need suffer greatly, and which every year is in a better position to help more people cope with sickness, and finally, death.

"Yet the moral pendulum has swung, and suicide is at the heart of the agenda. This wonderful book sheds extraordinary light and will help wake up the Christian community to the culture of death and at the same time give us the tools to convince our fellow-citizens that we should choose life."

Nigel M. de S. Cameron, Ph.D.
Provost, Trinity International University

"We have lost our footing on the slippery slope from abortion to voluntary euthanasia to involuntary euthanasia. This book confronts this dangerous cultural drift, giving legal, medical, and scriptural reasons for the sanctity of human life. My prayer is that all of us will read this book and get others to read it too. It's our future that is at stake."

Erwin W. Lutzer
Senior Pastor, The Moody Church, Chicago, Illinois

"Spend time with patients in a hospice, as I have recently, or in counseling those who have ended a life through abortion, or in comforting those who have lost a loved one through suicide. In each case, you're bombarded with questions. What I love about this book is that it gives challenging, scholarly, and distinctly Christian answers to why we should choose life, not death—even in the most difficult of circumstances."

John Trent, Author and Speaker

"Increasingly, in our secularized society, Christians will be faced with the ethical issues of suicide, physician-assisted suicide, and euthanasia. This landmark volume brings together the best legal, medical, biblical, theological, ethical, pastoral, personal, and practical wisdom on the subject. This volume will be must reading for every pastor and church leader in order to help Christians have a clear biblical perspective on an issue which is muddied by the godless, secular thinking that predominates American culture in general. I highly commend this volume."

Richard L. Mayhue
Senior Vice President and Dean
Professor of Pastoral Ministries
The Master's Seminary

"Suicide and euthanasia are two of the most pressing ethical issues today. Is is right for a person to take his own life? Is it right for physicians and family members to end the lives of people who want to die? This book by physicians, theologians, professors, pastors, and attorneys offers outstanding wisdom on these questions from legal, medical, theological, biblical, and pastoral perspectives. This is one of the most thorough treatments of these issues from conservative evangelical writers."

Roy B. Zuck
Professor of Bible Exposition Emeritus
Dallas Theological Seminary
Editor, *Bibliotheca Sacra*

SUICIDE
A Christian Response

SUICIDE

A Christian Response

Crucial Considerations for Choosing Life

Timothy J. Demy & Gary P. Stewart, editors

Foreword by Carl F. H. Henry

kregel
PUBLICATIONS

Grand Rapids, MI 49501

Suicide: A Christian Response

Copyright © 1998 by Timothy J. Demy and Gary P. Stewart

Published by Kregel Publications, a division of Kregel, Inc., P.O. Box 2607, Grand Rapids, MI 49501. Kregel Publications provides trusted, biblical publications for Christian growth and service. Your comments and suggestions are valued.

For more information about Kregel Publications, visit our web page at http://www.kregel.com.

Cover design: PAZ Design Group
Cover photo: Eric Dinyer/The Image Bank
Book design: Nicholas G. Richardson

All views expressed in this work are solely those of the authors and do not represent or reflect the position or endorsement of any governmental agency or department, military or otherwise.

Library of Congress Cataloging-in-Publication Data
Demy, Timothy J.
    Suicide: a Christian response / Timothy Demy and Gary Stewart.
        p.   cm.
    Includes bibliographical references and index.
    1. Suicide—Moral and ethical aspects. 2. Suicide—Religious aspects—Christianity. 3. Euthanasia—Moral and ethical aspects. 4. Euthanasia—Religious aspects—Christianity. I. Stewart, Gary (Gary P.) II. Title.
HV6545.D25   1997   261.8'3228—dc21   97-36028
                                                    CIP
ISBN 0-8254-2355-4

Printed in the United States of America

1 2 3 / 03 02 01 00 99 98 97

To our parents,
Millard and Pauline Demy
and
Darrell and Jean Stewart,
who have taught and showed us the value of life,
presently and eternally

CONTENTS

Part 3: Theological Reflections

Part 4: Biblical Reflections

CONTRIBUTORS

Darrel W. Amundsen, Ph.D., is Professor of Classics at Western Washington University, Bellingham, Washington; Adjunct Professor of Interdisciplinary Studies at Regent College, Vancouver, British Columbia; and Affiliate Professor of the History of Medicine in the School of Medicine, University of Washington, Seattle, Washington.

Daniel Avila, J.D., is contributing editor of *Issues in Law & Medicine* and Chief Staff Counsel, National Legal Center for the Medically Dependent and Disabled, Inc., Terre Haute, Indiana.

Charles Ballard, Th.M., D.Min. (cand.), is pastor of the Flagstaff Evangelical Free Church, Flagstaff, Arizona.

Francis J. Beckwith, Ph.D., is Associate Professor of Philosophy, Culture, and Law at Trinity Graduate School, Trinity International University (Deerfield, Illinois), Southern California campus.

James Bopp Jr., J.D., is an attorney with Bopp, Coleson & Bostrom, Terre Haute, Indiana, and President, National Legal Center for the Medically Dependent and Disabled, Inc., Terre Haute, Indiana. Additionally, he serves as General Counsel, National Right to Life Committee; and Editor-in-Chief, *Issues in Law & Medicine*.

J. Daryl Charles, Ph.D., is an Affiliate Fellow of the Center for the Study of American Religion, Princeton University, Princeton, New Jersey, and Assistant Professor of Religion and Philosophy, Taylor University, Upland, Indiana.

Fred C. Chay, M.S., Th.M., D.Min., is Associate Professor of Theology and Biblical Studies at Phoenix Seminary and serves as the South Central Director of the Christian Medical and Dental Society.

Mary Krumholz Clifford, R.N., B.A., is Associate Program Director for the Program in Human Rights and Medicine, University of Minnesota Medical School, Minneapolis, Minnesota; Staff Nurse, Med-Surg Float Pool.

Richard E. Coleson, M.A.R., J.D., is an attorney with Bopp, Coleson & Bostrom, Terre Haute, Indiana; Staff Counsel, National Legal Center for the Medically Dependent and Disabled, Inc.; and General Counsel, Indiana Citizens for Life.

Matthew E. Conolly, M.D., F.A.C.P., F.R.C.P., is Professor of Anesthesiology, Medicine, and Pharmacology at the University of California, Los Angeles Medical School.

Barry C. Davis, Ph.D., is Assistant Professor of Theology and Bible at Multnomah Bible College, Portland, Oregon.

John M. Dolan, Ph.D., is cochair for the Program in Human Rights and Medicine; Morse-Alumni Distinguished Teaching Professor of Philosophy at the University of Minnesota Medical School.

John S. Feinberg, Ph.D., is Professor of Biblical and Systematic Theology at Trinity Evangelical Divinty School, Deerfield, Illinois.

Edward R. Grant, J.D., is an attorney in Washington, D.C., and member of the board of directors of Americans United for Life.

John D. Hannah, Th.D., Ph.D., is Chairman and Professor of Historical Theology at Dallas Theological Seminary and Adjunct Professor of Church History at Westminster Theological Seminary.

Carl F. H. Henry, Th.D., Ph.D., is a visiting lecturer at Trinity Evangelical Divinity School and The Southern Baptist Theological Seminary. He is the founding editor of *Christianity Today*, the author and editor of more than thirty books, and an international lecturer and spokesman for evangelicalism.

Dennis P. Hollinger, M.Div., M.Phil., Ph.D., is Dean of College Ministries and Professor of Christian Ethics at Messiah College, Grantham, Pennsylvania.

H. Wayne House, Th.D., J.D., is Professor of Theology, Michigan Theological Seminary, Plymouth, Michigan, and a Professor of Law at Trinity Law School, Anaheim, California.

A. A. Howsepian, M.D., M.A., Ph.D. (cand.), is a resident physician at the University of California, San Francisco-Fresno (Central San Juaquin Valley Medical Education Program) Department of Psychiatry.

Stan R. Kellner, M.A., is Executive Director of Sheresh Ministries in Colorado Springs, Colorado.

John F. Kilner, Ph.D., is director of the Center for Bioethics and Human Dignity, Bannockburn, Illinois.

Barry R. Leventhal, Ph.D., is codirector of Ariel Ministries, Tustin, California, and Chairman, Mission and Ministry Department, Southern Evangelical Seminary, Charlotte, North Carolina.

Alister E. McGrath, D.Phil., is Research Lecturer in Theology at Oxford University, Research Professor of Systematic Theology at Regent College, Vancouver, and Lecturer in Historical and Systematic Theology at Wycliffe Hall, Oxford.

Eugene H. Merrill, M.A., M.Phil., Ph.D., is Professor of Old Testament Studies at Dallas Theological Seminary.

C. Ben Mitchell, Ph.D., is visiting professor of Christian Ethics at The Southern Baptist Theological Seminary, Louisville, Kentucky; Editor of the journal *Ethics & Medicine*; and consultant on biomedical and life issues for the Christian Life Commission of the Southern Baptist Convention.

J. P. Moreland, Ph.D., is Professor of Philosophy of Religion, Talbot School of Theology, Biola University, La Mirada, California.

Dónal P. O'Mathúna, Ph.D., is Associate Professor of Medical Ethics and Chemistry at Mount Carmel College of Nursing, Columbus, Ohio.

Robert D. Orr, M.D., is Director of Clinical Ethics and Associate Professor of Family Medicine at Loma Linda University, Loma Linda, California.

James S. Reitman, M.D., M.A., is Military Consultant for Medical Ethics to the U.S. Air Force Surgeon General; staff internist at Spangdahlem Air Force Base, Germany.

David L. Schiedermayer, M.D., is an Associate Professor of Medicine at the Medical College of Wisconsin, Milwaukee, Wisconsin.

Gary P. Stewart, M.Div., Th.M., D.Min., is a U.S. Navy chaplain in Chicago, Illinois.

Joni Eareckson Tada is the founder and President of JAF Ministries, Agoura Hills, California, an organization that accelerates Christian outreach in the disability community.

Timothy C. Tatum, M.Div., Ed.D., is a retired U.S. Army chaplain, an Adjunct Professor in Ethics and Theology at Capital Bible Seminary, Lanham, Maryland, and consultant for the Center for the American Family.

Jeffrey A. Watson, M.S., Th.M., D.Min., is Senior Pastor, Grace Bible Church, Seabrook, Maryland, and Adjunct Professor of Gerontology, Washington Bible College, Lanham, Maryland.

Gary P. Weeden, M.Div., is a U.S. Navy chaplain in Chicago, Illinois.

FOREWORD

WE LIVE IN A MOMENT IN HISTORY when many people, in the Western world at least, seem more deeply concerned over how they will die than over how they ought to live. For multitudes of people the meaning and zest of life has evaporated, and the possibility of a painful death seems to loom as a cardinal human concern. It is sheer irony that the Western Hemisphere that gave science to the world as a second god should now press the question of whether science may not be as much a supreme source of our destruction as a hopeful means of salvation.

Twenty-five years ago in Cambridge I heard the religious philosopher Donald MacKinnon score this point while reminiscing in a class at King's College.

"When I was a boy," said MacKinnon, "influenza was the old man's benevolent disease. It would overtake one by surprise and swiftly carry one away without great pain. But today almost nobody dies of the flu," he added. MacKinnon then went on to identify nearly a dozen diseases that modern medical science has conquered. "We have advanced to the point that we die only of the more violent afflictions." Then the Scottish philosopher, who was later to give the Gifford Lectures, added, "We shall soon conquer cancer," he said, "but what are we then likely to die of in its place?"

It is a commentary on our backslidden society that it focuses the fear of death not primarily in terms of the pangs of hell or of the moral and spiritual predicament of moderns. In the recent past some Christians refused powerful prescription drugs in the final stages of illness. They felt that the providence of God embraces lessons that can be learned at the height of physical anguish. This need not imply that prescription drugs are under all circumstances to be avoided. But our society wants instant cures from headaches to hiccups. The painless life is the nearest thing to heaven on earth.

A passage in John's gospel speaks of God's sovereign determination of our final destiny and notes that we glorify God by accepting the death He ordains. The risen Jesus speaks to Peter of impending crucifixion. Peter redirects the conversation to inquire concerning John, and Jesus replies, "If I want him to live until I come, what is that to you? Follow me!" (John 21:19).

The will of God in connection with the birth of the fetus and with the death of the aging seems almost unmentionable in secular society today. That is doubtless one reason for the contemporary loss of the meaning and worth of human life. No effort could be more timely than this preparation of essays that connect the issues of how we are to die with those of how we ought to live.

CARL F. H. HENRY

ACKNOWLEDGMENTS

THE EDITORS WISH TO THANK SEVERAL people who were instrumental in this project. Without their assistance, its completion would have been most difficult. Dennis Hillman, publisher at Kregel Publications, gave great encouragement and support for the book from the very beginning. He shared with us a burden for the topic and an enthusiasm for the book. Ken Gire, a marvelous Christian author and friend gave us wise counsel and has been a role model for both the Christian life and professional writing. Other friends and colleagues who have encouraged and guided us include Barry Bostrom, Carrie Gordon, John Trent, John Kilner, Neff Blackmon, Ken Hillard, and Jim Ellis. Some of the chapters have been published previously or have been updated and revised. Permission to use them is most appreciated. These include:

Chapter 8 revised from *Christian Scholar's Review*, March 1994: 349–59.

Chapter 9 from *Suffering and God* by Alister E. McGrath. Copyright © 1992, 1995 by Alister E. McGrath. Used by permission of Zondervan Publishing House.

Chapter 10 from *Ethics for a Brave New World* by John S. Feinberg and Paul D. Feinberg. Copyright © 1993, pages 99–127. Used by permission of Good News Publishers/Crossway Books, Wheaton, Illinois 60187.

Chapter 11 from *Bibliotheca Sacra*, April–June 1991: 214–30.

Chapter 16 from *Ethics & Medicine* 12, no. 3 (1996): 60–64.

Chapter 18 from *Ethics & Medicine* 12, no. 2 (1996): 34–40.

Chapter 21 from *Bibliotheca Sacra*, July–September 1991: 298–318.

Chapter 24 from *Ethics & Medicine* 12, no. 3 (1996): 55–60.

Chapter 25 from *Issues in Law & Medicine* 11, no. 2 (fall 1995): 159–86.

The volume contains articles that cross several academic disciplines and professions, and the views and opinions expressed are solely those of the individual contributor. Footnoting and documentation has been left largely to the style of the discipline represented rather than attempting a uniform style throughout the book.

A special thank you from Gary to Kitty Peterson—the flame that Christ ignited in your life continues in mine. I miss you!

Throughout this project, our wives, Lyn Demy and Kathie Stewart, have been encouragers who believed not only in us, but in the message of the book. Their patience with faxes, mail runs, late night phone calls, and numerous dinner conversations has been remarkable and commendable. Thank you.

INTRODUCTION

THE VOLUME YOU HOLD PROVIDES AN evangelical Christian response to the issues of suicide and euthanasia. Lawyers, doctors, philosophers, theologians, pastors, and others have joined together to address an issue that has far-reaching ramifications regarding the treatment of those who struggle in life, no matter what their malady and no matter what their race or religion. The toleration of suicide, whether self-imposed or accomplished with assistance, lessens the value a society places on the lives of its individual members. The weaker must give way to the stronger and more productive for the benefit of the whole—an unnatural product of natural selection. In a land where God is becoming more and more a phase or memory of humanity's "unenlightened years," selfless care and mercy for the weak and less fortunate is being replaced by a false sense of compassion and responsibility that justifies the evil of killing for personal and societal benefit. Suffering, though difficult and never desired, is by no means a reason to declare a war on life. Besides, just wars are declared to protect life, not destroy it!

The right to kill oneself or to be killed—who would have ever thought that this country, which has made life the most livable in the world, would now be involved in a controversy over whether life is productive or not and therefore unlivable? Is it possible that our search for human comfort has found its ultimate resting place in death itself? Most of Tim's and Gary's grandparents, parents, aunts and uncles, as well as those of the other contributors are now elderly or have passed away. Gary's mother recently fell and broke her shoulder, and Tim's dad died less than one year after a stroke that left him paralyzed on his right side and unable to express many of his thoughts without hand gestures. Simply because they became less "useful to society" than they once were did not make either of them (or any other person) of less value. In fact, in their struggling we both have learned what it means to genuinely love and honor our parents; we did not look for ways to rid ourselves of the difficulty that accompanied their care. We probably understand their value more today than we did in our younger years when we were all strong and healthy and life looked promising. They will reap the benefit of being our parents; we will reap the benefit of serving them as their grateful children. There is no question that both they and we have suffered, but the value of suffering cannot be understood through one's

21

emotions, which long to see it pass, but through sound principles that ever protect the value of one's life, which in its very genes displays the image of God. We feel their pain daily, and it is genuinely terrifying; we live to find ways to comfort and relieve the pain, not to eliminate them because of it.

As we move more toward personal autonomy, we move toward a world whose citizens will not or cannot care for one another. Those who might rely on us become burdens, reminders of our own fears and shortcomings, and thus expendable rather than given protection and deserving of love, honor, and support. We all struggle and we all age—do we discard people by creating some kind of subjective criteria that classify them as less human and condemn them for being less productive? Or should we value and protect life by committing ourselves to using technology to find better ways to relieve pain, sorrow, and suffering? It is precisely because all people are created in the image of God that we must embrace and encourage those who are sick and who struggle as well as those who are called to assist them. Our lives are not our own, they are a gift from God.

We hope that this volume will serve as a resource to help you solidify your thinking on this critical issue. Suicide and euthanasia are never going to solve the question of human suffering; in truth, they can only add to it. Until the Lord Himself comes for us in life or takes us in death, we must faithfully pray for and respectfully interact with those who have yet to understand or consider the uncompromising mandates of the Christian worldview.

PART 1

LEGAL AND MEDICAL REFLECTIONS

An Overview

The recent decisions of the Ninth and Second Circuit courts create the impetus for the divisive debates that are presently raging between proponents and opponents of euthanasia. Ignoring the unimpeachable legal tradition in American jurisprudence, these two courts are attempting to make euthanasia the "latest American constitutional right." This article is essential to understanding the background for the reflections presented in the remainder of this book. Read it carefully; life as we know it is genuinely in jeopardy.

Chapter One

SHAPING EUTHANASIA RIGHTS
Compassion in Dying v. Washington and Quill v. Vacco

Edward R. Grant[1]

COMPASSION IN DYING V. WASHINGTON[2] and *Quill v. Vacco*,[3] issued respectively by the Ninth and Second Circuit Federal appeals courts, framed the legal questions regarding assisted suicide and euthanasia for ultimate resolution by the United States Supreme Court (a resolution handed down June 26, 1997, shortly before the publication of this volume). Thus, while American society continues its vigorous and rapidly evolving debate on *euthanasia rights*,[4] it must also ponder the potential of a Supreme Court decision analogous in scope to the Court's decisions defining abortion rights.

The Ninth Circuit held that under the Due Process clause of the Fourteenth Amendment, there is a "liberty interest in controlling the time and manner of one's death."[5] The court found the Washington statute that prohibits "aid[ing] another person to attempt suicide" is unconstitutional "as applied to terminally ill competent adults who wish to hasten their deaths with medication prescribed by their physicians."[6]

In contrast, the Second Circuit expressly denied the existence of any such liberty interest. The court found that two New York statutes prohibiting assisted suicide "do not impinge on any fundamental rights nor can it be said that they involve suspect classifications."[7] However, because other aspects of New York law permit the withdrawal of life-sustaining treatment, which also may result in death, the court found the assisted suicide prohibition to be a violation of the Equal Protection clause: "[T]o the extent that [these statutes] prohibit a physician from prescribing medication to be self-administered by a mentally competent, terminally-ill person in the final stages of his terminal illness, they are not rationally related to any legitimate state interest."[8]

Despite these doctrinal differences, the opinions share three fundamental errors. First, the circuits' respective interpretations of the due process and equal protection clauses to invalidate long-standing state prohibitions against assisted suicide find no basis in American legal traditions or constitutional precedent. Second, both circuits undervalued and in some cases ignored the compelling interests of the State in preventing physicians from taking actions to directly cause the deaths of their patients. Third, while claiming to allow wide latitude for the states to regulate the practice of assisted suicide, the relief fashioned by the circuits is inherently elastic, and in future cases could be interpreted to include the direct euthanasia, not only of competent terminally ill patients, but of patients who are incompetent and not terminally ill. Only time will tell whether the Supreme Court corrects or compounds these errors.

HISTORY AND DUE PROCESS

Under the doctrine of "substantive due process," federal courts have interpreted the due process clause of the Fourteenth Amendment to protect individual rights not specifically enumerated in the Constitution. This interpretative device is not unfettered: the Supreme Court has held that "new" rights, to be protected, must be "implicit in the concept of ordered liberty"[9] and "deeply rooted in this Nation's history and tradition."[10] Citing these doctrines, the Second Circuit found that the asserted right to assisted suicide "finds no cognizable basis in the Constitution's language or design, even in the very limited cases of those competent persons who, in the final stages of terminal illness, seek the right to hasten death."[11] Far from endorsing such a right, the court noted, our legal traditions (both English common law and American statutes) have prohibited assistance in suicide. These prohibitions have continued even though suicide and attempted suicide were themselves decriminalized.

The Ninth Circuit took a more expansive view of its role in interpreting novel claims of constitutional right in the light of history. The court rejected the conclusion of an earlier Ninth Circuit panel that a right to assisted suicide was "unknown to the past,"[12] finding that the real history is far more "checkered."[13] The court gave shorter shrift to the common law and statutory prohibitions on assisted suicide, placing greater emphasis on other historical and literary traditions on the subject: the acceptance of suicide among certain ancient cultures; the deaths of Jewish resisters at Masada; the practices of the Sythians and Vikings; and the writings of Montesquieu, Voltaire, Hume, Donne, and Thomas More. While interesting, this rendition of the history of suicide demonstrates nothing new: that in spite of a millennia of philosophical, religious, and legal strictures on the duty to preserve life (including one's own), noteworthy examples of suicide are part of our history, and command study and reflection. They are not to be confused, however, with the Anglo-American legal tradition or American constitutional history. As the court acknowledged, under the English common law, suicide was a crime and subject to varying degrees of punishment from at least the thirteenth century and into the nineteenth century. Even as these penalties were withdrawn in the nineteenth and twentieth centuries, penalties against *assisted* suicide were codified and strengthened—a critical point that is at best glossed over by the Ninth Circuit.[14]

To the extent the court recognized specific legal bans on assisted suicide, it treated them as vestiges of the past. This also is an erroneous characterization. Numerous state courts have addressed difficult and controversial cases where the withdrawal of medical treatment would result in a patient's death. As these courts have noted, the right to be free of unwanted medical treatment is well-established in the common law, and is not tantamount to a right to suicide or assisted suicide.[15] "[T]here is a substantial difference between the attitude of a person desiring non-interference with the natural consequences of his or her condition and the individual who desires to terminate his or her life by some deadly means either self-inflicted or through the agency of another."[16] Recent legislative enactments also confirm this distinction and the current viability of sanctions against assisted suicide. In addition to those that have recently codified specific restrictions against assisted suicide, forty-five states expressly disapprove of mercy killing, suicide, or assisted suicide in statutes authorizing the use of "living wills" and durable powers of attorney for health care.[17]

The Second Circuit and the earlier panel of the Ninth Circuit were correct: a "right" to assisted suicide is foreign both to our legal traditions and our contemporary jurisprudence.

EUTHANASIA RIGHTS AND ABORTION RIGHTS

The argument regarding history and tradition would be far less relevant, of course, if Supreme Court precedent speaks authoritatively on the question. Many believe this to be the case: the decisions of the Court regarding the "right to privacy," specifically those involving abortion, should require states to recognize the right of a terminally ill patient to end suffering and die "with dignity." Others view the situation differently: the jurisprudential problems and bitter public controversy spawned by the "privacy" decisions of *Roe v. Wade*[18] and *Planned Parenthood v. Casey*,[19] should, if anything, make the federal courts more hesitant to carve out new constitutional rights that will result in the destruction of human life. The Ninth Circuit's consideration of this question clearly adumbrates one of the most critical questions that will face the Supreme Court as it takes up the issue of assisted suicide.

The Ninth Circuit's claim, that the decision to end one's life in order to avoid suffering "is highly personal and intimate" and thus subject to the same constitutional protection as a woman's decision to end a pregnancy, seems plausible on its face. But can the question be resolved so simply? The unique position of *Roe* and *Casey* in American constitutional law suggests that a facile equation of euthanasia rights and abortion rights is not warranted.

First, while abortion and euthanasia both concern matters of life and death, the Supreme Court's 1973 rationale for extending constitutional protection to abortion does not easily fit the 1996 claim of a right to assisted suicide. *Roe* was based on earlier decisions regarding procreation and childbearing, matters that are traditionally the province of the family. *Roe* specifically rejected the notion that one has an absolute right to do with one's body as one pleases. Suicide shares no such connection with the tradition of privacy in family matters; rather, it seems the ultimate example of the discredited claim of absolute autonomy over the person.

Roe also recognized that if the unborn child was regarded as a person, the State would have a compelling interest in protecting the life of the child, and the claimed right to abortion would collapse. Although *Roe* declined to so treat the unborn child, it is crystal clear that persons who would be subject to assisted suicide *are* constitutional persons, and thus merit the protection of the State until their natural death. The entire *Roe* framework of trimesters and evolving rights and interests is entirely irrelevant to the case of assisted suicide.[20]

The Ninth Circuit also relied on a selective reading of *dicta* in *Planned Parenthood v. Casey* to support its broad notions of autonomy. Admittedly, the language in *Casey* stating that "the heart of liberty is the right to define one's own concept of existence, of meaning, of the universe, and of the mystery of human life"[21] is capable of broad application. But this *dicta* should not be confused with constitutional doctrine and should not be reflexively applied to matters outside the scope of the narrow issue before the Court. To find the real constitutional meaning of *Casey*, one does not look to the "mystery passage," but to the issues before the Court: whether to overturn *Roe v. Wade*, and whether to strike down certain Pennsylvania regulations of abortion. Significantly, *Casey* declined to reverse *Roe* by the narrowest possible margin, 5–4. The Court's meditations on the extent of liberty (the "mystery passage" is from a "joint opinion" of only three Justices, those being Souter, O'Connor, and Kennedy) were offered as a defense of *Roe*, not as an invitation to the declaration of other novel constitutional rights.[22] In the same opinion, Justices O'Connor, Souter, and Kennedy agreed to curtail much of *Roe*'s constitutional progeny, effectively overruling, for example, the 1986 opinion in *Thornburgh v. American College of Obstetricians and Gynecologists.*[23] *Thornburgh*, ironically, had invalidated earlier Pennsylvania regulations of abortion quite similar to those eventually upheld in *Casey*. While affirming *Roe* (and this by a narrower margin than had originally decided *Roe*), *Casey* at once illustrated the latent weakness of the so-called constitutional right to abortion. *Casey* is hardly an auspicious departure point for another profoundly novel and controversial constitutional "right." It is best read, rather, as a constitutional salvage operation.[24]

In addition, *Casey* emphasized the singular position of its abortion decisions on the spectrum of constitutional law: referring to *Roe* as a "sui generis" extension of prior decisions on the family and procreation; characterizing abortion as a "unique act"; and describing the liberty interests of the pregnant woman "as unique to the human condition and so unique to the law."[25] These statements, ignored by the Ninth Circuit, are dispositive on the question of whether *Casey* mandates recognition of an asserted constitutional right to assisted suicide. Far from being "prescriptive" on the question, as the Ninth Circuit states, *Casey* is really of very limited precedential value.

Finally, the claimed right to assisted suicide illustrates the danger in literal application of the *Casey* dicta on the "meaning of life" to novel claims of constitutional right. In the panel decision for the Ninth Circuit, Judge Noonan demonstrated that if applied outside the abortion context, this language would be illimitable, i.e., without bounds. Criteria such as "suffering" are inherently subjective and clearly are not limited to the terminally ill. The disillusioned twenty-year-old and the depressed forty-year-old may find life just as burdensome as a terminally ill person in his sixties or seventies. If a right to assisted suicide is predicated on an individual's unrestricted right "to define one's own concept of existence . . . and of the mystery of human life," there is no principled basis on which exercise of the right could then be restricted to those who are terminally ill.

EUTHANASIA AND THE RIGHT TO
REFUSE MEDICAL TREATMENT

The Ninth Circuit and the Second Circuit both equated the right to assisted suicide with the right to refuse life-sustaining medical treatment. In doing so, they ignored the legislative enactments of virtually every state, and the unanimous judgment of the state courts that have ruled on this issue, that exercise of the common-law right to refuse even life-sustaining medical treatment is not tantamount to suicide. This disregard of precedent is all the more remarkable due to the vast professional literature and widespread public discussion of these issues since the decision of the New Jersey Supreme Court regarding Karen Quinlan twenty years ago.

There are obvious reasons to blur the distinction between withdrawing treatment and direct assistance in killing. Placing both practices under the all-encompassing rubric of a "right to die" avoids having to make the separate case for legitimating assisted suicide. Indeed, just as "pro-choice" has become the euphemism for advocacy on behalf of legal abortion, terms such as "physician aid-in-dying" have been coined by advocates of legalized euthanasia. It is one thing for social advocates to engage in such linguistic sleight-of-hand; it is quite another for our federal courts to adopt the practice, as has occurred in both opinions here.

Both courts gloss over the fundamental distinction between omission and commission, between allowing a patient to die and killing the patient. The Second Circuit used this equivocation to hold that under the equal protection clause in the Fourteenth Amendment, the State could not permit certain patients to die by refusing life-sustaining treatment, while denying others who are not dependent on such treatment an equivalent freedom to die. The Ninth Circuit used similar reasoning to buttress its analysis under the due process clause of the Fourteenth Amendment: since there is a right to refuse unwanted life-sustaining medical treatment, the court reasoned, there must be a corollary right to enlist the assistance of a physician in directly causing one's death. The Ninth Circuit in particular attempted to make the case that the prescription of lethal medication to a terminally ill patient should not even be considered as assistance in suicide, but merely as an effort to ensure that the patient's inevitable death will be humane and dignified.

Other legal authorities dismiss this point of view. Virtually without exception, the judicial decisions and statutes in this area have recognized the distinction between directly causing death by an affirmative act to end life and allowing death to occur by withholding or withdrawing life-sustaining medical treatment.[26] To deny this is to deny the ethical distinction between act and omission. When life-sustaining treatment is removed, it is the underlying fatal illness that causes death, not, as in the case of assisted suicide or euthanasia, the direct action of the physician. The law reflects this distinction as well. The common-law right to refuse medical treatment is properly classified as a *negative* right: the right *not* to be forcibly subjected to treatment, particularly treatment that is burdensome and carries an uncertain hope of benefit to the patient. The Ninth Circuit wrongly concludes that the judicial precedents in this area create a *positive* right on the part of patients to hasten their deaths; the clearest evidence that this is not the case is the repeated refrain in these cases that refusal of life-sustaining treatment is not tantamount to suicide or euthanasia.[27]

Finally, if the rationale of the Ninth Circuit were taken to its logical conclusion, every decision by a physician not to employ a life-sustaining medical treatment, or to withdraw such a treatment with the consent of the patient or family members, could constitute a form of homicide. As recognized by *Quinlan* and succeeding cases, however, the essential element of criminal *intent* is not ordinarily present in a medical decision to withdraw treatment. Homicidal intent is much easier to infer, of course, if the physician uses a lethal agent, the sole purpose of which is to cause death. On this point, law and ethics are in agreement: "[I]n ceasing treatment, the physician *does not intend the death* of the patient, even if death follows as a result. Rather, he seeks to avoid useless and degrading medical additions to the already sad end of a life. In contrast, in assisted suicide, the physician necessarily intends primarily that the patient be made dead."[28] Thus, the Ninth and Second Circuits notwithstanding, it is constitutionally permissible for the states to draw a clear line between omissions and acts—even if *some* of the permitted omissions may have the same result as *all* of the forbidden acts.

Both courts also misread *Cruzan v. Director, Missouri Dept. of Public Health*[29] to create an affirmative constitutional right to hasten death. In *Cruzan*, the Supreme Court presumed (but did not decide) that a competent patient has the right to refuse unwanted medical treatment and may refuse assistance in feeding, even if this will result in death. The Ninth Circuit held that in so ruling, the Supreme Court "necessarily recognizes a liberty interest in hastening one's own death."[30] The Second Circuit, relying in part on Justice Scalia's concurring opinion, declared that there can be no logical distinction between causing one's death by the refusal of treatment and causing one's death by more direct means.[31] The Second Circuit glossed over the facts (1) that Justice Scalia would permit the State far greater latitude in prohibiting decisions to withdraw certain forms of life-sustaining medical treatment, (2) that he would clearly uphold State decisions to prohibit active assistance in suicide, and (3) as a fundamental matter, he would reserve all such questions to the people and their elected representatives—the entire point of his *Cruzan* concurrence.

[T]he point at which life becomes "worthless," and the point at which the means necessary to preserve it become "extraordinary" or "inappropriate" are neither set forth in the Constitution nor known to the nine Justices of this Court any better than they are known to nine people picked at random from the Kansas City telephone directory. . . . It is quite impossible . . . that they will decide upon a line less reasonable.[32]

The Ninth and Second Circuits also give insufficient weight to *Cruzan's* recognition of the tensions between the right to refuse treatment and other important legal tradition. The premise that patients have the right to consent to or to refuse medical treatment reached judicial and legislative attention when medical science expanded its ability to sustain life through "artificial" means. As *Cruzan* recognized, these developments brought two legal traditions into potential conflict: the right to consent or not to consent to treatment, and the interest of State in preventing homicide, including assisted suicide. On this latter point, the Court's endorsement of State interest was unequivocal: "As a general matter, the States—indeed, all civilized nations—demonstrate their commitment to life by treating homicide as a serious crime. Moreover, the majority of States in this country have laws imposing criminal penalties on one who assists another to commit suicide."[33] The Court noted that the Constitution "protects an interest in life as well as an interest in refusing life-sustaining medical treatment."[34]

Cruzan's holding was narrow: to affirm Missouri's requirement that there be clear and convincing evidence of a patient's intent to refuse life-sustaining treatment. The Court placed no outer limits on the State's ability to assert its interest in sustaining life; indeed, *Cruzan* repeatedly stressed that where death is a potential consequence of an action, the recognition of a "liberty interest" in that action does not end the constitutional inquiry. Instead, "the dramatic consequences [death] involved in the refusal of such treatment would inform the inquiry as to *whether the deprivation of that interest is constitutionally permissible.*"[35] The Court specifically cited laws against assisted suicide as evidence of the measures traditionally taken by the states to affirm their interest in protection of human life. Finally, *Cruzan* specifically denied a central premise of the Second and Ninth Circuit opinions—that the State must tailor its interests in light of diminished life expectancy or human capacity. The State may assert an "unqualified" interest in the patient's life,[36] the Court held, and thus may require *heightened* procedures to protect life precisely because of the vulnerability of the patient's condition. The findings in *Quill v. Vacco* and *Compassion in Dying*[37] that the State has no legitimate interest in protecting the lives of terminally ill patients from the practice of assisted suicide are unsupported by and indeed directly contradictory to the opinion in *Cruzan.*

The Second Circuit also ignored the findings of the nonpartisan New York State Task Force on Life and the Law in its 1995 report on assisted suicide and euthanasia: as timely and comprehensive a defense of the current state of the law as one could bring to bear on the subject.[38] The task force was "particularly struck by the degree to which requests for suicide assistance by terminally ill patients are correlated with clinical depression or *unmanaged* [not unmanageable] pain, both of which can ordinarily be treated effectively with current medical techniques."[39] It noted studies that demonstrate that suicidal ideation is rare among terminally ill patients, unless those patients are also suffering from depression.[40] It also observed that the elderly and terminally ill are less likely to receive appropriate diagnosis and treatment for depression. The task force stated that, "[a]s a society, we can do far more to benefit these patients by improving pain relief and palliative care than by changing the law to make it easier to commit suicide or to obtain a lethal injection."[41] It also warned that the risks of legalizing assisted suicide "would be most severe for those whose autonomy and well-being are already compromised by poverty, lack of access to good medical care, or membership in a stigmatized social group."[42] States are clearly free to enact statutes against such dangers, and there is an equally clear, rational basis to do so.

THE ELASTICITY OF THE RIGHT TO ASSISTED SUICIDE

In contrast to *Cruzan*, the decisions in *Quill* and *Compassion in Dying* are anything but narrow in scope. Both courts, mindful of "slippery slope" and related arguments, contended that the right to assistance in suicide is limited to the ability of terminally ill and competent patients to hasten a death that is already imminent and inevitable. Even this allegedly narrow beachhead, however, provides ample cover for broadening the contours of the right to assisted suicide and extending protection to active euthanasia. The circuits' failures to distinguish between withdrawal of treatment and active assistance in death virtually ensures that euthanasia rights will be extended to the full range of patients (that is, virtually *any* patient) who currently have the right to refuse life-sustaining medical treatment.[43] In the words of Professor George Annas, "[t]his logical failure also helps explain why neither court could define the right they had discovered or persuasively limit its exercise to cases involving prescriptions written by physicians for competent, terminally ill patients, limitations that have no basis in constitutional law."[44]

The right to assisted suicide recognized in these decisions is in principle illimitable. It cannot be restricted to the mentally competent terminally ill, or more specifically, to those whose deaths are imminent. The Ninth Circuit stated that there is a "liberty interest in determining the time and manner of one's death."[45] Could such a broadly articulated liberty be denied to a patient upon initial diagnosis of an inevitably fatal disease, or of a degenerative condition such as Alzheimer's, merely because death is not imminent? Such patients could make a strong claim for assisted suicide in order to avoid a long process of physical decline and suffering. Their families and caregivers could thus be relieved of the burdens of care that often attend such conditions. The Ninth Circuit, in fact, endorses such thinking: "Faced with the prospect of astronomical medical bills, terminally ill patients might decide it is better for them to die before their health care expenses consume the life savings they planned to leave for their families, or, worse yet, burden their families with debts they may never be able to satisfy. . . . [W]e are reluctant to say that . . . it is improper for competent, terminally ill adults to take the economic welfare of their families into consideration."[46]

Terminal illness itself is also an arbitrary boundary. Ironically, patients who are *chronically* ill might well claim a denial of the equal protection of the laws if a state legalized assisted suicide only for the "benefit" of the *terminally* ill. If the right were extended in this fashion, it would be a small step to acceptance of assisted suicide for the handicapped, particularly those who are perceived to have a low "quality of life." The Ninth Circuit treats this concern with two responses: First, it asserted that the handicapped and disabled "are sufficiently active politically and sufficiently vigilant" to prevent actions that would pressure them into taking their own lives. Second, it suggested that "seriously impaired" individuals will be the *beneficiary* of the right to assisted suicide, because otherwise they will be compelled to "ensure unusual and protracted suffering."[47]

This effective endorsement of assisted suicide for the severely handicapped demonstrates that the "boundaries" established by the Ninth Circuit are inherently subjective—the "terminal illness" criterion carries an implicit judgment that some lives are not worth living and, hence, that it is reasonable that such lives be ended. For example, the Ninth Circuit concedes that the State *does* have an interest in preventing suicides by teens and young adults and "in preventing anyone, no matter what age, from taking his own life in a fit of desperation, depression, or loneliness or as a result of any other problem, physical or psychological, *which can be significantly ameliorated.*"[48] Thus, the court concluded, suicide is senseless for some; for others it is not. The distinction lies in the dangerous notion of "quality of life." The Second Circuit echoed this line of reasoning, referring to the "greatly reduced interest of the state in preserving life" in the case of a terminally ill patient. However, there is no issue in these cases of the State's requiring additional means to sustain life; the State's only claim is that the lives of the terminally ill, like those of all other citizens, be protected under generally applicable laws against assisted suicide.

The criterion of "suffering," often used to defend the right to assistance in death for the terminally ill, is similarly subjective. The New York State Task Force discussed this problem:

> [A]s long as the policies hinge on notions of pain or suffering they are uncontainable; neither pain nor suffering can be gauged objectively or subjected to the kind of judgments needed to fashion coherent public policy. Moreover, even if the more narrow category of terminal illness is chosen at the outset, the line is unlikely to hold for the very reason that it has not been selected by advocates of assisted suicide—the logic of suicide as a compassionate choice for patients who are in pain or suffering suggests no such limit.[49]

Both the Second and Ninth Circuit explicitly cite suffering as grounds for diminishing the State's interest in the lives of terminally ill patients. Neither adequately considers that the option of aggressive pain management is the reasonable response to such circumstances—or that the impetus to treat pain and suffering will diminish if the option of hastened death can be presented to the patient.

The criteria of competency and self-control in administering the means of death are also ineffectual limits. The Ninth Circuit has specifically endorsed the practice of assisted suicide, with the consent of a duly-appointed surrogate, in the case of an incompetent patient. The court left unanswered the question of how an incompetent patient can commit suicide; clearly, such cases would require the direct killing of the patient by the physician. While the court takes no position on this issue, it clearly indicates that the liberty interest "in controlling the manner of one's own death" would be broad enough to encompass such practices.

These points illustrate that, in the words of a report of the British House of Lords, assisted suicide is not "a discrete step which need have no other consequences." The Lords emphasized that "individual cases cannot reasonably establish the foundation of a policy which would have such serious and widespread repercussions." They concluded:

> It would be next to impossible to ensure that all acts of euthanasia were truly voluntary, and that any liberalisation of the law was not abused. Moreover to create an exception to the general prohibition of intentional killing would inevitably open the way to its further erosion whether by design, by inadvertence, or by the human tendency to test the limits of any regulation. These dangers are such that we believe that any decriminalisation of voluntary euthanasia would give rise to more, and more grave, problems than those it sought to address.[50]

The seeds of such expansion are well-cultivated in the opinions of the Second and Ninth Circuits.

ASSISTED SUICIDE AND HUMAN DIGNITY

The Ninth and Second Circuits contend that assisted suicide is necessary so that terminally ill patients can end their lives in a dignified and humane fashion. The Second Circuit asks: "What business is it of the state to require the continuation of agony when the result is imminent and inevitable?"[51] Like most rhetorical questions, this is designed not be answered, but the response is elementary: Laws against assisted suicide do not require that life be prolonged, merely that life not be shortened by deliberately lethal measures. The laws of New York State provide no obstacle to a decision by a competent, terminally ill patient to reject prolongation of life by medical means.[52] The following question is more appropriate: "What business does the State have in deciding that some lives are less worthy of the law's protection than others, and suggesting through legalization of assisted suicide that this is a 'rational' way for people to end their lives?"

There is perhaps a universal temptation to surrender to the stress and tension of a chronic, long-term illness, and to despair of any relief, to give up hope of recovery, to abandon the family member in need, and inevitably, to hasten the death of the chronically ill patient. Technology has not alleviated these concerns, but neither should technology be viewed as the sole source for aggravating them. It is because of human nature itself that there is an enduring need for the protection embodied in the common law and now codified in the law of most states.

Overturning this tradition on the basis of an unenumerated constitutional "liberty interest," or obliterating the historical distinction between act and omission, threatens the values that the law has long sought to protect. The House of Lords Committee spoke to the importance of laws prohibiting assisted suicide and euthanasia in protecting the dignity of the person.

> The right to refuse medical treatment is far removed from the right to request assistance in dying. We spent a long time considering the very strongly held and sincerely expressed views of those witnesses who advocated voluntary euthanasia. . . . Ultimately, however, we do not believe that these arguments are sufficient reason to weaken society's prohibition of intentional killing. That prohibition is the cornerstone of law and of social relationships. It protects each one of us impartially, embodying the belief that all are equal. We do not wish that protection to be diminished and we therefore recommend that there should be no change in the law to permit euthanasia.[53]

Against such a background, the fundamental errors of the Ninth and Second Circuits are clear. The decisions ignore an unimpeachable legal tradition of protecting the most vulnerable, a tradition firmly embedded in the common law and reinforced through the legal and medical reforms of the past twenty years. These decisions assume that the State and medical practitioners can effectively limit the practice of physician-assisted death only to those who are truly terminally ill, truly competent, and truly free of depression, duress, or other undue influences upon their decision. The decisions also presume that courts are the appropriate institutions to assess the wisdom of public policies on these questions and that their judgments should trump those of the elected branches of government. The Ninth and Second Circuit decisions are profoundly wrong on all three counts.

CONCLUSION

Euthanasia rights proponents would clearly disagree with the analysis in these pages of *Compassion in Dying* and *Quill v. Vacco*. They would argue that the impact of these decisions (if affirmed by the Supreme Court) will be modest, that American medicine will maintain a strong bias to preserve human life even in the face of terminal illness, and that the freedom of the dying patient to determine the time and manner of death is merely a narrow and logical extension of the rights patients now have to refuse life-sustaining medical treatment. Patients, families, and the medical profession, the argument goes, have as little to fear from the recognition of euthanasia rights as they did from the decisions in cases such as Karen Quinlan and Nancy Cruzan.

Which vision is correct will not ultimately be decided in these pages or even by the Supreme Court. But a close reading of the Ninth and Second Circuit decisions illustrates that something far more ambitious than a modest extension of existing health care rights is at hand. The popular images of this debate concur; the crusade of Dr. Jack Kevorkian bears little resemblance to the pleas of the Quinlans or Cruzans to withdraw their brain-damaged daughters from life-sustaining treatment. Those who argue that Dr. Kevorkian's activities demonstrate the need for *liberalization* of assisted suicide laws (on the grounds that they could then be subject to tighter regulation)[54] seem to miss an obvious point: If Kevorkian can't be stopped now, when assisted suicide is illegal, how could he or his like be stopped if the rulings of the Second or Ninth Circuits became the law of the land?[55]

ENDNOTES

1. A. B. Georgetown University; J. D. Northwestern University. Counsel, Judiciary Subcommittee on Immigration and Claims, United States House of Representatives. The views expressed herein are entirely those of the author, and do not necessarily reflect the opinions of any Member or staff of the Committee on the Judiciary. The author acknowledges the editorial comments and suggestions of Victor G. Rosenblum and Clarke D. Forsythe.
2. 79 F.3d 790 (9th Cir. 1996) (*en banc*), *superseding* 49 F.3d 586 (9th Cir. 1995), *rehearing denied*, 85 F.3d 1440 (9th Cir. 1996), *cert. granted sub nom. Glucksberg v. Washington*, No. 96–110 (Oct. 1, 1996).
3. 80 F.3d 716 (2d Cir. 1996), *rev'g Quill v. Koppell*, 870 F. Supp. 78 (S.D.N.Y. 1994), *cert. granted*, No. 95–1858 (Oct. 1, 1996).
4. Edward R. Grant and Paul Benjamin Linton, *Relief or Reproach?: Euthanasia Rights in the Wake of Measure 16*, 74 OREGON L. REV. 449, 451 (1995).
5. *Compassion in Dying*, 79 F.3d at 816.
6. 79 F.3d at 837.
7. *Quill v. Vacco*, 80 F.3d at 726.
8. 80 F.3d at 731.
9. *Palko v. Connecticut*, 302 U.S. 319, 325 (1937).
10. *Moore v. City of East Cleveland*, 431 U.S. 494, 503 (1977).
11. 80 F.3d at 724. "The Court is most vulnerable and comes nearest to illegitimacy when it deals with judge-made constitutional law having little or no cognizable roots in the language or design of the Constitution." Id., *quoting Bowers v. Hardwick*, 478 U.S. 186, 194 (1986).
12. *Compassion in Dying v. Washington*, 49 F.3d 586, 591 (9th Cir. 1995), *superseded*, 79 F.3d 790 (9th Cir. 1996) (*en banc*).
13. 79 F.3d at 806, 806–810.
14. For example, the court claimed that at the time of the passage of the Fourteenth Amendment, only 9 states had statutes against assisted suicide. This ignores, first, that at least 12 additional states had adopted the common law of crimes, which treated assisted suicide as a species of homicide, and second, that due to a clear trend of states codifying prohibitions against assisted suicide (including several that have done so in recent years), virtually all states forbid assisted suicide either by express statute (Iowa just became the 34th state do so), by judicial

decision, or by adopting the common law of crimes. *See* Grant and Linton, *supra* note 4 at 483–84.

15. Id. at 462–68.
16. *McKay v. Bergstedt*, 801 P.2d 617, 627 (Nev. 1990).
17. Grant and Linton, *supra* note 4 at 462–63.
18. 410 U.S. 113 (1973).
19. 505 U.S. 833 (1992).
20. The unique status of *Roe* is illustrated by the court's decision, in the same Term that *Roe* was decided, in *Paris Adult Theatre I v. Slaton*. There, the Court referred with approval to then-unchallenged laws banning, among other things, assisted suicide, "although these crimes may only directly involve consenting adults." 413 U.S. 49, 68, n.15 (1973).
21. 505 U.S. at 851.
22. The passage is preceded by a discussion of the constitutional protection given to marriage, procreation, contraception, and the rearing and education of children, thus tying this *dicta* to more firmly established (and much narrower) precedent. However, nearly 25 years after the ruling in *Roe*, neither the Supreme Court nor even some defenders of *Roe* genuinely accept that the decision to end the life of an unborn child is tantamount to a decision on whom to marry, or how to educate one's children.

> Abortion today is as American as free speech, freedom of religion, or any other practice protected by our courts. With this difference: unlike other American rights, abortion cannot be discussed in plain English. Its warmest supporters do not like to call it by its name. . . .

> If one abortion is not a bad thing, why are many abortions bad? What is it about abortion that is so troubling? The obvious answer is that abortion is troubling because it is a killing process. . . . Abortion has thus come to occupy an absurd, surrealistic place in the national dialogue: It cannot be ignored and it cannot be openly stated. It is the corpse at the dinner party (George McKenna, "On Abortion: A Lincolnian Position," *The Atlantic Monthly* [Sept. 1995]: 52, 54. *See also* Naomi Wolf, "Our Bodies, Our Souls," *The New Republic* [Oct. 16, 1995]: 26).

23. 476 U.S. 747 (1986).
24. Precedent, in the end, was what *Casey* was about. The Court repeatedly drew the distinction between the decision to overturn existing precedent and to fashion new precedent. This was seen most clearly in the Court's admonition that, even if *Roe* had been decided in error, principles of institutional integrity and the public's reliance on established doctrine militated against an abrupt reversal of the decision. These factors are clearly not present in the case of assisted suicide.
25. *Casey*, 505 U.S. at 852.
26. Grant and Linton, *supra* note 4 at 461–62.
27. Id. at 462–68.
28. Leon R. Kass, "Dehumanization Triumphant," *First Things* (Aug./Sept. 1996): 15–16. Courts have consistently recognized that the distinctions between omission and act apply even in cases where the withdrawal of treatment—i.e.,

the cessation of feeding—will most certainly result in death. Admittedly, such cases appear *close* to the actual causation of death, particularly if the patient's death is not imminent. But the courts have ruled that assisted feeding is a medical treatment and thus remains within the ambit of the common-law right of competent patient to consent to or to refuse. *See, e.g., In re* Gardner, 534 A.2d 947, 955–56 (Me. 1987); *In re* Grant, 747 P.2d 445, 455 (Wash. 1987), *modified* 757 P.2d 534 (Wash. 1988); *In re* L.W., 482 N.W.2d 60 (Wis. 1992).

29. 497 U.S. 261 (1990).
30. *Compassion in Dying,* 79 F.3d at 816.
31. *Quill v. Vacco,* 80 F.3d at 729.
32. 497 U.S. at 296.
33. 497 U.S. at 280.
34. 497 U.S. at 281.
35. 497 U.S. at 279.
36. 497 U.S. at 279–82.
37. The Ninth Circuit dismissed this aspect of *Cruzan* on the species rationale that if the state's "unqualified" interest is not always controlling because if it were, "the draft, as well as the defense budget, would be unconstitutional." 79 F.3d at 817, n. 72.
38. New York State Task Force on Life and the Law, *When Death Is Sought: Assisted Suicide and Euthanasia in the Medical Context* (1994).
39. Id. at ix.
40. Id. at 12–17, 127.
41. Id. at 9.
42. Id. at vii–viii.
43. *See* Edward R. Grant and Clarke D. Forsythe, "From "Natural Death" to "Aid-in-Dying": Reflections on the American Judicial Experience," in *Euthanasia: The Good of the Patient, the Good of Society* 151 (Robert I. Misbin, ed., 1992).
44. George J. Annas, "The Promised End—Constitutional Aspects of Physician-Assisted Suicide," 355 *New Eng. J. Med.* 683, 686 (1996).
45. *Compassion in Dying,* 79 F.3d at 816.
46. 79 F.3d at 826.
47. 79 F.3d at 825.
48. 79 F.3d at 820.
49. *When Death Is Sought, supra* note 38, at 15.
50. H.L. *Rep of the Select Comm. on Med. Ethics* 49 (U.K. 1994).
51. *Quill v. Vacco,* 80 F.3d at 730.
52. *When Death Is Sought, supra* note 38 at 49–53.
53. Id. at 48.
54. Timothy E. Quill and Betty Rollin, "Dr. Kevorkian Runs Wild," *New York Times,* 29 Aug. 1996, 25(A).
55. *See* Correspondence, "More Assisted-Suicide Laws, More Kevorkians," *New York Times,* 2 Sept. 1996, 20(A).

An Overview

The abuse of substantive due process used in *Roe v. Wade* created a pattern of decision making that has made it easier to pass legislation (or difficult not to pass legislation, depending on your perspective) favoring assisted suicide. Through this abuse, the courts have been able to stretch the original intent of the word *liberty* in the Fourteenth Amendment, a post-Civil War document, to create new rights and strip the people and the states of their constitutional role in determining legislation. James Bopp and Richard Coleson discuss the origin of substantive due process and trace its use from *Roe v. Wade* to the present day battle over the legality of assisted suicide.

Chapter Two

ROE v. WADE AND THE EUTHANASIA DEBATE

James Bopp Jr. and Richard E. Coleson

WHEN ABORTION WAS DECLARED A constitutional right in America, pro-life scholars declared that the nation had stepped on a slippery slope and predicted it would quickly lead to infanticide, assisted suicide, and active euthanasia. That prediction has proven true[1] because federal appellate courts in the Second and Ninth Circuits have found a constitutional right to assisted suicide.[2]

The prediction was based on the fact that societal approval of abortion constituted something even larger than approval of abortion. Implicit in the approval of abortion on demand was the principle that it is permissible to take innocent human life, even for reasons of convenience. Once that principle was accepted, it was but a short distance to societal acceptance of "baby Doe" cases and assisted suicide.

The slippery slope has been lubricated by the numbing effect of three decades of one and a half million abortions a year. Jack Kevorkian's relentless flouting of the law, coupled with the inability of prosecutors to gain criminal convictions against him, has further numbed public outrage at assisted suicide and created a malaise of perceived inevitability.

However, if America does not gain a toehold on the slippery slope before reaching legal approval of assisted suicide, it should not be expected that the slide will stop at assisted suicide. *The distance between assisted suicide and involuntary euthanasia is even shorter than that between abortion and assisted suicide.*

What is not appreciated by many (including those who support abortion rights but oppose assisted suicide) is the connection between the declared right to assisted suicide and the constitutional analysis employed by the United States Supreme Court in *Roe v. Wade.*[3] To change metaphors, *Roe v. Wade* (the case declaring a right to abortion) is the root, the reaffirmation of *Roe* in *Planned Parenthood of S.E. Pennsylvania v. Casey*[4] is the branch, and the right to assisted suicide is the fruit.

THE ROOT: *ROE v. WADE*

In 1973, the United States Supreme Court seized the abortion issue from the laboratory of the states (some of which had been experimenting with more permissive abortion laws) and secured it behind the pale of constitutional protection. The decision, known as *Roe v. Wade*, was vigorously criticized by constitutional scholars for abandoning all pretense of being constitutional law and imposing on the states by fiat a regime of abortion on demand.[5]

To understand the scholarly outrage, it is necessary to explore the debate over the shadowy realm of *substantive due process*. Substantive due process is the analytical device employed by the Court to declare constitutional rights not enumerated in the Constitution.

Of course, it was not intended by the framers of the Constitution that the Supreme Court find unenumerated rights. The Constitution was designed to create a limited government, with the federal government receiving only those powers and protecting only those rights ceded to it by the people. All other powers and the right to regulate all other matters were retained by the people and the states, as expressly set out in the Constitution.[6] The arrangement was only to be altered by formal constitutional amendment.

In the Constitution and its amendments, the people granted the federal government the power to protect certain rights, which were to be beyond the power of the federal or state governments to impinge. Those enumerated rights included the rights to free speech, free press, free association, free exercise of religion, and so on, as set out in the Bill of Rights.

Over the years, the High Court has had to apply these enumerated rights in changing contexts. For example, the rights to free speech and free press have been applied to an age of broadcast media and the Internet. However, such logical extension of enumerated rights was not a declaration of new rights.

Some justices have also been tempted to illegitimately stretch existing rights to encompass new ones that would surely be unrecognized as constitutional rights by the framers of the Constitution and its amendments. Where a newly declared right cannot be fairly traced to an enumerated right, the Court has engaged in a limited coup d'état by seizing power to control areas not granted to the federal government by the people.

The temptation of the Court to create federal constitutional rights in areas left to state control by the framers has been strong, because it allows the justices to decide the important issues of the day, rather than leaving them to the democratic process. When judges seek to decide matters not entrusted to them by the people, they arrogate to themselves the powers envisioned by Plato when he proposed his elite ruling guardians. Such judges do not limit themselves to the powers entrusted to them in the Constitution, which they swore to uphold. Rule by judges, rather than by the laws and Constitution duly enacted by the people, results in rule by man, not by law, a concept the framers clearly rejected when they rejected a monarchy and established a democratic republic.

Substantive due process, the tool the Court uses to create unenumerated rights, is based in the Fourteenth Amendment statement that a state may not "deprive any person of life, liberty, or property, without due process of law." The obvious intent of this post-Civil War amendment was to secure for all persons fair legal proceedings before they could be hanged, imprisoned, or fined.

However, the term *liberty* has beckoned justices seeking to declare new rights. If the Court could gain public acquiescence in its decision to define the term *liberty* beyond its original meaning, the Court would have the freedom to create new rights. "Liberty" would become an empty vessel that the Court could fill with its notion of proper public policy on a wide range of issues and thus control the direction of public policy on the major social issues.

The public has so far acquiesced. Despite the outcry of scholars against the creation of new rights, there have been no impeachments of activist justices. Presidents who appoint activist justices have suffered little, if any, political penalty. In fact, the dominant media hue and cry only arises when presidents attempt to appoint conservative justices who promise to interpret the laws, not make laws. Robert Bork, whose strong position against judicial activism has been articulated in his book *The Tempting of America: The Political Seduction of the Law* (1990), was found by the Senate to be outside the mainstream in his confirmation hearings because of his opposition to substantive due process. Thus, substantive due process has become part of the Supreme Court's armamenture, and Court control of social policy is governed only by the Court's self-control.

The Court showed a return to self-control briefly in the early 1960s when it repudiated prior use of substantive due process to strike down a variety of social legislation. That period was characterized by the most famous case of the period, *Lochner v. New York*,[7] a 1905 case in which the Supreme Court struck down state laws limiting the hours bakers could be required to work. The limitation (to a sixty-hour work week) was a traditional police-power regulation of the state designed to protect the health of bakers, but the Supreme Court used substantive due process to strike it down. The hot issue of the day was laissez-faire economics versus economic regulation and the Supreme Court read its philosophy into the "liberty" of the Fourteenth Amendment, finding a right to unfettered freedom of contract. Thus, the use of substantive due process to strike state legislation became known as Lochnering.

However, Lochnering was repudiated by scholars, dissenting justices, and finally by the Supreme Court in 1963, when the Court declared,

> There was a time when the Due Process Clause was used by this Court to strike down laws which were thought unreasonable, that is, unwise or incompatible with some particular economic or social philosophy. In this manner the Due Process Clause was used, for example, to nullify laws prescribing maximum hours for work in bakeries, outlawing "yellow dog" contracts, setting minimum wages for women, and fixing the weight of loaves of bread. This intrusion by the judiciary into the realm of legislative value judgments was strongly objected to at the time. . . . Mr. Justice Holmes said,
> "I think the proper course is to recognize that a state legislature can do

whatever it sees fit to do unless it is restrained by some express prohibition in the Constitution of the United States or of the State, and that Courts should be careful not to extend such prohibitions beyond their obvious meaning by reading into them conceptions of public policy that the particular Court may happen to entertain."[8]

The Court declared further that the doctrine "that due process authorizes courts to hold laws unconstitutional when they believe the legislature has acted unwisely, [had] been discarded."[9] "We have returned," the Court concluded, "to the original constitutional proposition that courts do not substitute their social and economic beliefs for the judgment of legislative bodies, who are elected to pass laws."[10]

Because of this declaration just a decade before *Roe v. Wade* was decided in 1973, one would have expected that no abortion right would have been declared on the basis of substantive due process. After all, abortion was not an enumerated right in the U.S. Constitution, so it was left to the states to regulate.

However, the lure of substantive due process was strong, and the Court once again succumbed. Reaching back to prior substantive due process decisions finding a right to privacy "founded in the Fourteenth Amendment's concept of personal liberty," the *Roe* Court declared that this right to privacy was "broad enough to encompass" abortion.[11]

By stretching the right of privacy—a right itself of questionable constitutional pedigree[12]—to encompass a new abortion right, the Court did not even apply the limitations it had previously created to circumscribe its discretion in creating new rights. Recognizing that the ability to find new rights in the "liberty" clause gave it broad discretion, the Court had created certain tests to give an air of legitimacy to the enterprise and prevent "judges from roaming at large in the constitutional field."[13]

The *Roe* Court even cited one of these tests: only those rights "implicit in the concept of ordered liberty" were "fundamental," i.e., protected by the liberty concept of the Fourteenth Amendment.[14] This test meant that if ordered liberty could not exist without abortion, then abortion must be a "fundamental" right that the states could not infringe. Of course this nation had enjoyed two centuries of ordered liberty while abortion was largely illegal, so the right to abortion was not truly a fundamental right under that test.

Because the "ordered liberty" test for fundamental rights was somewhat abstract, the Court had developed a more concrete "historical" test for fundamental rights.[15] The historical test asked whether a proposed right had been recognized as fundamental in the history and tradition of our people. Of course, an asserted right to abortion would have failed this test—because abortion has been largely illegal in common law and in state statutes since the founding of the republic—so the *Roe* Court ignored this test, too, and stretched the questionable privacy right to "encompass" a right to abortion.

The scholarly outrage at the *Roe* Court's decision to reembrace its old Lochnering ways was immediate, powerful, and sustained.[16] John Hart Ely examined *Roe's* logical poverty and pronounced it a "Lochnering" opinion more dangerous than other activist decisions of the Supreme Court. He declared it "a very bad decision . . . because it [was] *not* constitutional law and [gave] almost no sense of an obligation to try to be."[17]

Archibald Cox stated:

> My criticism of *Roe* . . . is that the Court failed to establish the legitimacy of the decision by articulating a precept of sufficient abstractness to lift the ruling above the level of a political judgment. . . . The failure to confront the issue in principled terms leaves the opinion to read like a set of hospital rules and regulations, whose validity is good enough this week but will be destroyed with new statistics upon the medical risks of childbirth and abortion or new advances in providing for the separate existence of a fetus . . . unless they can be stated in principles sufficiently absolute to give them roots throughout the community and continuity over . . . time. . . .[18]

Alexander Bickel commented, "The state regulates and licenses restaurants and pool halls and . . . God knows what else in order to protect the public; why may it not similarly regulate . . . abortion clinics, or doctor's offices . . . ? One is left to ask why." He continued, "[T]he Court never said. It refused the discipline to which its function is properly subject."[19]

Richard Epstein wrote that "*Roe* . . . [was] symptomatic of the analytical poverty possible in constitutional litigation."[20] He added that "we must criticize both Mr. Justice Blackmun in *Roe v. Wade* . . . and the entire method of constitutional interpretation that allows the Supreme Court . . . both to 'define' and to 'balance' interests on the major social and political issues of our time."[21]

THE BRANCH:
PLANNED PARENTHOOD OF S.E. PENNSYLVANIA V. CASEY

Because of the barrage of scholarly criticism and growing dissent on the Court, it was widely speculated that the Supreme Court might reverse *Roe v. Wade* when it decided *Planned Parenthood of S.E. Pennsylvania v. Casey* in 1992.[22] However, it chose to reaffirm *Roe* by a vote of 5 to 4, relying primarily on the legal doctrine of *stare decisis*, i.e., prior judicial decisions should generally be followed to provide stability to the law. In an effort to justify its reaffirmation of the *Roe* decision in the face of telling scholarly critiques, the Court resorted to an extremely broad and vague substantive due process analysis.

The *Casey* Court first rejected the history-and-tradition approach to deciding whether asserted constitutional rights should be declared fundamental and protected by federal courts. The Court declared, "Neither the Bill of Rights nor the specific practices of States at the time of the adoption of the Fourteenth Amendment marks the outer limits of the substantive sphere of liberty which the Fourteenth Amendment protects."[23]

The meaning, of course, was that the Court was declaring its independence from any limits on its ability to create rights. It would not be bound by the intent of the framers of the Constitution and its amendments, nor the history and tradition of our nation, nor by any neutral principle of law. It would be guided only by its own predilections. The Court put it more palatably:

> The inescapable fact is that the adjudication of substantive due process claims may call upon the Court in interpreting the Constitution to exercise that same capacity which by tradition courts always have exercised: reasoned judgment. Its boundaries are not susceptible of expression as a simple rule. That does not mean we are free to invalidate state policy choices with which we disagree; yet neither does it permit us to shrink from the duties of our office.[24]

Of course, if "reasoned judgment" is the only pole star for the Court, there is nothing stopping it from invalidating at will state policies with which it disagrees. There is no longer any neutral principle for decision or for evaluating the Court's decisions. We are left with the principle that constitutional law is merely whatever the Court says it is.

In an effort to justify its appeal to the right of privacy, the *Casey* Court defined the right of privacy extremely broadly. To understand how broad it was, it is helpful to understand the roots of the right of privacy.

Originally, the right of privacy had protected the right of families to make important decisions concerning the upbringing of their children, such as whether children could be taught German or be sent to a private school. The decisions were based on the fact that the family is an institution predating the Constitution and was revered and protected in the history of our civilization. From this little-debated protection of family sovereignty over children, the Court had expanded the privacy right to include a right to contraception, based on the idea that the state should not be searching marital bedrooms for evidence of such activity. However, this marital right was then extended to the right of unmarried persons to use contraception. From these discreet cases, the Supreme Court derived a right of privacy, which it has characterized as protection for "personal decisions relating to marriage, procreation, contraception, family relationships, child rearing, and education."[25]

Obviously, none of these had anything to do with killing children, born or unborn. Nor could it legitimately because killing children, born or unborn, had been a crime under common law and statutory law in America. Yet, the Supreme Court stretched this so-called privacy right to encompass abortion. In an attempt to justify in *Casey* what it had done in *Roe*, the Supreme Court characterized the right of privacy expansively in an apparent effort to make the declaration of a right to abortion appear reasonable. It declared:

> These matters, involving the most intimate and personal choices a person may make in a lifetime, choices central to personal dignity and autonomy, are central to the liberty protected by the Fourteenth Amendment. At the heart of liberty is the right to define one's own concept of existence, of

meaning, of the universe, and of the mystery of human life. Beliefs about these matters could not define the attributes of personhood were they formed under compulsion of the State.[26]

By broadly defining Fourteenth Amendment liberty, the Court intended to make its decree of an abortion right appear reasonable. However, it should be self-evident that with such a spacious definition of substantive-due-process liberty, the federal judiciary is without limits—other than the caprice of the Supreme Court—in pronouncing new constitutional rights.

The *Casey* Court also altered another aspect of traditional substantive due process analysis. Historically, once a fundamental right was identified (by whatever test), it was then weighed against asserted state interests to see if any were found to be "compelling."[27] If a state interest was found to be compelling, then it trumped the right and a state could regulate the activity. Of course, the Supreme Court ultimately decided whether or not a state interest was sufficiently compelling to override the free exercise of a fundamental right, so this provided no diminution of the Court's power to impose its view on public policy issues.

However, in *Casey* a new controlling analysis emerged. If a state statute constituted an "undue burden" on a woman's right to abortion, then the statute was unconstitutional.[28] Of course, the high court still determined what burdens were undue. The practical effect of these changes was to make abortion jurisprudence an even more freewheeling balancing enterprise by the Supreme Court.

THE FRUIT: ASSISTED SUICIDE

When advocates of legalized assisted suicide went looking for federal constitutional protection for a right to physician-assisted suicide, the *Roe/Casey* analysis was ready at hand. Judge Rothstein, of the United States District Court for the Western District of Washington, began her legal analysis by setting out the liberty interest described in *Casey* (as set out in the block quote *supra*).[29] She declared that "this court finds the reasoning in *Casey* highly instructive and almost prescriptive on the [issue of assisted suicide]."[30] "Like the abortion decision," she continued, "the decision of a terminally ill person to end his or her life 'involv[es] the most intimate and personal choices a person may make in a lifetime' and constitutes a 'choice central to personal dignity and autonomy.'"[31]

The district court then considered the interests asserted by the State of Washington to determine whether the state's criminal prohibition on assisted suicide constituted an undue burden on the right to assisted suicide. Judge Rothstein rejected traditionally recognized justifications for barring assisted suicide—preventing suicide and preventing undue influence and abuse—as insufficient to prevent the ban on assisted suicide from being an undue burden on persons who were terminally ill, competent adults.[32] Of course, based on the rationale employed, it is but a short step (and one legal challenge) from such limited assisted suicide to broadly available assisted suicide.

On appeal of the decision to the Ninth Circuit Court of Appeals, a three-judge panel first employed the traditional substantive due process analysis and reversed the district court.[33] The panel asked whether a right to suicide or assistance in suicide had been recognized as a fundamental right in the history and tradition of our nation. It noted that while suicide had been widely decriminalized because of the discovery that most suicides were due to competence-impairing ailments such as depression, neither suicide nor assisted suicide had ever been considered as fundamental rights. In fact, suicide was yet subject to social approbation and assisted suicide was illegal in most states. The panel continued, declaring that even if there was a right to assisted suicide, there remained compelling interests in protecting vulnerable persons from assistance in self-termination and protecting the ethics of the medical profession by keeping doctors out of the killing business.

However, this victory for traditional values, for a more responsible brand of substantive due process, and for vulnerable persons was short-lived. The Ninth Circuit decided to hear the case *en banc*, i.e., instead of the usual three-judge panel, eleven judges would hear the case.

The *en banc* Ninth Circuit vacated the ruling of the three-judge panel, affirmed the district court, and declared a constitutional right to physician-assisted suicide.[34] It did so with heavy and primary reliance on *Roe* and *Casey*. The Ninth Circuit extensively analogized the right to abortion and the right to assisted suicide and dismissed as insufficient the asserted state interests in preserving life, preventing suicide, avoiding the involvement of third parties, precluding undue influence, protecting family members, protecting the integrity of the medical profession, and avoiding adverse consequences (such as the Netherlands' slide into nonvoluntary euthanasia). It declared that it was "guided by the Court's approach to the abortion cases."[35] "*Casey* in particular provides a powerful precedent," it declared, adding that the fundamental message of that case lies in its statements regarding the type of issue that confronts us here: "These matters, involving the most intimate and personal choices a person may make in a lifetime, choices central to personal dignity and autonomy, are central to the liberty protected by the Fourteenth Amendment."[36]

CONCLUSION

As may be seen, there is a direct link between *Roe v. Wade* and the finding of a right to assisted suicide. The expansive substantive due process analysis embraced by the United States Supreme Court to justify its imposition of an abortion-on-demand regime has been employed by the Ninth Circuit to justify the proclamation of a right to assisted suicide. Interestingly, the Supreme Court of Michigan and the United States Court of Appeals for the Second Circuit have rejected any substantive-due-process right to assisted suicide, employing a more traditional (history and tradition) liberty analysis.[37] The Second Circuit, however, found a right to assisted suicide under the Equal Protection Clause of the Fourteenth Amendment, an equally suspect analysis earlier rejected by the Michigan Supreme Court.

At the time of this writing, the United States Supreme Court has been asked to review the cases from the Ninth and Second Circuits. It has the option of accepting or rejecting either or both cases. At issue is not only whether assisted suicide will become a right in all or parts of this nation, but also whether the federal judiciary will continue to impose its will on the republic without the accountability of neutral principles of law evenly applied. If the Court recognizes a right to assisted suicide, it will do so on the basis of the sort of flawed analysis that was employed in an effort to justify *Roe v. Wade*. If it rejects a right to assisted suicide, it will do so on the basis of an analysis that demonstrates once again how intellectually bankrupt was its decision in *Roe v. Wade*.

ENDNOTES

1. In a supremely ironic statement, Judge Reinhardt, author of the opinion declaring a right to assisted suicide in *Compassion in Dying v. State of Washington*, 79 F.3d 790 (9th Cir. 1996), insisted there were no legitimate slippery slope concerns with respect to declaring a right to assisted suicide. He opined that "[b]oth before and after women were found to have a right to have an abortion, critics contended that legalizing that medical procedure would lead to its widespread use as a substitute for other forms of birth control or as a means of racial genocide . . . The slippery slope fears of *Roe's* opponents have, of course, not materialized" (Id. at 830–31). He insisted this despite the facts that there are approximately 1.5 million abortions per year in America since *Roe* and that most of these are for convenience reasons (with well over 90 percent done for reasons other than to preserve the life or health of the mother or because of rape or incest). Judge Reinhardt asserted this even as he was in the very act of fulfilling the predictions he eschewed with his declaration of a right to assisted suicide on the basis of the analysis used in the abortion cases.
2. At the time of this writing, the Ninth and Second Circuit cases finding a right to assisted suicide are both before the United States Supreme Court on requests for the Court to review the decisions. The Ninth Circuit decision was *Compassion in Dying v. State of Washington*, 79 F.3d 790 (9th Cir. 1996). The Second Circuit decision was *Quill v. Vacco*, 80 F.3d 716 (2d Cir. 1996).
3. *Roe v. Wade*, 410 U.S. 113 (1973).
4. *Planned Parenthood of S.E. Pennsylvania v. Casey*, 505 U.S. 833, 112 S. Ct. 2791 (1992).
5. Some of these critiques are discussed in text *infra*.
6. The Ninth Amendment to the Constitution (1791) states: "The enumeration in the Constitution, of certain rights, shall not be construed to deny or disparage others retained by the people." The Tenth Amendment (1791) states: "The powers not delegated to the United States by the Constitution, nor prohibited by it to the States, are reserved to the States respectively, or to the people."
7. *Lochner v. New York*, 198 U.S. 45 (1905).
8. *Ferguson v. Skrupa*, 372 U.S. 726, 729 (1963) (footnotes and citations omitted).
9. Id. at 730.
10. Id. (emphasis added).
11. *Roe*, 410 U.S. at 153.

12. Scholarly criticism included comments by luminaries Epstein and Ely. Richard Epstein commented of the *Roe* Court's effort to distill a right of privacy from its prior decisions that "[i]t is difficult to see how the concept of privacy linked the cases cited by the Court, much less . . . explains the result of the abortion cases" (Richard Epstein, *Substantive Due Process by Any Other Name: The Abortion Cases*, 1973 SUP. CT. REV. 159, 170). John Hart Ely declared: "The Court has offered little assistance to one's understanding of what it is that makes [the privacy 'precedents'] a unit." (John Hart Ely, *Foreword: On Discovering Fundamental Values*, 92 HARV. L. REV. 5 [1978]).

13. *Griswold v. Connecticut*, 381 U.S. 479, 502 (1965) (Harlan, J., concurring).

14. *Roe*, 410 U.S. at 152 (citing *Palko v. Connecticut*, 302 U.S. 319, 325 [1937]).

15. *See Duncan v. Louisiana*, 391 U.S. 145 (1968); *Moore v. City of East Cleveland*, 431 U.S. 494 (1977).

16. The following discussion permits examination of only a few scholarly critiques of *Roe*. *See generally* James Bopp Jr. and Richard E. Coleson, *The Right to Abortion: Anomalous, Absolute, and Ripe for Reversal*, 3 B.Y.U. J. PUB. L. 181 (1989) (cataloging numerous critiques of *Roe* and discussing at length the flaws of abortion jurisprudence).

17. Ely, *The Wages of Crying Wolf*, 82 YALE L.J. at 947 (emphasis in original).

18. Archibald Cox, *The Role of the Supreme Court in American Government*, 113–14 (1976).

19. Alexander Bickel, *The Morality of Consent*, 27–28 (1975).

20. Epstein, *Substantive Due Process by Any Other Name*, 1973 SUP. CT. REV. at 184.

21. Id. at 185.

22. *Casey*, 112 S. Ct. 2791.

23. Id. at 2805.

24. Id. at 2806.

25. Id. at 2807.

26. Id.

27. Cf. *Roe*, 410 U.S. at 163.

28. *Casey*, 112 S. Ct. at 2820 (plurality opinion).

29. *Compassion in Dying v. State of Washington*, 850 F. Supp. 1454, 1459 (W. D. Wash. 1994).

30. Id.

31. Id. at 1460.

32. Id. at 1464–65.

33. *Compassion in Dying v. State of Washington*, 49 F.3d 586 (9th Cir 1995).

34. *Compassion in Dying v. State of Washington*, 79 F.3d 790 (9th Cir. 1996).

35. Id. at 801.

36. Id.

37. *People v. Kevorkian*, 447 Mich. 436, 527 N.W.2d 714 (1994), *cert. denied sub nom. Kevorkian v. Michigan*, 1995 WL 126365 (April 24, 1995).

An Overview

Not all proponents of assisted suicide take an "all or nothing" approach to the issue. Some desire moderation through the creation of legal and objective criteria through which an individual's life can be judged to be of value or of little value. This position is especially relevant and frightening to those with disabilities, who already have the sanctimonious pity of many in the nonhandicapped population. Could the disabled actually become targeted as a group that could "benefit" from legislation favorable to euthanasia? Have they become an economic burden requiring that they see themselves as frontline expendables? Daniel Avila describes the quandaries associated with a moderate assisted-suicide position, the critical concerns of the disabled, and the disparaging disposition of the Ninth Circuit Court.

Chapter Three

BRICK WALLS ON THE SLIPPERY SLOPE

*Reasonable Moderation or Unjust Discrimination
Against Persons with Disabilities?*

Daniel Avila

AUTHORITIES IN SAN FRANCISCO HAVE designed a new program to prevent suicidal individuals from jumping off the Golden Gate Bridge. Persons trained in suicide counseling patrol the bridge's walkways and are prepared to intervene whenever they suspect someone on the bridge is suicidal. As with any other suicide intervention program, the patrols treat all suicides as tragedies to be avoided. The goal is to save every human life.[1]

However, some mental health professionals no longer believe that every suicide should be prevented. One recent poll indicated that 81 percent of psychotherapists supported the concept of "rational" suicide. This prompted two authors to recommend changes in the current professional standards governing suicide intervention. Rather than prevent all suicides, mental health officials would assess whether the potential suicide victim is "psychologically competent" and "has an unremitting hopeless condition." This category would include persons with terminal illnesses, severe pain, debilitating or deteriorating levels of mental or physical health, or a "quality of life no longer acceptable to the [victim]." In such cases, *those desiring death would be abandoned to their destructive impulses while life-affirming care is extended to all other would-be suicides.*[2]

Such a proposal would impact the way the Golden Gate suicide patrols are conducted—and indeed alter the performance of *any* suicide prevention program run by other public authorities, the churches, or community-sponsored crisis lines. Suicide counselors would have to determine whether the person leaning over the water or threatening to swallow an overdose of pills has a terminal condition, is experiencing pain, or has rationally concluded that his or her existence lacks sufficient meaning. If the mental health assessment verifies any of these conditions, then a double standard is imposed by which some are left to die while others are saved.

Very few who believe that suicide can be "rational" would assert, at least publicly, that all suicides are rational. Instead, those urging legal or social reforms in this area refrain from demanding that the status quo be abolished entirely. Striving to appear moderate and attempting to strike a balance between the extremes of all or nothing, they explain that while an across-the-board ban is too restrictive for their tastes, unrestricted suicide is not their aim. They would, in effect, agree to the construction of brick walls on the slippery slope to accommodate both the hard cases and society's general abhorrence of intentional self-killing.

Yet such appeals for moderation almost always divide permissible from impermissible suicides according to the victim's proximity to death and quality of life. Like the suggested change in mental health policy described above, proposals for legal or social reform assume that the desirability of death can and should be measured against the desirability of life by referring to some objectively discerned criteria based on a person's physical and mental condition. No matter how desperate for death suicidal individuals may be and no matter how little they may value their own lives, their requests to die will be approved according to a social, not individual, estimation of the comparative values of their life and death. Consequently, the law and the community would sanction death not because the victim wants it, but because the victim who wants it happens to have a condition that the law and community deem unworthy of protection.

WE'RE NOT DEAD YET!

The calls for "moderate" reform on assisted suicide have not rested easily in the ears of the very persons for whom death is offered as a benefit. Persons with disabilities from across the country have created what they describe as a grassroots resistance group with the provocative name Not Dead Yet. The group endorses policies prohibiting assisted suicide, seeks qualified disability peer counseling for suicidal persons with disabilities, and promotes the inclusion of persons with disabilities on medical ethics committees.

According to one member,

> Many people believe they would rather be dead than be like us. So if one of us becomes depressed and suicidal, most people conclude that our feelings are rational. They don't try to understand or respond to whatever our real problem might be. Nowadays, with the rise of managed care and the popularity of Dr. Kevorkian, we can't afford to get depressed—some doctor might just help us die.[3]

Recent remarks by a prominent and influential medical ethicist validated these fears. Dr. Ronald Cranford was asked by the press to comment on the suicide of Joe Cruzan, known for his involvement in a legal battle to remove his daughter Nancy's feeding tube. Dr. Cranford observed that Mr. Cruzan had experienced severe clinical depression for several years "and he never came out of it." Dr. Cranford informed the press that Mr. Cruzan's death was "a rational suicide" because despite treatment for his depression, "he was never going to get better."[4]

In addition, Jack Kevorkian has reported that, "In my experience, which I think is difficult to match, only about five percent of the requests [for assisted suicide] come from people who are terminally ill. It's the chronically ill who want this service. And they will comprise the vast majority of people who request it."[5]

Rather than viewing the phenomenon of vulnerable persons seeking death as a cause for alarm, Jack Kevorkian and others might claim that it simply verifies the existence of a public demand for assisted suicide among a certain group. If persons facing imminent death or experiencing chronic disability want suicide assistance and are more likely than the rest of us to want it, then they should have it. Who are we to interfere?

During an April 1996 hearing before Congress, Not Dead Yet spokesperson Diane Coleman acknowledged that "[w]ith today's cutbacks in health care and the human safety net, and with growing isolation from the supports our families can no longer easily provide, people's fears of aging, illness, disability, and the dying process are understandably growing." Yet she claimed that "a right to physician-assisted suicide is not the answer." Instead,

> We ask all who care about social injustice to believe us when we state that disability-based discrimination in this culture is deep seated, virtually unconscious, pervasive, and overwhelming. This discrimination against millions of Americans must be acknowledged, understood, and reversed long before we can discuss expanding the ways in which society's unwanted can be killed.[6]

Persons with disabilities fear that by legalizing assisted suicide for the seriously ill society will stigmatize an entire class of persons as having lives unworthy of living. As disability advocate and White House consultant Paul Steven Miller has written,

> With society continually reinforcing its values through discriminatory cultural practices, it becomes difficult for a person with a disability, whether acquired or congenital, not to accept that stigmatized value system. People with disabilities are taught that the reason for their exclusion is their own inferiority. Thus, when people with disabilities make a "choice" to seek their right to die, they do so from the position of a society that fears, discriminates against, and stigmatizes disability as undignified. Facing a life of societal exclusion, prejudice, and fear, in conjunction with self-deprecation and devaluation based on those same irrational assumptions, is there really a choice at all?[7]

Joni Eareckson Tada has described her chilling vision of what society would be like for persons with disabilities if the law permits assisted suicide. According to Ms. Tada, the following trends would result:

> *The character of a helping society is beginning to disintegrate.* Euthanasia is now seen as a cure-all to societal problems such as rising public health-care costs

and limited facility space for elderly and debilitated people. It's easier to kill than cure, or even care. Society is now assigning no positive value to suffering and is becoming more oriented toward a culture of comfort. Discrimination against elderly and disabled people is beginning to run rampant—terms such as "useless victim" and "unfortunates to be pitied" reveal a growing cynicism and bigotry. Before euthanasia became legalized, hospice organizations and handicap associations had difficulty securing funding and volunteer support. Now, with the new law, these agencies are having more trouble than ever.[8]

The concerns raised by persons with disabilities have at times been ridiculed as farfetched or alarmist. For example, the U.S. Court of Appeals in the Ninth Circuit rejected the disability perspective in forceful, and even hostile, terms. In an opinion declaring assisted suicide to be a constitutional right for persons with terminal conditions, the majority of the court characterized the predictions of abuse and discrimination against persons with disabilities as "ludicrous on [their] face" and even "meretricious" (which Webster's defines as "of, pertaining to, characteristic of, or being a prostitute" and "alluring, by false show, gaudily and deceitfully ornamental").[9]

The court's derisive tone was matched only by its demeaning portrayal of the persons granted the right to kill themselves with a physician's assistance. According to the court, a person with a terminal condition "has a strong liberty interest in choosing a dignified and humane death rather than being reduced at the end of his existence to a childlike state of helplessness, diapered, sedated, incontinent." For such persons, "the decision to commit suicide is not senseless, and death does not come too early."[10] Furthermore, the court found that it would be quite reasonable for patients with terminal conditions to "take the economic welfare of their families and loved ones into consideration" and, when faced "with the prospect of astronomical medical bills," it is entirely commendable for them to kill themselves in order to relieve others from the responsibility of providing their care.[11]

Thus the court's substantive rationale for giving persons with terminal conditions the right to kill themselves with another's assistance evidences the very threat of biased policy-making feared by the disability community and dismissed by the court itself as unlikely. The court's ruling prompted Diane Coleman of Not Dead Yet to inform Congress that "the Ninth Circuit Court decision, in effect, recognizes assisted suicide as an acceptable solution to the economic burdens of health care. The so-called right to die has become the duty to die."[12]

WHEN "MODERATION" UNJUSTLY DISCRIMINATES

Discrimination *per se* is neither inherently immoral nor unlawful. One might reasonably believe that adults require less protection in certain matters than children, and draft laws or implement social policies that provide less protection to adults than is afforded to children. Such an approach will undoubtedly treat adults and children unequally but will do so without offending principles of justice. As long as the authorities base their different treatment on some relevant distinction between the two classes, then the resulting "discrimination" is permissible.

For example, we will allow adults to expose themselves to the risks of buying liquor or operating dangerous machinery while at the same time we withhold these privileges from children. Given the close association between one's age and level of maturity, it makes sense to enforce certain protections regarding children but not for adults. Moreover, we will permit life insurance companies to charge higher rates to older persons, persons in dangerous occupations, or persons with certain life-threatening conditions because of the close association between one's level of health, length of years or lifestyle and the resulting likelihood of having to pay out death benefits. Even in situations where the relationship between the reasons for making the distinction and the actual dissimilarities in the populations treated differently is not so close, more leeway will sometimes be appropriate to allow experimentation in social policy to take place.

Those who would limit assisted suicide to persons with terminal or physically painful conditions rarely explain why these classes are selected, even though it is obvious that difficult circumstances and a consequent wish to die can arise regardless of one's proximity to death or level of pain. About the only consistent response given for public consumption is that, well, we have to start somewhere.

For example, after the voters of Oregon approved a measure to decriminalize assisted suicide for persons with terminal conditions, the state attorney general defended the measure in court on the ground that it was the voters' prerogative to extend the "benefit" of legalized killing to some but not to others. Even though other classes of persons might "benefit" from legalized physician-assisted suicide and the lines drawn might be somewhat arbitrary, the voters should be free to take one step at a time in extending this new social experiment.[13]

In other contexts such a minimal defense might suffice, but a life and death matter involving the criminal code calls for a closer examination of why persons with terminal conditions are being singled out. The "moderate" policy at issue here would still punish those who assist in the suicides of members of the general population. Retaining an overall criminal prohibition evinces or demonstrates the belief that suicide is an especially bad thing both for the victim and society, and the prohibition, by threatening criminal punishment, deters those who might otherwise help others to die. When compared against such a norm, an exemption should be based on something more compelling than the bald assertion that assisted suicide itself is a benefit.

Otherwise, the majority could freely discriminate against members of a disfavored minority by granting them legal access to an activity deemed harmful to the majority, based only on the spurious claim that such license merely extends a special benefit. Consequently, voters could approve the use of cocaine just for ghetto residents or allow blacks but not whites to ride motorcycles without helmets. Yet, that some people consider it beneficial to have the freedom to abuse drugs or to ride without helmets should not obscure the underlying issue: Why is it okay for ghetto residents but not suburbanites to get high, or for blacks but not whites to risk head injury on the road? In the context of assisted suicide, why is it beneficial for persons with terminal or physically painful conditions but no one else to obtain lethal medications?

The question calls for a more compelling response because one can easily infer from the circumstances an invidious motive. A policy that permits lethal assistance for some but not for the majority implicates the view that those provided the lethal assistance are less worthy or deserving of protection and that their lives have less value under the law. While such a policy is ostensibly autonomy-based, it would fundamentally alter our country's commitment to equal protection.

As one commentator has written,

> [Our society's] liberal commitment to limited popular government requires a commitment to the equal worth of each person and to limits on the power of government that are contained in the teaching of inalienable rights, especially an inalienable right to life. This teaching forms the essential horizon of liberal theory and it is only within this horizon that liberal regimes and the policies they endorse can take shape. . . . Given the liberal commitment to equality as the precondition of liberty, the "new consensus" [proposing that certain suicides be sanctioned based on the assumption that some lives are less valuable than others] fails completely in its policy recommendations. The policies these writers wish to see adopted logically entail the creation of a public standard for determining when some lives are in fact not worth living anymore. However, this is a judgment that is fundamentally inconsistent with the premises of the very regime that is supposed to adopt this policy.[14]

For this reason, *the law should not abandon whole categories of individuals to their suicidal urges under the solicitous guise of protecting individual rights*. Instead, as concluded by the British Medical Association,

> the deliberate taking of a human life should remain a crime. This rejection of a change in the law to permit doctors to intervene to end a person's life is not just a subordination of individual well-being to social policy. It is instead, an affirmation of the supreme value of the individual, no matter how worthless and hopeless that individual may feel.[15]

In their bid to seize the middle ground between the summit and foothills of the slippery slope, proponents of "moderate" reform on assisted suicide would substitute one negative social consequence for another. To save society from the chaos of unrestrained autonomy that most assuredly would result from suicide on demand, they propose a limited right. They present their blueprints for constructing a long and winding wall around the mountain of shifting social policy, but such a wall could only be built with the bricks of prejudice and the mortar of bias. No longer would all lives be equally deserving of protection. In the end, the appearance of moderation would be purchased at too steep a price.

ENDNOTES

1. Carey Goldberg, "Golden Gate Bridge to Start Patrols to Prevent Suicides," *New York Times*, 25 Feb. 1996, Midwest edition, 10.
2. James L. Werth, Jr. and Debra C. Cobia, "Empirically Based Criteria for Rational Suicide: A Survey of Psychotherapists," *Suicide and Life-Threatening Behavior* 25 (Summer 1995): 231, 238.
3. Diane Coleman, "Not Dead Yet: The Resistance Meets Success," *Mouth* (Sept. 1996): 37.
4. Diane Gianelli, "Major Figure in Right-to-Die Debate Dies," *American Medical News*, 2 Sept. 1996, 8.
5. Jack Kevorkian, television interview on *Good Morning America*, 22 July 1992 (transcript on file with National Legal Center for the Medically Dependent & Disabled, Inc.).
6. Diane Coleman, oral testimony during hearing on "Assisted Suicide in the United States" before U.S. House of Representatives, Subcommittee on the Constitution, Committee on the Judiciary, 29 Apr. 1996 (unpublished transcript on file with National Legal Center for the Medically Dependent & Disabled, Inc.).
7. Paul Steven Miller, "The Impact of Assisted Suicide on Persons with Disabilities—Is It a Right Without Freedom?" *Issues in Law & Medicine* 9 (summer 1993): 54.
8. Joni Eareckson Tada, *When Is It Right to Die?: Suicide, Euthanasia, Suffering, Mercy* (Grand Rapids: Zondervan, 1992), 77.
9. *Compassion in Dying v. Washington*, 79 F.3d 790, 825 (9th Cir. 1996).
10. Ibid., 821.
11. Ibid., 826.
12. Coleman, congressional testimony.
13. Stephen K. Bushong and Thomas A. Balmer, "Breathing Life Into the Right to Die: Oregon's Death with Dignity Act," *Issues in Law and Medicine* 11 (winter 1995): 281–82.
14. Richard Sherlock, "Suicide and Public Policy: A Critique of the 'New Consensus,'" *Journal of Bioethics* 4 (1982–83): 62.
15. British Medical Association, *Euthanasia: Report of the Working Party to Review the British Medical Association's Guidance on Euthanasia* (1988): 69.

An Overview

The ethical dilemmas surrounding euthanasia and assisted suicide are not ethereal arguments, but questions faced daily in hospital rooms across our nation. For well-intentioned medical professionals, family members, and patients, the issues are very real. Through several illustrations, Robert Orr helps us understand the issues, definitions, and concerns faced by all of those involved in the decision-making process. Yet he compassionately argues that there are moral and ethical boundaries that we must not cross. The issue is not compassion or the lack of it, but rather the realization that pain, suffering, and the course of individual lives also have a spiritual dimension. We must not neglect spiritual treatment. We cannot take life; we can, however, offer hope, compassion, eternal life.

Chapter Four

THE PHYSICIAN-ASSISTED SUICIDE

Is It Ever Justified?

Robert D. Orr, M.D.

JENNIE WAS ONLY FORTY-EIGHT when she found the breast lump. The surgeon had been hopeful, but the pathology report showed the cancer was very aggressive and had already spread to the lymph nodes. Radiation and chemotherapy were completed; everyone wished for the best, hoping and waiting.

Sadly, the wait wasn't long. In only a few months, Jennie developed back pain. The cause: spread of the breast cancer to her spine. The disease seemed to gallop through her bones, liver, and lungs. She lost weight very rapidly, became depressed, and required large doses of morphine. The medication only partially relieved her severe pain. Any movement was excruciating.

It had been several weeks since she had smiled, desired food, or even enjoyed the brief visits of her loving children. Eventually her husband, Sam, asked, "Doctor, it's probably wrong to ask you this, but could you possibly give Jennie one large injection of morphine so that she won't suffer anymore? She's been in so much pain for so long. She just wants to get it over with."

Everyone was suffering: Jennie, Sam, the children, the nurses—yes, even the doctor suffered from his inability to control the patient's pain. All involved were ready for Jennie to die.

UNDERSTANDING THE ISSUE: TERMINOLOGY

Clear thinking, or meaningful dialogue, about any issue is only possible if the meanings of the terms under debate are agreed upon in advance. In relation to euthanasia and assisted suicide, several words require definition:

Homicide is the killing of one human being by another. It is a morally neutral generic term. Homicide may be deemed *justifiable* (by some) in cases of self-defense, capital punishment, or war. It is *accidental* if done without intention; *murder* if done with premeditation and malice, or *manslaughter* if done without express or implied malice.

Suicide is the voluntary and intentional killing of oneself. In some cultures, suicide has been morally acceptable or even honorable. Many early Greek and Roman philosophers felt that suicide was an honorable death (notable exceptions were Hippocrates, Plato, and Aristotle). The Hindu practice of *suttee* (where a widow would throw herself upon her deceased husband's funeral pyre), the Japanese act of *hari-kari*, and the Inuit practice of "going out on the ice" (where older individuals would voluntarily freeze to death when they felt they were a burden to their families) were also considered to be deaths with honor.

Our Western societal attitude condemning suicide has Judeo-Christian theological roots. In Judaism, killing oneself has traditionally been viewed as an abhorrent sin except when deemed necessary to glorify God. This narrow limitation would never justify self-interested suicide or voluntary euthanasia. This Jewish proscription against suicide has been carried over into both Christian and Islamic thought.

Although there is no specific scriptural admonition against suicide, most biblical scholars believe it is proscribed by the commandment against murder (Ex. 20:13). Christian tradition has taught that suicide is wrong because it is an arrogant and improper assertion of human will that violates the intention of a sovereign God. Augustine taught that suicide was even worse than murder because there is no chance for repentance. Thomas Aquinas judged suicide to be a failure in one's duty to oneself, to society, and to God.[1]

Western secular society accepted this negative attitude toward suicide. This began in canon law, evolved into common law, and eventually into statutory law. In generations past, a person who committed suicide was "punished" by being denied a religious burial, by being buried in isolation outside the city, or even by having a stake driven through the heart. In recent decades, laws against suicide have been revoked, but most jurisdictions retain laws that forbid assistance with suicide.

Modern philosophers have developed the concept of rational suicide, usually pertaining to someone who is terminally ill and suffering. In their view it is understandable and forgivable to voluntarily and actively end one's life to avoid further suffering. A parallel concept is altruistic suicide where a person takes his or her own life in order to avoid grave harm to others, including financial or emotional burden, or even the inconvenience of providing long-term care. The moral disapproval that once characterized Western society's view of suicide is gradually being eroded, and many medical professionals are beginning to accept this secular philosophy.

Assisted suicide is when one individual helps another take his or her own life because the latter lacks the knowledge, courage, or physical capacity to achieve the desired end.

Physician-assisted suicide occurs when a physician has provided information, prescriptions, or a "suicide machine," knowing that the patient's intention is suicide.

Euthanasia means "good death" (or an easy death). Classically, it refers to mercy killing—one person, motivated by compassion, intentionally and actively killing another in order to end that person's suffering. Most examples of mercy killing occur in the context of terminal disease (e.g., a husband gives an overdose of sleeping pills to his wife who is suffering the excruciating pain of bone cancer). Euthanasia is practiced by veterinarians, e.g., by giving a lethal injection to a severely injured or sick dog to "put it out of its misery." This is what Sam had in mind in his request to end Jennie's suffering: a deliberate act to bring about her rapid death. And this act of medical killing is what is meant throughout this chapter by the term euthanasia. *Voluntary euthanasia* means intentionally killing another person at his or her request, usually because of the latter's suffering. *Involuntary euthanasia* occurs when a competent person is deliberately and actively killed, without his or her request or consent, usually because another party has decided that this person's life is too burdensome. *Nonvoluntary euthanasia* occurs when it is applied to an incompetent patient.

Two other terms—*active* and *passive euthanasia*—are sometimes used, but the distinction they strive for is confusing and best avoided. *Active* euthanasia is defined as causing death directly by a deliberately fatal act, usually by lethal injection. But this is just another way to describe euthanasia. This redundant phrase's only function is, therefore, to act as an antithesis for its likewise unnecessary semantic cousin, *passive* euthanasia.

Passive euthanasia is commonly used to describe situations where life-sustaining treatments are withheld or withdrawn from a terminally ill patient, with the expectation that this omission will allow the person to die naturally. Use of the term suggests that forgoing treatment that might be burdensome or serve no therapeutic purpose except to prolong a person's dying is a form of mercy killing (euthanasia). But in such cases it is not an act or omission that causes the patient's death *but the underlying disease process*. We would say that withdrawing or withholding treatment or artificial means of life support from someone who is dying is not euthanasia at all—not even *passive* euthanasia—but acceptable, humane, and an often appropriate part of everyday medical practice. It is not euthanasia nor is it suicide for a terminally ill but competent patient to decline life-prolonging treatment that will only extend his or her period of suffering. Thus, *passive* euthanasia is not a necessary or helpful term.

PLAYING GOD?

The ethical dilemmas raised by euthanasia are complex. As technology provides more and more ways of prolonging life and as our society moves away from a Judeo-Christian value system, including its redemptive view of suffering, people are increasingly asking their physicians to end their lives. As the value of human life and the impact of a sovereign, loving, and all-wise God diminishes in importance, other rules such as autonomy and social justice become more powerful.

The ethical principle of self-determination (autonomy), it is claimed, affirms your "right to die" with dignity. However, there is no "right to die;" there is a clearly delineated legal right to refuse treatment, even if that refusal will lead to death. But there is no legal right to be made dead.[2]

Social justice (the greatest good for the greatest number) may further transform your "right to die" into a "duty to die" (if you're exhausting family or state resources). If it is your duty to die, is it then my duty as a physician (or family member) to help you fulfill your duty to die? It may even seem immoral of me to refuse. If one calls evil good long enough, good will seem to become evil.

Even sincere Christians, committed to the biblical truth that life is sacred and of inestimable value because man is made in God's image and He is sovereign, may find themselves requesting euthanasia when someone they love is dying and in great pain.

Sam (who loves God) requested that Jennie's life (he also loves Jennie) be ended by immediate overdose, which would be an illegal and immoral case of "active" euthanasia. But what if the physician, in administering enough narcotic to relieve the pain, should incidentally hasten her death through depressed respiration? Is this "double-effect euthanasia" more acceptable? The principle of double effect states that if there is an action that can produce both a good effect and a bad side effect, it is morally acceptable to perform the act as long as the intention is to produce the good effect. The bad side effect is then accepted as unavoidable, but unintended. This principle has been accepted by most philosophers and theologians for hundreds of years.

If you were Jennie, what would you want? Can it be the will of a loving God that His own children suffer terribly when there is medicine that would hasten death?

When ninety-five year old Mrs. Miller was admitted to the hospital suffering from a variety of illnesses and complications, her family requested "no heroics." The family was agreeable to providing normal sustenance (food and water) but was against providing other treatments that would only prolong her dying. Could a loving family allow Mrs. Miller to die without intensive care? On what basis would the medical team cooperate with the family's wishes? Would withholding life-sustaining treatments be more justified if Mrs. Miller herself requested it? Is it playing God to withhold the treatment, or is it playing God to give such treatment to a patient who may be dying a natural death?

TO KILL OR TO LET DIE?

Modern technology has developed remarkable means to prolong our living—and our dying. There is almost always something more that could be done. Someone has to decide when enough has already been done, when it is time to let the patient die. In recent years, many of these decisions have fallen to the courts, with one ruling amplifying another as the legal system has tried to grapple with these relatively new life-and-death decisions.

For example, in the case of *Rudolpho Torres*, the Minnesota Supreme Court ruled that the respirator sustaining his life could be disconnected because, as one writer put it, "Mr. Torres may well have wished to avoid . . . the ultimate horror not of death but the possibility of being maintained in limbo, in a sterile room, by machines controlled by strangers."[3]

Increasingly, the courts have allowed the withdrawal or withholding of life-sustaining treatments (including artificially administered nutrition and hydration) in cases broader than those where patients are terminally ill or in unrelenting pain. Although the trend is toward a broader interpretation of the right to refuse treatment, there is still a sharp division of legal, ethical, and medical opinion on the issue.

For committed Christians, what in theory may seem rather black and white can become rather gray in practice. When eighty-six year old Grandma Davis developed breast cancer, the family and doctor decided against aggressive chemotherapy. They favored less stressful hormonal treatment, knowing that while chemotherapy might prolong her life, it could also make her life miserable because of severe side effects, she might not understand the reason for the treatment, and she would be subjected to numerous injections, infusions, and blood draws. Less aggressive treatment would mean a shorter, but more peaceful life. As Grandma's death grew near, the doctor and family decided not to feed her artificially or treat her pneumonia with antibiotics or a ventilator. She died quietly at home a few hours after receiving a dose of pain medication, and she appeared to be comfortable and pain-free at the very end.

Grandma Davis' death was a "good death" if any death can be called good. It was certainly a better death than many others have experienced from cancer. But was it euthanasia? Were the decisions that were made good decisions? Because Grandma could not make her own decisions, the family had to make them for her. They chose not to aggressively treat her disease, for they didn't wish to delay the inevitable. In the end, they chose not to force-feed her, because they viewed the extension of her life a few more hours or days as inappropriate. Her physician agreed.

So Grandma Davis' death was not a case of euthanasia. Yes, there was that injection, given just hours before her death, to ease her struggle to breathe. But in euthanasia there is rapid and intentional death, and the time of death is determined by the choice of an intruder rather than by natural causes.

Grandma Davis was not killed; she died. This is an important point, because some philosophers argue that there is no difference between active and passive euthanasia.[4] This sort of confusion muddles the real issues of medical killing. The result is that euthanasia, which is evil, can be classified as acceptable if it is allowed to be redefined by qualifying the term as *passive*. Such designation is incorrect. Allowing Grandma Davis to die as she did is morally acceptable. The decision to forego life-sustaining treatment is not *passive euthanasia*. Euthanasia as classically understood is an active process of mercy killing. *Passive euthanasia* is a deceptive term used by proponents of physician-assisted death to suggest that there is little difference between euthanasia and decisions to forego life-sustaining treatment. If a term like *passive euthanasia* is acceptable today, it becomes much easier to accept the practice of *active euthanasia* tomorrow.

It is critical that we make a clear distinction between physician-assisted suicide and euthanasia on the one hand, and the practice of deciding to forego life-sustaining treatment on the other. In the former, the intention is death; in the latter, the intention is to stop postponing inevitable death. In the former, there is an attitude of control, or even arrogance; in the latter, an attitude of humility. In the former, the means of death is killing; in the latter, the means of death is withholding or withdrawing treatment. In the former, the agent of death is the physician; in the latter, the agent of death is the disease. Granted, both of these practices may lead to death, but the end does not justify the means.

THE MODERN EUTHANASIA MOVEMENT

Euthanasia in the Netherlands

Since proponents of euthanasia and physician-assisted suicide often point to the success of these activities in the Netherlands, let us look for a moment at the current practice in that country.[5] Voluntary euthanasia has been professionally practiced and societally accepted in the Netherlands for about ten years. Although killing and assisted suicide are still illegal in that country, physicians are immune from prosecution if they follow the 1984 guidelines proposed by the Royal Dutch Medical Association. All acts of euthanasia are supposed to be reported as such on the death certificate. All reported cases of euthanasia are then investigated by the police and the district attorney to see if the physician followed the professional guidelines. If he or she did follow those guidelines, the investigation stops and there is no prosecution. If the guidelines were not followed, the physician is charged with the illegal act and tried in court. The Royal Dutch Medical Association guidelines for mercy killing are as follows: (1) there is voluntary, competent, and durable request on the part of the patient; (2) the request is based on full information; (3) the patient is in a situation of intolerable and hopeless suffering (either physical or mental); (4) there are no acceptable alternatives to euthanasia; and (5) the physician has consulted another physician before performing euthanasia.[6]

In order to avoid these investigations and the possibility of prosecution, many physicians who have performed euthanasia, have reported the deaths as being of natural causes. In order to determine the actual frequency of euthanasia, the Dutch government appointed the Remmelink Commission in 1990 to study medical decisions concerning the end of life. Their thorough study was reported in the *Lancet* in September 1991.[7] Their methods included detailed interviews with 405 physicians, questionnaires mailed to physicians of 7,000 deceased persons, and the collecting of information about 2,250 deaths by a prospective survey. The results are sobering. They estimate that 1.8 percent of all deaths in the Netherlands are caused by euthanasia and 0.3 percent are a result of physician-assisted suicide, accounting for about 2,700 deaths in 1990. However, there were two other very disturbing features of the report. They found that 0.8 percent of all deaths in the Netherlands, over 1,000 deaths in 1990, were the result of what they called "life terminating acts without explicit and persistent requests." This is involuntary euthanasia; lethal injection of patients who were felt to be suffering, but who had not requested that their physician kill them. This is still clearly against the law and the accepted practice. This means that one death in every 30 in the country was induced by physicians, and greater than one quarter of those were involuntary. In addition to that, the report contains the unbelievable statistic that 17.5 percent of all deaths in the country are the result of large doses of medication used to alleviate pain and suffering. Well-trained hospice physicians will tell you that only rarely is it necessary to use a dose of narcotics so large that death is hastened even by minutes or hours. But the Dutch report that 17.5 percent of all deaths are a result of this! This indicates that either they are not being intellectually honest about their practices, or the slippery slope is really alive and well so that once euthanasia and physician-assisted suicide are accepted, it will be expanded quickly into other marginal areas.

Euthanasia in the United States

There has been a resurgence of interest in the legalization of euthanasia in this country for about ten years, spearheaded by the Hemlock Society and other "right to die" organizations. Voter initiatives to legalize physician-assisted death were attempted unsuccessfully in California (1988, 1992) and in Washington (1991). Such an initiative (Measure 16) was passed by a narrow margin of the voters in Oregon in 1994, but legal injunctions prevented its usage until October 27, 1997 when Measure 51 was introduced in an attempt to repeal Measure 16. Voters rejected Measure 51 by a 20 percent margin, thus reaffirming Measure 16. Oregon law now allows doctores to prescribe lethal drugs to terminally ill patients. Although death by lethal injection is banned by Measure 16, legislators have already begun talking about it as being a more humane method of termination (Gail Kinsey Hill, *This Week from the Oregonian*, November 6, 1997, on the internet). Supporters say that sufficient safeguards have been built into the legislation to prevent abuse, but opponents disagree. When the Oregon law will go into effect has not been determined at the time of this writing. Several other state legislatures are considering bills with a similar intent.

In addition to these legislative attempts, there have been successful legal challenges to the existing laws that forbid physician-assisted death in Washington, New York, and California. Two of these have been successfully appealed to Federal Courts of Appeals in the Ninth District (covering Washington and eight other western states) and Second District (covering New York and several northeastern states). It is anticipated that the United States Supreme Court will agree to hear final appeals.

ARGUMENTS PRO AND CON

A growing number of secular writers on the topic do not appeal to the rightness or wrongness of euthanasia but state that it should not be legalized because of the bad consequences of such a change in our society. Such bad consequences are (1) *abuse:* once it is considered right to end someone's life on request, it will be much easier to presume a "request" from others (the demented, comatose, etc.); (2) *error:* the inherent uncertainties in medicine will cause some to die unnecessarily; (3) *slippery slope:* once society accepts voluntary euthanasia, it can be predicted that very quickly allowance will have to be made for those who are unable to speak for themselves; (4) *distrust*: if the patient knows his doctor is allowed to kill him, there will be an erosion of the traditional trust between patient and doctor—the sick will become apprehensive, uncertain of what their doctor may do to them; and (5) *coercion*: elderly, handicapped, and dying people may feel subtly or directly encouraged to request their legal option of euthanasia.

Regardless of all the safeguards that could be built into legislation *for euthanasia*, it would be impossible to prevent its expansion from the proposed voluntary request of terminally ill patients. It could easily lead to coerced voluntary euthanasia where families pressure patients into requesting euthanasia for either good or bad motives. In addition, with our legal and judicial history in this country of allowing family members to make proxy medical decisions to withdraw life-sustaining treatment from incompetent patients, it would be virtually impossible to prevent a successful court challenge in which a family member could say, "I am sure that my father would want a lethal injection at this point in his life if he were able to talk to us." And it could easily expand to allowing requests from people who are suffering but are not terminally ill.

Derek Humphry, author of *Final Exit*,[8] a "self-help" volume on how to take your own life, freely admits that he believes we should be drafting legislation to permit such expanded practices, but he sees it to be politically expedient to first seek only legalization of voluntary measures.[9] It is not difficult to envision expansion within a short time to discriminatory involuntary euthanasia where incompetent patients who are a drain on the public purse would be euthanized to save money for society. Legalization of these measures would be bad public policy. These consequential arguments against euthanasia may be sufficiently convincing for some, but they cannot answer the basic question, "Is euthanasia wrong?"

Those who support euthanasia and physician-assisted death argue that competent patients who are terminally ill should have access to euthanasia or physician-assisted suicide. They claim at least three arguments for why these activities should be legalized. The first is autonomy, a person's right to self-determination; "I am the master of my destiny." However, if autonomy is overriding, why shouldn't we honor requests for assisted death from anyone whether they are terminally ill or not? Their second argument is compassion. If we really care for patients who are suffering and want to help them out of their suffering, we should be willing to take these drastic steps. "We shoot horses, don't we?" However, if compassion is over-riding, shouldn't we meet the needs of anyone who is suffering, whether they are competent and able to request it or not? And the third argument in favor is a pragmatic one: "It works in the Netherlands." However, the data presented above suggests that it is not working as envisioned; nearly one third of those euthanasized did not request this "service." The over-arching supportive reasoning is the utilitarian argument that the end justifies the means; if we have good motives and achieve good results, it doesn't matter what we do to get there.

There are at least two strong, and I think persuasive, arguments in opposition to euthanasia and physician-assisted suicide. The first argument in opposition is that of professional virtue. Killing patients has been outside the bounds of medical care for hundreds of years. When the Hippocratic Oath first proscribed these practices, anti-euthanasia was a position held only by a minority of physicians. However, it gradually became the accepted medical professional standard—a long-standing, absolute prohibition of physicians' taking their patients' lives or helping them take their own lives. If the current generation of medical professionals makes this a possibility, it would change the very character of the practice of medicine. The physician would no longer be purely a healer but would be an executioner as well. This would seriously undermine the doctor-patient relationship and the trust that is so necessary to that relationship. In addition, I believe it would also detract from our current efforts in palliative care. Although we are far from perfect, we are now doing a much better job with pain control and other aspects of hospice care than we did twenty years ago. If patients and doctors had the easy option of euthanasia, there would be less impetus to further improve end-of-life care. For these two reasons, bad consequences and professional virtue, the American Medical Association,[10] the American Geriatrics Society,[11] the British Medical Association,[12] the Christian Medical and Dental Society,[13] many other medical professional organizations, and a large majority of physicians strongly oppose the legalization of euthanasia and/or physician-assisted suicide.

The second, and I think the strongest argument, against legalization of these two entities is the theological argument based on the sovereignty of God and the sanctity of human life.[14] God has created humankind in his own image. We are special. We are different from animals. We are not totally autonomous, but accountable to a sovereign God who has said, "Thou shall not kill" and has also shown us the compassion of the Good Samaritan.[15] We must treat each other with the reverence and respect befitting vessels containing the image of God.

By saying that human life is sacred, I don't mean that human biological life is the supreme good. The supreme good is eternal, spiritual life with God, and that should be our primary goal. But because we are special, because our lives are sacred, because we have been placed on this earth and have been given stewardship over our lives, we must respect those lives and not snuff them out.

Another theological concept that bears on these issues but is even less popular in the secular realm, is the role of suffering in human endeavors. Many Christian writers have addressed the problem of pain and have pointed out that God may have a purpose for allowing suffering, even when that purpose is not evident.[16] He is still sovereign. But I still don't like pain. Nobody likes pain. Nobody likes to suffer. But Scripture teaches us that there may sometimes be a role for suffering in our lives. That does not mean that medical professionals should not try their best to alleviate human suffering; that is part of the calling. But it does mean that we must humbly recognize the finiteness of our human capabilities, and our reliance upon a loving and merciful God.[17]

BEYOND THE PAIN TO MEANING

People who support suicide and/or euthanasia appeal to compassion for the dying and a person's right to final self-determination. However, most terminally ill people do not choose suicide; if they do, it is out of desperation and despair. They take their own lives because they can no longer tolerate the physical or emotional suffering they are experiencing. "I am in too much pain. I am no use to anyone. I cannot live this way." Like Jennie, they just want to die. In their pain, suicide and euthanasia victims ignore an even more basic question: Is there any meaning or purpose to suffering? Is there really any alternative to pain and suffering? Viktor Frankl, Austrian psychiatrist imprisoned in Auschwitz for three years, says, "Suffering ceases to be suffering in some way at the moment it finds meaning."[18] Nietzsche said, "He who has a *why* to live can bear almost any *how*."[19]

Dr. Paul Brand, noted Christian surgeon, believes there is a purpose for physical pain in our material world. He found that his leprosy patients were injuring themselves because they lacked pain sensation in their hands and feet. He tried to develop an artificial pain system for his patients, but his attempts were unsuccessful because the patients always turned off or ignored the artificial pain system. They didn't understand their need for pain. He concluded that pain sensation is a marvel, a bioengineering masterpiece of warning and protection. Even if we don't want it, pain is necessary.[20]

But suffering is more than just physical pain. Suffering includes emotional pain (grief), social pain (loneliness), financial pain (poverty), and spiritual pain (guilt). A person may choose suicide or request euthanasia for any one or a combination of these components of "total pain."

We do not mean to glorify suffering. On the contrary, according to the biblical worldview, painful toil (for Adam) and increased pains in childbearing (for Eve) are a part of the curse that God imposed on human beings in the material world as a result of rebellion (Gen. 3:16–17). These painful experiences were in addition to the more basic spiritual pain of a fractured relationship with the Creator.

Christians can believe and rejoice that in the kingdom, "There will be no more death or mourning or crying or pain, for the old order of things has passed away" (Rev. 21:4). But we are still inhabitants of this fallen world— the "old order of things." If God promised us a pain-free existence on earth as a reward for following Him, people would choose to be "believers" for the wrong reason. He wants us to choose Him freely, not for what we can get out of Him. And we can't get out of pain anyway. It happens.

But what is the purpose of a specific pain in a specific person at a specific time? Is there a purpose, or is God just impulsive? Sometimes pain is corrective. God uses it to get our attention and make us realize we are walking our own path instead of His way: "But you have planted wickedness, you have reaped evil, you have eaten the fruit of deception. Because you have depended on your own strength . . ."(Hos. 10:13). Other times, pain is meant to help us grow and develop: "And the God of all grace, who called you to his eternal glory in Christ, after you have suffered a little while, will himself restore you and make you strong, firm and steadfast" (1 Peter 5:10). God sometimes allows suffering for His glorification. The disciples asked Jesus if it was the sin of the blind man or that of his parents that was the cause of his affliction. Jesus responded, "Neither this man nor his parents sinned . . . but this happened so that the work of God might be displayed in his life" (John 9:3).

Man's correction, man's development, or God's glorification. One, two, three purposes for pain; sounds nice and pat. But we know that other reasons are often hidden from us. Consider Jennie, the forty-eight-year-old woman dying of breast cancer in the prime of her life. Why? We know that the answer isn't always straightforward. We are not always able to see the big picture. We are reminded in Deuteronomy 29:29, "The secret things belong to the LORD our God, but the things revealed belong to us."

In the past, pain was accepted as a part of life; not glorified, but accepted. Today's attitude is more frequently that all pain must be stopped and eliminated. When someone is suffering and sees no meaning or purpose, and no hope for improvement, despair is the result. This can be the path to suicide attempts or requests for euthanasia.

A RESPONSE

What should be our response to someone who pleads, "I can't stand the suffering! Kill me or help me kill myself"? There are two valid responses, and both should be made available. One response is a h*ospice* answer: "I can't kill you, but I can still help you. Because I won't kill you, I have a great moral responsibility to ease your suffering. Let me treat your pain (medically) as effectively as I can; let me hold your hand; let me help you address your emotional, financial, and spiritual needs. Let me be your friend so that when you die you will not die alone." Hospice has demonstrated that physicians should be better educated about pain management and better equipped to treat pain effectively. More than 95 percent of cancer patients can be kept virtually pain free if they are given adequate doses of pain medication at appropriate intervals.

The other response is to try to help the person *gain insight into his or her suffering*, to find some meaning in the plight, to help the sufferer see that there is a sovereign, loving God who has allowed this situation for His purpose, a purpose that we may or may not be able to discern. This response involves letting God's love shine through us. Second Corinthians 1:4 reveals that He is our example: "The God of all comfort, who comforts us in all our troubles, so that we can comfort those in any trouble with the comfort we ourselves have received from God."

Above all, we can offer hope—the hope that pain is temporary, that glory is forever, that heaven is free of suffering and tears. And we can be with those who suffer, pray with them, and love them.

ENDNOTES

1. Robert D. Orr, "Suicide," *Decision*, July 1996, 31–35.
2. Joni Eareckson Tada, "A Right to Die?" *Christian Medical & Dental Society Journal*, 23 (1992) 4:20–24.
3. Beth Spring and Ed Larson, *Euthanasia* (Portland, Ore.: Multnomah Press, 1988), 137–38.
4. See James Rachels, *The End of Life: Euthanasia and Morality* (New York: Oxford University Press, 1986).
5. H. Jochemsen, "The Netherlands Experiment," in *Dignity and Dying: A Christian Appraisal*, ed. John F. Kilner, Arlene B. Miller, and Edmund D. Pellegrino (Grand Rapids: Eerdmans, 1996), 165–79.
6. R. L. Schwartz, "Euthanasia and Assisted Suicide in the Netherlands," *Cambridge Quarterly of Healthcare Ethics* 4 (1995): 111–21.
7. P. J. van der Mass, J. J. M. van Delden, L. Pijnenborg, C. W. N. Looman, "Euthanasia and Other Medical Decisions Concerning the End of Life," *Lancet* 338 (1991): 669–74.
8. Derek Humphry, *Final Exit* (New York: Dell, 1992).
9. Derek Humphry, "Limitations of Care; Limitations of Freedom," public presentation in Santa Ana, Calif., October 1991.
10. American Medical Association, "Euthanasia, Report 12, 1988," in *Reports of the Council on Ethical and Judicial Affairs* (Chicago: AMA, 1989).
11. American Geriatrics Society Public Policy Committee, "Voluntary Active-Euthanasia" (Position Statement), *Journal of the American Geriatrics Society*, 39 vols. (1991) 8:826.
12. British Medical Association, *Euthanasia: Report of the Working Party on Euthanasia*, (London: BMA, 1988), 80.
13. Christian Medical & Dental Society, "Euthanasia," in *Opinions on Ethical/Social Issues*, (Richardson, Tex.: Christian Medical & Dental Society, 1991), 17. See also Robert D. Orr, "Physician-Assisted Death," *New Issues in Medical Ethics* (Bristol, Tenn.: Christian Medical & Dental Society, 1995), 181–88.
14. See for example, Robert N. Wennberg, *Terminal Choices: Euthanasia, Suicide, and the Right to Die* (Grand Rapids: Eerdmans, 1989); Nigel M. de S. Cameron, "Theological Perspectives on Euthanasia," *Death Without Dignity* (Edinburgh, Scotland: Rutherford House Books, 1990), 37–46; and Edmund D. Pellegrino, "Euthanasia and Assisted Suicide," in *Dignity and Dying: A Christian Appraisal*, 105–19.
15. "The Good Samaritan and the Euthanasia Debate" in this volume.
16. C. S. Lewis, *The Problem of Pain* (New York: Macmillan, 1962).
17. E. Schaeffer, *Affliction* (Toronto: Welch, 1973); Philip Yancey, *Where Is God When It Hurts?* (Colorado Springs: NavPress, 1989); David B. Biebel, *If God Is So Good, Why Do I Hurt So Bad?* (Colorado Springs: NavPress, 1989); G. E. Pence, "Do Not Go So Slowly into That Dark Night: Mercy-Killing in Holland," *American Journal of Medicine*, 84 (1988) 1:139–41.
18. Viktor Frankl, *Man's Search for Meaning* (New York: Pocket Books, 1963), 179.
19. Ibid., 164.
20. See Philip Yancey's, *Where Is God When It Hurts?* (Grand Rapids: Zondervan, 1992).

An Overview

Pain, which through most of our lives functions as a friend in the sense of warning us that a physical problem may exist, can become the focal point of our greatest fear and the literal sting before death when age and terminal illness overcome us. In seeking to ease the pain that is so often a part of the process of dying, it is incumbent upon humanity to devote itself to the application and advancement of pain management techniques rather than shifting medicine's focus to alleviating pain through assisted suicide and euthanasia. Dr. Matthew Conolly provides needed insight into this critical concern for medicine as a profession through a discussion of the numerous drugs and surgical procedures presently available for the management of cancer pain, thus providing hope for many. The end of human life should come naturally; the role of medicine is to attack the pain rather than the sufferer.

Chapter Five

THE MANAGEMENT
OF CANCER PAIN

Matthew E. Conolly, M.D.

"Pain is a more terrible lord of mankind than even death itself."
—Albert Schweitzer

THE IMPACT OF INCURABLE MALIGNANCY

Once the diagnosis of incurability has been assimilated, most patients are plunged into an existential crisis. Awareness of their approaching death compels them to redefine life in stark and unacceptable terms, and the prospect of dying in unrelieved pain becomes a dominant concern. Too often, that fear becomes a reality, as many physicians offer woefully inadequate responses to the suffering over which they preside, ignoring the fact that pain is a complex issue with mental, social, and spiritual components as well as a physical one. If we ignore these other components, then no matter what we do about merely physical pain, the patient's suffering will not be relieved. Additionally, the sheer indignity of terminal illness, with loss of independence, mobility, and even continence, may reduce quality of life to wretched levels. The growth of the Hemlock Society, the emergence of Dr. Kevorkian, and repeated attempts to legalize euthanasia by means of ballot initiatives represent not only a desire to escape from pain, but also represent an attempt to exercise self-determination, choosing to die rather than continue enduring the "slings and arrows of outrageous fortune."

From a detached and theoretical Judeo-Christian position, we may believe that life has been entrusted to us by God and that we are not entitled to end it by suicide. We may be well aware of the potentially disastrous effects euthanasia might have on weaker members of society were it to be legalized, but it can be hard to sustain that posture at the bedside if such a patient really wants to die. We must approach such patients with deep humility, for we have not walked where they now tread. What we can do, what we *must* do, is to offer them all that we can to alleviate their sufferings and, having done all this, stand by their side, affirming their abiding worth as persons. In that way, we may, without words, present our best argument against euthanasia. With that in mind, this chapter on pain management is written.

THE PREVALENCE OF PAIN

Although about one-third of patients dying of cancer may have no pain, Bonica estimates that more than one million Americans experience cancer-related pain each year, of whom 25–30 percent have excruciating pain.[1] Worldwide, tens of millions of patients are so affected. That patients should suffer this much in the United States is a disgrace. It is not that we lack the means of alleviating suffering, but that, as individuals, we lack either the knowledge or the courage to properly use the tools available to us.[2]

A RATIONAL APPROACH TO PAIN

For a rational approach to the management of pain, the physician must understand the source of the pain. It has been pointed out that the physical pain encountered by cancer patients is commonly due to not one but to two, three, or even more processes going on simultaneously.[3] Moreover, not all pain is necessarily related directly to the malignancy. It is important for the treating physician not only to obtain a clear diagnostic view of the sources of pain at the outset, but to *frequently* reanalyze the situation, since the sources of pain may alter radically as the disease progresses.

THE IMMUNOLOGICAL CONSEQUENCES OF UNRELIEVED PAIN

Recent important studies have revealed that untreated pain may impair the body's immune system. It has been shown that the activity of natural killer cells, an essential component of this system, is depressed by unrelieved pain.[4] Most disquietingly, Ben-Eliyahu et al., have raised serious questions about the impact of pain on prognosis.[5] In their studies, experimental animals were subjected to implantation of tumor cells in the abdominal cavity. The animals were then subdivided into two groups, one of which was given adequate postoperative pain relief, while the other received none. In the animals with unrelieved postoperative pain, the tumor spread faster and grew more aggressively. While such data cannot be directly applied to humans, they raise extremely provocative questions about the importance of pain control in general, and about postoperative pain control in particular. One has to ask whether five-year survival figures after cancer surgery may not be worse where there has been failure to provide adequate postoperative pain relief.

REASONS FOR FAILURE TO CONTROL PAIN

Ignorance is the principal cause for our failure to control pain,[6] including ignorance of

- duration of action of the drugs used;
- dose equivalence, between one opiate and another;
- degree of absorption of drugs when given by mouth;
- the most appropriate way to schedule doses;
- realistic concerns regarding addiction;
- the legal consequences of prescribing large doses of narcotics;

- differences between patients in their susceptibility to pain; and
- the consequences of unrelieved pain.

Duration of action. This is directly related to the half-life of the drug in question. For the most part, the half-lives of commonly used morphine-like drugs (opiates) are in the range of 2–4 hours. If pain is to be controlled at all times, most opiates need to be given on a strictly four-hour basis, unless a sustained-release preparation is being used. For other agents such as the aspirin-like drugs (often called nonsteroidal anti-inflammatory drugs or NSAIDs), the half lives may be considerably longer, and a less frequent dosing schedule will suffice.

Dose equivalence. Frequently the need arises to change a patient from one opiate to another, perhaps because of side effects. Suitable conversion factors are well-described, but often ignored. A common scenario is for physicians to discharge a patient from a hospital, substituting, as they do so, an inadequate dose of an oral agent, like Percocet, for an infusion of morphine, on which the patient had been stabilized. Under these conditions, the resurgence of often quite intolerable pain is entirely predictable.

Bioavailability. Most opiates are rather poorly absorbed from the gut. This presents no problem so long as the physician makes suitable allowance when changing from infused or injected to oral dosage forms. For example, a patient receiving morphine intravenously at a rate of 10mg/hr might require 120mg every 4 hours by mouth. Many physicians fail to realize how great is the difference in dose.

Time-contingent administration. Analgesics for the cancer patient are almost universally prescribed to be given "as needed." However, it has been well established that once pain is allowed to break through, higher doses of pain medicines are required to regain control of the pain, and drug toxicity becomes more probable.[7] Further, the constant recurrence of pain (the condition necessary to trigger another dose) serves only to escalate the patient's level of anxiety and create a climate of conflict between the patient and the caregivers. Doses should be given at fixed and predetermined intervals, with additional doses being allowed for any breakthrough pain.

The myth of addiction. Common sense should dictate that, in patients with a fatal illness, addiction should be the last thing on anyone's mind. However, such is the societal fear of drug-related problems, that this is not the case.[8] There is, moreover, widespread ignorance of the difference between addiction (the overwhelming psychological craving for a drug in order to experience its euphoric effects) and physical dependence. The latter is a state in which abrupt cessation of an opiate leads to withdrawal symptoms. This latter state may occur not only with opiates, but also with quite dissimilar agents.[9] Physical dependence is an inevitable consequence of chronic exposure to drugs that work in the way that opiates do. It is not addiction.

The popular, but totally erroneous, belief is that once a patient receives opiates, addiction becomes likely, if not inevitable. This notion has its origins from surveys, carried out forty or more years ago, in which established addicts were asked about the source of their addiction. They commonly placed the blame on a physician's prescription of, say, postoperative pain medicines.[10] In more appropriate studies, where *normal* subjects requiring opiates have been examined before and after exposure to these drugs, an entirely different picture emerges. In one such, by Perry and Heidrich,[11] the records of 10,000 patients with significant burn injuries were studied. After drawn-out and painful courses that required prolonged treatment with opiates, only 22 out of 10,000 patients were considered to have a drug problem, and they had the problem before the injury occurred or any opiates had been prescribed. In another very brief report of 11,882 patients receiving opiates, Porter and Jick found only *four* patients who were thought to have developed any kind of drug problem, and in only *one* (out of 11,882) was it considered serious.[12]

The physician should be aware of "pseudo-addiction," in which the patient *appears* to be exhibiting drug-seeking behavior but, which, in reality, is a desperate quest, provoked by poor clinical management of the pain, for adequate analgesic therapy.

As Professor Patrick Wall in London has rightly pointed out, it has been "a disgraceful episode in the history of medicine that doctors and scientists allowed themselves to join a mass hysteria which confused the tremendous benefits of narcotics for the patient in pain with the social abuse of the same compounds."[13]

Respiratory depression is an acknowledged side effect of opiate overdose.[14] However, it has been shown that pain, which is a powerful stimulant to respiration,[15] is capable of counteracting the effect of opiates on respiratory drive. Thus, it is safe to give opiates in increasing doses, so long as the dose is increased only to the point at which the pain is obliterated.[16] (In a patient thus stabilized on opiates, should an invasive procedure be carried out to provide relief of pain, the previously tolerated dose of opiates would become an overdose, and, under those special conditions, respiratory depression could ensue.[17])

Legal barriers have played a major role in preventing many patients from obtaining the opiates they need to control their pain. These barriers usually take the form of fear on the part of the physician—of losing their license and of prosecution by overzealous governmental agencies[18]—who dares to prescribe narcotics. These fears are heightened by the very evident governmental surveillance embodied in the requirement, adopted by several states,[19] that narcotics be prescribed on special three-part (triplicate) prescription forms, of which the top copy goes to a police agency, and are further boosted by the watchdog mentality of some states' medical boards. Recent changes in the laws of California and Texas have provided some much-needed relief. The Texas statement that "quantity and chronicity of prescribing will be judged on the basis of the diagnosis and treatment of the targeted symptoms, and *neither of these factors are prima facie evidence of inappropriate or excessive prescribing*" [emphasis added][20] is commendably sensible. Still, more changes are needed, and some states are far behind in their understanding. It is very encouraging to note that despite the rapid increase in the medical use of morphine in this country, the diversion of legitimate morphine toward unlawful consumption is very small, being no greater than it was ten years ago.[21]

Difference in susceptibility to pain is a poorly studied phenomenon. However, it appears that tissue injury may lead to changes in nerve function within the spinal cord,[22] heightening the intensity of pain and widening the area in which it is perceived. From other animal studies, it also appears that, in some individuals, there is an inherited increased susceptibility to pain, traceable to a deficiency in opiate receptors.[23] With such factors as these in mind, it is to be expected that there will be widely differing reports on the part of patients as to how much opiate they require to control their pain. The temptation to label complainers as "drug seeking" should be subject to critical scrutiny.

The consequences of inadequately relieved pain are rarely considered, but the immunological considerations alluded to above must surely spur on every caregiver who becomes aware of them to achieve better pain control.

OPTIONS FOR TREATING PAIN

Direct Interventions for the Relief of Cancer Pain

Wherever possible, the pain should be attacked at its source. This may take the form of surgical intervention, be it draining an abscess, surgical repair of a pathological bone fracture, or relief of intestinal obstruction. At other times, a more appropriate intervention might be radiation therapy, which may be an extremely effective way of reducing pain from tumor deposits in bone (bony metastases) or from the perineal pain of recurrent recto-sigmoid cancer, to cite but two examples. Within the last two years, strontium 89 has been approved as a new form of radiotherapy. Being selectively taken up at sites of increased bone turnover, this b-emitting isotope is uniquely effective in concentrating radiation at the sites of bony metastases. It is specifically indicated in situations where the metastases are too numerous and widespread to permit conventional irradiation.

Pharmacology may sometimes provide a form of direct intervention. For example, some studies have suggested certain drugs may be helpful for the pain of bony metastases.[24] Muscle spasm is a common source of considerable pain, and this too can be treated with specific pharmacology rather than being blocked out by analgesics. Baclofen, given orally or by means of a spinal infusion (see below), may give dramatic relief.[25]

Even in those situations when surgical correction or radiation are not appropriate, other interventions may be considered, including nerve blocks, or neurosurgical procedures, as will be discussed. Fortunately, however, much can be achieved by means of pain medications without the discomfort and risk of invasive procedures.

The Pharmacological Control of Cancer Pain

In the majority of patients with incurable malignancy, it becomes necessary for the physician to draw upon the extensive pharmacological resources available for the control of pain. Analgesic (pain relieving) drugs fall into three categories: the nonopiate analgesics, the "adjuvant" analgesics, and the opiate analgesics.

1. The "Analgesic Ladder"

Frequent reference is made to the "analgesic ladder,"[26] which describes a sequential deployment of all three categories of analgesics, in a sequence supposed to represent increasing potency, in order to control the pain. While this approach may have some usefulness, it does not take into account the complexity of pain and the multitude of pain sources that may be active. A more thoughtful approach, based on careful repeated clinical assessments of the source or sources of the pain(s) and in full knowledge of the differing modes of action of the available drugs, will be more likely to produce the desired result.

2. Nonopiate Analgesics

Acetaminophen is a widely used analgesic of moderate potency. In conventional doses it is very safe, and it is often used for prolonged periods of time.[27] However, in high single doses it may actually destroy the liver. It is important to remember that not only is acetaminophen a common over-the-counter agent available in unlimited amounts, but it is also a component of many prescription analgesics. Some of these preparations may contain up to 750mg acetaminophen per capsule or tablet, so the potential for the unwitting consumption of a larger than intended dose of acetaminophen does exist.

Nonsteroidal anti-inflammatory drugs (NSAIDs) comprise a large and heterogeneous group of agents. It is important to recognize that they are derived from several dissimilar parent compounds, and individual patients react differently to the various groups of NSAIDs. Thus, if the response to one NSAID is not satisfactory, before abandoning this valuable class of drugs, the physician should try to utilize an NSAID from another chemical group.

NSAIDs may be extremely effective in providing pain relief, most especially that related to bony metastases. Among skilled hospice physicians, it is often found that in managing bony pain the appropriate use of NSAIDs may permit the use of opiates to be sharply curtailed or even, for a while, suspended (per a personal communication). Though NSAIDs are normally administered by mouth, and occasionally by suppository, in recent times one has been approved for intramuscular injection. A recent report of success with prolonged intravenous infusions of this NSAID in controlling the bony pain of a patient with disseminated prostatic cancer[28] suggests a more useful way of treating cancer pain.

There are numerous side effects associated with the use of NSAIDs. The most common is gastrointestinal irritation, or even ulceration, with attendant bleeding, which can be massive. This may occur regardless of the route of administration. Gasrointestinal irritation may be lessened by the administration of antacids or one of the drugs now available to reduce gastric acidity. This side effect is more common with some NSAIDs and less prominent with others, but it can occur with any NSAID and may occur without any warning symptoms.

Platelet function is compromised by many NSAIDs and may produce a risk of significant bleeding. Kidney function may sometimes become severely compromised by NSAIDs. Diuretic action may be inhibited, and fluid retention with dependent edema (leg swelling) can occur. Excretion by the kidneys of other important drugs may occur with the coadministration of NSAIDs. Also, these agents may interfere with the metabolism of warfarin, and thus potentiate its anticoagulant effect. A very few patients develop life-threatening asthma when exposed to even small doses of NSAIDs. Liver damage is rare with agents other than acetaminophen.

3. Adjuvant Agents

A heterogeneous group of agents has been found effective in reducing certain pains, particularly those associated with nerve damage, which is fortunate, as such pain may respond poorly to conventional analgesics, although some dispute this.[29] This collection of drugs includes some antidepressants, anticonvulsants, and neuroleptics (drugs used most often to treat schizophrenia). Though sometimes effective when used singly, it may be necessary to give two, or even all three types of adjuvant drugs in combination in order to gain the desired relief.

The antidepressants are usually the preferred agents since they have less toxicity than the other two groups, even though side effects are sometimes pronounced. They are said to be particularly effective against the burning pain associated with nerve damage. The dose may differ widely among patients because of the way the body eliminates the drug.[30]

The most problematic side effects, especially in older patients, are sedation, low blood pressure on standing (orthostatic hypotension), dry mouth, urinary retention, and severe constipation. Newer agents may have fewer side effects but seem to work less well in relieving pain.

Anticonvulsants may be the best agents to use for the shooting, stabbing pain that often accompanies nerve damage.[31] Toxicity is quite rare. Dose adjustment for each individual patient is necessary

Local anesthetics may be an important and underutilized resource, especially in treating nerve pain. Brose and Cousins recently reported the efficacy of subcutaneous infusions of lidocaine in three patients whose pain was refractory to all other interventions, including spinal infusion of opiates.[32] Good pain relief without significant toxicity was maintained for up to six months by this means.

4. Opiates

These agents have been in use for over five thousand years. Over the last several decades, we have developed numerous derivatives of the original compounds. Despite important individual differences, there are certain features common to all opiates.

1. All can cause nausea, which may be severe, so it is not uncommon to have to coadminister an anti-emetic. At times, the nausea can be intractable, and even new potent anti-emetics may not overcome it. One agent,

insufficiently recognized in the United States, is methotrimeprazine. It is orally active, though no oral preparation is marketed in this country. It can be given by intramuscular injection, or by intravenous infusion. In the United Kingdom, methotrimeprazine is not uncommonly mixed in the same syringe as the opiate and given by subcutaneous infusion by means of a portable infusion device.[33] It confers the added benefit of a quite considerable pain relieving effect.[34] The main disadvantage is that it is quite sedating, and it has some potential for causing orthostatic hypotension.

2. Constipation is an almost entirely unavoidable side effect, but it often becomes a major problem because of inappropriate use of laxatives. Stool softeners should first be used in adequate amounts. If this is insufficient, it can be supplemented with bowel stimulants, again, in adequate amounts. A bowel stimulant should not be given if the gut has not been prepared with a stool softener, since this may merely provoke regional bowel spasm, making a bad situation worse.

3. Tolerance may develop to a surprising degree, though it is never absolute, i.e., morphine will never totally "lose its effect" through prior use. Efficacy at low dose may be regained by changing to another opiate. Tolerance is the inevitable result of the prolonged administration of drugs that stimulate cell mechanisms (as opiates do). It is the basis of physical dependency and the well-known withdrawal reactions, but is **not** to be confused with the entirely different phenomenon of addiction.

4. Allergy may very rarely develop to the opiates. Not infrequently, patients may erroneously report allergy, when what they had experienced was flushing of the skin caused by histamine release.

5. Other side-effects include sedation, confusion, hallucinations, coma, and, in extremely high doses, muscle jerks and epilepticlike seizures.

6. There appears to be considerable variability in the response of any given patient to each individual opiate. No one opiate is inherently superior in all patients, since patients who fail to obtain adequate pain relief from one opiate given at the maximum tolerable dose may do so from another.[35]

Significant Features of the Individual Opiates

Codeine is widely used, despite its low potency as an analgesic. For convenience, it is usually given in combination with acetaminophen, because the combination is classified as a Schedule III drug (available on regular prescription forms), whereas, given singly, codeine is Schedule II (i.e., it must be prescribed on a triplicate prescription form). The disadvantage of such combinations is that the amount of narcotic that can be given without risk of acetaminophen-induced hepatotoxicity is limited. In the cancer patient, once significant pain has developed, codeine is too weak an analgesic to be of much use. Like all opiates, it can cause nausea, and it can constipate.

Propoxyphene, chemically related to methadone, is less potent than codeine and more expensive. It is supplied as a single agent and with acetaminophen.

Dihydrocodeine, though available in Europe for over thirty years, has only just been approved for oral use in the United States. It is available only in combination with acetaminophen and caffeine (DHC Plus), or with aspirin and caffeine (Synalgos DC). It may be twice as potent as codeine,[36] though this is open to question.[37] It is classified as a Schedule III drug.

Hydrocodone may be more powerful than dihydrocodeine, though exact potency ratios are unknown. It is most widely used in combination with acetaminophen or with aspirin. It is not available as a single agent. All hydrocodone-containing preparations are classified as Schedule III agents.

Diamorphine (heroin), the most controversial and maligned of all the major narcotics, is not available as a legal therapeutic agent in the United States. It is endowed with no spectacular analgesic properties since once it enters the body, it is rapidly transformed into morphine. Nevertheless, it does have certain advantages:

- It is more soluble than morphine and therefore more analgesic effect can be gained with smaller injections (of importance chiefly for intramuscular administration).
- Its oral absorption is significantly better than that of morphine, so fewer mistakes would be made in conversions from parenteral to oral dose forms.
- It is more lipid-soluble than morphine, so, when used subcutaneously, absorption is probably more reliable. When given spinally, there can be greater certainty that the drug will be absorbed into the spinal cord at the level at which it was inserted. Unfortunately, when the issue of legalizing heroin was discussed in Washington, D.C., some years ago, there were no really "clean" data for review, so the measure was not passed. While our patients would probably be better off with heroin than without it, the time and energy it would take to change the law is probably not justified, given the other options available to us. However, it should be noted that in the United Kingdom, where it is available, it continues to be widely used.

Fentanyl is available in the form of a transdermal patch as a medication for the ambulatory patient. For the transdermal patch to be effective, it must remain securely stuck to the skin. Many patients do not press around the edge of the patch firmly enough or long enough for the contact adhesive to form an adequate bond. The kinetics of this dosage form differ from other forms of opiate administration. It takes seventeen hours for the plasma level to reach its plateau (and correspondingly long for the level to decline once the patch is removed). There is, of course, no means of altering the dose at short notice to alleviate breakthrough pain.

Drug delivery is, to a large extent, regulated by the membrane within the patch, but skin blood flow, and therefore the prevailing room temperature, also influence the rate of removal from the skin. Patients with reduced skin blood flow will probably not absorb transdermally administered fentanyl quite as well as anticipated. These concerns, coupled with the relatively high cost of the patch, may limit its general acceptance. Nevertheless, for a selected subset of patients who are unable to take opiates by mouth and are unwilling to use an infusion device, transdermal fentanyl is a useful addition.

Levorphanol is about five times as potent as morphine, but its pharmacological profile is essentially the same. When given orally, it is slightly better absorbed than morphine.

Hydromorphone is an opiate of major importance. It has a higher potency than morphine. It is often possible to maintain good pain control with fewer undesirable side effects, such as sedation and hallucinations, than may be the case with morphine. It is regrettable that there is as yet no controlled-release formulation of this drug. The only tablet sizes available (2mg and 4mg) are inappropriately small, given the high doses sometimes needed in treating severe pain. A significant disadvantage of hydromorphone is that, while the oral form is about the same price as morphine, the powder needed to make up the drug for infusion is five times as expensive.

Meperidine is not a good drug for the control of pain in the cancer patient. It has a relatively low analgesic potency. Oral absorption is less than for morphine, while intramuscular injections are painful, produce extensive tissue damage, and result in erratic absorption. A serious problem associated with the use of meperidine in large doses or for prolonged periods of time, is that one of its breakdown products—with a long-half life (15–35 hrs.)—may accumulate[38] and can cause agitation, confusion, and major epilepsy, which is not reversed by the opiate antidote naloxone[39] and responds poorly to conventional anticonvulsants.

Methadone is a difficult drug to use because of the variable way in which it accumulates in the body. In acute single dose studies, it is as potent as morphine, but it is somewhat better absorbed from the intestine than morphine is.[40] When first administered, the half-life is between twenty-four and thirty-five hours, but with prolonged administration it may rise to about fifty hours.[41] This may create a trap for the unwary for if a patient achieves rapid pain control on a given dose and is then discharged from the hospital, within ten to fourteen days he or she may develop symptoms of opiate overdose as the drug accumulates. Methadone is extensively metabolized in the liver. Some other drugs may accelerate its metabolism, thus producing an acute withdrawal state[42] while others may reduce the rate of metabolism and lead to opiate overdose.[43] Although there are some patients who seem to do better on methadone than other opiates, most find that the prolonged half-life makes rapid dose adjustment difficult. Furthermore, central side effects are more common.

Morphine remains the gold-standard by which all other opiates should be judged. Inexpensive and available in a wide variety of dosage forms, it is without question still one of the most valuable drugs available for the control of severe pain. First and foremost, it should be considered as an oral agent. Although in former times it was given as a component of a pain "cocktail," such as the Brompton mixture (named after the Brompton Hospital in London), it is now usual to give it alone to begin with, either as an elixir or as an immediate release tablet. Once the dose required to achieve pain control has been established, it can then be given in the form of a controlled-release tablet. These are available in a range of dose sizes, which is important given the extremely wide dosage requirements seen among patients. In opting to use controlled-release morphine tablets, some caveats need to be kept in mind:

1. It is inappropriate to begin therapy with a controlled-release preparation. Initial dose titration requires an immediate-release form of the medication.
2. Controlled-release tablets cannot be crushed to facilitate swallowing or administration through a feeding tube, because this will disrupt the tablet matrix on which the controlled release depends.
3. Any preparation that releases its contents over a twelve-hour period necessarily requires a functionally normal intestinal tract. If a controlled-release tablet falls into an ileostomy bag with much of its contents undischarged, pain relief may disappear (Conolly, unpublished observation).

Morphine, more than the other opiates, has been utilized in a variety of patient-controlled analgesia (PCA) devices designed to deliver a constant background or basal infusion, together with the option of extra self-administered doses, of predetermined size at a predetermined frequency for breakthrough pain. Once programmed, the pump can be electronically "locked" to prevent deliberate or accidental maladministration. Absorption from the subcutaneous tissues is quite adequate, provided that no more that 2–3ml are infused per hour. An intravenous line is not required for such infusions unless more than 100mg/hr is required. This is one situation where heroin would be advantageous. It has been our experience with morphine that the infusion site needs to be changed every three days to prevent local irritation or infection. Given that modest level of care, we have been able to maintain patients at home for periods ranging from a few weeks up to four years, without difficulty. Although these pumps are expensive (costing up to $450/month to rent), they are extremely reliable and allow many patients to retain dignity, mobility, and a high degree of comfort far into the course of their disease.

Even with the most aggressive dose titration, there will be a small number of patients for whom adequate pain relief cannot be obtained with systemically administered opiates. For such patients, a recent technique has been developed, in the form of intraspinal opiate infusions (see below). Only morphine is FDA-approved for this purpose at the present time.

Oxycodone, as a single compound, is an underutilized, even little-known, opiate. Most practitioners know it in its combination forms. It is generally regarded as a weak opiate, but only because these fixed-dose combinations contain just 5mg oxycodone per tablet. If used as a medication in its own right, it has at least 60 percent of the potency of morphine[44] and often causes fewer central side-effects.[45] The current immediate-release tablet size (5mg) is far too small, but a controlled-release formulation that contains 10, 20, 40 or 80mg per tablet has recently been approved by the FDA.

Oxymorphone is available in parenteral and suppository form in the United States. It is approximately five to ten times more potent than morphine, but its pharmacological profile is otherwise similar.

"Narcotics for the dying patient" protocol

It is generally accepted (in theory) that terminally ill patients should be given whatever opiates they require to control their pain. It is also well understood that the popular notion that adequate pain control shortens life is a misconception. However, in practice, we have found that many physicians, especially among the ranks of the resident staff, have some difficulty in incorporating these two facts into their care of the terminally ill. Once or twice a year a dying patient is "revived" with naloxone, a narcotic antagonist, given in response to a slowed respiration rate. The resulting disruption of narcotic effects is predictably distressing for all concerned. In order to ease the minds of physicians caught up in this situation and to emphasize the fact that the patient is dying of the disease *regardless of the medication that is prescribed*, we place such patients on the hospital-approved "Narcotics for the Dying Patient" protocol,[46] which explicitly states that dying patients are entitled to the greatest degree of comfort that can be secured and that they are not to be denied narcotics because of changes in their vital signs.

"Barbiturates for the dying patient" protocol

Very rarely, especially so given the availability of spinal blocks, we do encounter patients who are not adequately relieved by opiates, even when pushed to the level of significant toxicity. In those very few cases, we have for several years employed a barbiturate infusion similar to that described by Truog, et al.[47] In essence, this requires giving the patient a general anesthetic and maintaining them in a state of coma until death supervenes naturally.

Anesthesiology Techniques for Control of Cancer Pain

Nerve blocks can serve both diagnostic and therapeutic purposes in the management of cancer pain. If an injection of a local anesthetic provides temporary relief of pain, chemical nerve destruction may be indicated. Opioids, administered directly into the central nervous system (usually spinally), may control pain when all other forms of treatment have failed.

1. Diagnostic Blocks

Local anesthetics interfere with the neural transmission of pain signals and can often provide immediate relief of pain.[48] This approach does not usually provide a long-term solution but may aid in localizing the origin of the pain. It may also provide further useful information in predicting the effects of procedures intended to be permanently destructive of neural structures. Such destructive procedures include injecting absolute alcohol or phenol, or surgically interrupting various nerve pathways. Temporary nerve blocks allow the patients to experience the sensations that they will encounter after the more permanent procedure is performed.[49] These temporary blocks are useful but not fully predictive of the long-term outcome, because the nervous system has the capacity to develop alternative pain pathways over a period of several months or years, eventually leaving the patient without permanent complete pain relief.[50]

2. Destructive Nerve Blocks (neurolysis)
Careful patient selection is the key to success with neurolysis.

- Diagnostic local anesthetic blocks should have demonstrated significant pain relief.
- Aggressive conventional pharmacological management should have failed because of lack of efficacy or intolerable side effects.
- The block should not exacerbate the underlying medical condition nor accelerate its course.
- Bodily functions important to the patient—such as bowel or bladder control, or ambulation—should not be compromised by the block.
- Contraindications to invasive procedures, such as abnormality of blood clotting or infection, should be ruled out.
- Nondestructive procedures, such as spinal infusion of narcotics, should be deemed inappropriate.

Patients should understand the risks and benefits of neurolysis. Realistic expectations should be fostered. These should be partially based on the outcome of the prognostic block and should also include the understanding that successful pain control does not treat the underlying disease process.

3. Sympathetic Blocks for the Treatment of Pain
Pain from internal body organs not amenable to other therapies may respond to blockade of the so-called sympathetic nerves. These nerves are involved in the automatic regulation of functions such as heart rate, blood pressure, and intestinal activity, and the basis for their involvement in pain is not well understood. The three most commonly used sympathetic blocks are the stellate ganglion, celiac plexus, and lumbar sympathetic blocks.

Stellate ganglion blocks interrupt sympathetic outflow to the head, neck, and arm as well as to the organs of the thorax. The ganglion lies at the base of the neck.

The technique of blocking the stellate ganglion involves injecting local anesthetic at the level of the sixth cervical vertebra. There are numerous important structures in this region, and great care is necessary to avoid inflicting significant local damage.

Problems responsive to stellate ganglion block include pain in the head, pain from a tumor at the top of the lung involving chest wall structures, and pain from vascular insufficiency in the upper limb. Neuropathic pain caused by tumor involvement, postshingles pain (post herpetic neuralgia), radiation therapy, and chemotherapy may also benefit from this procedure.

Celiac plexus block is one of the most common and effective nerve blocks used in the management of cancer pain.[51] This plexus is the largest of the great sympathetic plexus. It is wrapped around the aorta and is actually a diffuse complex of interconnected neural fibers embedded in fatty tissue. The plexus can transmit pain from the colon, small intestine, abdominal aorta, mesentery, adrenal glands, pancreas, spleen, liver, stomach, and diaphragm. Blocking the plexus may therefore interrupt pain impulses from all these organs.

The most common indication for performing a celiac plexus block is treatment of upper abdominal and referred back pain caused by pancreatic carcinoma. It is also useful for other cancer pain involving the upper- and midabdomen as well as acute and chronic visceral disease.

A common side effect is orthostatic hypotension. Other complications may include aortic or vena caval puncture resulting in intra-abdominal bleeding. Puncture of the lung, liver, spleen, pancreas, ureter, or kidney have been reported.

Lumbar sympathetic block is most useful for diagnosis and treatment of sympathetically maintained pain unrelated to cancer. Lower extremity pain of neoplastic origin is predominantly transmitted via normal sensory nerves. Often, however, in patients with rectal or cervical carcinoma, tumor involvement of the lumbar sympathetic nerves can give rise to painful situations. Radiation-induced fibrosis of the lumbar plexus can produce neuropathic pain, which mimics sympathetically maintained pain and actually may be treated successfully with lumbar sympathetic block.[52]

Common complications and side effects include orthostatic hypotension, spinal or epidural injection resulting in somatic block, injury to the kidney or ureter, and genitofemoral block.

4. Neuraxial Narcotics

Patients who do not derive adequate pain relief from systemic narcotics (usually because of dose-limiting side effects) have a further therapeutic option in the form of narcotics delivered directly into the spinal column (neuraxial narcotics). The drug may be infused into the space between the outer membranes surrounding the spinal cord (epidural) or directly into the cerebrospinal fluid, which bathes the cord itself (intrathecal). This technique is a valuable alternative to the irreversible destructive procedures outlined above, which may be associated with risks of loss of function and independence. Unlike specifically targeted nerve blocks, neuraxial narcotics may be used to treat multiple sources of pain, which are typically present in metastatic disease. This approach can provide dramatic improvement in cancer pain control when other approaches have failed. The reason for its singular efficacy lies in the fact that the greatest concentration of opioid-sensitive cells lies in that area of the spinal cord where the sensory nerves actually enter.[53]

Spinal drug delivery methods range from simple to highly sophisticated systems. The most simple technique involves the percutaneous placement of an exteriorized epidural[54] or intrathecal catheter, which is taped in place. This allows either intermittent or continuous spinal administration of the opiate. The most sophisticated system by which intraspinal narcotics can be administered is a totally implanted intrathecal catheter, which delivers medications from an implanted, externally programmable variable-rate pump.[55] These pumps can deliver either a constant infusion or may be set up to follow a complex sequence of steps in which different infusion rates are automatically delivered at set times of the day. Before such an elaborate and expensive system is implanted, it is essential that the patient have a trial injection of neuraxial narcotics to confirm efficacy and a lack of unacceptable side effects. Also, a psychological determination that the patient could adjust to "living with" such a permanent device is essential prior to implantation.

From time to time, the patient must attend the clinic for the pump to be refilled by percutaneous injection and for adjustments to be made to the infusion rate as necessary. Preservative-free morphine has been the drug of choice for continuous intrathecal infusion, and is currently the only narcotic preparation that is FDA-approved.

In the initial phase of enthusiasm for this technique, it was thought that tolerance would not develop when opioids were infused intrathecally. However, after several years of experience, tolerance has been recognized as a limitation of the efficacy of intrathecal opioid infusion.[56] Other opioids, such as fentanyl, may be used intermittently in place of morphine to lessen the development of tolerance, though none are FDA-approved for this purpose as yet. Overall, the reported efficacy of intrathecal infusion varies from 70 percent to 90 percent during a median follow-up time of six months.[57]

Both epidural and intrathecal narcotics have assumed a prominent role in the management of cancer pain. Epidural narcotics may be delivered from external pumps and can be mixed with dilute concentrations of a local anesthetic. Such external delivery systems offer certain advantages, such as easy changing of medication and easy refilling, coupled with sophisticated patient controlled analgesia. Major disadvantages are the need for a spinal catheter to be connected to an external device, with the inevitably increased risks of infection, and the limitations on activity necessary for protection of the catheter and its entry site. While these external systems have lower initial costs, in the long run they have higher monthly maintenance costs than internal systems.

Internal systems, which use implantable pumps built to extremely high specifications, are expensive. Currently, to place such a pump costs about $20,000. However, one has to set against the cost both the level of comfort that it alone may provide (coupled with the need to impose fewer restrictions on the patient's activity) as well as the rather considerable costs of providing a steady supply of medication cassettes for the external devices described above. Overall maintenance costs for the implanted devices may ultimately be lower that those of external pumps.[58]

Neurosurgical Aspects of Cancer Pain Control

Roughly one-third of the patients with cancer pain gain inadequate benefit from medical treatment. Severe side effects and poor pain control greatly impair the quality of life for these patients. Unfortunately, many physicians tend to refer such patients to a neurosurgeon very late in the course of their disease, when they are already severely debilitated and have become poor surgical candidates. The likelihood that they could then benefit from the neurosurgical procedure is very small.

Alternative approaches to pain management should always be considered as soon as it becomes clear that other less invasive treatments are failing to maintain the patient pain-free and functional. Nerve blocks performed by the anesthesiologist, as already discussed, often prove helpful and frequently serve as a diagnostic pointer for future neurosurgical intervention. The chief aim of any neurosurgical procedure is to provide the patient with a pain-free terminal phase, without the need for high doses of analgesic drugs that often impair cognition.

Neurosurgical procedures can be directed toward:

- alleviation of pressure on neuronal structures caused by encroachment on nerves by a tumor;
- delivery of drugs directly to the central nervous system;
- augmentation of pain-controlling pathways by electrical stimulation; and
- interruption of pain pathways.

These surgical options are discussed below.

1. Neuronal Decompression

The best approach to the treatment of pain is always removal of the causative factor. Tumor encroachment on neuronal structures, particularly of peripheral nerves and spinal cord, can cause excruciating pain that often responds very poorly to medical management. Decompression of these structures should be the first goal of the neurosurgeon.[59] Detailed work-up with imaging studies such as MRI and CT-scans must be performed before any surgical plan is developed.

Invasion of a vertebral body can cause vertebral collapse and instability at any level of the spine. Radiation therapy, with or without steroids, frequently controls pain. Surgery for decompression and stabilization and possibly reconstruction of the affected vertebra may be indicated and may completely alleviate both pain and instability.[60] In the thoracic region, instability is less common because of the rib cage.

Involvement of the thoraco-lumbar junction and lumbar spine is often a more difficult diagnostic problem. The pain takes on a more diffuse quality, frequently described as sacro-iliac pain. Plain X-rays, MRI, CT-scans and, if necessary, a myelogram may disclose tumor invasion of the spinal canal, root compression, vertebral collapse or dislocation. Surgical decompression followed by spine stabilization using metal supports may be the treatment of choice for such pain.[61] Every available spinal procedure for tumor resection and vertebral stabilization is indicated when the general medical condition of the patient permits and life expectancy is reasonable.[62] This decision must be made by the team taking care of the patient, including the medical oncologist, the pain management group, the anesthesiologist, and the neurosurgeon.

Pain involving limbs, shoulder or sacral region secondary to brachial, lumbar or sacral plexus infiltration is hard to treat. Techniques to expose these plexus to permit resection of tumor tissue have been developed but have yielded uncertain results.[63] Radiation therapy remains the best initial approach, although, unfortunately, its results diminish with time. Other neurosurgical approaches, as discussed below, might be required.

2. Delivery of Drugs Directly to the Central Nervous System

The least invasive procedures are obviously the most desirable for control of pain in patients in poor condition and with short life expectancy. Direct infusion of opioids intrathecally or epidurally (as described above) has gained popularity since its conception in the early 1980s. Poletti, et al. devised a method to permit continuous infusion of morphine into the subarachnoid space of the spine to control cancer pain.[64] The surgery is simple. The intrathecal catheter is placed transcutaneously and is connected to a continuous delivery system, which is buried in the abdominal subcutaneous tissue. The operation can be performed under light sedation and local anesthesia. Patients return every two to four weeks to allow the reservoir in the pump to be refilled.

Patients with upper neck and facial pain have been treated with infusion of opioids into anatomical brain cavities (ventricles).[65] Placement of an intraventricular catheter connected to an infusion system located in the subcutaneous tissue in the anterior chest wall is a relatively simple neurosurgical procedure. This approach has been rewarding, with a very low complication rate.[66] Intracranial hemorrhage related to catheter placement is extremely rare. Infection, pump malfunction, and catheter disconnection are possible complications. As in the case of intrathecal infusion at the spinal level, these problems should be suspected when analgesia fails. Plain X-rays usually show catheter disconnection, and MRI or CT-scan may disclose any intracranial mishap.

3. Augmentation of Pain Controlling Pathways by Electrical Stimulation

The idea of applying deep brain stimulation (DBS) to control pain has been developed over the past forty years.[67] Knowledge accumulated in the laboratory was quickly applied to the treatment of persistent pain in humans. The first trial in humans was performed in 1960 by Heath and Mickle,[68] who implanted electrodes in the septal area. Success with this technique has been reported to range from 22 percent to 94 percent.[69] This approach, although controversial, confers the benefit of avoiding permanent interruption of central nervous system pathways or destruction of nuclei, which must occur with ablative procedures. However, since the results obtained by this approach have been inconsistent, only a few centers throughout the world use these techniques.

Stimulation of somatosensory pathways to control pain is based on the gate theory of Melzack and Wall,[70] which postulates that stimulation of specific nerves will block the transmission of pain impulses to higher centers in the brain. This theory provides a mechanism not only for the effect of deep brain stimulation but also for pain control achieved by transcutaneous peripheral nerve[71] and dorsal column stimulation.[72] These procedures are apparently more successful for treatment of chronic pain of nonmalignant origin than cancer pain.[73] The use of electrical stimulation for cancer-related pain has been advocated for phantom limb pain, nerve injury pain, sympathetic dystrophies, and postherpetic neuralgia.[74]

The variability of the results may be merely the result of the lack of a dependable commercially available electrode or to selection of different targets on the part of the authors.[75] The data of Young and Brechner are encouraging. This technique may represent the solution for several cases of severe, diffuse cancer pain that responds poorly to systemic or intrathecal opioids[76] and certainly deserves further study.

4. Interruption of Pain Pathways in the Peripheral or Central Nervous System

Destructive procedures have been progressively abandoned over the years. The idea of impairing function, even when it represents abolition of pain, is not well accepted by the patient. This idea also induces in the surgeon a feeling of failure, since he or she is, in fact, destroying the nervous system. Nevertheless, neurosurgical interruption of pain pathways, or the limbic system, can provide pronounced relief of pain. Destructive surgery should be considered only when all other options for pain control have failed.

Cutting Nerve Roots

Rhizotomies represent peripheral interruption of pain pathways. The major disadvantage of these procedures is the complete loss of sensory function in the section of the body served by that nerve.

The surgeon shares with the anesthesiologist the percutaneous techniques for rhizotomy or ganglionectomy, such as alcohol, phenol, and glycerol injection.[77] Radiofrequency rhizotomy is usually performed by neurosurgeons. These procedures are performed under local anesthesia and with fluoroscopic guidance. The patient cooperates with the surgeon in identifying the roots that, when severed, will lead to pain relief.[78] When percutaneous procedures fail, surgical section under general anesthesia is undertaken. Rhizotomy can also cause loss of motor function if the particular nerve root carries motor fibers. Section of the posterior rootlets in the spinal canal or removal of the sensory ganglion (ganglionectomy) avoids motor compromise. However, when several roots or ganglia are involved at the upper or lower extremities level, motor function can become severely compromised by the concomitant loss of position sense. Rhizotomies and ganglionectomies are reserved for malignant pain related to sensory cranial nerves, thoracic wall, and somatic pain. The main drawback of rhizotomies and ganglionectomies is the short duration of pain relief, usually measured in months, and the possible later onset of severe deafferentation pain in the denervated area as alternative pain pathways develop.

Cordotomy and Myelotomy

Cordotomy is the most common destructive procedure performed for cancer pain. Pain relief after a cordotomy, with few exceptions, lasts up to eighteen months. Therefore, the life expectancy of the patient is an important factor in the decision to perform a cordotomy. The best candidates for cordotomies are patients with unilateral pain below the T12 dermatome. However, pain relief and analgesia up to the C5 dermatome can be obtained.[79] The technique was described by Spiller and Martin in 1912.[80] Since then, improvements in the surgical procedure and development of a technique for percutaneous cordotomy at the C2 level have made this procedure safe, and it can provide excellent control of cancer pain in up to 90 percent of the patients.[81] The complication rate increases dramatically when bilateral cordotomy is performed. Complications are urinary incontinence and partial paralysis. Death from respiratory arrest in cases of bilateral cordotomy performed above the C4 level may occur because of diaphragmatic paralysis. Obviously, complications related to open surgery, such as infection and cerebrospinal fluid leakage, can also occur.

Pain and temperature pathways are separated from those of touch and proprioception in the spinal cord. This unique anatomical distribution allows for obliteration of pain and temperature sensation in the site of the pain, with preservation of touch and proprioception, which are indispensable for motor function. After a cordotomy, patients must be warned to be careful with the extremity deprived of pain and temperature perception in order to avoid thermal injuries.

Intracranial Ablative Procedures

Bilateral disconnection of a part of the brain known as the limbic system usually affords control of cancer pain without somatic sensory loss,[82] and a remarkable decrease in opioids intake may be observed after such disconnection.[83] The affective ("suffering") component of the patient's distress is abolished, and, although still present, the pain no longer bothers the patient.[84] The site of choice for limbic system disconnection is the cingulate gyrus. Magnetic resonance imaging provides excellent visualization of the cingulate gyrus to guide the neurosurgeon in the placement of his "incision," which may be secured by radiofrequency thermocoagulation or by radiosurgery.[85]

Several other targets, which potentially might improve the control of cancer pain, have been described. Stereotactic guidance, supplemented by electrical stimulation to confirm the accurate localization of the desired target, makes the procedures anatomically reliable. However, although effective, pain relief by these central procedures is short lasting.[86]

THE IMPACT OF MANAGED CARE
ON CANCER PAIN MANAGEMENT

We have a new problem to deal with, in that managed care may add to the difficulties of caring for the dying. The essence of managed care is frugality. The function of a gatekeeper is to say "No" whenever possible. While most carriers have acted responsibly in the area of pain control, some have not, insisting that pain management is "not a covered benefit," especially when expensive forms of treatment such as the intrathecal pump is required.[87] Most frightful of all, I have encountered some patients with policies that allow a *lifetime limit* of only $1,000 for palliative care. Patients who are medically naïve can be excused for signing such a policy, but only the most cynical and callous of carriers would offer it.

CONCLUSION

We can do vastly more for our patients than is often done. Fear of unrelieved pain should not stalk our patients in the way that it does. In the truly good centers of palliative care, such as St. Christopher's Hospice in London, they control cancer pain in 95 percent of the patients they see. In the 5 percent where less than ideal control is accomplished, it is usually because the patients were presented too late for everything to be done before death occurs. Perhaps one reason why their results are so good is that they do not forget that pain is multidimensional. Mental, social, and spiritual pain are addressed along with the physical. This is hard to do because it often requires that the caregiver move far outside his or her comfort zone. Like the Good Samaritan, we have to get off our mount, get down in the ditch, and get our hands dirty. We must share our patients' grief and mourn with them, even as we seek to "bind up their wounds, pouring in oil and wine." Depression is a common accompaniment that also merits treatment, though it is beyond the scope of this chapter to discuss.

In order to ensure that patients do not endure unnecessary pain, we have an obligation to exploit to the full the knowledge and understanding and the many drugs and procedures now available to us. More than that, we need to strive to maximize the patient's quality of life. Our goal is not to provide relief in the form of a morphine-induced fog but to provide maximal pain relief with minimal side effects. For many patients, this approach can result in months or, depending on the actual malignancy, even years of happy and productive life. Where death is inescapable, conquest of pain is the last great service that we can render to our patients, and it is important that we succeed.

ENDNOTES

1. Bonica, J., ed. *The Management of Pain* (Philadelphia: Lea and Febiger, 1990), 402.
2. Von Roenn, J. H., Cleeland, C. S., Gonin et al. "Physician Attitudes and Practice in Cancer Pain Management." *Am Intern Med* (1993): *119*, 121–26.

3. Twycross, R. G. and S. Fairfield. "Pain in Far Advanced Cancer." *Pain* (1982): *14*, 303–10.
4. Liebeskind, J., "Pain Can Kill." *Pain* (1991): *44*, 3–4.
5. Ben-Eliyahu, S., Yirmiya, R. et al. "Morphine Attenuates Surgery-Induced Enhancement of Metastatic Colonization in Rats" *Pain* (1993): *54*, 21–28.
6. Bonica, *The Management of Pain*, 12–15.
7. Twycross, R. G., "Relief of Pain," *The Management of Terminal Malignant Disease*, Ed. C. M. Saunders (London: Edward Arnold, 1984), 64–90.
8. Clark, H. W., and Sees, K. L., "Opioids, Chronic Pain and the Law," *J Pain and Symptom Management* (1983): *8*, 297–305.
9. Conolly, M. E., Briant, R. H., George, C. F. et al. "A Cross-over Comparison of Clonidine and Methyldopa in Hypertension." *Eur J. Clin. Pharmacol* (1972) *4*, 222–227.
10. Friedman, D. P. "Perspectives on the Medical Use of Drugs of Abuse." *J Pain and Symptom Management* (1990) 5, Suppl. 1, S2–S5; and Portenoy, R. K. "Chronic Opioid Therapy in Nonmalignant Pain." *J Pain and Symptom Management* (1990) 5, Suppl. 1, S46–S62.
11. Perry, S. and Heidrich, G. "Management of Pain During Debridement; a Survey of U.S. Burn Units." *Pain* (1982) *13*, 267–80.
12. Porter, J. and Jick, H. "Addiction Rare in Patients Treated with Narcotics." *New Engl J Med* (1980) *302*, 123.
13. Wall, P. D. "Neuropathic Pain." *Pain* (1990) *43*, 267–68.
14. Jaffe, J. H. and Martin, W. R. "Opioid Analgesics and Antagonists." *The Pharmacological Basis of Therapeutics*. Eds. Goodman, A. G. and Gilman, L. S. (New York: Macmillan, 1985), 500–501.
15. Glynn, C. J., Lloyd, J. W., and Folkhard, S. "Ventilatory Response to Intractable Pain." *Pain* (1981) *11*, 201–11.
16. Hanks, G. W. and Twycross, R. G. "Pain, the Physiological Antagonist of Opioid Analgesics." *Lancet* (1984) *i*, 1477–78. See also Walsh, T. D., Baster, R., Bownman, K. et al. "High Dose Morphine and Respiratory Function in Chronic Cancer Pain." *Pain* (1981) Suppl. 1, S39.
17. Jaffe and Martin, "Opioid Analgesics," 507. See also Wells, C. J., Lipton, S., and Lahverta, J. "Respiratory Depression after Percutaneous Cervical Antero-Lateral Cordotomy in Patients on Slow-Release Oral Morphine." *Lancet* (1984) *i*, 739.
18. Stanley, R. "Legal Questions Over Pain Relief Worrying Medical Community." *Austin American Statesman*, October 31, 1992. See also Pulley, M. "Doctors Thrust, Consumers Parry Enforcement Issue." *Business Journal*, February 1993.
19. Jorenson, D. E. "Federal and State Regulation of Opioids." *J Pain and Symptom Management*, (1990) 5, Suppl. 1, S12.
20. Stasney, C. R. and Stratton-Hill, C. "Pain Control and the Texas State Board of Medical Examiners." *Texas State Board of Medical Examiners Newsletter* (1993) *15*, 1.
21. Joranson, D. E. "Availability of Opioids for Cancer Pain: Recent Trends, Assessment of System Barriers, New World Health Organization Guidelines, and the Risk of Diversion." *J Pain and Symptom Management* (1993) *8*, 353–60.
22. Woolf, C. J. "Functional Plasticity of the Flexor Withdrawal Reflex in the Rat Following Peripheral Tissue Injury." *Advances in Pain Research and Therapy*. Eds. Fields, H. L., Dubner, R., and Cervero, F. (1985) *9*, 193–201.

23. Mogil, J. S., Marek, P., O'Toole, L. A. et al. "Mu-opiate Receptor Binding is Up-Regulated in Mice Selectively Bred for High Stress-Induced Analgesia." Unpublished observations.
24. Hindley, A. C., Hill, E. B., Leyland, M. J. et al. "A Double-Blind Controlled Trial of Salmon Calcitonin in Pain Due to Malignancy." *Cancer Chemother. Pharmacol* (1982) 9, 71–74. See also Szanto, J., Jozsef, J., Rado, J. et al. "Pain Killing with Calcitonin in Patients with Malignant Tumors." *Oncology* (1986) 43, 69–72; Roth, A. and Kolaric, K. "Analgetic Activity of Calcitonin in Patients with Painful Osteolytic Metastases of Breast Cancer." *Oncology* (1986) 43, 283–87; Bloomquist, C., Elomaa, I., Porkka, L. et al. "Evaluation of Salmon Calcitonin Treatment in Bone Metastases from Breast Cancer—A Controlled Trial." *Bone* (1988) 9, 45–51. See also Ernst, D. S., MacDonald, R. N., Paterson, A. H. G. et al. "A Double-Blind, Crossover Trial of Intravenous Clodronate in Metastatic Bone Pain." *J Pain and Symptom Management* (1992) 7, 4–11.
25. Fodstad, H. and Ljunggren, B. C. A. "Baclofen and Carbamazepine in Supraspinal Spasticity." *J Royal Soc Med* (1991) 84, 747–48.
26. "Cancer Pain Relief." Geneva, World Health Organization (1986), 74. See also "Cancer Pain Relief and Palliative Care." Geneva, World Health Organization Technical Report Series 804 (1990), 75.
27. Bradley, J. D., Brandt, K. D., Katz, B. P. et al. "Comparison of an Anti-inflammatory Dose of Ibuprofen, an Analgesic Dose of Ibuprofen and Acetaminophen in the Treatment of Patients with Osteoarthritis of the Knee." *New Engl J Med* (1991) 325, 87–91.
28. Klein, D. S. and Edwards, L. W. "Continuous Intravenous Ketorolac Infusion for the Treatment of Cancer Pain." *Am J Pain Management* (1993) 3, 179–80.
29. Portenoy, R. K., Foley, K. M., and Inturrisi, C. E. "The Nature of Opioid Responsiveness and Its Implications for Neuropathic Pain: New Hypotheses Derived from Studies of Opioid Infusions. *Pain* (1993) 43, 273–86.
30. Sjoqvist, F., Borga, O., and Orme, M. L. E. "Fundamentals of Clinical Pharmacology." *Drug Treatment.* Ed. Avery, G. S. (Sydney: Adis Press, 1980), 32.
31. Swerdlow, M. "The Use of Anticonvulsants in the Management of Cancer Pain." *The Pain Clinic.* Eds. Erdmann, W., Oyamma, T., Pernack, M. J. (Utrecht, The Netherlands: VNU Scientific Press, 1985), 1, 9.
32. Brose, W. G. and Cousins, M. J. "Subcutaneous Lidocaine for Treatment of Neuropathic Cancer Pain." *Pain* (1991) 45, 145–148.
33. Baines, M. J. "Control of Other Symptoms." *The Management of Terminal Malignant Disease.* Ed. Saunders, C. M. (London: Edward Arnold, 1984), 109.
34. Bloomfield, S., Simard-Savoie, S., Bernier, J. et al. "Comparative Analgesic Activity of Levopromazine and Morphine in Patients with Chronic Pain." *Can Med Assn* (1964) 90, 1156–59. See also Beaver, W. T., Wallenstein, S. L., Houde, R. W. et al. "Comparison of the Analgesic Effects of Methotrimeprazine and Morphine in Patients With Cancer." *Clin Pharmacol Ther* (1966) 4, 436–46.
35. Galer, B. S., Coyle, N., Pasternak, G. W. et al. "Individual Variability in the Response to Different Opioids." *Pain* (1992) 49, 87–91.
36. Swerdlow, M. "General Analgesics Used in Pain Relief: Pharmacology." *Brit J Anaesth* (1967) 39, 699–712.
37. Seed, J. C., Wallenstein, S. L., Houde, R. W. et al. "A Comparison of the Analgesic and Respiratory Effects of Dihydrocodeine and Morphine in Man." *Arch Int Pharmacodynam* (1958) 116, 293–339.
38. Szeto, H. H., Inturrisi, C. E., Houde, R. et al. "Accumulation of Normeperidine,

an Active Metabolite of Meperidine, in Patients with Renal Failure or Cancer." *Am Int Med* (1977) *86*, 738–41.

39. Martin, W. R. "Pharmacology of Opioids." *Pharmacol Rev.* (1983) *35*, 283–323.
40. Jaffe and Martin, "Opioid Analgesics," 519. See also *US Pharmacopeia Dispensing Information* 12th Edition, Vol 1B, 2089.
41. Anggard, E., Nilsson, M. I., Holmstrand, J. et al. "Pharmacokinetics of Methadone During Maintenance Therapy: Pulse Labeling with Deuterated Methadone in the Steady State." *Eur J Clin Pharmacol* (1979) *16*, 53–57.
42. Jaffe and Martin, "Opioid Analgesics," 518.
43. Twycross, "Relief of Pain," 64–90.
44. Sunshine, A., Laska, E. M., Olson, N. Z. "Analgesic Effects of Oral Oxycodone and Codeine in the Treatment of Patients with Post-operative, Postfracture, or Somatic Pain." *Advances in Pain Research and Therapy, Opioid Analgesics in the Management of Clinical Pain*. Eds. Foley, K. M. and Inturrisi, C. E. (New York: Raven Press, 1986), 225–34.
45. Poyhia, R., Vainio, A., and Kalso, E. "A Review of Oxycodone's Clinical Pharmacokinetics and Pharmacodynamics." *J Pain and Symptom Management* (1993) *8*, 63–67.
46. McCarty, K., Rosemark, R., and Katz, R. L. "Narcotic Policy for Terminally Ill Patients." *Seminars in Anesthesia* (1991) *10*, 175–79.
47. Truog, R. D., Berde, C. B., Mitchell, C. et al. "Barbiturates in the Care of the Terminally Ill." *New Engl J Med* (1992) *327*, 1678–82.
48. Boas, R. A., Cousins, M. J. "Chronic Pain and Local Anesthetic Neural Blockade, Diagnostic Neural Blockade." *Neural Blockade*. Eds. Cousins, M. J. and Bridenbaugh, P.O. (Philadelphia: J. B. Lippincott, 1986), 885–98.
49. Bonica, *The Management of Pain*, 438, 1886.
50. Loeser, J. D. "Dorsal Rhizotomy for the Relief of Chronic Pain." *J. Neurosurg* (1972) *36*, 745–750.
51. Thompson, G. E., Moore, D. C., Bridenbaugh, P. O. et al. "Abdominal Pain and Alcohol Celiac Plexus Nerve Block." *Anesth Analg* (1977) *56*, 1–5.
52. Evans, R. J., Watson, C. P. N. "Lumbosacral Plexopathy in Cancer Patients." *Neurology* (1985) *35*, 1392–93.
53. Cousins, M. J. and Mather, L. E. "Intrathecal and Epidural Administration of Opioids." *Anesthesiology* (1984) *61*, 276–310.
54. DuPen, S. L., Peterson, D. G., Bogosian, A. C. et al. "A New Permanent Exteriorized Epidural Catheter for Narcotic Self-Administration to Control Cancer Pain." *Cancer* (1987) *59*, 986–93.
55. Waldman, S. D. and Coombs, D. W. "Selection of Implantable Narcotics Delivery Systems." *Anesth Analg* (1989) *68*, 377–84.
56. Yaksh, T. L. and Onofrio, B. M. "Retrospective Consideration of Doses of Morphine Given Intrathecally by Chronic Infusion in 163 Patients by 19 Physicians." *Pain* (1987) *31*, 211–23.
57. Coombs, D. W., Maurer, L. H., Saunders, R. L., and Gaylor, M. "Outcomes and Complications of Continuous Intra-spinal Narcotic Analgesia for Cancer Pain Control." *J Clin Oncol* (1984) *2*, 1414–20. See also Penn, R. D. and Paice, J. A. "Chronic Intrathecal Morphine for Intractable Pain." *J. Neurosurg* (1987) *67*, 182–86; and Yaksh, T. L. and Onofrio, B. M. (1987) op. cit.
58. Bedder, M., Burchiel, K., and Larson, A. "Cost Analysis of Two Implantable Narcotic Delivery Systems." *Journal of Pain and Symptom Management* (1991) *6*, 368–73.

59. Boraas, M. C. "Palliative Surgery." *Semin Oncol* (1985) *12*, 368–74.
60. Sundaresan, N., Galicich, J. H., Lane, J. M. et al. "Treatment of Odontoid Fractures in Cancer Patients." *J. Neurosurg* (1981) *52*, 187–92.
61. Sundaresan, N., Galicich, J. H., Lane, J. M. et al. "Treatment of Epidural Cord Compression by Vertebral Body Resection and Stabilization." *J. Neurosurg* (1985) *63*, 676–84.
62. Sundaresan, N., DiGiancinto, G. V., and Hughes, J. E. O. "Surgical Treatment of Spinal Metastases." *Clin Neurosurg* (1986) *33*, 503–22.
63. Sundaresan, N., DiGiancinto, G. V., and Hughes, J. E. O. "Neurosurgery in the Treatment of Cancer Pain." *Cancer* (1989) *63*, 2365–77.
64. Poletti, C. E., Cohen, A. M., Todd, D. P. et al. "Cancer Pain Relieved by Long-Term Epidural Morphine with Permanent Indwelling Systems for Self-Administration." *J. Neurosurg* (1981) *55*, 581–84.
65. Leavens, M. E., Hill, C. S., Cech, D. A. et al. "Intrathecal and Intraventricular Morphine for Pain in Cancer Patients: Initial Study." *J. Neurosurg* (1982) *56*, 41–45. See also Lobato, R. D., Madrid, J. L., Lorenza, M. D. et al. "Intraventricular Morphine for the Control of Pain in Terminal Cancer Patients." *J. Neurosurg* (1983) *59*, 627–33.
66. Obbens, E. A., Hill, S. C., Leavens, M. E. et al. "Intraventricular Morphine Administration for Control of Chronic Cancer Pain." *Pain* (1987) *28*, 61–68.
67. Olds, J. and Milner, B. "Positive Reinforcement Produced by Electrical Stimulation of the Septal Area and Other Regions of the Rat Brain." *J Comp Physiol Psychol* (1954) *47*, 419–27. See also Raynolds, D. V. "Surgery in the Rat During Electrical Analgesia Induced by Focal Brain Stimulation." *Science* (1969) *164*, 444–45nvbnv; and Hammond, D. L. "Control Systems for Nociceptive Afferent Processing. The Descending Inhibitory Pathways." *Spinal Afferent Processing*. Ed. T. L. Yaksh (New York: Plenum Press, 1986), 363–90.
68. Heath, R. G. and Mickle, W. A. "Evaluation of Seven Years Experience with Depth Electrode Studies in Human Patients." *Electrical Studies on the Unanesthetized Brain*. Eds. Ramey and O'Doherty (New York: Hoeber, 1960), 214–47.
69. Richardson, D. E. and Akil, H. "Long Term Results of Periventricular Gray Self-Stimulation." *Neurosurgery* (1977) *1*, 199–202. See also Hosobuchi, Y., Admans, J. E., and Linchitz, R. "Pain Relief by Electrical Stimulation of the Central Gray Matter in Humans and Its Reversal by Naloxone." *Science* (1977) *197*, 183–85; Mazars, G., Merienne, L., and Ciolocca, C. "Comparative Study of Electrical Stimulation of Posterior Thalamic Nuclei, Periaqueductal Gray, and Other Midline Mesencephalic Structures in Man." *Adv Pain Res Ther* (1979) *3*, 541–46; Boivie, J. and Meyerson, B. A. "A Correlative Anatomical and Clinical Study of Pain Suppression by Deep Brain Stimulation." *Pain* (1982) *13*, 113–26; Lazorthes, Y., Siegfried, J., Gouarderes, C., Bastide, R., Cros, J., and Verdie, J. C. "Periventricular Gray Matter Stimulation Versus Chronic Intrathecal Morphine in Cancer Pain." *Adv. Pain Res Ther* (1983) *5*, 467–75; Meyerson, B. A. "Electrical Stimulation Procedures: Effects, Presumed Rationale, and Possible Mechanisms." *Adv. Pain Res Ther* (1983) *5*, 495–534; De Salles, A. A. F., Katayama, Y., Becker D. P., and Hayes, R. "Pain Suppression Induced by Electrical Stimulation of the Pontine Prabrachial Region." *J. Neurosurg* (1985) *62*, 397–407; Baskin, D. S., Mehler, W. R., Hosobuchi, Y. et al. "Autopsy Analysis of the Safety, Efficacy and Cartography of Electrical Stimulation of the Central Gray in Humans." *Brain Res* (1986) *371*, 231–36; and Young, R. F. and Brechner,

T. "Electrical Stimulation of the Brain for Relief of Intractable Pain Due to Cancer." *Cancer* (1986) *57*, 1266–72.

70. Melzack, R. and Wall, P. D. "Pain Mechanisms: A New Theory." *Science* (1964) *150*, 971–978.

71. Barolat, G. "Percutaneous Retroperitoneal Stimulation of the Sacral Plexus." *Stereotac Funct Neurosurg* (1991) *56*, 250–57. See also Nashold, B. S. and Goldner, J. L. "Electrical Stimulation of Peripheral Nerves for Relief of Intractable Chronic Pain." *Med Instrum* (1975) *9*, 224–25.

72. Holsheimer, J., Struijk, J. J., and Rijkhoff, N. J. M. "Contact Combination in Epidural Spinal Cord Stimulation. A Comparison by Computer Modeling." *Stereotact and Funct Neurosurg* (1991) *56*, 220–33.

73. Long, D. M. "Surgical Therapy of Chronic Pain." *Neurosurgery* (1980) *6*, 317–28.

74. Sundaresan, DiGiancinto, and Hughes, (1989) op cit.

75. Boivie and Meyerson, (1982) op cit.

76. Young and Brechner, (1986) op cit.

77. Singler, R. C. "Alcohol Neurolysis of Sciatic and Femoral Nerves." *Anesth Analg* (1981) *60*, 532–33. Sahni, K. S., Pieper, D. R., Anderson, R. et al. "Relation of Hypesthesia to the Outcome of Glycerol Rhizolysis for Trigeminal Neuralgia." *J. Neurosurg* (1990) *72*, 55–58.

78. Tobler, W. D., Tew, J. M., Cosman, E. et al. "Improved Outcome in the Treatment of Trigeminal Neuralgia by Percutaneous Stereotactic Rhizotomy with a New, Curved Tip Electrode." *Neurosurgery* (1983) *12*, 313–17.

79. Batzdorf, U. and Weingarten, S. M. "Percutaneous Cordotomy: A Simplified Approach to Management of Intractable Pain." *Western J Med* (1970) *112*, 21–26.

80. Spiller, W. G. and Martin, E. "The Treatment of Persistent Pain of Organic Origin in the Lower Part of the Body by Division of the Anterolateral Column of the Spinal Cord." *J Amer Med Assoc* (1912) *58*, 1489–90.

81. Mullen, S. "Percutaneous Cordotomy." *J. Neurosurg* (1971) *35*, 360–366. See also Levin, A. B. and Cosman, E. R. "Thermocouple-Monitored Cordotomy Electrode." *J. Neurosurg* (1980) *53*, 266–68; and Batzdorf, U. and Bentson, J. R. "Use of Metrizamiade for Percutaneous Cordotomy." *J. Neurosurg* (1983) *59*, 545–47.

82. Folz, E. L. and White, L. E. Jr. "Pain Relief by Frontal Cingulumotomy." *J. Neurosurg* (1962) *19*, 89–100.

83. Hassenbush, S. J., Pillay, P. K., and Barnett, G. H. "Radiofrequency Cingulumotomy for Intractable Cancer Pain Using Stereotaxis Guided by Magnetic Resonance Imaging." *Neurosurgery* (1990) *27*, 220–23.

84. Hurt, R. W. and Ballantine, H. T. "Stereotactic Anterior Cingulate Lesions for Persistent Pain. A Report on 68 Cases." *Clin Neurosurg* (1974) *21*, 334–51.

85. De Salles, A. A. F. and Hariz, M. "Functional Radiosurgery." *Stereotactic Surgery and Radiosurgery*. Eds. De Salles, A. A. F. and Goetsch, S. J. (Madison, Wis.: Medical Physics Publishing, 1993), 390–406.

86. Laitinen, L. V. "Functional Stereotactic Surgery for Movement Disorder, Pain and Behavioral Disorder." *Stereotactic Surgery and Radiosurgery*. Eds. De Salles, A. A. F. and Goetsch, S. J., 95–106.

87. Lagnado, L. "But Who Will Pay for the High Cost of Relief?" *Wall Street Journal*, 20 August 1996.

An Overview

Two deaths, one an international figure and the second an unidentified young woman, form the basis for this essay. The death of Sigmund Freud and an incident reported in a brief medical journal article provide fertile ground for reflection on suicide, physician-assisted suicide, and the potential course of medical practice in our society. Values have consequences, and ultimately the choices we make as individuals and a society stem from our worldview. Hopefully, it will be one that is Christian.

Chapter Six

SUICIDE AND THE RIGHT TO DIE (WITH HELP)

The Cases of Sigmund Freud and JAMA's *Debbie*

David L. Schiedermayer, M.D.

THE LINES WE SO CAREFULLY DRAW on paper between pain control, suicide, and active euthanasia tend to blur in real cases. One need not appeal to recent court decisions (*Quill v. Vacco* [State of New York], 2nd Circuit Court of Appeals, 9th Circuit Court of Appeals) to illustrate this blurring; old cases suffice. One of the most interesting I have found involves the treatment of Sigmund Freud, the great unriddler of human enigmas, who died of head and neck carcinoma. I leave it to you to decide if Freud's death involved suicide, physician-assisted suicide, or active euthanasia. Let me tell you his story, drawn largely from the excellent biography of Freud by Peter Gay,[1] and then discuss the concepts of withdrawal of treatment, physician assisted suicide, and active euthanasia, and conclude with the story of Debbie.

THE CASE OF SIGMUND FREUD

Sigmund Freud was born May 6, 1856, the son of Jacob Freud, a Jewish wool merchant. Sigmund studied medicine at the University of Vienna and exhibited physical and moral courage in fighting racial bias and anti-Semitism while growing up. In 1896, he began to develop psychoanalysis, the study of the id, superego, and ego, and began writing his prodigious volumes. In mid-February 1923, Freud detected "leukoplakia on my jaw and palate." He was afraid to tell his personal physician because he had been previously told to stop smoking. He consulted, instead, a dermatologist, Max Steiner, who did not ask Freud to give up smoking, but instead trivialized the clinical findings.

On April 7, 1923, Felix Deutsch Freud's internist, called on him. At first glance, Deutsch saw that the lesion was cancer, but Deutsch merely called it a "leukoplakia." Freud's grandson had recently died, and he was distraught. His fragile emotional state was one reason his physicians lied to him. Freud was a doctor surrounded by famous doctors, but he didn't see an eminent specialist for his first and most crucial ENT surgery. Instead, he turned to a local rhinologist, Marcus Hajek. Something went wrong during the surgery.

Freud bled heavily in his hospital room. His only company was his roommate, a mentally handicapped dwarf. The dwarf saved Freud's life. When Freud bled, becoming too weak to even call for help, the dwarf ran to get the nurse, and the bleeding was stopped. Hajek subsequently prescribed X-ray and radium treatments.

The pain continued. On October 4, 1923, Freud finally saw a good specialist. Professor Pichler, an eminent surgeon, reoperated twice and fed Freud through a nasogastric tube. Freud was fitted with a prosthesis between his mouth and his nasal cavity. Nonetheless, the cancer remained. Pichler suggested reoperation in November of 1923. From 1923–30, Freud had thirty more operations, some minor, including fittings and refittings of his prosthesis. Through it all, he continued smoking.

In 1929, Freud had a first meeting with his personal physician, Max Schur. Dr. Schur became very close to Freud and was a central character in Freud's life. Freud had only two complaints regarding Schur's treatment: first, that Schur's bills were too low; and second, that Schur stop advising that Freud give up his beloved, necessary cigars.

At their first meeting in March of 1929, Freud said, "Dr. Schur, promise me also: when the time comes, you won't let them torment me unnecessarily." Schur promised, and the two men shook hands. By the spring of 1939, the time had almost come to keep the promise. Freud was eighty-two years old. He'd had cancer since age sixty-six. The Nazis had reached Austria, and Freud fled reluctantly—finally persuaded that he could not stay. He wrote, "I have come to England to die in freedom." In January of 1939, Freud noticed new swellings in his mouth. He wrote, "My condition is threatening to become interesting. Since my operation in September I have been suffering from pains in the jaw which are growing stronger slowly but steadily, so that I cannot get through my daily chores and my nights without a hot water bottle and sizeable doses of ASA." He was not certain whether this was a harmless process or "progress in what I have been battling for years."

In late February 1939, Dr. Antoine Lacassagne came from Paris to examine Freud in Schur's presence; he applied radium, but the pain persisted. Freud then made a quality of life statement to his friends, when another consultant thought that a mixture of x-ray and radium would "add some weeks or months of life." Freud was not sure it was worth the effort, saying, "I don't deceive myself about the chances of a final result at my age. I feel tired and exhausted by all that they do to me. As a way to the unavoidable end it is as good as any other, although I would not have chosen it myself." On February 28, 1939, he had a biopsy of the cancer far back in his mouth—positive; X-ray treatments suppressed the cancer, surpassing Schur's expectations.

In June of 1939, Freud's pain increased again. His prosthesis became hard to use. The smell from his cancer ulcerations increased, but Freud still kept a couple of hours each day for his analytic practice. On August 27, Freud made his last journal entry: "War Panic," he wrote. The end was now near. Freud's dog would not go near him because the smell was so bad. Freud was very tired, and it was hard to feed him. But while he suffered greatly and the nights were especially hard, he did not want any sedation. He could still read, and his last book was Balzac's mysterious tale of the magic shrinking skin, *La Peau de Chagrin*. When he finished the book he told Schur, casually, that this had been the right book for him to read, dealing as it did with shrinking and starvation.

Schur was agonized by his inability to relieve Freud's suffering, but on September 21, as Schur was sitting by Freud's bedside, Freud took Schur's hand and said to him, "Schur, you remember our 'contract' not to leave me in the lurch when the time had come. Now it is nothing but torture and makes no sense." Schur indicated he had not forgotten. Freud gave a sigh of relief, kept his hand for a moment, and said, "I thank-you." Then, after a slight hesitation, he added, "Talk it over with Anna, and if she thinks it right, then make an end of it."

Anna Freud wanted to postpone the moment, but Schur insisted that to keep Freud going was pointless, and she submitted to the inevitable, as had her father. The time had come; he knew and acted; this was Freud's interpretation when he said he had come to England "to die in freedom."

Schur was at the point of tears as he witnessed Freud facing death with dignity and without self-pity. He had never seen anyone die like that. On September 21, Schur injected Freud with thirty milligrams of morphine—he considered the normal dose for sedation to be twenty milligrams in Freud's case—and Freud sunk into a peaceful sleep. Schur repeated the injection when he became restless, and administered a final injection on the next day, September 22, 1939. Freud lapsed into a coma from which he did not awake. He died at three in the morning, September 23, 1939. Nearly four decades earlier, Freud had written what he would do "when thoughts fail or words will not come . . . I tremor before this possibility. That is why, with all the resignation before death that suits an honest man, I have one wholly secret entreaty: only no invalidism, no paralysis of one's powers through bodily misery. Let us die in harness, as King Macbeth says."

As Gay points out, Freud had made certain that his secret entreaty would be fulfilled. The old stoic kept control of his life to the end.

EUTHANASIA VS. WITHDRAWAL OF TREATMENT

Euthanasia may be defined as a "good death." While the distinction between passive euthanasia and active euthanasia may be difficult to make, passive euthanasia may be defined as allowing patients to die by withdrawing or withholding therapy—for example, stopping a patient's respirator. Active euthanasia is the administration of a drug to bring about the rapid death of a patient—for example, large doses of phenobarbital, curare, or morphine. The euthanasia debate is very ancient. The question, after all, is an old one, not easily settled. The Hippocratic oath states, "I will neither give a deadly drug to anybody if asked for it nor make a suggestion to that effect." Socrates said, "The chief task of philosophy is to prepare one to die."

The death of a patient can be one of the most guilt and anxiety provoking aspects of medicine. It can also be one of the events physicians remember as personally meaningful and significant. At a recent national seminar on important stories of medical practice, most of the stories were about physicians attending patients at their deaths.

Let me tell you some of the ways we attend patients at their deaths. I will first discuss passive euthanasia, then active euthanasia. Note that even in defining the actions this way, the definitions blur. I wish that weren't the truth, but is seems to me that the bright lines ethicists often seek to draw fail to delineate the reality.

There are several different forms of passive euthanasia: withholding treatment, withdrawing treatment, and double effect. Withholding life-sustaining medical treatment is a common occurrence in the medical setting. A study of renal failure on dialysis patients showed that 10 percent of these patients die from nontreatment—that is, nondialysis.[2] A study of nontreatment of fever in nursing home patients showed that antibiotics are commonly withheld, as is hospitalization.[3]

Sometimes, the form of withholding treatment can be very subtle. For example, when a patient's blood pressure drops, physicians sometimes keep the medicine to raise the blood pressure at a predetermined level rather than raise the medicine in response to the worsening pressure. These medicines, called pressor agents, are kept at a fixed level and higher doses are withheld from the patient. The doctor's order is something like this: "Keep the dopamine at 8mcs even if the pressure drops." Dialysis, ventilators, and medications are withheld from patients at the request of the patient, or the family, or sometimes at the medical judgment of the physician. In passive euthanasia situations, the purpose of these withholdings is to allow the patient to die a more natural or quicker death.

In withdrawal situations, we take the technology out; we stop the feeding and remove the feeding tube. We don't maintain our pressor agents at a steady level, we just stop them. We withdraw the respirator. We can also withdraw care in more subtle ways. For example, doctors sometimes withdraw intensive care from patients.

The doctrine of double effect takes it one step further. This ancient doctrine holds that if the physician intends to control pain but the unintended result is also death, the physician's action is ethical. Pain control and death are double effects of the action that *intended only pain control*, not death.

Most physicians are comfortable, depending on the medical situation, with performing "passive euthanasia"—withholding or withdrawing various therapies and/or allowing the patient to die. Most physicians are now also comfortable with "double effect" euthanasia.

EUTHANASIA AND PHYSICIAN-ASSISTED SUICIDE

The controversy now concerns active intervention—physician-assisted suicide—by providing medications, which the patient takes himself or herself. But the lines are not as clear as my definitions would suggest. Freud's doctor gave him fairly large doses of morphine, but by no means certainly lethal doses (which are probably in excess of two hundred milligrams). Was Freud's death active euthanasia? Or was it good pain control with the unintended double effect of death? Or was it perhaps physician-assisted suicide?

The ethical underpinning of the modern active euthanasia movement is that the whole enterprise is based on the voluntary consent of the patient who would request to be rapidly killed. Physicians in the Netherlands perform active euthanasia at the patient's request. While euthanasia is illegal in the Netherlands, it is societally sanctioned and physicians are rarely prosecuted. Estimates are that Dutch physicians have performed euthanasia on as many as eight thousand patients.[4] Many Dutch physicians who perform euthanasia inject patients with fatal doses of phenobarbital and curare.

I have had the chance to talk in detail on several occasions with a physician from Holland who performs euthanasia. He told me that euthanasia is a "forced measure" and that it is sometimes the only way to relieve intractable suffering. In addition, he assured me that physicians in Holland follow strict guidelines. (To review these guidelines, refer to Dr. Robert D. Orr's article which appears earlier in this book.)

Most of the arguments for active euthanasia are based on intractable patient suffering. It is true that physicians need to better ease the suffering of patients; the data show that we need to be better educated about narcotic use and more aggressive in the treatment of terminal patients who have severe pain.[5] There is an implicit right to die (in the end, we all get this right, whether we want it or not!). The problem is stretching the concept of death with dignity to include the right to be killed by others upon request. There are several arguments against performing active euthanasia on competent patients.

First, medical perspectives on healing stress the importance of the individual life and eschew the notion of an autonomy so radical it would permit one to request to be killed by a doctor. Second, the Hippocratic Oath speaks out strongly against such action (even if requested). Third, it is not certain that philosophical distinctions about consent can avoid potential abuses in practice. A group of leading physicians and ethicists have reported that there are documented cases in the Netherlands of cryptic and uninvited killing by doctors. Currently, right to die advocates are concerned about Kevorkian's excesses here in the United States. Derek Humphry noted, after the Michigan doctor's thirty-eighth assisted suicide, it is "time to change the law and regulate Kevorkian style deaths."[6]

Easier said than done because the bright lines between all these forms of assisted death are really difficult to see in real practice. For example, consider a case of what might have been active euthanasia in America.

JAMA'S DEBBIE

It is the middle of the night on a quiet hospital ward. A tired young physician has been called by the nurse to see Debbie, a young woman with metastatic ovarian cancer. Debbie is nauseated and short of breath; she weighs a mere eighty pounds; her only words to the doctor are, "Let's get this over with." The physician calculates what he or she thinks is a lethal dose of morphine, walks over to the bedside, and injects the contents of the syringe into Debbie's intravenous line. Debbie dies minutes later.

Is this an act of compassion or the scene of a crime? Did Debbie want relief of her pain, nausea, and shortness of breath, or did she request a fatal injection? If Debbie was requesting aid-in-dying, should this aid have been administered in the middle of the night by an exhausted doctor who was unfamiliar with her case and who failed to consult Debbie's family, attending physician, or the hospital ethics committee? Was this an assisted suicide, or double effect, or was it in fact euthanasia.

These are not merely hypothetical questions: the scene described was published anonymously in the January 8, 1988 edition of the *Journal of the American Medical Association* (*JAMA*).[7] The title of the article was, "It's Over, Debbie." Cook County State's Attorney Richard M. Daley unsuccessfully subpoenaed *JAMA* to release the writer's name.

George Lundberg, then editor of *JAMA*, invoked the Illinois Reporter's Privilege Act to shield the author's identity. The American Medical Association, prominent physicians, lawyers, journalists, theologians, civil libertarians, philosophers, and the media have also entered the fray. All this uproar was caused by an unsolicited, undocumented, anonymous piece less than five hundred words long, a brief vignette that is rich in ambiguity and raises far more questions than it answers!

Why did the doctor write the article, why did Lundberg publish it, and why all the fuss? There are several simple answers and several more complex answers. The physician who wrote the piece felt ambivalent, guilty, or curious about the response of other physicians to his actions. He wanted to stir up controversy: he did. Lundberg, a shrewd editor, decided that the time was ripe for the euthanasia controversy. He thought the article would attract widespread attention to the issue and to his journal: it did.

More is at stake, however, than the motives of a tired young physician or a savvy old editor. The debate goes right to the heart of our modern problem, put succinctly by Willard Gaylin: "Nothing in life is easy anymore, not even the leaving of it."

Many physicians oppose giving a lethal injection to patients like Freud or like Debbie for the express purpose of killing them. They reason that such an act is simply not part of the doctor's job description because killing patients goes against several thousand years of medical ethics. The effects of widespread euthanasia on the doctor-patient relationship are predictable and negative in the long run. Margaret Mead reported that in societies where doctors actively kill patients, the sick are apprehensive. What will their doctor do to them? "Debbie" demonstrates that physicians may act quickly and unilaterally to bring patients' lives to an end.

The outcome of the Netherlands' experience with active euthanasia is still too early to assess: their culture is very different from ours. Promoting euthanasia in a rapidly aging, cost-conscious society like ours may present policy problems. Our medical system is too fragmented and is undergoing too much economic and structural upheaval to make euthanasia a prudent policy choice. Finally, the euthanasia movement would largely ignore the great progress made in pain control and in compassionate hospice care. Why not provide care for the dying instead of killing them?

Even if we decide euthanasia is ethically permissible, should we advocate euthanasia when our definitions of death, terminal illness, and suffering continue to change? Might we stop the lives of patients who literally have months or years of good life left to live? Should we close off the future for them at an arbitrary point, and if so, how can patient and doctor choose such a point? Or should nonphysicians—"Thanatos (death) technicians"—be allowed to do euthanasia?

As a Christian physician I am troubled by the little piece in *JAMA*. I am sympathetic to the acts of Freud's physician, but I am also troubled by the intention behind the injections, even though the plan was "prearranged" in a competent patient. As someone who might very well be a cancer patient in the future, I can appreciate cancer and other patients' plights. How and when will they die? Will it be with dehydration, or with infection, or perhaps a pneumonia? Will their pain be treated aggressively, or will they be abandoned in their suffering? Will they be alone, short of breath, and frightened, or will they be cared for and comforted? These basic questions—which are medical, philosophical, theological, and so personal—are the real ones raised by the deaths of Sigmund Freud and *JAMA*'s Debbie.

One last irony: Freud was apparently depressed and perhaps suicidal at the end of his life. Perhaps the greatest psychiatrist of our age was suffering from mental illness when given three large shots of morphine by his personal physician. No single shot was enough to clearly cause his death, but, given his already weakened condition, the three together had a cumulative effect. Debbie, who was even weaker than Freud, died more quickly. Given Oregon's physician-assisted suicide law, the votes in Washington and California, the euthanasia legalization in the Northern Territories of Australia, it seems we are only at the beginning of this debate.

Once physician-assisted suicide is legalized or even societally condoned, we will move on to address the euthanasia question. But again, the issues will not be new. We have been there before, and I am more and more convinced, as I see the debate rage, that it comes down to a basic worldview issue.

Is life a gift, or better, a loan from God? As Jesus would say, "If you answer that question for me then I will answer yours": "Is suicide, or assisted death, in any of its categories, right or wrong?" Are we children of the earth or of the Father? Once again, If you answer that question then I will also answer yours: "Is there a right to die (with help)?"

ENDNOTES

1. Peter Gay, *Freud: A Life for Our Times* (New York: W. W. Norton, 1988).
2. Steven Neu and Carl M. Kjellstrand, "Stopping Long-Term Dialysis: An Empirical Study of Withdrawal of Life-Supporting Treatment," *N Engl J Med* 314 (1986): 14–20.
3. N. K. Brown and D. R. Thompson, "Nontreatment of Fever in Extended Care Facilities," *N Engl J Med* 300 (1979):1246–50.
4. F. E. Pence, "Do Not Go Slowly Into that Good Night: Mercy Killing in Holland," *Am J Med* 84 (1988): 139–41.

5. S. H. Wanzer et al., "The Physician's Responsibility Toward Hopelessly Ill Patients—A Second Look," *N Engl J Med* 320 (1989): 844–49.
6. D. M. Gianelli, "Right-to-Die Advocates Seek Distance from Dr. Kevorkian," *American Medical News*, 39, no. 34 (September 9, 1996).
7. Anonymous, "It's Over, Debbie," *JAMA* 259, no. 2 (1988): 272.

An Overview

The provision of medical care and the debate regarding physician-assisted suicide has many facets and affects many people. One critical dimension of treatment and care is that of nursing. In this essay, Mary Krumholz Clifford emphasizes the life-affirming nature of nursing. Those who advocate physician-assisted suicide must logically and ultimately abandon the strong and compassionate foundation of nursing. Nurses are an integral part of the health-care continuum and their affirmation of life is essential in our society today.

Chapter Seven

A NURSE'S PERSPECTIVE ON EUTHANASIA

Mary Krumholz Clifford

THIS ESSAY IS A DISCUSSION of euthanasia (particularly, euthanasia by dehydration and starvation), assisted suicide, and "living wills," and their impact on the health care professions and on society. Consideration is also given to the question, "What should be the Christian response to the proposal that these practices are appropriate solutions to pressing social and economic problems?"

As a nursing student, I learned that the basic goal of the nursing profession is the facilitation of health (physical, mental, emotional, and spiritual health) in fellow human beings with whom one has entered into a nurse-patient relationship. The nurse, I was taught, accepts each patient as a unique individual positioned at a given point on a theoretical continuum between "high-level wellness" and terminal illness, and assists the patient to realize the maximal health and well-being possible at that point.[1] In my classes on nursing theory, no notion was put forward that a part of the nurse's charge is to assist in deciding whether a patient's health is worth promoting. Neither was I taught that causing a person's death could be a way to assist him or her to maximize well-being. Rather, I learned that even when a patient's position on the "wellness continuum" is in the terminal illness range, the nurse devotes his or her theoretical and technical knowledge and all appropriate resources (including compassion and respect) to the task at hand: in this case, assisting the patient to achieve the highest level of comfort possible.

My first nursing position was at a forty-two bed rural community hospital, and it provided broad experience of many aspects of nursing. I cared for children with asthma, teenagers injured in car accidents, middle-aged farmers with heart attacks, and geriatric patients who had experienced strokes. Among my most memorable experiences were the births—sometimes with no doctor present—and my first encounters with death. I then took a position at a large, urban teaching hospital on a cardiac and pulmonary medical-surgical floor. I enjoyed the new experience of specializing, but my concept of nursing remained the same one I had held at the small rural hospital, and it continued to serve me well enough until one night in 1987.

I was assigned to care for an elderly woman whose family had decided to stop her medical treatment and to withdraw her food and water, which were being given via a feeding tube. The woman had had a stroke and was showing no clear signs of recovering cognitive function after one month of intensive treatment. The patient's level of awareness was a matter of question; some of us thought she was aware of being touched, of discomfort, and of sounds. She was partially paralyzed and could not be fed orally. She probably would have required the services of a long-term-care facility for the remaining months or years of her life. But she was not dying.

Her family said she had "suffered enough." They professed to love her and appeared to believe they were doing the right thing, the compassionate thing. They claimed that her disability and the perceived diminishment of her "quality of life" were evils from which they had a right and an obligation to deliver her, even at the cost of her life itself—even at the cost of taking responsibility for intentionally causing her death. As one of her nurses, I was expected to participate. In fact, I was told I had no right to refuse to participate (which turned out not to be the case, according to hospital policy). As I looked around her that night, from the pictures of her family and her garden, to her fine features and her beautiful white hair, I felt queasy. She was alive, and we were planning deliberately to allow her to dehydrate until she died. In a "high-tech" hospital, in a wealthy country, with simple means available for feeding and hydrating swallowing-disabled patients, this patient would starve and dehydrate because her family wanted death for her as the alternative to a life they saw as unworthy.

I refused to be involved. Another nurse, aware of the possibility of recourse, reported the situation to an adult protection agency. However, once satisfied that the withdrawal of sustenance was authorized by the patient's family, the agency declined to intervene. Five days after her food and water were withdrawn, the woman died.

The incident left me stunned and sickened. I instinctively felt that nursing that participates in dehydrating and starving patients is no longer truly the profession of nursing. The very word, "nurse," is derived from the Latin word for "nourish." I think patients or families who reject nourishment reject such an integral element of the practice of nursing that, in a real sense, they are rejecting nursing care. The question legitimately can be raised: if one rejects medical treatment and nursing care, on what basis can one seek admission to a hospital or nursing home?

In the move to legitimize the starvation and dehydration of certain patients, the nursing profession has followed the lead of the medical profession. In 1986, the Ethical and Judicial Council of the American Medical Association classified the administration of food and water to certain patients as "medical treatment," which (the council asserted) it is ethically permissible for a physician to withhold or withdraw, *even in the absence of terminal illness*. The only clear exception to this judgment, in practice, is the case of patients who are fully willing and able to take in adequate calories by themselves without the assistance of spoon, tube, or intravenous feeding by nurses, nursing assistants, or family members.[2]

But what is "medical treatment?" Are food and water, by definition, medical treatment? Physicians order administration and restriction of food and water in various ways for medical purposes, as when a physician prescribes dietary restrictions for a patient with congestive heart failure, limiting the patient's sodium and water intake for the purpose of decreasing the workload on the patient's heart. Other substances and conditions necessary to life, such as oxygen and heat, are also used in such a way that they treat disease or injury, relieve pain, and improve or preserve health, in addition to their primary function of supporting life. But such use does not change the nature of these things as basic requirements of life. Clearly the physician's use of oxygen, warmth, light, food, and water in medical treatment is a use over and above their primary use; it is a refinement of the primary usefulness of these basic elements. It does not make them essentially or primarily medical treatments. The art and science of the physician does not supplant nature; medicine is, at its best, a studied, skillful, creative enhancement of the natural healing processes, which operate most effectively when the basic requirements of life are properly provided.

One might reasonably wonder about the status of tube-feeding solutions prepared in pharmacies (most are not), colored with blue dye, administered through a silicon tube, and regulated by a machine according to doctors' orders (based on dieticians' recommendations). It is very easy for the lay person to believe that such solutions are medical treatment, especially when the AMA says so.[3] But Webster's defines "food" as "any substance taken into and assimilated by a plant or animal to keep it alive and enable it to grow. . . ." The human body does not discriminate between an artificially colored, chemically flavored, "blueberry" milkshake served in a fast-food restaurant and a tube-feeding solution; it digests and assimilates both mixtures in the same way. There is nothing about the tube-feeding solution that makes it essentially different from other foods, either in purpose, form, content, or the way it is used by the human body. Such solutions are not medical treatment, even if they may constitute a restricted diet and may be said to improve and preserve health. They contain real calories and real water, and their primary purpose is simply to sustain life and enable growth. Tube-feeding solutions are food.

What about the tube and the machine that regulates the flow of the feeding through it? Do these qualify as examples of the "tyrannical new technology" portrayed by many as the adversary in the patient's quest for a peaceful, natural death? As a nurse who has fed a number of patients with the assistance of feeding tubes over the past fourteen years, I strongly believe they do not. First, there is nothing peaceful or natural about death by dehydration and starvation. No one can say with absolute certainty what an individual nonverbal patient is experiencing during the process of such a death. However, in my clinical experience, I have observed such a patient in apparent distress during the eleven days it took him to die of dehydration and starvation. Second—and this cannot be overemphasized—tube feeding is not "high-tech": *no machine is necessary.* Feeding solutions can be administered perfectly well by means of gravity. The machine is primarily for the convenience of caregivers. Third, the most commonly used naso-gastric feeding tube is quite small, about three-sixteenths of an inch in diameter, and neither the naso-gastric feeding tube (used for short-term feeding) nor the gastrostomy tube (used for long-term feeding) are painful or particularly burdensome. The benefit derived from the use of a feeding tube outweighs any small unpleasantness that the tube may cause. It does not treat a person's inability to swallow or lack of appetite. Neither does the tube, in itself, relieve pain or preserve health. The feeding tube is simply an assistive device that makes up for the inability to take in adequate food and water, so that the patient's basic requirements for life can be met.

To withhold tube feeding from a person who depends on it is to withhold a basic requirement for life. The deliberate withholding of tube feeding—by physicians, nurses, or families—from a patient not on the verge of death,[4] with the realization and expectation that this will cause the patient's death, is an act of euthanasia. In the case where such withholding is directed by a "living will," the act in question is either assisted suicide or euthanasia. (One usually cannot be certain, at the point of the withholding, that the author of the will is still in agreement with its contents.) Many people disagree that the withholding of food and fluids is euthanasia. Many think that not feeding, or discontinuing feeding, is simply "allowing to die." But inaction, or the cessation of action, is an action—an act of omission, when the action omitted or stopped is owed to someone by those withholding it, when the action omitted is practically and ethically possible, and when the omission is deliberate. And when those committing such an act of omission know that it will certainly cause the death of an innocent human being, the act of omission is an act of murder[5] (the socially unacceptable term for "mercy" killing).[6]

At minimum, families and health care facilities owe dependent members and patients adequate food, clothing, and shelter. To argue that disability in a vulnerable person relieves the people *charged with guarding that person's welfare* of basic obligations toward the person is to argue in favor of discrimination on the basis of disability.

Does God honor the murder of the innocent when the motive is empathy? In Proverbs 6:17 we are told that the Lord hates "hands that shed innocent blood"—we are not told that our motivation mitigates God's hatred of murder. In Matthew 15:18–19 Jesus says murders defile a man—He does not say murders committed out of hatred defile a man. In Deuteronomy 5:17 God says, "Thou shalt not kill," better translated as "Thou shalt not murder," the central cases of which are the deliberate killing of the innocent.[7] He does not say, "Thou shalt not kill except when it seemeth right to you." We are warned in Proverbs 14:12 (among other places) that "There is a way which seemeth right unto a man; but the end thereof are the ways of death." I think this verse must be pondered very carefully by persons of faith who live in what has become a society lacking in faith. We must continually scrutinize our positions on current issues and ask God to free us from those ideas that genuinely seem right to us, partly due to our social conditioning, but are contradicted by His Word.

Euthanasia is a Greek word that means "good death" or "happy death." Groups such as the Hemlock Society consider a "good death" to be one over which human persons have total control. But Christians have a Source, infinitely superior to that of the Hemlock Society or the ancient Greeks, from which to form an idea of what constitutes a "good" death—or a good life. Our Source leads us to reject both the idea of total human control and the current notion that death can, in itself, be good.

There is a trend now to view death ambiguously, as something that can in itself be positive, not as a clear evil out of which can arise, against all appearances, an infinite good. This notion is expressed through a subtle shift of emphasis in the way death is presented and is often promoted by half-truths asserted in public statements by apparently credible and compassionate professionals. For instance, the oath taken at some medical schools is a replacement for the Hippocratic oath and states that "death is not always an enemy." This is an ominous statement for a group of doctors to make, and it deserves more critical consideration than it may be given by the graduates and the family members and friends in whose presence they take this updated oath. From a biological point of view, death certainly is always the enemy of the living organism. Death and life, not to mention death and health, are incompatible by nature. What kind of physician is it who does not see death as "always an enemy" of the human organism?

Often the intended—and perceived—implication of a statement such as "death is not always an enemy" is that "death is sometimes a friend," that "the lesser evil" is the same thing as "the greater good," a conclusion that does not follow. An important question not addressed by the nontraditional oath is this: If death is "sometimes a friend," are we then justified in pursuing it for a particular patient at his or his family's request, or even at our own discretion? And if, under newly "enlightened" standards of "reasonable medical practice," death is viewed as the highest good for some of the patients some of the time, on what basis can we argue that we are not sometimes obligated to "provide" death as a "treatment" for suffering?

Christians must think especially clearly about this: death was not a part of God's original intention for mankind. Death is a result of sin, and as such it is never a good in itself; it is never a "friend." Death in itself is an evil, as disease and aging are evils—the destruction of God's handiwork. In view of the Fall, we can understand the existence of evils in the world, and we know that God can bring good out of them; yet in themselves they remain evils. The notion that we may or should do evil "that good may come" is condemned by St. Paul as a scandalous misrepresentation of Christian teaching (Rom. 3:8).

As citizens, also, we must think critically about medically "provided" death. Starting from its acknowledged status as a lesser evil under certain circumstances, it does not logically follow that death is sometimes the highest good, or even a good at all. We should admit that medical murder is an evil some are willing to tolerate in an attempt to ease the burdens, perceived and real, of individuals and society. This is a utilitarian approach and, to many thinking people, an incredibly brutish, elitist, and shortsighted utilitarianism at that.[8] We ignore at our peril the deep disorder that historically has resulted when societies have resorted to doing evil.

What, then, should be the Christian position in the face of human suffering and economic pressures? We must first consider some central questions. What kind of life does God consider worthy to be lived? How does God want us to approach death? And how, then, are we to bear witness to God's position on these issues? In the answer to these questions lies the antidote to the poisonous messages being circulated throughout our culture. For the Christian, the simplest way to state God's answer to these questions is, "in Christ." God considers a life lived in Christ to be a life worth living, and He wants us to approach death in the same way—in Christ. One of the most striking things about the earthly life and death of Jesus Christ was that He lived—and died—to do the will of His Father. He made it clear that this was His primary motivation. Our life and death in Christ must be, as his were, in accord with his Father's will.

Many people say, "Surely God would not will that I [or my loved ones] should live with intolerable discomfort, or in a condition that would make life meaningless to me." No, God does not will suffering or disability, in themselves. But God does will that we show our love and reverence for Him by trusting Him enough to accept what He allows, or causes, to happen in our lives for His own high purposes, which sometimes include our purification.

Long before Jesus Christ gave us our supreme example of submission to God's will, Job said, in the midst of intense tribulation, "the LORD gave, and the LORD hath taken away; blessed be the name of the LORD," and "shall we receive good at the hand of God, and shall we not receive evil?" (Job 1:21 and 2:10). Job also said, "when he hath tried me, I shall come forth as gold" (Job 23:10). And God was pleased with Job's response to calamity, calling him "a perfect and an upright man, one that feareth God, and escheweth evil," noting that "he holdeth fast his integrity, although thou [Satan] movedst me against him, to destroy him without cause" (Job 2:3).

Job was in severe physical and emotional discomfort and felt his life to be a terrible burden, a miserable existence compared to which death would be preferable. Yet, in spite of his suffering, he maintained his will to submit: "All the days of my appointed time will I wait, till my change come" (Job 14:14). Job understood his position in relation to the Creator of the universe, "in whose hand is the soul of every living thing, and the breath of all mankind" (Job 12:10), and he did not presume to take his situation into his own hands. Neither did he ask his wife or his friends to take the situation into their hands. Job prayed to God for death, but that is as far as he ventured in the direction of his own will.

Some churches frequently emphasize the demands of justice in selected cases, such as in the relationships between the rich and poor and between powerful and vulnerable countries. It is disturbing, however, that the same people who will sacrifice enthusiastically for justice in such contexts often seem blind to the requirements of justice in other equally compelling ones, for instance, in the case of abortion on demand or, now, in the case of euthanasia—cases in which those being oppressed are unable to cry for justice.

Many will tolerate no interference with what they believe to be their absolute rights, including the heavily promoted "right to die." The majority of respondents to polls on the subject do not seem to appreciate the arrogance of throwing God's continuing gift of life back in His face at the point when, according to human opinion, its quality has become unacceptable. How far we have descended from the frame of mind in which one says, in the face of loss, "The LORD gave, and the LORD hath taken away; blessed be the name of the LORD."

Psalm 104:27 says that God gives all creatures food "in due season." God has blessed us, as individuals and as a nation, with abundant food. What right have we to withhold it from the most vulnerable, most dependent among us, whether that be the child in the inner city or the disabled person in a nursing home? In Matthew 25:42, 45 Jesus says, "I was an hungered and ye gave me no meat: I was thirsty, and ye gave me no drink. . . . Inasmuch as ye did it not to one of the least of these, ye did it not to me."

In 1984, Ella Bathurst, a physically dependent, but conscious, elderly woman was starved and dehydrated to death at Abbott-Northwestern Hospital in Minneapolis, Minnesota, at her daughter's request (the case is a matter of public record). A couple visiting her roommate while this was happening to Mrs. Bathurst heard her calling out weakly; at the time they had thought she was calling, "Walter, Walter!" Later, while watching a television program on medical ethics in which the topic of withholding food and fluids was discussed, the couple remembered that Ella was never given anything to eat or drink during the considerable time they spent visiting their own family member. They realized Ella might actually have been crying out for "Water!" They reported the case to authorities, but by then Ella Bathurst, certainly one of the "least" among us by societal standards, was dead.[9]

Americans today, often at the urging of professional and advocacy organizations, are demanding medically managed deaths and total control over their bodies. Scripture does not support these demands. In 1 Corinthians 6:19–20, St. Paul says, "Know ye not that your body is the temple of the Holy Ghost which is in you, which ye have of God, and ye are not your own? For ye are bought with a price: therefore glorify God in your body, and in your spirit, which are God's." The teachings that we do not own ourselves, that our bodies can be temples of the Holy Spirit, and that we are bought with a price bear directly on the question of whether euthanasia, suicide, or assisted suicide are ever permissible. The answer must be "no." For even if we should enter a comatose state, or become unable to interact with our environment, or lose our ability to comprehend our circumstances, our lives would still have immeasurable meaning and value. We would still retain the image and likeness of God in our beings. We would still be the same persons[10] who were bought at an awesome and appalling price: the incarnation and death of the Son of God.

What believer in the Incarnate Word would claim that Jesus did not die for the severely retarded individual or for the person who is considered to be in a "persistent vegetative state?" Jesus died for each one of us, for the entirety of your life, for the entirety of my life. If I lose my memory or I am injured in an accident, it makes no difference. And even in the case of the most severe disability possible, my body is still that of a believer, the dwelling-place of God the Holy Spirit. I can conceive of no greater argument against killing a human being: it is sometimes the razing of a temple of God and always the desecration of an image of God. Even where the Spirit is absent, who but God can know whether a particular person may not yet turn to Him? Some people thought to be lacking cognitive function actually do have it, and situations in which people are confronted with their absolute powerlessness and neediness— sometimes for the first time—often cause them to turn to God. *Who knows what the Spirit of God may be doing in the mind of an unconscious patient?*

A true Christian does not say to the Father, "Sorry, Lord, it's not enough that you gave your only Son over to death to redeem my body, soul, and spirit, which you sustain throughout my life and in which your Spirit has come to dwell. I'm going to make sure that if I ever become dependent, don't look the way I'm accustomed to looking, am viewed with pity and embarrassment by other people, and lose the ability to have meaningful social interactions, someone will put me out of my misery. It's not enough for me just to be your living temple, Lord. I know you don't approve of killing, but in my opinion such a case has to be an exception." It is so easy for us, facing a situation we deem unbearable, to believe that God's will is in line with ours. We need to pray the more fervently, in such situations, that "this mind be in [us] which was also in Christ Jesus" (Phil. 2:5), so that He may, rather, bring our wills into alignment with that of His Father.

What should be the position of physicians and nurses in regard to the idea that causing patients' deaths or assisting with patients' suicides is part of our calling? We should vigorously fight such a notion for the sake of human dignity, professional integrity, and logic, even on grounds of utilitarian ethics. The corruption of the concept of healing is the beginning of the destruction of the medical, nursing, and other professions. Doctors cannot heal the sick by exterminating them. Nurses cannot nourish human beings by destroying them. To think otherwise is to expose a shallow concept of human personhood, a deficient sense of wonder, an unjustified reliance on human understanding, and a menacing "liberation" from reality. It is, all in all, a lack of reverence for life.

Professional organizations in the health care field are currently rewriting— or have already rewritten—the ethical guidelines of their respective professions to allow for, or even to exhort their practitioners toward, compliance with people's requests for death, in certain cases, in the name of respect for patient autonomy.[11] The identities of the health care professions are in danger of becoming hopelessly confused.[12] Christian doctors, nurses, medical social workers, chaplains, and others should realize that this deadly confusion is not from God. We must urge our colleagues, at each opportunity, to reconsider these life-and-death issues with minds open to the requirements of logic, morality, justice, and true compassion. We need to speak out at seminars and staff meetings and risk being thought fools for our refusal to go along with the latest "professionally correct" viewpoints. We can make an effort to become members of committees that set institutional policies on "withdrawal of treatment" and related issues. We can attempt to influence our professional organizations to reverse themselves where they have taken irrational and unethical positions. We must pray for members of our professions who are advocating ungodly policies, and we must pray for the institutions in which we practice.

The church also needs to promote pro-life principles in society by living as a fruitful witness of Jesus Christ. We must be ready to minister to society in concrete and visible ways, with prayer support, respite care services, and more hospital and nursing home ministries. The church must support those who take a stand for pro-life principles, first of all by praying for them. We must work for better nursing homes and for better services for people living with disabilities, which will enhance their sense of dignity and well-being (antidotes to the depression and despair that can lead to a suicidal mind-set). Pro-life media programs that profess a Christian response to the challenges of aging, disability, and terminal illness are another way the church can be "salt and light" in our society. But we must be careful that our message is clear in its uniqueness, in its dissimilarity to the message the world is pushing—for in the distinctiveness of our message lies the "saltiness" of our witness, and we know that we are good for nothing if the salt of our witness loses its savor (Matt. 5:13).

We must show that the church really does value and care for the elderly, the mentally ill, those with disabilities, and those with terminal illnesses. We can model the love Christ has for these people by taking our own elderly parents, or ill or disabled family members, into our homes when they are no longer able to live independently. The church can develop programs, such as parish nursing programs, to encourage members to consider making such commitments. If dependent family members need more care than, upon prayerful consideration, we can provide, we can maintain a close involvement with them as they are cared for by others. We need more outreach initiatives for sharing the love of God with the residents of long-term-care facilities. Many of these people are hungry for personal contact; we can put them in contact with Someone who can give them joy and abundant riches in spite of their losses.

If we do not, by God's grace, succeed in stemming the pro-death tide (and we may not), what lies ahead for our society? Those who promote euthanasia generally insist it will not get out of hand, it will be strictly voluntary, there will not be "abuses." Any prediction of a Nazi-like slide down the "slippery slope" is categorically rejected, by some, with open derision. But the average person accepts as common wisdom that killing begets killing, and that it is self-destructive for a nation to become—as ours is—desensitized to the gravity of killing. We have killing in the heat of passion, killing in the heat of compassion, killing to protect career interests, killing out of covetousness, killing as entertainment. A killing-saturated society soon becomes dehumanized, and dehumanizing.

We must remember that the medical profession in Germany, between 1939 and 1945, engineered the euthanasia of more than 275,000 "defectives"— retarded, mentally ill, senile, and physically disabled men, women, and children—by means of sedatives, starvation, and poisonous gas both prior to and concurrent with its participation in the Holocaust.[13] Leo Alexander, in an article published by the *New England Journal of Medicine* in 1949, noted that the gradual progression of physician-supervised killing in Nazi Germany began with a "subtle shift in emphasis," which is identical with the one we see in America today, in our medical and nursing professions and elsewhere.

> Whatever proportions these crimes finally assumed, it became evident to all who investigated them that they had started from small beginnings. The beginnings at first were merely a subtle shift in emphasis in the basic attitude of the physicians. It started with the acceptance of the attitude, basic in the euthanasia movement, that there is such a thing as a life not worthy to be lived. This attitude in its early stages concerned itself merely with the severely and chronically sick. Gradually the sphere of those to be included in this category was enlarged to encompass the socially unproductive, the ideologically unwanted, the racially unwanted, and finally all non-Germans. But it is important to realize that the infinitely small wedged-in lever from which this entire trend of mind received its impetus was the attitude toward the nonrehabilitable sick.[14]

What if Hitler had won the war? Perhaps, among other things, the world would by now have progressed farther in the direction in which we ourselves are headed.

Jean Rostand, a French biologist, described very clearly the type of society Hitler would have gloried in—one for which our generation is already willing to kill.

> If eliminating "monsters" became common practice, lesser defects would come to be considered monstrous. There is only one step from suppression of the horrible to suppression of the undesirable. If it became customary to thin out the ranks of people over ninety, those in their eighties would begin to seem very decrepit, and then those in their seventies. Little by little the collective mentality, the social outlook, would be altered. Any physical or mental impairment would diminish the right to live. Each passing year, each stress, each illness would be felt as an exclusion; the sadness of aging and deteriorating would be combined with a kind of shame at still being there. . . . Such a cleansed and purified society would be more dynamic, invigorating, wholesome, and pleasant to look at than our own. Pity would be obsolete, and the idea of gaining insight through suffering would be considered absurd. Waste and inefficiency would be banished, and the normal and the strong would benefit from all the resources formerly devoted

to the abnormal and the weak. Such a society would represent a return to the spirit of Sparta and would delight disciples of Nietzsche. But I am not sure that it would still deserve to be called a human society."[15]

There are no statistics to tell us how often euthanasia and assisted suicide are occurring in our country. In the Netherlands, which has embraced voluntary euthanasia-by-lethal-injection, an estimated six thousand to twenty thousand persons (out of a population of fifteen million) are killed by their doctors each year.[16] This estimate includes cases of involuntary euthanasia, which also occurs regularly in Holland.[17] Almost 80 percent of Dutch general practitioners have now had "experience with" euthanasia.[18] Many physicians refuse, on ethical and religious grounds, to kill their patients; those who do kill "often report nightmares afterwards."

> You have to conquer something in yourself to do it. It is not a natural act, said Dr. Cornelius van der Meer, who for years was in charge of internal medicine at Amsterdam's Free University Hospital. Physicians are warned never to drive alone to perform the procedure, and to seek counseling before and after. "I think it will always be regarded as a necessary evil," said Henk J. Leenen, a law professor at Amsterdam's Institute of Social Medicine, who has been a "cautious, but active, supporter."[19]

In the United States, many bioethicists, physicians, and even clergy are promoting assisted suicide and living wills, as well as euthanasia. We read constantly about economic pressures on health care providers, and these pressures will certainly increase.

Living wills, however, are not the answer to the problems we face.[20] First of all, they are not necessary; people already have, and have had, the right to refuse medical treatment, and families have traditionally had the right to make treatment decisions on behalf of incompetent family members. And even when there is disagreement within the family over what should be done in a particular situation, the majority of physicians will not attempt to push heroic or minimally beneficial treatment on patients. Secondly, it is premature to make life-and-death decisions, months or years ahead of time, based on imagined scenarios, which may be rendered moot by advances in medical science or may not in any case correspond with the real events of one's life as they unfold. People should certainly talk with their families and friends about what kind of treatment they would or would not want in various possible situations. But the best treatment decisions will be made in the actual situations, with all the variables known, rather than guessed.

It should be noted that, in the wake of the passage of the Patient Self-Determination Act in 1990, many groups and individuals concerned for the welfare of vulnerable people are endorsing protective versions of a type of document usually referred to as a "durable power of attorney for health care," which enables people to indicate a proxy decision-maker for health care, in anticipation of a time in their life when they may become incompetent to make decisions.[21] These are not living wills; there is no attempt made to imagine all possible health care scenarios and anticipate all possible choices within the imagined situations. The purpose of these documents is to ensure that a person of one's own choosing will have clear legal standing as the decision-maker if the need arises. A person who has reason to believe that family members (or health care providers) may not share his values might do well to investigate such documents. Careful consideration should also be made regarding which family members or friends have the respect for one's values, the emotional balance, the intelligence, the knowledge of health care, and the courage to stand up for one's welfare in complex and intimidating situations.

Our culture is increasingly fascinated with death; the pro-death movement—spurred on by a coalition of the elite from the spheres of bioethics, health care, law, politics, and religion—is developing faster than most people realize. Mary Senander, nationally known anti-euthanasia activist, has uncovered very disturbing information about the promotion of suicide as a rational alternative even for teenagers in certain situations and for the elderly (of course) as a remedy for the fear of being without the necessities of life in advanced old age.[22]

We are engaged in a struggle that represents one crucial battle in the current war for the preservation of our culture, a relatively life-giving culture rooted in Western, Judeo-Christian civilization. This war is itself part of a larger war—the war of history: the conflict between good and evil, between those who are willing to bend the knee to their Creator, and those who are not. As we encounter those who present murder as a humane and ethical solution to human problems, it is prudent to remember that "we wrestle not against flesh and blood, but against principalities, against powers, against the rulers of the darkness of this world, against spiritual wickedness in high places" (Eph. 6:12).

The death peddlers will continue relentlessly to push their agenda. Only the grace and power of God are sufficient to overcome the lust for death. To that end, that the powers of death be "swallowed up in victory," we must fast and pray. We must repent for our nation; we must cry out to God for mercy. We must pray for our own sanctification, that we may become better witnesses of the Way, the Truth, and the Life to this lost and deceived generation, a generation dying, if not already on the verge of death.

We would do well as a society to reflect upon the challenge of Moses to the Israelites shortly before his death: "I call heaven and earth to record this day against you, that I have set before you life and death, blessing and cursing: therefore choose life, that both thou and thy seed may live: That thou mayest love the Lord thy God, and that thou mayest obey his voice, and that thou mayest cleave unto him: for he is thy life, and the length of thy days" (Deut. 30:19–20).

ENDNOTES

1. Dunn, H., *High Level Wellness*, R. W. Beatty, Ltd., 1961; cited in "Conceptual Framework and Curriculum Guide," Austin Community College Nursing Program, revised 1980–81, pp. 1–2, 5, 7.

2. Here I make two references. The first is to the American Medical Association Ethical and Judicial Council's 1986 opinion, which states in part that "Life-prolonging medical treatment includes . . . artificially or technologically supplied . . . nutrition or hydration," which can be withheld or withdrawn from patients who, though not dying, are judged to be permanently unconscious. This opinion is widely cited and has been pivotal in the push toward the legalization of euthanasia, yet the AMA House of Delegates never voted on the opinion, and the Ethical and Judicial Council, which formulated it, had only seven members. See "Current Opinions of the Council on Ethical and Judicial Affairs of the American Medical Association—1986," Nancy W. Dickey, et. al., AMA, Chicago, 1986, Opinion 2.18 "Withholding or Withdrawing Life-Prolonging Medical Treatment," 12–13.

   The second reference is to Dr. Ronald Cranford's testimony as an expert witness in the Cruzan case that "even spoon-feeding of a person in Nancy Cruzan's condition should be considered 'medical treatment' and, therefore, optional. This marks the first time that medical testimony has favored the withholding of oral feeding from a severely disabled, non-terminally ill person." This quote is from the February 1990 International Anti-Euthanasia Task Force (IAETF) newsletter, commenting on trial testimony in *Cruzan v. Harmon and Lampkins*, Transcript Vol. 1, pp. 228–229, 3/03/88. (The IAETF newsletter is, to my knowledge, the most comprehensive source of current information, with pro-life commentary, on the status of euthanasia in the United States and elsewhere. The newsletter is published by The Human Life Center, P.O. Box 760, Steubenville, OH 43952.)

3. Nancy W. Dickey et al., note 5., par. 1.

4. I took the phrase "on the verge of death" from John M. Dolan's "Death by Deliberate Dehydration and Starvation: Silent Echoes of the Hungerhauser," *Issues in Law and Medicine* 7, no. 2 (fall 1991), 184, note 31; he refers to a conversation he had with Charles Geach, in which Mr. Geach pointed out the linguistic error represented by the phrase "imminently dying."

5. Ibid., 184–185, 189.

6. G. E. M. Anscombe, Chapter III, "Murder and the Morality of Euthanasia," in *Euthanasia and Clinical Practice: Trends, Principles, and Alternatives, Report of a Working Party* (The Linacre Center, 1982), 24–36.

7. John M. Dolan, "Lethal Medicine," 12–14.

8. See Dolan; "Lethal Medicine," cited above, and "Death by Deliberate Dehydration and Starvation: Silent Echoes of the Hungerhauser," 189–93.

9. David O'Steen, "Climbing Up the Slippery Slope," Chapter 10, in *Window on the Future, the Pro-Life Year in Review* (Washington, D.C.: The National Right to Life Committee, 1986), 76.

10. Dolan, "Death by Deliberate Dehydration," 193–94.

11. As an example of the revisions taking place, compare the following two formulations of nursing ethics. I see the second as a break from, rather than a refinement or expansion of, the profession's ethical base. In 1978, Leah Curtain, then editor of the journal for nursing, *Leadership and Management*, addressed the ethical nature of nursing in an article entitled "Nursing Ethics: Theories and Pragmatics," *Nursing Forum* 17, 1978 no. 1, pp. 4–11. She wrote, "The claim that nursing is a moral art emphasizes nursing's commitment to care for, as well as to the care of, other human beings. It is a particularly intense form of general moral commitment (the intensity is directly derivative of the degree of vulnerability of the patient) . . ." (p. 5). She identifies "the nurse's concern for,

and commitment to, the individual patient, his/her integrity, human rights, and needs" as the "central ethical commitments of nursing" (p. 7). She also quotes from the "American Nursing Association Code for Nurses With Interpretive Statements" (1976), in reference to the nurse's ethical responsibility for his or her actions: "Neither physicians' orders nor the employing agency's policies relieve the nurse of ethical or legal accountability for actions taken and judgments made" (p. 9).

In contrast, in a 1989 press release put forth by the American Nursing Association (ANA), the ANA and the American Association of Nurse Attorneys assert that the Missouri Supreme Court's 1988 decision denying Nancy Cruzan's parents' request that tube feeding be withdrawn from her "would require professional nurses to violate the most fundamental ethic of nursing practice: *the obligation to ascertain and carry out the wishes of their patients*" (emphasis added). Lucille A. Joel, then ANA president, stated in the same piece that "As nurses, we are ethically bound to assist our patients in maintaining *control over their lives*, to help them preserve their dignity and self-esteem."

In the first case, the ethical commitment of the nurse is to care and advocate for the patient, who possesses inherent rights and dignity by virtue of his humanity. The patient with diminished ability to exercise autonomy has a "particularly intense" moral claim on the nurse in his or her role as a patient advocate, especially in cases where physicians' orders or institutional policies— or the patient's own confused or uninformed wishes, for that matter—might threaten the patient's welfare and human rights.

In the second case, the patient's dignity resides in his or her ability to maintain control over his or her life, his or her ability to *exercise* his or her right of autonomy. This has in fact become such an overriding value, that it is seen virtually as a prerequisite for the granting of dignity to the human person. This faulty premise leads to the bizarre conclusion that in the case of the patient who is unable to exercise autonomy, it is to be exercised for him or her, even in the absence of clear and convincing evidence of the patient's wishes, and even in a manner inimical to the goal of meeting the patient's most basic needs: food, clothing, shelter, respect, love. It is, in fact, to be exercised in such a way that the patient's "dignity deficit" is resolved definitively, by the elimination of his or her "autonomy incapacity"—even when the only means to do so is to eliminate *the patient*.

12. See John M. Dolan, "Fatal Blunders," 5–7; read at the April 1989, conference on "Human Rights in Clinical Practice: Abortion, Euthanasia, and Vulnerable Patients," sponsored primarily by the Program in Human Rights and Medicine, a division of the University of Minnesota's Human Rights Center.

13. Opening statement of the prosecution, Brigadier General Telford Taylor, 9 December 1946, "The Medical Case," 1:27, 28, 68–74; cited by William Brennan in *Medical Holocausts I*, (Houston: Nordland Publishing International, 1980), 51 n. 30.

14. Leo Alexander, "Medical Science Under Dictatorship," *New England Journal of Medicine* 241 (July 14, 1949): 39–47. See also Ben Mitchell, "Nazi Germany's Euphemisms," in *Dignity and Dying: A Christian Appraisal*, eds. John Kilner, Arlene B. Miller, and Edmund D. Pellegrino (Grand Rapids: Eerdmans, 1996), 123–34.

15. Jean Rostand, *Humanly Possible*, trans. Lowell Blair (New York: Saturday Review Press, 1973), 92–93. I am indebted to Dr. Joseph Stanton for this quote; he included it in a speech he gave at the Town and Country Club in St. Paul,

Minnesota, in 1989. When I thanked him for the wonderful quotations he used in his talk, he promptly and generously handed them over to me.

16. "Voluntary Euthanasia Common, Accepted in the Netherlands," The *Washington Times*, 6 April 1987, cited by IAETF in an information sheet on "Aid-in-Dying: Holland."

17. The Remmelink Committee report, released on 9/10/91, titled "Medische Beslissingen Rond Het Levenseinde" (Medical Decisions About the End of Life), the Hague, reported in the IAETF "Networker Update" 5, no. 5 (September–October 1991): 1.

18. "Do Not Go Slowly Into That Dark Night: Mercy Killing in Holland," *The American Journal of Medicine* 84 (January 1988): 140.

19. "Thousands of Dutch Choose Euthanasia's Gentle Ending," *The Washington Post*, 5 April 1990; reprinted in the *Minneapolis Star Tribune*, 9 April 1990, sec. A, p. 2.

20. See Peter L. Jaggard, "Advance Directives: The Case for Greater Dialogue" in *Bioethics and the Future of Medicine: A Christian Appraisal*, eds. John F. Kilner, Nigel M. de S. Cameron, and David L. Schiedermayer (Grand Rapids: Eerdmans, 1995), 250–62.

21. Under the terms of the Patient Self-Determination Act, *every* health care facility or program receiving federal funds is required to ask *all* adult patients, on admission to the facility or program, if they have a living will, and also is required to furnish patients with information about such documents. As a result of this act, many persons who would not otherwise have considered signing an "advance directive" will no doubt do so, unaware of the dangers inherent in the typical versions of such a document, and without sufficient reflection on the grave moral issues involved.

    For a copy of an alternative to the living will, see the "Patient Self-Protection Document." Interested persons may contact: Illinois Right to Life Committee, 11244 South Western Avenue, Chicago, IL 60643, (773) 239–6457, or Center for Pro-Life Studies, P.O. Box 166, North Troy, VT 05859, (802) 988–4041.

    The IAETF has also developed a protective alternative to "living will"-type documents. It is called the "Protective Medical Decisions Document" (PMDD), and "directs that the signer receive food and water unless death is inevitable AND truly imminent or [the signer] is unable to assimilate food and fluids. It further specifies that, 'even in the face of death,' the signer be provided with ordinary nursing and medical care, including pain relief and comfort care appropriate to his/her condition." For further information, write to IAETF at P.O. Box 760, Steubenville, OH 43952.

    A similarly protective alternative to the "living will," the "Will to Live," is available through the National Right to Life Committee. For a free copy of the document, interested persons should send a stamped, self-addressed, business envelope to: Will to Live Project, Suite 500, 419 Seventh Street, NW, Washington, D.C. 20004.

22. Margaret P. Battin, *The Washington Times*, 13 March 1987, sec. A, p. 6, cited by Mary Senander, in "Suicide, Living Wills, and the Will to Live," an IAETF position paper.

PART 2

PHILOSOPHICAL REFLECTIONS

An Overview

The decisions made today regarding physician-assisted suicide must be approached from the theological foundation of yesterday to ensure that sound ethical decisions are made tomorrow. John Kilner clearly develops a scenario to explain the lure of physician-assisted suicide, compassionately deals with the wholistic needs of those who experience pain and suffering, and concisely describes the shortcomings of physician-assisted suicide and the potential distrust of the medical profession that accompanies it. Each of us has a responsibility to assist one another in alleviating pain and suffering, but these must never be alleviated at the expense of God's will. Today's struggles must be channeled through divine guidance to ensure hope and blessing tomorrow.

Chapter Eight

PHYSICIAN-ASSISTED SUICIDE
Today, Yesterday, and Tomorrow

John F. Kilner

IN ORDER TO ASSESS THE WISDOM of embracing physician-assisted suicide as an answer to tomorrow's troubles, we would do well to investigate why people are turning to it today and what counsel we can gain from the experience of yesterday. Accordingly, this chapter will begin with an exploration of the current predicament—examining both the challenges faced by a particular family (of composite characters) and the broader social trends that these challenges illustrate. It will then draw upon the wise counsel of yesterday—not only the direct teaching of Scripture but also the lived experience of the One who exemplifies who we are to be and what we are to do: Jesus Christ.[1]

A GOOD DEATH FOR GLEASON?

Even a year later C. J. wondered if they had made the right decision. His father's death had been quite an ordeal. But, then, so had his father's life. Born to poor African-American parents in the rural Southern United States, Gleason had headed north before completing high school. Working two low-paying jobs in inner-city Chicago hadn't been easy, but C. J. never recalled his father complaining. Gleason was proud that he had been able to raise three children and that his wife Cassie had never had to work full-time outside the home. Theirs was a blessed family in a neighborhood where two-parent families, not to mention employed fathers, were far from the norm. Blessed indeed—that is, until the illness.

Gleason had just turned sixty-five, amid kidding by friends and family alike that he was an old man now, when he began to feel pains in his chest. He didn't talk about them with the family, but C. J. could see that something was not right with his father. As the eldest of three children, C. J. felt a special sense of responsibility for his aging parents. But he was reluctant to press his father too aggressively when Gleason insisted that he felt fine. It wasn't until later that C. J. learned from the doctor how much pain his father had endured before collapsing at work and being rushed to the hospital.

Gleason had revived quickly and some medication had been prescribed for a heart problem Gleason didn't really understand. C. J. doubted in hindsight that his father had taken the medication, and the disease got rapidly

129

worse. Gleason's lungs as well as his heart were soon seriously compromised. Upon being hospitalized, Gleason was found to have a form of pneumonia that proved resistant to treatment. Three times he had to be placed on a respirator to maintain breathing while the pneumonia was treated. Each time he was progressively weaker after the respirator was removed, and each treatment was less effective in combating the pneumonia. Gradually the disease did such damage that Gleason obviously was experiencing frequent chest pain. Even now, a year later, C. J. could clearly recall the sight of his father's deteriorating body.

In light of Gleason's worsening condition and the family's evident concern, Gleason's doctor, Angela Perkins, called a meeting to discuss continued treatment. C. J. could picture the circular table as if it were yesterday. He sat wedged between Dr. Perkins and his mother, with his brother, Jesse, and sister, Roberta, on his mother's other side, and Rev. Wilson leaning back in his chair between C. J.'s sister and the doctor. The decision belonged to someone else, C. J. thought, and he felt awkward being thrust into the middle of the discussion.

Who was he to decide whether his own father was to live or die? Did they think he was God or something? If somebody had to play that role, the pastor clearly was the man for the job. Or why didn't the doctor just tell them what to do? That's what she was there for. C. J. felt totally unprepared to say anything. Certainly his education in the public school system had not equipped him for this day. Nor had over four decades at Ebenezer Baptist Church. Or perhaps that was going too far. He did have a curious sense of support as he inwardly cried out to God without knowing the words to use. "Leaning on the everlasting arms," they would have called it at Ebenezer. But that didn't answer the questions at hand.

Dr. Perkins explained to the group her inability to arrest the progress of the heart and lung deterioration. When asked by Jesse if a heart or heart-lung transplant he had heard about on TV had been considered at any point in the course of treatment, the doctor indicated that Gleason was not a good transplant candidate "for a variety of medical, economic, and social reasons." What did the doctor mean by that, C. J. had wondered after the meeting. Everyone had been so fixated on what the doctor was going to recommend, he reasoned, that they had not wanted to interrupt her explanation. Now in hindsight the question seemed much clearer and more imposing: Had there, after all, been a way available to save his father's life? And what had she meant by "social reasons"? Spared from addressing that issue by the family's passivity, the doctor instead went on to help the family members envision the suffering that both they and Gleason would experience during Gleason's final weeks. Reverend Wilson confirmed that what she was saying was accurate.

At this point two questions arose. Should Gleason be resuscitated if his heart stopped? Should he be placed on a respirator again if his lungs deteriorated further? Explaining that these actions would extend Gleason's life a week or two at most, Dr. Perkins recommended "passive involvement" (i.e., no treatment except to provide comfort care) should the need arise for such emergency actions as resuscitation or starting Gleason on a respirator.

Cassie turned to Rev. Wilson to ask what she should do. While the pastor seemed to share the burden of her sorrow, he told her it was her decision to make. She then turned to her children. C. J. and Jesse suggested that the doctor knew best what to do. C. J. was shocked, though, by what his sister had to say. Roberta was so concerned by the suffering that lay ahead for all and by the mounting medical bills, that she inquired about the possibility of physician-assisted suicide or even so-called "active euthanasia"—painlessly inducing her father's death right away for his and the family's sake. While the doctor acknowledged that either could easily be accomplished, using an overdose of the right pills or intravenous potassium chloride, she refused to consider these options. So Cassie told Dr. Perkins to follow the course of passive involvement she had suggested. Nevertheless, Cassie had an uneasy feeling that the reasons for considering a more active role in facilitating her husband's death had not been given sufficient attention.

At the same meeting, C. J. recalled, the doctor, family, and pastor had also considered whether or not to discuss the chosen course of passive involvement with Gleason himself. Gleason had consistently maintained his determination to overcome his illness. Cassie in particular felt that Gleason would maintain this attitude to the end—for the family's as well as his own sake—but that he would in fact appreciate the doctor's deciding not to prolong the dying process. Everyone present agreed. So they decided not to discuss the matter with Gleason. The doctor proceeded to order that no emergency measures be taken to maintain Gleason's life and that only standard comfort care be provided.

The decision had made things easier for the family at first. No one wanted to face Gleason's impending death. But C. J. began to sense a distance developing between the family and his father almost immediately. Had his father really known he was dying without being told? Would his dying days have been better if he and the family could have spoken together freely of his coming death and the end-of-life treatment decisions that needed to be made? Looking back a year later, C. J. felt much less comfortable than he had at the time with the family's decision not to discuss the predicament with his father.

Shortly after this family meeting with the doctor and pastor, Gleason's condition began to deteriorate rapidly. Three days following the meeting, his heart stopped beating. No attempt was made to revive him. During Gleason's final days, C. J. and the rest of the family had been increasingly disturbed by the sight of his wasting away. Although he had been receiving pain medication, he had frequently asked for more, to no avail. While no steps had been taken to speed up Gleason's death, even C. J. had begun to wonder near the end if something should have been done to bring a quicker end to his father's suffering.

MEETING PEOPLE'S NEEDS

When we consider the needs of people like Gleason and his family, it is no wonder that physician-assisted suicide appears to be an attractive option.

First, people need adequate health care, which includes a way to *pay* for adequate health care. The lack of sufficient health insurance for Gleason is one of the key considerations that moved his daughter Roberta to consider ending her father's life. But Gleason is far from alone. In the United States, thirty-five to forty million people lack any health insurance whatsoever, and many more are underinsured. Studies now indicate that those with insufficient coverage end up receiving less health care than others and end up less healthy as a result.[2] Although physician-assisted suicide might appear to be a plausible alternative in the face of suffering that accompanies inadequate health care, a much better alternative would be to provide people with the health care that they need.

Providing health care is not necessarily sufficient to meet the needs of those who are ill, however, if what is provided does not meet a second need: the need for effective pain management. As in Gleason's case, many patients today receive inadequate pain control.[3] This may be due to insufficient physician training in how to manage pain effectively.[4] Pain management is not curative care, so there has been a tendency to de-emphasize it in a medical environment that emphasizes and rewards acute care more than chronic care or symptom relief. Alternatively, inadequate pain management may result from a lack of respect for the patient's responsibility to determine when the risk of diminished alertness or of addiction to pain-relieving drugs is outweighed by the horror of having to endure great pain. The prospect of significant pain again renders the attraction of physician-assisted suicide understandable. However, moving too quickly to this "final solution" risks not only overlooking the possibility of providing more effective pain management but may instead even undermine current efforts to do so.

Even when patients have access to sufficient health care, including effective pain management, there can be serious unmet needs. There can, for instance, be significant suffering, for suffering and pain are not the same. *Pain is a physical sensation, whereas suffering involves a threat to one's identity and sense of worth.* It may be caused by pain or by a variety of other aspects of a person's illness, such as the limitations illness imposes.[5] Physicians may be effective in meeting patients' physical needs. However, they rarely have the time available to meet the needs of the whole person—including body, mind, and spirit—not to mention the needs of the family. It does not appear that Gleason's or his family's needs were well met, so contemplating how to end the suffering as soon as possible is quite understandable. However, there are alternatives. As physicians make more room for multi-disciplinary teams to take major responsibility for treating their patients, not only clergy (as in Gleason's case) but also social workers, nurses, and others can play more significant roles in alleviating suffering. This approach represents one of the strengths of the hospice movement, where alleviating suffering in all its forms becomes even more important an agenda than treatment decisions.[6] All too often, as in Gleason's situation, the hospice alternative is not known or seriously considered.

Even patients who know about and can pay for all that health care has to offer, however, may have unmet needs. Having witnessed others who were barraged with unwanted treatments, they fear that they, too, will lose control of their lives. They know that there is such a fear of death—such a desperation to win the battle with death—that treatment will sometimes be instituted with little prospect of benefit, and that stopping treatment already begun can be next to impossible. Patients need to know that their values and wishes will be respected in the dying process—not only when they have the mental capacity to express them but also after they lose it.

Living wills, as traditionally conceived, have been anything but confidence-building in this regard. The traditional approach has been to develop forms with detailed options for choosing and refusing treatment—or simply to ask people to detail such choices and refusals on their own. People have known that they are not covering all of the possible bases and that they are not medically competent, in any case, to prescribe and rule out treatments for most medical conditions.[7] Whereas some like Gleason are left out of the process entirely by families and physicians who make decisions for them, others do not consider living wills worth executing. Indeed, a relatively small percentage of people in the United States have living wills, and studies suggest that patients' wishes recorded in living wills are often disregarded.[8] In such an environment, the best way to assert control can understandably appear to be through ending life itself by insisting on physician-assisted suicide.

Again, though, better alternatives are available. For example, a different type of advance directive, the durable power of attorney for health care, allows patients to designate the person most in touch with their values to make health care decisions for them when they lose their mental capacity. Within this may helpfully be incorporated a statement of the patient's goals for health care ("I want anything that will keep me alive," or "I want anything that will keep me alive and conscious," etc.)[9]—as long as the designated decision-maker is explicitly given the authority to interpret how the patient's goals apply in particular situations.

Physician-assisted suicide, then, addresses a variety of patient needs, but in a way that undermines efforts to address those needs in a life-affirming way. It encourages the individual to grab the ultimate quick-fix in a fast-food, throwaway society. *Society needs to be challenged to take more responsibility for the needs of its members, not be absolved of them.*

The allure of physician-assisted suicide would be problematic enough if it just undermined society's efforts to meet patients' needs. However, it also creates new needs—new fears for patients—at the same time. Patients have always been able to trust that their physicians are wholeheartedly committed to sustaining their lives. Physicians diagnose their problems and suggest options for treatment and/or supportive care, which patients can accept or reject. Introducing a new role for physicians, fostering death, means that physicians would begin to weigh in their minds whether life or death is best for the patient. Patients could no longer count on the physician's historical commitment to sustain life.

To be sure, at first physicians would not make independent judgments concerning whether to foster the patient's life or death. They would intend merely to assist the patient in pursuing whatever course of action the patient wanted. However, once fostering death became an acceptable and appropriate part of physicians' responsibilities, they would want to be consistent in exercising that responsibility. If patients could not express their wishes about continuing to live, then the physician would have to make that judgment for them (perhaps in consultation with others). Once such decisions were made for such patients, it is reasonable to expect that they would soon be made for patients like Gleason under circumstances such as those surrounding the end of his life.

Is there any way to confirm whether or not such a scenario is likely? There is, in fact, one country in the world where physician-assisted suicide has virtually been legalized: the Netherlands. The practice is still technically illegal, but the courts have formulated guidelines within which cases of physician-assisted suicide and euthanasia (death caused by the physician rather than the patient) will not be prosecuted. One such guideline is that the patient must explicitly consent to the death.[10]

The first official government study documents not only cases where consent was obtained, but also nearly six thousand cases where patients were killed without their consent. Moreover, in nearly a quarter of these six thousand cases, patients were still mentally competent.[11] So the one test case available suggests that patients' fears about involving physicians in fostering death are warranted.

Are such fears more or less warranted in the United States as compared with the Netherlands? It would appear that they are more so. The United States has already demonstrated a much greater willingness to leave patients unattended. Whereas the Netherlands insures health care for all, the United States is not so committed to insure that all receive care. As noted earlier, tens of millions of people are left without any financial coverage to insure that they receive the health care they need. Especially in the current cost-conscious environment, physician-assisted suicide will appear to be a much easier and cheaper way to handle those with serious health problems than providing them with the full range of care that they require.

Physician-assisted suicide, then, not only fails to address the most important needs of patients like Gleason. It also exacerbates the needs of many by undermining trust and instilling fear. Some individual patients who want physician-assisted suicide will applaud having the option, but the price to be paid by all of the rest will be unacceptably high.

A THEOLOGICAL PERSPECTIVE

The experience of today has already begun to chart a course for us regarding physician-assisted suicide. Does the wise counsel of yesterday confirm this direction? Neglecting and exacerbating human need is indeed a serious matter from many perspectives, including a biblically-grounded theological approach. As I have argued elsewhere,[12] meeting human need is an essential component of the biblical mandate to do justice. Justice stands alongside of other mandates of God, including freedom and life, as a guide for ethical human action. There is much more to ethics, to be sure, than following such guides; however, these guides arguably constitute an essential context within which other dimensions of ethics are to be pursued. The guides of freedom and life, for instance, generate two key questions that are among those that need to be asked as care-giving options are being evaluated with or for patients who are seriously ill: (1) Is the patient willing? and (2) Is death intended?

The question of the patient's willingness is so important because God has given people the freedom and responsibility to make major choices regarding their lives. If these choices even encompass the nature of their eternal life, it is not surprising that choices about their temporal life should also be entrusted to them. One implication of this perspective is that life-or-death decisions must not be made *for* patients but *by* patients, when they have the mental capacity to make them.

This affirmation made in the context of the biblical writings, however, means something very different from what it would mean in a public, nontheological context. First, the understanding of freedom on which it rests is fundamentally different from the concept of autonomy commonly invoked in the public sphere. Autonomy (literally "self-law") suggests not only that people have responsibility for making choices, but that the choices they make are right by virtue of the fact that they made them. A more biblical understanding of freedom rejects the latter notion, insisting instead that there are standards of right and wrong that are independent of people's own wishes and desires. People may make wrong choices. God allows them the freedom to do so, but that does not mean that the choices are right. So while moral decisions must reflect patients' choices where they can be ascertained, other questions must also be addressed before the morality of an action can be determined.[13]

With regard to physician-assisted suicide, a further key question concerns whether the action in view intends life or death. The biblical materials address not only what people do, but also the intentions behind their actions, among other ethical concerns. Repeatedly, life and death are contrasted, and people are called upon to "choose life."[14] Life is understood wholistically; it includes material and nonmaterial dimensions, which, in most texts, are not separated. Death, including physical death, is often associated with disobedience and selfishness; it entered the world when people disobeyed God, went their own way, and were separated from God's life-giving power. Death is portrayed as a defeated enemy—as the last enemy to be destroyed when the world ends.[15] *As an enemy, it is not to be facilitated—people are to choose life.* Since death is an ultimately defeated enemy, however, people need not fear death or desperately resist it. Nevertheless, it remains an enemy, and people are not to embrace it, not to choose it.[16]

But what of the cruel suffering that often attends dying? For many this is the crucial issue. Is suffering not an evil to be avoided if possible? Indeed it is, but not at all costs. The biblical accounts make this vital point, first of all, by challenging the idea that what life is about is trying to maximize one's own happiness. People belong to God and have been created for a purpose. It is only by "losing," or giving, one's life, as God directs, that one finds it and finds fulfillment in it.[17] The hedonistic outlook so common today, according to which pursuing one's own happiness and eliminating suffering are more important than any other pursuits, reduces people to mere bundles of pleasure and pain. According to the biblical materials, however, people have much greater dignity, associated with a very different agenda. While relieving suffering is an important goal, it is to be pursued in accordance with God's purposes as best those can be known—i.e., pursued in the service of life, not in the service of death.[18] To eliminate suffering by eliminating the sufferer is to fail to make an important distinction between them.

A GOOD LIFE AND DEATH FOR JESUS?

One way, then, that the biblical accounts affirm that suffering is not to be avoided at all costs is by providing ethical guides that establish a contextual framework for faithful living. Another way is through the stories the Bible tells of people who have wrestled with the temptation to avoid suffering or maximize happiness by forsaking God's sometimes difficult agenda. While many such stories could be told, two from the life of Jesus, one from the beginning and one from the end of His ministry, are indicative.

The first appears in the fourth chapter of Luke (vv. 2–12), where the wilderness temptations of Jesus are narrated.

> For forty days he was tempted by the devil. He ate nothing during those days, and at the end of them he was hungry. The devil said to him, "If you are the Son of God, tell this stone to become bread." Jesus answered, "It is written: 'Man does not live on bread alone.'" The devil led him up to a high place and showed him in an instant all the kingdoms of the world. And he said to him, "I will give you all their authority and splendor, for it has been given to me, and I can give it to anyone I want to. So if you worship me, it will all be yours." Jesus answered, "It is written: 'Worship the Lord your God and serve him only.'" The devil led him to Jerusalem and had him stand on the highest point of the temple. "If you are the Son of God," he said, "throw yourself down from here. For it is written: 'He will command his angels concerning you to guard you carefully; they will lift you up in their hands, so that you will not strike your foot against a stone.'" Jesus answered, "It says, 'Do not put the Lord your God to the test.'"

This story is sometimes invoked to suggest that Jesus considers such matters as hunger relief or political involvement to be unimportant. However, this is to miss the heart of what the temptations and story are about. The essence of each temptation can be recognized by noting precisely what Jesus responds to in it. The common thread in all three is that the Devil is trying to drive a wedge between Jesus and the Lord God. *In each case the Devil offers Jesus something that addresses His legitimate needs and desires, but in a way that requires Him to forsake God or God's ways.* The crucial and difficult choice that

Jesus makes three times is to reject the pursuit of a legitimate concern when it pushes Him beyond God's purposes for how He should live.

While each of the three temptations thus bears on the present discussion of suffering and physician-assisted suicide, a closer look at the first temptation will suffice to elaborate the main point. Jesus objects to the Devil's insinuation that "bread alone" should be His concern. His point is not that bread is unimportant, but that such material concerns can become all-encompassing and distract people from other aspects of God's agenda. They should be pursued only in the larger context of that agenda, which means that there will be circumstances in which they cannot be satisfied. Whether the suffering in view is that of ravaging hunger or end-of-life illness, the story suggests that suffering per se does not justify every effort to eliminate it. People must be careful lest efforts to eliminate suffering carry them outside of God's will.

This point is illustrated even more forcefully at the end of Jesus' ministry (Mark 14:32–42), this time in a garden rather than a desert.

> They went to a place called Gethsemane, and Jesus said to his disciples, "Sit here while I pray." He took Peter, James and John along with him, and he began to be deeply distressed and troubled. "My soul is overwhelmed with sorrow to the point of death," he said to them. "Stay here and keep watch." Going a little farther, he fell to the ground and prayed that if possible the hour might pass from him. "Abba, Father," he said, "everything is possible for you. Take this cup from me. Yet not what I will, but what you will." Then he returned to his disciples and found them sleeping. "Simon," he said to Peter, "are you asleep? Could you not keep watch for one hour? Watch and pray so that you will not fall into temptation. The spirit is willing, but the body is weak." Once more he went away and prayed the same thing. When he came back, he again found them sleeping, because their eyes were heavy. They did not know what to say to him. Returning the third time, he said to them, "Are you still sleeping and resting? Enough! The hour has come. Look, the Son of Man is betrayed into the hands of sinners. Rise! Let us go! Here comes my betrayer!"

The suffering of Jesus portrayed here is about as intense as suffering gets. He is "overwhelmed with sorrow to the point of death." His response is to recognize suffering for the evil that it is and to voice His desire to escape it. Yet He acknowledges a more important agenda—God's agenda—which He is committed to follow no matter how great the suffering that must be endured.

The challenge of this story is particularly great for those wrestling with the possibility of physician-assisted suicide. It suggests that when one recognizes that something as central to God's purposes as "choosing life" is at issue, no amount of suffering justifies forsaking it. In most circumstances of life, one pursues God's agenda by alleviating suffering, and one's ultimate allegiance is not truly tested. End-of-life suffering is different, for alleviating suffering may be possible only by forsaking God's agenda. Such is not always the case, as noted earlier. Ironically, by embracing physician-assisted suicide too quickly as a way to alleviate suffering, other (life-affirming) ways to alleviate that suffering may be undermined. But when no alternative is available, people can find themselves in Gethsemane with Jesus, facing the ultimate test of their allegiance.

Although Jesus had to make the final decision Himself, He did not intend to face it alone. He not only brought the disciples to Gethsemane with Him, He brought three of them even closer to His place of prayer so that they could support Him by watching and praying. He was understandably grieved when they fell asleep.

People today facing serious illness and wrestling with the possibility of requesting physician-assisted suicide are in just as much need of support—perhaps in greater need. Jesus was able to choose God's way in the face of overwhelming suffering, even without the support of others. Most people are not so strong. Only with the kinds of support discussed earlier in relation to Gleason's experience can people be expected to remain faithful in the midst of great suffering. There are very few things in the New Testament that are overtly acknowledged to have the force of law. Providing people the support they need to remain true to God is one of them. In one of the many places where the importance of such support is affirmed, Paul writes, "Carry each other's burdens, and in this way you will fulfill the law of Christ."[19] In effect, Paul's admonition is the same as the one that often concludes Jesus' stories of caring and healing: go and do likewise.[20]

ENDNOTES

1. This essay has been adapted from John F. Kilner, "Physician-Assisted Suicide: What's the Story?" *Christian Scholar's Review* 23 (1994) 3:349–59.
2. Office of Technology Assessment, Congress of the United States, *Does Health Insurance Make a Difference?* (Washington, D.C.: U.S. Government Printing Office, 1992).
3. Mildred Solomon et al., "Decisions Near the End of Life: Professional Views on Life-Sustaining Treatments," *American Journal of Public Health* 83 (January, 1993): 14–23.
4. Kathleen M. Foley, "The Relationship of Pain and Symptom Management to Patient Requests for Physician-Assisted Suicide," *Journal of Pain and Symptom Management* 6 (July 1991): 239–97. Also Richard A. McCormick, "Physician-Assisted Suicide: Flight from Compassion," *Christian Century* (December 4, 1991): 1132–34.
5. William R. May, *The Patient's Ordeal* (Bloomington, Ind.: Indiana University Press, 1991).
6. Nina M. Fish, "Hospice: Terminal Illness, Teamwork and the Quality of Life," in *Social Work in Health Settings,* ed. Toba Kerson (New York: Haworth Press, 1989), 449–69.
7. Allan S. Brett, "Limitations of Listing Specific Medical Interventions in Advance Directives," *Journal of the American Medical Association* 266 (August 14, 1991): 825–28.
8. Solomon et al., "Decisions." See also David J. Doukas et al., "The Living Will: A National Survey," *Family Medicine* 23 (July 1991): 354–56.

9. A document explaining this approach can be obtained from the American Medical Association, 515 North State Street, Chicago, IL 60610. For further discussion, see Jean De Blois et al., "Advance Directives for Healthcare Decisions: A Christian Perspective," *Health Progress* 72 (July–August 1991): 27–31.

10. "Final Report of The Netherlands State Commission on Euthanasia: An English Summary," *Bioethics* 1 (1987): 163–74.

11. Richard Fenigsen, "The Report of the Dutch Governmental Committee on Euthanasia," *Issues in Law and Medicine* 7 (winter 1991): 339–44.

12. John F. Kilner, *Life on the Line: Ethics, Aging, Ending Patients' Lives, and Allocating Vital Resources* (Grand Rapids: Eerdmans, 1992).

13. For a discussion of freedom as release not only *from* restriction but also *for* a life in accordance with God's will, see Jacques Ellul, *The Ethics of Freedom* (Grand Rapids: Eerdmans, 1976); cf. Kilner, *Life on the Line*, 57–59.

14. Deut. 30:15–20; Prov. 8:35–36; Jer. 21:8; Matt. 7:13–14; Rom. 8:6; 1 John 3:14–15.

15. Gen. 2:16–24; Job 18:14; Isa. 25:7–8; Rom. 5:12; 1 Cor. 15:20–26, 54–55; Heb. 2:14; Rev. 20:10–14; 21:3–4.

16. For a fuller discussion, see Paul Ramsey, "The Indignity of 'Death with Dignity,'" in *Death Inside Out*, eds. Peter Steinfels and Robert Veatch (New York: Harper and Row, 1974), 81–96; cf. Kilner, *Life on the Line*, 97–103.

17. Jesus' paradoxical statement about how to gain life receives an emphasis in the Gospels unlike any other statement. It appears in all four gospels and in two of them more than once (Matt. 10:38–39; 16:24–25; Mark 8:34–35; Luke 9:23–24; 14:26–27; 17:33; John 12:25).

18. For a discussion of the close connection between suffering, on the one hand, and life and hope, on the other, see J. Christian Beker, *Suffering and Hope* (Philadelphia: Fortress Press, 1987); cf. Kilner, *Life on the Line*, 103–8.

19. Galatians 6:2. In other contexts, carrying one another's burdens is a manifestation of love. Love fulfills God's law in that it encompasses all of God's intentions for how people are to live (see Rom. 13:8–10; 1 Cor. 9:21; Gal. 5:14). See also John F. Kilner, "Not Caring Enough," *Perspectives* 8 (April 1993): 3–4; and Arthur J. Dyck, *Rethinking Rights and Responsibilities: The Moral Bonds of Community* (Cleveland, Ohio: Pilgrim Press, 1993).

20. For more information on physician-assisted suicide, contact The Center for Bioethics and Human Dignity, 2065 Half Day Road, Bannockburn, Illinois 60015 USA; phone 847–317–8180; fax 847–317–8141; E-mail cbhd@banninst.edu; World Wide Web site http://www.bioethix.org. Among other resources the Center has a multimedia resource packet on assisted suicide and euthanasia, which includes pithy issue overviews, a list of relevant biblical passages with brief commentary, a case study with discussion guide, a Bible study with leader's guide, a sample sermon, an annotated bibliography, eight helpful articles, John Kilner's book *Life on the Line*, an audio tape of Washington pastor Dennis Hollinger discussing the church's responsibility, and an audio tape of a public debate on physician-assisted suicide featuring Dr. Jack Kevorkian's lawyer and spokesman, Geoffrey Fieger, and prominent Christian physician, Edmund Pellegrino. The Center also has a supplementary packet containing many more key articles, a video of the debate, an audio tape of Dutch ethicist Henk Jochemsen discussing the Dutch euthanasia experience, and Nigel Cameron's book *The New Medicine*. For additional material, see the Center's book: John F. Kilner et al., eds., *Dignity and Dying: A Christian Appraisal* (Grand Rapids: Eerdmans; and United Kingdom: Paternoster, 1996).

An Overview

Why do we suffer and how does it affect the value and meaning of life? Suffering does not make life meaningless or valueless. Its effect can be quite the opposite. It can bring about maturity, creativity, compassion. It also, however, reminds us of the limitations of our freedom and humanity. While we are created in the image of God, we live our days in a world fallen and marred by sin. Ultimately, pain and suffering are part of that experience. They are part of the price we pay for being human.

Chapter Nine

THE PRICE OF LIFE

Alister E. McGrath

I ARRANGED TO MEET an Oxford colleague, whom I had not seen for some time, for lunch one day. We talked about our lives, swapped news, and discussed our mutual friends—the sort of things any friends do when they get together after a period of absence. My friend then told me a story about a young woman who had been seriously injured in a traffic accident. Although she survived the accident, she would have to endure a degree of pain for the remainder of her life.

My friend was in a reflective mood. I remember his saying something like, "She was so badly hurt, that she is probably going to be in some pain for the rest of her days. You know, if she had been an animal—a horse or a dog—she would have been put to sleep." That remark stayed in my mind, even though (I have to confess) I have forgotten just about everything else we talked about that day.

Suffering is the price we pay for being alive. More than that, it is the price we pay for being human. We are willing to terminate the life of an animal to prevent suffering, but human life is different. Human existence seems to be something priceless. Suffering does not make life meaningless or valueless. Suffering is not an add-on feature, which we can dispense with, but a vital aspect of our existence as humans. To live without suffering would be to live in a pretend world, under permanent sedation not only from its trials and tribulations, but also from its joys and pleasures.

But there is more to it than this. Suffering brings us to maturity. We learn through suffering. There is much truth in the old Greek saying, *pathemata mathemata* "suffering is education." Suffering makes us more sensitive and compassionate people, more aware of the needs and anxieties of others. It brings out the full power of human creativity. It is no accident that some of the best art seems to arise from situations of pain or hardship. Van Gogh's paintings echo his personal sadness. Some of Beethoven's greatest music dates from the period of his life when he was devastated by the thought of becoming deaf and thus being cut off from the musical world of his own making.

Suffering often brings out the full potential of human beings, unleashing a creativity that is too easily stifled by smugness and security. Orson Welles is merely one of many writers to note that material well-being and affluence seem to suppress the power of the human imagination. Renaissance Italy, with all its struggles and suffering, produced some of the finest works of art humanity has ever known. But what, Welles asked, has pampered, neutral, and prosperous Switzerland ever contributed to the history of human culture? The cuckoo clock.

To be human is to want to be free. Freedom matters to people. Think of how many wars have been fought in order to preserve, or restore, the freedom of nations. Think of the great civil rights protests, which demanded freedom for the citizens of these nations. The yearning for liberty seems to be a basic feature, not merely of human civilization, but of human nature itself.

I remember once hearing an interview with a prominent politician in a small eastern European nation that was demanding freedom from its much larger neighbor, then known as the Soviet Union. The interviewer pressed him on a significant point. What about the economic consequences? Wouldn't it spell economic ruin to break away from its larger neighbor? "Maybe—but we want to be free to make our own mistakes!" was the indignant reply.

Children leave their parental home, setting to one side its familiarity and security. Why? Partly because they want to break free from it. However much they may value their parents, they want to live their own lives, to make their own decisions, and to learn from their own mistakes. Deep down, all of us know of our need to learn things for ourselves. We don't want to accept everything on authority. That seems too much like a lapse into blind and mindless dictatorship. We want to check things out for ourselves. And that means having the freedom to do so.

But what is the price of this freedom? Freedom implies that we are free to make mistakes, to do things that hurt others, to cause evil. Jean-Paul Sartre, easily among the most perceptive of the existentialist writers, spoke of humans as being "condemned to freedom." In other words, we have no choice but to be free and to live with the consequences of that freedom. If we were simply a form of machine or computer, programmed to do only things that we found acceptable, there would be no problem about evil. We wouldn't do wrong things. We wouldn't be allowed to do them. We wouldn't cause suffering or evil. But then we wouldn't be free, either. So we have two options: to be free in a restricted sense of the word (only to do good), or to be free in a fuller sense of the word (including the worrying possibility of being free to make mistakes and do evil). The first is fraught with the risk of paternalism: "Don't do this. It wouldn't be good for you." The original sin of Genesis chapter 3 is based on a rejection of precisely this sort of freedom. The first man and woman were free to do exactly what they pleased, providing they did not do something, which they were told was forbidden.

But they did it. They didn't want to be told what was off limits and what wasn't. They wanted to be like God, free to decide what was right and what was wrong. They wanted to set their own limits and live within them. The Christian tradition has seen in this demand for autonomy the root of all suffering. It seems that a central element of fallen human nature is a rugged sense of independence: We do not like being told what we may and may not do.

So we have freedom—a freedom to do evil, a freedom to avoid and disobey God. God leaves us room to be human. He makes space for us to make mistakes. God pulls Himself back from His creation in order to allow it to exercise the freedom that He chose to allow it. (It is pointless to speak of God's endowing His creatures with freedom, only to refuse to allow them to exercise that freedom.) Yet in the exercise of that freedom, we may see the origins of much of the tragic suffering of the world.

But would we rather be without that freedom? Paradoxically, it is something that we can never abandon, even though we find it difficult to live with its results. As Sartre rightly saw, to be human is to be free to commit evil and to inflict suffering. Part of our problem with suffering is that we are reluctant to allow that there is something wrong with human nature that allows us to abuse our God-given freedom. Yet the casualty of this observation is not God; it is humans who persist in their deluded and naive belief about the goodness of human nature.

There is another aspect of suffering that we need to note here. That is the sheer tragedy of the human predicament. In everyday use, the word *tragedy* tends to mean something like disastrous, pitiful, or pathetic. But here it means more than that. It points to our powerlessness to change things. It hints at our lack of control over our own destiny. It declares our inability to change things or to change our sense of anger, mingled with despair, at the way things are. Part of the offense of suffering lies in the fact that we cannot control it. Suffering is part of the chaos and disorder of sin. We have been able to master the skills of putting people on the moon and discovering the hidden secrets of the most distant planets, yet we cannot put an end to human suffering on earth. One of the reasons why modern human beings find suffering so offensive is that its existence points to the limits of human achievement. Despite all human advances in civilization, suffering remains unmastered and untamed.

Many cultures have developed ways of coping with the tragic side of life. They know that nature is difficult to control and to predict. Suffering takes its place among the changes and chances of life. Suffering does not seem to have been a major philosophical problem in the Middle Ages, nor is it today for countless millions in Africa and Latin America. But in the highly developed societies of the West, suffering is a problem, perhaps because these societies have long lost sight of cultural resources for coping with suffering. It is not so much a theological, as a cultural, issue. So how has this problem arisen?

In the West, and especially in the United States, a form of "cultural Pelagianism" has gained the upper hand. Pelagianism was a movement, based in Rome in the early fifth century, that asserted that human beings were in total control of their situation, including their relationship to God. This overconfident worldview overlooked the tragic side of human nature with its obvious weaknesses and failings. Pelagianism was, at heart, a delusion, but a delusion that many people passionately wanted to believe in. They didn't want to face up to the hard facts of life, which suggested that human beings were not in control of things and needed the grace of God if they were to survive and prosper.

Just as Pelagius declared that human beings had total control over themselves and their destinies, so modern Western society wants to believe that it can control every aspect of life. Yet although it is enormously technologically advanced, Western society has discovered that it cannot defeat death any more than it can control suffering.

Suffering thus causes offense by pricking this bubble of optimism. It is a painful reminder of the limitations of human nature and human culture. Suffering hurts because it points to definite and disconcerting limits to human abilities. At least some of the theological fuss about suffering reflects this sense of outrage and offense. This explains the paradox that Westerners, who are among the most privileged of the human race, who enjoy standards of living that are astonishing by other standards, and who, through excellent medical services, suffer less than anyone else, make suffering into a bigger theological problem than it need be.

So how should Christians respond to this? Partly, by asking that we recover our awareness of our limitations as human beings. Suffering is threatening because it is a reminder of our powerlessness to control our world. We need to accept those limitations and realize that, on account of them, suffering will be an inevitable part of human existence. It is the price we pay for being human.

An Overview

The debate regarding euthanasia entails many definitions, nuances, and presuppositions. Without a clear understanding of what is being said and what is at stake in the debate, individuals risk being swept along by emotions, clichés, and misinformation. John Feinberg provides readers with clear and concise definitions in the context of an extensive and technical critique of the biblical and theological issues. The issues discussed as well as the cases involved require hard decisions. What we decide in the future will be based upon what we think about today. We must think through the issues responsibly, and we must solicit divine guidance as we do so.

Chapter Ten

EUTHANASIA
An Overview

John S. Feinberg

ON AUGUST 26, 1981, CLARENCE HERBERT had a routine operation to remove a colostomy bag. During the first hour in the recovery room, he suffered a massive loss of oxygen to his brain, became comatose, and was put on a respirator. Though the brain still performed some lower brain functions, his wife was told he was brain dead, and she agreed to remove him from the respirator. On August 29 he was removed from the respirator, but he did not die. On August 31 the doctor ordered removal of all intravenous feeding. On September 6 he died from dehydration and pneumonia.[1]

Was this mercy or murder? In October 1983 the California Court of Appeals decided that the doctors did not commit murder. The court claimed that Herbert's comatose condition was "terminal illness," and argued that intravenous nutrition and water is "medicine" that can be withdrawn or denied if it does not cure the patient's disease or even make him better.[2]

Janet Adkins was fifty-four years old, but she was diagnosed with Alzheimer's disease. Informed about the course of this disease, she decided she did not want to live for years in this progressively deteriorating condition. She decided to kill herself, but she wanted a quick, painless death. She enlisted the aid of Dr. Jack Kevorkian of Michigan, inventor of the infamous suicide machine. On June 4, 1990, Dr. Kevorkian hooked her up to a heart monitor and intravenous tube. She pushed a button that released chemicals that killed her in five minutes. A murder charge was filed against Kevorkian, but it was dismissed because Michigan's law against assisted suicide is vague. However, the court ordered Kevorkian not to use the device again or assist any more suicides. Despite warnings, Kevorkian later revealed that on October 23, 1991, he helped Shery Miller, forty-three, and Marjorie Wantz, fifty-eight, commit suicide. These incidents raised even greater complaint than the Adkins case, because neither Miller nor Wantz was suffering from a terminal disease. Miller had multiple sclerosis, and Wantz had a painful pelvic disease that was not terminal.[3] At the time of this writing, Kevorkian continues to assist in suicides and has been present at more than three dozen.

In the United States twenty-seven states ban assisted suicide, and four ban suicide or assisted suicide. A new law in Michigan, which outlaws what

Kevorkian is doing, was due to be in force March 30, 1993. In the meantime, Kevorkian continued to help others commit suicide. As a result, on February 25, 1993, the Michigan legislature voted to enforce the law immediately. He has subsequently been tried and acquitted twice.

Should Kevorkian be charged with murder? Is it immoral to seek Kevorkian's help to commit suicide?[4] What about those who "do it themselves" with instructions from the recent best-seller *Final Exit?* These cases raise a whole series of questions that in contemporary discussions relate to the issue of euthanasia. Questions involved include the following: Is mercy killing ever morally permissible or justifiable? If euthanasia is morally justifiable, are there cases where it would be morally obligatory to remove a patient's suffering? Is requesting a lethal dose of a drug equivalent to asking for help in committing suicide? If voluntary euthanasia is suicide, is suicide ever morally justifiable? Is there any moral difference between killing and letting someone die?[5]

Advancements in medical technology that allow doctors to prolong life have raised these and many more ethical and legal problems. The problems are exacerbated by cases such as the Karen Ann Quinlan case, for which neither the medical nor legal profession was prepared.[6] Problems are heightened by the rapidly increasing numbers of people living well beyond sixty-five into their eighties and nineties. Statistics from the Census Bureau tell the story in America. In 1940, 365,000 Americans were eighty-five or over (.3 percent of the population). In 1982, 2.5 million (1.1 percent) were in that category. The bureau predicts that by the end of the twentieth century this group will top 5.1 million (almost 2 per cent), and by 2050 more than sixteen million men and women will be eighty-five or over (5.2 percent of the population).[7] It is estimated that one fourth of all people who have ever reached sixty-five were alive as of 1975.[8] Since 1900, average life expectancy has increased more than 50 percent, from forty-nine to almost seventy today.[9]

Just because Americans are living longer does not mean they always remain in good health.[10] Increase in medical expenses as one grows older suggests a decline in health. It is estimated that per-capita hospital spending of the sixty-five-and-over group is more than 250 percent higher than that of the under-sixty-fives, and the eighty-five-or-over group is 77 percent higher again.[11] All of these factors contribute to a climate in which many are calling for legislation to legalize and regulate various forms of euthanasia.

Debates over euthanasia are not of modern invention. In the ancient world, Pythagoreans opposed euthanasia, whereas Stoics favored it, especially in cases of incurable disease.[12] Plato approved it in cases of terminal illness.[13] Under the influence of Christianity, the Western attitude toward euthanasia and suicide has been negative, though some have advocated it.[14] Moreover, euthanasia is not unique to the West. For example, Indian sacrifices of the incurably ill to the Ganges and the Balinese practice of burning widows for the benefit of a dead chief are all well documented.[15]

In more modern times debate over euthanasia has been quite lively.[16] In 1935 the Euthanasia Society of England was formed to convince the public that adults suffering severely from incurable fatal illnesses should be allowed a painless death if they requested it. The society's other goal was to promote legislation to that end. Despite the society's efforts, in both 1936 and 1969 bills to legalize euthanasia were defeated in the British House of Lords. In 1969 the British Medical Association passed a resolution that the medical profession has a duty to preserve life and relieve pain, but it condemned euthanasia.[17]

Holland has one of the most liberal attitudes toward euthanasia. Though the Netherlands has had a specific law against euthanasia that dates from the nineteenth century,[18] euthanasia was basically a nonissue until the early 1970s when a Dutch doctor killed her terminally ill mother with a lethal injection. The doctor was convicted, but the court suspended sentence and ruled that in cases where death is imminent and the patient has requested death, the physician could commit euthanasia.[19] Prior to 1993, euthanasia was still illegal in Holland, but Dutch courts were favorable to doctors who practiced it so long as they met the following guide lines: (1) the patient must be terminally ill, suffering unbearably, and must request it; (2) it must be a case in which no other treatment is possible; (3) the patient must consider the decision at length; and (4) only a physician in consultation with another physician can perform the act.[20] It is estimated that in Holland as many as six thousand people per year are put to death by euthanasia. Opinion polls show that about 60 percent of the Dutch population approve and only 12 percent of Dutch doctors oppose it. Moreover, surveys show that 80 percent of the doctors have been involved in euthanasia cases. One of the most telling facts about Dutch acceptance of euthanasia is that in Holland no surviving relative has filed a lawsuit against a doctor for performing euthanasia.[21]

In February 1993 the Dutch parliament voted to legalize doctor-assisted suicide and active euthanasia of terminally ill patients who request it. The guidelines governing these practices fundamentally follow those that were in use prior to the Dutch parliament's decision.

In the United States, the Euthanasia Society of America was formed in 1938. Public opinion and American law have generally reflected opposition to any form of euthanasia, but in more recent years the trend has been shifting.[22] For example, in 1973 a Gallup Poll asked if in cases of incurable disease, doctors should be allowed to end the patient's life by some painless means if the patient and his family request it. Of those responding, 53 percent said yes. When the same question was posed in 1950, only 30 per cent had answered yes.[23] A Harris Poll (1981) found that 78 percent of all polled would prefer not to suffer pointless life prolongation. That is, the majority preferred to reject life-prolonging care when there was no hope of recovery.[24]

Several events in recent years have really captured the attention of Americans, polarized views on the euthanasia question, and galvanized many to action. One is Dr. Kevorkian's suicide machine, and another is the book *Final Exit*. But undoubtedly the right-to-die case of Nancy Cruzan has been the most significant factor in raising people's awareness and "temperature" on this issue. Because of its importance, we briefly sketch the details of this case.

On January 11, 1983, twenty-five-year-old Nancy Cruzan was in an automobile accident in the Ozarks in southwestern Missouri. Paramedics arrived and restarted her breathing, but she had been without oxygen for so long that she never regained consciousness. On February 5, 1983, doctors implanted a feeding tube in Nancy's stomach. Apart from this apparatus, she was not on life support systems. Over the next years Nancy did not die, but she did not improve. She seemed to be in what is called a permanent vegetative state. As a result, in October 1987 Nancy's parents went to court to get permission to remove the feeding tube and let her die as they believed she would want. On July 27, 1988, the Jasper County (Missouri) judge granted them permission to remove the tube. However, the case was appealed to the Missouri Supreme Court, and on November 16, 1988, the court, in a 4–3 decision, overturned the lower court ruling, claiming there was no legal authority to grant the Cruzans' request.

The Cruzans appealed the case to the United States Supreme Court. It was the first time the Supreme Court ruled on a right-to-die case. In a 5–4 decision on June 25, 1990, the Court ruled to deny the Cruzans' request. However, the decision was not based on a belief that food and water could not be removed because they are basics of patient care and are not medicine. Nor was it based on a belief that patients do not have a right to choose to die. Instead, the ruling came because there was no "clear and convincing evidence" that Nancy would have wanted to stop artificial nutrition.[25] Had she signed a living will to that effect or granted power of attorney to her family to make decisions on her health care, the petition would have been granted. But she had done neither, and once comatose she obviously couldn't. Though the Cruzans' request was rejected, the Supreme Court in essence affirmed a patient's right to die under certain circumstances so long as there is a living will specifying those situations or a power of attorney granting decision-making power to a surrogate.

On August 30, 1990, the Cruzans went back to the Missouri judge and asked for another hearing, claiming they had new evidence that their daughter had once told three people she would rather die than live in a persistent vegetative state. In light of the Supreme Court's ruling that clear evidence of her desire to die was necessary to remove the tube, and in view of the new testimony to that effect, on December 14, 1990, the judge ruled that Cruzan's parents could remove her feeding tube. Shortly thereafter, that was done, and Nancy Cruzan finally died.[26]

As a result of cases like the Cruzan case, many are resorting to a living will. The first United States state to enact a Natural Death Act (living will legislation) was California (1976). As of 1990, forty-one states and the District of Columbia had living will laws.[27] The document, signed while a person is in good health and spirits, states that if a time comes when the individual cannot take part in decisions about his/her future, and if there is no reasonable expectation of recovery from physical, mental, or spiritual disability, he/she asks to be allowed to die rather than to be kept alive by artificial means or heroic measures.[28] In some states living wills are not legally binding, but those who sign them hope friends and family will feel morally bound to honor them. In addition, by 1990 some thirteen states had power-of-attorney laws that allow individuals to name a proxy to make health care decisions if the individual becomes incapacitated.[29]

Further developments have also occurred since the Cruzan case. For example, on September 26, 1991, Governor Jim Edgar of Illinois signed a right-to-die law. This law calls for naming a surrogate from a list of relatives and friends who will have the right "to decide when to end life-sustaining treatment for patients who are comatose, terminally ill or unable to decide for themselves, instead of leaving the matter to strangers in the legal system."[30] This law is considered especially important because two years earlier the Illinois Supreme Court had ruled that "without further direction from the legislature, such matters needed to be decided in court."[31] Of no small import in the drafting and passage of this law was the case of Rudy Linares. Linares' fifteen-month-old son was on life support systems at Chicago's Rush-Presbyterian St. Luke's Medical Center. The child was not going to get better, so Linares sought permission to withdraw life support. When the hospital denied permission because of legal concerns, in April 1989 Linares got a gun and unhooked his comatose son's respirator while holding police at bay. Linares was charged with murder, but a Cook County grand jury would not indict him. The right-to-die law should eliminate such problems in the future, since it provides medical workers legal immunity if they are strictly following the surrogate's decisions.

Permission to withdraw life-support systems from a terminally ill patient is one thing. Permission to help a terminally ill patient commit suicide is another. In California there was an attempt to get on the November 1988 ballot the Humane and Dignified Death Act. The measure would allow a patient to ask a doctor for help in committing suicide. The bill defined aid in dying as "any medical procedure that will terminate the life of the qualified patient, swiftly, painlessly, and humanely."[32] The bill would require two physicians to certify that the patient's death would occur within six months. Helping a patient under these conditions would protect doctors from any legal liability. The urgency of the bill stems from the increasing number of AIDS patients who choose to commit suicide and want help from a doctor to perform a successful suicide. Sponsors of the bill failed to get enough signatures to put the measure on the ballot, but they said public opinion polls showed nearly 60 percent approval of the measure, and they intended to get the measure on the ballot in 1990.[33] They were not successful in 1990, but a similar measure was on the November 1992 ballot in California. The previous bill would have allowed a surrogate to make the decision for someone who is mentally incompetent. The new bill removed that provision and stipulated that the person making the request must be a mentally competent adult (eighteen years or older) and must ask for this action on at least two consultation visits with the physician. Thankfully, that bill was defeated, but it will likely appear again since forces favoring it are very persistent.

A similar aid in dying bill was voted on in the state of Washington on

November 5, 1991. The bill was defeated there, but only by a close margin. Reflecting on the import of this proposed legislation, as well as the recent decision by the Dutch parliament to legalize doctor-assisted suicide, one is struck by how far medicine has strayed from the foundational principle incorporated in the Hippocratic Oath that a doctor will not use medicine to harm his patients.[34]

CLARIFICATION OF TERMINOLOGY

The term *euthanasia* is derived from two Greek words—*eu* meaning "well" or "good," and *thanatos* meaning "death." In contemporary discussions, it stands for a wide variety of practices. Terminology in regard to euthanasia can be divided into four different categories, each adding another dimension to the discussion.

Voluntary/Involuntary

This distinction focuses on whether or not the patient requests death. *Voluntary euthanasia* refers to cases where a patient requests death or grants permission to be put to death. It is often considered equivalent to suicide. Euthanasia is *involuntary* when someone is put to death without requesting it or granting permission. This distinction is crucial to many doctors and ethicists who think euthanasia can be morally justified if requested (voluntary), but not otherwise.

Active/Passive

These terms focus on the kind of action taken to bring about death.[35] *Active euthanasia* refers to taking some purposeful action to end a life whereas *passive euthanasia* refers to the withholding or refusal of treatment to sustain life.[36] Passive euthanasia may also involve withdrawing treatment already begun.[37] The distinction is often equated with the ideas of commission (active) and omission (passive), and some see it as the difference between killing (active) and letting someone die (passive). Giving a lethal dose of drugs to someone diagnosed with AIDS is active euthanasia. Removal of Clarence Herbert's feeding tube is an example of passive euthanasia.

Upon minimal reflection, one can see that both active and passive euthanasia can be either voluntary or involuntary. What ethicists often debate is whether there is any morally significant difference between killing and letting die.

Direct/Indirect

These terms denote the role played by the person who dies when his life is taken. *Direct euthanasia* refers to cases where the individual himself carries out the decision to die. *Indirect* refers to situations where someone else carries out the decision. These terms are not equal to *voluntary/involuntary*. Those terms refer to whether the individual requests or permits the act, but not to the actual doing of the act. *Direct/indirect* refers to whether the individual does the act himself or not.

Death with Dignity, Mercy Killing, and Death Selection[38]

These terms focus on the ultimate intended goal to be achieved through the act of euthanasia. *Death with dignity* refers to allowing the patient to die a truly humane death. Rather than using extraordinary means (such as hooking the patient up to a machine) to forestall death (which is said to be dehumanizing), the patient is allowed to die "naturally." Basic needs such as food and drink are met, but there is an attempt to avoid the dehumanizing effects of isolating a dying patient from family while making him or her little more than a body hooked up to a machine. Though this kind of euthanasia is often voluntary, rarely is it equated with suicide, since the patient is incurably ill and no medical procedure would heal him.

In *mercy killing*, the intent is to release someone who is suffering excruciating pain and has no other way of escape but death. It is seen as an act of mercy.[39] Mercy killing may involve using medical technology to hasten or cause death, or it may involve using ordinary means to bring death. The case of Janet Adkins is an example of mercy killing. Shooting someone who is trapped in a burning car, cannot escape, and is in terrible pain is another example. Often voluntary mercy killing is equated with suicide. Whereas the goal with mercy killing is ostensibly the removal of individual pain and suffering, the goal with *death selection* is the deliberate removal of persons whose lives are no longer considered socially useful. People in this category need not be ill; they need only be deemed useless, a bother to society, expendable. This kind of euthanasia might fall on groups such as "hardened" criminals, the mentally retarded, or (as in Hitler's Germany) whole ethnic or racial groups.[40]

CONTEMPORARY DEBATE OVER EUTHANASIA

Arguments in the debate about euthanasia can be divided into broad categories. For example, some attempt to justify euthanasia generally, without focusing on a specific form. Others attempt to justify both active and passive euthanasia, and still others focus on involuntary euthanasia. From these perspectives we shall present the case for euthanasia and then offer what we believe is an appropriate Christian response. We reject euthanasia in general, but we think there are some cases where euthanasia may be permissible. After considering arguments on both sides of the question, we shall turn to the difficult issue of decision making in specific cases.

In Favor of Euthanasia Generally

Personhood

The issue of personhood is crucial to the abortion debate, and it is equally important in debates over euthanasia. We have already noted contemporary criteria for determining personhood (criteria used in both the abortion and euthanasia debates), so we need not repeat them here.[41] Those who use the argument to support euthanasia propose that though an individual once possessed personhood, does not as his or her life nears its end, and has no potential of regaining it. Thus, someone in an irreversible coma, for example, is no longer a person but only a biological organism. There is no need to maintain biological life that does not sustain personal life. "Pulling the plug" on a comatose person neither increases nor relieves his suffering, since he feels nothing anyway. However, pulling the plug may relieve the agony of those who grieve over their relative and friend.[42] The obvious decision should be to pull the plug.

Several points become clear from this line of argument. For one thing, the mere possession of biological life is not enough to warrant one's continued existence. However, without personal life, life may be disposed of whether by abortion, infanticide, suicide, or any form of euthanasia. Unfortunately, as it has been noted in the case of abortion, the criteria of personhood are extremely ambiguous, and under some interpretations none of us qualify as a person. Nonetheless, proponents of euthanasia believe the criteria are specific enough and use this line of argument to justify euthanasia.

Quality of Life Ethic

Preserving life at all costs, no matter what the condition of that life, is what Joseph Fletcher has called the "vitalist fallacy," the fallacy that all life is valuable and is to be maintained no matter what. Instead, a certain quality of life (as defined by criteria of personhood) is necessary to warrant continued existence.

Proponents of euthanasia further argue that the question of euthanasia is not always clear-cut even for those espousing a sanctity of life ethic. For example, if a person in an irreversible coma continues biological life without artificial means (e.g., Clarence Herbert and Karen Quinlan once the respirator was unplugged), does the sanctity of life principle require that such life go on? In cases of unrelenting and unrelievable suffering with no chance of recovery, does a sanctity of life ethic stand in the way of removing such pain by death? In other words, regardless of one's ethic, is there not a time when enough is enough, or must life always be preserved at all costs?[43] Those holding a quality of life ethic say that when sanctity of life proponents agree that sometimes enough is enough, they at least implicitly recognize that quality of life does matter. Of course, medical technology can prolong biological life way beyond a time when there is any significant quality of life. In virtue of that fact, and since the sanctity of life proponent agrees that sometimes enough is enough, must we not after all make decisions on the basis of quality, not sanctity, of life?[44]

Perception of God

Atheists and theists alike are using their views about God as a basis for supporting euthanasia. For example, the *Humanist Manifesto*, which presupposes atheism, sees man as the measure of all things and in control of decisions about life and death. If there is no God, all arguments against euthanasia on grounds that God is the owner of life are automatically ruled out.[45] Moreover, if one believes as atheists do that there is no life beyond the grave, that everything happens by pure chance, and that all creatures are subject to the whims of blind fate, then all humans can do is treat one another with sympathy and kindness. That means, of course, that if someone faces hopeless suffering and unbearable pain, we should do what we would do to an animal, have pity and remove the pain by helping him or her die.[46]

As for some theists, a changed perception of God underlies their advocacy of euthanasia. For example, Joseph Fletcher still believes in God, but not the traditional one. Fletcher knows that many think modern medicine is "playing God" with the new technology. Fletcher admits this is true, but claims the real question is "which or whose God are we playing?"[47] Man used to believe in a God who was in charge of birth and death, believing that man had no responsibility and no right to tamper in these areas. When man did not understand matters relating to life and death, he appealed to this God who knew all and was in control. Now men have grown up spiritually as their knowledge of life and death has increased, and they are turning to a God who "is the creative principle behind things, who is behind the test tube as much as the earthquake and volcano."[48] Fletcher says this God can be believed in, not a God who prohibits freedom to choose our manner of birth and death or inhibits our research. According to Fletcher, the traditional God who allowed no tampering with matters of life and death is dead.[49]

Utilitarian Concerns

Invariably, proponents of euthanasia argue their case on consequentialist (usually utilitarian) grounds. Joseph Fletcher blatantly admits holding this ethic and sees it as a support for euthanasia. Fletcher asks whether we should ever hasten someone's death out of compassion or mercy. One's answer depends on whether he thinks the end justifies the means. Fletcher adamantly asserts that the end does justify the means. In fact, he asks what else could.[50] However, the key question in Fletcher's mind is what justifies the end. Fletcher responds "that human happiness and well-being is the highest good or *summum bonum*, that therefore any ends or purposes that that standard or ideal validates are just, right, good. This is what humanistic medicine is all about; it is what the concepts of loving concern and social justice are built upon."[51] This is unabashed consequentialism. If the consequences are acceptable, the means to those ends are morally justified.

Not only is utilitarianism often the underlying ethic, but frequently euthanasia is justified in virtue of utilitarian concerns. For example, some ask whether a family can afford the expense of "heroic" means of medical care. Others note that medical resources generally are limited, and some medical procedures (e.g., an artificial heart operation) are extremely expensive. The real dilemma arises when more than one person needs the expensive care. Paul Brand, former missionary to India, argues that we must ask whether $100,000 for a single operation is the best use of that money. Moreover, if more than one person needs special care, but there is only money or hospital resources for one, how does one decide who gets the medical attention?[52] A decision to let some die would be necessary, and who dies might be decided on the utilitarian ground of who is perceived to be of most use to society.

Freedom of Choice, Cruelty, and Euthanasia

Some argue that those who qualify as persons should be free to choose the kind of death they want. Submitting to "whatever God brings," even though it may involve the depersonalization of hooking up oneself to a machine, is not to act as a person.[53] For this reason the "living will" is favored. Removing choices about the end of life from the free control of the individual is dehumanizing.[54]

Anthony Flew agrees that freedom of choice *per se is* crucial, but he supports it as well on other grounds. Flew notes that some people suffering unbearably want to die quickly. He thinks it immoral to refuse legal grounds for them to do so. Any law that prevents them from doing so, and "usually thereby forces other people who care for them to watch their pointless pain helplessly, is a very cruel law."[55] We extend mercy to animals to put them out of their misery. Why be less merciful to humans?[56] Flew appeals here to the principle that it is immoral to be cruel, and he thinks that in the cases mentioned, denying requests to die is cruel. Marvin Kohl goes even further. Some might *reject* euthanasia on the ground that *it is* cruel. Kohl says the difference between the two sides centers on what constitutes cruelty and whether or not avoiding cruelty is morally sufficient. Opponents of euthanasia define cruelty narrowly to refer to *causing* unnecessary pain or harm deliberately. They overlook the broader sense, which means to cause or *allow* harm or pain deliberately. The narrower sense of cruelty tolerates human misery. However, this is contrary to the ideal of the Good Samaritan, who not only avoided cruelty, but actively went out of his way to help the suffering person. Merely taking care not to cause cruelty is insufficient. That tells us what not to do, but not what to do. Only a notion of cruelty broad enough to include the obligation to help remove the suffering is adequate.[57]

Euthanasia and Abortion

Joseph Fletcher argues that if abortion can be morally justified, so can euthanasia. Fletcher has in mind cases where the individual no longer qualifies as a person. He says, "It is ridiculous to give ethical approval to the positive ending of subhuman life *in utero*, as we do in therapeutic abortions for reasons of mercy and compassion, but refuse to approve of positively ending a subhuman life *in extremis.*"[58] This in itself does not prove that either eugenic abortion or mercy killing is morally right, but it does demand consistency in one's position. Fletcher, of course, thinks eugenic abortion is moral, and argues that termination of the lives of those suffering unbearably follows with logical inevitability.

Other Concerns

Three other considerations are raised to legitimize euthanasia generally. One appeals to the doctor/patient relationship. Normally, a patient expects his doctor to act in accord with his duty to preserve life. Of course, the doctor's duty is also to alleviate suffering. Sometimes those duties conflict, and such conflicts underscore the fact that a doctor's fundamental obligation is to his patient, not to a principle of preserving life. Thus, the morality of voluntary euthanasia becomes a question of whether a patient can expect a doctor to honor the patient's requests to end life.[59] If it is morally permissible for the patient to request euthanasia, then given the doctor's obligation to the patient, the doctor can also morally grant the request.

Another argument rests on a distinction between ordinary and extraordinary means of prolonging life. Even Roman Catholic thinking, for example, holds that when a patient faces imminent death from incurable disease, he must prolong life by ordinary means, but in good conscience may refuse treatment that is extraordinary.[60] Despite the fact that one generation's extraordinary means may be another generation's ordinary means, many ethicists still think the distinction is legitimate, even if category boundaries cannot be perfectly drawn.[61]

A final argument supporting euthanasia in certain circumstances appeals to the double effect doctrine. When a patient is terminally ill, will not recover, and is in terrible pain, many hold that giving that person medication to relieve pain is morally acceptable, even if the medication will also speed death.[62] The argument is that the directly intended effect of relieving pain is a good; the coincident effect of shortening life is only an inescapable, but unintended effect of the action.[63] Thus, such instances of hastening death are morally justifiable.

Biblical and Theological Considerations

Sixth Commandment Not Absolute

An initial biblical consideration used to support euthanasia appeals to the sixth commandment (Ex. 20:13), "Thou shalt not kill." Many use this as a prohibition against all forms of euthanasia, but others question its validity. Ought this commandment be absolutized? Some think it wrong to do so, because the absolutizing of biblical commands is inconsistent. For example, Das and Mabry note that in India there is a tendency to absolutize this commandment but not to absolutize Jesus' teaching in Matthew 6:2–4 about giving to those who beg from you. How does one decide which teachings to absolutize and which not?[64]

Moreover, the command against killing cannot be absolute, for those who invoke it against euthanasia typically favor capital punishment, war, and killing in self-defense. The prohibition in the sixth commandment seems to be against vengeful killing, not all killing. If so, then clearly some forms of voluntary and even involuntary euthanasia are permissible if no other considerations rule them out. Erickson and Bowers note that Old Testament teaching on killing reveals that there was condemnable killing (murder), excusable killing, and even mandatory killing (capital punishment). Murder is characterized as intentional, premeditated, malicious, contrary to the desire or intention of the victim, and against someone who has done nothing deserving of death. Voluntary euthanasia fits the first two and the last criteria, but does not always fit the third and fourth.[65] Even involuntary euthanasia would not always meet all these criteria, for in many cases no malice is intended. Patient benefit is the aim. Thus, euthanasia in general cannot be excluded by appeal to the sixth commandment.

Perspective on Death and the Afterlife

Scripture portrays death as the natural and appointed end of everyone (Heb. 9:27). Some claim it should be accepted as a good gift from God, not an enemy.

Through death man enters into the fullness of God's glory.[66] Paul's words summarize things for believers: "For to me, to live is Christ and to die is gain" (Phil. 1:21). Clearly, death is not an enemy to avoid at all costs. Some agree that death benefits those who go to heaven, but it does not make things better for those who wind up in hell. For example, Anthony Flew claims that the strongest argument against euthanasia would be the existence of hell, if there were one.[67] Robert Wennberg disagrees. Christians usually portray hell as a place of horrible torment. Wennberg says we need not assume this is so. Symbolic imagery characterizes many biblical descriptions of heaven and hell, so the punitive aspect of hell need not include literal physical suffering. We cannot conclude that no matter how much one has suffered in this life, hell will be worse. Moreover, if one rejects euthanasia on the ground that a person will be worse off in hell no matter how much he suffers in life, one must also endorse prolonging life as long as possible regardless of the patient's condition in order to keep people from slipping into hell. Most would be uncomfortable with that position.[68]

Suffering as Valueless

Many think the book of Job illustrates that God often uses affliction to mature people spiritually. Thus, it should be accepted. On the contrary, Das and Mabry claim Job did not willingly accept suffering, nor did he ever understand why he suffered. If Job teaches anything, it is not confident acceptance of suffering, but the refusal of a pious man to yield to the temptation to reject God. "Thus we do not see in Job, nor in the Bible generally, a counsel to passively accept suffering. Rather, the general course of the Bible is in the other direction—to relieve suffering, to show mercy, to help the helpless.[69] Though one can learn through affliction, Scripture never guarantees that sufferers will respond properly. Suffering cannot justify continuing life at all costs, especially when suffering is solely for the sake of suffering. Scripture never sanctions that kind of suffering.[70]

Self-Sacrifice

Self-sacrifice for others is a value of the highest order. Jesus' death illustrates it, and His words (John 15:13) commend it as the highest form of love. When a patient suffers unbearably from an incurable disease, others suffer emotionally and even physically as they view their loved one. Depending on the cost of medical care, the family may also suffer financial hardship. In such cases some argue that the principle of self-sacrifice on others' behalf warrants the voluntary ending of the patient's life. In fact, if done to relieve the pain inflicted on family and friends, the act qualifies as a praiseworthy act of self-sacrifice.[71]

Voluntary Euthanasia and Suicide

Many think that most, if not all, cases of voluntary euthanasia (whether direct or indirect) are tantamount to suicide. Thus, for them to justify voluntary euthanasia, they must also justify suicide.[72] Historically, one of the best-known defenses of suicide comes from David Hume. For Hume the crucial issue was whether suicide violates one or more of the following obligations humans normally have: obligations to self, others, and God. As to God, Hume argued that life is not God's property just because He created it. Life and death are governed by natural causes, so one need not appeal to God to explain life and death. Moreover, if causal laws collectively constitute the divine order, then we should never do anything to control the natural order. Of course, that would be absurd, for unless we resisted some natural events (like extreme heat and cold), life could not exist. Thus, just as one may divert the course of a river to avoid a flood, so one may, for example, rightly divert the flow of blood from its normal course to prevent the evils of shame, dishonor, or constant suffering. Some might reply that since God has sovereign control over whatever happens, deserting one's position in the universe by suicide is rebellion against God. However, Hume thought this a worthless objection to suicide, for if God is so in control of life that nothing happens without divine consent, then neither does suicide happen without God's consent. When someone prefers death to life because of pain and anguish, that person must conclude that God is recalling him from his station in life.[73]

As to responsibility to society, Hume reasoned that committing suicide might actually better fulfill one's obligations than staying alive. If one cannot promote the interests of society and instead is a burden to it, or at least to those who care for him, rather than meeting societal needs, then committing suicide would better fulfill one's obligations to society than not.[74]

In regard to self-love, some assert that suicide, rather than deserting obligations to oneself, indulges one's own wishes. In fact, some suicides are condemned as supreme acts of selfishness. Thus, it can hardly be maintained that someone who commits suicide has no concern for his own well-being. As to scriptural considerations, Erickson and Bowers (though not advocating suicide) question whether Scripture really rules out suicide so clearly as one might think. Citing the cases of Abimelech (Judg. 9:50–57), Saul (1 Sam. 31), Samson (Judg. 16:28–30), and Judas Iscariot (Matt. 27:5), they note that Scripture merely reports these suicides but does not evaluate them. David grieved over Saul's death, but the reason offered (2 Sam. 1:4–16) is that God's anointed had died, not that suicide was involved. Erickson and Bowers conclude that the morality of euthanasia cannot be determined simply by treating it as suicide and arguing that Scripture clearly prohibits suicide.[75]

Active/Passive—Killing/Letting Die
James Rachels has argued that there is no moral difference between active

and passive euthanasia (killing and letting die). For one thing, sometimes active euthanasia is more humane than passive. For example, if it is morally right not to operate on a Down's syndrome child with intestinal obstruction, it is actually preferable to kill the child directly rather than allowing a slow death. The key issue is Down's syndrome, not the intestines (which could be repaired by surgery); so the moral justification for the child's death will have to come in regard to the Down's. But then the more rapid death is more humane.[76]

Rachels's other line of argument rests on two cases that show there is no moral difference between killing and letting die. Let us say that Smith and Jones, who have six-year-old cousins, will each receive a large inheritance if their cousins die. Smith drowns his cousin while his cousin is bathing. Jones plans the same fate for his cousin, but as Jones enters the bathroom, his cousin slips, hits his head and falls facedown in the water. Jones stands by and lets the child drown. We are not inclined to think Jones more praiseworthy than Smith. Rachels argues that this shows there is no difference morally between killing and letting die.[77]

Gerald Hughes claims that even when no ill intent is involved, there is no significant distinction between killing and letting die. He offers two cases, one involving a patient on life-support systems without which he will die, and the other involving a terminally ill person who will die in a few days. In the first case, the doctor can switch off the machine and "allow the patient to die." In the second, the doctor can give a lethal injection, which will work as quickly as pulling the plug will end the first patient's life. Since the intentions are the same, in these cases there is no difference between killing and letting die.[78]

For one who accepts this line of argument, active and passive euthanasia can be equally justified because there is no morally significant difference between killing and letting die.

Involuntary Euthanasia

Several lines of argument can be used to justify involuntary euthanasia. The first appeals to arguments favoring euthanasia generally. Arguments about extending mercy and avoiding cruelty apply whether a person requests death or not. Moreover, on consequentialist views of ethics such as utilitarianism, one can justify any form of involuntary euthanasia, including death selection.

Second, the Jones/Smith cases can be used to support both active and passive involuntary euthanasia because both cases are instances of involuntary killing. Anyone who agrees with the Jones/Smith argumentation can agree that there is no moral difference between active and passive involuntary euthanasia.

A final argument stems from Richard McCormick and Robert Veatch's discussion of Joseph Fox. Fox was put on a respirator after going into a coma during an operation. McCormick and Veatch note the reasoning behind the decision to remove the respirator. Judge Robert Meade granted permission because Fox had made his wishes known previously. In discussing the Quinlan case, Fox stated that if he were in a similar condition, he would not want to be kept alive artificially. The judge granted permission to uphold what he claimed was Fox's right to self-determination.

McCormick and Veatch disagree. They note that many people never express their wishes about such a situation. If one were forced to adopt Meade's reasoning, such people would have to remain indefinitely on a respirator. That would be unacceptable. Moreover, McCormick and Veatch note that some people even from birth are incompetent to render a decision on this issue. McCormick and Veatch suggest another set of principles for cases where the person is incompetent or has never expressed his wishes. The first and major principle is patient benefit. Someone must make a decision about the patient's best interests. The second principle is that the "someone" should be a family member or family surrogate. Thus, they claim that when the individual does not or cannot express his wishes (involuntary), the matter of patient benefit as determined by a family member can be used not only to decide what to do for the patient but to justify morally what is done, even if what is done brings about the death of the individual.[79]

A CHRISTIAN RESPONSE TO EUTHANASIA

Against Euthanasia Generally

Sanctity of Life Ethic

Opponents of euthanasia argue that life is so valuable that it should be terminated only when unusual considerations dictate an exception. Some exceptions such as a just war and self-defense are enumerated in the Bible. Scripture does not say the list is complete, but with no clear indication of other exceptions, one should not look for others, but should rather uphold the sanctity of life principle. In cases where life is less than most would call human, the person involved seldom can maintain life on his or her own anyway. No active means are needed to end life; refusal of unusual means of care will suffice.[80] Some might think this approach too liberal, but what actually is being urged rules out active euthanasia in favor of the sanctity of life principle while ruling in passive euthanasia *only* in cases where the person would die anyway with ordinary care.

Biblically speaking, human life is sacred. It is sacred because man is made in God's image (Gen. 1:26–27; 5:1). As we have argued in our discussion of personhood,[81] even someone severely deformed or wracked with pain from a terminal illness so that he or she cannot interact with his or her environment still bears the image of God. That alone suggests care in decision making concerning such people.[82]

Life is sacred as well because God has given it and sustains it. Because it is His gift, we must treat it with care and not discard it. To treat it lightly is a supreme act of ingratitude, but it also suggests that we think we own our life, when in fact God gave it and owns it.[83] Christians have traditionally used this argument against suicide. It seems relevant as well to euthanasia in general.

Finally, a further biblical indication of the sanctity of life is the prohibition against life-taking. Killing is condemned both in the Old Testament (Ex. 20:13) and the New Testament (Matt. 5:21; 19:18; Mark 10:19; Luke 18:20; Rom. 13:9). While there are exceptions to the rule (e.g., killing in self-defense, capital punishment, just war), what is unexceptional is the prohibition against the deliberate, intentional taking of innocent life. In most cases, euthanasia is the deliberate taking of innocent life. Biblical teaching renders those cases morally unacceptable.[84]

Anticonsequentialism

As already noted, much argumentation for euthanasia rests on consequentialist concerns. Deontologists respond that ends do not justify means. Some who espouse biblically based ethics claim that scriptural precepts are deontological, grounded in the nature of God, and not consequentialist, grounded in the ends sought.[85] Moreover, some note that consequentialism also undercuts the difference between acts and omissions, a very important distinction in any case of letting die. Since the consequence in cases of killing and letting die is the same, consequentialism generally sees no moral difference between the two. This is unacceptable to anyone who sees a legitimate distinction between killing and letting die.[86] In our thinking, all of these considerations and more are serious problems with consequentialism. Once consequentialism is rejected, justification for many instances of euthanasia evaporates.

The Wedge Argument

Sometimes referred to as the slippery slope argument, this argument warns against opening the door even to the seemingly most innocuous instances of euthanasia. Appeal is often made to what happened under the Nazis. They began with mercy killing in limited cases to relieve suffering, but later genocide eventuated. Once a country starts down the slope of killing, it gradually becomes more comfortable with euthanasia, and it becomes much easier to accustom people to even more inhumane and unwarranted killing.

We believe Arthur Dyck states the wedge argument most convincingly. He notes that a wedge argument need not predict that certain practices will follow from others. The key to a wedge argument is the form or logic of moral justifications or actions.[87] One might want to limit the breadth of the category of people who qualify for euthanasia, but once it is decided that certain people are to die, it is hard to find any logical grounds for keeping others alive. For example, if the category includes those lacking the dignity of human beings, this can include many not terminally ill, nor in pain, nor desirous of death. They may simply fail to meet some ambiguous standard of what it means to be human. Proponents of euthanasia invariably guarantee that it will be used only in rather narrowly defined cases. The wedge argument says that "there is no logical or easily agreed upon reason why the range of cases should be restricted"[88] to what might appear at first sight as paradigm cases. The wedge argument assumes that killing is wrong generally and that there should be as few exceptions as possible to the command to preserve life. Realizing where it could lead, why make a wedge in the door for any euthanasia?

Medical Concerns

Several medical considerations cause many to hesitate before encouraging euthanasia. First, a request to execute a natural-death directive may be based more on fear or misinformation than anything else. The patient may think his situation far worse than it actually is and ask to die. Once the patient dies, the mistake cannot be undone.

Second, a cure for a supposedly incurable disease may be found. Medical history is filled with examples of people thought to have an incurable disease who were later healed when medicine progressed.[89] Medical science advances very rapidly, but new cures cannot be offered to a dead person.

Third, those who think patients must choose between terrible suffering and relief through death have overlooked a third option. Even in terminal cases, modern medicine can provide measures sufficient to reduce pain to a bearable level or even remove it altogether.[90] In most cases one need not choose death as the sole release from pain.

A final medical matter relates to a doctor's involvement in euthanasia. Many note that when a doctor takes the Hippocratic Oath, he promises to use medicine to help the sick and never to injure or wrong them. The doctor also promises never to give poison to anyone, even if asked to do so.[91] Some claim the Oath no longer applies in our times, but those who think otherwise have serious problems in squaring the Oath with aiding euthanasia.

Additional Biblical and Theological Concerns

Value in Suffering. Though suffering is neither enjoyable nor to be sought, that does not mean it cannot have any positive function in a person's life. Romans 5:3–5; 1 Peter 1:6–9; 2 Corinthians 4:17; 12:10; and the book of Job, for example, speak of the potential benefits to be gained from suffering. While afflictions are evils, God can and does use them to work good in our lives. Suffering need not be seen as valueless, something to be escaped at all costs.

Perspective on Life, Death, and the Afterlife

Initially, we must underscore biblical teaching that God is in control of life and death. The humanist may dislike it, but passages such as Job 14:5; Ecclesiastes 3:2; and James 4:13–15 teach that no one can add or detract even one second from his life beyond what God has decided. Moreover, those who try to extend life endlessly, regardless of the patient's condition, are reminded by Ecclesiastes 3:2 that there is a time to be born and a time to die. Man's manipulations cannot overturn God's control.

As to the biblical portrayal of death, we agree with those who claim it is quite different from views that "glorify death" as a beautiful friend of man, greatly to be desired when suffering intensely. The biblical perspective is that death is not natural; it entered the world as a result of sin (Gen. 3:14–19; Rom. 5:12). Moreover, the process of dying is itself often very painful, and Scripture does not portray it otherwise. Death is not a friend; it is the last enemy to be overcome (1 Cor. 15:26). As Paul Ramsey aptly states, we should not talk of the beauty of death or even of death with dignity. Death is the final indignity to man, and Scripture presents it that way.[92]

Douglas Stuart contends that the biblical perspective on life and death is seen in part by how biblical saints considered death. Those who asked God for a "good death" (e.g., Balaam, Num. 23:10; Simeon, Luke 2:26, 29) showed no desire for an early death. In cases where someone is in agony or near death (e.g., Pss. 22:19–21; 88), death is not welcomed or desired. Instead, the plea is for deliverance and restoration to a full, active life.[93] All these facts suggest the preciousness of life and the disdain with which Scripture views death and dying.

Some think Paul forbids sorrow over death (1 Thess. 4:13). However, he is not suggesting we should rejoice when someone dies. He only mandates that as believers grieve, they should not grieve *as those who have no hope*. This is hardly an endorsement of death. In fact, Paul sees the Christian's hope not as a death that releases from suffering, but as resurrection to life, which occurs at Christ's return (1 Thess. 4:13–18). Proponents of euthanasia may reply that our portrayal of scriptural teaching on death contradicts the biblical teaching that dying is gain for the believer (e.g., Phil. 1:21). However, the contradiction is apparent, not real, as can be seen by properly distinguishing (1) the cause and nature of dying, from (2) what happens after death; from the perspective of (1) death is negative, as our immediately preceding comments indicate, to (2) the outcome of death is negative for the nonbeliever, for he or she is consigned to eternal punishment. For the believer, the outcome is positive (2 Cor. 5:8; Phil. 1:21, 23). However, nowhere does Scripture encourage the believer to do something to "speed up" his entry into the Lord's presence. The time of his departure is in God's hands.

The biblical perspective on life, death, and the afterlife is incomplete without the teaching of the resurrection of the body. Scripture does not teach that death ends it all. Rather, it tells us that for believers and nonbelievers alike, following death there is disembodied conscious existence and eventually resurrection of the body (Luke 16:19ff.; Rom. 8:18ff.; 1 Cor. 15:20–23; 2 Cor. 5:8; Rev. 20:4–5, 11–15). Among other things, this means for the Christian that his ultimate hope for escaping pain and suffering is not physical death, but resurrection of the body.[94]

Other Concerns

Two other considerations are noteworthy. Some emphasize that learning from affliction is not the only biblical alternative to euthanasia. The other is healing. There are even cases of dead people being resurrected (e.g., 1 Kings 17:22; John 11; Acts 20:10). This does not mean anyone has a right to miraculous healing or that he should expect it. It does mean that we have a right to ask God to heal and then wait to see what He does. Biblically, this is acceptable, whereas taking matters into our own hands and deciding in favor of euthanasia is not.[95]

Finally, what about biblical teaching to extend mercy to those in need? Many reply that mercy to the sick and dying does not include granting their wish to die. However, it does include proper care for their needs. Proper care involves giving drugs to relieve pain. Kerby Anderson appeals to Proverbs 31:6 as a moral justification for giving pain-relieving drugs. He also cites Galatians 6:2 to urge believers to provide counsel and spiritual care for dying patients.[96]

Suicide

There are various biblical and common-sense arguments against suicide. Despite the fact that Scripture simply records the occurrence of suicides without offering an evaluation of them, it is safe to conclude that the biblical perspective on suicide is negative. Scripture directly forbids taking the innocent life of creatures made in God's image. This regulation applies whether the life is someone else's or one's own.

An additional biblical consideration is that Christians are commanded not only to love others but to love themselves (Matt. 22:39; Eph. 5:28–29, 33). However, suicide is not an act of self-love but of self-hatred. As such it disobeys biblical commands.[97]

Those who claim to the contrary that the suicide of someone suffering greatly is an act of self-indulgence, not an act of self-hate, confuse issues. One must distinguish between response to a particular situation and overall evaluation of one's life. There are many stop-gap solutions that one can apply at the moment that in the long run will have very negative effects on the person's overall well-being. Though suicide may bring immediate relief in difficult circumstances, it cannot help but communicate a low view of the worth of the life (one's own) taken.

In light of these moral principles that rule out suicide, we find especially troublesome talk of a patient's right to die. Granted, a government may legislate such a right, but that does not mean there is a *moral* right to die. In fact, given moral principles against taking life, we cannot see how there could be a moral right to die, if by "right to die" is meant a right to commit suicide. Undoubtedly, some who speak of this right are really asserting a right to have control over their own body via the right to privacy. However, the right to do what one wants with one's body cannot be an absolute right, especially if so doing breaks moral rules.

We suspect that those who speak of a right to die are not thinking of voluntary euthanasia and suicide so much as they are thinking of cases such as that of Nancy Cruzan. But what was really at stake there was not a right to die (and there is no moral right to do so anyway), but rather a right not to be kept alive indefinitely by artificial means in a permanent vegetative state. The Cruzan family wanted natural processes to run their course, since attempts to forestall those processes could not have cured their daughter or even enhanced her ability to interact with the environment. While we are sympathetic with such desires, they have nothing to do with a right to die construed as a right to voluntary active euthanasia or suicide. They relate to passive euthanasia and hence have nothing to do with a right to take one's life.

Several common-sense objections to suicide are also noteworthy. Some contend that committing suicide is an act of cowardice. Of course, in some cases the motives are not cowardly, but when they are and when one is obligated to act bravely in the midst of affliction, suicide is wrong.[98] Second, some think about suicide but later regain their zest for living and are thankful they did not commit the irrevocable act of suicide. What seems insufferable today may dissipate tomorrow. Common sense suggests hoping for a better day rather than doing what cannot be undone.[99] P. F. Baelz thinks the most compelling common-sense argument against suicide is that it injures others. He admits that the amount of harm may vary from case to case. He also grants that on a utilitarian ethic some acts of suicide would be morally obligatory because they are acts of self-sacrifice that benefit those who are left. However, the utilitarian principle has limits. In human relationships there are what Baelz calls "canons of loyalty" which should guide our moral decisions, and these are more fundamental than utilitarians are willing to admit. These canons that govern relationships with one another and God must be considered when contemplating suicide.[100]

Finally, Hauerwas and Bondi reject both euthanasia and suicide on the ground that they involve the erosion of community. Suicide is the final sign of abandonment both by the individual and the society. The individual refuses any longer to fulfill his or her duties to society and expresses his or her feeling of being abandoned by it. As for voluntary euthanasia, it is akin to suicide. Involuntary euthanasia signals society's abandonment of its responsibility for the patient.[101] In ancient and medieval cultures the key issue was how people collectively could realize the true human good. In modern society the key matter is to ensure that individuals are safeguarded from interference by others as they pursue their own concerns. The problem is that this modern concern involves concern with individual rights (including the "right" to commit suicide), and an overemphasis on such individual rights has seriously damaged the concepts of community and obligation to others.[102]

Active/Passive—Killing/Letting Die

Some claim that for a consequentialist, the distinction between killing and letting die is not morally significant. For consequentialism, what matters is the end envisioned. Since both Jones and Smith in the example case intended the same end and since the same end was achieved, there is essentially no moral difference between the two cases.[103] On the other hand, deontologists, who are more likely to be concerned about means, might think there is a morally significant difference between the two cases.

From our perspective, this issue is not so simple as just suggested. In fact, we believe the consequentialist and the deontologist could agree on whether there is any moral difference between killing and letting die, despite their different ethical theories. Let us explain.

We begin by noting that headway can be made if one remembers what makes an act and an agent moral or immoral, and also recalls the principle that moral accountability presupposes acting freely. With those matters in mind, we believe we can show that in some cases there is not and in others there is a moral difference between active and passive euthanasia. Consider cases where I could refuse to kill or let die without harming myself (i.e., I am free to reject euthanasia), but I *choose* to kill/let die anyway. Whether my intention is to disobey a moral rule I am obliged to obey (deontology) or to achieve a certain end (teleology), the death of my friend, whether I kill him or let him die, makes no moral difference. In both cases I choose the same thing and carry it out. The Jones/Smith cases are good examples. Jones and Smith were free to preserve life or kill. They chose death even though they knew it was morally wrong. In cases like these, despite the different means, the acts are immoral acts, and the agents were immoral because their motives were wrong.

Consider, however, a different set of cases where the difference between active and passive does make a moral difference. Suppose I desire to but cannot save a dying individual through medicine or medical technology. My failure to use such means is not morally reprehensible. I do not preserve life, but since I am not free to do so, I am not guilty for letting someone die. On the other hand, if I know a patient is incurable and I freely decide to kill him, I am guilty. In this case I could avoid killing him, but I kill him anyway, even though this breaks a moral command. The fact that I break the command out of compassion for the sufferer does not overturn the fact that I freely broke the command. I am guilty. In sum, in the first case I cannot avoid breaking the command to preserve life, but in the second I am free to refuse to kill, but I kill anyway. The act of killing (active) is immoral, whereas the letting die (passive) is not. This analysis would fit whether one held a teleological or deontological ethic. The reason is that the moral difference stems not from one's ethical theory, nor from different means used in an attempt to reach ends, nor from different intentions in the two cases. *The difference is the freedom to act in the latter case as opposed to the inability to act in the former.* The upshot of this discussion is that in some instances passive euthanasia is not as morally condemnable as active euthanasia. The key in assessing cases such as those sketched is the intent behind what the physician, family, or friends do or do not do and their ability to do otherwise. Each case of killing or letting die must be evaluated individually.[104]

Voluntary/Involuntary Euthanasia

Most who favor euthanasia argue for voluntary euthanasia alone. The implicit assumption is that it is morally permissible to take someone's life so long as he grants permission. Despite how entrenched this idea is in the thinking of so many, we disagree. If it is wrong to take innocent life, it is wrong whether the individual in question grants permission or not.

In elaborating our position, several things must be said. First, that moral evaluation of acts of euthanasia does not depend on the voluntary/involuntary distinction is evident from our discussion elsewhere about what makes an *act* right or wrong.[105] How one determines whether an act is moral depends on one's overall ethical theory, not on the voluntary/involuntary distinction. For consequentialists, the rightness or wrongness of an act depends upon the results. Thus, if euthanasia benefits the one who dies (and/or others as well), the act is right, regardless of whether the deceased asked to be killed or not. Nonconsequentialism holds that the morality of an act depends on something other than consequences, but not on whether people affected by the act did or did not request it. Whether one is a consequentialist or nonconsequentialist, his or her justification or condemnation of acts of euthanasia will not depend on the voluntary/involuntary distinction.[106]

Is the voluntary/involuntary distinction, then, irrelevant to ethics generally and euthanasia in particular? We think it is relevant, but not so as to justify voluntary euthanasia. The distinction is significant, because some acts cannot even be done unless they are done *without* permission. The classic example is theft. The very notion of stealing involves the victim's desire that his possessions *not* be taken. Thus, if I want you to take 100 dollars of mine and you take it whether I am looking or not, it is dubious that I could rightly accuse you of stealing. Stealing is wrong not just because someone takes something that is not theirs, but because permission is not granted to take it. If I grant permission to take something of mine, that is gift giving, not theft.

Is murder like theft in this respect? That is, can it only be committed when the victim does not ask or consent to be killed? We think not. Murder involves the intentional taking of the innocent life of someone made in God's image. If that is the definition of murder, obviously murder can be committed whether the victim asks to be killed or not. Murder, unlike stealing, can be committed with or without the victim's permission. Thus, the voluntary/involuntary distinction matters in the way suggested to some acts like theft but not to others like murder.

There is another way voluntary and involuntary euthanasia differ, but again not so as to justify the former and condemn the latter. Both forms of euthanasia are wrong, because they ignore the obligation to preserve life. In addition, involuntary euthanasia is wrong, because it ignores the freedom of choice of the one killed (obviously, this comment pertains to cases where an individual can choose). So, involuntary euthanasia is still wrong. The difference is only that with voluntary euthanasia one less right has been abridged.

From the preceding, we conclude that when acts of euthanasia are wrong, they are wrong whether done voluntarily or involuntarily. In cases of death with dignity, for example, we might feel better about pulling the plug if the comatose patient left a living will, but the living will *per se* cannot determine whether pulling the plug is morally right or not. That evaluation must be made on other grounds.

MORAL DECISION MAKING AND
FORMS OF EUTHANASIA

Up to this point we have argued that euthanasia is generally unacceptable. However, how does one decide which cases are the exceptions? In what follows we shall note items that must be considered when making a decision in specific cases. Then we shall apply those guidelines as much as possible to death with dignity, mercy killing, and death selection.

Considerations in Decision Making

In addition to all the preceding argumentation, we suggest that as one confronts individual situations five items will help in making decisions. They do not solve all problems but are helpful in many cases. The first is the proper understanding of death. Frequently, death is thought to be an event that occurs at a particular moment and involves separation of man's immaterial from his material part.[107] This sounds good, but modern medicine has shown that death is really a *process*. Moreover, doctors demand some kind of empirical evidence of the soul's departure from the body.

In our opinion, at present the best one can do is invoke criteria set forth by an ad hoc committee of the Harvard Medical School. The committee defined brain death—irreversible coma—by four criteria. They are (1) unreceptivity and unresponsivity (no stimuli of any sort evoke any kind of response); (2) no movements or spontaneous breathing for at least an hour; (3) no reflexes, and fixed dilated pupils; (4) flat brain wave (flat EEG) for at least ten minutes, preferably twenty. All four must apply, and they must still be true of the patient twenty-four hours after first tested.[108]

A second consideration in decisions about euthanasia is one's overall ethical stance. Consequentialists will give greatest weight to arguments that emphasize the outcome of actions or omissions. Nonconsequentialists will determine what is right on other grounds. For nonconsequentialists like us, relevant divine commands will be paramount in decision making.

Third, one's understanding of personhood is critical. We have espoused a view of personhood defined in biological terms, not in quality-of-life terms. Whatever is or potentially is genetically a person counts as a person and has a person's rights. This does not solve all problems in all cases, but it offers criteria far more objective than those proposed by those who hold a quality-of-life view of personhood.

Fourth, in assessing moral praise or blame for what is done with a patient, one must remember that only actions done (or omitted) freely are morally accountable. Finally (and related to the freedom point), there is the double effect doctrine. We are obliged both to preserve life and to relieve pain.[109] Sometimes it may be impossible to do both. If it is impossible to preserve the life of the terminally ill, we are not immoral if we do not. Of course, there is still the obligation to relieve pain and suffering. If we do what we can to relieve pain and in the process hasten death, there is still no moral blame, since we could not preserve life.

The Morality of Death with Dignity, Mercy Killing, Death Selection

Is euthanasia ever moral? We have rejected euthanasia in general, but are there exceptions? From the preceding study we conclude that anyone holding an ethical theory such as ours cannot morally justify any cases of death selection. In cases of death selection, the individual does not deserve to die and is not suffering from a disease that warrants ending his life. The only considerations are matters of social utility. For a nonconsequentialist, such concerns can never outweigh the prohibition against taking innocent life.

With mercy killing and mercy dying, matters are more difficult, but some general guidelines are possible. For example, when someone is not brain dead and there is no evidence that death will come within hours or even days but he or she is suffering intensely, we have a dual obligation—to preserve life and do everything possible to relieve pain. If some known medical procedure would improve the situation (even produce a cure), and we know the patient could undergo it without it killing him or her, it seems morally obligatory to use it. Likewise, the patient should not refuse treatment. On the other hand, if it is unclear that the medical procedure would improve the patient's condition, and it might harm him or her instead, there is no moral obligation to undertake the new treatment. For each person there is a time to die, and that must be accepted. Use of such procedures (extraordinary or otherwise) is certainly morally permissible, but not obligatory.

From these guidelines, we suggest the following for someone suffering terribly with a terminal illness: do whatever is possible to relieve pain, and do not force the patient to undergo procedures or take medicines already proven ineffective or that have no foreseeable benefit. However, because of the commandment not to take life, do not kill or aid the patient in committing suicide. If painkillers hasten death, but the intent is to relieve pain, giving pain medicine is morally acceptable. The principle of double effect applies.

Death with dignity cases are especially difficult, and part of the problem is evident when one understands what happens physiologically as someone dies. Traditionally, death was thought to involve cessation of heart beat and respiration. Today it is common knowledge within medicine that the heart continues beating for a few minutes after breathing ceases. Thus, artificial respiration can sometimes restore life. Respiration depends on reflex nervous activity, which is governed from a center in the brain stem. Reflex action stops quickly if the oxygen supply to the brain fails. This information became especially important when techniques of mechanical respiration were invented. The respirator allows oxygenation of the brain to continue even if the reflex center or its connecting nerves are irreparably damaged. As a result, one may be kept biologically alive by means of a respirator. If the reflex center will not function autonomously and one pulls the plug on the respirator, oxygen will not reach the brain, and the person will die.[110]

This is not the end of the story, however. Superimposed on the brain stem is the cerebral cortex, which gives rise to consciousness and thought. As long as there is evidence of no more than minor cortical damage, doctors normally try to keep a person alive by whatever means are possible. What complicates matters is that there are cases where the heart-lung brain stem complex can be maintained while cortical functions are so terribly damaged that evidence of personhood is hardly apparent.[111] Writing in 1976, James Mathers explained that in practice doctors tend to "accept responsibility for caring for the life of such 'cortical cripples' so long as the heart-lung-brain stem complex continues to function autonomously. It is when the complex can only be maintained artificially, while the cortex appears to be severely and irrecoverably damaged, that the dilemma of whether to turn off the switch appears in its most acute form."[112]

Mathers describes three situations that illustrate the problems in determining death and knowing what to do with a patient. In the first, circulation is maintained by a machine, but there is no evidence of brain activity (flat EEG). In the second, breathing and circulation continue without artificial help, but the cortex is severely damaged and the patient deeply unconscious. In the third, there is prolonged unconsciousness, evidence of great cortical damage, and circulation can only be maintained by machine. In the first case, the patient is presumed dead, in the second alive, and in the third, it is debatable whether the organism is a *person*, even though biologically there is life.[113] In the first case where a flat EEG indicates death, a decision to unplug the machine poses no moral predicament. The latter two cases involve obvious moral dilemmas. There is biological life, and the criteria for death are not met, but could the individual ever regain consciousness? Is cortical damage too severe to know? In either of those cases, who really knows if the immaterial part has left the body?

Though cases of death with dignity are very difficult, we offer the following generalizations: if a person is terminally ill (even hooked up to a machine), but according to the best medical opinion would not die within hours or even days, the obligation to preserve life takes precedence.[114] This does not obligate the use of means whose benefit to the patient is dubious. It does mandate not leaving the person to die without any care and not deliberately killing him. On the other hand, if the patient is terminal and according to the best medical judgment will die within hours regardless of what is done, attempts to maintain life at all costs seem tantamount to refusing to accept the fact that it is that person's time to die. In those cases, allowing the person to die is morally acceptable.

CONCLUSION

We close this chapter with three final comments. First, in all potential cases of death with dignity and mercy killing, it is crucial to consult the best medical opinion of a pro-life doctor and make decisions in light of his advice and the Holy Spirit's leading. Second, despite the advances of modern medicine and regardless of how pro-life a doctor is, there will be cases where it is impossible to predict when a patient will die or what the outcome of a medical procedure will be. In such cases, our obligation is to do what is reasonable and moral to preserve life and relieve pain, and then leave the outcome in the hands of

Him who ultimately controls matters of life and death. Finally, though we believe the most acceptable view is that euthanasia is wrong in general, we grant that some forms in some instances may be acceptable. It has been said that hard cases make for bad rules. The problem in decisions about euthanasia is that so many cases are hard cases. We must solicit divine guidance!

ENDNOTES

1. Bonnie Steinbock, "The Removal of Mr. Herbert's Feeding Tube," *Hastings Center Report* 13 (October 1983): 13.
2. Martin Mawyer, "Court Decision Paving the Way for Euthanasia," *Fundamentalist Journal* 3 (July–August 1984): 60.
3. For the details of this case see Sharman Stein, "Physician Aids in Suicide," *Chicago Tribune*, 6 June 1990; Stephen Chapman, "Assisting Suicide: Whose Painful Life Is It Anyway?" *Chicago Tribune*, 7 June 1990; Michael Hirsley and Karen Thomas, "'Doctor Death' Puts New Focus on Right-to-Die Debate," *Chicago Tribune*, 25 October 1991. For discussion of these cases see George J. Annas, "Killing Machines," *Hastings Center Report* 21 (March–April 1991). For discussion of another case of doctor assisted suicide, see the report of Dr. Timothy E. Quill in the March 1991 *New England Journal of Medicine*.
4. Hirsley and Thomas, "'Doctor Death' Puts New Focus on Right-to-Die Debate."
5. Consider also the case of Ida Rollin who was dying of cancer. She underwent repeated chemotherapy to no avail. She would die soon, but not an easy death. Wracked with unremitting pain, she asked her daughter and son-in-law to find out what dosage of sleeping pills would kill her. Seeing absolutely no hope for relief or recovery, they reluctantly agreed. Betty Rollin recounts how her mother unflinchingly carried out her own suicide, and she tells how friends and family alike applauded the bravery and "wisdom" of this act when they heard how her death occurred. Is suicide under such conditions morally justifiable? Are Ida Rollin's family members accessories to a murder, or should they be applauded for their compassion in granting their dying mother's last wish? See Betty Rollin, "My Mother's Last Wish," *Good Housekeeping* (October 1985) for details of this story.
6. Examples of articles that discuss various details of this case include Tabitha M. Powledge and Peter Steinfels, "Following the News on Karen Quinlan," *Hastings Center Report* 5 (December 1975); Richard McCormick and Robert Veatch, "The Preservation of Life and Self-Determination," *Theological Studies* 41 (June 1980); and Kenneth L. Woodward, "To Live and Let Die," *Newsweek* 96 (July 7, 1980): 80.
7. Alan L. Otten, "The Oldest Old," *The Wall Street Journal* (March 30, 1984): 1.
8. Sid Macaulay, "Euthanasia: Can Death Be Friendly?" *Christianity Today* 20 (November 21, 1975): 37. Macaulay reviews various books on euthanasia.
9. Otten, "The Oldest Old," 1.
10. Ibid. It is estimated that occurrences of dementing illnesses roughly double every five years after age sixty-five: 1 percent show it at sixty-five, 2.5 percent at seventy, 5 percent at seventy-five, 12 percent at eighty, between 20 and 30 percent at eighty-five, and 40 percent to 50 percent in the nineties. Other diseases that strike with increasing frequency and severity as old age progresses

are arthritis, limiting heart conditions, hypertension, and problems with hearing and vision.

11. Ibid., 2. As of 1984, the U.S. government estimated that only 6.4 percent of the seventy-five to eighty-four-year-olds are in nursing homes, while 21.6 percent of the eighty-five-or-over group are.
12. Teodoro Dagi, "The Paradox of Euthanasia," *Judaism* 24 (spring 1975): 157.
13. Plato, *Republic*, 111:405.
14. D. C. Overduin, "Euthanasia," *Lutheran Theological Journal* 14 (December 1980): 114. Overduin (pp. 115–16) notes that in Thomas More's fictional utopian society, euthanasia was encouraged for the terminally ill who granted their permission. The English philosopher Francis Bacon (1561–1626) in *Advancement of Learning* claimed that a physician should use medicine not only to restore health, "but to mitigate pain and dolors; and not only when such mitigation may conduce to recovery, but when it may serve to make a fair and easy passage." In addition, many have advocated certain forms of euthanasia for religious purposes. For example, the Papal Bull *Summi desiderantes* of December 5, 1484, introduced the practice of witch finding and witch burning. Some claimed there were women who cohabited with the Devil. As a result they would be pregnant with monsters who were thought by people like Luther not to have a soul. These women were killed to prevent the birth of such monsters. The practice was permitted in some countries until the first half of the nineteenth century. Self-induced euthanasia and suicide were also supported by such philosophers as Voltaire and Rousseau, though rejected by Kant.
15. Ibid., 114.
16. Ibid., 117. Some claim that the modern debate over voluntary euthanasia really began in 1873 with the publication of L. A. Tollemache's "The New Cure for Incurables," Fort R. Moreover, the real medical debate is said to have begun when Dr. Killick Millard gave his Presidential Address on euthanasia to the Society of Medical Officers of Health in 1931.
17. Ibid., 117–18.
18. This came as a result of a case involving an Amsterdam barmaid who was so shamed by her pregnancy that she hired a man to kill her. He complied, but he not only slit her throat; he also chopped off her fingers in order to steal her rings. As a result of this case, a law was passed against euthanasia, and the penalty was twelve years in prison. For details see Tim Harper, "Dutch Accept, Regulate Suicides Aided by Doctors," *Chicago Tribune*, 3 November 1991.
19. Overduin, 117–18.
20. Reported on a "Nightline" program on euthanasia on the U.S. network ABC in January 1987. See also Harper, "Dutch Accept, Regulate Suicides Aided by Doctors," who lists slightly different conditions, though ones that are consistent with those reported on "Nightline." He says doctors are not prosecuted "if the patient repeatedly and consistently requests death; the doctor has extensive consultations with the patient, the patient's family and at least one other doctor; the patient's suffering cannot be averted by any accepted medical treatment; and the illness is terminal, even if death is not 'imminent.'"
21. Harper, "Dutch Accept, Regulate Suicides Aided by Doctors." In the "Nightline" interview in 1987, Dr. Pieter Admiraal of Holland, when asked about euthanasia for those in a coma who had not requested it, stated emphatically that it would not be performed in such a case. Even if the family asked, that would not matter. Admiraal, who admitted performing euthanasia

on many occasions, urged its legalization. He argued that without legalization, the government will not be able to regulate it, and it will be abused.

22. The Karen Quinlan case, in which her parents went to court and won the right to remove her comatose body from the respirator, is quite famous, but it is hardly the only such case. Moreover, in 1983 the Virginia senate passed a bill that would allow terminally ill people to order the discontinuance of life-support systems. According to the bill, when "a reasonable degree of medical certainty" exists regarding a patient's imminent death, a previously signed document allows the physician (with one concurring opinion) to stop life-preserving procedures. One doctor noted that though there was debate over the bill's wording, the bill was really unnecessary, for doctors do all the time what the bill proposed to make legal. Taken from "Natural Death Act Passes Virginia Senate," *Fundamentalist Journal* 2 (May 1983): 62.

23. Robert C. F. Cassidy, "Euthanasia: Passive *and* Active?" *St. Luke's Journal of Theology* 20 (December 1976): 7. It is safe to say that attitudes have changed even more since that poll in 1973, especially in view of the Karen Ann Quinlan case. In 1980 Donald Granberg ("What Does It Mean to Be 'Pro-life?'" *Christian Century* 99 [May 12, 1982]: 566) surveyed almost nine hundred members of the National Right to Life Committee and the National Abortion Rights Action League. He asked not only about abortion but about a series of other "pro-life" issues, including various forms of euthanasia. When asked if a doctor should be allowed to end a patient's life in cases of incurable disease if the patient and family so request, 97 percent of the NRLC people polled said no, whereas only 11 percent of the NARAL people responded negatively. When asked if a person with an incurable disease had a right to end his or her own life (suicide), 94 percent of NRLC respondents said no, while only 6 percent of NARAL members polled said no.

24. Stephen Wise, "The Last Word—Whose?" *Christian Century* 98 (September 16, 1981): 895. Wise notes that although Catholic pronouncements tend to be more conservative than Protestant viewpoints, in 1957 Pope Pius XII ("The Prolongation of Life") stated that neither the doctor nor patient is bound to use anything other than "ordinary" means of prolonging life. Thus, a doctor may properly remove artificial respirator apparatus before blood circulation completely stops. In 1980 Pope John Paul II essentially reiterated this position when he said, "When inevitable death is imminent in spite of the means used, it is permitted in conscience to take the decision to refuse forms of treatment that would only secure a precarious and burdensome prolongation of life, so long as the normal care due to a sick person in similar cases is not interrupted."

25. Interestingly, at about the same time the Cruzan case was decided before the Supreme Court, Belle Greenspan was granted permission by the Cook County (Illinois) Circuit Court to withdraw the feeding tube from her husband Sidney, who had been in persistent vegetative state since 1984. Her request was approved because she was able to give the judge conclusive evidence that her husband would not have wanted to remain in that state. For details, see Barbara Brotman, "Man's Life Is Put on Display So He May Be Allowed to Die," *Chicago Tribune*, 27 September 1990; and "Six Years of 'Living Hell,'" editorial in the *Chicago Tribune*, 5 October 1990.

26. For details of this case, see the following: Glen Elsasser, "Justices Will Decide on Right to Die of Long-Comatose Woman," *Chicago Tribune*, 4 July 1989, and "Court Blocks 'Right-to-Die' Bid," *Chicago Tribune*, 26 June 1990; Ronald

Kotulak, "Doctors Rip 'Right to-Die' Edict, Say More Suicides Could Result," *Chicago Tribune*, 26 June 1990; Michael Tackett, "Judge OKs Removing Comatose Woman's Feeding Tube," *Chicago Tribune*, 15 December 1990. As Elsasser reported in his June 26 article, this case was watched closely by both medical and religious groups, especially because an "estimated 10,000 Americans are being maintained in a persistent vegetative state in care centers around the country."

27. Elsasser, "Court Blocks 'Right-to-Die' Bid." Despite the enthusiasm of many for living wills, not everyone is convinced. For an interesting discussion of some of the problems with living wills, see Richard Hughes, "Ethical Problems in Living Will Legislation," *Journal of Religion and Aging* 5 (1988).

28. Paul D. Simmons, "Death with Dignity," *Perspectives in Religious Studies* 4 (summer 1977): 140–41.

29. Elsasser, "Court Blocks 'Right-to-Die' Bid." The Illinois power-of-attorney form for health care "grants the designated person power to make all decisions on personal care, medical treatment, hospitalization and health care including withdrawal of treatment, even if death could result" (see Jean L. Griffin, "Hospitals Confronting the 'Right-to-Die' Issue," *Chicago Tribune*, 26 July 1990). In addition, the Cruzan case and others like it have occasioned much debate over whether food and water should be administered to the person in the persistently vegetative state. For interesting discussions of this topic, see Thomas A. Shannon and James J. Walter, "The PVS Patient and the Forgoing/Withdrawing of Medical Nutrition and Hydration," *Theological Studies* 49 (1988); Thomas D. Kennedy, "Eating, Drinking, and Dying Well," *Christian Scholar's Review* 20 (1991); and Lisa Cahill, "Bioethical Decisions to End Life," *Theological Studies* 52 (March 1991).

30. Hugh Dellios, "Edgar Signs Law Giving Patients a 'Right To Die,'" *Chicago Tribune*, 27 September 1991.

31. Ibid.

32. "Nightline," March 1988, quoting from the proposed bill.

33. In a phone conversation with the law office of Robert Risely (in Los Angeles), author of the bill, I learned that approximately 370,000 signatures were needed to get the measure on the ballot. Sponsors had only 150 days to get the signatures and got approximately 150,000. However, Risely claimed that polls showed about a 58 percent approval of the measure.

34. For an excellent treatment of medicine in the Hippocratic mold and the history of the move away from that paradigm, see Nigel M. de S. Cameron, *The New Medicine* (Wheaton, Ill.: Crossway Books, 1991).

35. Jonas Robitscher, "Living and Dying: A Delicate Balance," *Engage/Social Action* 1 (October 1973): 42.

36. Douglas K. Stuart, "'Mercy Killing'—Is it Biblical?" *Christianity Today* 20 (February 27, 1976): 9.

37. Dagi, "The Paradox of Euthanasia," 161.

38. Thomas St. Martin, "Euthanasia: The Three-in-One Issue," in *Death, Dying and Euthanasia*, eds. Dennis Horan and David Mall (Frederick, Md.: University Publications of America, 1980), 596–97.

39. Ibid., 596.

40. Ibid., 596–97. Though it is imaginable that someone might request this kind of euthanasia, this form is usually involuntary.

41. See our chapters on abortion in *Ethics for a Brave New World* (Wheaton, Ill.: Crossway Books, 1993).

42. Robert Wennberg, "Euthanasia: A Sympathetic Appraisal," *Christian Scholar's Review* 6 (1977): 297–98.
43. James Childs, "Euthanasia: An Introduction to a Moral Dilemma," *Currents in Theology and Missions* 3 (April 1976): 69.
44. For further discussion of recent literature on the matter of quality of life considerations, see James J. Walter, "Termination of Medical Treatment: The Setting of Moral Limits from Infancy to Old Age," *Religious Studies Review* 16 (October 1990): 303–6; and Shannon and Walter, "The PVS Patient and the Forgoing/Withdrawing of Medical Nutrition and Hydration," 634–37.
45. Humanist Manifesto II, as discussed in Joseph R. Stanton, "From Feticide to Infanticide," in *The Zero People: Essays on Life*, ed. Jeff Hensley (Ann Arbor, Mich.: Servant Books, 1983), 188–89.
46. Greville Norburn, "Euthanasia," *The Modern Churchman* 16 (April 1973): 179.
47. Joseph Fletcher, "Ethics and Euthanasia," in *Death, Dying and Euthanasia*, eds. Dennis Horan and David Mall, 296.
48. Ibid.
49. Ibid.
50. Ibid., 300–301.
51. Ibid., 301.
52. Paul Brand's comment in an interview with three other scholars. The article reporting the interview is "Biomedical Decision Making: The Blessings and Curses of Modern Technology," *Christianity Today* 30 (March 21 1986): 8.
53. Joseph Fletcher, *Morals and Medicine* (Boston: Beacon Press, 1960), 213–15.
54. Childs, 68–69. The same point is also made in Anthony Flew, "The Principle of Euthanasia," in *Euthanasia and the Right to Death*, ed. A. B. Downing (Los Angeles: Nash Publishing, 1970), 33. See also Eike-Henner Kluge, *The Practice of Death* (New Haven/London: Yale University Press, 1975), 178–79, who argues that euthanasia is allowable in all cases where the individual asks to be killed or allowed to die because he/she finds life physically or psychologically unbearable, and there is no other way to relieve the pain. Of course, the person must be fully aware of what he/she is doing. Kluge notes that murder involves infringement of rights, but in the cases he/she mentions the individual gives up his/her right to live.
55. Flew, 33.
56. Ibid., 33–34.
57. Arthur Dyck, "Beneficent Euthanasia and Benemortasia: Alternative Views of Mercy," in *Death, Dying and Euthanasia*, eds. Dennis Horan and David Mall, summarizes Kohl's point on pp. 353–54.
58. Fletcher, "Ethics and Euthanasia," 297.
59. P. F. Baelz, "Voluntary Euthanasia," *Theology* 75 (May 1972): 250–51.
60. While the distinction seems intuitively correct, as Milton Sernett shows ("The 'Death With Dignity' Debate: Why We Care," *The Springfielder* 38 [March 1975]: 270), difficulties arise in trying to specify the difference between ordinary and extraordinary means of treatment. He says physicians define ordinary means as the standard, recognized, orthodox, or established medicines and procedures of that time-period at that level of practice and within limits of availability. On the other hand, many moralists define it to include not only normal food, drink, and rest, but also all medicines, treatments, and operations that offer reasonable hope of patient benefit and that can be obtained and used without excessive expense, pain, or other inconvenience. Obviously, words such as *reasonable hope*

and *excessive* are ambiguous. As to extraordinary means, Sernett explains that many physicians include any medicine or procedure that might be fanciful, bizarre, experimental, incompletely established, unorthodox, or not recognized. He claims that for many moralists, extraordinary means are all medicines, treatments, and operations that are excessively painful and expensive or produce other inconveniences for the patient and others and/or are treatments that offer no reasonable hope of benefit to the patient.

61. Ibid. Those who use the distinction agree with Pope Pius XI's 1957 statement to anesthesiologists that it is ethically correct not to employ such extraordinary means. For further discussion of this issue, see Shannon and Walter, "The PVS Patient and the Forgoing/Withdrawing of Medical Nutrition and Hydration," 643–45.

62. Dyck, 356.

63. Cassidy, 8. For further discussion of the principle of double effect, see A. Van Den Beld, "Killing and the Principle of Double Effect," *Scottish Journal of Theology* 41 (1988). As Van Den Beld shows, the principle of double effect states that the bad effect must not be the means to the good effect. The good effect must be logically (if not also chronologically) prior, even though it leads to a bad effect, and the good effect must be what the agent intends. In other words, if one does evil to do good, that is not moral by the principle of double effect. Nor is it moral to do good to accomplish evil. One must do good for its own sake, even though the doing of good also eventuates in an evil.

64. Somen Das and Hunter Mabry, "Human Rights and the 'Mercy-Killing Bill,'" *Religion and Society* 29 (June 1982): 18–19. (The authors cite Matt. 5:4, which says nothing about giving alms. Matt. 6:2–4 deals with alms, but doesn't quite say what they claim. Their more general claim, though, is clear, apart from reference to specific verses.)

65. Millard Erickson and Ines Bowers, "Euthanasia and Christian Ethics," *Journal of the Evangelical Theological Society* 19 (winter 1976): 17.

66. Simmons, 142, 153.

67. Flew, 46.

68. Wennberg, 299–300.

69. Das and Mabry, 20.

70. Ibid., 28.

71. Ibid.

72. Glenn Graber (cited in Donald S. Klinefelter, "The Morality of Suicide," *Soundings* 67 [fall 1984]: 338) defines suicide as doing "something that results in one's death in the way that was planned, either from the intention of ending one's life or the intention to bring about some state of affairs (such as relief from pain) that one thinks it certain or highly probable can be achieved only by means of death."

73. Klinefelter, 340–42.

74. See Baelz's citation (p. 241) of David Hume's "On Suicide."

75. Erickson and Bowers, 19. For further argumentation to the effect that Christians who oppose suicide really do not have a very good case, see Kenneth Boyd, "Terminal Care, Euthanasia and Suicide," *The Modern Churchman* NS 30 (1988): 12–14. See also Walter, 306.

76. James Rachels, "Active and Passive Euthanasia," in Tom Beauchamp and Seymour Perlin, eds., *Ethical Issues in Death and Dying* (Englewood Cliffs, N.J.: Prentice-Hall, 1978), 241–42.

77. Ibid., 243.

78. Gilbert Meilander, "The Distinction Between Killing and Allowing to Die," *Theological Studies* 37 (September 1976): 467. Wennberg (pp. 284–85) speaks of the supposed difference between withholding treatment (at the patient's request) and stopping treatment begun (at the patient's request). Generally, the former is less objectionable than the latter, because the latter involves "doing something," whereas the former involves refraining from doing something. Wennberg thinks there is no difference. If it was wrong to start treatment, the error is compounded by refusing to stop it. He says (p. 285), "The decision to unplug a life-support system is no more serious a decision—though every bit serious as—the decision not to plug it in to begin with."

79. McCormick and Veatch, 390–95.

80. Erickson and Bowers, 21–22.

81. See our section on personhood in chapter 2 of *Ethics for a Brave New World*.

82. J. Kerby Anderson, "Euthanasia: A Biblical Approach," *Bibliotheca Sacra* 144 (April–June 1987): 215.

83. See Klinefeiter on Aquinas, 340 and Robert Nelson, "Euthanasia: A Dilemma for Christians," *Engage/Social Action* 13 (April 1985): 33–34.

84. In an interesting article, Leon Kass argues that despite what some claim, it is possible to uphold the sanctity of life principle and at the same time favor death with dignity. See Leon R. Kass, "Death with Dignity & the Sanctity of Life," *Commentary* 89 (March 1990).

85. David J. Atkinson, "Causing Death and Allowing to Die," *Tyndale Bulletin* 34 (1983): 207–8. This does not mean God does not care about what happens to us or that consequences of actions are irrelevant to him. It only means that for those committed to biblical ethics, the moral justification of an action has traditionally been understood along nonconsequentialist lines.

86. Ibid.

87. Dyck, 351.

88. Ibid., 352.

89. M. Pabst Battin, "The Least Worse Death," *Hastings Center Report* 13 (April 1983): 14; and Nelson, 37. See also Battin's argument that those who desire a natural and peaceful death cannot guarantee it even with euthanasia.

90. "Nightline," March 1988. Because of this fact, even some with AIDS who consider suicide choose to live on with pain-killing medication. See also Erickson and Bowers, 23.

91. Robitscher, 44.

92. Paul Ramsey, "The Indignity of Death with Dignity," in *Death, Dying and Euthanasia*, eds. Dennis Horan and David Mall, passim.

93. Stuart, 10.

94. Ibid., 11. Stuart also argues that in view of biblical teaching on the Resurrection, "the events of this life, whether miserable or joyful, are placed in a very different perspective. This life is seen as by definition temporary and transitory (James 4:13), and its miseries are not ends in themselves but are potentially beneficial."

95. Ibid. Here the case of Jackie Cole is a beautiful example of what God can do. Her husband relates how she was in a coma as a result of a massive stroke. He sought legal permission to remove her life-support systems but was denied. Six days after permission was denied, Jackie miraculously opened her eyes and has been on the road to rehabilitation since then. Though this case is extraordinary and one cannot expect a miracle in every situation, this case does underscore

the need to be patient enough to allow the Lord to do what he chooses. For details of this compelling story see Harry A. Cole, "Deciding on a Time to Die," *Second Opinion* 7 (March 1988).

96. Anderson, 217.
97. Ibid., 216.
98. Baelz, 241–42.
99. Ibid., 242.
100. Ibid., 242–43.
101. Stanley Hauerwas and Richard Bondi, "Memory, Community and the Reasons for Living: Theological and Ethical Reflections on Suicide and Euthanasia," *Journal of American Academy of Religion* 44 (1976): 449–50.
102. Ibid., 450–51.
103. James Childs Jr. makes this point nicely in citing Joseph Fletcher's belief that there is no moral difference between active and passive euthanasia. See James M. Childs Jr., "Ethics at the End of Life," *Currents in Theology and Missions* 15 (April 1988): 168–70.
104. Because of the different kinds of cases that can arise in regard to killing and letting die, Michael Philips ("Are 'Killing' and 'Letting Die' Adequately Specified Moral Categories?" *Philosophical Studies* 47 [1985]) thinks this proves that the categories of killing and letting die are not adequately specified. Philippa Foot ("Commentary," *Hastings Center Report* 9 [October 1979]: 20) thinks the distinction between active and passive is relevant in cases where rights are in question. A person's right to noninterference usually extends farther than his/her right to receive care. Thus, even if we may not interfere to bring a certain result (active), it does not follow that we may not allow it to come about (passive). On the other hand, in some cases active and passive make no difference. Foot states that if someone grants permission to kill a person for his/her own good, it makes no moral difference whether we kill him/her or let him/her die. If one is moral so is the other; and if one is immoral, so is the other. In other words, *voluntary* active and passive euthanasia are morally the same.

Only when euthanasia is *involuntary* is there any moral difference between active and passive. Here we disagree, for if it is wrong to kill or let die, it is wrong to do either, regardless of whether the patient requests it or not. Moreover, we have also shown cases where there is a moral difference between killing and letting die, and those differences remain regardless of whether the patient does or does not give permission for killing or letting die. See also Michael Wreen, "Breathing a Little Life into a Distinction," *Philosophical Studies* 46 (1984): 400–401; and J. P. Moreland, "James Rachels and the Active Euthanasia Debate," *Journal of the Evangelical Theological Society* 31 (March 1988) for further discussion of this issue.
105. See chapter 1 of *Ethics for a Brave New World*. Here the emphasis is not on what makes the agent moral in doing the act, because the voluntary/involuntary distinction focuses not on the one who does the act but on the one who requests the act. Therefore, the key category for moral assessment is the act itself.
106. We note here that our point is also true for those whose theory of moral obligation mixes deontological and teleological concerns.
107. See, for example, comments in *Christianity Today* 30 (March 21, 1986): 7, on biomedical decision making.
108. "A Definition of Irreversible Coma: Report of the Ad Hoc Committee of the

Harvard Medical School to Examine the Definition of Brain Death," *The Journal of the American Medical Association* 205 (August 5, 1968): 337–40.

109. Here the obligations might be stated as duties to relieve pain and not to take a life. From scriptural injunctions against murder, one can see that there is a duty not to take a life. One might wonder, however, if there is also a positive duty to preserve life. We believe there is and that it stems from the principle of benevolence. It is commonly agreed upon by ethicists that if one is in a position to do benefit to others without exposing oneself to harm, one is morally obliged to do so. In a case where someone is in danger of losing life, the moral principle just stated translates into an obligation to preserve that life, unless our life would be endangered by doing so. The point about the double effect principle can be equally made in the case mentioned in the text, regardless of whether one focuses on the duty to preserve life or the duty not to take a life.

110. James Mathers, "'Brain Death' or 'Heart Death'? Reflections on an Ethical Dilemma," *Expository Times* 87 (1976): 328.

111. Ibid.

112. Ibid., 328–29.

113. Ibid., 329.

114. Some might think this means that in cases where a person is comatose but hooked up to a machine, life will last indefinitely. This is not so. Even someone hooked up to a machine can die while on the machine.

An Overview

What are some of the moral questions surrounding suicide? An understanding of how the issues are being addressed from both inside and outside the Christian community is vital to those who want to influence public and private thought on the subject. A concise analysis and evaluation of the various positions is here offered, which demonstrates the complexity of some ethical aspects of suicide. Issues of the morality of suicide are closely tied with worldview considerations. Where one rests on the philosophical and theological spectrum will determine the opinions and options held on the subject.

Chapter Eleven

THE MORALITY OF SUICIDE

Issues and Options

J. P. Moreland

ON DECEMBER 2, 1982, SIXTY-TWO-YEAR-OLD Barney Clark became the first human to receive a permanent artificial heart. In addition he was given a key that could be used to turn off his compressor if he wanted to die. One of the physicians, Dr. Willem Kolff, justified the key by stating that if Clark suffered and felt that life was not enjoyable or worth enduring anymore, he had the right to end his life. Clark never used the key. He died fifteen weeks after the operation.

This case illustrates the growing importance of ethical reflection regarding suicide. Today it is the tenth leading cause of death in the general population, and the suicide rate is on the rise in groups ranging from teenagers to the elderly. The purpose of this article is to clarify important issues and options involved in the ethical aspects of suicide.

It is crucial that pastors and other Christian leaders understand how these issues are being argued, apart from reference to the biblical text. This will enable the Christian community to argue in a pluralistic culture for positions consistent with the Bible and to understand how others are framing the debate. This article focuses on three issues: the definition of suicide, the moral justifiability of suicide, and moral problems involved in paternalist state intervention to coercively prevent people from committing suicide.

THE DEFINITION OF SUICIDE

Before discussing the morality of suicide, two preliminary issues must be examined. First is whether the term *suicide* should be used in a purely conceptual, descriptive manner or in a normative, evaluative manner. Second is the need to define suicide to show how suicidal acts differ from other self-destructive acts.

Is Suicide a Descriptive or an Evaluative Term?

Should suicide be defined in a purely conceptual, descriptive manner or in normative, evaluative terms? Suppose one person said suicide is sometimes morally permissible and another said suicide is always wrong. It would be possible for these two people to agree over substantive moral issues regarding suicide and differ merely in their definition of what counts as suicide. For example, two people could agree that a Jehovah's Witness who refuses a blood transfusion (see case six discussed below) was morally justified in his action; one arguing that it was a morally justifiable suicide, the other that it was not a suicide at all but a case of martyrdom. Thus definitions are important in clarifying where agreement and disagreement lie in a moral discussion.

Beauchamp and Childress have argued that one should opt for a stipulative definition of suicide that is conceptual, descriptive, and nonevaluative.[1] They propose this definition: an act is a suicide if and only if one intentionally terminates one's own life, no matter what the conditions or precise nature of the intention or the causal route to death. Their argument for this stipulative definition is that an ordinary language definition is evaluative and carries with it an attitude of disapproval. If an act is a suicide, many say, then it is wrong. But, according to Beauchamp and Childress, this prejudices one's understanding of suicide and removes objectivity from the conceptualizing of the term. If an act of self-caused death is morally appropriate, one should hesitate to label it a suicide because of the evaluative nature of the term.

Hauerwas has argued against Beauchamp and Childress, claiming that the evaluative use of moral terms is preferable to mere stipulative, descriptive uses.[2] Hauerwas points out that the idea of a normatively "uncorrupted" definition of suicide distorts the very grammar of the term. He agrees that the definition of suicide itself cannot settle how and why suicide applies to certain kinds of behavior and not to others. But this is because the use of moral terms of appraisal like "suicide" derives from broad worldview considerations of the culture in question. Within one's worldview a person finds the factual and moral beliefs that are necessary to make judgments about when a range of life-ending behavior is morally inappropriate. So the way one understands "suicide" already incorporates moral judgments and factual beliefs about the world in general.

In this writer's judgment, Hauerwas is right. By their nature, moral terms are evaluative, they are intended to guide behavior, and the normative component of a moral term derives its applicability from worldview considerations of the community that uses the term to praise or blame behavior. Thus an "uncorrupted" definition fails to weight properly the evaluative component of the term *suicide*, and it would be revisionary in nature and could therefore effect the way the morality of specific behaviors is perceived.

What Is Suicide?

When an ethical term is being defined, a proposed definition should explain the ordinary language intuitions of people of good will regarding clear and borderline cases of what to count as acts of suicide. Thus cases are important guides in defining ethical terms.

Examination of Cases

The following cases may be noted:

1. An elderly man, despairing of life, leaves a note behind and jumps off a bridge.
2. A soldier captured in war takes a capsule in order to avoid a torturous death and to hide secrets from the enemy.
3. A truck driver, foreseeing his own death, drives off a bridge in order to avoid hitting children playing in the road.
4. A hospitalized cancer patient with six months to live shoots himself in order to save his family from unneeded psychological and financial suffering.
5. A terminally ill patient, realizing death is imminent, requests that she not be resuscitated again if another heart failure occurs.
6. A Jehovah's Witness refuses a simple blood transfusion for religious reasons and subsequently dies for lack of blood.

Case one above (the elderly man jumping off the bridge) is clearly a case of suicide. Suicide clearly involves at least a person's death and that person's involvement in his or her own death. In a suicide, a person must willingly bring about his or her own death. This insight is expressed in what might be called the standard definition of suicide: a suicidal act involves the intentional termination of one's own life. But this definition needs clarification in light of the other cases listed.

Consider first, the issue of intention. Some understand intention to be the notion that a person has the power to avoid a foreseen death, and yet willingly and knowingly chooses not to do so. On this view, all six cases above would be suicides. But most people would not agree with this usage, e.g.; cases two, three, and five do not appear to be suicides at all.

A different understanding of intention defines the act in terms of what someone is trying to do. The intent of an act specifies what the act itself is, and an intent can be clarified by the reasons or motives for doing the act. (In the truck driver case above, the ultimate intent of the act seems to be sacrifice for the preservation of the life of others. In this case the truck driver did not desire to die, but permitted his own death to accomplish an act of lifesaving). This second sense of "intent" seems more in keeping with the common usage of "suicide," so it is to be preferred to the first sense.

Case two raises a second issue, that of coercion. The soldier terminated his own life because he knew he would be killed by means of prolonged torture, and because he did not wish to reveal his country's secrets. Some have argued that this is not an example of suicide because it involves (a) coercion and (b) other-directed rather than self-directed motivation. If the soldier were not under coercion but terminated his life anyway, this would most likely be classified as a suicide. Thus if an act is coerced, it probably does not count as a suicide.

What about self-destructive acts for the sake of others, such as cases two and three? Some hold that these are not suicides because they involve other-directed and not self-directed motivation. When considering then, a third issue, that of motivation, these are sacrificial acts, not suicides. Here death is not desired, but one's own life is taken for the sake of others.

Some philosophers add the stipulation that other-directed acts are suicidal if they are done for animals or nonpersonal states of affairs (e.g., wealth). Thus case four, though an act of self-destruction for others (a cancer patient shoots himself to save others economic and psychological distress), should still be classified as a suicide because it is not done to save the lives of others, but to realize a nonpersonal state of affairs.

The Jehovah's Witness case could be treated similarly. If God does command that no blood be taken and if a blood transfusion violates this command, then refusing a blood transfusion would be not a suicide but a sacrificial act of martyrdom. (An important issue in this case is whether the Jehovah's Witness' interpretation of Scripture is accurate. Most biblical scholars do not think so and thus would have a factual problem with case six.)

What about a Buddhist monk who sets fire to himself in protest of a war? Some would argue that this is not a suicide because it is self-sacrifice for the lives of others. Beauchamp disagrees and believes that such an act is suicidal because the monk himself directly and intentionally causes the life-threatening condition (the fire) that brings on the death.[3] According to Beauchamp, most people would judge such an act as suicidal, and this shows that usage of the term *suicide* turns on the fact that the agent creates the conditions for death, not on the notions of sacrifice or martyrdom.

But even if one grants that the monk's act is a suicide, all that follows is that there are different ways an act counts as suicidal, and in addition to the issue of self-versus other-motivation, there is also the issue of direct causation of death. It would seem then that all things being equal, an act of martyrdom or sacrifice for the lives of others is not a suicide.

However, Beauchamp's point does raise a fourth issue of direct causation and active means used by the individual. This writer considers case four a suicide but not case five. If a sick but nonterminal person died as a result of refusing to eat or take medication, that would be considered a suicide. These insights indicate that a self-destructive act is a suicide if the person is nonterminal and death is intentionally and directly caused as a means to some other end. In case five, death is foreseen but not directly and intentionally caused. Thus, this is an example of passive euthanasia. In case four, however, death is directly and intentionally caused by a gunshot, and this is what makes the act a suicide.

A Definition of Suicide

From these deliberations about the cases listed above, fundamental intuitions about suicide, embedded in ordinary language, become clearer. On the basis of these deliberations the following definition of suicide can be formulated: An act is a suicide if and only if a person intentionally and/or directly causes his or her own death as an ultimate end in itself or as a means to another end (e.g., pain relief), through acting (e.g., taking a pill) or refraining from acting (e.g., refusing to eat) when that act is not coerced and is not done sacrificially for the lives of other persons or in obedience to God.[4]

This attempt to define suicide does not mean that all nonsuicidal acts of self-destruction are considered morally permissible. For example, a daredevil, foolishly performing an unnecessarily risky stunt for money or fame, jumps to his death. Such acts can be wrong for several reasons: they harm others (e.g., loved ones left behind) by removing a member of the community, they manifest a disrespect for human life, they can contribute to similar acts, and so on.

IS SUICIDE MORAL?

Before discussing different views regarding the morality of suicide, two preliminary points should be made. First, this discussion of the morality of suicide focuses on the morality of a suicidal act done by a rational, competent decision-maker. Such a person can effectively deliberate about and understand different courses of action and the ends they accomplish, as well as different means to accomplish those ends.

Second, some ethicists argue that the subjective and objective aspects of the morality of suicide should be distinguished. The former refers to the guilt incurred by the person who commits suicide, the latter refers to the morality of suicide considered objectively as an act in itself. The idea behind this distinction is that some persons who commit suicide may be in such a state of distress (e.g., they are severely depressed, acting on false information, etc.) that their act may be objectively wrong but the individuals themselves may not be blameworthy. The act may be called a serious mistake, but excusable.

However, this distinction is a questionable one, because in such cases it could be claimed that the person was not acting rationally and because it is not clear how an act can be at once morally wrong but not blameworthy. Perhaps the act is not blameworthy in the weak sense that one can easily understand and empathize with it. But the act would still be morally blameworthy if it is a morally wrong act, and it is the moral sense of blameworthiness that is of chief interest in ethics. In any case the focus here is on the "objective" side of the morality of suicide: Can a suicidal act as such be morally justifiable when it is done by a rational, competent decision-maker?

The Liberal View:
Suicide as Such Can Be Morally Justifiable

Advocates of the liberal view hold that an act of suicide may be morally justifiable even if that act does some harm to others, provided that the act does not do *substantial damage* to others and that it is in keeping with the individual liberty of the agent. Even if a person has some duty to others, say, family members, the suicide can still be morally acceptable provided the distress to others caused by the suicide does not outweigh the distress to the person who refrains from committing suicide. No person is obligated to undergo extreme distress in order to save others from a smaller amount of distress.

There are two major approaches to the morality of suicide within the liberal camp: the utilitarian approach and the autonomy approach. These views are not necessarily mutually exclusive.

The Liberal Utilitarian Position

Richard Brandt defines suicide as the intentional termination of one's own life and argues against the view that suicide is always immoral.[5] It may be appropriate, he says, to take one's own life to avoid catastrophic hospital expenses in a terminal illness and thus meet one's obligation to one's family. It may also be the case that a person may maximize his or her long-range welfare by bringing about death.

A person who is contemplating suicide is making a choice between "world-courses"—a world-course that includes his or her immediate suicide and several possible world-courses that contain his or her death at a later point. These alternatives are to be understood as world-courses, Brandt says, not as future life-courses, which refer only to the alternatives for the individual alone. This is because one's suicide or failure to commit suicide impacts the rest of the world, and the morality of suicide must take into account the welfare of all relevant parties, not just the welfare of the person contemplating suicide.

A person contemplating suicide must attempt to take into account all the relevant information, including all his or her own short- and long-term desires. Brandt argues that though one can never be certain of all these factors, one must not let this fact stand in one's way. A person contemplating suicide should compare the world-course containing his or her suicide with the best alternative. If the former world-course maximizes utility, all things being considered, then it would be rational and morally justifiable to commit suicide.

Among the reasons regarded as good and sufficient reasons for suicide are these: painful, terminal illness; some event that has made a person feel ashamed or caused a loss of prestige and status; reduction from affluence to poverty; the loss of a limb or of physical beauty; the loss of sexual capacity; some event that makes it seem impossible to achieve things deemed important; loss of a loved one; disappointment in love; and the infirmities of increasing age. If a person experiences these or other serious blows to prospective happiness, suicide may be justified if such an act maximizes the net amount of utility compared to alternative acts. In cases of morally justifiable suicide, others are morally obligated to assist in executing the decision, says Brandt, if the person needs help.

The Liberal Autonomy Position

A second liberal approach to the morality of suicide is the autonomy position. Major advocates of this view are Tom L. Beauchamp and James F. Childress.[6] They state that persons should be allowed to be self-determining agents who make their own evaluations and choices when their own interests are at stake. If a person is a competent, rational decision-maker, that individual has a right to determine his or her own destiny even if others believe that a course of action would be harmful to that individual.

The principle of beneficence states that one should seek to benefit others and oneself, and the principle of nonmaleficence expresses the duty to not harm others or oneself. In a case of rational suicide, there may be a conflict of duties between autonomy on the one hand, and beneficence and nonmaleficence on the other hand. In such cases autonomy should take precedence over other moral considerations. Disrespect is shown to individuals and the principle of autonomy is violated if the right to commit suicide is denied when, in their considered judgment, they ought to do so and no serious adverse consequences for others would result (such consequences do not necessarily present overriding grounds for opposing suicide).

The autonomy view is consistent with both a utilitarian ethic and a deontological ethic. If the autonomy view is utilitarian, then the principle of autonomy is justified on the grounds that accepting this principle maximizes utility compared to rejecting autonomy and acting on alternative rules. In this case the autonomy view becomes a way of expressing a utilitarian approach to the question of suicide.

If the autonomy view is deontological, then it becomes an alternative to the utilitarian approach. Here autonomy is seen as an expression of an intrinsic duty to respect persons and the priority of autonomy vis-à-vis beneficence and nonmaleficence becomes an attempt to emphasize individual liberty and quality-of-life considerations regarding suicide.

The Conservative View:
Suicide as Such Is Not Morally Justifiable

The conservative view holds that suicide as such is not morally justifiable. A number of reasons have been offered for this view: It violates one's sanctity-of-life duty to respect oneself as an end and not a means; it violates a natural law principle that man's very nature is such that he has an inclination to continue in existence and he has a moral duty to act in keeping with that nature; it violates man's duty to God as the Giver and ultimate Owner of life; it violates one's duty to one's community by injuring that community in some way.

According to Hauerwas, an ethics of autonomy (where the principle of autonomy overrides all other moral considerations) implies that suicide is not only rational, but also that it is a moral right.[7] This shows, Hauerwas says, how inadequate a minimalistic ethic of autonomy and a nonnaturalistic view of rationality really is as an overall approach to morality, suicide included. An ethic of autonomy has an insufficient view of the good life—the life of the virtuous person and community that each person ought to seek. As a result an ethic of autonomy fails to explain why anyone should decide to keep on living in the face of difficulties.

First, Hauerwas argues, suicide is wrong because life is a gift bestowed by a gracious Creator. While there are other reasons against suicide, any examination of suicide must consider the rational support given for the factual belief that human lives are gifts from God. Because life is a gift, man is obligated to his Creator to live. Living is an obligation, in that man is to go on living even when he is far from figuring out why things happen as they do. This obligation expresses the rational belief that God gives purpose to life even in the midst of hardships.

Second, Hauerwas states that one should not commit suicide because of one's duty to others in the community. People should not be viewed as atomistic individuals who are unconnected to others. Rather, people live in systems. A person's existence depends on his or her interaction with other lives in community. Their willingness to live in the face of pain, boredom, and suffering is (a) a moral service to one another; (b) a sign that life can be endured; (c) an opportunity to teach others how to die, how to face life, how to live well, and how a wise person understands the connection between happiness and evil (e.g., one does not obtain joy or live a good life only when one avoids hardship, but when one learns to live with it); and (d) a way of refusing to give the community a morally unhelpful memory of the person who committed suicide, which could hurt those left behind in their attempt to live well as individuals and in community with others. An act of suicide signals the failure of the community to be present to care for the suicidal person in his or her time of need, and it signals the person's lack of care for the community.

Third, Hauerwas argues that suicide is inconsistent with the very nature of medicine, especially the authority of medicine. Medicine is not to be defined merely as a technological field. The authority of medicine is not just that of a technologically skilled group of people. It is the authority of a virtuous profession wherein people in a community signal the virtue of being present for one another in time of need. The medical professional expresses a commitment to be present to heal or to care for the weak and sick when care cannot be reciprocated. The sick person signals his or her desire to place trust in the community's representative—the medical personnel—and allow the community to care for that sick person in time of need. Suicide signals a break in this value to be present for one another in time of need, and thus suicide is inconsistent with the presuppositions that make medicine itself intelligible.

Assessment of the Views

Broad Worldview Considerations

The debate about suicide clearly surfaces *two* fundamentally different *sets of presuppositions* about how to approach broad issues such as the purpose of life; the nature of morality, community, medicine, and persons; the ultimate ownership of life. Thus the debate about suicide is difficult to separate from broad worldview considerations. What is the good life, what is the point of life, and how does one's answer to these questions inform one's perspective about the nature and purpose of suffering? Is life sacred? Should life be treated as a gift? Is utilitarianism a better approach to ethics or is a deontological view a better approach? Is a quality of life or a sanctity of life approach to suicide preferable? Should persons be ultimately viewed atomistically, as individuals, or should they equally and irreducibly be seen as members of a community to which they are responsible? Is medicine to be understood along the traditional lines as presented by Hauerwas, or should it be seen as a contractual arrangement between patient and physician wherein medical goods and services are obtained so long as the patient wishes to have them?

The liberal and conservative views tend to answer these questions differently. Their competing views on the morality of suicide express deep differences on these basic, worldview questions. It is beyond the scope of this chapter to attempt a broad analysis and evaluation of these different outlooks, apart from some brief, specific considerations to be offered shortly. One's views are an expression of one's general worldview, and it is in the discussions about the morality of suicide that a Judeo-Christian worldview becomes especially precious and relevant.

The statements of the liberal and conservative views already presented above outline some of the specific arguments relevant to assessing these positions. Further, the arguments against the liberal views function as arguments for the conservative view. Therefore the following pages focus directly on criticisms of the liberal position. These criticisms show that the liberal view is morally inadequate and the conservative view is to be preferred.

Criticisms of the Liberal Utilitarian View

First, the liberal, utilitarian view is problematic because of the difficulties inherent in utilitarianism in general (e.g., the failure to treat people as ends in themselves and the failure to recognize the fact that some moral rules are intrinsically right). Further, if a utilitarian justification is offered for a specific act of suicide, it goes beyond justification, making the act of suicide permissible; it makes it morally obligatory. Why? Because one is morally obligated to maximize utility, and if an act of suicide maximizes utility, then it would be morally obligatory. But any view that makes a suicide obligatory is wrong.

Utilitarians respond to this argument in two ways. First, they argue that under certain circumstances, a rule requiring suicide would not be morally wrong. Deontological ethicists argue that this rule would dehumanize persons by treating them as a means to an end and by elevating a quality-of-life standard above a sanctity-of-life standard. It should be clear that one's evaluation of this debate will turn on one's opinion regarding the relative merits of utilitarianism versus deontological ethics and quality of life versus sanctity of life.

Second, utilitarians argue that a rule requiring suicide in certain circumstances might turn out to be wrong because adopting such a rule may itself fail to maximize utility. Deontologists respond by pointing out that utilitarians cannot rule out the possibility that such a rule may maximize utility, and in any case the moral impermissibility of a rule requiring suicide is not grounded in utility considerations but in the moral inappropriateness of requiring someone to treat himself or herself as a means to an end.

Criticisms of the Liberal Autonomy View

Other criticisms can be raised against the autonomy model that apply to the utilitarian model as well. For one thing, the liberal view in both forms violates a person's duty to him- or herself. This has been expressed in several ways.

1. To take one's own life is to deny its intrinsic value and dignity. It is to assume wrongly that man is the originator and therefore the controller of life.
2. Some have offered a natural law argument to the effect that everything, human nature in particular, is naturally inclined to perpetuate itself in existence. In response, it has been pointed out that suicidal persons do not have this inclination to continue existing. But this response fails to recognize that the notion of inclination used in natural law arguments is not to be understood as a psychological preference for life, but as a normative, natural urge grounded in one's nature as a human being.
3. Suicide is wrong because it involves the direct, intentional killing of human life. Such an act treats persons, who have intrinsic value, as means to ends.
4. Suicide is also a self-refuting act, for it is an act of freedom that destroys future acts of freedom; it is an affirmation of being that negates being; it serves a human good (e.g., a painless state) but, as a means to that end, violates other, more basic human goods (e.g., life itself); it is an act of morality that gives up on all other moral responsibilities and rejects the moral way of life.[8]
5. Suicide runs the risk of being an inappropriate way of entering life after death. Even if one does not believe in life after death, such a state is possible and perhaps reasonable in light of arguments that can be raised in support of it. Either way, it is unwise to risk entering life after death in a morally improper way.

As Hauerwas has pointed out, the autonomy model fails to capture the importance of community, the traditional understanding of medicine as a morally authoritative vocational expression of the community's respect for life, and a virtuous understanding of the good life and suffering. Suicide fails to explain adequately why one should continue to live when one no longer wishes to, and thus it is inappropriate from a moral point of view.

PATERNALISM AND SUICIDE INTERVENTION

General Statement of the Views

Is it justifiable for some agent of the state to coercively prevent a suicide or to compel a competent adult to take life-saving medical treatment? Opinions differ on these questions. The libertarian view opposes such paternalistic interventions because they are considered a violation of individual liberty, patient autonomy, and the respect for persons that presents an obligation to respect the wishes and desires of competent, adult decision-makers (provided of course that no overriding harm is done to others). In this view people have a right to commit suicide.

The second view, the beneficence model, is generally in favor of such interventions to keep the person from serious and irrevocable harm. Society has a duty to prevent people from harming themselves in acts of suicide.

Important Definitions

Paternalism is the refusal by an agent to accept and go along with a person's wishes, choices, and actions for that person's own benefit. Paternalism is rooted in the idea that the community as represented, say, in a physician, has better insight into what is good for a patient than does the patient, and thus can do what is medically good for the patient even if it is not judged good by the patient's own value system.

Strong paternalism involves overriding the competent, rational wishes, choices, and actions of another. Individual liberty is overridden because of benefit to the individual, even though that individual is not impaired as a decision-maker. *Weak paternalism* involves acting in the best interests of a person who is impaired as an actor or as a decision-maker. There is little disagreement that weak paternalism is morally justifiable. In fact most ethicists do not see it as paternalism at all, because it involves acting or deciding for a person who is incapable of doing so. Often such interventions eventually restore patient autonomy and liberty.[9]

The principle of *respect for persons* requires that persons be treated as ends in themselves and never as a means only. Respect is shown for the intrinsic worth and dignity of a person. The principle of *autonomy* requires that individuals should respect the self-determination of others by not doing for others what they would not want done to themselves and doing for others what they would wish done to themselves. The principle of *beneficence* says that people have a duty to benefit others and to act in their best interests. Beneficence comes in degrees: one ought not inflict harm on others, one ought to prevent harm, one ought to remove harm, and one ought to do good.

Exposition and Evaluation of the Views

The Libertarian View

According to Engelhardt, in the present secular society, moral pluralism must prevail.[10] Individual communities may share a substantive vision of the good life (and the good death), but a peaceable secular state must remain pluralistic and must respect rights that preserve individual liberty. Peace is maintained only by respecting the principle of autonomy as the supreme moral principle. Autonomy prevails in every situation, provided of course, that autonomous actions do not cause overriding harm to others. Beneficence is important, says Engelhardt, in that it gives content to different individual or community visions of the good life. Thus beneficence preserves autonomy.

Regarding suicide, a rational, competent decision-maker has the autonomous right to refuse life-saving treatment or to commit suicide without interference. Further, such individuals have a right to be assisted in suicide by others. In a peaceable, secular state, it is wrong to interfere with the moral authority expressed in free choices of individuals or those who assist them in refusing treatment or in committing suicide. In such a state, autonomy reigns supreme and paternalistic interventions are unjustifiable.[11]

Several strengths have been claimed for the libertarian view. First, it is important to respect the principle of autonomy, individual rights, and the privacy of individuals, and the libertarian view attempts to express this respect. Second, respecting the autonomy of a person can be part of what is needed to cure that person, so violations of patient autonomy can do harm. However, when it comes to suicide, this point is not applicable. Third, the libertarian view is a reaction to class dominance, and in a pluralistic society, legal moralism (liberty is limited to prevent a person from acting immorally) can easily be an oppressive tool in the hands of an elite. Forcing someone to live against his or her own will can be oppressive and fails to respect persons, so the argument goes, by failing to honor his or her self-determination.

In spite of these strengths, a number of weaknesses in the libertarian view have been surfaced. First, this view easily degenerates into an inordinate individualism that fosters, under the guise of respect for autonomy, disinterest in the plight of others and premature abandonment of a patient in time of need. Honoring autonomy is not always the best way to exhibit respect, especially when an individual is autonomously choosing to disrespect him- or herself in a serious way. Suicide is a serious act of disrespect for oneself, even when chosen autonomously, and so honoring a suicide disrespects a person. Freedom is not a bare, formal principle. People are free to do what they *ought* to do, they are not entitled to do anything they *want* to do, and suicide violates the sanctity of life.

Second, the libertarian view fails to recognize that decision making is an interpersonal process. The physician-patient relationship, the family-individual relationship, and other important relational systems (e.g., friendships) should be part of decision making. Usually when a person is contemplating suicide, the others in that person's system will argue against it out of respect for the sanctity of life and the desire not to lose the suicidal person. Admittedly this may not be true in all cases. But the libertarian model does seem to individualize decision making inordinately and fails to guard adequately against hasty decisions that may not be morally justifiable.

A third related point is that the libertarian view, in its retreat to private morality, treats people as atomistic individuals. Thus it fails to come to grips with the common good, the nature of community and how community constitutes part of what it is to be a person, and the community's interests in preserving the sanctity of life.

This atomistic view of individuals also distorts the patient-physician relationship by viewing it as an autonomous contractual agreement for the exchange of services that both parties enter freely. But the patient-physician relationship is a commitment between unequal parties (the patient needs healing), and that commitment must be present in order to heal. This involves altruistic but authoritative beneficence on the part of the physician, and trust on the part of the patient. This model can be abused, but it does seem to capture the real nature of the patient-physician relationship. The physician is committed to healing, and suicide is an act against that commitment.

Fourth, as Callahan has pointed out, the libertarian view expresses a minimalistic ethic (one may morally act in any way one chooses if one does not harm others).[12] The libertarian view, as a minimalistic ethic, has a number of features that make it barren and inadequate as a social ethic. It confuses a useful principle for government regulation with the broader requirements of the moral life; it inappropriately draws a sharp line between the public and private spheres with different standards for each; it has a shriveled notion of public-private morality in its reduction of interpersonal, moral obligations to a simple honoring of those agreements people have freely and voluntarily entered; it fails to account for the moral importance of communal life, the common good, and shared values; it tends to view all interventions into autonomous adult decision making in a negative light.[13]

Fifth, the libertarian view utilizes the wrong notion of rationality, that is nonnormative rationality: the ability to competently understand options and their consequences, formulate means to ends, and so on. Such a view of rationality in morality tends to reduce substantive ethics to procedural ethics: one arrives at a morally correct outcome if he uses the correct procedure in reaching that outcome. In the case of suicide, if a rational procedure was followed in the deliberation process, the choice of suicide is correct.

A more adequate view of rationality is a normative one: one is morally rational if one has the ability (perhaps through the cultivation of virtue) to gain insight into what is morally true and good. This view of rationality emphasizes the substantive aspects of ethics. It is true that men of good will frequently differ over what is in fact morally true and good. But the solution to this is an emphasis on argumentation and virtue, not a retreat to nonnormative rationality and procedural ethics. The libertarian view does the latter and for that reason is inadequate.

The Beneficence View

Advocates of the beneficence view are more sympathetic to the legitimacy of limiting individual liberty, including the right to commit suicide, in order to (a) benefit the individual and prevent him or her from serious and irrevocable harm, (b) preserve the common good and the community's interest in the sanctity of life, and (c) preserve the beneficent, healing, covenantal model of medicine.

It may be best to view the libertarian-beneficence debate as a continuum, with the former emphasizing quality of life, individual autonomy, and nonnormative rationality, and the latter emphasizing sanctity of life, beneficence, the common good, and normative rationality. Not all advocates of the libertarian view would sanction every act of rational suicide and not all advocates of the beneficence model would hold that a line is never crossed where a person should be permitted to commit suicide. Some advocates of the beneficence model hold that all acts of suicide require intervention, while others would severely limit the permissibility of suicide but agree that in some rare and extreme cases it may be allowed.

Two main advocates of the beneficence model are Edmund Pellegrino and David Thomasma.[14] They argue that autonomy should not always win in medical conflicts, and that in general, beneficence should be ranked higher than autonomy. This ranking is grounded in a virtue approach to ethics, which involves respecting the sanctity of life, the traditional view of the physician as a beneficent healer, and the common good.

Pellegrino and Thomasma express their views about suicide in the context of the Elizabeth Bouvia case. In 1983 Elizabeth Bouvia, a twenty-six-year-old who was virtually quadriplegic, dependent on others for her bodily functions, and suffering from intense pain, entered a California hospital and stated that she wanted to starve to death. A lower court rejected her petition and authorized involuntary tube feedings. In April 1986 the California Supreme Court granted removal of a nasogastric feeding tube from Bouvia on the grounds that she was a rational, competent decision-maker and that her request was in keeping with patient autonomy and privacy.

Pellegrino and Thomasma agree that a competent person has a moral right to refuse life-sustaining systems, but assisted suicide is clearly wrong and once a feeding tube was given Bouvia, its removal was wrong because it involved a clear intent to bring about death. By contrast other advocates of the beneficence model would not agree that Bouvia had a moral right to refuse life-sustaining treatment. Thus, advocates of these views of beneficence are more conservative than those of the libertarian view, but they differ over the right of a nondying patient to refuse life-sustaining treatment.

SUMMARY

The morality of suicide clearly surfaces how broad worldview considerations are important for understanding and evaluating different moral positions. *In the final analysis one's approach to suicide is determined largely by the worldview one brings to the issue.* Christian leaders should study the general arguments involved in suicide and other ethical issues of broad cultural concern. When they do, they will be in a better position to discuss the issues while being sensitive to the secular, pluralistic nature of the culture. Also they will have excellent opportunities to present the Gospel of Christ at intellectually appropriate places in the discussion.

ENDNOTES

1. Tom L. Beauchamp and James F. Childress, *Principles of Biomedical Ethics*, 2d ed. (New York: Oxford University Press, 1983), 93–95.
2. Stanley Hauerwas, *Suffering Presence: Theological Reflections on Medicine, the Mentally Handicapped, and the Church* (Notre Dame: University of Notre Dame Press, 1986), 103–5.
3. Tom L. Beauchamp, "Suicide," in *Matters of Life and Death*, ed. Tom Regan (Philadelphia: Temple University Press, 1980), 75–77.
4. Some add the qualification that death must occur fairly quickly after the action

or omission. See *Life-Sustaining Technology and the Elderly* (Washington, D.C.: U.S. Government Printing Office, 1987), 150. But the time factor is extremely controversial and an act could be suicidal even if death did not occur for some time.

5. Richard B. Brandt, "The Morality and Rationality of Suicide," reprinted in *Biomedical Ethics*, eds. Thomas A. Mappes and Jane S. Zembaty, 2d ed. (New York: McGraw-Hill Book Co., 1986), 337–43. See also, Beauchamp, "Suicide," 78–96.

6. Beauchamp and Childress, *Principles of Biomedical Ethics*, 93–101.

7. Hauerwas, *Suffering Presence: Theological Reflections on Medicine, the Mentally Handicapped, and the Church*, 100–13.

8. This type of argument is offered by Albert Camus, "An Absurd Reasoning," in *The Myth of Sisyphus and Other Essays* (New York: Vintage Books, 1955), 3–48.

9. For further distinctions regarding paternalism, see James Childress, *Who Should Decide? Paternalism in Health Care* (New York: Oxford University Press, 1982), 12–21.

10. H. Tristram Engelhardt Jr., *The Foundations of Bioethics* (New York: Oxford University Press, 1986), esp. chaps. 1–3 and pp. 301–20.

11. A less extreme libertarian view is expressed by Childress, *Who Should Decide?* esp. pp. 28–76, 157–85. Childress grounds his argument against paternalism not in the principle of autonomy, but in the principle of respect for persons. Thus respect for a person may require nonintervention if that honors a person's wishes, choices, and actions. Childress holds that paternalism is altruistic beneficence and generally ranks beneficence below autonomy because the latter may more clearly express respect for persons. However, it could be argued that in an act of suicide, a person actually disrespects him- or herself, and while allowing a suicide may in one sense respect a person, yet because of the finality of suicide, such an act shows overriding disrespect for the individual. Thus it shows more respect for persons to interfere with an autonomous suicide than to allow it.

12. Daniel Callahan, "Minimalistic Ethics," *Hastings Center Report* 11 (October 1983): 19–25.

13. Ibid. For more on the contrast between liberal and conservative approaches to abortion, infanticide, euthanasia, war, and capital punishment, see J. P. Moreland and Norman Geisler, *The Life and Death Debate: Moral Issues of Our Time* (Westport, Conn.: Praeger Books, 1990).

14. Edmund D. Pellegrino and David C. Thomasma, *For the Patient's Good: The Restoration of Beneficence in Health Care* (New York: Oxford University Press, 1988).

An Overview

The ever-present and penetrating existence of evil in the lives of all people, Christian and non-Christian alike, and its coexistence with a sovereign God is often difficult to accept and understand for both the world at large and for many who profess Jesus Christ as Lord. As a result, the issue of suffering is confused and from it is formed the basis for the thinking of discouraged and depressed people who consider or commit suicide, euthanasia, or assisted suicide. C. Ben Mitchell discusses the consequences of suffering in a society that embraces the worldview of the inherent goodness of man and of a God who is unable or unwilling to intervene for humankind. However, a biblical understanding of God and the presence of evil in our society inspires hope and eliminates despair; it is in the sanctuary of our God that we discover the peace that surpasses all understanding.

Chapter Twelve

SUICIDE AND
THE PROBLEM OF EVIL

*Why Bad Things Cause People
to End Their Lives*

C. Ben Mitchell

ON MY BOOKSHELF IS A FAVORITE two-frame cartoon strip. In the first frame a little man is shown standing in a torrential downpour, eyes lifted to heaven, saying, "Why me?" In the last frame, a voice calls down from the dark sky, "Why not?" In that simple exchange is a profound lesson we frail human beings find extraordinarily difficult to learn. I will suggest in this chapter that the failure to learn that lesson is the fundamental cause of many, if not most, suicides. Furthermore, I will offer what I hope are helpful prescriptions for preventing suicide among those who find themselves under a deluge of providence.

What causes people to want to kill themselves? There may be as many answers to that question as there are attempts to commit suicide. In his monumental study, *Why People Kill Themselves: A 1990s Summary of Research Findings on Suicidal Behavior,*[1] David Lester, of the Center for the Study of Suicide, discovers very few helpful conclusions from the ubiquitous literature on suicide. Studies among twins have failed to demonstrate a clear genetic correlation to suicide. Neurobiological causes of suicidal tendencies are notoriously difficult to prove. While there is an obvious linkage between depression and suicide, the studies on the connection are largely unilluminating. The literature of suicidology suggests that for the majority of individuals who kill themselves some form of psychiatric illness is present. For instance, one study of attempted suicides in Edinburgh, Scotland, found that nearly 70 percent of those who attempted to poison themselves suffered from a diagnosable psychiatric illness.[2] But what about the other one-third of attempted suicides? Moreover, we have good reasons to believe that at least some diagnoses of psychiatric illness are, in fact, misdiagnoses of coping problems associated with sinful decisions or improper behavioral patterns rather than organic dysfunction of the brain.[3] Thus, perhaps the majority of those who attempt suicide have no identifiable organic or psychiatric disorder that accounts for their decision to end their own lives.

One thing appears to be clear. Persons who attempt to kill themselves view themselves to be in some sort of extreme circumstance. The sense of being *en extremis* explains many attempts, successful and unsuccessful, to commit suicide. For example, G. F. Felstein found that suicide was common after plant shutdowns and relocations.[4] The recent American embrace of assisted death (of euthanasia and assisted suicide) is largely explained by the anticipation of suffering which individuals feel they might experience in the final days of their earthly existence. One study found that at an urban Pittsburgh high school, seven students attempted suicide after two students committed suicide within a four-day period.[5] Some researchers have indicated that "adolescents who kill themselves after a much publicized suicide are frequently those who perceive themselves as contending with similar life circumstances and situations."[6] Indeed, for many with suicidal thoughts, whether adolescents or adults, "circumstances" or "situations" are at the heart of their desire to put an end to their lives.

WHY ME?

Undoubtedly, some persons do find themselves in profoundly difficult, painful, and traumatic circumstances. A Christian wife of unflagging devotion to her husband learns that he is cheating on her and plans to move in with his partner in adultery. Faithful Christians are laid off in corporate downsizing, despite their hard work and loyalty to their employers. A godly nurse who has given her life in service to the weak and ill finds herself the victim of Lou Gehrig's disease. A spiritually mature couple prays to have a baby for ten years and invest tens of thousands of dollars in infertility treatments, all with no results. In one of the most painful and emotionally charged of all experiences, children of Christian parents are abducted, sexually abused, and brutally murdered by repeat offenders.

In the face of these kinds of personal disasters, non-Christians sometimes appear to (and indeed do) prosper in the world. Many seem to have very few personal and familial tragedies. They do not get sick appreciably more often than Christians. Automobile accidents seem to be no respecter of persons. Christians do not seem to have any advantage over non-Christians with respect to the experience of disease, disaster, and death.

On the surface, it just does not seem fair. Why do bad things happen to people who do not seem to have brought these tragedies on themselves? Why do Christians suffer? Why do children suffer? Intractable pain. Emotional torture. Mental delusion. Natural disaster. Physical trauma. Often, non-Christians escape these trials while Christians suffer.

When tragedy strikes, many are tempted to cash it all in. The question becomes intensely personal: "Why me?" In the midst of such pain, suicide, as the song goes, seems painless. In their despair, many choose to end it all. The suffering is too fierce, the pain too acute. Circumstances are simply too hopeless.

Quite apart from any organic brain disorder, quite apart from any hereditary predisposition, quite apart from the effects of social conditions— when tragedy strikes an individual personally and singularly, the knee-jerk reflex is to ask, "Why me?" The apparent impossibility of making sense of suffering drives many to the edge of the precipice with no obvious solution but to hurl themselves into the abyss.

Asaph, one of the psalmists, put it this way,

> But as for me, my feet had almost slipped;
> I had nearly lost my foothold.
> For I envied the arrogant
> when I saw the prosperity of the wicked.
> They have no struggles;
> their bodies are healthy and strong.
> They are free from the burdens common to man;
> they are not plagued by human ills. . . .
> Surely in vain have I kept my heart pure;
> in vain have I washed my hands in innocence.
> All day long I have been plagued;
> I have been punished every morning.
> —Psalm 73:2–5, 13–14

Do you hear the wracking anguish in the psalmist's words? He is plagued by his own circumstances and perplexed by the apparent prosperity of the wicked. "Why me?" he asks. "Why should I be in such awful pain? Life is pointless; no, it's worse than pointless. It is positively evil. I might as well end this suffering."

POSITING THE UN-GOD

In the midst of such intense agony, we are tempted to question the very existence of God. Even if we do not question His existence, we are at least tempted to question whether God is in fact the God we have been told He is. This is the heart of the so-called problem of evil. If evil exists and, more precisely, if it impacts believers, how can God be who God is supposed to be? I will not digress into a deep philosophical discourse on the microscopic details of the problem of evil. Others have done so quite admirably.[7] Yet, it is crucial, if we are to understand why many attempt suicide—and more importantly, to know what we can do to prevent such attempts—that we at least dissect down to the skeleton and tendons. What I hope to do is demonstrate the existential importance of the problem of evil as it impacts individuals who are thinking about committing suicide.

Classical Jewish and Christian theology have understood God's essential attributes to include His omnipotence, omniscience, and omnibenevolence. That is to say, God is all-powerful, all-knowing, and all-good. When confronted with the evil in the world, especially when it falls upon us like an anvil, we are tempted to doubt that God is . . . well . . . God. How can God be God and the righteous still suffer? How can God be God and wickedness run helter-skelter in the world? Perhaps we have misunderstood God. Perhaps God is not all those things Christians and Jews say He is.

Well, some might say that God is not, in fact, omnibenevolent. The eighteenth-century philosopher René Descartes actually considered the possibility that God might be an altogether evil being whose only goal was to deceive His creatures. But even Descartes could not prove to himself that God was like that. There was no good reason to think that God is evil. Such a view was both inconsistent with pure reason and daily experience. If there is a God, He must be good.

Furthermore, the uniform testimony of Scripture is that God is and that God is good. John the apostle reminds his readers of the teachings of Jesus, when he says, "This is the message which we have heard from him and declare to you: God is light; *in him there is no darkness at all*" (1 John 1:5, emphasis mine). Again, the apostle is the one who in staccato voice declares, "God is love" (1 John 4:16b). If there is a God, He must be good. A God who is not good is not God, but very *un-God*.

Few, then, are willing to believe that God is not good. Some argue, instead, that God must be ignorant of some things. God must be like us—limited in knowledge, unable to foresee all the contingent events of the future. Think about what that would mean. If God is unable to see in the future, then God is likewise unable to fashion the future. If God is unable to fashion the future, then God is unable to ensure anything in the future. If God is unable to ensure anything in the future, then this world is whirling out of control—or at least out of God's control. Again, this view is inconsistent with the biblical revelation of God. The God of the Bible is the God who knows the end from the beginning. The apostle Paul, for instance, makes it perfectly clear that everything is working "according to the plan of him who works out everything in conformity with the purpose of his will" (Eph. 1:11). God is a purposive being. The testimony of Scripture is that God not only knows the end from the beginning, but that, mysteriously but certainly, everything is working in accordance with His divine plan. Even though we sometimes quote Romans 8:28 flippantly, its truth remains powerful: "And we know that in all things God works for the good of those who love him, who have been called according to his purpose."

Others, unwilling to believe that God is ignorant of future events, posit that God is not all-powerful. That is, God has limited power. Either through self-limitation or some kind of incomplete divine evolution (as in some forms of process theology), God is less than fully capable of doing everything God wants to do. God's will is thwarted by circumstances, the human will, or some other limiting factor. On this view, God is just not able to help us except in certain, discrete situations. While such a notion might appear to provide comfort to those who are wrestling with evil in the world, in fact, such a view leads only to further despair. If God is not able to help, who can? Again, the testimony of God's own revelation of Himself is that His power is limitless.

Does this make sense? Could this be? Is there any evidence that God knows about and is involved in this present evil age? Or is God aloof and uninvolved in the events around us? Where would we look to find the answers to such questions?

We cannot look to the circumstances themselves. We ourselves are so limited in perception that we cannot possibly see every contingency. So how can we expect to see the hand of God clearly in every event? Where is God when bad things happen? Can God do anything about those bad things?

Returning to the anguished psalmist, we get answers to some of these questions.

> When I tried to understand all this,
> it was oppressive to me
> till I entered the sanctuary of God;
> then I understood their final destiny.
> —Psalm 73:16–17

Asaph declares that he was unable to understand the apparent prosperity of the wicked and his own depression, *until he entered the sanctuary of God.* That is to say, Asaph's despair had theological roots. Once he understood that God was in control and that His justice would prevail, in spite of what appeared to be the case (cf. vv. 18–20), he was able to recover. He even provided his own diagnosis.

> When my heart was grieved
> and my spirit embittered,
> I was senseless and ignorant;
> I was a brute beast before you.
> —Psalm 73:21–22

PRESCRIPTION: BIBLICAL THEOLOGY

There seem to be two primary theological misunderstandings that often lead to deep depression and subsequent thoughts of suicide: (1) the idea that God is absent, impotent, or unconcerned; and (2) the idea that we human beings are essentially good and do not deserve to experience evil in the world. Neither of these notions find quarter in the Bible.

God is. God is good. God is omnipotent. God is omniscient. These are the confessions of biblical Christianity. More than that, *these are the only grounds of hope in this present evil age.* The un-God described above provides no hope for individuals undergoing adversity. It makes little difference that God empathizes with us, unless God is superintending our experience. Similarly, there is little hope generated by the knowledge that God merely feels our pain. If God is powerless to control our circumstances, then God is under the same limitations as we ourselves. If this is so, then God can provide little more than empathy or moral support in the midst of our trials. There is no hope in a God who can do nothing about our circumstances.

I recently heard a pastor preach on Job's trials. He painted vividly the picture of Job's suffering. He accurately analyzed the false counsel of Job's so-called friends, Eliphaz, Bildad, and Zophar. Then the pastor cited Rabbi Kushner's best-selling, but woefully unbiblical, *When Bad Things Happen to Good People.*[8]

Kushner's God is impotent. Says Kushner, "God does not want you to be sick or crippled. He didn't make you have this problem, and He doesn't want you to go on having it, but He can't make it go away. That is something which is too hard even for God."[9] So what does God have to do with our trials? Kushner's answer: "Fate, not God, sends the problem. . . . And in the knowledge that we are not alone, that God is on our side, we manage to go on."[10] Here is the empathetic yet powerless God. And, worse, "Fate" is in control. Perhaps, then, we should seek help, not from God, but from some psychic network or some other medium that understands or manipulates fate. Kushner would leave us in the cruel hands of metaphysical forces, naturalistic processes, or blind luck. Where is the hope embraced by Asaph?

> Yet I am always with you;
> you hold me by my right hand.
> You guide me with your counsel,
> and afterward you will take me into glory.
> Whom have I in heaven but you?
> And earth has nothing I desire besides you.
> My flesh and my heart may fail,
> but God is the strength of my heart
> and my portion forever.
> Those who are far from you will perish;
> you destroy all who are unfaithful to you.
> But as for me, it is good to be near God.
> I have made the Sovereign Lord my refuge;
> I will tell of all your deeds.
>
> —Psalm 73:23–28

Asaph's God is the sovereign Lord, the God of great *deeds*. Asaph's hope rested in the God of history and providence, the God who works all things after the counsel of His own will. He did not learn (or relearn) this truth until he entered into the sanctuary. Asaph had to turn away from his narcissism (excessive love of self) and turn to the God who is there.

Likewise, for many who are suffering under a dark providence, their help and hope will only revive when they trust the sovereign Lord. God is. God is good. God is omnipotent. God is omniscient.

Furthermore, the God of Asaph is a purposive God. Everything God does works toward His own purpose. Even what we regard as bad things somehow fit into the plan and purpose of God. This fact is evident in one of the hard sayings of the Old Testament. When Moses offered his excuse for disobedience, telling God that he could not speak to Pharaoh because he was "slow of speech and tongue" (Ex. 4:10), God responded to Moses by reminding him that He superintended every human event. "The Lord said to him, 'Who gave man his mouth? Who makes him deaf or mute? Who gives him sight or makes him blind? Is it not I, the Lord?" (Ex. 4:11). No doubt God's providence is sometimes mysterious. But either God is in control or He is not. The uniform testimony of Scripture and the experience of many believers of the past is that God is sovereign over all the events of our lives.

I recall the story of a woman who lost her husband and daughter in a tragic airplane crash. In the midst of her grief, one well-meaning friend wrote her a note saying, "God must really trust you to bear these things for His glory." Another friend, on hearing the contents of the note, was livid. "How could they write such a thing! God didn't have anything to do with that!" The newly-widowed woman replied, "But that's my only hope. If God didn't have anything to do with that; if there is no purpose behind what happened, I might as well blow my brains out." When we try to defend God, we steal the only real hope an individual may possess. Nihilism reigns supreme and nothing matters.

Relatedly, the other contributor to the depression and despair that leads to suicidal thoughts is the view that human beings are basically good and do not deserve to suffer. The doctrine of human depravity has been lost in this age of self-love. In fact, however, the Scriptures teach that every human being and the entire cosmos has been subjected to the consequences of sin. God's original creation was good, but, in a sense, fragile. When the first man and woman, Adam and Eve, sinned in the Garden of Eden, the results were cosmically catastrophic. Genesis 3 is a catalogue of some of those results. Disease and death were repercussions of our progenitors's sin. Not only so, but the whole created order pays the price for original disobedience. Nevertheless, the apostle Paul rejoiced in the hope of the glory that is to come in the future.

> I consider that our present sufferings are not worth comparing with the glory that will be revealed in us. The creation waits in eager expectation for the sons of God to be revealed. For the creation was subjected to frustration, not by its own choice, but by the will of the one who subjected it, in hope that the creation itself will be liberated from its bondage to decay and brought into the glorious freedom of the children of God.
>
> For we know that the whole creation has been groaning in the pains of childbirth right up to the present time. Not only so, but we ourselves, who have the firstfruits of the Spirit, groan inwardly as we wait eagerly for our adoption as sons, the redemption of our bodies. (Rom. 8:18–23)

We live, as the old theologians used to say, in a fallen world and we ourselves are fallen creatures. Much of the suffering and many of the trials we experience are endemic to life in a fallen world. Because Western culture has largely forgotten or rejected the biblical worldview, including the fallenness of creation, we are surprised by suffering when it comes. We almost reflexively look for someone to blame for our circumstances and become a culture of victims. Or we seek through alcohol and other drugs a means of dulling our senses to the pain we feel and become a culture of hedonists. Or, finally, when our hope has been veiled by our ignorance of God, our perverted sense of justice, or our own selfishness, we opt for ending our lives. Instead, the question, "Why me?" should immediately evoke the answer, "Why not?"

Why *should* we be exempt from suffering? Suffering is the universal experience of humanity. In fact, some of the most devout saints in history suffered the most. Most of Jesus' own apostle's were martyred for their faithfulness. William Cowper, author of that splendid hymn, *There is a Fountain*, suffered intense agony of soul. The great evangelist George Whitefield died after an extended bout with a deteriorating illness. Charles Spurgeon, the "prince of preachers," suffered from painful gout and died at a relatively young age. The faithful of our day fare no better!

CONCLUSION

My contention has been that suicidal thoughts are more often than not attributable to bad theology. I fully realize that my argument runs the risk of being too simplistic. Let me hasten to add, therefore, that I think there is a place for biblical counseling and, in some cases, for psychotropic medications for those who are having suicidal ideations. However, my argument does entail that suicides can be prevented by attending to theology. That is to say, the prophylactic or precautionary treatment for suicide is good theology.

The problem of evil, more or less well articulated, is at the root of most thoughts of suicide. Individuals either think that their circumstances are hopeless or undeserved. Yet, when one understands that (1) God is sovereign and benevolent, and (2) that no one is exempt from suffering, *the impetus to commit suicide either vanishes or is significantly diminished*. Since God is in control and works everything to His own glory and for our ultimate benefit, we can persevere through suffering. Since suffering is the universal lot of humanity in a fallen world, we are not surprised when it comes. We may even be able to begin to anticipate how we will endure it for God's glory.

Sadly, many Christians and non-Christians alike lack the fundamental theological categories to understand and handle suffering. In fact, contemporary evangelicals have largely bought into either a nascent process theology or the therapeutic model. Instead of committing ourselves to the sovereign God and His good pleasure, we succumb to a maudlin sentimental deity who feels our pain but is helpless to defend us against the forces of fate. Instead of identifying with the common experience of suffering, we choose to see ourselves as victims of some malevolent and unjust force.

If we would save future generations from the soaring numbers of suicides, we must recover a vision of a sovereign God who rules and over-rules all things for His own glory. Evangelical preaching and pastoral counseling has become sufficiently weakened to produce men and women without theological vertebrae. If we would save individuals from becoming morbid statistics in the future, we must recover a biblical anthropology.

ENDNOTES

1. David Lester, *Why People Kill Themselves: A 1990s Summary of Research Findings on Suicidal Behavior*, 3rd ed. (Springfield, Ill.: Charles C. Thomas Publisher, 1992).

2. Cited in Margaret Pabst Battin, *Ethical Issues in Suicide* (Englewood Cliffs, N.J.: Prentice Hall, 1995), 8.
3. Paul C. Vitz, *Psychology as Religion: The Cult of Self-Worship*, 2d ed. (Grand Rapids: Eerdmans, 1994); William Kirk Kilpatrick, *Psychological Seduction: The Failure of Modern Psychology* (Nashville: Thomas Nelson, 1983); Jay E. Adams, *The Christian Counselor's Manual* (Nutley, N.J.: Presbyterian and Reformed, 1973).
4. G. F. Felstein, "Current Considerations in Plant Shutdowns and Relocations," *Personnel Journal* 60 (1981): 369–72.
5. Cited in Robert J. Myatt and Milton Greenblatt, "Adolescent Suicidal Behavior" in *Suicidology: Essays in Honor of Edwin S. Shneidman*, ed. Antoon A. Leenaars (Northvale, N.J.: Jason Aronson, Inc., 1993), 197.
6. Ibid., 198.
7. C. S. Lewis, *The Problem of Pain* (New York: Collier Books, 1962); R. Douglas Geivett, *Evil and the Evidence for God: The Challenge of John Hick's Theodicy* (Philadelphia: Temple University Press, 1993); Peter Kreeft, *Making Sense Out of Suffering* (Ann Arbor: Servant Books, 1986); and Jerry Bridges, *Trusting God* (Colorado Springs: NavPress, 1988).
8. Harold S. Kushner, *When Bad Things Happen to Good People* (New York: Avon Books, 1981). For a helpful rejoinder to Kushner see Warren W. Wiersbe, *Why Us? When Bad Things Happen to God's People* (Old Tappan, N.J.: Revell, 1984).
9. Ibid., 129.
10. Ibid.

An Overview

The wasteland of modernity and postmodernity is littered, in part, with those who, in despair and trauma, chose suicide as a means of physical and psychological release from their anguish and burdens. What critique should Christians provide and what solutions can they proclaim for a culture that so readily embraces death? This essay dispels the myth of autonomy and clearly shows that suicide is a worldview issue. The human dilemma with all of its ramifications is clearly addressed by the Christian view of reality. Christians are in the unique position of staunchly proclaiming the only lasting and healing message to a world straining to hear a word of hope. The message is a timeless one, and its moral realism penetrates the pain, monotony, and despair that are a part of the human dilemma.

Chapter Thirteen

CHRISTIANS AND
A CULTURE OF DEATH

Affirming Moral Accountability in an Amoral World

J. Daryl Charles

ABOUT THE TIME THIS WRITER was asked by the editors to contribute to this volume, the nation was jolted by the news that the U.S. Navy's Chief of Naval Operations, Admiral Jeremy "Mike" Boorda, had taken his life. Admiral Boorda's suicide left the press utterly dumbfounded and noticeably embarrassed, with news reports all cut from the same swath: Mike Boorda was extremely well liked, energetic and resourceful, the quintessential American success story. Having joined the navy at age sixteen, he worked his way up through the enlisted ranks, ultimately attaining the navy's highest official post.

Because of the social stigma attached to self-inflicted death by a gunshot wound, in the immediate aftermath of Boorda's death members of the media were extremely reticent to use the "S" word, and that only with the qualifier "alleged." It goes without saying that the press made no mention of the hellish nightmare and lifelong emotional scars that Boorda's suicide had freshly inflicted upon a wife and four children. Moreover, no one dared conjecture the immensely demoralizing effect Boorda's suicide would have on the millions of our nation's servicemen, irrespective of rank. Was it now preferable for officers and nonofficers alike, following Boorda's lead, to take their own lives, given the demands associated with serving national interests? (While unearned combat decorations and hypersensitivity to political criticism—factors adduced as contributing to Boorda's suicide—indeed raise important questions regarding leadership, they are not our present concern.)

What frequently goes unsaid in discussions of suicide is in some respects more significant than what is said. And as with other "quality of life" issues such as euthanasia,[1] the legal-moral aspects of self-inflicted death are often couched in morbidly comical euphemisms,[2] as society reels to evade both social stigma and the moral implications of the immoral act.[3] To consider suicide as a moral-legal right, as Herbert Hendin perceptively writes, is

> to parody the illusion of control that suicide confers on the . . . individual. Death and physical decline challenge our capacity for control and the

grandiosity in all of us, but suicide provides for some the illusion of maintaining omnipotent control through the ability to determine the when and how of death. In this control oriented culture, we delude ourselves that we can perfect a mode of dying and thereby gain control over the pain of life and death. Ironically, in this effort, those who suffer most from a need for control that is antagonistic to pleasure and to life—the suicidal—are being held up as prophets of a better world. . . . Death . . . [by] suicide is often the climax of a script, a drama, a communication launched at others. When society encourages such behavior it fails to exert any leavening effect and may unleash more than it intends. Discouragement of suicide, coupled with care and concern, can prevent the spread of suicide among the vulnerable."[4]

While Admiral Boorda's death is not the focus of this essay, it does illustrate with particular force that (a) all human acts have moral consequences (some of which are unspeakably tragic), and (b) our actions are conscious or unconscious expressions of a prevailing world- and life-view. Even the nonreligious individual's supposed autonomous (a)moral acts are shown in the end not to be suspended in a moral vacuum. Rather, as the Boorda incident tragically demonstrates, the ripple effect can be shown to have enormous moral ramifications. With Nietzschean tenacity one may choose to deny until one's dying breath the possibility of a moral universe. The wife and children of Mike Boorda, however, know differently. Theirs is a lot no human being should have to suffer; theirs is a scar no family should have to bear.[5]

The focus of this essay—part cultural critique, part apologetic—bypasses a discussion of statistics, demographics, and theories that seek to identify markers of the suicidal condition. It proceeds by building on the fundamental assumption that we presently live in what John Paul II has called a "culture of death."[6] This conviction by no means diminishes our sympathy toward those who in tendency are suicidal. Contrarily, it is our belief that with a better understanding of the moral-philosophical underpinnings of culture, the Christian community can with compassionate truth assert hope through a robust biblical theism, even amidst the most extreme social pathologies. This life-view is tethered to the conviction of two reconcilable philosophical-theological poles: human creation in the *imago Dei* and human moral accountability rooted in a created moral universe. Whether American Christianity can profoundly and sensitively address a cultural climate that fosters tragedy like that of Mike Boorda remains to be seen. Its first priority, however, is, like the men of Issachar, to understand the times in which we live.

THE SUICIDE OF THOUGHT

Although suicide is a personal response to the pressures of a life deemed not worth living, its thought germinates in a social climate in which a collapse both of the intellect and of faith has already taken place. Its seedbed is a cultural context of intellectual and spiritual amputation—a cultural environment whose dominating philosophies contain a strain of suicidal mania.

Though nearly a century removed from the gangrene that calls itself "postmodernism," one celebrated British writer and humorist offered a sturdy and timeless antidote to the monotony, pain, and despair that contribute to suicidal thought in the late twentieth century. Whether debating George Bernard Shaw and Sigmund Freud or critiquing Marxian and Nietzschean theory, G. K. Chesterton was able to speak with clarity and force to the fundamental issues of life as few in this century have. Chesterton seemed to write equally for friend and foe, for the Christian and the anarchist, for the hopeful and the despondent, as he contended for "the permanent things."

"The Maniac" and "The Suicide of Thought" constitute the first two chapters of an autobiographical *apologia* titled—somewhat dauntingly— *Orthodoxy*.[7] Therein Chesterton moves back and forth between the insane asylum and supposed sanity. Despite the collapse of the intellect endemic even to his own day, Chesterton could argue on the one hand that to all people disease is not beautiful, and on the other hand that even the wildest poetry of insanity can be enjoyed solely by the sane. Thus viewed, mental disorder does not necessarily impair one's reason; rather, it manifests itself as reason without root. That is to say, the mad or the forlorn are not the individuals who have lost reason; rather, they have lost everything except reason. It was Chesterton's belief that the "clean and well-lit prison" of "one idea sharpened to one painful point"—namely, that life as one knows it should cease—is present in most modern thinkers. Moreover, this disease has extended itself to modern culture at large.[8] This is a world in which all that surrounds the person

> has been blackened out like a lie; when friends fade into ghosts, and the foundations of the world fail; then when the man, believing in nothing and in no man, is alone in his own nightmare, then the great individualistic motto shall be written over him in avenging irony. The stars will be only dots in the blackness of his own brain; his mother's face will be only a sketch from his own insane pencil on the walls of his cell.[9]

From the Chestertonian perspective, the individual who thinks without the proper "first principles" goes "mad"; that is, he or she thinks and moves in the wrong direction. What is it precisely in Chesterton's opinion that drives the individual to extinction? Or, for that matter, that preserves one's sanity? For Chesterton, it was the ability to acknowledge life's mystery—having one foot on earth and one in the transcendent realm—that results in psychological health. Thereby the tension between fate and free will, divine sovereignty and human moral agency, is understood to be accounted for and, ultimately, reconciled. Mystery can be seen to breed lucidity; at the same time, free will ever acknowledges the existence of the mystery. Whereas the plethora of philosophies and religions of the world retain as their symbol the circle (which may be emblematic of both reason and madness), the cross, argued Chesterton, though it has at its core "a collision and a contradiction," extends its four arms "forever without altering its shape. Because it has a paradox in its center it can grow without changing."[10] The circle returns upon itself and is bound, while the cross, to use Chesterton's words, "opens its arms to the four winds; it is a signpost for free travelers."

The peril of the human psychological dilemma—a phenomenon not new under the sun—is that human volition is free to annihilate itself. Amply tragic testimony to this possibility can be found in both twentieth-century history and philosophy. In accounting for human volitional freedom,[11] Christian philosophers not infrequently speak of the integration of faith and reason. By this they wish to emphasize that the life of faith is not divorced from the pursuit of knowledge, that faith and the intellect are not to be dissociated. Perhaps a more accurate rendering of this relationship, which must be understood in the context of *worldview*, is to concede that *reason itself* is a matter of faith. For is it not an act of faith to assert—or even suggest—that our own thoughts bear any relation to reality whatsoever? Indeed, if life is without design, then even delayed suicide—on *everyone's* part—is an act of intellectual dishonesty, insofar as this delay expresses a false hope that in and of itself was a manifestation of misdirected "faith."[12] But such is perhaps too harsh a verdict, particularly for the despairing individual who wrestles with suicidal tendencies. Nevertheless, while from the outset acknowledging the psychological prison in which some find themselves, we shall attempt to examine suicidal thought as an expression of humanity that is in revolt against its Maker. This revolt has manifestations both ancient and modern.

THE MORAL WORLD OF GRECO-ROMAN PAGANISM

It has been said that Nietzsche ("The thought of suicide is a great source of comfort: thereby a person makes it through many a bad night.") well represents the archetype of intellectual violence that spawns suicidal thought. Such at least was the conviction of a contemporary of Nietzsche, stated with utmost clarity, when perhaps with a grain of harshness:

> The softening of the brain which ultimately overtook him was not a physical accident. If Nietzsche had not ended in imbecility, Nietzscheism would end in imbecility. Thinking in isolation and with pride ends in being an idiot. Every man who will not have softening of the heart must at last have softening of the brain.[13]

Whether or not Nietzsche may be so credited with paving the way to personal Armageddon, he is by no means the first to champion radical human autonomy. Roughly contemporary with the New Testament era, the Roman Stoic Lucius Annaeus Seneca (4 B.C.–A.D. 65) argued—and embodied—the principle that humans possess the ability and right to end their lives upon choosing: "Reason, too, advises us to die, if we may, according to our taste; if this cannot be, she advises us to die according to our ability, and to seize upon whatever means shall offer itself for doing violence to ourselves."[14] Quality of life rather than existence in and of itself justified, in Seneca's view, escape from the evils of human depravity.[15] It was with this Stoic outlook, dominant among the moral philosophers of the late Hellenistic era, that the early Christians were in regular contact. The basic assumptions undergirding the moral world of the early church are not without attestation in the pages of the New Testament. They can be glimpsed upon—however incompletely— in Luke's narrative recorded in Acts 17, where the reader finds a portrait of Paul's encounter with Athenian culture.

Specifically in Paul's address to the Council of the Areopagus,[16] the strategy of the Apostle to the Gentiles exhibits two notable characteristics. Both (1) an understanding and critique of pagan culture, and (2) a responsible, culturally relevant application of Christian truth are part of the apostle's intellectual arsenal. Moral relativism and hardened skepticism concerning moral accountability after death are twin peaks that Paul doubtless was prepared to encounter among sophisticated and cosmopolitan Athenians— beliefs shared to a greater or lesser extent by Epicureans and Stoics. By Paul's day, belief in the Olympian pantheon was no longer strong, the emperor cult was a foremost political phenomenon, and mystery cults sought to fill the remaining moral-spiritual vacuum of Hellenistic culture.

The intellectual atmosphere of first-century Athens might be characterized as mildly promiscuous, both in a religious and nonreligious sense. A relatively large percentage of the city's population had been initiated into the Eleusinian mysteries.[17] Religiously speaking, the city had no discernible knowledge of Old Testament revelation. Lacking the seriousness of intellectual and moral conviction that had typified the classical era, Athens, by Paul's day, exhibited a somewhat indiscriminate, almost casual approach to life issues. Several of the church fathers allude to Athens as a city of talkers, a people possessed of curiosity.[18] According to one ancient source, Athenians were particularly fond of lawsuits.[19] With hermaphrodites (commonplace at house doors) and innumerable symbols of phallic worship and sexual obsession on public display throughout the city (to some of which were attached religious significance), one can easily understand the dislocation in the Apostle's spirit (Acts 17:16) as he witnesses a culture in decline.[20]

Against the materialist-rationalist worldview of his audience at the Areopagus,[21] Paul adjusts reigning presuppositions regarding material creation. In his disputation he presumes a monotheistic outlook and seeks to validate divine revelation by introducing the notions of *creatio ex nihilo* and bodily resurrection, the core of Christian truth-claims, both of which cut against contemporary views of the universe, the body, and the soul. In the Areopagus speech, an apologetic bridge to the pagan mind is employed by the Apostle: nature itself. In Pauline thought, it is impossible to miss the connection between creation, the moral order, and human accountability. Although this line of reasoning is not developed in Acts 17 as it is in Romans 1, it is nonetheless present in both. "Natural theology" in Acts 17 has the function of pointing to human moral accountability. To the extent that Athenians have no Christocentric understanding, Paul's use of the creation motif at the Areopagus serves as a necessary pedagogical-missionary preamble of sorts. The phenomena of creation are accessible to all; knowledge of the

Creator is innate, and, therefore, all share a basic awareness of moral accountability. Pagans "know" because of creation and conscience; their ignorance, ultimately is "without excuse."[22]

As evidence that epistemological ignorance is *not* bliss, even among pantheists, the "one true God" has ordained "a day" on which the world is to be judged (Acts 17:31). Thus Paul dismantles the Stoic view of universal continuum, which denies an eschatological day of reckoning. The Judeo-Christian understanding of history, which begins and ends with divine fiat, marks a radical discontinuity with the worldview of Paul's audience. At this point in the address, one can imagine among Paul's audience polite tolerance turning into seething indignation (v. 32a). Paul's declaration, an intellectual and moral stumbling-block for his listeners, is that "one Man" will judge the cosmos. Things will not go on perpetually in the Stoic sense.

AN EARLY CHRISTIAN PERSPECTIVE
ON MORAL ACCOUNTABILITY

Several of the twenty-one New Testament epistles reflect a social situation in which the Christian community represents a minority social grouping in pagan Hellenistic culture. Hence it is not surprising that in most of these letters the subject of ethics presses to the fore. One notable example is 2 Peter, the destination of which remains uncertain but which is addressed most probably to a Christian community that is struggling to keep from being absorbed into a surrounding climate of pervasive moral skepticism.[23] The emphasis on ethics in 2 Peter can be seen by the extent to which the letter is suffused with ethical language, moral exhortations, moral paradigms, and caricatures of the moral reprobate. Furthermore, the writer incorporates motifs that contain important touch-points between Christian and Stoic thought.

Following the epistolary greeting, in which the recipients are reminded of the abundance and accessibility of divine resources for "life and godliness" (1:3), the author utilizes a catalog of virtues (1:5–7), a rhetorical device commonly employed by Stoic moral philosophers of the last three centuries B.C. and first century A.D. The catalog is intended to outline the contours of this "life and godliness" and incorporates commonly cited features from standard Stoic virtue lists—for example, moral excellence, knowledge, self-control, endurance, piety and brotherly affection. These features are adapted in the letter to the Christian hortatory tradition. The letter's greeting clarifies and highlights divine grace, the basis for building a virtuous life. This presupposed grace represents an acute departure from the Stoic view of ultimate things. While both Christian and Stoic ethical doctrine compel moral progress, the former can be understood to be less rigorous since it is predicated on the operation of divine grace and not human achievement or merit per se.

Following the catalog of virtues, the author uses highly repetitive reminder terminology to stir the Christian community to reaffirm moral truth that they already know (1:12–15). Theirs is not to be a life void of moral fiber; rather, the distinctly Christian ethic is to shine forth in bold contrast to surrounding culture. Tragically, in the author's view, some have disregarded the divine "promises" (1:4), and, as a result of their intercourse with Hellenistic society, have "forgotten" their inheritance. What's more, some in the community are even aggressively propagating the notion that there is *no* moral authority before which they must account (2:1; 3:3–5).

The second chapter of the letter is constituted by moral typology and a vivid sketch of the morally destitute. What are the marks of the moral struggle in the community? Among those listed are licentiousness, a reviling of truth, selfishness, and deception (2:1–2). In broader terms, these are said to "deny the sovereign Lord" (2:1). The moral paradigms that follow (2:4–10a) underscore through lessons of history the tragedy of denying moral truth. Allusions to the fallen angels, the contemporaries of Noah, and Sodom and Gomorrah serve dual purposes. On the one hand, they underscore the imminence and accountability of divine judgment. The angels, Noah's contemporaries, and the cities of the plain were judged for their rejection of moral authority. Their destiny is meant to admonish those in the community who would choose a similar course. On the other hand, the examples serve to remind the faithful that they can expect a merciful God to deliver them despite enormous social obstacles facing them.[24] The catchword "savior" throughout the epistle[25] is intended to have more than a christological thrust. God visits and saves those who place their trust in Him. The tenor of 2 Peter, in spite of the announcement of divine judgment, is not merely condemnatory. The letter contains the assurance of rescue from the midst of the cultural furnace. And if the reader imagines the author to be promulgating some sort of "perfectionistic" ethic, he or she should take heart, for in 2 Peter the righteous model in Sodom and Gomorrah is Lot. Lot in the Old Testament, it should be remembered, is anything but a model of faithfulness and righteousness.[26] Contrast, not essential nature, is the point of the Lot typology in 2:6–9. Important touch-points exist between the social environment of the readers and the contemporaries of Noah and Lot; the rhetorical force of these examples is easily lost on the modern reader.

Following the moral paradigms, the description in 2:10bff. accorded those denying moral authority (see 2:10a) is graphic, concise, and breathtaking. The individuals act as irrational beasts, they slander, they revel in their corruption. They are arrogant, irreverent, disobedient and scornful. Moreover, they are adulterous, insatiable in their lusts, and seductive. The Balaam typology in 2:15–16 is aimed at those in the community who over time became ethically divorced from the moral truth they had prior received. The downfall of a man of God is a singular phenomenon. In the end, the psychology of apostasy is such that moral skepticism and cynicism cause one to loathe what was once acknowledged. That there are divinely enforced limits to rejecting moral authority is emphasized in 2:20–22. The proverbial imagery in these verses of the dog returning to its vomit and a pig returning to the mud is meant to shock the readers.

The final stroke of the author's literary strategy is to caricature the hardened moral skeptic. Doubtless the Christian community struggles to maintain its religious and moral convictions amidst a Hellenistic cultural environment in which the notions of creation, a moral universe, providence, and eschatological judgment are ridiculed. Following the portrait in 3:3–5 of the moral skeptic, the fact of divine visitation is stressed.[27] This is to counter the fatal assumption that "everything goes on as it has since the beginning" (v. 4), which is to say, there is no moral universe, no divine judgment, no eschatological day of reckoning beyond the grave. The author's response is intended to remove the skeptic from the realm of illusion and into the sphere of reality: *there is a day of moral reckoning that looms ahead*. On this basis, hortatory language can be inserted once more in the letter to pose the unavoidable question, "What kind of people ought you to be?" (3:11).

The affirmation of cosmic renewal in 3:13 mirrors the interplay of pagan and Judeo-Christian cosmology, behind which stands a fundamental question—What is the relation of man to matter? And yet behind this question stands an even more fundamental question, namely: What is the relation of *moral* man to matter? Cosmology and eschatology, in the strictest sense, are not being showcased in 2 Peter 3; rather, this material is part of a response to the moral skeptic who is championing self-determination and denying moral universals. The point of the teaching in 2 Peter 3 is not foremost theological; it is to emphasize the *fact* of a day of reckoning as the ultimate expression of a cosmic *judicial* process. Ethics, not doctrine, is being emphasized.[28]

A unitary reading of 2 Peter leads us to certain conclusions. Strongly suggested in the epistle is an audience whose social setting is marked by a denial of moral self-responsibility. Such an environment, which can hardly be viewed as atypical of first-century Hellenism, calls for a sober and thoughtful response. Either the recipients live autonomously, as self-creations and without any higher purpose,[29] or they are part of a created moral order where actions in the present life have consequences for both now and beyond.[30] In 2 Peter, the reader is reminded that the former life-view has consequences that are indeed fatal.

REFLECTIONS ON THE CHRISTIAN TASK

Even for the hardened moral skeptic (or, the despairing pessimist), it is impossible not to intuit that life in this world is imbued with some purpose. If indeed there is a purpose, as the Judeo-Christian view of reality maintains, then there stands behind it a Person. If there is "story," then there must exist a Storyteller.

The dreary wasteland of modern and postmodern life, void of what Chesterton called "mystery," must be kept in proper perspective. As a conscious or unconscious explanation of life, it possesses no ultimacy in and of itself. It may exhibit a particular disdain for history, intergenerational wisdom, moral universals, indeed even the very notion of meaning itself. Nevertheless, history, wisdom, morality, and existential meaning endure outside the modern experience. The mystery, as it were, lives on.

In rejecting the falsehood that resides in both optimism and pessimism, Chesterton describes autobiographically the breakthrough of Christian hope that seemed to smash both idolatries:

> I had often called myself an optimist, to avoid the too evident blasphemy of pessimism. But all the optimism of the age had been false and disheartening for this reason, that it had always been trying to prove that we fit in to the world. The Christian optimism is based on the fact that we do *not* fit in to the world. I had tried to be happy by telling myself that man is an animal, like any other which sought its meat from God. But . . . I had learnt that man is a monstrosity . . . The modern philosopher had told me again and again that I was in the right place, and I had still felt depressed even in acquiescence. But [then] I had heard that I was in the wrong place, and my soul sang for joy, like a bird in spring. The knowledge found out and illuminated forgotten chambers in the dark house of infancy.[31]

Psychospiritual health does not reside with the optimist, whose loyalties are false and thus indefensible; neither does it lie with the pessimist, who knows no loyalties at all. Rather, it is to be found in the moral realist. The realist lives with one foot planted in the kingdom of heaven, the other in the kingdom of this world. Christian philosophers since the time of Augustine have maintained this two-tiered concept of moral realism. It is precisely this view of ultimate things that historically has distinguished martyrdom from suicide—two phenomena, which, despite their resemblance, stand literally worlds apart. But how might we account for the difference between the two?

Put simply, the one expresses loyalty—absolute loyalty—to something greater than itself; the other is the expression of an absolute lack of loyalty—to anything. The martyr yields up his or her life so that something—or someone—might live. The suicidal, by contrast, reflects little or no concern for anything—or anyone—else. Martyrdom and suicide then are opposites. The one sows seeds of life, while the other destroys—oneself and others. The latter act at its root is selfish; the former, selfless.

Among all world- and life-views, the peculiarity of Christianity is that it addresses the human dilemma, with its monotony, pain, and despair. It simultaneously humbles the proud and arrogant while raising the lowly and bowed down with an inner dignity. It engenders not human moral perfection but trust in a transcendent yet personal God of moral perfection. To the Stoic of the first century, the Christian view of reality—though it shared at some points a common moral grammar—was a stumbling block, a scandal to the rational-minded and self-determinist.

The Christian response to a culture filled with strains of death remains one of grace. It also entails reminding society around us that humans are fashioned in the image of a Creator who has framed a moral universe, and that all human actions have moral consequences. Contrary to the prevailing *Zeitgeist*, Christian realism purports not to be one among many life-views. It claims rather to be the solution to the human dilemma—the dilemma that confronts the Mike Boordas of this world. And it contains the healing balm that grieving families left behind so desperately need.

ENDNOTES

1. In calling suicide "autoeuthanasia," Herbert Tonne asks, "Why not go the logical step of granting suicide the acceptance we give euthanasia . . . ?" ("Suicide Is a Sign of Civilization," in *Problems of Death* [St. Paul: Greenhaven Press, 1981], 107).

2. The perversion of language in ethical debates is illustrated by relativist Joseph Fletcher: "Christian Europe started moving from pagan Rome's compassionate regard for the dignity of free persons to the savagery of an indiscriminating condemnation of all suicide in the Middle Ages . . . " ("In Defense of Suicide," in *Suizid und Euthanasie*, ed. A. Eser [Stuttgart: Ferdinand Enke Verlag, 1976], 237–38).

3. As with euthanasia, we increasingly see suicide framed as a fundamental human right, of which Thomas Szasz has been an articulate spokesperson (*Law, Liberty, and Psychiatry: An Inquiry into the Social Uses of Mental Health Practices* [New York: Collier Books, 1968]; *The Second Sin* [Garden City: Anchor Books, 1974]; and "The Ethics of Suicide," *Antioch Review* 31 [1971]: 7–17).

4. H. Hendin, *Suicide in America* (New York/London: W. W. Norton, 1982), 226–27.

5. American playwright Arthur Miller said it well: suicide kills two people; therein lies its purpose.

6. This expression surfaces in John Paul's more recent writings, notably in the two encyclicals *Veritatis Splendor* and *Evangelium Vitae*.

7. First published in 1908, *Orthodoxy* has been reissued several times, most recently in 1994 by Harold Shaw Publishers of Wheaton, Illinois.

8. Ibid., 18.

9. Ibid., 23.

10. Ibid., 25.

11. There is an inseparable connection between truth and freedom. Ethical relativism removes the moral reference point, turning human nature into a beast. The moral reference point, on the other hand, guarantees justice—individual and social. On this connection, see W. B. Smith, "No Truth, No Freedom," *Crisis* (November 1993): 28–31.

12. The logic of social Darwinism, as Hendin points out, would require us to cease our efforts to help and encourage people who are disabled, chronically ill, handicapped, or even depressed. Writes Hendin: "We need not believe that suffering is good for the character in order to understand that the capacity to deal with adversity, including illness, is one of the features of psychosocial stability" (*Suicide*, 213).

13. *Orthodoxy*, 41.

14. Taken from Seneca's essay "On the Proper Time to Slip the Cable," in volume 2 of *Epistulae Morales*, Loeb Classical Library, trans. R. M. Gummere, (Cambridge: Harvard University Press, 1920).

15. Following his exile to Corsica for eight years under the reign of the emperor Claudius, Seneca was reinstated and made a tutor to Nero. In the later years of Nero's rule, he was condemned as a coconspirator in an imperial plot and chose to take his life.

16. In the book of Acts there are three speeches of Paul recorded—one to a Jewish audience (13:16–41), one to a Christian audience (20:17–35), and one to a pagan audience (17:16–34). Surely this distribution is not by chance. For this reason, Paul's work in Athens raises important questions regarding Christian proclamation and the church's relation to culture—particularly to educated pagan culture, as I. Howard Marshall has noted in *Acts*, Tyndale New Testament Commentaries, ed. Leon Morris (Leicester/Grand Rapids: InterVarsity/Eerdmans, 1991), 281.

17. H. Koester, *History, Culture, and Religion of the Hellenistic Age*, vol. 1 of *Introduction to the New Testament* (Philadelphia/Berlin/New York: Fortress/W. de Gruyter, 1984), 180. Phyla, located near Athens, was the site of a mystery sanctuary.

18. Note Luke's depiction in Acts 17:18, 21.

19. *Charito* 1.2.6 (cited in H. Conzelmann, *Acts of the Apostles* [Philadelphia: Fortress, 1987], 139).

20. Writing one hundred years earlier, Cicero observed that in spite of its political decline, Athens still enjoyed "such renown that the now shattered and weakened name of Greece is supported by the reputation of this city" (*Pro Flaccia* 26.62). On the moral and intellectual atmosphere confronting Paul, see P. Parente, "St. Paul's Address before the Areopagus," *Catholic Biblical Quarterly* 11 (1949): 142–48, and J. D. Charles. "Engaging the (Neo)Pagan Mind: Paul's Encounter with Athenian Culture as a Model for Cultural Apologetics (Acts 17:16–34)," *Trinity Journal* 16NS (1995): 50–52.

21. Since the midthird century B.C., the council of the Areopagus functioned as an authoritative body in civil-legal and educational matters.

22. Cf. Romans 1:18–20. A prominent theme in the Areopagus speech is human "ignorance" (note, for example, vv. 23, 30). Not only is the Apostle in a city of great learning (along with Alexandria and Tarsus, one of three "university" cities of renown), the council of the Areopagus was composed of thirty of the most literate men of Paul's day. Although the most extensive background material on the Areopagus is available only in German, one of the most useful resources in English is B. Gaertner's The *Areopagus Speech and Natural Revelation* (Uppsala: Almquist, 1955).

23. This view is persuasively argued by T. Fornberg, *An Early Church in a Pluralistic Society: A Study of 2 Peter* (ConBNT 9; Lund: CWK Gleerup, 1977); J. N. Neyrey, "The Form and Background of the Polemic in 2 Peter," *Journal of Biblical Literature* 99 (1980): 407–31; R. Riesner, "Der zweite Petrus-Brief und die Eschatologie," in *Zukuenftserwartung in biblischer Sicht. Beitraege zur Eschatologie*, ed. G. Maier (Wuppertal: Brockhaus, 1984), 124–43; and more recently, J. D. Charles, *Virtue Amidst Vice* (Sheffield: Sheffield Academic Press, 1997).

24. Noah's generation is prototypical of a faithless generation in Jesus' teaching as well (Matt. 24:37–39; Luke 17:26–28). In Luke's gospel Noah's and Lot's generations appear side-by-side, where both are united by a common thread: life proceeding as normal in spite of pending judgment. For a thorough examination of the use of flood typology in both Jewish and Christian literature, see J. P. Lewis, *A Study of the Interpretation of Noah and the Flood in Jewish and Christian Literature* (Leiden: Brill, 1968). On Noah and Lot as types in the synoptic tradition, see J. Schlosser, "Les jours de Noe et de Lot. À propos de Luc xvii, 26–30," *Revue Biblique* 80 (1973): 13–36.

25. 1:1, 11; 2:20; 3:2, 18.

26. Genesis 13 and 19.
27. In 2 Peter 3, not the *timing* of the Parousia but its *fact* is being asserted.
28. This point is developed more fully in J. D. Charles, *Virtue Amidst Vice*.
29. The individual cannot be said to belong to himself, not even to society; he/she belongs to God. To deny God the right of life and death is the ultimate in rebellion against the Creator. By eradicating myself I rid myself of His sovereignty. This is the grand illusion of "autonomy."
30. John Paul II, in his 1993 encyclical *Veritatis Splendor*, takes to task moral philosophers who argue that human acts, including suicide, depend on the proportion of good between the end sought and the means needed to accomplish it. In the section "The Moral Act," he writes, "Human acts are moral acts because they express and determine the goodness or evil of the individual who performs them [cf. *Summa Theologiae* I-II, q. 1, 3]. They do not produce a change merely in the state of affairs outside of man but, to the extent that they are deliberate choices, they give moral definition to the very person who performs them. . . . The morality of acts is defined by the relationship of man's freedom with the authentic good. This good is established as the eternal law by divine wisdom, which orders every being toward its end. . . . Consequently, the moral life has an essential 'teleological' character, since it consists in the deliberate ordering of human acts to God, the supreme good and ultimate end (telos) of man (71–72). (For the complete text of the encyclical, see "Veritatis Splendor," *Origins* 22 [October 14, 1993]: 297–334.)
31. *Orthodoxy*, 82–83.

An Overview

This thought provoking and insightful article exposes four major inconsistencies with the popular notion of absolute personal autonomy. At its core, absolute personal autonomy decimates any concept of theistic reality or sovereignty and diminishes a critical deterrent to chaos—the social responsibility of the individual. Understanding the fallacy of this untenable principle is necessary to understanding its improper use by the courts and Dr. Kevorkian to promote physician-assisted suicide.

Chapter Fourteen

ABSOLUTE AUTONOMY AND PHYSICIAN-ASSISTED SUICIDE

Putting a Bad Idea Out of Its Misery

Francis J. Beckwith

PERHAPS THE MOST SIGNIFICANT and influential contribution that contemporary bioethicists have made to the medical community is their affirmation that a fundamental principle of medical ethics is the principle of respect for autonomy (or patient autonomy).[1] The implementation of this principle, though not entirely unproblematic,[2] has been instrumental in empowering patients and moving medicine away from physician paternalism.

Dr. Jack Kevorkian and his attorney, Geoffrey Fieger, have made much of the principle of autonomy in their defense of physician-assisted suicide. Fieger, in a talk given at a National Press Club luncheon on July 29, 1996, states:

> I have been at the center of this along with Jack Kevorkian for the last six years, and I am telling you, I have never heard a rational argument why a mentally competent, sick or dying person does not have an absolute right, under certain controlled circumstances, to end their suffering without government. I don't see how rationally you can make an argument in this country, where over twenty years ago, it was declared a fundamental right for a woman to control her own uterus and make decisions about an unborn child.

At the same luncheon, in a reply to a question posed by the moderator, Ms. Sonja Hillgren, Dr. Kevorkian was much more candid than his attorney:

> MS. HILLGREN: Many questioners have asked about your religious beliefs. I think you've articulated them, describing yourself as an agnostic. Can you tell us your underlying philosophical belief?

> DR. KEVORKIAN: Yeah, it's quite simple: Absolute personal autonomy. I'm an absolute autonomist. Do and say whatever you want to do and say at any time you want to do or say it, as long as you do not harm or threaten anybody else's person or property.

This exchange was followed by audience applause. Although Dr. Kevorkian claims to perform physician-assisted suicide on suffering people with terminal illnesses,[3] his application of the principle of autonomy, which he calls absolute autonomy, allows him to practice his specialty on a much larger constituency, including the depressed, the downtrodden, and the emotionally vulnerable, that is, pretty much any "rational" person who wants to exercise his or her right to absolute autonomy. This is not to say that Dr. Kevorkian in fact has helped or will help terminate such people. It just means that Dr. Kevorkian's lone moral principle, if it is truly the only legitimate moral principle, justifies such behavior.

Although there are some bioethicists who believe that physician-assisted suicide in some cases may be morally permissible, they employ other ethical principles in their moral decision making and conclude in many cases that physician-assisted suicide is morally impermissible.[4] These other ethical principles include the principles of beneficence, nonmaleficence, and justice. However, the view that Kevorkian and his attorney defend seems to not take this nuanced approach. It is crass and absolutist.

The principle of respect for autonomy, though a legitimate moral principle of medical ethics, if affirmed unrestrained by any other consideration, logically entails absolute personal autonomy, resulting in absurd counterintuitive consequences. Absolute autonomy trumps every other moral principle, every view of the human person that does not enshrine autonomy, as well as any concern, interest, or values of the community. In short, Kevorkianism is a dangerous and narrow dogma crushing in its path, in the name of tolerance and openness, every thoughtful notion or value that its proponents find disagreeable.

Although I believe that a good moral and legal case against physician-assisted suicide can and has been made,[5] my concern in this essay is the misuse of the principle of respect for autonomy by Dr. Kevorkian as well as the courts.

ABSOLUTE AUTONOMY AS A CONSTITUTIONAL RIGHT

Contemporary jurisprudence is headed in a troubling direction. Although many see Kevorkianism as an ethical aberration, there is reason to believe that absolute autonomy is becoming the primary dogma by which courts, especially the U.S. Supreme Court, adjudicate issues of great moral and social importance.

In the 1992 case that held *Roe v. Wade* (1973) as precedent, *Planned Parenthood v. Casey*, the Court departed from its 1973 appeal to the right to privacy and instead grounded abortion rights in an appeal to near absolute autonomy, which it believes it has found in the Fourteenth Amendment of the U.S. Constitution:

> Our law affords constitutional protection to personal decisions relating to marriage, procreation, family relationships, child rearing, and education. . . . These matters, involving the most intimate and personal choices a person may make in a lifetime, choices central to personal dignity and autonomy, are central to the liberty protected by the Fourteenth Amendment. At the

heart of liberty is the right to define one's own concept of existence, of meaning, of the universe, and of the mystery of human life. Beliefs about these matters could not define the attributes of personhood were they formed under compulsion by the State.[6]

Although political philosopher Hadley Arkes says that "this is the kind of sentiment that would ordinarily find its place within the better class of fortune cookies,"[7] this passage from *Casey* was taken to heart by Judge Stephen Reinhardt of the Ninth Circuit Court of Appeals, in the March 6, 1996 ruling of *Compassion in Dying v. Washington*, in which the judge not only affirmed a constitutional "right to die," but also called the state's motivation for banning physician-assisted suicide "cruel": "Not only is the state's interest in preventing such individuals from hastening their deaths of comparatively little weight, but its insistence on frustrating their wishes seems cruel indeed."[8]

Two years prior to this ruling, Judge Barbara Rothstein of the U.S. District Court in Seattle struck down the state's ban, employing the logic of *Casey*:

Like the abortion decision, the decision of a terminally ill person to end his or her life "involves the most intimate and personal choices a person can make in a lifetime," and constitutes a "choice central to personal dignity and autonomy."[9]

In supporting this decision, philosopher Ronald Dworkin makes a similar appeal, though emphasizing the state neutrality articulated in *Casey*:

Our Constitution takes no sides in these ancient disputes about life's meaning. But it does protect people's right to die as well as live, so far as possible, in the light of their own intensely personal convictions about "the mystery of human life." It insists that these values are too central to personality, too much at the core of liberty, to allow a majority to decide what everyone must believe.[10]

What makes these decisions particularly troubling is that they concerned a case in which a pro-euthanasia organization, Compassion in Dying, had sued the State of Washington over a statewide 1991 referendum in which the voters "had reaffirmed the provision of the criminal code that outlawed persons in its jurisdiction from 'knowingly causing or aiding other persons in ending their lives.'"[11]

Consider also a New York case, *Quill v. Vacco*, decided in the Second Circuit Court of Appeals. In that case, the court ruled that "the state of New York violates the equal protection clause of the Fourteenth Amendment with its prohibition of assisting suicide. By permitting patients to refuse treatment at the end of life, but not allowing physician-assisted suicide, the state unfairly treats similarly situated persons." The court did not take seriously the traditional distinction between passive (letting die) and active (killing) euthanasia. Like the Ninth Circuit and the District Court in Seattle, the

Second Circuit appealed to *Casey*. Writing for the majority, Judge Miner asked the question, "What concern prompts the state to interfere with a mentally competent patient's 'right to define [his or her] own concept of existence, of meaning, of the universe, and of the mystery of human life,' when the patient seeks to have drugs to end life during the final stages of a terminal illness?" The answer, according to Judge Miner, is "None."[12]

Philosopher Russell Hittinger, a critic of the case, explains the judge's reasoning: "[G]iven two patients, each of whom can define the meaning of the universe, the state of New York violates equal protection when it allows one to 'define' himself by having treatment withdrawn [i.e., passive euthanasia] while it forbids the other to 'define' himself by requesting that a physician assist his suicide [i.e., active euthanasia]."[13]

The courts are apparently saying that the community, moral considerations, and/or certain views of what it means to be a human person, however well-grounded philosophically and/or historically, are to be discarded and replaced with "absolute autonomy." The courts also seem to be saying that the people, whether through the legislature or through referendum, have no legal means by which to fashion the moral and social parameters of their communities or redress what they perceive as harmful to the public good as well as to their character-shaping institutions (e.g., the family, medicine, school curricula, the arts, higher education), since there is no objective good, only the unencumbered individual armed with his absolute autonomy.

Because these cases were decided in federal appeals courts on matters of constitutional law, they are legally significant, for they are, in the words of Hittinger, "authoritative renderings of the fundamental law."[14]

WHAT'S WRONG WITH ABSOLUTE AUTONOMY?

There are many reasons why absolute autonomy is flawed, both legally and morally, some to which I have previously alluded. Consider just the following four:

(1) *Absolute autonomy is based on a dogma for which its proponents typically provide no reason.* Remember Dr. Kevorkian's comments at the National Press Club luncheon: "I'm an absolute autonomist. Do and say whatever you want to do and say at any time you want to do or say it, as long as you do not harm or threaten anybody else's person or property." Although many people believe this, why is it any better than alternative dogmas, such as this one?: "Do and say whatever you want to do and say at any time you want to do or say it, as long as you do so consistent with what is morally correct and with living in a community of other persons, including one's family, neighborhood, and church, synagogue, or mosque."

Of course, Kevorkian and Fieger may find this alternative too constraining. But why should that matter? After all, maybe this dogma truly describes what really is while Kevorkianism does not. And if that is the case, then Kevorkianism puts people in bondage to an autonomy that is wholly unnatural, since human freedom may not be freedom at all if the will is antiseptically amputated from moral and social obligations and institutions that inform, empower, and nurture personal virtue. Consequently, what Kevorkian and Fieger find as liberating may in fact lead to cold and unnatural solitude, denying to the good doctor's patients the perspective that human life in community is much more than isolated individuals making choices for their unencumbered selves.

Recall Mr. Fieger's bold confession: "I have never heard a rational argument why a mentally competent, sick or dying person does not have an absolute right, under certain controlled circumstances, to end their suffering without government." Well we have yet to hear and are still awaiting Mr. Fieger's and his client's rational argument for absolute, unrestrained, unencumbered personal autonomy. Evidently, Mr. Fieger believes that mere assertion rather than rational argument is sufficient to justify his position, though it is not adequate for his opponents. Although Fieger and the courts would like us to think otherwise, Kevorkianism is not the default position. It too must be supported by rational argument.

(2) *Kevorkianism is counterintuitive.* In order to appreciate this flaw, consider the following fictional scenario: Imagine that you are a physician working the emergency room at a large urban hospital. Three paramedics wheel in an unconscious thirty-three-year-old man who has taken an overdose of barbiturates. Other than his drug overdose, he is in excellent physical condition. You tell your colleagues that he can be saved if his stomach is pumped immediately. As you are preparing the patient for the procedure, a nurse shows you a note that she had found in the young man's pocket. The note reads:

> If you find me before I die, please do not pump my stomach. I know exactly what I'm doing. My girlfriend, Rebecca, has broken up with me and life no longer has any meaning. I read somewhere that life's meaning and purpose is subjective, so you have no right to judge whether the reason for killing myself is serious or silly. Also, I recently read in a book by a Michigan pathologist, and during law school the legal briefs of his attorney, that each of us has a right to absolute personal autonomy. During my years in law school I also studied numerous U.S. Supreme Court and Federal Court decisions. One of them, *Planned Parenthood v. Casey*, said that "at the heart of liberty is the right to define one's own concept of existence, of meaning, of the universe, and of the mystery of human life." So, according to my concept of existence, life only has meaning if Rebecca loves me. Rebecca doesn't love me. So life has no meaning *to me*. Now that may seem like a dumb reason for me to kill myself. But I have absolute autonomy to do whatever I want with my body. I choose to kill my body. If you pump my stomach, you violate my autonomy. If I survive, I will sue you for violating my Fourteenth Amendment right to absolute autonomy and to define my own concept of existence, of meaning, of the universe, and of the mystery of human life.

Do you pump the young man's stomach? If you say yes, then you believe that it is perfectly appropriate for people, such as physicians, to make judgments about what sort of reasons are good or bad when another person is trying to justify killing himself. Although you may believe that in some circumstances physician-assisted suicide is justified, you don't believe that the principle of respect for autonomy is absolute and that nothing else should be considered.

On the other hand, if you say no, then you must take the counterintuitive position that nothing counts except personal autonomy. You have to assert that medicine as a profession has no purpose other than to facilitate the wants of patients no matter how fanciful or foolish they may appear to most people. You must also assert that the individual has no obligations to others, such as family, friends, and community that should be enforced by law and/or custom, since such an enforcement would violate the individual's absolute autonomy. Also, you must hold that family, friends, and community should not be encouraged by law and/or custom to consider how the individual's actions, such as committing suicide for foolish reasons, affect the moral ecology of important social institutions, such as medicine and family, and the future generations that will inhabit these institutions, as well as how such actions may affect the spiritual and/or moral well-being of the individual who commits them. The person who says no to pumping the young man's stomach is forced to admit that there is no such thing as public and private virtue that transcend the desires of the individual. He is also forced to say that there is no good to which society should strive, that human life is not inherently sacred, and that no view of human nature is correct if it does not allow for absolute autonomy; there are simply unencumbered autonomous selves exercising choices in light of their "own concept of existence, of meaning, of the universe, and of the mystery of human life." This view is so counterintuitive it is incredible that otherwise intelligent people should even consider it a viable alternative in social ethics.

(3) *When courts appeal to absolute autonomy as a "neutral position," they violate their primary reason for this appeal.* Recall the Supreme Court's assertion from *Casey*:

> At the heart of liberty is the right to define one's concept of existence, of meaning, of the universe, and of the mystery of human life. Beliefs about these matters could not define the attributes of personhood were they formed under compulsion by the State.

The Court is asserting the primacy of personal autonomy over the metaphysical question of personhood in order to affirm that the state should remain neutral when it comes to ultimate philosophical questions. The problem, of course, is that this appeal to autonomy is far from neutral, for it assumes a view of reality, a view of the person in particular, which is secular,[15] anti-communitarian,[16] and metaphysically libertarian. That is to say, the Court is answering some ultimate philosophical questions in a way that is consistent with the Court's own metaphysical predilections, which are far from neutral. If the Court's members were not so philosophically untutored (with the exception of Justices Scalia and Thomas), it would not be unreasonable to say they were intentionally trying to hoodwink their constituency.

Consider an ironic example. By affirming that human beings are the sort of beings that can be autonomous, the court apparently is presupposing a libertarian view of human freedom, which can be defined in the following way:

> [G]iven choices A and B, I can literally choose to do either one, no circumstances exist that are sufficient to determine my choice, my choice is up to me, and if I do one of them, I could have attempted to have done otherwise. I act as an agent who is the ultimate originator of at least some of my own actions.[17]

But this libertarian view of human freedom, which is apparently a necessary condition for the Court's view of personal autonomy, seems to be best established philosophically by a particular view of the human person, substance dualism,[18] a view that, many philosophers have argued, is inconsistent with mind-body physicalism[19] and property dualism,[20] two views of the human person that deny the independent existence of the soul (or mind). Yet if this is the case, then the court must presuppose a particular view of the human person, which *by definition* excludes other views from the purview of constitutional consideration. Ironically, according to some scholars, substance dualism entails the pro-life (anti-abortion) view that the fetus is a human person. Therefore, one could argue that the Court cannot get its "personal autonomy" justification of abortion rights (or for that matter, physician-assisted suicide, if it chooses to justify it on the same basis as abortion rights) without at the same time implicitly passing negative judgment on certain views of the human person that are associated with secularism and atheism (i.e., mind-body physicalism and property dualism) while implicitly establishing a view of the human person that is not only associated with theistic perspectives (i.e., substance dualism) but also seems to lend support to the claim that fetuses are human persons and that abortion is therefore homicide.[21] Other ethicists have argued that substance dualism also counts against physician assisted suicide as well as active euthanasia in general.[22]

The Court, therefore, in holding up personal autonomy as the basis for deciding not to overturn *Roe*, which it may employ to support physician-assisted suicide as a constitutional right, made a philosophical assumption about the nature of the human person that is *inconsistent with* mind-body physicalism and property dualism, both of which deny libertarian free will,[23] even though the Court claimed that beliefs about such things could not be "formed under compulsion by the State."

It seems, then, that when the courts affirm absolute autonomy in the name of neutrality they are not being neutral at all, but rather, violate their primary reason for this appeal.

(4) *Since Kevorkianism is based on the dubious presumption that suicide ends suffering, Dr. Kevorkian's patients may not be truly acting autonomously.* Mr. Fieger

states in his National Press Club speech: "Make no bones about it; we're involved in a fight here. This is not the right to commit suicide. This is not the right to obtain the right to suicide, physician-assisted suicide. It is the right not to suffer."

Don't forget that Dr. Kevorkian is an agnostic when it comes to questions of ultimate concern. Thus, he does not deny the existence of God or the afterlife, he merely claims that he doesn't know if there is a God or an afterlife. But according to the major Western religious traditions, including the orthodox versions of Christianity, Islam, and Judaism, there is a place of eternal torment for those who are not redeemed. And according to Dr. Kevorkian, since he is an agnostic, there *may be* such a place. In the gospel of Matthew (chap. 25), Jesus says it is reserved for the Devil and his angels as well as those Christ never knew, which may include a large percentage of Dr. Kevorkian's patients. If that is the case, then by assisting in their suicides, the good doctor may be leading them into greater suffering, violating, according to Mr. Fieger, their "right not to suffer." And since Dr. Kevorkian is doing so while admitting he is totally ignorant of the spiritual requirements for entering, let alone knowing the existence or nonexistence of the afterlife, one wonders if one can truly say that his patients are acting autonomously, i.e., making free choices with informed consent.

CONCLUSION

Even though it has support in both the federal courts and the popular culture, Dr. Jack Kevorkian's appeal to absolute autonomy to justify physician-assisted suicide, whether in the social or legal arena, is fatally flawed for at least four reasons: (1) absolute autonomy is based on a dogma for which its proponents typically provide no reason; (2) absolute autonomy is counter-intuitive; (3) when courts appeal to absolute autonomy as a "neutral position" they violate their primary reason for this appeal; and (4) since the appeal to absolute autonomy is motivated by the dubious presumption that suicide ends suffering, Dr. Kevorkian's patients may not be truly acting autonomously.

ENDNOTES

1. For a defense and explanation of the principle of respect for autonomy, see Tom L. Beauchamp and James Childress, *Principles of Biomedical Ethics*, 3d ed. (New York: Oxford, 1989), 67–119.

2. See, for example, Edwin R. Dubose, Ron Hammel, and Laurence J. O'Connell, eds., *A Matter of Principles?: Ferment in U.S. Bioethics* (Valley Forge, Pa.: Trinity Press International, 1994).

3. The question of what constitutes suffering as well as the question of pain management and how each relates to the moral and legal justification of physician-assisted suicide are outside the scope of this paper, though they are vitally important questions. For an informative discussion on these questions as they relate to the legal and political debate, see Robert Spitzer, "The Case Against Active Euthanasia," in *Life and Learning IV: Proceedings of the Fourth*

University Faculty for Life Conference, ed. Joseph Koterski (Washington, D.C.: University Faculty for Life, 1995), 80–97.

4. For example, Beauchamp and Childress write: "Although respecting autonomy is more important than biomedical ethics had appreciated until the last two decades, it is not the only principle and should not be overvalued when it conflicts with other values. . . . In many clinical circumstances the weight of respect for autonomy is minimal, while the weight of nonmalfeasance or beneficence is maximal. Similarly in public policy, the demands of justice can outweigh the demands of respect for autonomy" (Beauchamp and Childress, *Principles of Biomedical Ethics*, 112).

5. See, for example, Spitzer, "The Case Against Active Euthanasia"; John J. Conley, "Libertarian Euthanasia," in *Life and Learning IV*, 73–79; Victor Rosenblum and Clark Forsythe, "The Right to Assisted Suicide: Protection of Autonomy or an Open Door to Social Killing?" in *Do the Right Thing: A Philosophical Dialogue on the Moral and Social Issues of Our Time*, ed. Francis J. Beckwith (Boston: Jones & Bartlett, 1996), 208–21; J. P. Moreland, "James Rachels and the Active Euthanasia Debate," in *Do the Right Thing*, 239–46; and Patricia Wesley, "Dying Safely: An Analysis of 'A Case of Individualized Decision Making' by Timothy E. Quill, M.D.," in *Do the Right Thing*, 251–61.

6. Justices Sandra Day O'Connor, Anthony Kennedy, and David Souter in "Planned Parenthood v. Casey (1992)," in *The Abortion Controversy: A Reader*, eds. Louis P. Pojman and Francis J. Beckwith (Boston: Jones & Bartlett, 1994), 54.

7. Hadley Arkes, "A Pride of Bootless Friends: Some Melancholy Reflections on the Current State of the Pro-Life Movement," in *Life and Learning IV*, 19.

8. As quoted in Russell Hittinger, "A Crisis of Legitimacy," *First Things: A Monthly Journal of Religion and Public Life* 67 (November 1996): 26.

9. As quoted in Timothy Egan, "Federal Judge Says Ban on Suicide Aid is Unconstitutional," *The New York Times*, 5 May 1994, sec. A, 24.

10. Ronald Dworkin, "When Is It Right to Die?" *The New York Times*, 17 May 1994, sec. A, 19.

11. Hittinger, "A Crisis of Legitimacy," 26.

12. Ibid.

13. Ibid.

14. Ibid. In his article, Hittinger cites other cases as well as showing how the courts have arrived at their present state. See also Robert H. Bork "Our Judicial Oligarchy," in *First Things: A Monthly Journal of Religion and Public Life* 67 (November 1996): 21–24; and Hadley Arkes, "A Culture Corrupted," in *First Things: A Monthly Journal of Religion and Public Life* 67 (November 1996): 30–33.

15. The Supreme Court's bias in favor of secularism is made clear in recent comments made by Justice Anthony Kennedy, who said that it is a religious belief to hold that "there is an ethic and morality which transcend human invention" (as quoted in Hittinger, "A Crisis of Legitimacy," 27). It is not very difficult to imagine the Court, using Justice Kennedy's reasoning, to dismiss out of hand any ethical position which does not assume naturalism as a worldview on the basis that it violates the Establishment Clause of the First Amendment. The Court could then ignore, rather than take the time to refute, the arguments put forth by the proponents of a nonnaturalistic ethical position. So, in theory, the Court, on the basis of metaphysical bias alone without the benefit of reasoned argument, can dismiss an ethical view that may be more philosophically and

constitutionally justified in comparison to its rivals merely because it does not presuppose the truth of naturalism. This is intellectual fascism.

16. In his critique of John Rawls' political philosophy, Michael Sandel makes a similar point by arguing that Rawls' view of the person (which Sandel refers to as "the unencumbered self"), far from being the neutral view that Rawls claims, is anti-communitarian. See Michael Sandel, *Liberalism and the Limits of Justice* (New York: Cambridge University, 1982). See also Sandel's popular treatment of how this view of the self has negatively affected American political discourse, *Democracy's Discontent* (Cambridge, Mass.: Harvard University Press, 1996), as well as Mary Ann Glendon, *Rights Talk: The Impoverishment of Political Discourse* (New York: The Free Press, 1991).

17. J. P. Moreland, "A Defense of the Substance Dualist View of the Soul," *Christian Perspectives on Being Human: A Multidisciplinary Approach to Integration*, ed. J. P. Moreland and David M. Ciocchi (Grand Rapids: Baker, 1993), 71.

18. On this matter, John Mitchell and Scott B. Rae write that "a necessary condition for libertarian free will is the existence of an agent (e.g., agent-causation or noncausal agent theory); and a substance ontology of the agent is arguably a necessary condition for agency theory" (John A. Mitchell and Scott B. Rae, "The Moral Status of Fetuses and Embryos," in *The Silent Subject: Reflections on the Unborn in American Culture*, ed. Brad Stetson [Westport, Conn.: Praeger, 1996], 22). Because a defense of substance dualism is outside the scope of this paper, see Moreland, "A Defense of the Substance Dualist View of the Soul," and J. P. Moreland, "A Contemporary Defense of Dualism." In *Philosophy: The Quest for Truth* (3d ed., ed. Louis P. Pojman [Belmont, Calif.: Wadsworth, 1996], Moreland defines substance dualism in the following way: "Substance dualism holds that the brain is a physical substance that has physical properties and the soul is a mental substance that has mental properties. When I am in pain, the brain has certain physical (e.g., electrical, chemical) properties, and the soul has certain mental properties (the conscious awareness of pain). The soul is the possessor of these experiences. It stands behind, over, and above them and remains the same throughout my life. The soul and the brain can interact with each other, but they are different entities with different properties" (Moreland, "A Defense of the Substance Dualist View of the Soul," 61).

19. Mind-body physicalism is the view that the human person is merely a physical brain with no mental properties as well as no underlying nonphysical substance or human nature. "The only things that exist are physical substances, properties, and events. When it comes to humans, the physical substance is the body or brain and central nervous system. The physical substance called the brain has physical properties, such as weight, volume, size, electrical activity, chemical composition, and so forth" (Moreland, "A Defense of the Substance Dualist View of the Soul," 58–59).

20. Proponents of property-dualism assert that "there are some physical substances that have only physical properties. A billiard ball is hard and round. In addition, there are no mental substances. But there is one material substance that has both physical *and* mental properties—the brain. . . . The brain is the possessor of all mental properties. I am not a mental self that *has* my thoughts and experiences. Rather, I am a brain and a series or bundle of successive experiences themselves" (Moreland, "A Defense of the Substance Dualist View of the Soul," 60).

21. For a defense of substance dualism as it pertains to the human personhood of the fetus, *see* Mitchell and Rae, "The Moral Status of Fetuses and Embryos";

and J. P. Moreland and John Mitchell, "Is the Human Person a Substance or a Property-Thing?" *Ethics & Medicine* 11 no. 3 (1995): 50–55.

22. For a defense of substance dualism as it pertains to the question of physician-assisted suicide, see J. P. Moreland, "Humanness, Personhood, and the Right to Die," *Faith and Philosophy* 12, no. 1 (January 1995): 95–112; and Scott B. Rae, "Views of Human Nature at the Edges of Life: Personhood and Medical Ethics" in *Christian Perspectives on Being Human*, 235–56.

23. On this matter, Moreland points out that "if physicalism is true, then determinism is true as well. If I am just a physical system, there is nothing in me that has the capacity to freely choose to do something. Material systems, at least large scale ones, change over time in deterministic fashion according to the initial conditions of the system and the laws of chemistry and physics" (Moreland, "A Defense of the Substance Dualist View of the Soul," 71). Concerning property dualism, Moreland states that since this view maintains that mental properties are the result of physical causes (whether one takes an epiphenomenal or a state-state causation view), mental states (or mental agents) do not cause anything but are themselves caused by physical events. Consequently, human beings are not truly free moral agents (ibid., 71–73).

An Overview

The contemporary cultural trend toward the acceptance of physician-assisted suicide and euthanasia represents a major philosophical shift in the understanding and practice of medicine. This shift, if fully accepted, will have far-reaching ramifications, which will affect everyone. Though advocates speak of "choice" and "autonomy," they do so to the neglect or abandonment of such principles as "justice" and "equality." Those who advocate and practice physician-assisted suicide, whatever their motive, abandon the foundational principles of society, medicine, morality, and theology. The result is, then, not healing medicine, but homicidal medicine. It is lethal not only to individuals but to the very foundation and structure of society. Such beliefs have consequences and this one affects us all.

Chapter Fifteen

HOMICIDAL MEDICINE

John M. Dolan

IT IS A CURIOUS AND FRIGHTENING circumstance that some of the most dramatic changes in our social order in recent decades have altered the conditions under which it is deemed legitimate for one human being to declare another dead, to allow another person to die, to hasten another person's death, or, indeed, directly to cause another person's death. One example of these striking changes is the widespread adoption of brain-death criteria of death, motivated in part by the goal of facilitating the use of organs in the best possible condition from donors declared dead, a goal that comprehends the more specific aim of sanctioning the removal of a beating human heart from one person in order to transplant it into the body of another.[1] The legalization and widespread practice of induced abortion is another example of the radical changes here at issue, and the headlong rush toward routinized euthanasia and assisted suicide is still another.

One task of philosophy is to step back from the turbulent surge of events around us in order to strive for a more accurate understanding than is achievable in the midst of the rush of our daily lives. In the present essay we accept this task. Another task of philosophy is to search for insight into the ways in which we should order our lives. As Plato writes in Book 1 of his *Republic*, "No light matter is at issue; the question concerns the very manner in which human life is to be lived."[2] Embracing this second task as well, we shall set forth an analysis of euthanasia and assisted suicide, the aim of which is to illuminate a specific fundamental disorder essentially involved in those practices.

Among the most radical of the changes alluded to above are those that involve altering or completely abandoning long-standing prohibitions of lethal assaults against human life. Tinkering with such prohibitions is plainly grave business since prohibitions of lethal assaults against human life are fundamental in morality and in the legal systems of every social order. The depth at which such prohibitions lie is powerfully brought out by a passage in Thomas DeQuincey:

> If once a man indulges himself in murder, he thinks little of robbing and from robbing he comes next to drinking and Sabbath-breaking and from thence to incivility and procrastination.[3]

Here is a dreadful downward spiral indeed! From murder to robbery. From robbery to drinking and Sabbath-breaking. From drinking and Sabbath-breaking to the very depths of depravity: incivility and procrastination! These are grave dangers indeed! The hilarity of being warned against murder on the ground that it can lead to incivility and procrastination underscores the fundamental character of the prohibition against murder. The laughter DeQuincey's passage provokes teaches us that as we approach the prohibition of murder, we approach moral bedrock.

Very briefly, the plan of the present essay is first to argue that our usual homicide statistics are at fault, omitting many deliberate killings that must be taken into account by anyone hoping to form an accurate picture of our present practices. After presenting some evidence concerning one of many hundreds of thousands of deliberate killings omitted from the usual statistics, we carry out some rough calculations that shed light on the distance we have traveled toward becoming what might be termed a "homicidal society." Next, we consider a particular line of argument frequently used to justify one class of deliberate homicides: the appeal to reciprocity. We argue that the appeal in question is illegitimate. Next, recalling arguments and analyses we have set forth at greater length elsewhere,[4] we examine a peculiar blunder committed in efforts to involve physicians in such practices as euthanasia and assisted suicide. Having done that, we develop a novel argument concerning euthanasia and assisted suicide that underscores a painful dilemma faced by advocates of those practices. Finally, after remarking on an astonishing feature of the various movements toward legalizing brain death criteria, induced abortion, euthanasia, and assisted suicide, namely, their stark inegalitarianism, we draw the present essay to a close.

We turn, first, to consider the question whether there may be a fault in the manner in which we keep our death statistics.

OUR STATISTICS ARE AT FAULT

If we consult one of the most recent and authoritative volumes on the topic of homicide, Carl Malmquist's *Homicide: A Psychiatric Perspective*,[5] we discover at the outset a definition of homicide derived from the *Uniform Crime Report* (UCR):[6] "the willful, non-negligent killing of one human being by another person or group." This definition excludes what some would designate "auto-homicide," or suicide. As elaborated and interpreted in the *Uniform Crime Report*, the definition also excludes deaths due to negligence, attempted but failed killings, assaults that unintentionally lead to death, accidental deaths, and justifiable homicides (homicides carried out in the course of legitimate self-defense or as executions of prisoners convicted of capital offense).

Adopting this definition for the purpose of his investigations, Dr. Malmquist cites the *Uniform Crime Report*'s figure for the number of homicides in the United States each year: 22,000 to 24,000. But, this figure is, unfortunately, not even a remote approximation of the truth. In the course of his celebrated "Resistance to Civil Government," Henry Thoreau writes,

> Our statistics are at fault: the population has been returned too large! How many men are there to a thousand square miles in this country? Hardly one.[7]

Thoreau makes his point with hyperbole. But it is possible to speak here with (apologies for the expression) deadly literalness if we say:

> Our statistics are at fault: the homicide figure has been returned too small! How many homicides are there each year in this country? Vastly more than the 24,000 reported by the *Uniform Crime Report*.

The grounds for this assertion have nothing to do with a kind of case that intrigues readers of murder mysteries: one in which a homicide is carried out but disguised so that it resembles an accidental death or a death from natural causes. Undoubtedly such homicides take place. For obvious reasons, the exact figure is unknown. It is what sociologists call "a dark number." But the number of such cases is dwarfed by the total of the homicides omitted by our usual statistics. The homicides omitted by the *Uniform Crime Report* far outstrip those actually recorded in the *Report*. The omitted homicides belong to a vast class of deliberate killings that prompt the oxymoronic title of the present essay: "Homicidal Medicine."

A STUNNING SUICIDE

On 17 August in 1996, a man went into the carport of his modest home in Missouri and hung himself. That suicide was directly linked to a homicide of the sort omitted by the *Uniform Crime Report*. The man who killed himself in August of 1996 had, over a prolonged period of time and in a very public manner, fought for the right to perform what his opponents regarded as a rather disgusting act of homicide. Joe Cruzan, who was 63 when he killed himself, had battled in the courts for the right to bring about the death of his daughter Nancy Beth by means of dehydration and starvation. The case went to the Supreme Court, which dealt Mr. Cruzan a setback by ruling in 1990 that a state has the right to require, as Missouri does, that a standard of clear and convincing evidence be satisfied before anyone acts on the presumption that a patient would have wanted food and water cut off.[8] By a miracle, after the court ruled against Cruzan, witnesses were located who, apparently having been in some form of prolonged hibernation during the long nationally publicized battle over Nancy Beth's fate, stepped forward and provided testimony to the effect that, yes, they had heard quite definite and carefully considered statements from Nancy, which entailed that she would have preferred to be put to death by dehydration and starvation rather than live in a state of severe disability. On the basis of this new testimony, a Missouri court ruled that Joe Cruzan could proceed with his lethal project, and just after Christmas 1990, Nancy Beth Cruzan died of dehydration and starvation. In recent years, Mr. Cruzan had expressed public doubts about the rightness of what he had done to his daughter. It is possible that his suicide represents his final grim verdict on his earlier decision. A man who elects to solve even one problem by killing may find John Updike's observation to be true: "Death, once let in, leaves his bloody footprints everywhere."[9]

If Joe Cruzan did come to view his cutting off his daughter's food and water as murder, his hard-won and belated perception amounts to a recognition of the soundness of a judgment Pietr Admiraal passed when he was in this country seven years ago. Admiraal, one of the leading advocates of euthanasia in the Netherlands, a man who has killed many patients, upset bioethicists and hospital ethics committee members in Minnesota in the course of a visit in 1989 by turning out to be more conservative and protective of human life than were they. They were shocked to hear him say that he would not kill an incompetent patient, a practice they had long since accepted as morally permissible, indeed, desirable. Hearing that Admiraal would not kill a patient incapable of consent, one of the local physicians, a man who, by his own reckoning, can boast of a fairly substantial body count, exclaimed: "But, they're the ones that suffer the most!" Admiraal further upset his Minnesota audience by telling them that the American practice of causing death by deliberate dehydration and starvation is just as much killing as his killing by lethal injection, but that it is a cruel and inhumane method of homicide that he would never use. His auditors could have sat with comfortable smirks on their faces had such a condemnation of their preferred method of euthanasia been delivered by Mother Teresa or a priest or rabbi, but coming from a self-acknowledged killer whose moral coarseness matched their own, it stung.

Now it is interesting and important to ask: "How many homicides like the one that claimed Nancy Beth Cruzan's life take place each year in the United States?" How many persons die in the United States each year because they are severely disabled or otherwise gravely afflicted and someone decides to cut off their food and water in order to cause their deaths, or to withhold treatment, or to administer a lethal dosage of drugs? That is, how many people die each year in the United States as the result of an act of euthanasia? In order to eliminate unclarity concerning the question that is being asked here, we recall the definition of euthanasia we have presented (and defended at length) elsewhere: "Euthanasia is any act or deliberate omission undertaken with the specific intention of causing the death of another creature and actually causing that death, where the agent acts or deliberately forbears from action on the basis of a conviction that the death being caused will be good for the creature who is being killed." [10]

SOME DISTURBING EVIDENCE

Quite obviously, enormous problems (conceptual, methodological, legal, and so on) attend the task of obtaining accurate information about the current euthanasia rate in the United States. The inevitable disagreements over which deaths to count as deaths by euthanasia would stem from many sources. Many reasonable observers would naturally count the death of Nancy Beth Cruzan as death from euthanasia. Others would insist that it was merely a case of "discontinuing treatment" (the provision of food and water) in accordance with what was known of the wishes of the patient. Joe Cruzan, who had six years to contemplate the reality of his "discontinuing his daughter's treatment," appears to have found himself unable to continue believing the propagandistic descriptions of his deed, which were circulated by those who were his allies in his lethal project. Propagandistic talk about "discontinuing treatment," "choice in dying," "death with dignity," and "allowing Nancy to die" cannot cancel some simple truths. His daughter was alive. He waged a fight to cut off her food and water. He won his fight. Her food and water were cut off. And his daughter died, slowly from dehydration and malnutrition. ("Those who die from famine, die by inches.") One who refuses to count Nancy Beth Cruzan's death as a homicide is faced with the daunting task of deciding on a correct entry for her death certificate.

It is worth observing that any remotely plausible guess we arrive at concerning the euthanasia rate in the United States is likely to be nearer the truth than the implicit estimate of the *Uniform Crime Report*. That implicit estimate is zero, a figure we would know to be false even if our knowledge were confined to newspaper reports and court cases. Had we the resources of intellect required to emulate that master of cunning estimates—Enrico Fermi, the celebrated physicist who frequently astounded colleagues by producing remarkably accurate estimates of figures he had no right to know—we could produce a masterly argument defending a precise estimation of the euthanasia rate in this country. But, fortunately, it is not necessary to possess the extraordinary skill of Fermi, to outdo the *Uniform Crime Report*.

The episode mentioned above, in which physicians and ethics committee members in a typical American city were unhappy to discover that a medical killer from abroad was more conservative and more protective of innocent human life than they and unwilling to employ their favored method of euthanasia (deliberate dehydration and starvation), is itself a strong piece of evidence concerning the extent to which euthanasia was already fairly routinized in the United States in the year that meeting took place, 1989.

A great volume of additional relevant evidence has reached the present author simply because he happens to be an officer of a medical ethics program that studies the status of vulnerable persons under various health care systems and is known in its community to do so. Here we will set forth a tiny fraction of that additional evidence bearing on the prevalence of euthanasia.

One of the first death's by deliberate starvation and dehydration that reached public consciousness did so in mid-1985 and took place in the Minneapolis-St. Paul area. It was the death of Ella Bathurst, which had taken place in October of 1984. A young couple from St. Paul (with whom this writer later had a chance to converse) witnessed the killing. They had been horrified when they entered their grandmother's hospital room and saw that her roommate, Ella Bathurst, had no IV line or other tubes, was brought no trays of food at mealtimes, wasn't even being given water, and was, from time to time, moaning a word that was not the name "Walter," as they first thought, but rather, the word "water." Still, because they were seeing all this in a prestigious hospital, it did not occur to them that they might be witnessing a murder. We know about the homicide only because the young couple were prompted to report it after seeing a television program on euthanasia in June of 1985 and realizing the death of Ella Bathurst by dehydration and starvation, which they had witnessed, had been a case of homicide in a medical setting. They contacted one of the pro-life persons they had seen on the television program, and that individual assisted them in making reports to various governmental bodies responsible for the protection of vulnerable patients. One of those bodies, the Office of Health Facilities Complaints, responded by carrying out an investigation, which confirmed the young couple's report. What action was taken? The hospital was held by the Office of Health Facilities Complaints to have acted wrongly in two respects: (1) it did not have a written "supportive care only" policy; and (2) in the case in question, the patient had not been involved in her health care plan. Calling a plan to cut off food and water from a patient who is not terminally ill a "health care plan" is like calling the aerial bombardment of a city "an urban renewal project." Orwell, in his most satirically inventive moments, could not have created more bitterly ironic "Newspeak." What cause of death was written on Ella Bathurst's death certificate? "Respiratory failure." A hospital staff carries out a deliberate killing by dehydration and malnutrition, a procedure resulting in the death of an innocent and defenseless elderly woman who never consented to such mistreatment. And what is the response of the Office of Health Facility Complaints? It censures the hospital for not having a written "supportive care only" policy and for failing to involve the victim in her "health care plan." Ella Bathurst was, indeed, not involved in the formulation of the "health care plan" that caused her death and was intended to cause her death. One can be confident that the hospital at which she was killed formulated a written "supportive care only" policy very soon after being called to task for lacking one. One can be equally confident that, over the past thirteen years, other patients have, under that policy, met the same fate as Ella Bathurst.

Another episode sheds dramatic light on the rapidity of change that is underway. It took place at a disability rights conference in 1991. There the present author and a colleague conducted a session devoted to ethical evaluation of the practice of withholding food and water from nonterminally ill patients. A woman in attendance at that session arose during the discussion period and identified herself as a speech therapist who, after some years working in nursing homes, had taken an extended leave to bear and raise children and had returned to her professional work that spring when her youngest child had joined the older ones in attending school for full-day sessions. She stated that she was shocked to discover the changes that had taken place since she last worked in nursing homes. "They're cutting off tube feeding and not even bothering to test whether the patient's swallow reflex can be restored." Tube feeding is often initiated, not because the nursing home resident is incapable of swallowing, but because tube feeding is easier and less expensive to carry out (and also avoids the risk of aspiration attendant on manually assisted feeding). If a nursing home resident's swallow reflex has been weakened by prolonged tube feeding, that reflex can usually be restored without much difficulty. The newly instituted practices, which so troubled the returning speech therapist, were clearly not simple decisions about how best to care for a patient on tube feeding. They amounted to the adoption of a method of euthanasia rejected even by such a person as Pietr Admiraal.

Still another episode, which took place after the one just mentioned, gives a more startling glimpse of the distance we have traveled down the path to routinized euthanasia. This episode involves a fairly well-attended conference devoted to medical ethics, which took place in Minnesota. At one of the sessions, a medical social worker explained to a largely sympathetic audience that the staff at her nursing homes found families generally willing to cut off tube feeding. The sticking point for a number of them, she reported, was cutting off hydration. Many families, she said, were "uncomfortable" about cutting off water. But she was pleased to report that she and her colleagues had discovered a way to overcome this discomfort.

> We've found that it's best to leave the IV in place and ask the family "What level of hydration are you comfortable with? 10 cc an hour? 10 cc a day?"

This is breathtaking. One recalls a time when medical workers spoke of placing a patient on a "Hollywood Code," which meant that the staff was to go through the motions of responding if the patient went into cardiac arrest but was to do so in slow motion, to make a show of responding while the patient, in fact, died. Now we have entered a new era, an era in which patients are provided with "Hollywood Hydration." Moreover, cutting off food and water is such a common event that the staff of one nursing home has developed an effective technique for overcoming reluctance or moral "discomfort" on the part of families and gaining their consent to the procedure of killing their loved one by dehydration. The patient is in fact killed in this way, while the staff makes a show of providing water. Even worse, the current atmosphere is such that the medical social worker has not the slightest compunction about describing this technique for getting families to consent to killing by dehydration to an audience of health professionals at a conference open to anyone prepared to pay a modest registration fee. The entire remainder of the space allotted to this essay by the editors could be filled with further accounts comparable to those just set forth, but we must draw our narration of these episodes to a close.

SOME SOBERING CALCULATIONS

Studies conducted by Carl Kjellstrand and other nephrologists suggest that one-fifth to one-quarter of all deaths in dialysis patients in the United States and Canada result from deliberate cessation of dialysis and that, in a significant number of those cases, the patients are not in a position to consent to the cut-off. Here, it is important to bear in mind that, even those cases where consent was at least a theoretical possibility, it may not have been obtained and, in any case, even if it was obtained, it may have been imperfect or to some degree coerced. A chronically ill patient may be denied the full respect of the staff, may be feeling a "burden" on his or her family, and may be subject to a host of tacit and explicit pressures to "get out of the way." This means that the task of posthumously determining whether or not euthanasia figured in a given death is extremely difficult and that the death rate from nonvoluntary cessation of dialysis may, in fact, be considerably higher than the rate reported by Kjellstrand and others. The Remmelink Report in the Netherlands in 1990 asserted that the euthanasia rate in the Netherlands was 2.6 percent, but the actual data accompanying the report made clear that the actual euthanasia rate in that country was at least 20 percent in the year in question. And once again, that figure is probably low, since deaths that do not seem to be instances of euthanasia on their face might, upon inspection, turn out to be cases of euthanasia. If the current euthanasia rate in this country is at the level recorded in the Netherlands in 1990, that form of homicide is claiming 430,000 lives here each year. Even if the euthanasia rate at this moment is half the rate in Holland seven years ago (probably a wildly optimistic hope), euthanasia is claiming 215,000 lives each year, or *nine times* the UCR's figure for homicide.

To form a rough idea as to our present circumstances, let us take the most recent year for which relevant health statistics are available, 1994. In that year, according to the standard sources for such information, we had the following figures concerning life and death in the United States:

Total Deaths:	2,268,553[11]
Total Births:	3,952,767[12]
Total Suicides:	31,142
Total Homicides:	23,400[13]

The total of 2,268,553 deaths supplied by the National Center for Health Statistics omits certain deaths. Indeed, it omits a very large number of deaths likely to be of interest to a student who is as interested in the moral health of a society as in the degree of physical well-being enjoyed by its members. The total in question does not take into account deaths caused by induced abortion, deaths due to miscarriage, or deaths due to euthanasia.

One of these figures is available from other public health census data, namely, the total number of induced abortions in any given year. In 1994, the figure was 1.2 million, which is both surprising and encouraging, since induced abortions had been averaging about 1.5 million a year for quite a while in the United States. In 1993, there was an unexpected drop to 1.3 million. The drop in 1994 is equally unexpected.

The second of the three figures customarily omitted from the death statistics is the total of spontaneous abortions or miscarriages in a given year, the number of natural deaths in utero. This is a figure we must take into account if we want ultimately to calculate the ratio of deliberate killings to natural deaths, since a spontaneous abortion or miscarriage is simply a natural death in utero. The total of such deaths can be calculated with at least a rough degree of accuracy if we know the total births in a given year and have a plausible approximation of the rate of miscarriage in the year in question. The most recent year for which we have the statistics is 1994. The total number of live births that year was 3,952,767. We'll treat that as 3.95 million. An assumed spontaneous abortion rate of 20 percent means that 3.95 million is 80 percent of the actual number of pregnancies in 1994, which implies that there were, in fact, a total of 4.94 million pregnancies that year. This, in turn, suggests that there were about .988 million miscarriages that year. This estimate of the number of miscarriages in 1994 is, very likely, conservative. Rounding off, we have the following figures for 1994:

Total Induced Abortions: 1,200,000
Total Miscarriages: 1,000,000

These figures imply that an unborn child stands a substantially greater risk of being deliberately killed in utero than of dying a natural death there. In fact, these figures teach us the alarming fact that more than a third of the children conceived in the United States die or are deliberately killed while in the womb.

It remains for us to venture a guess as to the number of persons who died as a result of euthanasia in 1994. This is more difficult. We have already seen that some of our doctors are killing patients and even employing a method of killing rejected by one of the leading medical killers in the Netherlands. Suppose we adopt the somewhat optimistic hypothesis that the euthanasia rate in the United States in 1994 was half the rate that had obtained in the Netherlands four years earlier. This is to adopt the hypothesis that the euthanasia rate in this country was 10 percent in 1994. Notice that this figure is less than half the euthanasia rate reported in studies of deaths in U.S. dialysis patients. On this reckoning, the number of deaths in 1994 due to euthanasia would be 230,000, or about ten times the total of homicides recorded in the *Uniform Crime Report*. If the euthanasia rate in the United States in 1994 was the same as the rate that had obtained in the Netherlands four years earlier and thus at the lower end of the level reported for U.S. dialysis patients, then the death toll from euthanasia in 1994 was 460,000 or roughly twenty times the number of homicides reported in the *Uniform Crime Report*.

Working with the more optimistic assumed euthanasia rate of 10 percent, we have the following figures for deliberate homicides in the United States in 1994:

Abortion Deaths: 1.2 Million
Euthanasia: 230,000*
Suicide: 31,000
Homicide (UCR):   23,000

Total 1.5 Million

If the euthanasia rate in 1994 was 20 percent, then the totals for deliberate homicides that year were:

Abortion Deaths:	1.2 Million
Euthanasia:	460,000*
Suicide:	31,000
Homicide (UCR):	23,000

Total 1.7 Million

These are large numbers. Given the reliability of the abortion figure, they make clear that deliberate homicide is the leading cause of death in the United States, and they convey the chilling portend that we may be on a path taking us to a point at which an absolute majority of all deaths in a given year will be the result of deliberate homicide. Consider the figures just set out in the context of the total number of deaths in utero and ex utero in 1994. That total is, roughly, as follows:

Total Deaths: 1.2 million (induced ab) + 1 million (spon. ab) + 2.3 million (other) = 4.5 Million

Thus, even taking the more conservative and optimistic of the two euthanasia rate estimates, we have the result that one-third of all deaths in 1994 were deliberate killings. On the less conservative, and possibly more accurate assumption of a 20 percent euthanasia rate, we have the result that 38 percent of all deaths in 1994 were deliberate killings. Pope John Paul II's description of current societies as embodying a "Culture of Death"[14] seems grimly warranted by these figures. And what name should be bestowed on a society that achieves the sinister distinction of reaching a point where more than half of its deaths each year are the result of deliberate killings? Perhaps the title "Homicidal Society" would be in order.

Now that federal judges in the Second and Ninth Circuits have invalidated assisted suicide laws on constitutional grounds and one of them (the ninth)—in a headlong effort to establish the *Roe v. Wade* of euthanasia, asserting that there is an absolute constitutional right to physician-assisted suicide,—and the Supreme Court is about to decide whether or not the constitution is, in the phrase of Daniel Avila, some form of suicide pact,[15] it might be in order to carry out the hard work needed to determine the actual euthanasia rate in this country. In any case, no thoughtful observer can be complacent in the face of the vast (if not yet accurately calculated) number of deliberate homicides and of a climate in which people are clamoring loudly to increase the number of deliberate homicides and pretending to find constitutional grounds for the murder of those already born to match the fictitious legal grounds already constructed to justify the destruction of the unborn.

THE LIMITS OF RECIPROCITY

We turn now to an idea that pervades parables, religious scriptures, stories, poetry, novels, epistles, proverbs, folk tales, legends, legal briefs, opinion pieces, letters to the editor, sermons, editorials, ethical treatises, philosophical monographs, and the rest of the world's moral, religious, and political literature. The idea is that the mark of justice is reciprocity. According to this idea, the test of the justice of an action is the question whether the agent would be willing to be on the receiving end of the deed he or she is performing. Moral agents are invited to view and to assess moral transactions from the perspectives of each of the several persons involved in them, each of the persons participating in or affected by them.

The most familiar and perhaps the most ancient formulation of the doctrine of reciprocity in our Western tradition is the Golden Rule:

Do unto others as you would have them do unto you.

In the Old Testament book of Judges, Samson is questioned as to why he slew a large number of Philistines; according to the King James translation, he replies,

As they did unto me, so have I done unto them." (Judg. 15:11)

This reply suggests that the idea of reciprocity as a standard of justice is already a commonplace, although Samson's specific formulation is closer to a deformed version of the Golden Rule we shall consider below than to the standard version quoted above. A formulation of the Golden Rule in Luke 6:31, reads: "As ye would that men should do to you, do ye also to them likewise" (KJV). Another, even more ancient, version of the Golden Rule is submerged amid the treasures of Chinese civilization. It is known as the "Silver Rule"[16] and states as follows: "Do *not* do unto others what you would find hateful if it were done to you."

Each of these rules clearly involves counterfactual reasoning for its application. To decide what you *should* do now, you must consider what you *would want* to be the case if you were, contrary to present fact, in the circumstances of one of the other parties in the transaction that is underway.

Observe, further, the contrast in thickness between the two rules. The Golden Rule is the thicker of the two in that it requires the conferral of positive benefits in cases where you *would* desire the conferral of benefits were the tables turned. The Silver Rule does not require the conferral of benefits: it bids us to *abstain* from actions that we *would* find hateful if they were directed against us.

The idea of reciprocity is also at work in a maxim sometimes attributed to Americans Indians: "Do not judge a man until you have walked a mile in his moccasins." And Abraham Lincoln writes,

As I would not be a slave, so I would not be a master. That expresses my idea of democracy.

Many readers of the present volume are familiar with the spectacular application of reciprocity in Matthew 25:40, which invites the agent to imagine, not that he or she is in the place of the other party, but rather that Christ is in that place:

> Inasmuch as ye have done it to one of the least of these my brethren, ye have done it unto me. (KJV)

The concept of reciprocity plays a central role in the theories of the philosopher John Rawls.[17] According to Rawls, the question whether a social system is just is answered by carrying out a vast thought experiment. His test requires you to view the social system whose justice is in question from the perspective of each of the social roles or offices defined within it. You are required to consider the question: If I were in this position, what would my prospects be and would I be willing to accept them? Would I find them acceptable? Only if you are willing to accept the lot that would be yours within each of the representative positions within the social system can you call the system just. Readiness to accept the treatment that a social system accords each of the representative persons under it can be expected, according to Rawls, only when the system satisfies what he calls the "Difference Principle,"[18] which holds that inequalities in the distributions of any of the goods that arise from social cooperation (income, wealth, privileges of office, and so on) are unjust and, thus, unacceptable, unless they arise from a system that maximizes the expectations of the least advantaged representative persons.

Most readers will have encountered various "deformed" versions of the Golden Rule. On some occasions, these sinister-sounding formulations are put forward in a spirit of jest. On others, they are uttered in deadly earnest. One deformed version reads: "Do unto others *before* they do unto you." Another, not a moral rule but rather an observation concerning human affairs, states: "He who has the gold, rules."

Two high-ranking American officials advanced a deformed "Golden Rule" in dead earnest. Walter Isaacson reports that, in the course of a conversation with Golda Meir, Richard Nixon, whose policies in Southeast Asia are viewed by some as war crimes and who resigned the presidency over a minor burglary at a Washington apartment building, said, "My rule in international affairs is 'Do unto others as they would do unto you,'" at which point, Henry Kissinger, also complicit in the United States aggression in Southeast Asia, promptly interjected, "Plus ten percent."[19]

The most daring application of the idea of reciprocity known to the present writer is inscribed on a gravestone in England. The inscription reads,

> Here lies Martin Engelbrodde
> Ha'e mercy on my soul, Lord God,
> As I would do were I Lord God,
> And Thou wert Martin Engelbrodde.[20]

This is bold. It seems clear that Martin Engelbrodde was either an atheist or a man with great confidence in God's sense of humor.

Now the connection between reciprocity and euthanasia that concerns us in the present context is this: Again and again in the debate on euthanasia and assisted suicide, you find individuals justifying lethal assaults by making a particularly perverted application of reciprocity. Because their hatred and fear of disability are so powerful that they are convinced that they themselves would wish to be destroyed if a certain degree of disability were ever to afflict them, these individuals are convinced that they are acting with perfect justice if they advocate or carry out euthanasia or assisted suicide. Their belief that they would wish to be destroyed if they ever become severely disabled may well be wrong, as a matter of fact. But, anyway, they are convinced that they would rather be dead and would seek their own destruction if they were ever seriously disabled. Notice that, even if we assume that they are correct about the degree of their own fear and hatred of disability, nothing whatever follows about their gaining authority to destroy anyone who is in a state of severe disability.

> Do *not* do unto others as you would have them do unto you if your fear and hatred of disability are so severe that you are convinced that you would seek your own destruction if you ever became disabled.

Whatever its utility in other areas of human conduct, the standard of reciprocity is an unreliable guide when we approach the decisions and judgments called for by the cases that prompt some persons to opt for euthanasia or assisted suicide. In this particular vast range of cases, reciprocity is a most unreliable guide to the requirements of justice.

CONTRAFACTUM INTERRUPTUM

Before we proceed to consider a fascinating dilemma faced by those who are bent on institutionalizing euthanasia and assisted suicide, it will repay our time to look at the language of all those who participate in arguments over euthanasia and assisted suicide. Irrespective of the side they take in the controversy, these participants talk about "the doctor," "the physician," "the patient," "medicine." But, if euthanasia or assisted suicide is at issue, the deliberate ending of a human life, how do *doctors* get into the act?

It is remarkable that nearly everyone, whether in favor of assisted suicide or opposed to it, agrees with Viktor Brack, one of the architects of the Nazi euthanasia program, that "the needle belongs in the hand of the doctor."[21] Both sides of the assisted suicide debate make clear that what they are arguing for or against is a practice in which physicians are involved in killing or arranging for the killing of patients. But the assumption that any established practice of euthanasia or assisted suicide will necessarily place physicians in a central role involves an interestingly flawed use of counterfactual reasoning. Our task in the present section is to describe that flawed counterfactual reasoning.

To begin with, we can ask *why* the Nazi Brack and everyone else contemplating euthanasia and assisted suicide naturally assumes that "The needle belongs in the hand of the doctor." If the killing is going to go on, doctors will do it or at the very least oversee and supervise. Why?

The fact that doctors have technical skills that could, theoretically, enable them to kill people is a poor candidate as an explication. It would be a mistake to expect physicians to be especially good at killing; the task conflicts too radically with their pledged aim. We could expect to find a great deal more straightforward killing capacity if we were to turn to former members of Central American death squads, retired underworld hit men, or even veterinarians (who have some training at least in the task of killing large mammals). The circumstance under which a doctor's technical skills might admit of lethal perversions does not explain why so many people assume that a practice of assisted suicide would involve killing by doctors. Neither is this curious assumption explained by the circumstance that the overwhelming majority of deaths now occur in institutional settings (nursing homes and hospitals) with the result that doctors are often on the scene or in the vicinity when death takes place. This fact, by itself, cannot explain why some people want to assign the task of killing to doctors. Many professions are represented in the institutional settings where most deaths occur: nurses, social workers, chaplains, administrators, janitorial staff, and even attorneys and philosophers. Yet one hears no outcry for any of these persons to assume the role of killer.

Astonishingly, hilariously, heartbreakingly, a principal reason why people want to assign the task of killing to doctors is this: *We trust them.* For millennia, physicians have dedicated themselves to the maintenance, protection, restoration, enhancement, and preservation of human health and life. For millennia, we have turned to them for counsel when facing solemn decisions affecting life and death. But adducing these facts as grounds for entrusting the authority to kill to doctors involves a spectacular blunder of thought, a blunder overlooked by logicians in the course of the centuries as they assigned compact, vivid names to various blunders of reasoning in order to help us remember and avoid them. The catalog of blunders that has grown up is most impressive: the fallacy of division," "denial of the antecedent," *argumentum ad hominem,* "the fallacy of reasoning *post hoc ergo propter hoc,*" and so on,[22] but it omits the blunder to which we are calling attention here.[23] Before we give the fallacy in question a definition and a name,[24] we might look at a few additional illustrations of it. One of Lewis Carroll's characters says, "I don't like asparagus and I'm very glad I don't, because if I did I should eat them and I can't bear them!"

The present writer once found his youngest brother, then perhaps six years of age, struggling to get a sneaker on his foot. He was lying on the floor, his foot over his head, saying, "This sneaker doesn't fit me! And even if it did, I can't get it on!" In the preface to "Man and Superman," George Bernard Shaw writes, "A lifetime of happiness! No man alive could bear it. It would be hell on earth."

We call this fallacy *contrafactum interruptum* and define it as follows:

Definition. The fallacy of reasoning *contrafactum interruptum* occurs when, reasoning about a counterfactual state of affairs, we enter in thought the counterfactual situation that concerns us and, in the midst of our reasoning about it, forget the counterfactual premise that defines the state of affairs in question and draw conclusions that are flatly excluded by that premise.

Interestingly, this fallacy can be found infecting some recent work in analytical philosophy, such as David Lewis's work on "counterpart theory"[25] and work, since disowned, by David Kaplan on the false "problem of identity across possible worlds."[26]

But what matters for us in our present investigation is this: the fallacy of *contrafactum interruptum* is precisely the fallacy committed when anyone reasons as follows: "We can't give the awesome authority to assist in the destruction of innocent persons to just anybody. Let's give it to the doctors! They have been single-mindedly committed for thousands of years to the protection, restoration, and maintenance of human health and life. Surely we can trust them!" This is straight *contrafactum interruptum*. The common assumption that assisted suicide should carried out by physicians rests on the fallacy of *contrafactum interruptum* reasoning.

A DILEMMA FACING ADVOCATES OF
EUTHANASIA AND ASSISTED SUICIDE

Given that the state enjoys its monopoly in the exercise of lethal force solely because it has assumed the task of protecting the innocent from unjust assault,[27] it is inevitable that any effort to institute a socially sanctioned practice of murder will turn out, on close examination, to involve deep incoherence and paradox. Consider the task before those who are attempting to persuade the rest of us to admit the deliberate killing of the ill and disabled into our practices, or, more accurately, to grant the sanction of law and legitimate authority to the killings already underway. They are asking us to carry out *two* spectacular acts of vandalism: first, that we abolish long-standing prohibitions of lethal assault against innocent persons; and second, they are asking us to transform, indeed *derange*, the medical profession in order to establish the practices they are so eager to establish. For they are asking physicians to renounce a central clause in the definition of the office of physician, namely, the strict prohibition of euthanasia and assisted suicide, the clause that the Hippocratic Oath phrases, "Neither will I administer a poison to anybody when asked to do so, nor will I suggest such a course."[28] Opponents of euthanasia and assisted suicide would do well to emphasize again and again the double vandalism involved in the "reforms" being urged upon us. One way of achieving this would be for some of those opponents to organize an initiative to place on the ballot in some state a bill calling for the legalization of attorney-assisted suicide or philosophy professor-assisted suicide or, best and most realistic, veterinarian-assisted suicide. Such a measure would make the advocates of euthanasia and assisted-suicide unhappy. For one thing, it is clear that such a measure would have no chance of gaining a victory at the polls. Second, it is clear that even if, contrary to all rational expectation, such a measure did win at the polls, it would be extremely difficult to get people to take advantage of the new "choice" now open to them. No matter how convinced the members of a certain family might be that it would be a "good thing" if Grandma were to die, it is immensely unlikely that they would be willing to take her to a vet.

So one way of phrasing the dilemma facing advocates of euthanasia and assisted suicide is this: *either* the practices they are so eager to establish have such strong merits that they deserve establishment even if the killing that is their central feature is not carried out by physicians, *or else*, if the practices are undesirable and even dangerous when the role of killer is assigned to anyone but the physician, they must acknowledge that the achievement of their goal is possible only by the effective dissolution of the one profession that has been single-mindedly devoted to the protection, enhancement, restoration, and preservation of human life and health for two-and-a-half millennia and that deforming the practice of medicine in the way proposed may yield a new breed of "physicians" who turn out to be as dangerous as attorneys or philosophy professors or veterinarians would be in the role of sanctioned killer.

A "reform" that can be achieved only by the profound derangement of a precious cultural heritage is a "reform" most citizens would oppose. So we must press advocates of euthanasia and assisted suicide with the question "What exactly is wrong with veterinarian-assisted suicide?" Unlike physicians, veterinarians are already trained in the task of killing large mammals by relatively painless methods. Having the vets do the killing, thus, has two advantages: first, it will not be necessary to change medical school curriculums by inserting practicums on killing; and second, and far more important, a practice of veterinarian-assisted suicide would, whatever its other defects and dangers, leave intact the precious practice of medicine, which has cost our species millennia of effort and pain and devotion and which is one of our proudest achievements.

"By all means, bring on euthanasia and assisted-suicide!" we can say to the unballasted advocates of those practices, "But," we will swiftly add, "let us put the task of killing into the proper hands and let us leave the practice of medicine intact!" Three cheers for attorney-assisted suicide! Three cheers for veterinarian-assisted suicide! But, by all means, hands off medicine!

INJUSTICE AND INEGALITARIANISM TRIUMPHANT

It is disquieting to observe and reflect on a pattern in the "reforms" that have been recently carried out and that activists are attempting to extend even further. Whether it is the physician declaring a patient with a beating heart dead or a nursing home staff disconnecting the feeding tube of a patient who is not terminally ill but presently unable to feed himself or herself, or a woman deciding to abort her developing baby, or a physician deciding to withhold or withdraw care from a patient on the ground that the patient's "quality of life" does not warrant further treatment, we are faced in each instance with an action that fits a striking pattern: in each instance someone who is stronger is acting against the interests of someone considerably weaker. There are two important words missing from the slogans of the ideological movements that have already brought us legalized abortion and are on the verge of bringing us legalized euthanasia and assisted suicide. The activists in those movements talk of "choice," and "individual autonomy," and "reproductive rights," and "the right to die." The words missing from their rhetoric are "justice" and "equality." The movements in question are bringing about one of the most massive and successful anti-egalitarian shifts in human history, an inegalitarian shift vehemently defended by armies of intellectuals who speak enthusiastically about "individual liberty," "choice," "autonomy," and "individual rights," while steadily averting their faces from the fates of the vulnerable persons whose misfortune is to die when the stronger kill the weaker.

CONCLUSION

It is well known that the majority of people who commit suicide or who attempt suicide are suffering from (treatable) clinical depression. That is, we know that anyone desperate enough to contemplate destroying himself or herself needs love and support and care, not assistance with the lethal project to which his or her desperation is leading. We know that suicide is always "a permanent 'solution' to a temporary problem." We know that when the killers, in cases of euthanasia and assisted suicide, tell us that they are only doing for their victim what they would want done to themselves were they in similar circumstances, we are being given an attempted justification that is morally invalid. We know that involving physicians in lethal action against human life places them at complete opposition to the aim of medicine and deranges one of our most precious cultural heritages.

When we are prepared to authorize policeman to carry out crimes, when we are ready to authorize attorneys to incriminate their clients, when we are prepared to authorize firemen to engage in arson, when we are ready to permit lifeguards to carry out deliberate drownings, the time will have arrived to consider the merits of physician-assisted suicide.

In the meantime, we will remember that we were taught that "Inasmuch as ye have done it unto these the least of my Brethren, ye have done it unto me." Perhaps we will draw inspiration from Mother Teresa who said in simple modesty, "We do not do great things; we do small things with great love."

ENDNOTES

1. For information concerning this topic, the reader can consult the article, "Brain Death—An Opposing Viewpoint," by Paul A. Byrne, Sean O'Reilly, and Paul M. Quay in the *Journal of the American Medical Association*, 242, no. 18 (1979): 1985–90, whose arguments and analysis remain unrefuted. The interested reader might also consult Paul A. Byrne, "Understanding Brain Death," American Life

League, 1990; and Josef Seifert, "Is 'Brain Death' Actually Death?," *The Monist*, 76, no. 2 (1993): 175–202.

2. Plato, "The Republic," Book 1, *The Dialogues of Plato*, vol. 1, trans. Benjamin Jowett (New York: Random House, 1937).

3. Thomas DeQuincey, *Supplementary Papers.*

4. John M. Dolan, "Is Physician-Assisted Suicide Possible?" *Duquense Law Review*, 35, no. 1 (fall 1996): 355–93.

5. Carl P. Malmquist, *Homicide: A Psychiatric Perspective* (Washington, D.C.: American Psychiatric Press, 1996).

6. *Uniform Crime Reports*, United States Department of Justice, Federal Bureau of Investigation (Washington, D.C.: U.S. Government Printing Office, 1991).

7. Henry David Thoreau, "Resistance to Civil Government," *Reform Papers*, ed. Wendell Glick (Princeton, N.J.: Princeton University Press, 1993), 70.

8. "*Cruzan v. Director*, Missouri Department of Health," 497 U.S. 261, 110 Supreme Court 2841, 111 L. Ed. 2d 224 (1990).

9. I am indebted to Nancy Koster for calling this striking quotation to my attention.

10. Dolan, "Is Physician-Assisted Suicide Possible?" 355–93.

11. G. K Singh, K. D. Kochanck, and M. F. MacDorman, "Advance Report on Final Mortality Statistics, 1994," *Monthly Vital Statistics Report*, 45, no. 3 (National Center for Health Statistics, 1996): supp., p. 15.

12. S. J. Ventura, J. A. Martin, T. J. Mathews, and S. C. Clarke, "Advance Report on Final Mortality Statistics, 1994," p. 28.

13. Bureau of Justice Statistics/Federal Bureau of Investigation as of October 13, 1996.

14. Pope John Paul II, "Evangelium Vitae," March 1995.

15. See Daniel Avila, "Is the Constitution a Suicide Pact?" *Duquense Law Review*, 35, no. 1 (fall 1996): 201–59.

16. I owe my knowledge of the existence of this rule to one of the few men on the planet with a deep knowledge both of the rich traditions of Chinese philosophy and of contemporary analytical philosophy: David Nivison, professor of philosophy emeritus at Stanford University.

17. See John Rawls, *A Theory of Justice* (Cambridge: Harvard University Press, 1971), 11–12, 118–92.

18. Ibid., 75–83.

19. Walter Isaacson, *Kissinger* (New York: Simon & Schuster, 1992) cited by Thedore Draper in a review of the book in *The New York Times Book Review*, 6 September 1992, 21.

20. Amartya K. Sen quotes this "celebrated epitaph" in *Collective Choice and Social Welfare*, (New York: Holden-Day, Inc., 1970), 132. He cites Kenneth Arrow, *Social Choice and Individual Values*, 2d ed. (New York: John Wiley & Sons, 1963).

21. See 177 of chapter 7, "The Destruction of 'Lives Not Worth Living,'" in *Racial Hygiene: Medicine Under the Nazis*, Robert N. Proctor (Cambridge: Harvard University Press, 1986).

22. For a discussion of the traditional fallacies see chapter 8 of John M. Dolan, *Inference and Imagination* (Minneapolis: Archimedean Point Press, 1994).

23. At any rate, the tradition overlooked this fallacy until Saul Kripke carried out his penetrating investigations of modality and reference, which exposed a wide range of fallacies in the context of modal reasoning. Kripke does not bother to confer formal labels on any of the modal misunderstandings he examines, but it is clear that several of the thinkers whose reasoning he dissects are in fact committing

the fallacy under discussion here. See Saul A. Kripke, *Naming and Necessity* (Cambridge: Harvard University Press, 1981), especially 49–53.

24. Or more accurately, recall the definition given in chapter 8 of the present writer's book, *Inference and Imagination*, 153–55.

25. See, for example, his article, "Counterpart Theory and Quantified Modal Logic," *Journal of Philosophy*, 65 (March 1968): 110–28; and his book, *Counterfactuals* (Cambridge: Harvard University Press, 1973).

26. See his 1967 article, "Trans-World Heir Lines," in *The Possible and the Actual*, ed. Michael Loux (Ithaca, N.Y.: Cornell University Press, 1979), 88–109.

27. In her paper, "On the Source of the Authority of the State," G. E. M. Anscombe argues persuasively that the source of the State's authority and the basis of its exclusive right to wield deadly force is its assumption of the task of protecting the innocent from unjust attack. This leads her to conclude that "there is one consideration here which has something like the position of absolute zero or the velocity of light in current physics. It cannot possibly be an exercise of civic authority deliberately to kill or mutilate innocent subjects" (*Ethics, Religion, and Politics*, vol. 3 of *The Collected Philosophical Papers of G. E. M. Anscombe* [Oxford: Blackwell, 1981], 155).

28. *Hippocrates*, vol. 1, trans. W. H. S. Jones, Loeb Classical Library (Cambridge: Harvard University Press, 1923), 299.

PART 3

THEOLOGICAL REFLECTIONS

An Overview

We live in a society that, apparently indifferent to seeking balance, lives on the extreme edges of life's issues. The acceptability of suicide and euthanasia is found in an unbalanced philosophy that sees death as only a friend and not a foe, and suffering as something that must always be alleviated rather than a challenge to persevere. Rather than seeking balance between divine providence and human stewardship, proponents of suicide and euthanasia lean heavily toward the human responsibility to solve human tragedy at the expense of divine providence. At the other extreme are those who espouse a position that supports the maintaining of life at any cost, i.e., vitalism. Dennis Hollinger delineates the importance of understanding the balance that is found by investigating and accepting both of the extremes that create the tensions prevalent in death and suffering. A theologically balanced understanding of death helps us to avoid faulty and dangerous conclusions.

Chapter Sixteen

A THEOLOGY OF DEATH

Dennis P. Hollinger

THERE ARE MANY FORCES THAT SHAPE our ethical judgments and moral actions in the issues surrounding death and dying. But perhaps none is greater than our worldview. Moral reflection and choices are not only determined by the virtues espoused or principles utilized, but also by the larger perceptions of reality in which those virtues or principles reside. Our worldview is reflected in both the stories we tell and the discursive constructs we set forth about the nature of things.[1] Our views of reality, however, are not merely descriptions of the way things are but also embody moral oughts and character obligations.

When we deal with death and dying issues, we are immediately confronted with worldview, and hence theology. Definitions of death, judgments about treatment termination or futility, and moral arguments surrounding euthanasia and suicide are deeply intertwined with our theological assumptions. It is nearly impossible to grapple with these ethical issues without significant engagement in matters such as the nature of life, the nature of death, the meaning of suffering, the meaning and limits of human agency, and the nature and actions of God. How we describe these theological/worldview issues or what narratives we utilize to reflect them, provide the major context for determining our moral choices in death and dying, including the issue of suicide.

When one begins to construct a theology for the ethical issues of death and dying, one is struck by the paucity of theological engagement with death. If death is a topic in systematic theologies, it is usually very brief and lacking in the same depth that accompanies other theological topics.[2] But the contemporary ethical issues that attend the end of life call for clear theological reflection. In particular they beckon us to theological analysis of the nature and meaning of death, the nature of suffering, and the role of human agency or stewardship in relationship to God's providence and power. Our theological commitments on these matters directly determine our ethical stance on suicide.

In reflecting on these three theological issues, it seems to me that they are best understood in creative tensions. That is, in the Bible sometimes several tenets are held together and ought not to be severed from each other. As we work at ethical issues like suicide, treatment termination, or euthanasia, these theological tensions give us perspective and boundaries. Most of us don't like tensions, whether it be in relationships or in thought. But when Holy Scripture holds together two theological verities, we should not sever them; we must uphold the tension. Specifically, we will examine three theological tensions as guidelines and boundary markers for our work in ethical issues of death: death as friend and foe, suffering as challenge to persevere and opportunity to overcome, and divine providence in relation to human stewardship.

DEATH AS FRIEND AND FOE

Many Christians see death only as foe. For these people death is not only the great enemy that will one day be destroyed, but the great enemy that we face now in life. This view is set forth by Larry Richards and Paul Johnson when they write, "Theologically death is so intimately entwined with our sinful condition, both as a result of sin and as an evidence of its relationship-destroying power, that we can never lightly view its approach or even welcome death as a doorway to eternity."[3] There are also secular versions of this view of death, such as the work of Thomas Hobbes, who built his philosophy on the premise that death is the greatest of all evils.[4] The ethical implication of such a theology is medical vitalism, the view that we must use all means at our disposal to ward off death. If death is only the enemy, acceptance will be difficult whether as a patient, health care practitioner, or ethicist. The logical conclusion is to always use every means possible to keep the dying person alive.

For other thinkers, mostly non-Christians, death is only a friend. It is simply a part of nature that we ought to regard with indifference, as the ancient Stoics put it, or with natural acceptance in the journey of life as some modern therapists put it. In our era this view of death is exemplified by the death and dying movement led by psychologists such as Elizabeth Kubler-Ross, Avery Weisman, and Edwin Shneidman. Death in this perception is primarily an opportunity for growth and should not be accompanied by fear or sadness. Humans should see and experience death, according to Kubler-Ross, as a "peaceful cessation of the functioning of the body. Watching a peaceful death of a human being reminds us of a falling star; one of the million lights in a vast sky that flares up for a brief moment only to disappear into the endless night forever."[5] Such a worldview is part of a larger school of psychology focusing on human potential or self-actualization, and reflects what Donald Browning has called a "culture of joy."[6] The ethical implications of this view are to openly accept death without qualification or to even hasten death when reasons for living are no longer apparent. The logical connection between this view of death and physician-assisted suicide or an autonomous act of suicide are obvious.

Neither of these perspectives on death, taken by themselves, are adequate, for neither does justice to the whole of biblical teaching. Biblically and theologically we must view death as friend and foe and not isolate one from the other.

Human death as foe is of course quite evident in the biblical story. Death is generally understood by Christians to be the separation of the physical body and the soul,[7] but that separation is intimately linked to human sin. In the Garden of Eden, Adam was told that he "must not eat from the tree of the knowledge of good and evil, for when you eat of it you will surely die" (Gen. 2:17). In the New Testament the apostle Paul makes a clear connection between the sin of Adam and human death: "Sin entered the world through one man, and death through sin, and in this way death came to all men, because all sinned" (Rom. 5:12). In arguing for the reality of Christ's resurrection as a foretaste of the believer's future resurrection, Paul says, "For since death came through a man, the resurrection of the dead comes also through a man" (1 Cor. 15:21). As a result, "The sting of death is sin," and "The last enemy to be destroyed is death" (1 Cor. 15:56, 26).

There has been some theological debate as to whether these passages mean that there would have been no physical cessation of life without the human fall into sin. Some have argued that the entrance of sin changed the nature of death and certainly brought spiritual death, but that even without the fall there would have been the natural biological process of the life cycle, which moves from the inception of life, through various stages, to its conclusion. That is, even without sin humans would have ended their biological life in time and space. Karl Rahner, the Roman Catholic theologian, has spoken of "a death without dying" which would have been "pure, apparent and active consummation of the whole man by an inward movement, free of death in the proper sense, that is, without suffering any violent dissolution of his actual bodily constitution through a power from without."[8] Other theologians, however, have contended that physical death per se, not just its sinister components, is the result of sin. Millard Erickson, for example, believes that passages like Romans 6:23, "The wages of sin is death," have been misused to support the linkage of physical death and sin, but nonetheless "physical death was not an original part of man's condition."[9]

Whatever our perspective on that theological debate, we must acknowledge that the Scriptures are clear in their linkage of sin and death. Death, at least as we all experience it in human life, is antithetical to God's original intention and to the resurrected life yet to be experienced. Therefore, death is a foe that is associated with despair (Ps. 88:15), anguish (Ps. 116:3; 2 Sam. 22:5–70), fear (Heb. 2:15), and the valley of the shadow (Ps. 23:4). Before death we tremble and stand in awe of its mysterious, haunting power.

But death in the Bible is also a friend. Though the friendship language may overstate the case, death is portrayed as the natural end of life, albeit in a fallen condition. It is being "gathered to my people" (Gen. 49:29, 33; 25:8), "breath[ing] his last . . . at a good old age" (Gen. 25:8; 35:29), and returning to the ground, for "dust you are and to dust you will return" (Gen. 3:19). Death is "the destiny of every man" (Eccl. 7:2; cf. Heb. 9:27) and the time for one's "departure" after having "fought the good fight" (2 Tim. 4:6). These and other texts seem to connote that death is a natural process that comes after we have journeyed through life.

At times in the Bible, death is viewed as hope and longed for with great expectation of entering into the presence of God. The psalmist could write, "Precious in the sight of the LORD is the death of his saints" (Ps. 116:15), and the apostle Paul contemplating the possibility of his own death expressed a sense of feeling torn between living and dying: "For to me, to live is Christ and to die is gain. If I am to go on living in the body, this will mean fruitful labor for me. Yet what shall I choose? I do not know! I am torn between the two: I desire to depart and be with Christ, which is better by far; but it is more necessary for you that I remain in the body" (Phil. 1:21–24). Paul's perception of death as friend is not a death wish because his physical condition overwhelmed him, but is rather a longing to see his Lord. It is this "hope" for the believer that makes death the enemy more than just palatable, but at times an experience of great joy amidst the sorrow of leaving this temporal world.

The early church was therefore able to live with both the tragedy and victory of death. As Peter Davids writes, "The death of martyrs could be celebrated and the death of the faithful, while sorrowful, could be spoken of with confidence and joy. . . . Death was not denied nor sorrow suppressed, but death was seen as hopeful, an event in Christ, an event for which one could prepare."[10] In a similar vein, C. S. Lewis, contrasting the Christian view of death with common natural understandings, argues that there is an "ambivalent" perspective in Christianity: "It is Satan's great weapon and also God's great weapon: it is holy and unholy; our supreme disgrace and our only hope; the thing Christ came to conquer and the means by which He conquered."[11]

What does it mean for contemporary ethical issues that death is both friend and foe? Holding the two in creative tension precludes any radical answers to moral issues such as treatment termination or suicide. On the one hand it precludes the vitalist assumptions, which err on the side of maintaining physical life through burdensome treatment long past the point where there is any real benefit to the dying patient. Because the medical profession is trained to heal and thwart death, there are clearly times when heroic measures have gone way beyond the point of benefit and have unnecessarily prolonged life or even caused greater suffering. Refusing to allow death to come in the course of time is every bit as much "playing God" as attempting to control the timing and means of death. Withholding or terminating treatment when death is imminent (and the medical procedures would unduly prolong the person's life), is distinct from actively inducing death, for there is a clear recognition that ultimately, "The LORD gave and the LORD has taken away" (Job 1:21). Medical vitalism then is wrong because it upholds the foe side of death, but not the friend side.

But the creative tension of death also precludes active euthanasia and suicide in any form. Euthanasia and suicide advocates have embraced death as friend but have lost sight of death as enemy. They have too readily embraced death as being merely the natural end of life. Suicide proponents not only usurp God's sovereign control over life and death, but fail to recognize that death is a powerful, mysterious enemy that is not welcomed without qualification. It fails to affirm not only the biblical teaching regarding the "last great enemy," which will one day be destroyed, but to acknowledge the experience of people in the face of death—it is an enemy that vexes our deepest emotions, sets asunder our dearest relationships, and leads us to our most profound encounter as we stand face-to-face with the creator of the universe to receive reward or judgment.

A theology of death for moral issues must hold together death as friend and foe. Such a theology is beautifully set forth by John Donne in one of his most well known sonnets.

> Death, be not proud, though some have called thee
>   Mighty and dreadful, for thou art not so;
> For those whom thou think'st thou dost overthrow
>   Die not, poor death, nor yet canst thou kill me.
> From rest and sleep, which but thy pictures be,
>   Much pleasure, then from thee much more must flow,
> And soonest our best men with thee do go,
>   Rest of their bones, and soul's delivery
> Thou art slave to fate, chance, kings, and desperate men,
>   And dost with poison, war, and sickness dwell,
> And poppy, or charms can make us sleep as well
>   And better than thy stroke; why swellst thou then?
> One short sleep past, we wake eternally,
>   And death shall be no more; death, thou shalt die.[12]

SUFFERING AS A CHALLENGE TO PERSEVERE AND AN OPPORTUNITY TO OVERCOME

The death and dying process inevitably involves suffering, and how we view suffering is a major factor in our ethical positions surrounding death and dying. There is an intimate connection between our theology of suffering and our ethic of suicide.

Suffering has long been a major source of philosophical and personal anxiety. The issue of theodicy raises questions about the character of God, for if our maker is all-powerful and all-loving why do pain and suffering exist? While the theodicy issue is extremely important for our trust in God and His Son, Jesus Christ, our focus here is a bit different. It is not the philosophical question of why a good, powerful God allows suffering, but rather the biblical/theological issue of how we respond to suffering.

John Kilner has noted two commonly accepted assumptions about suffering that can profoundly shape one's approach to health care. "One is that suffering is an unqualified evil; the other is that suffering should be removed at all costs."[13] Both, however are far removed from the biblical understanding in two ways. First, each view is too drastic and extreme, and second each is divorced from the other. These distortions in worldview or theology lead, of course, in two moral directions: a too rigid acceptance of suffering which may unnecessarily prolong suffering and death or a too easy acceptance of death as the remedy for suffering. In contrast to these approaches, Christian theology upholds suffering as a challenge to persevere and an opportunity to overcome.

Suffering in the Bible is seen as a challenge to endure and persevere, for out of the affliction comes potentially good results for the person, society, and God's kingdom. This does not mean that humans are to seek suffering or trials and tribulation, but we are encouraged to find joy in the midst of them, for "you know that the testing of your faith develops perseverance. Perseverance must finish its work so that you may be mature and complete, not lacking anything" (James 1:3–4). We are called to persevere in suffering, because it can result in spiritual growth, depth of character, and courage for living. In and of itself suffering and pain are not moral goods, for they are clearly results of the Fall. But as an inevitable part of life that all humans know, suffering in the hands of God's providence can be used for good. While this is an explicit understanding of Christian theology, it is an insight that goes far beyond the scope of Christianity and special revelation; humans through experience have recognized the potential benefits of affliction and difficulty.

The book of Job is, of course, the most powerful rendition in the Bible of the mystery of suffering. Job in his physical suffering, and then interpersonal anguish through his "friends" accusatory advice, never receives a philosophical response to the age-old question of why God allows suffering or why he personally has experienced such calamity and physical pain. His speculations continue on. But in the end, after God has spoken out of the storm and given him a tour of his majesty and glory in the universe, Job comes to a new understanding of God and life: "I know that you can do all things; no plan of yours can be thwarted" (Job 42:2). Job has come to experience something of what the apostle Paul says in Romans 5:3–5: "We know that suffering produces perseverance; perseverance, character; and character hope. And hope does not disappoint us, because God has poured out his love into our hearts by the Holy Spirit, whom he has given us."

Such texts do not mean that suffering is easy. But they do imply that the external or physical conditions of our being are not to be the primary determiners of our own contentment and meaning in life (cf. Phil. 4:11–12). Paul knew the anguish of trying physical and relational circumstances and even asked the Lord to remove such suffering ("thorn in my flesh") from his life. But God's response was the hope given to all who live in this fallen world with its inevitable thorns and thistles: "My grace is sufficient for you, for my power is made perfect in weakness" (2 Cor. 12:9). We are assured, therefore, that no matter how painful the physical, mental, or social malady, God's merciful power will enable us to withstand. Moreover, such circumstances do not destroy the essential reason for living or nullify the givenness of life granted by God. Suffering is a challenge to perseverance.

At the same time, the Bible also implies that suffering is an opportunity to overcome. Suffering is to be persevered with joy on the one hand, but there are clearly examples of prayers to remove and healings to alleviate painful sickness. Even our Lord in the face of his own death cried out to the Father to, if possible, remove the suffering: "Abba, Father . . . everything is possible for you. Take this cup from me. Yet not what I will, but what you will" (Mark 14:36; cf. Heb. 5:7–9). Though he was fully God, Jesus being fully human entered into our sufferings even to the point of the cross. But his own endurance reflected what we all desire in the moments of pain, a possibility to overcome it.

The biblical teaching on healing is a clear example of the point that suffering is an opportunity to overcome. The healings by Jesus and the apostles were on the one hand "signs and wonders" to validate the inauguration of the kingdom. But they were also clear expressions of mercy and love to people undergoing the trials of physical pain and illness. When a man with leprosy came to Jesus desiring healing of the dreaded disease, Jesus, "filled with compassion . . . reached out his hand and touched the man" (Mark 1:41).

Divine healing is accomplished in various ways. First, God heals through the natural process in that he has created our bodies and minds in such a way that there are built-in mechanisms to bring health and healing. When we have a wound or cut, the blood normally clots or coagulates to stop the bleeding. This is divine healing, for God made us this way. Second, God heals through the healing arts, the insights that humans have garnered over the years. Since all truth is God's truth, discoveries about the body, the mind, nutrition, and medicine constitute a form of divine healing. Third, God heals through direct intervention. This is the kind usually designated divine, but here God directly intervenes into the ailment and brings healing in a miraculous way. And fourth, God heals through spirituality. In this type, health and healing come to the mind and body by utilizing the spiritual resources available to us. Because we are whole beings, what happens in the spiritual domain affects the physical and the emotional.

All of these are theologically valid forms of healing, and all demonstrate that God is active in the world to alleviate suffering and pain. We too, as "cocreators" with God, are able to participate in his healing ministry, which is a direct affront to the agony of pain and suffering.

To be sure there are many mysteries that surround suffering and physical pain. We may not fully understand why God allows it or why God brings healing relief to one person but not another. But we must hold in creative tension the biblical teachings that suffering is a challenge to persevere and an opportunity to overcome. As J. P. Kenny puts it, "Christian morality freely admits that man may employ all the resources of nature to alleviate or to suppress physical pain. But it also maintains that suffering is not purely negative. Physical suffering can have religious overtones and supernatural value."[14]

What does this theological tension mean for the ethics of death and dying? Like our first theological tension regarding death, this one precludes both euthanasia/suicide and the needless suffering of vitalism. Euthanasia and suicide proponents say yes to the one side of our tension, suffering as opportunity to overcome. They argue that actively inducing death is one of the ways to alleviate that suffering. But such thinking obscures the other side of the tension; namely, that suffering is a reality of life that presents us with a challenge to perseverance.

Similarly, vitalism gives credence to one side of our tension, suffering as challenge to persevere. But in neglecting the other side it prolongs needless suffering. When both sides of the tension are upheld, we can work to alleviate suffering in the dying patient and even welcome its alleviation through death. But we will not cause the death as a means of mitigating the suffering.

DIVINE PROVIDENCE AND HUMAN STEWARDSHIP

Moral issues surrounding death and dying are intimately linked to our views of the interaction of God's power and human action. Some believe that humans have been granted the freedom and right to regulate the world, including matters of life and death. In such a worldview suicide is often readily accepted on the grounds that it reflects our humanness. While it is a very modern view on the one hand, it is also very old for the Stoics argued much the same. As Seneca put it, "As I choose the ship in which I sail and the house which I shall inhabit, so I will choose the death by which I leave life."[15]

Others believe that God is in total control of the affairs of this world and humans have virtually no legitimate say over what transpires regarding life and death. Ideally, in this world we will not have to make decisions that affect death for such decisions belong to God alone. Taken to its logical conclusion, this view would find it difficult to "pull the plug" on a dying patient for such decisions are not the domain of human beings.

When we examine the biblical teachings we find an affirmation of both divine providence and human stewardship.[16] Providence is the understanding that God is continually at work in preserving and guiding the created order toward its divine end and fulfillment. It need not imply, as is sometimes assumed, that all human and historical effects are directly caused by God. Rather it means that He is ultimately and finally in control. While humans can temporarily thwart the divine plan, providence assures us that God is at work even amidst the tragic elements of life, which result from the Fall, so that ultimately His plan is brought to fruition.

God is thus the ultimate giver and culminator of human life, as is exemplified in Hannah's prayer for a son, "The Lord brings death and makes alive; he brings down to the grave and raises up" (1 Sam. 2:6). Providence is the theological assertion that our times are in God's hands (Ps. 31:15) and that finite creatures cannot usurp the role of an infinite all-knowing God.

But the Bible also portrays a theology of human stewardship. Though finite and fallen, humanity is given the task of being the caretaker of the earthly garden (Genesis 1–2). Because we have been made in His image, God has granted to us the responsibility of maintaining the created world, which is simultaneously upheld by His own hand. The creation mandate was to "rule over the fish of the sea and the birds of the air and over every living creature that moves on the ground" (Gen. 1:28). The psalmist reflecting on God's majestic creation puts it this way: "When I consider your heavens, the work of your fingers, the moon and the stars, which you have set in place, what is man that you are mindful of him, the son of man that you care for him? You made him a little lower than the heavenly beings and crowned him with glory and honor. You made him ruler over the works of your hands; you put everything under his feet" (Ps. 8:3–6).

Humans are called to be caretakers and decision-makers who must exercise wisdom in the use and allocation of all the resources that God places into our hands. Because of our fallenness, we often misuse our freedom and create tragedy, ambiguity, and chaos. But nonetheless we are moral agents to whom much has been given and much will be required. As theologian Millard Erickson puts it, "God's creative activity includes not only the initial creative activity, but also his later indirect workings. Creation does not preclude development within the world; it includes it. Thus God's plan involves and utilizes the best of human skill and knowledge in the genetic refinement of the creation. Such endeavors are our partnership with God in the ongoing work of creation."[17]

Holding together human stewardship and divine providence, like the other two tensions we've examined, leads us to reject both suicide and vitalism. Suicide and euthanasia proponents accentuate human stewardship and agency, but negate providence. Conversely vitalism accentuates providence, but negates stewardship. The creative tension of divine providence and human stewardship can help us, as Richard McCormick put it, "to walk a balanced middle path between medical vitalism (that preserves life at any cost) and medical pessimism (that kills when life seems frustrating, burdensome, useless)."[18]

CONCLUSION

The moral issues of death and dying will not go away. Increased medical technologies will only exacerbate the dilemmas as we face new capabilities for extending life far beyond what was possible in the past and what is possible even in the present. Simultaneously, we will increasingly have at our disposal the possibilities of taking the initiative to end life. Control over life and death, once clearly the domain of God, is now, through medical technology, in the hands of a fallen humanity.

Our response to the moral dilemmas is, and indeed as Christians should be, deeply rooted in our worldview. When Christians differ with secularists over the issue of suicide, it is fundamentally a worldview or theological difference. It is therefore imperative that Christians grapple with the moral dilemmas from within an explicitly Christian framework. As we seek to make a dent in the culture, we will of course need to utilize broader forms of argument to preserve God's intentions for the human race. But our own reflections must begin with the biblical story and assertions that form the worldview of believers.

In the face of death and dying issues, such as suicide, we must hold together what humanity tends to pull apart: death as friend and foe, suffering as challenge to persevere and opportunity to overcome, and the dual affirmation of divine providence and human stewardship. These theological assertions do not solve every dilemma a physician or family of a dying patient faces. But they do provide a framework that can guide us to make wise decisions amidst the complexity and ambiguity we often face in death and dying issues. On the one hand they preserve us from playing God in ethics, but on the other hand they also prevent us from abdicating our responsibilities as human stewards made in the very image of an all-powerful God.

ENDNOTES

1. This has been particularly articulated by narrative theory, which is currently popular in a number of disciplines including biblical studies, theology, literature, and the social sciences. Narrative theology can be useful if it is not divorced from the propositional or discursive statement of the Bible and theology. For a helpful balanced view of narrative thought, see David K. Clark, "Narrative Theology and Apologetics," *Journal of Evangelical Theological Society* 36, no. 4 (1994): 499–515.
2. Karl Rahner, for example, notes, "It cannot be said that the theology of death usually receives in scholastic theology the attention which the theme deserves" (Karl Rahner, "Death," *Sacramentum Mundi: An Encyclopedia of Theology*, vol. 2 (New York: Herder and Herder, 1968), 58.
3. Larry Richards and Paul Johnson, *Death and the Caring Community* (Portland: Multnomah Press, 1980), 30.
4. See, for example, his best known work *Leviathan*, where he writes, "A law of nature . . . is a precept, or general rule, found out by reason, by which a man is forbidden to do that which is destructive of his life, or taketh away the means of preserving the same, and to omit that by which he thinketh it may be best preserved" (1.14).
5. Elizabeth Kubler-Ross, *On Death and Dying* (New York: MacMillan, 1969), 276.
6. Donald Browning, *Pluralism and Personality* (Lewisburg, Pa.: Bucknell U. Press, 1980), 195. For a further analysis of these psychologists and their view of death see Bonnie J. Miller-McLemore, *Death, Sin and the Moral Life: Contemporary Cultural Interpretations of Death* (Atlanta: Scholars Press, 1988).
7. See, for example, Ecclesiastes 12:7 and James 2:26. The future resurrection of the physical body in the eschaton is further evidence of this definition of death.
8. Karl Rahner, *On the Theology of Death* (New York: Herder & Herder, 1961), 42. For an overview of others who hold Rahner's view but on different grounds see the critical evaluations of John Kilner, *Life on the Line* (Grand Rapids: Eerdmans, 1992), 99–103.
9. Millard Erickson, *Christian Theology* (Grand Rapids: Baker, 1983), 1170. Erickson believes this and passages such as Ezekiel 18:4, 20 are really about spiritual death and not physical death.
10. Peter H. Davids, "Death," *Evangelical Dictionary of Theology*, ed. Walter Elwell (Grand Rapids: Baker, 1984), 300.
11. C. S. Lewis, *Miracles* (New York: Macmillan, 1947), 130.
12. John Donne, "Holy Sonnets, 10," *The Norton Anthology of English Literature* (New York: Norton, 1968), 520.
13. Kilner, *Life on the Line*, 103.

14. J. P. Kenny, "Euthanasia," *New Catholic Encyclopedia*, vol. 5 (New York: McGraw-Hill, 1967), 640.

15. Seneca, *Laws* 9.843.

16. Holding together divine providence and human stewardship can be a significant corrective to some recent theological attempts to redefine a theology of God. Process philosophy and theology, for example, portray a bipolar theism in which one pole of God is limited and dependent upon actions within history. The creative tension can also be seen as potentially a corrective to some recent evangelical attempts to redefine God. See, for example, Clark Pinnock et al., *The Openness of God* (Downers Grove, Ill.: InterVarsity Press, 1994).

17. Erickson, 385–86.

18. Richard McCormick, "To Save or Let Die: The Dilemma of Modern Medicine," in *Ethical Issues in Death and Dying*, ed. Robert Weir (New York: Columbia University Press, 1977), 178.

An Overview

At what level in a society's psyche must we deal in order to effect lasting change philosophically and morally? And what measures must we take to secure these changes? In a discussion of the history of the suicides at Masada and their societal impact on the nation of Israel, Barry Leventhal discusses the ingrained mythical consequences that have developed in modern day Israel since the suicides were uncovered in 1963. He concludes with four suggestions for bringing lasting change that work as seeds of hope to sway the tide of suicide when it is tolerated in Israeli society or any other society.

Chapter Seventeen

THE MASADA SUICIDES
The Making and Breaking of a Cultural Icon

Barry R. Leventhal

"MASADA SHALL NOT FALL AGAIN!" "Remember Masada!" "Never again!" Up until recently, most Israeli military recruits, especially the paratroopers and soldiers of the armored units, confessed these solemn words with their lips and also embraced them with their hearts. These confessional affirmations comprised a major part of each recruit's oath of allegiance. For many years this military induction ceremony was conducted upon the ancient Judean desert rock-fortress of Masada. Why this place? Why Masada? The answer is bound up in one of the major cultural icons of the modern state of Israel. In Israel's collective national psyche, no better place could be selected to solemnize such a sacred moment, a moment that quite possibly could lead to these young recruits' laying down their lives in defense of this ancient biblical land.

In order to grasp the meaning and significance of Masada, as well as the making and breaking of this Israeli cultural icon, one must not only delve into the Masada of history, but also into the Masada of mystery.

THE MASADA OF HISTORY

For almost nineteen hundred years Masada lay buried and hidden from all eyes but those of the Divine. Of course, the Jewish historian Flavius Josephus (ca. A.D. 37–100) had recorded a detailed contemporaneous account of the rise and fall of Masada.[1] But the actual discovery and eventual excavation had to wait until the years of 1963 to 1965, under the direction of Professor Yigael Yadin, the distinguished Israeli military leader and archaeologist.[2] As the story of Masada began to unfold, the haunting echoes of the 960 men, women, and children who had committed suicide in A.D. 73 materialized out of the obscure past, seemingly begging for the birth of a national and cultural icon. But that takes us back to Herod the Great and his now famous mountain fortress of Masada. Two great periods laid the foundation for the Masada of history: first, the Herodian building period, and second, the Zealot revolt period.

The Herodian Building Period

King Herod the Great (47–4 B.C.) was a demented genius who first ruled as Governor of Galilee (47–37 B.C.) and then as "King of the Jews" (37–4 B.C.).[3] He played a significant role in the illustrious Herodian dynasty that traced its roots back to the struggle between Hellenism and Judaism, climaxing in the Maccabean or Hasmonean revolt against Antiochus Epiphanes (168–143 B.C.). With the Maccabean victory in 163 B.C. and beginning in 142 B.C., the Jews became more or less an independent nation under the rule of the Hasmoneans.

During the reign of Alexander Janneus (103–76 B.C.) the Herodians' influence in leadership began to be felt. Herod the Great's grandfather, Antipater I (or Antipas), was appointed governor of Idumea by Alexander (Josephus, *Ant.*, 14.1.3 [10]).[4] With the eventual defeat of Jerusalem under the Roman general Pompey in the autumn of 63 B.C., Jewish independence, as well as the Hasmonean house itself, came to an end (142–63 B.C.).

After Julius Caesar defeated Pompey in Egypt (48 B.C.), Herod the Great's father, Antipater II, attached himself to Caesar's party, eventually being made a Roman citizen with all of the proper benefits. Caesar also appointed Antipater II procurator of Judea, which soon led to his official recognition as administrator of Judea. It was not long before Antipater II was seized with dynastic ambitions, first appointing his son Phasael as governor of Jerusalem and then his second son Herod (the Great) as governor of Galilee in 47 B.C.

Herod the Great ruled as governor of Galilee from 47 to 37 B.C. Through his leadership and governing skills, he gained a proud reputation both with the Galilean Jews as well as with the Roman officials of Syria. Through the ensuing, internal Roman political and military machinations, Jerusalem again came under Roman siege, this time under the generalship of Herod himself (in the spring of 37 B.C.). Jerusalem fell in the summer of 37 B.C., and with it, the Hasmonean rule came to its final end, and Herod the Great became the King of the Jews. He had already been designated the King of Judea before the siege of Jerusalem in the spring of 37 B.C.

Herod the Great reigned as King of the Jews from 37 through 4 B.C. His reign is usually divided into three definite periods: (1) the period of consolidation (37–25 B.C.); (2) the period of prosperity (25–14 B.C.); and (3) the period of domestic troubles (14–4 B.C.).[5] During this first period of consolidation (37–25 B.C.), Herod eliminated his four major adversaries: the populace and the Pharisees, the aristocracy, the Hasmonean family, and Cleopatra of Egypt. This not only removed potential threats to his rule, it also insured him the loyalty of his subjects. This bloody period, both from without and from within the house of Herod, also overcame two other obstacles to Herod's successful reign, especially among the Jews: he was an Idumean or half-Jew (an Edomite or descendant of Esau) and, even worse, he was a friend of the Romans. His strategic conquests during this period of consolidation proved that these two obstacles need not stand in the way of his future dreams of political power and prestige.

During the period of prosperity (25–14 B.C.), though also times of distress, Herod left his mark of splendor. This period of prosperity was marked by three areas of advancement: (1) cultural development (e.g., the growth of Hellenistic education; the rebuilding of key areas of the city of Jerusalem, especially the Jewish [Herodian] temple, which he began in 20 B.C. and that was completed in A.D. 63, long after his death;[6] the development of Greek games, theaters; etc.); (2) domestic changes (e.g., his marriage in late 24 B.C. to Mariamne [later to be designated as Mariamne II], the daughter of Simon, whom Herod had appointed as high priest (23–6 B.C.); the sending of his two sons, Alexander and Aristobulus, to Rome for their formal educations, where they were personally received by Caesar himself, and who later returned to Judea and married, etc.); and (3) political advances (e.g., Augustus [Octavius's newly acquired title] Caesar's giving large areas of political control to Herod; Augustus also making the procurators of Syria accountable to Herod for all their actions; Herod's formidable tax cuts; etc.).

The period of domestic troubles (14–4 B.C.) relates directly to the violent years of Herod's reign. The last ten years of Herod's life were marked by family and political intrigue, bringing the Great One to the very precipice of anxiety and hysteria. Alongside of his growing older, there was the intense infighting between the many sons of his ten wives, each contending for his own share of the aging Herod's kingdom and power. In his growing dementia the aging Herod trusted no one—all were suspect, all supposedly out to seize his throne. No one escaped his paranoiac accusations and attacks, not even his wives and children.

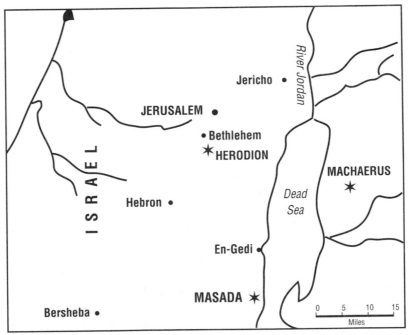

✳ Herod's defensive fortresses

Figure 1

It was during his first years of consolidation (37–25 B.C.) that Herod built
his magnificent mountain fortress of Masada, between the years of 36 and
30 B.C. According to Yadin, "The rock of Masada, at the eastern edge of the
Judean desert with a sheer drop of more than 1,300 feet to the western shore
of the Dead Sea, is a place of gaunt and majestic beauty."[7] In order to protect
himself both from within his own house as well as from without, Herod the
Great fortified three major defensive fortresses, to which he could flee at any
time in a moment's notice (see fig. 1): (1) Herodium (Herodion) in Cisjordan
to the north; (2) Machaerus in Transjordan to the east; and (3) Masada in the
Dead Sea area to the south.[8] These fortresses also served as "vacation spots"
for Herod and his entourage. It is believed that he visited Masada, the isolated
cliff overlooking the Dead Sea on the edge of the Judean Desert, only for
about one week each year.

The reason for the extensive fortifications of the impregnable rock of
Masada was explained by Josephus:

> For it is said that Herod furnished this fortress as a refuge for himself,
> suspecting a twofold danger: peril on the one hand from the Jewish people,
> lest they should depose him and restore their former dynasty to power; the
> greater and more serious from Cleopatra, queen of Egypt.[9]

The fortification of Masada was not only extensive but also magnificent.
The sheer grandeur of the mountain-rock itself, apart from any of Herod's
fortifications, again was well described by Josephus:

> A rock of no slight circumference and lofty from end to end is abruptly
> terminated on every side by deep ravines, the precipices rising sheer from
> an invisible base and being inaccessible to the foot of any living creature,
> save in two places where the rock permits no easy ascent.[10]

Masada, therefore, is an isolated rock bluff or table mountain ten miles
south of En-gedi on the western shore of the Dead Sea, opposite el-Lisan
("the tongue") peninsula. The rock is separated from the cliffs that border
the western shore of the Dead Sea by deep wadis on the west and south, the
top rising to some 193 feet above sea level. It also rises to a height of about
1300 feet above the surrounding land. Masada itself is about 1900 feet from
north to south and 650 feet from east to west, pointed at each end, with almost
sheer sides. The top, with an area of about twenty acres, is flat, somewhat
lower at the southern end, so that to one approaching from the north it
resembles a large ship.[11]

Herod's constructions were both immense and stunning. Yadin summarized
the work done by King Herod the Great:

> Between the years of 36 and 30 B.C., Herod built a casemate wall round the
> top, defense towers, storehouses, large cisterns filled ingeniously by occasional
> rain water, barracks, arsenals and palaces. It was these fortifications and

buildings which served the last band of Jewish fighters in their struggle against the Romans some seventy-five years after Herod's death.[12]

The Zealot Revolt Period

All of Herod the Great's work done at Masada laid the groundwork for the culmination of the First Jewish Revolt. The First Jewish Revolt against Rome began in A.D. 66 and ended with the downfall of Masada in A.D. 73. Yadin marked Masada as "the site of one of the most dramatic episodes in Jewish history."[13] He then went on to describe the details of this dramatic episode:

In the 1st century A.D. Palestine was under the occupation of the Romans, who had overthrown the Jewish Maccabean kingdom in the middle of the previous century. Periodic rebellion by the inhabitants, who sought to regain their freedom and sovereignty, had been quickly crushed. But in the year 66 A.D. the Jewish revolt flared up into a full-scale countrywide war, which raged with fierce bitterness for four years, the Romans having to bring in legion after legion of reinforcements to suppress the insurgents. In 70 A.D. the Roman general Titus conquered Jerusalem, sacked the city, destroyed the Temple, and expelled the bulk of the Jewish survivors from the country.

One outpost alone held out till 73 A.D.—the fortress of Masada. . . .

At the beginning of the 66 A.D. rebellion, a group of Jewish zealots had destroyed the Roman garrison at Masada and held it throughout the war. They were now—after the fall of Jerusalem—joined by a few surviving patriots from the Jewish capital who had evaded capture and made the long arduous trek across the Judean wilderness, determined to continue their battle for freedom. With Masada as their base for raiding operations, they harried the Romans for two years. In 72 A.D., Flavius Silva, the Roman Governor, resolved to crush this outpost of resistance. He marched on Masada with his Tenth Legion, its auxiliary troops and thousands of prisoners of war carrying water, timber and provisions across the stretch of barren plateau. The Jews at the top of the rock, commanded by Eleazar ben Yair, prepared themselves for defense, making use of the natural and man-made fortifications, and rationing their supplies in the storehouses and cisterns.

Silva's men prepared for a long siege. They established camps at the base of the rock, built circumvallation round the fortress, and on a rocky site near the western approach to Masada they constructed a ramp of beaten earth and large stones. On this they threw up a siege tower and under covering from fire from its top they moved a battering ram up the ramp and directed it against the fortress wall. They finally succeeded in making a breach.

This was the beginning of the end. That night, at the top of Masada, Eleazar ben Yair reviewed the fateful position. The defensive wall was now consumed by fire. The Romans would overrun them on the morrow. There was no hope of relief, and none of escape. Only two alternatives were open: surrender or death. He resolved "that a death of glory was preferable to a life of infamy, and that the most magnanimous resolution would be to disdain the idea of surviving the loss of their liberty." Rather than become slaves to their conquerors, the defenders—960 men, women and children—thereupon ended their lives at their own hands. When the Romans reached the height next morning, they were met with silence. And thus says Josephus at the end of his description:

"And so met (the Romans) with the multitude of the slain, but could take no pleasure in the fact, though it were done to their enemies. Nor could they do other than wonder at the courage of their resolution, and at the immovable contempt of death which so great a number of them had shown, when they went through with such an action as that was."[14]

And so the "heroic suicide" was carried out.[15] Each man was dispatched to his own family, executing his own women and children. Then ten men were chosen by lots to kill the rest. The last remaining man, before taking his own life, set fire to the palace, leaving the food and rations gathered together in the center of the fortress, in full view of the soon-arriving conquerors, the Romans: clear and profound testimony that they had not been able to starve out the Jewish patriots. As it turned out, two women and five children escaped the fate of the rest, being hidden by the man of their house. Later they reported the whole scenario to Josephus and the Romans.

And so, with the final strokes of the blade, the Masada of mystery was conceived. But the day of its birth must wait for the year 1965, when it will arise out of the Judean wilderness to meet its chosen appointment with destiny.

THE MASADA OF MYSTERY

How did the Masada of *history* become the Masada of *mystery*? The answer is deceptively simple: in the same way that the making of a cultural icon eventually becomes the breaking of that same cultural icon. When mystery grows beyond the truth of history and takes on its own fictional reality, it is bound for self-destruction. In other words, when the reality devolves into myth, it is doomed to ultimate failure. The mystery of Masada must be traced through three stages: Masada as a sacred symbol, a broken icon, and finally, a moral lesson.

Masada as a Sacred Symbol

It was inevitable that Masada would become a sacred symbol, especially for the newly founded and struggling state of Israel. Eleazar ben Yair's own words were not just enough to ignite the valor of his own compatriots, but also of another, future generation, when he resolved "that a death of glory was preferable to a life of infamy, and that the most magnanimous resolution would be to disdain the idea of suffering the loss of their liberty."[16] Josephus' lofty manner of describing the fall of Masada should have been a further hint of the eventual movement of Masada toward a sacred symbol. Words like, "the courage of their resolution," "the immovable contempt of death," etc.,[17] are clearly destined for the sacred symbol category—just awaiting the right cultural moment. It is not surprising then to see even a scholar like Yadin following after the footsteps of Josephus. His words like, "the site of one of the most dramatic episodes in Jewish history," etc.,[18] also make Masada prime for the rank of sacred symbol.

Anthropologist Clifford Geertz has devoted the greater part of his life and studies to the relationships between any given culture's ethos, worldview, and its sacred symbols. His research has a direct bearing on the making and breaking of Masada as a cultural icon. First, Geertz distinguishes between a culture's "ethos" and its "worldview":

> In recent anthropological discussion, the moral (and aesthetic) aspects of a given culture, the evaluative elements, have commonly been summed up in the term "ethos," while the cognitive, existential aspects have been designated by the term "world view." A people's ethos is the tone, character, and quality of their life, its moral and aesthetic style and mood; it is the underlying attitude toward themselves and their world that life reflects. Their world view is their picture of the way things in sheer actuality are, their concept of nature, of self, of society. It contains their most comprehensive ideas of order . . . ; the ethos is made intellectually reasonable by being shown to represent a way of life implied by the actual state of affairs which the world view describes, and the world view is made emotionally acceptable by being presented as an image of an actual state of affairs of which such a way of life is an authentic expression.[19]

Second, Geertz describes how the meanings of a culture's ethos as well as its worldview must be "stored" in sacred symbols if that given culture is to conserve the fund of meanings that it holds of value and by which each individual interprets his or her experience and organizes his or her conduct:

> But meanings [of value and reality] can only be "stored" in symbols: a cross, a crescent, or a feathered serpent. Such religious symbols, dramatized in rituals or related myths, are felt somehow to sum up, for those for whom they are resonant, what is known about the way the world is, the quality of the emotional life it supports, and the way one ought to behave while in it. Sacred symbols thus relate an ontology and a cosmology to an aesthetics and a morality: their peculiar power comes from their presumed ability to identify fact with value at the most fundamental level, to give to what is otherwise merely actual, a comprehensive normative import.[20]

The insights of Geertz and other anthropologists have direct implications for Masada as a sacred symbol in today's Israeli society. If it is true, as Geertz has demonstrated, that a society's sacred symbols uphold, support, and align its ethos and worldview—i.e., its personal, social, and moral view of itself as well as its cognitive and existential perspectives of reality—then Masada has played a major role in Israeli culture and society, for in 1948 Israel was born as a modern state, cast, as it were, from the womb of God's providence right into the fiery furnace and hostility of the Middle East. In other words, from its inception, the modern state of Israel has had to defend itself to the teeth, in the face of insurmountable odds and the reality of virtual national annihilation as a daily threat. With this kind of ethos and worldview, it is no wonder that Israel has, up until recently, so readily embraced Masada as a sacred symbol and cultural icon.

Masada, the sacred symbol, speaks of valor, honor, commitment, sacrifice, persistence, heroism, etc.—"stored" symbols that have guided, sustained, and inspired Israel in her most desperate hours. It is doubtful whether Israel could have survived these recent years without a cultural icon like Masada, as well as other like symbols, such as the Holocaust, etc. "Masada shall not fall again!" "Never again!" "Remember!"

It is also to be noted that recent Holocaust scholars have continued to define Masada as a sacred symbol, portrayed as one of two different models for facing Nazilike aggression.[21] The Masada model is the active model of power and militancy, of turning outward and against the aggressor, facing him in all of his fury and then robbing him of his expected victory. Caesar could not be trusted. Suicide was better than surrender. The other model was being laid about the same time as the Masada model. If Eleazar ben Yair and his Zealot followers were responsible for laying the Masada model, it would be left to Rabbi Yochanan ben Zakkai and his rabbinic colleagues (spiritual heirs) to lay the foundations of the Yavneh model.

Following the destruction of Jerusalem in A.D. 70, along with the 1,197,000 Jews who were killed or taken captive by the Romans,[22] a remnant of surviving Jewish religious leaders, guided by Rabbi Yochanan ben Zakkai, gathered at the town of Yavneh to discuss the very survival of religious Judaism, now that their temple, priesthood, sacrifices, Sanhedrin, etc. were all no longer functional. The ensuing Yavneh model was in most respects diametrically opposed to the Masada model. The Yavneh model is the passive model of surrender and submission, of turning inward and away from the aggressor, allowing him to vent his wrath and then trusting God to save a surviving remnant of the faithful. Caesar could be trusted. Surrender was better than suicide and annihilation. At least in this way Judaism would survive and its religious heritage could be passed on to the next generations. Obviously the early Zealots bitterly opposed Zakkai's policy of submission to the Romans.

Ben-Yehuda summarized the two conflicting models: "Moreover, as the Great Revolt [the First Jewish Revolt against Rome, A.D. 66-73] was reaching its end, two cultural legacies remained: Masada and Yavneh. Masada meant death, whereas Yavneh represented life."[23] Rubenstein and Roth also summarized the competing models in somewhat more detail:

> At Masada the Zealots preferred death to life in a world where their lives would be entirely dependent upon the whim of hostile strangers. By contrast, the rabbis [of Yavneh] were prepared not only to accept the risks of powerlessness but to create a religious culture predicated upon the disciplined renunciation of the use of force. Such a policy entailed the necessity of submitting at regular intervals to acts of murderous aggression. Yochanan and his spiritual heirs trained the Jews so to live that their defenselessness became their only defense.[24]

So two models were born in the inferno of A.D. 70, both still surviving down to this very day, especially in Israel.

Masada as a Broken Icon

Cultural icons have a unique staying power; they seem to endure as if thrust ever forward by a life-energy of their own making—until reality hits and a paradigm shift occurs.[25] Masada is just such a cultural icon. Having seen the making of Masada as a cultural icon, it is also necessary to focus on the breaking of Masada as a cultural icon.

There are numerous reasons why Masada has endured as a cultural sacred symbol.

One of the most important reasons has been related to a concept called "cognitive dissonance."[26] Psychologists have defined "cognitive dissonance" as a sort of emotional static produced in the psyche of persons when they are confronted with information telling them that they are wrong, especially in an area of one's life where there has been considerable personal investment in terms of time, money, and energy.[27] It is the all too human tendency to avoid change, especially where the evidence is totally convincing that change (in thought, word, or deed) is required. The psychic pain is too great, and change is all but impossible. It is the power of a preconceived idea, so ingrained that one almost has to be blasted out of his or her psychological rut. New ideas, even with conclusive supporting evidence, or old ideas, with contrary conclusive proof, are too revolutionary to be embraced at an intellectual level and too painful to be embraced at an emotional level. The consequences are too lethal to consider: submission to the truth with the obvious required transformation in both worldview and ethos.

To dismiss Masada as a cultural icon is no easy matter, even with mounting evidence that Masada may have been more myth than truth, more mystery than history.[28]

The sacred symbol of Masada is deeply entrenched in the Israeli collective memory and psyche. To dismiss it as mere myth is to invite a cognitive dissonance that strikes directly at the heart of Israeli identity, meaning, purpose, and values. This is no small matter.

Despite such cognitive dissonance, Masada seems to be cracking at its very foundations. Israeli sociologist Nachman Ben-Yehuda goes to great lengths to describe these cracks in Masada's foundations. His following four pieces of evidence in support of such a crumbling of the Masada icon seem to relate most directly to our thesis: (1) Masada is a truly mythical narrative ("invented history") rather than true history;[29] (2) Masada was a useful sacred symbol during a unique period of Israeli history (the early 1940s to the late 1960s), fulfilling the quest for symbols of heroism within the emerging new nonreligious Jewish identity (i.e., the new "Zionist mentality"); therefore, Masada was "a heroic myth";[30] (3) Masada and its "collective suicide" (i.e., the "Masada Complex" or "Masada Syndrome") is a dangerous model for Israeli society, especially for new military recruits[31]; and (4) Masada legitimized the unrestrained use of force by the earlier secular Zionists, as well as emphasizing current Zionistic national power and aggression (to insure that another Masada suicide will never occur again).[32]

Of particular interest to our theme, of course, is Ben-Yehuda's third piece of evidence above: the inherent power of persuasion in any culturally sacred symbol or icon that elevates suicide. The cultural glorifying or honoring of either a collective or individual suicide, in the nature of the case itself, will inevitably undermine that culture's national ethos and worldview.[33]

Within Judaism suicide is generally frowned upon at a personal level and rejected at a moral level.[34] Rabinowicz summarized the rabbinic law on suicide:

> Although suicide is not regarded in the Mishnaic Code as a felony, nevertheless, where it is committed with full deliberation and by somebody unquestionably of sound mind, it is regarded as a usurpation of the Divine prerogative and a trespass against both God and man. . . .
>
> In many cases, however, suicide is not an act of wanton self-destruction but a manifestation of intense despair. In the whole of the Bible there is mention of only a few people who took their own lives, and in each case the circumstances were exceptional. Each incident took place in a time of despair or when death by hostile hands was imminent. . . .
>
> A suicide is called in Hebrew *me'abed atzmo ladaat* (one who knowingly destroys himself) [*Semachot* 4]. The rabbis have never shared the opinion of Seneca (31 B.C.E.-30 C.E.) that the "eternal law that has assigned a single entrance to this life has mercifully allowed many exits. Any death is preferable to servitude."[35]

Lamm reinforces this strong rabbinic approach to willful suicide, when he maintained:

> Man is the magnificent creation of an all-wise and all-merciful God. The awesome determination of life and death is not given to man. As it is God's prerogative to grant life, so it is His sole decision to take life: "Perforce were you born," say the rabbis of the Talmud, "and perforce must you die" (*Ethics of the Fathers*, chapter 4). One who takes his own life is a murderer, as is one who takes another's life. "I will seek your blood for your souls," is applied by the *midrash* to one who destroys his own soul. The suicide, in effect, denies the lordship, the supreme mastery of God, when he decides that he is the lord of his own soul. He is then committing not only an act of violence; he is guilty of sacrilege.[36]

Other so-called mitigating factors have been applied by the rabbis in order to legitimize any particular kind of suicide:[37] (1) in the case of martyrdom (*Kiddush ha-Shem*), which, under certain circumstances, is the greatest *mitzvah* [a religious good work that merits favor with God] of Judaism; (2) in the case of mental derangement or an unsound mind; (3) in the case of a minor, which is always considered as the result of an unsound mind; (4) in the case of undue "duress" (e.g., the compulsion or necessity to kill oneself rather than surrender to the enemy [i.e., the heathen], even the possibility of the *subjectively* reasonable despair of life or the identification with a person who just died; etc.); and (5) in the case of violating any of God's laws, especially under external compulsion, one must kill himself or let himself be killed rather than commit any of those crimes forbidden by the Divine (e.g., forced or unforced conversion, idolatry, adultery, murder, etc.).

The fourth mitigating factor above, of course, has a direct bearing on the Masada suicides, as the rabbis have well noted. In fact, the question of "duress" does not even arise as in the case of Masada, etc., since choosing to die rather than surrendering to the heathen is highly praiseworthy according to rabbinic tradition.

In summary, although Masada as a cultural icon or sacred symbol seems to be collapsing because of various factors (e.g., historical, psychological, sociological, etc.), the whole issue of suicide in a society like Israel is anything but resolved. No moral consensus seems possible when so many conflicting ethical traditions and worldviews are struggling for cultural preeminence (e.g., secular humanism, various religious and political traditions, philosophical and educational ideologies, the individual quest for personal autonomy, and materialism, etc.).

Masada as a Moral Lesson

In order to conclude properly, we must view Masada as a moral lesson. What can we learn from Masada in general? And further, even more to the point, what can we learn from Masada in the particular area of suicide?

According to missiologist David J. Hesselgrave, "There is a consensus among most anthropologists that a cosmology or world view is at the core of culture. It is out of that core that the rest of culture emanates."[38] He then goes on to cite Christian anthropologist G. Linwood Barney as the one who has proposed a "four-layered" diagram of culture in which worldview (cosmology and basic belief system) is at the center (see fig. 2).[39]

LAYERS OF CULTURE

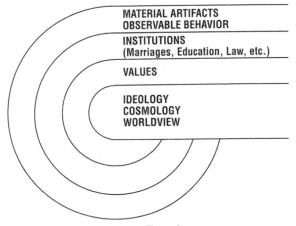

**MATERIAL ARTIFACTS
OBSERVABLE BEHAVIOR**

**INSTITUTIONS
(Marriages, Education, Law, etc.)**

VALUES

**IDEOLOGY
COSMOLOGY
WORLDVIEW**

Figure 2

Hesselgrave explains the significance of Barney's diagram when he asserts, "From a Christian perspective the important thing to learn from this is that change becomes more and more difficult to effect as one moves from the outer layers to the inner core."[40] In other words, it will be easier to remove the actual material artifacts and observable behavior associated with Masada and its suicide than to change the Israeli institutions associated with Masada (e.g., the military, the schools, the politics, the courts, the religions, the media, the tourism, etc.). Likewise, these Israeli institutions will be easier to change than to reform the Israeli value system that undergirds Masada (e.g., its morals, ethics, goals, purposes, standards, etc.). And finally, it will be easier to reform the Israeli value system than to transform its ideology, cosmology, and worldview that are associated with and determinative of Masada (e.g., its view of God, of truth, of the universe, of man within such a universe, of its own nationhood as well as other nations, the sanctity of human life—both at the beginning [e.g., the abortion question, etc.] and at the end [e.g., the euthanasia question, etc.], etc.).[41]

The real question, then, is: How can we begin at the center of Barney's "four-layer" diagram, at the very core? What must we do to see a real transformation of Israeli society (or for that matter, any society) at the worldview level, so that the Masada-driven icon of suicide will ultimately disappear?

We conclude with four suggestions for penetrating Israeli society, or any other society, at the core level of its very existence. First, we must know the cultural issues and how they have developed and penetrated any given culture. It will do us, others, and God no good whatsoever by sitting back and taking potshots at cultural icons like Masada. Any efforts at change aimed merely at the outer layers of a society will only be short-lived. Therefore, we must know the issues and know them well, from the outer layers and especially to the inner core.

Second, we must examine our own cultural issues, especially assuming a cut-throat approach to the core stuff in our own lives, families, and churches. Knowing and living "the whats" (our practices in life) is good. Knowing and living "the how to's" (our principles for life) is better. But knowing and living "the whys" (our philosophy of life) is the best and absolutely critical for any kind of transformation around us. It must begin with us.

Third, we must penetrate any given society at the personal level. This means praying regularly and persistently for that society and going to that society, or if that society has come to us (e.g., as immigrants, migrants, refugees, students, tourists, etc.), welcoming it into our midst through opening our homes, churches, and hearts to it with the love of God. Transformation at the core layer never takes place from a distance. It must be visible, personal, and intimate—just like the Incarnation. We have to earn the right to speak. When love is felt, the message will be heard.

And fourth, we must know the Gospel well enough to live it out on a daily basis as well as to share it on a collective or individual basis when God opens the door. It is still true today as it has always been: "For God so loved the world that He gave His one and only Son, that whoever believes in Him shall not perish but have eternal life" (John 3:16 NIV). Yes, sacred symbols rise and fall, but the Gospel of our God stands eternal. We will always see the making and breaking of cultural icons—man's best effort to hack out his own meaningful life apart from God—but let us pray for and work toward the day that we see the coming of the kingdom of God in our own day, the one reality that will live on forever.

ENDNOTES

1. For Josephus as the principal source of the historical incidents of Masada, see his *Jewish War* and Books 13–20 of his *Antiquities of the Jews*, plus, for one very definite period, the time at the beginning of the Jewish War, his so-called *Life*. For the authenticity and accuracy of the Josephus corpus on Masada, see Martin Hengel, *The Zealots: Investigations into the Jewish Freedom Movement in the Period from Herod I until 70 A.D.*, trans. David Smith (Edinburgh: T. & T. Clark, 1989), 6–18; and S. G. F. Brandon, *Jesus and the Zealots: A Study of the Political Factor in Primitive Christianity* (New York: Charles Scribner's Sons, 1967), passim.

2. For a detailed account of the excavation, see Yigael Yadin, *Masada: Herod's Fortress and the Zealots' Last Stand* (New York: Random House, 1966).

3. For a detailed portrait of the life and times of Herod the Great, see William J. Gross, *Herod the Great* (Baltimore: Helicon Press, 1962); and Harold W. Hoehner, *Herod Antipas* (Grand Rapids: Zondervan, 1972, 1980).

4. *The International Standard Bible Encyclopedia*, rev. ed., ed. Geoffrey W. Bromiley, 1979–88, s.v. "Herod," by Harold W. Hoehner, 2 (1982): 688.

5. Ibid., 690–94.

6. Of course, Herod's greatest achievement in construction was his massive additions to the Jewish temple in Jerusalem, which took well over forty years to complete (see John 2:20; cf. Josephus, *Ant.* 15.11.1–6 [380–425]). This temple was first rebuilt in the postcaptivity period, under the leadership of Ezra, Nehemiah, etc.; this original rebuilding took place seventy years after the destruction of the Solomonic temple by Nebuchadnezzar and the Babylonians in 586 B.C. Concerning the Herodian temple (i.e., the second temple period), the rabbis taught, "He who has not seen the Temple of Herod has never seen a beautiful building" (Babylonian Talmud, *Baba Bathra* 4a).

7. Yadin, *Masada*, 11.

8. Map taken from Yadin, *Masada*, 9.

9. *The Jewish War*, 7.8.4 [300f.].

10. Ibid., 7.8.3 [280].

11. *The International Standard Bible Encyclopedia*, rev. ed., ed. Geoffrey W. Bromiley, 1979–88, s.v. "Masada," by William Sanford LaSor, 3 (1986): 273.

12. Yadin, *Masada*, 11.

13. Ibid.

14. Ibid., 11–12. One of the ironic notes of history is that although Masada has taken on mythical and symbolic status, Gamla (northeast of the Sea of Galilee), although now known as the "Masada of the North," never achieved this kind of status. And the real note of irony is that, according to Josephus, 4,000—of the original 10,000 men, women, and children—were killed in battle by the Romans in A.D. 67, while 5,000 others committed suicide by jumping off of a

cliff to their deaths; only the women survived. See Josephus, *The Jewish War* 4.20–26, 64–67, 76, 80; Ben-Yehuda, 35, 42, 76, 90, 162, 254, 330n36; also, for recent excavations and historical insights into Gamla, see Danny Syon, "Gamla: Portrait of a Rebellion," *Biblical Archaeology Review* 18 (January/February 1992): 21–37, 72.

15. Ibid., 232–37 [in Josephus' own words].
16. *Supra*, 6.
17. *Supra*, 7.
18. *Supra*, 6.
19. Clifford Geertz, "Ethos, World View, and the Analysis of Sacred Symbols," in *The Interpretation of Cultures: Selected Essays by Clifford Geertz* (New York: Basic Books, 1973), 126–27.
20. Ibid., 127.
21. See Richard L. Rubenstein and John K. Roth, *Approaches to Auschwitz: The Holocaust and Its Legacy* (Atlanta: John Knox Press, 1987), 30–37ff., 177; also Ben-Yehuda, *Approaches to Auschwitz*, 49, 101, 156, 229–31, 330n38, 331n39, etc.
22. Rubenstein and Roth, 35.
23. Ben-Yehuda, *Approaches to Auschwitz*, 230.
24. Rubenstein and Roth, 37.
25. For a detailed study on this paradigm shift phenomena, see Thomas S. Kuhn, *The Structure of Scientific Revolutions*, 2d ed. (Chicago: University of Chicago Press, 1970).
26. For a thorough analysis of "cognitive dissonance" and its application to the field of apologetics, see Gershon Robinson and Mordechai Steinman, *The Obvious Proof: A Presentation of the Classic Proof of Universal Design* (New York: C. I. S. Publishers, 1993).
27. Ibid., 16; also see 15–48, etc.
28. For the most recent scholarly work on this, see Nachman Ben-Yehuda, *The Masada Myth: Collective Memory and Mythmaking in Israel* (Madison: The University of Wisconsin Press, 1995).
29. Ibid., passim. Ben-Yehuda asks the following question, "So how might we conceptualize a myth within the context of the present study?" (p. 282). He then answers the question in the following words: "A myth is a particular portrayal of a sequence of events (real or imaginary) characterized by a number of attributes distinguishing this sequence from a regular historical account" (p. 282). His list of attributes includes (1) an attitude of sacredness; (2) a high degree of symbolization; (3) a dimension of morality, of an instructive lesson; (4) a frequent demand for action from the listener, either immediately or in the future; (5) a conscious "choice" of specific events and a disregard of others, distinctly different from the historical context; (6) a simple narrative: the moral world is painted simplistically in terms of "good" and "bad"; (7) in addition, an impressive site, with an impressive environment, attached to the mythical tale provides a great advantage (pp. 282–83).
30. Ibid., 9, 14 ("a symbol for a heroic *last stand*"), 15–16, 23, 40–45, 72–110 passim, 119–22, 232–38, 288–96.
31. Ibid., 14, 156 ("educating people to commit suicide"), 157–58, 159 ("Hence the [recent] commanders wanted to use Masada as a vehicle by which to instill what they felt were important values in their new recruits: a willingness to fight to the end, non-surrender, a renewed link to the past, an identification with ancient

Jewish warriors, a love of freedom, a readiness to sacrifice."), 160, 229–30, 231 ("... Yavneh [i.e., renewed religious Judaism] and love of life should be the national symbols, not Masada, doomed Zealots, and death."), 243–49.

32. Ibid., 16, 63, 73, 132, 157, 222, 270, 312.
33. Geertz, "Ethos, World View, and the Analysis of Sacred Symbols."
34. For Judaism and its views on suicide, see *Encyclopaedia Judaica*, 16 vols., 1972, s.v. "Suicide," by Haim Hermann Cohn, 15:489–91; Maurice Lamm, *The Jewish Way in Death and Mourning* (New York: Jonathan David Publishers, 1969), 215–17; Tzvi Rabinowicz, *A Guide to Life: Jewish Laws and Customs of Mourning* (Northvale, N.J.: Jason Aronson, Inc., 1989), 65–68; Jack Riemer, ed., *Jewish Insights on Death and Mourning* (New York: Schocken Books, 1995), 223–59; and Fred Rosner, ed., *Medicine and Jewish Law* (Northvale, N.J.: Jason Aronson, Inc., 1990), 29, 118.
35. Rabinowicz, *A Guide to Life*, 65. It should be noted that six suicides are recorded in the Bible: (1) Abimelech (Judg. 9:54); (2) Samson (Judg. 16:30); (3) Saul (1 Sam. 31:4); (4) Ahithophel (2 Sam. 17:23); (5) Zimri (1 Kings 16:18); and (6) Judas (Matt. 27:5).
36. Lamm, *The Jewish War*, 215.
37. See *Encyclopaedia Judaica*, 489–91.
38. David J. Hesselgrave, *Scripture and Strategy: The Use of the Bible in Postmodern Church and Mission*, Evangelical Missiological Society Series Number 1 (Pasadena: William Carey Library, 1994), 49.
39. Ibid.; for Barney's "four-layered" diagram (figure two) and its development, cited by Hesselgrave, see G. Linwood Barney, "The Supracultural and the Cultural: Implications for Frontier Missions," in *The Gospel and Frontier Peoples: A Report of a Consultation December 1972*, ed. R. Pierce Beaver (Pasadena: William Carey Library, 1976), 48–57.
40. Hesselgrave, *Scripture and Strategy*, 50.
41. For further development of these and other "world view" themes, see James W. Sire, *The Universe Next Door*, rev ed. (Downers Grove: InterVarsity Press, 1988); R. C. Sproul, *Lifeviews: Understanding the Ideas That Shape Society Today* (Old Tappan, N.J.: Revell, 1986).

An Overview

Should suicide and martyrdom be viewed as synonymous acts in church history? Though some sociologists, historians, and judges have argued such, the author clearly shows that such an interpretation is a distortion of Christian history and theology. Recent secular scholars, applying a sociological model of suicide have compounded the confusion, but their studies have been accepted with little critical appraisal. The issues surrounding physician-assisted suicide necessitate precise language and accurate historical representation. The historical distortions that have now become part of legal records, such as those of Dr. Jack Kevorkian, may become part of future public discussion and debate.

Chapter Eighteen

DID EARLY CHRISTIANS "LUST AFTER DEATH"?

A New Wrinkle in the Doctor-Assisted Suicide Debate

Darrel W. Amundsen

MANY CHRISTIANS, AS WELL AS OTHERS, assume that the Bible and church history have consistently condemned self-murder, or what is commonly known as suicide.[1] However, because this assumption generally has not been defended with great rigor, most people who accept this assumption are not prepared to support it when it is called into question.

Recently some scholars have argued that the Christian tradition has not always condemned suicide and that martyrdom is a form of suicide that has been applauded in church history. This distortion is being offered by judges as well as historians as a basis to support the cause of doctor-assisted suicide, made popular in recent years by the work of Michigan pathologist Jack Kevorkian. It has become crucial that Christians, as well as other pro-lifers, be prepared to respond to this pseudo history.

Secular activists in the right-to-die movement typically campaign for a right of the ill to procure the assistance of others (usually physicians) in expediting their deaths. This is an issue that expanding numbers of voters are facing and on which judges are increasingly asked to rule.

THE JUDGE AS HISTORIAN

When Dr. Jack Kevorkian, charged with the felonious act of assisted suicide, appeared in Michigan Circuit Court, Wayne County, on December 13, 1993, he insisted that a right to commit suicide is fundamental to those liberty interests protected by the Fourteenth Amendment. In his opinion on Michigan's law that forbids assisted suicide,[2] Judge Richard C. Kaufman wrote, "The prosecutor argues that a right cannot be deemed fundamental, and thus entitled to protection through the 'liberty' provision of the Fourteenth Amendment, unless it is based upon our Nation's history and tradition. In contrast, the defendant [Kevorkian] insists that history and tradition can be completely ignored in distilling the existence of a fundamental liberty interest. This Court rejects both approaches."[3]

En route to rejecting both approaches, Judge Kaufman felt compelled "to analyze whether the claimed right is 'deeply rooted in this Nation's history and traditions.'"[4] Although perhaps a competent legal scholar, Judge Kaufman proved himself to be an inept historian, relying exclusively on one questionable secondary source for his understanding of the history of the ethical/theological (as distinct from legal) dimensions of suicide. That secondary source was Alfred Alvarez,[5] whom Judge Kaufman clearly regarded as a reliable and authoritative "historian." Nonetheless, Alvarez is not a historian but a poet, literary critic, and writer of fiction, nonfiction, and screenplays.

After quoting some of Alvarez's comments on the openness of pagan classical culture to suicide, Judge Kaufman admits that "the teachings of mainstream Christian and Judaic faith find suicide anathema." But then he repeats Alvarez's unfounded claim that "the idea of suicide as a crime comes late in Christian doctrine. . . . It was not until the sixth century that the Church finally legislated against it, and then the only Biblical authority was a special interpretation of the Sixth Commandment: 'Thou shalt not kill.' The bishops were urged into action by St. Augustine; but he, as Rousseau remarked, took his arguments from Plato's *Phaedo*, not from the Bible."[6]

Judge Kaufman adopts Alvarez's view "that when the Christian Church decided to adopt a prohibition on suicide it had a difficult time in supporting this new position on the basis of the Scriptures." Supposedly, it was difficult for the church to justify its ban on suicide because the Bible does not directly condemn it.[7]

Judge Kaufman next asserts that Christianity's emphasis on the afterlife and its supposed emphasis on the unimportance of this life were a powerful incitement to suicide. This, according to the judge, led Christians to welcome death and thus to commit suicide by means of martyrdom. But the church had to stop the practice. He writes: "Although theologically rooted in the concept of the sanctity of life, the change in Christianity's attitude toward suicide was, as Alvarez persuasively argues, primarily motivated by practicalities. He explains that the cult of martyrdom led to a rapid increase of actual suicide in the name of religion. In order to preserve its numbers the early Church needed to stop this practice."[8]

Judge Kaufman then suggests, "As can be seen from this historical analysis, attitudes towards suicide in Western civilization evolved with radical changes." Quoting Alvarez he concludes, "An act which during the flowering of Western civilization had been tolerated, later admired, and later still sought as a supreme mark of zealotry, became finally the object of intense moral revulsion."[9] According to Alvarez, it was Augustine who was responsible for this profound change.

WHAT OTHER "AUTHORITIES" SAY

If written during the last several decades, assessments of early Christianity's view of suicide—whether by sociologists, anthropologists, psychologists, or philosophers—typically are consistent with those of Alvarez. For example, in his *The Sanctity of Life and the Criminal Law*, the noted legal scholar and philosopher Glanville Williams writes,

> There is no condemnation of suicide in the New Testament, and little to be found among the early Christians, who were, indeed, morbidly obsessed with death. . . . The Christian belief was that life on earth was important only as a preparation for the hereafter; the supreme duty was to avoid sin, which would result in perpetual punishment. Since all natural desires tended toward sin, the risk of failure was great. Many Christians, therefore, committed suicide for fear of falling before temptation. It was especially good if the believer could commit suicide by provoking infidels to martyr him, or by austerities so severe that they undermined the constitution, but in the last resort he might do away with himself directly.[10]

Influence of Emile Durkheim

Because Western culture is so thoroughly severed from its moral roots and from its Judeo-Christian heritage, it is not surprising that scholars in a variety of fields arrive at conclusions that are simply an articulation of their erroneous presuppositions regarding the very essence of historical Christianity. These scholars base their opinions about early Christianity neither on an examination of early Christian theology nor on an investigation of the historical evidence.

In discussions of suicide, the conceptual influence comes from the father of academic sociology in France, Emile Durkheim, who obscured some basic issues. In his *Le suicide: étude sociologique*, published in 1897 but not translated into English until 1951,[11] he created three categories of suicide: (1) egoistic suicide, which results from a lack of social integration; (2) anomic suicide, which is precipitated by the destabilizing effects of sudden negative or positive social change; and (3) altruistic suicide, which results from overintegration, especially when the individual is completely controlled by religious or political groups.

Durkheim formulated his definition of suicide so as to render immaterial the question whether the individual intended his own death: "All cases of death resulting directly or indirectly from a positive or negative act of the victim himself, which he knows will produce this result."[12] It is suicide if the individual believes that his positive or negative action(s) will result in his own death. Accordingly, Durkheim classifies as (altruistic) suicides the deaths of Christian martyrs who,

> without killing themselves, voluntarily allowed their own slaughter. . . . Though they did not kill themselves, they sought death with all their power and behaved so as to make it inevitable. To be suicide, the act from which death must necessarily result need only have been performed by the victim with full knowledge of the facts. Besides, the passionate enthusiasm with which the believers in the new religion faced final torture shows that at this moment they had completely discarded their personalities for the idea of which they had become the servants.[13]

Thus, dying for one's beliefs is suicide, and since the person who commits suicide is a victim of pathological social phenomena, a martyr is a victim not of those who put him to death but of his religion's demand for excessive integration of the individual into the group.

Two Liberal Theologians Compound the Confusion

When secular scholars apply Durkheim's grid to the history of early Christianity, it results in predictable distortions. Hence, when two theologians trained in Old and New Testament history and in patristics recently published a book entitled *A Noble Death: Suicide and Martyrdom among Christians and Jews in Antiquity*, it was reasonable to hope for some clarification and correction. Unfortunately, these scholars, Arthur J. Droge and James D. Tabor, have further compounded the confusion. They eschew the word *suicide* as "a recent innovation and pejorative term, preferring instead the designation *voluntary death*. By this term we mean to describe the act resulting from an individual's intentional decision to die, either by his own agency, by another's, or by contriving the circumstances in which death is the known, ineluctable result" (emphasis in original).[14] After acknowledging the similarity of their definition of voluntary death to Durkheim's definition of suicide, they say that theirs is "intended to be morally neutral, since our enterprise is not one of moral (or clinical) judgment but an attempt to understand the ways in which voluntary death was evaluated in antiquity."[15]

Droge and Tabor insist that the concept of voluntary death is a much more objective grid than suicide for the historian (and theologian as well). Their avowed intention was "to deconstruct the 'linguistics of suicide' by examining the precise terms and formulations employed in antiquity to denote the act of voluntary death."[16] They correctly assert that the English word *suicide* (as well as the post classical Latin *suicidium* from which it is derived) is of recent vintage and that it is a pejorative term. Not only is it almost always used negatively, but it is also semantically and conceptually ambiguous. They also contend that *martyr*, a generally favorable term, is as semantically and conceptually ambiguous as suicide. They think that they have reduced the ambiguity and confusion by calling suicide and martyrdom voluntary death. They want to be morally neutral; so does Durkheim. But since Durkheim views suicide as a result of various social pathologies, he conveys a negative view of suicide. Droge and Tabor convey a positive view of voluntary death since, as the title of their book proclaims, a voluntary death is a noble death. Is the result credible history?

After analyzing the suicides of Abimelech, Saul and his armor-bearer, Samson, Ahithophel, and Zimri, Droge and Tabor say of Elijah's request that God take his life (1 Kings 19:4-5), "Though no act of self destruction is involved, we might term this a 'voluntary departure' or perhaps even a 'voluntary death.'"[17] Aaron's "death is voluntary in the sense that he submitted to God's decision" that it was time for him to die![18] They speculate that "whether Moses himself took a hand in his own death or not is left unclear, though it might well be implied," and then say, "The point we want to emphasize here is that the distinctions tend to be blurred between a request that God take one's life, God's determining the time of death, and one's taking a hand to carry out such a choice or decision."[19] The blurring is Droge and Tabor's doing. They prove to be even more adept at blurring distinctions when they deconstruct New Testament and patristic texts.

"It is a profound irony of Western history," they maintain, that Christian theologians, beginning with Augustine, "condemned the act of voluntary death as a sin for which Christ's similar act could not atone. . . ."[20] Later in the book they carry this argument further: "Despite the claim of Augustine and later theologians, the New Testament expresses no condemnation of voluntary death. . . . Yet, to say only that the writers of the New Testament did not condemn voluntary death is to miss the positive significance they attached to the act. The authors of the Gospels created [sic] a Jesus who died by his own choice, if not by his own hand."[21] Jesus' "voluntary death" is a theme central to their argument. They ask, "Was it the legal execution of a criminal, an example of heroic martyrdom, or a case of suicide?"[22] Irrespective of how that rhetorical question is answered, "The Jesus created by his earliest followers became the paradigm for Christians to imitate."[23]

Martyrdom in the early church supplies Droge and Tabor with abundant examples of "voluntary death": "The martyrs are portrayed as going to their death in one of three ways: either as a result of being sought out, by deliberately volunteering, or by actually taking their own lives. On the basis of the evidence that has survived, it would appear that the majority of Christian martyrs chose death by the second and third means."[24] The accuracy of the last sentence is highly questionable.[25]

One example of the first category that they give is Bishop Pionius who, arrested around A.D. 250, reminded his fellow Christian prisoners that Jesus had "departed from life at his own choice." Droge and Tabor emphasize that Pionius could easily have escaped death by offering sacrifices to the pagan gods. But he chose to follow Christ's example.[26] They fault as "anachronistic and without textual support" Robin Lane Fox's comment that "Pionius shared the Church's execration of suicide, a death, naturally, which was quite distinct from martyrdom."[27] (It is, of course, their own faddish linguistic deconstructionism and historical revisionism that, by their very nature, do violence to the texts and are inevitably anachronistic.) "On the contrary," they maintain, "Pionius insists that Jesus . . . 'departed from life at his own choice.' In other words, Jesus' death, like Dionius's, was *voluntary!*" (emphasis in original).[28]

But, according to Droge and Tabor, so was Judas's death: "In the *Umwelt* of early Christianity the act of taking one's life was judged to be acceptable and, in certain circumstances, noble. . . . This was Matthew's implicit judgment on Judas's death. Judas was condemned for betraying the Messiah, not for killing himself. According to Matthew, Judas's act of self-destruction was the measure of his remorse and repentance."[29]

Convinced that Paul "lusts after death,"[30] they dwell on his "fascination with death and his desire to escape from life."[31] The only reason, they say, that Paul did not end his life with his own hand (see Phil. 1:21–25) was that the time was not opportune. "That Paul was not opposed to voluntary death is clear from his famous panegyric to *agape* in 1 Corinthians 13, where he classified self-destruction with other *worthy* but ineffectual approaches to salvation" (emphasis in original).[32] They further suggest that "for Paul, an individual could kill himself and be 'glorifying God with his body' by doing so."[33] Indeed, "In a world-negating system like the apostle Paul's, the question became how to justify continued existence in the world rather than voluntary death,"[34] for, as their book' s final words emphasize, "voluntary death was one of the ideals on which the church was founded."[35]

RELEVANCE FOR THE DOCTOR-ASSISTED SUICIDE DEBATE

People may disagree about the relevance to the doctor-assisted suicide debate of the history of suicide as an ethical issue. All should agree, however, that inaccurate history cannot be relevant. Judge Kaufman's flawed historical and theological perceptions suffer from Alvarez's adoption of Durkheim's definition of suicide, amplified by inaccurate theological presuppositions. Sad to say, sources similar to Alvarez abound on the shelves of libraries. The entry of trained theologians into the discussion has further muddied the waters.

Droge and Tabor's work has typically been greeted as a significant contribution to the current debate.[36] This suggests that the advocates of active voluntary euthanasia are, by arguing that principles of respect for, and sanctity of, human life are far from consistent and fundamental features of Christian tradition, seeking to preempt Christian efforts to inform moral discussion. How may this distortion of early Christian theology and history be countered?

First, we must recognize that the issues are extremely complex. Is there a moral difference in a terminally ill patient's (1) insisting that extraordinary means not be initiated or be discontinued so that "nature" may take its course; (2) requesting palliative medications for pain even though the patient is aware that, as a secondary effect, his or her death may be expedited; or (3) asking for means that either the patient or someone else will employ directly to bring about immediate death? Typically the third is regarded as suicide, a moral category under which are subsumed extremely diverse variables.

Second, we must insist on conceptual and semantic precision. An entirely objective and consistent definition of suicide will never be made to everyone's satisfaction. Robert N. Wennberg, in his book *Terminal Choices: Euthanasia, Suicide, and the Right to Die*, presents a compelling answer to the question posed as the title of chapter 2, "Suicide: What Is It?"[37] He maintains that "a suicide is someone who *intends* to die, either as a means . . . or as an end" (emphasis in original).[38] His definition would exclude martyrs who did not seek death but were willing to die rather than deny their faith, even if they had a "strong, unwavering desire to die and be ushered into the presence of the God [they] had faithfully served all [their lives]."[39] Intent is for Wennberg the crucial and decisive factor. But not for Durkheim, whose broad sociological definition of suicide glosses over and distorts ethical, theological, and historical issues.

The differences are so significant between, for instance, hanging oneself after being jilted by one's lover, burning oneself to death as a public protest against a government's policies, sacrificing one's life to save others' lives, and being executed for refusing to renounce one's most deeply held convictions, that to label them all as "voluntary death" and then insist that anyone who approves of any of them approves of all forms of "voluntary death," flies in the face of even the most basic logic and common sense.

At least one reviewer of Droge and Tabor's book understands this. William Birmingham observes that "the authors' perhaps unconscious tendency to legitimate one form of voluntary death, suicide, by too closely associating it with others—death for the sake of honor, martyrdom for the sake of faith—blurs ethical lines and vitiates readers' confidence in their handling of evidence. . . ."[40]

Nevertheless, we do no service to the truth if we deny that there have been some aberrations and excesses in the history of Christianity. Some early Christians intentionally provoked pagans to martyr them. It may be perverse obstinacy to insist that such were not suicides. Furthermore, Christian women who killed themselves to avoid sexual defilement, especially during times of persecution, were venerated by their fellow Christians. Were they suicides? Although the philosophical principle of double effect (i.e., distinguishing between results that are intended and consequences that are foreseen and even inevitable but not desired) may be marshaled in support of the contention that they were not, only those who are willing will be convinced by such an approach.

Finally, asceticism as a Christian virtue became a form of daily martyrdom, especially after Christians ceased to be a persecuted minority. Although the church quite consistently condemned asceticism if based on dualistic heresy or if practiced to excess, some Christians undoubtedly brought on an early demise through immoderate mortification of the flesh. Were they suicides? Here again one may resort to double effect. Intent is then the criterion. Severe asceticism was practiced not in order to expedite one's death but to purify one's soul.

I bring up these matters to emphasize that there are some gray areas. We should argue strongly against the proposition that early Christians lauded self-murder per *se*, but we should not weaken our argument by being inflexible regarding those questionable areas that were never normative for Christian practice.

Third, we must reject a presentistic treatment of ancient texts. Scholars such as Droge and Tabor maintain that since neither Greek nor Latin had a specific word for suicide, we risk reading our preconceptions into the past if we apply our word, with all of its conceptual baggage, to ancient texts. While there is some validity to their concern, even if Greek or Latin had an exact equivalent of our word suicide, it would be fraught with the same ambiguities; hence it would still demand precise contextual interpretation. Extant Greek texts employ over 160 different terms or phrases to denote the taking of one's own life; Latin over 170.[41] Ancient Greeks and Romans, whether pagans or

Christians, were quite able to distinguish between various circumstances, motives, and methods of self-killing.

Self-killing encompasses a range of actions and choices involving complex issues that, as I have asserted above, will never be untangled to everyone's satisfaction. This did not prevent the ancients from making most of the same distinctions that we do among a wide variety of motives for taking one's own life, including escape from grinding chronic suffering or painful terminal illness. Suicide by the ill is frequently discussed as an ethical issue in pagan classical texts and was quite commonly practiced. Indeed, classical literature is rife with examples.[42]

Physicians regularly assisted in such suicides (as well as in suicides by those not suffering from illness or disabilities). Those relatively rare examples of physicians' refusing to assist in suicide are particularly striking (e.g., in the so-called Hippocratic Oath).

Although early Christians lived in a secular milieu in which suicide to escape from illness was frequently practiced, I am unaware of any discussion of the issue in the entirety of patristic literature. Nor can I find one example of a Christian during the first five centuries of Christianity taking his own life to escape from the suffering of terminal or other illness. The only ethical issues raised by illness in patristic literature were (1) the propensity of Christians to seek the help of physicians without first considering the spiritual significance of their sickness, (2) their resorting to occult healing practices; and (3) their sometimes frantic efforts to cling to any slim hope of recovery. By actively caring for the sick, early Christians, in Henry Sigerist's words, introduced "the most revolutionary and decisive change in the attitude of society toward the sick. . . . The social position of the sick man thus became fundamentally different from what it had been before. He assumed a preferential position which has been his ever since."[43] There is absolutely no evidence that this preferential position of the sick encouraged an expedited "final exit."[44]

It could be maintained that the absence of any discussion or examples of suicide by the ill in patristic literature supplies at best an argument from silence. Such an absence can best be explained, however, by noting those aspects of life and belief in the early church that militated against suicide to escape from illness.

Consider the theology of martyrdom. There was much dispute within the Christian community regarding the propriety of seeking martyrdom. We can with confidence assert that those who condemned it would also condemn the intentional killing of oneself. And those who approved seeking martyrdom did so for a variety of reasons (e.g., the spiritual benefits thought to derive from such a death, the "protest value" of dying dramatically for one's faith), none of which could apply to suicide to escape from illness.

Furthermore, whereas martyrdom is the ultimate act of suffering and sacrifice for one's beliefs, suicide—unless it is an act of protest—is the ultimate act of escape from suffering. Suicide in the face of illness can be seen as analogous to martyrdom only if God is viewed as either significantly less than sovereign or as an oppressive tyrant. So foundational are the goodness and sovereignty of God in patristic theology and so consistently is patient endurance of affliction stressed as an essential Christian virtue, that it is not at all surprising that patristic texts do not refer to suicide by the ill.[45]

My fourth and final suggestion for a Christian response to this distortion of history moves the issue to an individual level: every Christian must be thoroughly grounded in Scripture. Even if you are never involved in any aspect of this debate, would doctor-assisted suicide be a morally acceptable option for you, as a Christian, if you were terminally ill?

Although Scripture nowhere refers to doctor-assisted suicide, it does provide a relevant theological framework for the consideration of those moral issues that it does not specifically address. God's Word enables us to formulate a theology of life and death, sin and holiness, joy and suffering, and, most importantly, a theology of the sovereignty of God.[46]

I was compelled to do that in a highly personal sense when I recently agreed to write an article for a new journal. I presented my argument under six headings: (1) "You were bought with a price"; (2) "If you love Me, you will keep My commandments"; (3) "Whether we live or die, we are the Lord's"; (4) "Waiting eagerly for our adoption as sons, the redemption of our body"; (5) "That I may know Him and the power of His resurrection and the fellowship of His sufferings"; and (6) "Precious in the sight of the Lord is the death of His godly ones." I thus concluded the paper: Jesus is my Sovereign. He has bought me with His blood. I have been called into a fellowship of suffering with Him. I cannot claim to understand this fully, either intellectually or experientially. Perhaps it will be in my dying that my comprehension of His marvelously condescending love will be enriched when, in ways of which my experiences thus far are but adumbrations, the Holy Spirit will be my Comforter and Jesus my Comfort. To take my life—or to ask another to—in order to escape from the final act of my personal drama that He has written and is directing, would be worse than rebellion. It would be for me a failure of love and a breach of trust.[47]

If we are not markedly different from secularists in our dying, we are of all people most to be pitied. Bombarded as we are by sometimes blatant, sometimes subtle secularism, we must not only strive to live as Christians but be prepared to die as Christians. Although we shall not know death experientially until we have entered its portals, it is incumbent upon us to be equipped to understand and withstand those temptations that are unique to that realm.

ENDNOTES

1. Historic Christianity's wrestling with the moral ambiguities of suicide precipitated by depressive or other mental illnesses lies outside the parameters of this article.
2. *1993 WL 603212* (Mich. Cir. Ct.).
3. Ibid., 6.

4. Ibid., 7.
5. Judge Kaufman's quotations are from Alfred Alvarez's "The Background," in *Suicide: The Philosophical Issues*, ed. M. P. Battin and D. J. May (New York: St. Martin's, 1980), 7-32, which is chapter one of Alvarez's very influential book, *The Savage God: A Study of Suicide* (New York: Random House, 1970).
6. *1993 WL 603212* (Mich. Cir. Ct.), 9.
7. Ibid.
8. Ibid., 9–10.
9. Ibid., 10.
10. Glanville Williams, *The Sanctity of Life and the Criminal Law* (1957; reprint, New York: Knopf, 1970), 254-55.
11. Emile Durkheim, *Suicide: A Study in Sociology*, trans. J. A. Spaulding and G. Simpson (Glencoe, Ill.: Free Press, 1951).
12. Ibid., 44.
13. Ibid., 227, cf. 67.
14. Arthur J. Droge and James D. Tabor, *A Noble Death: Suicide and Martyrdom among Christians and Jews in Antiquity* (San Francisco: HarperCollins, 1992), 4.
15. Ibid.
16. Ibid., 187.
17. Ibid., 61–62.
18. Ibid., 62.
19. Ibid., 63.
20. Ibid., 5.
21. Ibid., 125.
22. Ibid., 114.
23. Ibid., 119.
24. Ibid., 156.
25. Still the best treatment is W. H. C. Frend, *Martyrdom and Persecution in the Early Church* (Oxford: Blackwell, 1965).
26. Ibid., 153.
27. Robin Lane Fox, *Pagans and Christians* (San Francisco: Harper & Row, 1986), 480.
28. Droge and Tabor, 164–65, n. 124.
29. Ibid., 125.
30. Ibid., 122.
31. Ibid., 119.
32. Ibid., 123.
33. Ibid., 124.
34. Ibid., 187.
35. Ibid., 189.
36. Derek Humphry, founder of the Hemlock Society and author of a well-known suicide manual, exclaims on the dust jacket of Droge and Tabor's book, "This book will upset traditional Christian views about the right to choose to die." A fellow founding member of the Hemlock Society, Gerald A. Larue, adjunct professor of gerontology and emeritus professor of biblical history and archeology at the University of Southern California, writes that Droge and Tabor "have shown in their careful analysis of all relevant biblical passages [that] there is no condemnation of, or negative comment on, what they prefer to call 'voluntary death'" (*Playing God: Fifty Religions' Views on Your Right to Die*

[Wakefield, R.I.: Moyer Bell, 1996], 19). Reviews of Droge and Tabor's book typically have been overwhelmingly favorable.

37. Robert N. Wennberg, *Terminal Choices: Euthanasia, Suicide, and the Right to Die* (Grand Rapids: Eerdmans, 1989), 16–38.

38. Ibid., 22.

39. Ibid., 28.

40. William Birmingham, review of Droge and Tabor's *A Noble Death* in *Cross Currents: The Journal of The Association for Religion and Intellectual Life* 42 (1992): 273–74.

41. See "Appendix C: Suicidal Vocabulary of Greek and Latin," in Anton J. L. van Hooff, *From Autothanasia to Suicide: Self-Killing in Classical Antiquity* (London: Routledge, 1990), 243–50.

42. See, e.g., Danielle Gourevitch, "Suicide among the Sick in Classical Antiquity," *Bulletin of the History of Medicine* 43 (1969): 501–18.

43. Henry Sigerist, *Civilization and Disease* (Chicago: University of Chicago Press, 1943), 69–70.

44. See Darrel W. Amundsen, *Medicine Society and Faith in the Ancient and Medieval Worlds* (Baltimore: Johns Hopkins University Press, 1996), especially chapters 1, "Body, Soul, and Physician," and 4, "Suicide and Early Christianity."

45. It should be noted that Augustine (354–430) was not the first church father to condemn suicide. Furthermore, he based his condemnation essentially on the same theology as did earlier church fathers who condemned the act: Justin Martyr (ca. 100–165), Clement of Alexandria (ca. 155–220), Tertullian (ca. 160–220), the anonymous *Epistle to Diognetus* (late second century), the anonymous Clementine *Homilies* (late second/early third century), Lactantius (ca. 240–320), Ambrose (ca. 339–397), Jerome (ca. 345–419), and John Chrysostom (349–407). For references and discussion see ibid., 70–126.

46. The writings of Joni Eareckson Tada are an excellent starting point. Most pertinent to the doctor-assisted suicide debate is her *When Is It Right to Die? Suicide, Euthanasia, Suffering, Mercy* (Grand Rapids: Zondervan, 1992). The easy readability of her writings belies their theological depth and spiritual richness.

47. Darrel W. Amundsen, "Suffering and the Sovereignty of God: One Evangelical's Perspective on Doctor-Assisted Suicide," *Christian Bioethics* 1 (1995): 305.

An Overview

Margaret Pabst Battin's attempt to make certain forms of suicide a fundamental right includes an effort to discredit the Christian influence in the discussion; an influence she believes does not have a legitimate play in a pluralistic setting. Does Christian teaching, as Battin claims, actually invite the faithful to commit suicide? And is the Christian prohibition against suicide merely a reaction designed to eliminate suicide attempts? A. A. Howsepian reveals the numerous weaknesses in Battin's argument and hermeneutics, discloses her subjective understanding of what constitutes human dignity, and provides a response to Battin's unsupportable claim that suicide is a natural or fundamental right.

Chapter Nineteen

SOME RESERVATIONS
ABOUT SUICIDE

A. A. Howsepian, M.D.

I

IN "SUICIDE: A FUNDAMENTAL HUMAN RIGHT?" Margaret Pabst Battin argues that certain forms of suicide are constitutive of human dignity and, therefore, that the commission of such suicides is a fundamental human right.[1] In another essay, "Prohibition and Invitation: The Paradox of Religious Views about Suicide," she argues that a universal moral prohibition against suicide based upon Christian moral teaching can have no proper role to play in the contemporary pluralistic discussion.[2] She claims that, on the one hand, there are deep and irreconcilable tensions in the Christian tradition concerning the morality of suicide—tensions that culminate in her surprising thesis that, for the Christian, not only is suicide on occasion morally permissible, but that in fact sometimes suicide is morally obligatory—and that, on the other hand, the tradition's best arguments for there being such a universal prohibition are unconvincing. Battin's arguments are intended to play a pivotal role in the contemporary discussion concerning physician-assisted suicide and other forms of euthanasia.

Although I acknowledge the fact that several popular arguments for there being a universal moral prohibition against suicide are unconvincing, I here attempt to show that some religious arguments against the moral permissibility of suicide are invulnerable to Battin's specific criticisms of them. In addition, I argue that the deep tensions that she perceives in the Christian tradition regarding suicide are, in large part, illusory. Along the way, I draw attention to Alasdair MacIntyre's reservations concerning the very grounds for there being natural rights. If MacIntyre is right, then *contra* Battin, not only do we have no natural right to suicide, but we have no natural rights at all. Finally, in connection with Battin's discussion of dignity and suicide, I briefly introduce Jorge Garcia's apt reflections on whether or not it is possible for one to be better off dead.

II

"[A]rguments against suicide" according to Margaret Pabst Battin, "originated within religious contexts" (p. 205). And, she continues, "it is

Christianity's opposition to suicide that is the basis of much of our cultural and legal disapprobation of [it]" (p. 205). But, she claims, the scriptural, theological, and rational foundations for an absolute moral prohibition against suicide within the Christian tradition are demonstrably inadequate, and this in two ways. First, Battin claims that religious arguments for such an absolute prohibition against suicide are seriously defective. Although Battin does not go so far as to claim that an adequate religious argument for the absolute moral prohibition against suicide *cannot* be constructed, she does suggest that all such arguments of which she is aware are unsuccessful.

Second, Battin argues that, in the light of the perceived inadequacy of Christian conceptual foundations invoked in support of a universal moral prohibition against suicide, the primary reason for the unreasonably strong moral stance against suicide found in the Christian tradition is that Christian teaching actually *invites* the faithful to commit suicide. In order for the faithful to resist this impulse, she hypothesizes that Christian teaching prohibiting suicide has grown increasingly, albeit unreasonably, forceful. "Christianity," she writes, "*invites* suicide in a way in which other major religions do not; it is for this reason, we may suppose, that Christianity has been forced to erect stringent prohibitions against it" (p. 206).

Battin begins by enumerating and criticizing a series of arguments prohibiting suicide to which there have been explicit appeals made within the Christian tradition. Almost all of these arguments, she states, "presuppose the existence of a divine being, as well as the meaningfulness of such concepts as salvation, retribution, and sin; and almost all of these arguments could be defeated by denying these beliefs" (p. 206). It is, to say the least, exceedingly odd to claim that an argument can be *defeated* by denying certain of its premises. If this were so, then one could easily defeat a whole host of arguments (including W. V. O. Quine's arguments for the radical indeterminacy of translation and the inscrutability of reference) with almost no effort at all. At any rate, Battin refuses to take this low road to "victory." Rather, she intends to presuppose many of those traditional theological beliefs to which the Christian tradition appeals and only then attempts to defeat the arguments in question on other grounds.

Battin divides the arguments for there being a universal moral prohibition against suicide in the Christian tradition into four principal groups: (1) arguments based on biblical grounds; (2) arguments based on analogies to ordinary objects and relations; (3) natural law arguments; and (4) arguments that rely on the role that suffering is thought to play in the Christian life. She begins her analysis of the biblical text-based arguments by stating that "there is no explicit prohibition of suicide in the Bible . . . [n]or is there any passage in either the Old or New Testament that can be directly understood as an explicit prohibition of suicide" (p. 207). She continues, "[T]hose passages that are often taken to support such a prohibition require . . . a considerable amount of interpretation and qualification" (p. 207). This is all quite puzzling. Evidently, the word *directly* is doing a lot of work for Battin here. Even if it were granted, as Battin claims, that "there is no word anywhere in the Bible

. . . that is equivalent to the English term suicide [*sic*]," certainly there are either explicit biblical passages themselves or their clear entailments that can plainly be understood as being prohibitions of suicide, if only because there are passages that *have* plainly been so understood by scholars in the Christian tradition; and, as the saying goes, "if it's actual, it must be possible."

It is true, but not in itself interesting, that some biblical passages are more complex and more difficult to understand than others. Devising methods for elucidating the meanings of these more difficult passages is what the discipline of hermeneutics strives to perfect. Many scientific texts contain passages that require a great deal of interpretive skill and proper qualification. What is supposed to follow from this? It has often been pointed out that neither the term *Trinity* nor the term *incarnation* is found in the biblical texts, yet the clear interpretations of several biblical passages leave no plausible conceptual space for the claim that the Christian Scriptures teach neither that God is a Trinity nor that Jesus is God incarnate.

Battin claims that,

> The Christian use of the Sixth Commandment as the basis for the prohibition of suicide originates with St. Augustine; prior to the early fifth century A.D., the church had no unified position on the moral status of suicide, and was widely divided on whether various forms of self-killing, including deliberate martyrdom and religiously motivated suicide, were to be allowed. (p. 210)

She then argues that this commandment "does not serve as a general prohibition of self-killing, since self-killing may not always be wrongful killing" (p. 210) and that the sixth commandment (as numbered by Protestants) is best translated "Thou shalt do no wrongful killing," or perhaps "Thou shalt do no murder." She goes on to say that the sixth commandment is

> almost universally relaxed to permit the killing of plants and animals, . . . [and] the killing of human beings in self defense, capital punishment, and war. However, one might argue, if under this commandment the killing of human beings is permitted in these situations, it is hard to see why [*sic*] it should not also be permitted in the case of suicide. Indeed, suicide would seem to have a stronger claim to morality, since suicide alone does not violate the wishes of the individual killed. (p. 210)

We must first attend to the fact that it is simply false that "suicide alone does not violate the wishes of the individual killed" (p. 210). Some persons who commit suicide do not, in any ordinary sense of the term "wish" to kill themselves: sometimes suicide is seen, whether rightly or wrongly, as the only way out of an otherwise unbearable situation. Suppose, for example, that a terrorist demands that Jones kill himself or else he (the terrorist) will summarily execute Jones's family. Now Jones in no way wishes to die *and* he in no way wishes for his family to die. Whether rightly or wrongly, Jones chooses to kill himself in this situation for the sake of preserving the life of his family, but it would surely be inappropriate to insist that some of Jones's deepest wishes were not violated in this circumstance. On the other hand, it is obvious that certain *non*suicidal forms of killing also do *not* violate the deepest wishes of those individuals who are killed. Some faithful Mormons, for example, who have been found guilty of murder have uncompromisingly demanded that they undergo capital punishment (specifically by firing squad) in order to help atone for those sins for which, according to orthodox Mormon doctrine, Christ's sacrificial death alone was inefficacious.

Battin's claim that the sixth commandment has been "relaxed" in order for the Christian church to have permitted the killing of plants and animals is quite puzzling. I am unaware of any plausible historical or textual reason for thinking that the sixth commandment could *possibly* have been properly applied to the killing of plants and animals, and thus was in need of "relaxation," especially in light of the culture-of-sacrifice into which the commandments were introduced. It seems most plausible to view the biblical injunction expressed by the sixth commandment not as "Thou shalt do no wrongful killing," but as Battin's other tentatively advanced suggestion, viz. "Thou shalt not murder." All murders are, after all, wrongful killings of certain sorts, namely, those wrongful killings that are constituted by one's intentionally bringing about the deaths of innocent persons. (One cannot, for example, murder walking sticks, iguanas, or thrips.) On this understanding of the commandment, there would be no "relaxation" involved when permitting the killings of plants, sheep, fish, thrips, or other humans whether in self-defense, for capital crimes, or in just wars if, in fact, certain instances of these latter varieties of human killing are not murderous killings.

This does not, of course, settle what it is precisely that constitutes an act as a murderous killing, or even what constitutes an act as a nonmurderous wrongful killing of, say, innocent human persons. It is one of the most conspicuous defects in Battin's essay on religious views of suicide that she nowhere gives a careful, satisfying analysis of what suicide *is*. Her claim that there are a total of eleven suicides chronicled in Scripture (including two in the Apocrypha) suggests that she has adopted an idiosyncratic understanding of this notion, an understanding that is not, to my mind, philosophically current, morally significant, or conceptually satisfying. This becomes clear when one examines the examples of alleged suicides that she adduces from the biblical texts. One such example involves "Samson, who in destroying the Philistines pulled the temple down upon himself" (p. 208). What is Battin's justification for so confidently proposing this as an example of suicide? Nowhere in the biblical texts does it imply that Samson intended to take his own life as a result of this act. Surely it is critical to suicide (just as it is critical to murder generally) to *intend* the death of the one killed. Even if Samson were to have known that his destroying the temple would result in his death, there is no reason to think that his death was the result of a suicide. Battin, of course, might not see it this way, but she really *must* see it this way if she intends to address what, in fact, constitutes the traditional Christian prohibition of suicide, for this traditional Christian prohibition involves only *intentional* self-killings, not just any act that results in one's death. (Unintended self-killings may be properly handled by the doctrine of double effect.)

This troubling feature of Battin's piece, i.e., the conspicuous absence of a conceptually subtle, intellectually satisfying characterization of what suicide is, surfaces repeatedly. For instance, Battin's discussion of St. Augustine's distinction between "private killing" and divinely ordered killing is also undertaken in a context in which the notion of suicide appears to be infelicitously characterized. The principal problem with which Augustine[3] struggles is how to understand those scriptural passages in which God commands the taking of human lives. Private killings of human beings, i.e., killings of human beings by one's own authority are, according to Augustine, intrinsically evil and hence never permissible. But, he argues, perhaps not all human self-killings are private killings. There may be cases in which God, for instance, authorizes a self-killing. In such a case, not only is the self-killing morally permissible, it is also morally obligatory. From this Battin concludes that, according to Augustine, "Suicide is permitted under divine command; otherwise, it is not" (p. 211).

But the inference from "some self-killings are morally permissible" to "some suicides are morally permissible" is as misshapen as the inference from "some killings of other human beings are morally permissible" to "some murders are morally permissible." For not all self-killings are suicides; just as not all killings of others are murders. In fact what Battin appears to have overlooked is that suicide—that human act that is universally prohibited in traditional Christian moral theory—is just a form of *murder*, viz. self-murder. Insofar as this is the case, a large number of self-killings discussed by Battin under the rubric of suicide have been egregiously misclassified.

Battin first addresses what she feels are the inadequacies of the religious analogy arguments against suicide frequently invoked within the Christian tradition. One such argument draws on an analogy between life and a gift from God. The argument states that "because life is a gift of God, one ought not destroy it by suicide" (p. 217). This argument, according to Battin,

> is open to a very simple objection, first formulated by the eighteenth-century Swedish philosopher, Johan Robeck . . . who . . . argued that if life is a gift, then it becomes the property of the recipient, who may therefore do with it as he or she wishes. In giving a gift, the donor relinquishes his or her rights and control over the gift item; if he or she does not, then the item is not a genuine gift. (p. 217)

Battin appears to recognize the thinness of this objection as it stands. "We are, of course, aware of circumstances in which it would indeed be wrong to destroy a gift—for instance, if it is an object like a peck of wheat, a warm coat, or a fifty dollar bill" (p. 217). But, she argues, "these counter-arguments show only that it is wrong to destroy an item if it is useful to someone else, or if it has intrinsic value of its own; they do not show that it is wrong to destroy something *because it is a gift*" (p. 217). Battin does, though, explicitly acknowledge the personal relation of gratitude, which appears to be quite proper in such gift-giving contexts, and, given the assumption that the gift of life is given by God, suicide may thereby be viewed as an expression of extreme and ultimate ingratitude toward God.

However, argues Battin, ingratitude toward the giver of a gift—whether the giver be merely human or divine—can be appropriate in cases where the gift given is "unattractive, ill-fitting, or spoiled . . . damaging to one's health or one's value . . . unnecessary, burdensome, or embarrassing" (p. 218). "Gratitude, in such a circumstance," claims Battin, "might seem impossible or perverse" (p. 218). She goes on to conclude:

> Thus, the potential suicide who, because his or her life is so excruciatingly painful to live, considers discarding the "gift" that an omniscient and omnipotent God has given him or her, in effect asserts that it is the donor's and not his or her own intentions that are subject to moral questions. If he or she does commit suicide, it is God who is at fault and not the person: God clearly is not a benevolent God, and one has no obligations to be grateful to the uncaring or even malevolent donor of a horrid and painful "gift." Read in this way, the original gift argument against suicide seems to backfire, and to legitimize suicide wherever life involves unfortunate, deeply unwanted circumstances. (p. 219)

Battin has here chosen to wade in deep and treacherous waters. Her appeal to the problem of evil in this context is ill-conceived, if only because she has failed to appreciate both the nature of the problem and the strategies for its containment. Battin appears to be aware that a satisfactory solution to the problem of evil would go a long way toward rebutting her objections to the gift analogy adumbrated above. For an all-loving, all-powerful, and all-knowing God who has a good reason for instantiating this world will also have a good reason for giving the gift of life to all on whom he bestows it, whatever form this gift of life happens to take. Battin implies though that there can be no such good reason. She asks, "Why would God, who is not only omniscient and omnipotent but perfectly good, give to some individuals the gift of good lives, and to some others desperate or painful ones?" (p. 219). Battin then outlines what she calls "[t]hree principal strategies . . . traditionally used to answer the problem of evil" (p. 219), viz. the ultimate harmonies defense, the free will defense, and the soulmaking defense. "There are" she claims, "other theodicies, of course, but it is these three that have been central in the traditional discussions of philosophy of religion" (p. 220).

It needs first to be pointed out that Battin has confused the distinction between the notions of theodicy and defense. The former is, in part, an attempt to answer Battin's above question. The latter is simply an attempt to show that the existence of God, as he is conceived for example in the Christian faith, is compatible with the existence of those evil states of affairs that happen to obtain.[4] Providing a successful theodicy guarantees a successful defense; providing only a successful defense does not, though, guarantee a successful theodicy.

Battin's general purpose in having brought up the topic of theodicy in this context is as follows:

> [T]he answer to the overriding question of whether gratitude to God is appropriate or morally required, even when the life He has bestowed is unsatisfactory, depends on the type of theodicy we employ. But there is no easy agreement among philosophers of religion or theologians as to which, if any, of these theodicies is successful; all of them are open to considerable objection. If none of them is sound, we may be led to conclude either that God does not exist, or that He does not have all three attributes of omnipotence, omniscience, and perfect benevolence. (p. 220)

But Battin appears clearly to be mistaken here. There *is* something of a general consensus among philosophers of religion that the freewill defense against the deductive problem of evil presented by Alvin Plantinga (1980) is, in fact, successful. But this is neither here nor there. Even if there were no such consensus, in the absence of any plausible argument that there *is* a genuine conceptual problem for the traditional Christian theist here, there is no good reason that I can see that would make it irrational to believe both in the existence of evil and in the traditional God of Christianity. One must, of course, do more than simply *state* (as J. L. Mackie was wont to do) that the traditional Christian theist is faced with a conceptual problem here.

Battin's characterization of the concept of omnipotence is likewise misaligned. She states,

> But gratitude for the intentions and affections of *a* given despite the unsatisfactoriness of the gift can be expected only in a situation where the giver is subject to limitations . . . Life, however, is the gift of a giver who has no limitations: it is the gift of an omnipotent, omniscient being, one who has, presumably, the ability to fashion for any individual a pleasant and attractive life, including a healthy body, a sane mind, and comfortable circumstances. (p. 219)

But Battin appears to presume too much. Her apparent unfamiliarity with Molinism in general and with Plantinga's free-will defense in particular leads her to presuppose that the consensus among philosophers of religion is that to be omnipotent is to have the ability to do anything at all. This is not, though, a view of omnipotence that is widely held. In fact, the standard view is that God is omnipotent insofar as he has no *nonlogical* limitations. The Molinist's gloss on this class of limitations includes God's inability to cause person S libertarian freely to perform action A in circumstance C at time t *if* the following counterfactual of creaturely freedom is true of S: If S were to be in C at t, then S would libertarian freely perform non-A at t. *Contra* Battin, then, an omnipotent God does *not* have the ability to fashion for individuals all of the features of their lives that Battin imagines. If Molina was right, then it is a matter of contingent fact—a contingency that depends upon the counterfactuals of creaturely freedom that happen to be true (that God is *unable* to so fashion them).

Battin's criticisms extend to other analogy-based arguments as well, for example to the argument that "suicide is wrong because, according to the biblical text, man is made in the image of God" (p. 221). In response, Battin points out "that while destruction of an image . . . may be an insult to the model when the likeness is a good one, it may be an act of respect when the likeness has become distorted" (p. 221). This is especially so, says Battin, if one interprets the term "'likeness' . . . as is customary in Catholic theology, as the conformity of the human will to the will of God," for "then the tacit premise of the underlying analogy—that one ought not destroy an image or likeness of someone—no longer exerts its initial precritical pull" (p. 221).

But clearly the image of God in Catholic theology, or Christian theology more broadly construed, is not, as she claims, "the conformity of the human will to the will of God" (p. 221), for if that were so, human embryos would not be divine image bearers. Certainly, the human embryo's will is not in conformity with the will of God, because the human *embryo* does not (and arguably *cannot*) will. In virtue of being an ensouled rational being, the powers of its soul include the power to will, but it is not simply in virtue of possessing a certain power to will, *thereby willing*, much less willing in conformity with God's will.

Battin further errs in thinking that God's image in us can somehow be *destroyed* in the manner that she suggests. This thought betrays a fundamental misunderstanding of what it means to be a divine image-bearer. Humans are *essentially* divine image bearers according to the Christian tradition. To destroy the divine image in us is to destroy us; we could not, that is, both survive and lack God's image. Even human zygotes possess this image, for to be a divine image-bearer is simply to share with God those powers of will and intellect— powers that for us are powers of the soul—necessary for acting freely (including loving freely) and for thinking rationally.

One of Battin's most egregious errors in this context is embodied in her concluding statement: "If, when contrasted with the lives of other human beings, one's own life seems to be an example of a good craftsman's uncharacteristically bad workmanship, ordinary practices suggest that it would not be wrong or disloyal to destroy it" (pp. 221-2). It would appear to follow from this that the lives of many of those who struggle with mental illness are lives that, according to Battin, it would not be wrong for the mentally ill themselves to destroy. Those who, in virtue of psychic pain, struggle daily against suicidal impulses generated by how their lives presently seem, would do no wrong, it seems, to give in to these impulses and take their lives. Perhaps she would rest comfortably knowing that, on her prompting, many suicides have been effected by those large numbers of mentally ill persons whose lives seem to be products of uncharacteristically bad workmanship. Note the gradient of the slope on which Battin is presently sliding. Rather than requiring a *veridical* perception of how badly constituted one's life happens to be, a *mere seeming* on the part of the potential suicide is justification enough.

Battin's inadequate grasp of Christian theology is again here apparent. What does she mean when she says that certain lives are examples of "a good craftsman's uncharacteristically bad workmanship"? (p. 222). According to Battin, such shoddy workmanship is such that "ordinary practices suggest that it would not be wrong or disloyal to destroy it" (p. 222). Traditional Christian thought concerning suffering, disfigurement, and dying is intimately bound up with an understanding of such disorder as the unfortunate consequence of that primary source of agential evil that we call sin. God is not the one who has wrought this disorder; it is the result of misuse of the will on the part of human and nonhuman agents. According to traditional Christian teaching, then, there simply is no disordered state of affairs for which one can seriously hold God responsible in the sense suggested by Battin.

III

Battin next examines arguments against suicide based upon natural law. She correctly points out that such natural-law based arguments have been favored by the medieval and later Christian tradition as offering an *explanation* for what it is that is wrong with suicide. She proceeds by enumerating and expounding upon three different interpretations of what is meant by the claim that suicide violates natural law: (1) suicide is a violation of (descriptive) natural physical law; (2) suicide is a violation of (descriptive) biological law; and (3) suicide is a violation of (prescriptive) natural law. I shall focus only on the third of these proposed interpretations, *viz.* suicide as a violation of prescriptive natural law and, hence, as a derivation of humankind's natural end.

This latter sense of natural law, as it is understood in much of the Christian tradition, presupposes that human beings have a natural end, a *telos*, the fulfillment of which is constitutive of human happiness. According to Battin, this means that "it is natural for humans to live and to engage in specifically human activities: thought, communication, the performance of morally good acts, and other actions that promote the fulfillment of humankind's highest potential" (p. 229). "Suicide," she says, "is wrong because it precludes these activities" (p. 229). But this could not be right the way it stands. It is here that Battin's imprecise characterization of what counts as suicide again becomes a serious issue. One is tempted to read Battin as saying that just *any* activity that precludes these aforementioned activities is wrong. But it would then follow that acting in a way (*any* way) that gets one martyred for the sake of Christ is to act wrongly; or that acting in a way (*any* way) that eventuates in one's death is to act wrongly. This, I dare say, is preposterous. No traditional natural law adherent would affirm that performing *just any* act that gets one martyred or otherwise eventuates in one's death is to act wrongly. The problem with suicide, according to dominant Christian concepts of natural law, is not simply that it precludes one's performing distinctively human acts, but that intending or attempting or succeeding in the performance of suicide, precisely understood, is to act in a manner that is directed *against* one's nature; it is, in short, to act in a manner that is intended to *divert one* from one's natural end.

Battin goes on to claim that natural law arguments are "directed, so to speak, only to the able-bodied and to those of sound temperament; . . . [they do] . . . not say how persons ought to act who are . . . unable to perform 'the natural' functions of human beings," for "[e]ven if we were to grant that it is 'natural' and therefore morally obligatory for human beings to think, communicate, and perform morally good acts for one another, there can be circumstances for individual human beings in which they are not able to do these things" (p. 230).

Precisely what is Battin meaning to ask when inquiring about how, according to natural law, persons ought to act who are unable to perform functions natural to human beings? The obvious answer to a query of this kind is that all voluntary acts that they perform ought to be acts that are in accord with their nature. It is, of course, a rather banal truth that some "[p]eople in severe and unremitting pain or subject to severe mental disturbance . . . may be unable to reason or think in any coherent way" (p. 230) and may thereby be rendered temporarily unable to perform any distinctively human acts at all. Some persons in deep sleep or under deep general anesthesia are also in this predicament. Is Battin further suggesting that, according to natural law, one is transiently freed from the obligation to live life in accord with one's nature simply in virtue of having fallen into a very deep sleep?

IV

Battin's above attempts at demonstrating the failures of traditional Christian arguments for there being an absolute moral prohibition against suicide are not successful. It does not, of course, follow from this that Battin is mistaken in thinking that suicide is morally permissible under some circumstances. In this light, in a second essay, "Suicide: A Fundamental Human Right?" Battin argues for the positive conclusion that human beings have a fundamental human right to commit suicide. Such fundamental rights are thought to attach to human beings simply in virtue of the fact that they are human beings. Other rights held to be fundamental in the same sense by Battin are the rights to life, liberty, freedom of speech, worship, education, political representation, and the pursuit of happiness.

Battin properly acknowledges that the success of this move allows her to evade certain consequentialist objections to there being a specifically *liberty* right to suicide, i.e., a *prima facie* right to suicide that, depending on the circumstances, can be overridden. If suicide is merely a right in this sense, then, claim its consequentialist critics, there may be numerous circumstances in which the calculated outcome of one's consequentialist calculus turns out to be unfavorable, and, hence, there may be frequent circumstances in which the *prima facie* right to suicide is overridden. Such unfavorable outcomes might consist, for example, of generally untoward effects of one's suicide on others. Were suicide to be a *fundamental* human right, though, no such defeators could succeed in overriding it. "If," states Battin, "what had appeared to be a liberty right to suicide turns out to be a *fundamental* right, the force of ordinary utilitarian arguments against it will collapse" (p. 279).

Battin argues for suicide's being a(n) (unequally distributed) fundamental human right by attempting to show that some suicides are constitutive of human *dignity*. "'Human dignity,'" states Battin, although difficult to define, "is a notion rooted in an ideal conception of human life, human community, and human excellence" (p. 280). According to Battin, it typically involves autonomy, self-determination, responsibility for one's acts, self-awareness, rationality, self-expressiveness, and self-respect.

One would have expected that Battin would next have argued that some specified range of *values* should be attached to each of the aforementioned features that comprise human dignity in order that one might judge when one's or another's life does or does not possess the requisite measure of dignity. One would think that it would be upon this basis that one could differentiate between suicides compatible with dignity and those that are not. It is here that Battin takes an unexpected turn. Rather than basing judgments concerning dignity on certain *objective* features of human beings, she bases judgments concerning human dignity explicitly on *subjective* foundations. These allegedly dignified suicides, says Battin, are based on "a self-ideal; a conception of one's own value and worth, beneath which one is not willing to slip" (p. 284). It is these "threat[s] to one's self ideal[s]" (p. 284) from pain (whether somatic or psychic) and physical illness from which one escapes in the act of dignified suicide.

Battin's view entails that if one's self-ideal were, like Christ's, to exemplify unsurpassable moral excellence in this life and if one were to realize that one is not going to reach this self-ideal and that life is not worth living unless this self-ideal were ultimately attained, then one's suicidal response to this realization would be an act that is constitutive of one's human dignity. This would be so even if one *were* in fact morally excellent in the manner desired, for Battin's proposal makes the alleged dignity of some suicidal acts depend upon a certain *perception of* one's value or self-worth, not on one's *actual* value or self-worth. This view has the absurd consequence of converting a potential nondignified suicide into a dignified suicide simply by virtue of convincing the potential suicide that his life, no matter how it is *actually*, is not and probably never will be the kind of life that will approximate to his self-ideal. This might be done either by changing the potential suicide's view about his life or by changing his self-ideal. Note that the former method allows for the added absurdity that convincing one, through deception if need be, of a *false* view of one's life can effect the intended reorientation toward dignity; and that the latter method invites one to convince the potential suicide of a self-ideal that is logically impossible, convincing him both of this logical impossibility and of the view that life is not worth living if this self-ideal is not attained and, thereby, insuring that the suicide in question would, on Battin's grounds, be constitutive of human dignity.

V

There is a more direct route than the path that I have trod above to showing that Battin's attempt at demonstrating that suicide is a fundamental human right fails. The first step on this path is simply to point out that nowhere does Battin *argue* for there being *any* fundamental human rights at all. She simply presupposes that there are. "It is rarely disputed," she claims, "that persons have a right to freedom, since it is very widely assumed that freedom contributes to human dignity" (p. 280). Although *rarely* disputed, it certainly *has been* disputed that persons have a natural right to freedom, most notably by those who deny that there are any natural (or what Battin calls "fundamental") rights at all. I, for example, count myself among those who do not countenance the existence of natural rights.

Alasdair MacIntyre[5] has mounted an impressive case for being suspicious of there being anything like fundamental human rights. If MacIntyre is right then, *contra* Battin, suicide is not a fundamental human right in virtue of the fact that there are no fundamental human rights at all. This is presently not a popular position. Nevertheless, I believe that there is much to recommend it.

MacIntyre has pointed out that there does not appear to be a term that can properly be translated "a fundamental human (or natural) right" in any language prior to the close of the middle ages. He also supplies a plausible reason for why this is so, namely, that claims to the possession of natural rights in fact presuppose the instantiation of particular, local socioculturally established sets of rules. "Such sets of rules," claims MacIntyre, "are in no way universal features of the human condition" (p. 67). Rather, states MacIntyre, the objection that friends of natural rights must meet "is precisely that those forms of human behavior which presuppose notions of some ground to entitlement, such as the notion of *a* [natural] right, always have a highly specific and socially local character, and that the existence of particular types of social institution or practice is a necessary condition for the notion of a claim to the possession of a right being an intelligible type of human performance" (p. 67).

Those historical particularities that gave rise to a belief in human rights appear not to have been properly formed until relatively recently in human history. Neither in Old Testament Hebrew nor in classical or New Testament Greek, for example, does there appear to be expressions that can properly be translated "a natural right." It appears, then, that the rich and thick ethical developments contained within the primary texts of Judaism and Christianity progressed to their present state unaided by any natural rights language.[6] The same could, of course, be said of Aristotle's ethical views as well as the ethical theories embodied within Plato's dialogues and, if MacIntyre is to be believed, any piece of moral philosophy or moral theology written in any language, including classical or medieval Latin or Greek until circa A.D. 1400. These considerations, in conjunction with the fact that no one has yet devised a cogent, positive argument for the existence of such rights, are reason enough, claims MacIntyre, confidently to reassert that "the truth is plain: there are no such rights, and belief in them is one with belief in witches and in unicorns" (p. 69). "The best reason," states MacIntyre, "for asserting so bluntly that there are no such rights is indeed of precisely the same type as the best reason which we possess for asserting that there are no witches and the best reason that we possess for asserting that there are no unicorns: every attempt to give good reasons for believing that there *are* such rights has failed" (p. 69).

For one, therefore, who is suspicious of the whole conceptual framework within which the notion of fundamental human rights has been conceived, Battin's presupposition that there are such rights and her claim that suicide is one of these rights is not in the least bit persuasive. What she needs is an *argument* for why one ought to take this notion of fundamental human rights seriously. I, like MacIntyre, am presently unaware of there being any such argument.

VI

Although Battin is not explicit about this, she appears to believe that certain humans are, in some sense, better off dead. Perhaps this is what she means, in part, when she says that some forms of suicide are constitutive of human dignity. Perhaps, that is, Battin believes that some human lives have become relatively undignified but that, should one commit suicide, some of this dignity would be restored. It appears then that, according to Battin, the postsuicide state is *ceteris paribus* better than the presuicide state for some individuals in virtue of the dignity that accrues to them in virtue of having committed suicide.

Can one's dying be a good thing for some human beings? Can one be more dignified in death than one was in life? Can a human person be better off dead than alive? Jorge Garcia has recently argued that an affirmative answer to at least this latter question is at best seriously doubtful.[7] One is struck, in fact, with the strong suspicion that this latter question is unintelligible. What, after all, could it possibly mean to claim that a human being is off dead?

Suppose, for the sake of argument, that at our deaths we cease to be. If this were so, then at our deaths *we* shall no longer exist. In what sense, then, could death be better for *us*, for there simply is no *us*, on this view, for whom death could be a benefit?[8]

On a traditional Christian view, the problem is no less difficult. As Garcia correctly points out, there is nothing in traditional Christian theology that "entails that humans survive death, in effect, that we are immortals" (p. 86). The intervening period between the moment of my death and the moment of my resurrection is not a period in which Howsepian the human being survives. If anything survives, it is Howsepian's disembodied soul that survives. But this disembodied soul is not a human being. If Howsepian the human being were to survive what is commonly called "death," there would be nothing for God to resurrect. It is, of course, only the dead that can be resurrected.

The point is that on neither of the two above-adumbrated views does it appear to be intelligible to speak of death as being a benefit to one. Those sorts of goods that Battin believes are attained through suicide, e.g., freedom from physical pain, psychic suffering, disfigurement, despondency, immobility, and dependency are, as Garcia points out, "good for us only insofar as they are *parts of human life*. They are goods when and because they are attained in life. Being free from such troubles as anxiety, physical pain, and despondency is good inasmuch as it yields a less troubled life" (pp. 85-6). What Battin lacks, therefore, and what she must supply prior to any *argument* for the claim that some forms of suicide are constitutive of human dignity is a clear *explication* of the mere intelligibility of that claim. Although it is true, as Battin (1994) avers, that "one cannot promote one's own *dignity* by destroying the dignity of someone else" (p. 283), what she has failed to see is that to destroy oneself is to destroy one's own dignity and, therefore, that one also cannot promote one's own dignity by destroying oneself.[9]

ENDNOTES

1. In Margaret Pabst Battin, *Least Worry Death: Essays in Bioethics on the End of Life* (New York: Oxford University Press, 1994), 205–53.
2. Ibid., 277–88.
3. St. Augustine, *Concerning the City of God Against the Pagans* Bk. 1, Ch. 21, ed. David Knowles, trans. Henry Bettenson (Harmondsworth, Middlesex, England: Penguin, 1972).
4. See Alvin C. Plantinga's *God, Freedom, and Evil* (Grand Rapids: Eerdmans, 1980), 28.
5. Alasdair MacIntyre, *After Virtue: A Study in Moral Theory*, 2d ed. (Notre Dame, Ind.: University of Notre Dame Press, 1984).
6. Battin herself takes it to be significant that "there is no word anywhere in the Bible, either in Aramaic, Hebrew, or Greek, that is equivalent to the English term suicide [*sic*], either in its nominal or verbal form, nor is there any idiomatic way of referring to this act that suggests that it is a distinct type of death" (p. 207).
7. J. L. A. Garcia, "Better Off Dead?" *APA Newsletters* 92, 1 (spring 1993): 858.
8. Battin herself appeals to a similar argument in her many-faceted attempted refutation of the "life as a gift" argument against suicide. "For instance, it is often claimed that life is a gift from God, and therefore ought not be destroyed. But this invites us to ask who it is who receives God's gift, if that individual does not yet have life; mainstream Christian theology does not assert the antecedent existence of nonliving individuals upon whom such gifts might be bestowed" (p. 216). She later calls this a "trivial" objection.
9. This essay was presented at an international conference on "Dignity and Dying" at Trinity Evangelical Divinity School in Deerfield, Illinois (July 1995).

PART 4

BIBLICAL REFLECTIONS

An Overview

Although the Old Testament does not make a direct value judgment concerning suicide, a thorough understanding of its teaching regarding death and the legitimate, accidental, and illegitimate means by which death occurs provides clear guidance concerning the appropriateness of suicide. During a time when many are attempting to find justification for the acceptance of suicide by appealing to Scripture's apparent silence about the issue, Eugene Merrill provides a sound theological argument against this untenable and precarious position.

Chapter Twenty

SUICIDE AND THE CONCEPT OF DEATH IN THE OLD TESTAMENT

Eugene H. Merrill

DEATH, ONE OF THE INESCAPABLE REALITIES of human existence, is very much at the forefront of Old Testament (hereafter OT) interest. The biblical story has barely begun when death intrudes, first as the promised penalty should mankind sin (Gen. 2:17) and then as a fact when Cain murdered his brother Abel (Gen. 4:8). This first recorded human death—all the more tragic because of its violence—inaugurates a monotonous and tiresome refrain: "and then he died." Beginning with Adam himself (Gen. 5:5), this brief and somber epitaph occurs no fewer than nine times in five chapters. Like a drumbeat it punctuates the human predicament—as surely as one lives, so surely will he die. But though death is the common lot of all in the biblical record, its causes, modes, and aftermaths vary from instance to instance and from individual to individual. There is "natural" death from illness or old age, death in famine or war, death by manslaughter or murder, or death at one's own hand. The purpose of this chapter is to examine the last of these—suicide—against the backdrop of the whole notion of death in the OT, especially death as the result of homicide.

BIBLICAL TERMS FOR DEATH

The Hebrew vocabulary for dying or death is almost exclusively limited to the intransitive verb *mût* and its derivative noun *māwet*.[1] The verb occurs about 780 times in the OT. In its basic stem (565x) it means simply "to die." Otherwise it is rendered "kill" (D stem, 9x; Hi stem 137x) or "be killed" (Ho stem, 68x). The noun is attested about 160 times, all of which may be translated "death." Several other verbs are employed to speak of the act of killing, whether the victim be human or animal. These include *'ābad, hārag, hāram, kārat, nākâ, pāga', rāṣaḥ,* and *šāḥaṭ.* Of these *hārag* and *šāḥaṭ* are most commonly used of animal slaughter (though not exclusively so); *pāga'* is very rare; and *'ābad, hāram,* and *kārat* usually speak of judgment resulting in death, particularly by the Lord or a divine agent. Of the remaining two verbs, *nākâ* regularly occurs to describe homicide in general whereas *rāṣaḥ* is to be construed almost always as murder. By definition, murder is premeditated and therefore, suicide, as a premeditated self-killing, also may at times be considered murder.[2] It will be helpful, then, to limit the discussion to occurrences of *rāṣaḥ* and/or *roṣēaḥ* ("murderer") and to the few instances where other terms also speak of murder and/or suicide. This will be undertaken in the course of examining texts where suicide is described in the OT.

In the modern world, the thought of death is so disconcerting and even repugnant that a panoply of euphemisms have been coined to sanitize its discussion. Thus, one hears of "passing away," "passing on," "departing," "going to heaven," "going to one's reward," and the like. A common Christian circumlocution is to speak of the deceased as having "gone to be with the Lord." While these speak truth (albeit evasively), they clearly are intended to soften the impact of the bald statement, "X died." But such euphemism is to be found in Scripture as well. We read that so and so "slept" or "I shall go to him" (David with reference to his dead baby; 2 Sam. 12:23) or "rested with his fathers" (a common description of the death of a king; cf. 1 Kings 11:43; 14:20, 31; 15:8; etc.).

THE OLD TESTAMENT UNDERSTANDING OF DEATH

The inevitable, unexceptional fact of death as an everyday reality and one that could and must be observed and addressed, produced what might be called a phenomenological understanding or interpretation of death. Death, that is, is an "act" that takes place, one that can be noted empirically and about which practical conclusions can be drawn. On the other hand, the innate recognition of the uniqueness of humankind and the impossibility of its potentiality being exhausted in mortality, in this life, raised reflection about death to another dimension altogether, one that refused to limit death to a mere biological function. Mankind must be more than just another animal species and so his death must be qualitatively different from that of the subhuman world. When divine revelation is added to these natural intuitions, a picture of death in the OT develops that is incomparably in advance of anything known in the surrounding world of the time.

It will be helpful to look at these two viewpoints, then: (1) the phenomenological and (2) the revelatory or theological.

At its most fundamental level, death is the cessation of life so whatever it is that makes a thing appear to be alive (warmth, breath, movement, pulse, response to stimulus) is lacking in the state of death. This is certainly the case, at least, when all five of the signs of life just listed cease to be operative. When viewed this way, it is apparent that there is no apparent difference between human beings and animals, especially those of the higher orders, with respect to biological or "clinical" death. Phenomenologically, they are one and the same. There are many narrative texts that speak of persons dead or dying but without comment as to biological and/or spiritual implications. These, of course, have no value to our discussion. Our attention then must be directed to those that are reflective, that draw conclusions about the death experience and its aftermath from a "clinical" perspective. By and large, texts of this kind are limited to the wisdom corpus, and most particularly to Ecclesiastes.

In a remarkable statement Qoheleth (the Preacher) proposes that "the day of death [is] better than the day of birth" because one can learn more about real life in the presence of death and mourning that he can in laughter and celebration (Eccl. 7:1–3). What this asserts is that death is inexorable, inflexible, and to be taken most seriously because of its finality.[3] Death's inevitability is further affirmed by the sage when he says that "no one has power over the day of his death" (8:8). But his most philosophical assessment of death appears in Qoheleth's observation that "the same destiny [death] overtakes all" (9:3) and that "a live dog is better off than a dead lion" (v. 4). The reason is that "the living know that they will die, but the dead know nothing" (v. 5). In another place he muses that "Man's fate is like that of the animals; the same fate awaits them both: As one dies, so dies the other" (3:19). He concludes with the rhetorical question, "Who knows if the spirit of man rises upward and if the spirit of the animal goes down into the earth?" (v. 21). The point is that phenomenologically speaking, death is death—the cessation of life.

Something of this sentiment appears in the Psalms as well. Even David laments, "No one remembers you [Lord] when he is dead" (Pss. 6:5; cf. 88:10). And he compares the death of human beings to the withering away of green plants (37:2). Similarly, Psalm 90 suggests that mankind is like the morning grass, which, "though in the morning it springs up new, by evening it is dry and withered" (v. 6). So much, then, for human life and its vaunted glory! When God takes away people's breath "they die and return to the dust" (104:29) where it is impossible for them any longer to praise God (115:17).

In common with other ancient Near Eastern concepts of death and the hereafter, popular Hebrew thought also imbibed certain philosophical or even mythical ways of articulating their realities.[4] Structurally, creation was perceived to be three-tiered: heaven (or the heavens), earth, and the netherworld. The last ambivalently swung between something as immediate and apparent as the grave, to a realm of departed entities, only semi-corporeal, whose precise location was uncertain but perhaps deep within the earth. A reconciling viewpoint was one that postulated the grave as an anteroom to a dwelling place of a more mysterious and yet more permanent nature.

The first text that comes to mind with respect to the condition of the dead is the narrative of Saul's consultation with the necromancer of Endor (1 Sam. 28:3–25). The pericope opens with the laconic statement that Samuel was dead and buried (v. 3). Having ordered all mediums to be executed, Saul was hard pressed to find one who could put him in touch with the deceased prophet. By itself the desire to do so presupposes a popular belief that the dead lived on, albeit in a different place. That place must be "down" for Saul requests the witch to bring Samuel "up" (v. 8; cf. v. 11). To her great surprise she is able to conjure up a recognizable facsimile of Samuel and when asked by Saul (who cannot see the apparition) what she sees, she replies, "I see a spirit coming up out of the ground" (v. 13). "Samuel" then speaks and indignantly asks, "Why have you disturbed me by bringing me up?" (v. 15).

The brevity of this chapter will not allow a full discussion of this episode, but what must be noted is that Samuel is identified as 'elōhîm, that is, a mighty or even "godlike" one, and four times is said to have been below and in need of being brought up.[5] This singular occurrence should certainly not be construed as a paradigm of ancient Israelite thought, particularly given its pagan overtones, nor should it in any sense be viewed as divine revelation about the state of the dead. At most it is a unique concession by the Lord to Saul, an unrepeated (and unrepeatable?) means of communicating a word of judgment to the fatally flawed king of Israel.

A second relevant passage is Isaiah 14:3–20, the prophecy of the demise of the king of Babylon. Drawing upon language and imagery appropriate to the fall of Satan in primordial times, Isaiah describes the overthrow of the Babylonian ruler as a descent into Sheol. In fact, he personifies the place of the dead as he depicts the king's death:

> The grave (Sheol) below is all astir
>   to meet you at your coming;
> it rouses the spirits of the departed to greet you—
>   all those who were leaders in the world;
> it makes them rise from their thrones—
>   all those who were kings over the nations.
>
> Isaiah 14:9

Then, with clear allusion to mythic contest, Isaiah designates the Babylonian king as the "morning star, son of the dawn" (v. 12; Heb. *hēlēl ben šāḥer*), the one Jesus referred to as Satan (Luke 10:18). Like this pagan deity, ultimately patterned after Satan himself, the wicked king will die and descend "down to the depths of the pit" (v. 15). The whole scene is one of consciousness in a place of the dead, but life at best of a nebulous, "ghostly" kind. In any case, the mythopoetic nature of the passage precludes its being taken as a normative revelation concerning the hereafter.

The OT is not silent about death and its aftermath, however, though it lacks the fullness and eloquence of New Testament revelation. Job, after struggling with a tentative hope that man, once dead, might live again (Job 14:13–14), bursts out at length in exuberant conviction:

> I know that my Redeemer lives,
>   and that in the end he will stand upon the earth.
> And after my skin has been destroyed,
>   yet in my flesh I will see God;
> I myself will see him
>   with my own eyes—I, and not another.
>
> Job 19:25–27

The dogmatism of this assertion leaves little doubt that Job is not "whistling in the dark" but is responding to clear revelation on the matter.[6] Lingering skepticism that such a view is theologically premature should be put to rest by David's confidence that "[God] will not abandon [him] to the grave, nor will [he] let [his] Holy One see decay" (Ps. 16:10). That is because David has been set on "the path of life," one that results in "eternal pleasures at [God's] right hand" (v. 11). These truths, so out of keeping with ancient Near Eastern concepts and even with OT popular theology, can be explained only as revelation.

The prophets pick up the theme and go beyond the sages and poets in some respects in articulating a theology of death and the hereafter. Isaiah declares in bold resurrection language:

> But your dead will live;
>   their bodies will rise.
> You who dwell in the dust,
>   wake up and shout for joy.
> Your dew is like the dew of the morning;
>   the earth will give birth to her dead.
>
>   Isaiah 26:19

He had earlier declared that God "will swallow up death forever" (Isa. 25:8), a promise Paul puts to use in his great resurrection apologia (1 Cor. 15:54). Hosea, contemporary with Isaiah, makes the astonishing declaration (also appropriated by Paul in 1 Cor. 15:55),

> I will ransom them from the power of the grave;
>   I will redeem them from death.
> Where, O death, are your plagues?
>   Where, O grave, is your destruction?
>
>   Hosea 13:14

This intense use of personification in which Sheol is viewed as a captor and death as a persecutor is consonant with Isaiah's similar description already discussed. Finally, it is important to include the witness of Daniel, who delivers the unambiguous revelation that "multitudes who sleep in the dust of the earth will awake: some to everlasting life, others to shame and everlasting contempt" (Dan. 12:2). This high-water mark in the OT understanding of death and its ultimate outcome clinches the proposition that death, *though mysterious as an observable phenomenon, is under God's control and therefore has an ultimate resolution.*

THE TERMINATION OF LIFE

In addition to "ordinary" occurrences of death by old age, disease, famine, and the like, the OT attests to premature and/or violent death through either legitimate, accidental, or illegitimate means. Examples of legitimate death are those through war, especially "holy war," and as acts of justice. Accidental death, defined here as manslaughter as opposed to death through one's own unaided carelessness or misfortune, occupies a position between legitimate and illegitimate circumstances of death and must be treated separately. Finally, illegitimate death includes murder and true suicide. The last of these is the proper subject of this chapter so it must receive a disproportionate share of attention in the ensuing discussion.

Death Through Legitimate Means

Mankind's tragic fall into sin and out of fellowship with the Creator resulted in death, both physical and spiritual. This had been the promised consequence (Gen. 2:17) and the narratives of biblical history are replete with evidences of fulfillment. Fallen people, not chastened and humbled by the fact of their own mortality, began to become the agents of death of their fellow creatures, killing and maiming one another with no respect for their common identity as the image and likeness of a holy God. This took the form of murder on the individual level (cf. Gen. 4:8) and war on a grander scale (cf. Gen. 14:1–4).

Most wars throughout history have had no valid justification. They have been fought in the interest of territorialism, imperialism, acquisition, and national pride. Only occasionally have they been just, waged in order to overthrow despotic and cruel regimes, to repel hostile threats or acts of aggression, or to achieve some noble humanitarian objective such as the deliverance of an enslaved or threatened minority. This is the pattern that emerges from the OT record as well. Over and over again war dominates the scene and usually war with flimsy justification at best. Rarely is there an exception to this in the ordinary course of international relations, and such exceptions are invariably defensive actions undertaken to counteract aggression instigated in the first place on less than legitimate grounds.

Standing apart, however, is war authorized by the Lord in pursuit of the protection of his saints and the guarantee of their conquest and occupation of the land granted to them as an element of the ancient patriarchal covenants. "Protective war" is defensive, and, though rarely mandated, there are some examples (cf. Gen. 14:2; Ex. 17:8–9; Judg. 11:4–6; 1 Sam. 17:1; 2 Kings 6:8; etc.). War of conquest by Israel is well attested, however, but *only* in achieving acquisition and domination of the land of Canaan. This kind of war springs out of the theological principle that Canaan is fundamentally the territory of the Lord, the inheritance he had chosen and prepared for his elect people Israel. All other occupants are therefore squatters who must be removed in order for Israel to take its rightful place there (Gen. 12:1; 13:14–18; 15:18–21; 17:8; Deut. 8:1–10; 11:8–12). Since it is apparent that the nations already living there will not simply pack up and move out without a struggle, war would become a practical necessity, war designed, instigated, undertaken, and brought to successful conclusion by the Lord himself. Such war is called "holy war" or, more recently, "Yahweh war."[7] War under these strict definitions is offensive but with limited objectives: It is to be waged against only the Canaanite nations that persist in laying claim to Israel's inheritance and only until these nations are expelled or annihilated.

The text that spells out the prosecution of such war and that sets forth the stipulations that govern it is Deuteronomy 20:16–20 (cf. 7:1–5).[8] Here the Lord commands the extermination of the occupants of the land and for two reasons:

to make the land available to Israel and to remove forever the temptation to Israel to emulate the idolatry of these hopelessly corrupt people. A subset of holy war, one authorized against non-Canaanites and presumably of a defensive nature, finds regulation in Deuteronomy 20:1–15. In such conflict, terms of peace will be offered to the aggressors (v. 10), failing which, the males of the enemy must be slain (v. 13) but the women and children spared and made subservient (v. 14). Both kinds of war not only allow but demand death under carefully prescribed circumstances. It is clear, therefore, that violent death in these situations is theologically and morally justifiable. How that relates to the modern world, particularly in a nontheocratic politic, is a matter beyond the purview of this chapter. Christian consensus for the most part is that defensive war is at least permissible if not specifically authorized.

The taking of life as a matter of justice (capital punishment), though a matter of considerable debate in the contemporary world, has clear OT support. Cain feared human vengeance for his crime of murder (Gen. 4:14) and Noah is clearly told in a covenant context:

> Whoever sheds the blood of man,
> by man shall his blood be shed;
> for in the image of God has God made man.
> Genesis 9:6

The allusive association of this entire pericope (Gen. 9:1–18) with the covenant made with the whole human race at its creation (Gen. 1:26–28) puts beyond doubt the fact that the Noahic injunction has universal and timeless import. Murder (which is the issue here) demanded and still demands *lex talionis* in its most severe form—a life for a life. In the more limited framework of the so-called Mosaic covenant this penalty for murder continues to be upheld, precisely because the underlying principle is so inviolable and unqualifiable (cf. Ex. 21:12; Lev. 24:17; Num. 35:30–33). Other occasions that call for capital punishment in the theocratic community are somewhat tangential to our purpose of looking at suicide as an aspect of murder in the OT, and therefore will receive no further attention.

Death Through Accident

Under this category only homicide will be explored since "ordinary" fatal accident usually carries no outside culpability in biblical law. But homicide is not necessarily the result of malice aforethought and, though resulting in the taking of human life, is ameliorated by its unintentionality. This kind of violent death—put euphemistically in the phrase "God lets it happen" (Ex. 21:13)—was unplanned and perpetrated by one who had no history of ill will toward the victim (cf. Deut. 19:4). However, the act did carry legal consequences for the slain, a precious human being, and the perpetrator presumably could and should have been more careful in the circumstances in which the death occurred (cf. Num. 35:22–23; Deut. 19:4–5). To prevent the normal resort to vengeance by the kinfolk of the deceased, the individual accused of manslaughter must flee to a city of refuge to await trial. If proven innocent of murder, he must remain there until the incumbent high priest of Israel died and then he could return home. If convicted, however, he must suffer the prescribed penalty for murder, the surrender of his own life (Num. 35:22–28). Though manslaughter did not demand *lex talionis* the very fact that it necessitated virtual imprisonment and exposed the agent to family vengeance underscores the heinousness of homicide in any form.

Death Through Illegitimate Means

Enough has been said to this point to make clear that there are legitimate as well as accidental circumstances in which human life may be taken with little or no culpability and punishment. It has also been intimated that murder— the intentional and premeditated destruction of another human being—falls outside these categories and is unqualifiedly repugnant to a holy God who therefore demands its punishment measure for measure. The reason for such harsh measures is to be found not ultimately in jurisprudence but in theology. The willful taking of a human life is indescribably reprehensible because all human beings are the image of God. The wording "are the image of God" is deliberately chosen over against "in the image of God" because the springboard text—Genesis 1:26–27—favors that view in our opinion.[9] In any event, the sacredness of human life lies precisely in its association with the nature, character, and function of God himself. He created man to represent him on the earth and to rule through him. To slay a person is, in effect, to attempt the egregious, almost incomprehensible act of slaying God the Creator. It is the ultimate act of hubris, a blasphemy of incalculable proportions.

In more legal terms, murder may be defined as unqualified manslaughter.[10] That is, it is an act of violence lacking the mitigations that make other kinds of homicide different in both essence and repercussions. The OT provides its own lexicon of terms to clarify the matter. The Mosaic law states that "if a man schemes and kills another man deliberately" he is a murderer (Ex. 21:14). Or he is a murderer if he "with malice aforethought shoves another or throws something at him intentionally so that he dies or if in hostility he hits him with his fist so that he dies" (Num. 35:20–21). The killer is presumptively guilty if he or she only has a stone or club in his or her hand that is designed to function as a weapon and uses it to kill (as opposed to an implement or tool clearly not made for the purpose of killing) (Num. 35:17–18). A history of ill will also adds to the distinction between murder and other homicide, especially when accompanied by ambush or other unexpected encounter (Deut. 19:11).

If murder is marked out, then, by (1) previous hostility on the part of a person who (2) schemes (3) with malice aforethought to (4) waylay another and (5) strike him or her with an object designed to do harm (or any part or permutation of these), what is to be said of suicide, by definition a self-murder in certain circumstances? Is it, in fact, murder by OT standards?

Murder is normally an act of violence by one person against another and not against him- or herself. So much so is this a fact that the OT says not a word in legal texts about suicide. Yet suicide is the taking of a human life, and so it clearly falls at least under the rubric of manslaughter. The question is, does it meet the criteria that distinguish murder as a subcategory of manslaughter? The answer appears to be an unequivocal yes. Suicide usually is committed (1) premeditatedly by one who (2) schemes to do so (3) with malice aforethought by (4) a stratagem or means (5) designed to do harm. The difference, of course, is that suicide, if successful, carries with it no practical repercussions of penalty at law.

SUICIDE AS AN OLD TESTAMENT PHENOMENON

The OT is, among other things, a record of war, bloodshed, murder, and mayhem. Yet, and perhaps amazingly, there are only a handful of instances of suicide, all in narrative texts. Undoubtedly a general reverence for life, fear of death and its aftermath, and the self-evident inability to repent of suicide may be contributing factors in the apparently low incidence of suicide. Other reasons may also have been at work but, if so, are not clear from the reported accounts.

The first of these is the story of Abimelech, son of Gideon, who, upon his father's death, led a failed attempt to make himself king of Israel (Judges 9). When it came to nought and he was mortally wounded by a stone dropped from the tower of Thebez, he commanded his aide-de-camp to kill him with a sword, a favor the young man granted (v. 54). The situation calling for suicide was certainly exacerbated by Abimelech's having been wounded by a woman (v. 53), but most of the bases for suicide as listed above are missing in this instance.[11]

The most famous case is the suicide of Saul, king of Israel, whose instrument of choice was also a sword (1 Sam. 31:1–6). Like Abimelech, Saul asked his armor-bearer to kill him but this time the request was denied. Saul therefore fell upon his own sword (v. 4). The extenuating circumstance was Saul's own likely death at the hands of the Philistines, a fate that had already befallen three of his sons. There is no embarrassment at the root of Saul's action but a fear that the Philistines would "abuse" him (v. 4), a particularly abhorrent thought because they were uncircumcised pagans.[12]

A third example is the self-inflicted death of Ahithophel, counselor to David and Absalom. When his advice to Absalom was spurned, "He put his house in order and then hanged himself" (2 Sam. 17:23). The businesslike, methodical manner in which this is reported suggests that most if not all the criteria of suicide are there. To "put his house in order" is to presuppose careful, deliberate, and time-consuming attention to detail. Ahithophel's suicide, triggered by his public humiliation, is no spur-of-the moment deed— he thinks through his options and concludes that self-destruction is his best.

The only other recorded instance of suicide in the OT is that of Zimri, king of Israel for seven days, who burned his palace down around him (1 Kings 16:18). Like Saul, Zimri was afraid to fall into enemy hands alive so he chose what to him was the lesser of the two evils. Unlike Saul, however, his suicide most certainly resulted in the death of others for the palace was a public building in which others, too, must have sought refuge. Suicide always leaves pain in its wake, but less often does it carry with it the physical destruction of unwitting participants.

The four examples of suicide in the OT record teach very little about the theological ramifications of the act but they do share certain things in common that may be worth pointing out: (1) none is viewed in a favorable light, as a viable option to be emulated in difficult times; (2) all were responses to crises, either in fact or in perception: Saul and Zimri certainly would have died at enemy hands in any event, Abimelech was dying from injury, and Ahithophel was "dying" from chagrin and loss of face; (3) all chose suicide with varying degrees of readiness or planning. Ahithophel thought through all that was involved in the deed and its aftermath, Zimri arranged, with some strategy, to torch the royal palace, and Abimelech and Saul, though acting peremptorily, clearly did so with due consideration of other possible alternatives. The major differences among the four, in fact, are the choice of means—two by sword, one by hanging, and one by immolation.

CONCLUSION

The OT witness is mute as to the propriety, significance, and consequences of suicide except as suicide can be viewed as a category of murder, i.e., the willful and planned termination of a human life. In only four narrative passages does it appear at all and then only reportorially, with little or no assessment or value judgment. One may be inclined, then, to dismiss the OT as having nothing to contribute to this painful issue. This would be a serious mistake, however, for it is precisely because suicide is self-murder and murder is a matter of great biblical moment that discussion as to its theological and pastoral ramifications must begin here, in the Hebrew Scriptures.[13] It is immediately apparent from the OT that murder is unspeakably abhorrent for at least two reasons: (1) It is the irremedial and permanent destruction of life, the most precious possession an individual can ever have; (2) It is an assault upon God Himself, for every human being without exception is an image-bearer of his Creator; in fact, every man and woman is a vice-regent of the King of Glory who brought them into being to have dominion over all things. There is not only inherent value in humanity—there is imputed value as well.

Such an assessment of murder per se would meet with little objection in society at large, even among those who oppose capital punishment. But suicide, many would argue, is different because it is an act against oneself only and therefore is within the realm of freedom of choice. Only the self is really hurt, and as a moral agent, one has the right to hurt oneself if one so chooses.[14] The full implications of the ethics inherent in this argument are dealt with elsewhere in this volume, but the OT view will not for a moment permit that argument to stand. The ineluctable and necessary fact that every human being is of priceless worth to God means that any human effort to terminate a life—even one's own—is an affront of the most serious magnitude to God.

But sin—any sin—can be forgiven! This is the good word of grace that shines through even the apparent inflexibility and rectitude of OT law. No better example can be given than that of David. Convicted of murder and adultery by his own admission (2 Sam. 12:5–6; Ps. 51:1–4), he, fully repentant, heard also the prophetic word, "The LORD has taken away your sin. You are not going to die" (2 Sam. 12:13). One may respond, of course, that the suicide cannot repent and therefore cannot be forgiven. But the OT Word silences that objection with a message of infinite grace. The same psalmist who confessed his sin of murder and pleaded for forgiveness was also able to say:

> You have made known to me the path of life;
> you will fill me with joy in your presence,
> with eternal pleasures at your right hand.
> (Ps. 16:11)

Thank God for the overarching umbrella of His grace that extends not only from eternity past to eternity to come but from life even into death, no matter how that death may come about.[15]

ENDNOTES

1. See my article "Death" in *New International Dictionary of Old Testament Theology and Exegesis*, ed. Willem A. VanGemeren (Grand Rapids: Zondervan, 1997).
2. Emile Durkheim, in his *Negatives: The Limits of Life*, states that "Suicide is applied to all cases of death, resulting directly or indirectly from a positive or negative act of the victim himself, which he knows will produce this result" (cited by Tom L. Beauchamp, "Suicide," in *Ethical Issues in Death and Dying*, eds. Tom L. Beauchamp and Seymour Perlin [Englewood Cliffs, N.J.: Prentice-Hall, 1978], 92). Of course, not all self-destructive acts are suicide in the technical sense and therefore are not murder. For many examples see J. P. Moreland, "The Morality of Suicide: Issues and Options," in this volume, and also in *BibSac* 148 (1991): 216–19. The view of the Western church equating suicide with murder is attributed primarily to Augustine. See Robert N. Wennberg, *Terminal Choices: Euthanasia, Suicide, and the Right to Die* (Grand Rapids: Eerdmans, 1989), 53–57.
3. As Garrett puts it, "Those who [reflect soberly on death] realize that the same end awaits them, and their hearts are turned from folly." Duane A. Garrett, *Proverbs, Ecclesiastes, Song of Songs*, NAC 14 (Nashville: Broadman, 1993), 318–19.
4. Nicholas J. Tromp, *Primitive Conceptions of Death and the Nether World in the Old Testament*, Bib. et Or. 21 (Rome: Pontifical Biblical Institute, 1969); and Alexander Heidel, "Death and the Afterlife," in *The Gilgamesh Epic and Old Testament Parallels* (Chicago: University of Chicago Press, 1949), 137–223.
5. An excellent analysis of this difficult pericope is that of Ronald F. Youngblood, "1, 2 Samuel," in *The Expositor's Bible Commentary*, ed. Frank E. Gaebelein, vol. 3 (Grand Rapids: Zondervan, 1992), 776–85.
6. R. Laird Harris, "The Doctrine of God in the Book of Job," in *Sitting with Job*, ed. Roy B. Zuck (Grand Rapids: Baker, 1992), 177; reprinted from *Grace Journal* 13 (1972): 3–33.
7. The authoritative study is still that of Gerhard von Rad, *Der heilige Krieg im alten Israel (The Holy War in Ancient Israel)* (Göttingen: Vandenhoeck und

Ruprecht, 1965). See also Peter C. Craigie, *The Problem of War in the Old Testament* (Grand Rapids: Eerdmans, 1978).

8. Eugene H. Merrill, *Deuteronomy*, NAC 4 (Nashville: Broadman & Holman, 1994), 281–87.

9. William J. Dumbrell, *Covenant and Creation* (Nashville: Thomas Nelson, 1984), 33–34.

10. Marvin Wolfgang, "Crime: Homicide," *International Encyclopedia of the Social Sciences*, ed. David L. Sills (New York: Macmillan & Free Press, 1968), 3:490. Wolfgang distinguishes between first degree murder, which is premeditated, and second degree, which is not.

11. Moore goes so far as to say that, to Abimelech, "To perish by the hand of a woman was an ignominy worse than death . . . " (George Foot Moore, *A Critical and Exegetical Commentary on Judges*, ICC (New York: Scribner's, 1895), 268.

12. The nature of the abuse is not clear but the stem of the Hebrew verb (*'ālal*) used here appears at least once elsewhere to refer to sexual abuse (Judg. 19:25). However, the more common meaning of the verb is "to mock" or "ridicule" and the context favors that here, especially since the "uncircumcised" Philistines had previously been mocked by Jonathan (1 Sam. 14:6) and David (1 Sam. 17:26, 36) by this description. See Ralph W. Klein, *1 Samuel*, WBC 10 (Waco, Tex.: Word, 1983), 288.

13. Wennberg, *Terminal Choices*, 45–48.

14. For an interesting discussion of suicide and personal freedom of choice, see Annemarie Pieper, "Ethical Arguments in Favour of Suicide," in *Suicide and the Right to Die*, eds. Jacques Pohier and Dietmar Mieth (Edinburgh: T. & T. Clark, 1985), 39–49.

15. It is well to recall the words of Dietrich Bonhoeffer in this instance: "Many Christians have died sudden deaths without having repented of all their sins. This is setting too much store by the last moment of life" (cited by Wennberg, *Terminal Choices*, 55).

An Overview

Solomon's realistic and moving pictures of the aging process and the awfulness of inevitable death provide the framework for his call to live life to its fullest. Rather than proposing a reason to escape the pain and suffering associated with the aging process through some form of suicide, Solomon admonishes us to live faithfully and productively during the years we have our strength (Eccl. 12:1, 13–14), for it is during this period that we accomplish the most for God. Barry C. Davis ably supports the thesis that Solomon's difficult depiction of the reality of death is not the morbidity of an aged and frustrated man, but the impetus to commit oneself to live to the glory of God. The inevitability of death demands an investment in life.

Chapter Twenty-One

DEATH, AN IMPETUS FOR LIFE
Ecclesiastes 12:1–8

Barry C. Davis

IN THE BOOK OF ECCLESIASTES THE AUTHOR described his search for the key to the meaning of life. That search, however, became an exercise in futility because the more he sought for the answers to life, the more he discovered that life itself is unfair, that human wisdom is woefully insufficient, and that death continually laughed in his face. Furthermore, he realized that of those three barriers—injustice, ignorance, and death—death by far is the most devastating. As Fuerst wrote, "Death is clearly the major problem, which intensifies and exacerbates all others; the specter of death mocks the brave plans of the living. Man cannot argue with this specter, and cannot combat it. It will win in the end."[1]

Death has a voracious, insatiable appetite. Much like a vicious animal, it silently stalks its prey and then strikes with great fury and often little warning. It tears asunder hopes and dreams, and declares that life itself is "vanity," "futility," "meaninglessness," or "emptiness" (הֶבֶל). Thus death "can make a man hate life, not because he wants to die, but because it renders life so futile."[2]

Since death cannot be circumvented, Solomon argued that the key to life and living is to be found in facing death and dying. Going to a wake will help one become awake to the realities of life (7:2, 4). Perhaps to his surprise, Solomon discovered that the meaning of life can be found only by facing the inevitable reality of death.

Ecclesiastes includes numerous references to death and dying.[3] The most thorough treatment on the process and finality of death is in 12:1–8, a passage that graphically depicts the decay of life with its frailty, fear, and ultimately its finality. Before discussing this passage, six principles on death and life will be presented.

PRINCIPLES ON THE DEATH-LIFE PHENOMENON

Principle One: All die (2:14–16; 3:19–22; 9:3). There is an inescapable finality to death; "the inclusiveness of the grave [is] universal."[4] Whether human or animal, wise or foolish, righteous or unrighteous, clean or unclean, sacrificer or nonsacrificer, good or bad, swearer or the one who refuses to swear oaths,

329

each one must face the fate of death. Being a human may have its advantages over being an animal, and being wise may have its advantages over being foolish in being able to live longer. Yet ultimately death functions as the great equalizer. Thus, the one certainty of life is death.[5]

Principle Two: Death has certain advantages over life (4:1–3; 7:1–2, 26). In life, wickedness abounds; in death, there is no suffering and there are no snares to entrap a person. In life, there is constant oppression, often with none to offer comfort; in death, there is a sense of escape. For the living, there is seldom relief—the innocent are unable to "throw off an oppressive yoke, and in the absence of hope, life becomes intolerable."[6] Contemplating these truths, Solomon concluded that death is to be preferred to life and nonexistence to either death or life.[7]

The quest to find meaning to life by investigating life itself, therefore, becomes a hopeless and vain effort.[8]

Principle Three: Death cannot be avoided, but it is best not to act foolishly and to rush it (3:2; 6:6; 7:17; 8:8, 12–13; 9:11–12). Humans desire to control death, and, to a limited extent, they are able to forestall it. They are capable of acting in ways that would seem to hasten death on the one hand or to extend life on the other (7:17; 8:12–13). Yet typically death happens without regard to people's plans. In the ultimate sense, it is controlled by God (3:2; 9:11–12).

Remarkably, despite principle two (that death has certain advantages over life), the author of Ecclesiastes never encouraged the shortening of life, by either unintentional or intentional means. To the contrary, he urged people to refrain from wickedness or foolishness that conceivably could hasten the end of their lives (7:17). Furthermore, he avoided offering suicide as an option—that which "would seem irresistible for one who hates life and falls into despair's vice-like grip."[9] Avoiding such extremes, he offered principles four and five as positive affirmations of life in the face of death.

Principle Four: Studying the reality of death can be instructive on how to live life to the fullest (7:4; 12:1–7). "The heart of the wise is in the house of mourning" rather than in "the house of pleasure" (7:4). Such a perspective forces the individual to face the reality of death, toward which all life inevitably points. A soberness or an attitude of reflection thereby is thrust on the individual. "Sorrow penetrates the heart, draws the thought upwards, purifies, transforms."[10] By advocating the study of death, Qohelet challenged his readers to face life in light of their mortality. Also he urged them to consider their fate early in life (12:1) while there is still time to make a difference in how they live. The longer the delay, the more old age will rob them of the ability to make changes necessary to live life to the fullest to the glory of God (vv. 1–5).

Principle Five: Life has certain advantages over death (9:4–6, 10). While one is alive, there is a hope of finding meaning to life and the possibility of attaining success in life that carries beyond the grave. Qohelet illustrated this truth by maintaining that even the lowest of the low (i.e., the dog)[11] that is alive is better off than the greatest of the great (i.e., the lion)[12] that is dead (v. 4). By this contrast he reinforced the superiority of life to death. Whereas life offers hope, death shatters all dreams. Death allows no further opportunity for obtaining any reward in this life or the next.

Principle Six: Living solely for this life is meaningless (5:15–16; 6:3–5; 8:10). Securing all possible physical possessions (wealth, health, and family) and religious credits does nothing to ensure an enduring reward or a meaningful existence after the grave. Riches in fact deceive the individual who places his or her trust in them (5:13–16). They are inherently unsatisfying—they are never enough; someone always desires to take them away; and they produce worry and misery in this life. Riches also are temporary—they provide no true security. They cannot be taken into the next life; they are as fleeting as the wind.

Having a long life with many descendants (6:3–5) does not guarantee earthly satisfaction, much less eternal rewards. The joy of children's laughter may fade through the years, and children's love for their father may turn to resentment or apathy—the resultant tragedy being that none of a man's children may care enough even to save face by giving him a decent burial.[13] Such a man, as Kidner states, would "have the things men dream of—which in Old Testament terms meant children by the score, and years of life by the thousand—and still depart unnoticed, unlamented and unfulfilled."[14]

These tragic situations are compounded by the fact that even if an individual is religious, he is quickly forgotten after he dies (8:10).[15] The seemingly solid permanence of this life fades quickly into the shadowy, elusive specter of the next.

AN INTRODUCTION TO 12:1–8 ON DEATH AND LIFE

Many attempts have been made to unify Ecclesiastes 12:1–8 under one analogical scheme.[16] Some scholars have advocated that the passage describes physiological changes. Others have suggested that it pictures a funeral, and still others have indicated that it depicts a ruined house. The wisest approach seems to be that suggested by Gordis who maintains that "most plausibly, old age is pictured here without one line of thought being maintained throughout."[17] Fuerst concurs, stating that "it is better not to insist on . . . the presence of just one dominant figure of speech."[18] Perhaps Solomon saw death and dying as such debilitating and devastating events that he determined to portray them through a multiplicity of analogies with great rapidity to ensure that the thrust of his message was clearly understood.

Because of the diversity of illustrative material in the passage, it is necessary to analyze each of the images separately to determine its specific point of reference.[19] In doing so, the various conundrums will be clarified and the integrity of the passage maintained.[20]

The passage is framed by references to God as the Originator of life. Despite the inequities of life and the terrors of death, God is ever the Creator of both the living (v. 1)[21] and the dead (v. 7). God's sovereignty is thus recognized as a regulating element in all human activities. If God is present at the beginning and the ending of life, He most certainly is there throughout the totality of life. God thus can give meaning to an otherwise meaningless existence; He can even help individuals make sense out of the senselessness of death.

To aid the flow of thought through the passage, Qohelet employed three times the temporal marker עַד אֲשֶׁר ("before") (vv. 1–2, 6) to denote the transitions between the temporal-psychological shifts in the passage. While signaling a new thought, the words also recall the command of verse 1, "Remember also your Creator." The primary activity to undertake throughout all phases of life is to consider God and His involvement in the life-death phenomenon.

THE DAYS BEFORE THE END (12:1)

"Remember also" (זְכֹר) provides a transition from the injunction to live life to the fullest because it is short and the future is uncertain (11:1–10) to a serious enjoinder to live life wisely precisely because it is short and the future is certain (12:1–7). That future certainty is the fact that every individual will die. Furthermore the process of dying is an experience filled not with pleasure but with sorrow.

"Remember" (זכֹר) is the most appropriate choice for this solemn religious adjuration.[22] Though the Qal form of this verb normally refers "to inner mental acts, either with or without reference to concomitant external acts,"[23] the context of this passage (and of the entire book) implies that action subsequent to the mental activity must be undertaken. Readers are challenged to remember, not for the sake of reminiscing but for the purpose of revolutionizing their lives, bringing them into conformity with God's eternal and sovereign plan.

Various commentators have sought to emend בּוֹרְאֶיךָ ("your Creator") in the Masoretic Text to read "your well" or "your cistern"—euphemistic terms for one's wife.[24] These commentators argue that the verse is recommending "the enjoyment of marital relations."[25] Others have suggested "your pit" as a possible alternative, thereby implying the grave. Still others have offered "your vigor, well-being."[26] These options are similar in phonics but not in orthography.[27]

Though there is no textual support for these alternative readings,[28] those who recommend an emended text do so because they believe that an "allusion to God the Creator ill fits this context."[29] However, strong arguments based on the context may be made in favor of the reading "your Creator." First, in 11:5, God is first mentioned since 9:7. Then the Person of God is kept before the minds of the readers in the concluding verses of the book (11:5, 9; 12:1, 7, 13–14). Second, the reference to God provides an effective inclusion to the discussion of death, picturing God both as the One from whom life comes (12:1) and as the One to whom life returns (12:7). Third, though in 11:9–10 Qohelet urged his readers to enjoy the pleasures of life, he counterbalanced that charge by a solemn warning to remember the judgment of God. To shift away from that God-oriented perspective in 12:1 to encourage the embracing of one's wife would be contrary to his argument.[30] Fourth, remembering one's "grave" or one's "well-being" might be shown to fit the context of 12:1–7, but their use would weaken the impact of the text.

In contrast to the alternative renderings, the term בּוֹרְאֶיךָ, a probable plural of majesty,[31] is highly appropriate in this context. Since the theme of 12:1–8 is death, the end of physical life, what better way is there for expressing the nonfinality of that death than to remind the readers that God is Creator? Death is pictured not as the end but rather as the beginning of an everlasting existence.

Readers are to remember God early in their lives ("in the days of your youth")[32] because childhood and the prime of life are fleeting (11:10). As the days of one's youth pass quickly, the onset of the aging process brings with it a decline that impacts the vigor and drive of one's life.[33] Pleasure and hope are inversely proportional to age. Thus people ought to turn to God while there is still time to discover the meaning of life and alter the course of their lives.[34] Goldberg suggests the intent behind Qohelet's concern as follows: "We are encouraged . . . to commit ourselves to our Creator while we have our wits about us, while we can still enjoy life, and before we lose the fullest capacity to even think of God's purposes and desires."[35]

In verse 1 the first of the three עַד אֲשֶׁר ("before") temporal clauses, "before the evil days come," highlights the time of life before the onslaught of death's decay is noticeable. This summarizes in an overview fashion what is described in detail in verses 2–7, namely, that in his dying the individual will have no delight.

To what do "the evil days" refer? Rather than being a reference to moral perversion[36] or the darkness of Sheol,[37] as some suggest, "evil days" is synonymous with "old age, in which there is no pleasure."[38] Such a view is contextually appropriate because of its contrast to "in the days of your youth" and because of its continuation of the argument (11:6–10) that the early years of life provide opportunities for enjoyment whereas the later years do not.

Furthermore the closing chapter of one's life reduces dramatically the opportunity for accomplishing the desires of one's heart. They are in fact times of "no delight"—times in which there is an absence or impossibility[39] (אֵין) of delight. This "delight" (חֵפֶץ) is an emotion-laden word that implies an attraction to some object, hence a "desire" or a "longing" for something.[40] It conveys the idea of "delight" or "pleasure" and may be used "in reference to a person's great interest."[41]

The fact that an individual will lose his delight in life seems to indicate that he may tend to focus too much on his infirmities to the detriment of enjoying what God has created.[42] He will have lost the proper perspective on life and will have run counter to the commands to rejoice while growing up, to follow the impulses of one's heart and the desires of one's eyes, and to enjoy life with one's own spouse (9:9; 11:9). As Hengstenberg perceptively summarizes this message: "How mournful a thing must it be to pass into the ranks of those who are here described, without having tasted of the feast of joys prepared by the Creator for all those who remember Him."[43]

THE DAYS OF THE ENDING (12:2–5)

The second thematic marker (עַד אֲשֶׁר, "before") shifts the reader's thinking from that time of life before the individual is fully aware of the aging process to that time when he is painfully aware of his personal decay. Verses 2–5 include a series of metaphors that reveal that the signs forewarning old age are no longer mere warnings; they have become realities.

The beginning metaphor is that the sun, the light, the moon, and the stars are darkened (v. 2). Because the passage speaks of aging and the dying process, this verse should not be thought of as referring to the future cosmic judgment in which the sun, moon, and stars will be destroyed (Rev. 6:12–13). In addition, this clause should not be considered a reference to the loss of one's family, drawing on the symbolism of Genesis 37:9–10 (i.e., the sun meaning father, the moon meaning mother, and the stars meaning brothers). Rather, it should be understood as being generically suggestive of one or more of the following: "a time of affliction and sadness,"[44] "the fading capacity for joy,"[45] "the more general desolations of old age,"[46] or the failing of one's eyesight "so that the lights of all sorts become dim."[47] Most simply,[48] the clause is expressing metaphorically the loss of joy and excitement in life.[49]

Solomon next pictured old age as clouds that return after the rain.[50] Delitzsch succinctly describes the Hebrew concept of the cloud image when he states, "A cloudy day is = a day of misfortune, Joel 2:2, Zeph. 1:15; an overflowing rain is a scourge of God, Ezek. 13:13, 38:22."[51] Ecclesiastes 12:2 may have in mind a Middle Eastern winter rainstorm, which is normally followed by blue skies that promise good weather. However, "the unexpected return of the clouds soon after a storm, once more shutting out the light, is a bad sign and brings gloom, both literally and psychologically."[52] This imagery is not depicting gradually failing eyesight or the onset of glaucoma,[53] but rather the repetitive gloom into which the elderly may be prone to fall as they encounter setback after setback in the final years of their lives. Much as an elderly person recovers from one injury or illness only to be subjected to another, the individual's hopes and dreams are continually being dashed. Thus, as Kidner comments, "the clouds will always gather again, and time will no longer heal, but kill."[54]

The metaphors in verse 3 have been variously interpreted by some as "a household falling into decay or house struck by a violent storm."[55] Other commentators understand the verses to be picturing the deterioration of the human body as it ages[56]—the watchmen representing the arms, the mighty men the legs, the grinding ones the teeth, and those at the window the eyes.[57] The uncertainties in these images, therefore, result in a general lack of agreement among scholars regarding how best to depict each individual image.[58]

What can be noted, however, is that Qohelet did not play favorites. He did not picture the decaying process of old age as solely the lot of one sex as opposed to the other. In fact, of the four metaphors in this verse, he relates two of them to the male population and the other two to females. Thus the terrors associated with dying are a reality of life for all people.

"The watchmen of the house" who "tremble" are those who preserve, protect, and guard the house. Their function is to ensure that everyone within the house is safe and secure. Yet these men "tremble," "quake," are "in terror," or "quiver."[59] What might cause this trembling is the degeneration of the nervous and muscular system of the body[60] or a powerful outside force that greatly intimidates the watchmen, causing them to cower in fear.

What then is the impact on the house? What is the impact on the elderly when the guardians tremble? Protection against a dreaded enemy decreases. Vulnerability to attack increases and there is a subsequent increase in the potential for catastrophe or ultimate destruction to occur.

The second of the two male-oriented metaphors is that "mighty men stoop." Because חַיִל ("mighty") has a broad semantic range including strength, efficiency, ability, wealth, force, army, and virtue,[61] determining exactly who these men are is difficult. They undoubtedly are men of high standing, at least in the house, if not in the city. Whybray indicates that they "may be masters, but are probably the stalwart men-servants."[62]

Why would such honorable (and perhaps strong) men stoop? Are they doing so because of old age or are they bending over in abject submission to some outside force? The verb עָוַת ("stoop," here in the Hithpael form) is best translated "bend themselves,"[63] and therefore would seem to favor the latter position. They are not naturally bent over nor do they choose to be, but rather forces working contrary to their will impose conditions to which they finally succumb.

The next metaphor states that "the grinding ones [feminine form] stand idle because they are few." An often held view of this metaphor argues that "the grinding ones" (הַטֹּחֲנוֹת) are teeth. If this is true, then Delitzsch is correct when he states that "they [the teeth] stand no longer in a row; they are isolated, and (as is to be supposed) are also in themselves defective."[64] This view, however, does not seem to fit the pattern of development in this verse. The other three metaphors in the verse are more easily understood as references to actual people rather than as references to body parts.

A second view of this metaphor presents "the grinding ones" as women (i.e., female servants) who make flour for the household's bread.[65] This metaphor thus suggests that the women are no longer able to complete their work because they are few in number and apparently need a full complement of laborers to function properly.[66] Though this view is plausible, it has one major weakness, as Crenshaw points out. Would not one expect the grinders to work even more diligently if they are few in number, unless the implication is that the residents of the house are also few in number and have little need for food?[67]

If Crenshaw's implication is correct, then the metaphor changes its focus from the visible grinders to an unspecified group of people in the house who no longer possess the wherewithal to support a flourishing household. Whereas such a shift of focus is possible, it would seem to lessen the impact of the metaphor, making the reference to the aging process indirect rather than direct.

An alternative suggestion is that the grinders themselves have become few through attrition due to old age, incapacitation, or death. Under such conditions, there would be much sadness among the remaining grinders because so many of their friends are no longer around to make their work a joy. So the remaining grinders, themselves too weary to carry on, have just given up.

The fourth metaphor in this verse (and the second one directed toward women) states that "those who look through windows grow dim." Most commentators agree that "those who look through windows" is a reference to the women of the household who, according to Middle Eastern custom, were not allowed to mingle with the men in the business of the household, and so they peered through the latticework of the house.[68] That they "grow dim" means either (a) that others outside the house have a more difficult time seeing them in the windows because they go to the windows no more,[69] (b) that it has become dark,[70] or (c) that they themselves have a harder time seeing, for their eyes have lost their brilliance.[71] In each case, the women are becoming progressively isolated from the outside world, shut off from whatever joys and pleasures they once knew.

The writer continued this isolation-fear imagery as he began verse 4 by stating that for the aging person "the doors on the street are shut." Immediately the reader grasps the idea that life is not as it once was or as it should be. What once allowed people or objects to go in or out no longer does so. The doors are closed—perhaps through fear, perhaps through inattentiveness or a lack of care by those responsible for opening them, or perhaps through their own inability to be opened any more.

"Doors" (דְּלָתַיִם) is a dual form meaning "literally 'double doors,' only found at the entrance to cities, temples and exceptionally grand houses,"[72] most houses apparently having had only one door.[73] The doors may remain shut as a picture of a self-enclosed, self-isolated group of people or may refer symbolically, as many suggest, to the lips or the ears.[74]

"The sound of the grinding is low" because few people are working there (cf. v. 4 NASB). Such a condition would be discouraging to the elderly because what they remember as a cheerful indicator of the exciting activities of business is now more and more being shut out of their lives. They in turn find themselves "increasingly cut off from the hum of daily life."[75]

The Hebrew of 12:4, however, does not isolate the metaphor of the grinding mill from the previous metaphor of the doors on the street being shut. Rather, it uses the sound of the mill being low to explain why the doors are closed. The ב in בִּשְׁפַל ("as . . . low") functions as a temporal preposition indicating that the doors on the street are shut "when" or "at the same time as" the activity of the grinding mill decreases dramatically. If the grinders in verse 3 are understood as a reference to teeth, then that lends credibility to the view that "doors" here refer to lips. On the other hand if the grinders in verse 3 are women who prepare flour for bread, then the house imagery better fits the closing of the doors in this verse. This latter view seems preferable.

Having completed what Fredericks observes is a chiasm beginning with verse 3b and ending with verse 4a,[76] the symbolism shifts to picture death from still another angle, the chirping of birds—"one will arise at the sound of the bird." Whybray offers two possible interpretations for this illustration:

"either that the elderly get up early in the morning . . . or that their voice becomes high like that of a bird."[77] What is so discouraging or sad about arising when birds sing or about the pitch of one's voice being elevated? The latter would be merely a statement of fact and therefore not necessarily a source of worry, but simply rather a reminder that one has aged. The former (rising when birds sing) only becomes a matter of dread if it implies that one is awakened by every little sound. Kidner points out, however, that if the previous metaphors imply that deafness accompanies old age, then the elderly person would "hardly be wakened or startled by the sparrow."[78]

The music metaphor is continued in the final portion of verse 4: "all the daughters of song will sing softly" (NASB). This may refer to female singers, to song birds, or to musical notes.[79] That they "will sing softly" may mean that the sound is faint to the ears of the elderly,[80] that for the elderly "all singing as well as all appreciation of singing is a thing of the past,"[81] or that the singers themselves have lost the ability to sing.[82] A further possible interpretation is that the singers sing softly for fear of waking the elderly who have difficulty sleeping and who arouse easily, even at the sound of the birds chirping. No matter which view is correct, the disheartening fact is that those who have aged in this way are no longer able to enjoy what was once a pleasure to them.

The quiet sadness of the metaphors in verse 4 changes in verse 5 into what Crenshaw terms "a full measure of existential Angst."[83] Fear now runs rampant. Those who have grown old "are afraid of a high place and of terrors on the road." A straightforward rendering of these two pictures of fear best expresses their meaning. To a person who is old, feeble, and defenseless, the world looms as a place of great risks and physical dangers. Delitzsch equates this fear to that of the sluggard of Proverbs 22:13:

> As the sluggard says: there is a lion in the way, and under this pretence remains slothfully at home . . . so old men do not venture out; for to them a damp road appears like a very morass; a gravelly path, as full of neck-breaking hillocks; an undulating path, as fearfully steep and precipitous; that which is not shaded, as oppressively hot and exhausting—they want strength and courage to overcome difficulties, and their anxiety pictures out dangers before them where there are none.[84]

The remaining three metaphors in Ecclesiastes 12:5 are difficult to interpret. The two primary views are that the imagery symbolizes either the rapid growth of spring or the deterioration of the human body. The former contrasts the downfall of the house, which will never rise again, with the fresh renewal of nature, which offers a wellspring of hope. The latter understands that the words focus on the gradual encroachments of old age.[85]

Regarding the first of these three images—"the almond tree blossoms"—most commentators say the symbolism refers to the white hair of an elderly person. This view is favored because the almond blossom, which exhibits a pink color when it blooms in January, very soon thereafter becomes white at the tip, only to fall to the ground later like white snowflakes.[86]

Hengstenberg, however, offers a different perspective. He contends that both the context and the etymology of the word for almond tree (שָׁקֵד) support the notion that the tree is "a symbol of that watchfulness with which old age is visited."[87] The word for almond tree is similar to the verb "be watchful" (שָׁקַד).

For the second of the three metaphors—"the grasshopper drags himself along"—the following views are most often suggested: (a) the stiffness of the joints; (b) the bent figure of an old person; (c) the enormous appetite of the locust, which, becoming weighted down by its full stomach, moves awkwardly; (d) the inability of the male sex organ to function as it should in old age; and (e) an emblem of smallness, indicating that even the smallest object is a burden to carry.[88]

The first two explanations (stiffness and being hunched over) and possibly the fifth suggestion (difficulty in burden-bearing) offer the more reasonable suggestions of the meaning of the grasshopper illustration. The overeating view (view c) functions at cross purposes to imagery regarding the elderly's loss of ability to eat (if grinders in verses 3–4 refer to teeth) and to the picture of the elderly's loss of a desire to eat in the caperberry metaphor below. Furthermore the diminished sexual capacity view (view d) requires that a double entendre be understood—a suggestion about the grasshopper not observed elsewhere in Scripture.[89]

The third metaphor in verse 5, "the caperberry is ineffective," is easier to interpret than the other two. Caperberries were used in ancient times as a "provocative to appetite."[90] This implies, therefore, that in old age, not even an artificial stimulant can move the individual to do what in years gone by would have been done with gusto and relish.[91]

Verse 5 concludes with a straightforward presentation of the fact of death: "For man goes to his eternal home while mourners go about in the street." The verb הָלַךְ ("goes") is used euphemistically in typical Hebrew fashion to express the concept of dying.[92] "To his eternal home" indicates that the end of that "going" is the individual's final resting place.

As a common designator of the grave,[93] the "eternal home" is "a 'home' for successive generations of a family [that] spans an endless period of time."[94] It should not be thought of as expressing anything more than the grave, nor should it be assumed that it introduces the nascent underpinnings of a theology of the afterlife. As Youngblood states, "OT references to the afterlife are, for the most part, shrouded in darkness when compared to the fuller revelation of the NT."[95]

The final clause of this section, "while mourners go about in the street," reveals one last insult that the dying process has in store for the aged. The irony of the clause should not be missed. While the man dies, and even before he is dead, professional mourners gather around in front of the dying man's house seeking employment to engage in the practice of mourning (cf. Jer. 9:16–20; Amos 5:16). Little thought, if any, is given to the one who has suffered the mockery and misery of death. As Gordis concludes, the tragedy of this man's death "constitutes merely one more professional routine for the hired mourners—the vanity of life is climaxed by the vanity of death!"[96]

THE END OF DAYS (12:6–8)

The beginning of this final analysis of death again employs the temporal marker עַד אֲשֶׁר ("before"), the third such usage of this Hebrew phrase in the verses under study.[97] The first (v. 1) places the individual under the indictment of death but seemingly (though not actually) far removed from it. The second (v. 2) dramatically portrays the rapidly deteriorating conditions of life and the fast approach of death. Finally, here, the last act of life (i.e., death) is played out. There is no timidity about death when it comes and there is no escape for the individual whom death attacks. Ultimately what is discovered is that both the body and the spirit of the dead man return to their place of origin—the body to the ground and the spirit to God (v. 7).

In verse 6, Qohelet portrayed the end of life by three graphic metaphors: the crushing of a lamp, the shattering of a jar, and the breaking of a wheel. Each presents an irreversible destruction, symbolizing the suddenness and finality of death. Furthermore each picture may be thought of as suggestive of a different type of life that is taken in death. The rich imagery of the lamp made up of the cord and bowl appears to reflect the fact that even the wealthy do not escape death. The pitcher illustration, by contrast, seems to show that those who are fragile and helpless also do not escape death. And the wheel at the cistern pictures apparently the strong, utilitarian type of person as still another category of individuals who are unable to avoid death.

The two metaphors—the silver cord being broken and the golden bowl being crushed—are in reality only one,[98] for the cord and the bowl are parts of one lamp. Once the cord is cut, the bowl drops to the ground and is irreparably damaged. So too, when the cord of life is cut, the individual falls to the ground never to rise again.

The final two images in this verse—the pitcher and the wheel—may also, according to certain commentators, be two components of one metaphor. Gordis suggests that Levy is correct when he states, "One end of the cord has a pitcher, the other a metal ball . . . as a counterweight. When the cord is torn, ball, pitcher and wheel all fall to the bottom and are broken."[99]

Other commentators, however, view the two as separate metaphors.[100] The fragile, easily broken pitcher suggests the fragile life of the elderly. It, like they, needs only to be struck once and then it is of no use to those who are under the sun.[101] Likewise, the crushing of the wheel is assumed to symbolize the total destruction of life at the point of death.

Concluding these dramatic illustrations of devastation, Solomon moves from what to many has been a series of indistinct metaphors in verses 2–6 to a picture that is unmistakably clear in verse 7. Death, simply and finally, is the separation of body and spirit.

An important point to note, however, is that the purpose in verse 7 (and throughout the book of Ecclesiastes) is not to present a theology of the afterlife. The goal was not to have readers understand the details of life after death, but rather to have them recognize the fact of the existence of an afterlife so that they might live eternally purposeful lives here and now. Wright states this thesis in this way:

The dead have run their course. They are waiting in Sheol for the judgment. They do not, like the living, know what is happening on the earth. They have no further opportunities of earning the Master's reward. Their bodies, the vehicles of the emotions of love and hatred and envy, have gone to dust, and no more can they share in life under the sun.[102]

Verse 7 begins by stating that "the dust will return to the earth as it was." "Dust" (עָפָר) refers symbolically to the physical nature of the individual. This is a favorite term employed by Old Testament writers to remind the reader of his or her earthly origin (Gen. 2:7; 3:19; Job 10:9) and physical weakness (Ps. 103:14).[103] The human body, being in essence dust, returns to dust when the individual dies.[104] Fuerst presents the perspective of life and death in Ecclesiastes as follows: "Migration from dust to dust, with a brief moment for wisdom and striving and reflection, is the fate of man."[105]

Verse 7 ends by differentiating the disposition of the human spirit from the dissolution of the human body. Despite the interplay between the two during life, there is no absorption of the one by the other in death. Each has a separate destiny. Whereas the body goes back to the earth as dust, the spirit returns to God who gave it.

To his credit, though he understands the finality of death to be a tragic disruption of human life, Solomon neither condemns that fact nor reproaches God for making life "a temporary gift which God would one day withdraw."[106]

As the body and spirit of the dead person return to their origins (v. 7), so the author in verse 8 returns to his original remarks in 1:2: "'Vanity of vanities,' says the Preacher, 'all is vanity!'" These words seemingly declare that all in life and in death is "futile"[107] (הֶבֶל). Crenshaw is led to assert that "one cannot imagine such a conclusion if the allusion to breath's return to God contained the slightest grounds for hope. In truth, divine support of life has vanished for Qoheleth."[108] Crenshaw's pessimistic position, however, fails to recognize that the statement "all is futile," is thoroughly steeped in Qohelet's positive understanding of the significance of life as he presents it throughout the book.

In line with this view of life and in light of the reality of death, individuals are challenged to live to the fullest and at the same time to be ever mindful of the transitory nature of life and of the sudden, irreversible coming of death. Qohelet urged individuals, moreover, to remember their Creator in the days of their youth (12:1) and to "fear God and keep His commandments" throughout all the days of their lives (v. 13). This therefore presents a balanced picture of life: "Man should enjoy what he can, be circumspect and pious, and fear the Lord; but [at the same time recognize a sense] of helplessness because the inexorable round of life finally does come to an end."[109]

CONCLUSION

Based on this study of death and dying in Ecclesiastes, including an examination of 12:1–8, the final and most extensive passage in the book on the subject, several conclusions may be drawn about the life-death phenomenon.

1. Everyone must turn to God while there is still time, because the end of days will come swiftly.
2. The aging, dying process, though in no way to be considered beautiful, does post warning signs of impending doom—signs that need to be heeded to ensure a successful life now and a proper reward after death.
3. Laying up treasures in this world is futile, because death will come for the individual, and the world will continue on as though he or she never existed.
4. No matter how long one lives or how much preparation one makes for dying, death comes suddenly and without fail.
5. Life after death does exist, and one needs to live now in such a way as to be ready to meet one's Maker.

Hengstenberg summarizes well this philosophy of life and death in Ecclesiastes:

> Since all things are vain, man, who is subject to vanity, should do all in his power to enter into a living relation to Him who is the true absolute Being, and through fellowship with Him to participate, himself, in a true eternal being. All being vanity, man should not further vex himself about a "handful of vanity"—he should not care much whether he have [sic] to suffer a little more or a little less, but [should] attach importance alone to that which either hinders or favours his fellowship with Him who is the true absolute, personal, Being.[110]

"Vanity of vanities, all is vanity"; yet with God there is hope.

ENDNOTES

1. Wesley J. Fuerst, *The Books of Ruth, Esther, Ecclesiastes, The Song of Songs, Lamentations: The Five Scrolls* (Cambridge: Cambridge University Press, 1975), 151.
2. J. Stafford Wright, "The Interpretation of Ecclesiastes," in *Classical Evangelical Essays in Old Testament Interpretation*, ed. Walter C. Kaiser Jr. (Grand Rapids: Baker, 1972), 143.
3. 2:14–16; 3:2, 19–22; 4:1–3; 5:15–16; 6:3–4, 6; 7:1–2, 4, 17, 26; 8:8, 10, 12–13; 9:2–3, 4–6, 10–12; 12:1–7.
4. J. Barton Payne, *The Theology of the Older Testament* (Grand Rapids: Zondervan, 1971), 453.
5. Ecclesiastes does not soften the harsh reality of death. In fact little by way of a theology of the afterlife is presented, leaving it to be understood primarily as a mystery. Moreover, when the subject of the afterlife is addressed (9:5–6, 10), it is presented as a contrasting existence to the present life, as a place where all earthly experiences cease (Michael A. Eaton, *Ecclesiastes: An Introduction and Commentary* [Downers Grove, Ill.: InterVarsity Press, 1983], 129). Furthermore even though at death the human spirit returns to God (12:7), no one is able to show what that existence will be like (3:21).

6. James L. Crenshaw, "The Shadow of Death in Qoheleth," in *Israelite Wisdom*, ed. John G. Gammie et al. (Missoula, Mont.: Scholars Press, 1978), 208.

7. Qohelet's conclusion regarding the preference of nonexistence over present existence appears on the surface to be at variance with the Old Testament Israelite's aversion to Sheol, the place of the dead. Knudson states that "the Israelites looked forward to it [Sheol] with unconcealed dread. Almost any kind of earthly existence was to be preferred to it" (Albert C. Knudson, *The Religious Teaching of the Old Testament* [New York: Abingdon, 1918], 390). Qohelet, however, did not embrace the place of the dead as the place to be. Rather, he preferred nonsuffering as the "place" to be. The dead and the never-alive do not face the miseries of this life. Their fate, moreover, is not a question mark but a reality; it is not something to be feared by the child of God but something to be experienced. (Compare principle five in which Qohelet argued that there are advantages to being alive when compared to being dead.)

8. J. Coert Rylaarsdam, *The Proverbs, Ecclesiastes, The Song of Solomon*, The Layman's Bible Commentary (Richmond, Va.: John Knox, 1908), 110. See Ecclesiastes 1:13–2:11.

9. Crenshaw, "The Shadow of Death in Qoheleth," 210.

10. Franz Delitzsch, *Commentary on the Song of Songs and Ecclesiastes*, Biblical Commentary on the Old Testament, trans. M. C. Easton (Grand Rapids: Zondervan, 1988), 315.

11. Crenshaw describes the Hebrew view of "dog" as follows: "The lowly cur [9:4b], restricted to a life of scavenging on the perimeters of human existence, functioned as a term of opprobrium. The epithet 'dog,' was hurled in the faces of male prostitutes, who belonged, in the speaker's opinion, outside the domain of human beings (Deut. 23:18–19). The term also became a means of self-abnegation, particularly in the presence of nobility (1 Sam. 24:14)" ("The Shadow of Death in Qoheleth," 209).

12. In direct contrast to the dog, which was despised by the Hebrews, the lion enjoyed an exalted status. "To the Jews the lion was the mightiest of beasts, having a king's regal bearing (Prov. 30:29–31). Thus it symbolized leadership (Gen. 49:9, 10; Num. 24:9)" (Walter A. Elwell, ed., *Baker Encyclopedia of the Bible*, 2 vols. [Grand Rapids: Baker, 1988], 1:107–8).

13. Eichrodt argues that the Israelites attached much significance to having a proper burial. He states that they saw a direct relationship between the absence or inadequacy of a burial and the realization of a less desirable position in the afterlife (Walther Eichrodt, *Theology of the Old Testament*, trans. J. A. Baker, 2 vols. [Philadelphia: Westminster, 1961, 1967], 2:212).

14. Derek Kidner, *A Time to Mourn, and a Time to Dance* (Downers Grove, Ill.: InterVarsity Press, 1976), 59.

15. This verse may be understood either as focusing solely on the wicked who in some way make a pretense of being religious or as presenting the wicked in the first half and the righteous in the second half. For a discussion of these two positions see Delitzsch, *Commentary on the Song of Songs and Ecclesiastes*, 345–47; and Crenshaw, *Ecclesiastes: A Commentary* (Philadelphia: Westminster, 1987), 154.

16. For a discussion of some of the more common approaches toward unification, see Delitzsch, *Commentary on the Song of Songs and Ecclesiastes;* and Robert Gordis, *Koheleth—The Man and His World* (New York: Schocken Books, 1968).

17. Gordis, *Koheleth—The Man and His World*, 339.

18. Fuerst, *The Books of Ruth, Esther, Ecclesiastes, The Song of Songs, Lamentations: The Five Scrolls*, 152.
19. R. N. Whybray, *Ecclesiastes*, The New Century Bible Commentary (Grand Rapids: Eerdmans, 1989), 163–64.
20. Kidner, *A Time to Mourn, and a Time to Dance*, 101.
21. See below for a discussion of the arguments for and against בּוֹרְאֶיךָ as a reference to God as Creator.
22. Gordis, *Koheleth—The Man and His World*, 340.
23. *Theological Wordbook of the Old Testament*, ed. R. Laird Harris, Gleason L. Archer Jr., and Bruce K. Waltke, 2 vols. (Chicago: Moody Press, 1980), s.v. "זָכַר," by Andrew Bowling, 1:241.
24. Proverbs 5:15, 18 presents this euphemistic use of the term בְּאֵרֶךָ.
25. Both Whybray and Gordis discuss and reject this view that requires an emended text (Whybray, *Ecclesiastes*, 163, and Gordis, *Koheleth—The Man and His World*, 340).
26. Crenshaw discusses these various alternatives and selects "your wife" as his preferred translation (*Ecclesiastes: A Commentary*, 184–85).
27. Kidner, *A Time to Mourn, and a Time to Dance*, 100.
28. Eaton, *Ecclesiastes: An Introduction and Commentary*, 148.
29. Crenshaw, *Ecclesiastes: A Commentary*, 184.
30. Qohelet commended spousal love-making in 9:9 in a somewhat less somber context. To reintroduce it here would be an unnecessary (and incongruous) redundancy.
31. Whybray suggests that בּוֹרְאֶיךָ is a plural of majesty (*Ecclesiastes*, 163); Gesenius says that the singular should be read (*Gesenius' Hebrew Grammar*, eds. E. Kautzsch and A. E. Cowley, 2d Eng. ed. [Oxford: Clarendon Press, 1910], 399).
32. Qohelet did not define the age of "youth," except as a contrast to what follows (12:2–5). Furthermore he did not indicate that an older person cannot or should not remember his God, but rather he seems to imply that the older an individual becomes, the more difficult it is to change his life when he does remember.
33. Eaton, *Ecclesiastes: An Introduction and Commentary*, 148.
34. Interestingly Qohelet did not suggest that the act of "remembering" God acts either as a deterrent to or as a cosmetic against the ravages of old age; it is not an elixir from the mythical fountain of youth. The assumption is that everyone who lives long enough will experience the natural debilitating effects of the aging process.
35. Louis Goldberg, *Ecclesiastes*, Bible Study Commentary (Grand Rapids: Zondervan, 1983), 132.
36. Eaton, *Ecclesiastes: An Introduction and Commentary*, 148.
37. George A. Barton, *A Critical and Exegetical Commentary on the Book of Ecclesiastes*, International Critical Commentary (Edinburgh: T. & T. Clark, 1908), 185–86.
38. Gordis, *Koheleth—The Man and His World*, 341.
39. *Theological Wordbook of the Old Testament*, s.v. "אַיִן," by Jack B. Scott, 1:37.
40. Francis Brown, S. R. Driver, and Charles A. Briggs, *A Hebrew and English Lexicon of the Old Testament* (Oxford: Clarendon Press, 1955), 343.
41. *Theological Wordbook of the Old Testament*, s.v. "חָפֵץ," by Leon J. Wood, 1:311.
42. H. C. Leupold, *Exposition of Ecclesiastes* (Grand Rapids: Baker, 1968), 274.
43. Ernest W. Hengstenberg, *A Commentary on Ecclesiastes* (Minneapolis: James and Klock, 1977), 245.
44. J. M. Fuller, ed., *Proverbs-Ezekiel*, The Bible Commentary (Grand Rapids: Baker, 1972), 111.

45. Eaton, *Ecclesiastes: An Introduction and Commentary*, 148.
46. Kidner, *A Time to Mourn, and a Time to Dance*, 101.
47. Barton, *A Critical and Exegetical Commentary on the Book of Ecclesiastes*, 186.
48. Simplicity and caution are perhaps the best guides in attempting to understand these and the following analogies regarding old age. Kidner agrees: "If some obscurities in these lines can be clarified, so much the better for kindling our imagination; but so much the worse if they tempt us into treating this graceful poem as a laboured cryptogram, or forcing every detail into a single rigid scheme" (*A Time to Mourn, and a Time to Dance*, 101).

   Furthermore stepping beyond the bounds of simplicity and caution may lead to an allegorical hermeneutic. The reader must be wary of commentators who pull from these analogies more than can be justifiably proven. For example Plumptre states that "the sun may be the Spirit, the Divine light of the body, the moon as the Reason that reflects the light, the stars as the senses that give but a dim light in the absence of the sun and moon" (E. H. Plumptre, *Ecclesiastes: or the Preacher, with Notes and Introduction* [Cambridge: Cambridge University Press, 1881], 214). Delitzsch, though decrying various attempts at interpreting these figures and calling those attempts "wholly or for the most part unfortunate," also oversteps the bounds of careful hermeneutics. He suggests that the sun, light, moon, and stars may be understood as alluding, respectively, to the spirit, the light of self-examination, the soul, and the five senses (*Commentary on the Song of Songs and Ecclesiastes*, 403–5).
49. Leupold states, "In the Scriptures 'light' is quite generally a symbol of joy and, when it is sent by God, a token of favor. Just as clearly the Scriptures let darkness be synonymous with judgment and punishment, cf., Joel 3:4; 2:10; Amos 8:9; Isa. 13:10; 5:3; Jer. 4:33; Ezek. 32:7; Rev. 6:12" (*Exposition of Ecclesiastes*, 276–77).
50. Eaton suggests that אַחַר ("after") may mean "with," though he recognizes that such a translation is not normally associated with אַחַר (*Ecclesiastes: An Introduction and Commentary*, 148, n.).
51. Delitzsch, *Commentary on the Song of Songs and Ecclesiastes*, 405.
52. Whybray, *Ecclesiastes*, 164.
53. Crenshaw, *Ecclesiastes: A Commentary*, 185.
54. Kidner, *A Time to Mourn, and a Time to Dance*, 102. Fredericks suggests that the returning clouds are representative of "the despair and terror of imminent death" that the individual faces "at the close of those miserable years" (Daniel C. Fredericks, "Life's Rise and Demise in Ecclesiastes 11:1–12:8," paper presented to the Evangelical Theological Society, San Diego, Calif., November 18, 1989, 19).
55. Whybray, *Ecclesiastes*, 164.
56. The words found in the Egyptian Ptah-hotep's preface to his *Instruction* to his son may be of interest at this point. He wrote, "Feebleness has arrived; dotage is coming. . . . The eyes are weak, the ears are deaf, the strength is disappearing. . . . The heart is forgetful. . . . All taste is gone" (cited by R. B. Y. Scott, *Proverbs, Ecclesiastes*, The Anchor Bible [Garden City, N.Y.: Doubleday, 1965], 255). See also 2 Samuel 19:35 for Barzillai's description of his physical deterioration at the age of eighty.
57. Fuller, *Proverbs-Ezekiel*, 111, and Rylaarsdam, *The Proverbs, Ecclesiastes, The Song of Solomon*, 132.
58. Crenshaw, *Ecclesiastes: A Commentary*, 186.
59. Brown, Driver, and Briggs, *A Hebrew and English Lexicon of the Old Testament*,

266; and *Theological Wordbook of the Old Testament*, s.v. "זוע," by Andrew Bowling, 1:238.

60. Plumptre suggests that the trembling may be caused by "the unsteady gait of age, perhaps even of paralysis" (*Ecclesiastes: or The Preacher, with Notes and Introduction*, 214–15).

61. Brown, Driver, and Briggs, *A Hebrew and English Lexicon of the Old Testament*, 298-99; and *Theological Wordbook of the Old Testament*, s.v. "חול," by Carl Philip Weber, 1:271–72.

62. Whybray, *Ecclesiastes*, 164.

63. Brown, Driver, and Briggs, *A Hebrew and English Lexicon of the Old Testament*, 736.

64. Delitzsch, *Commentary on the Song of Songs and Ecclesiastes*, 407.

65. Whybray, *Ecclesiastes*, 164.

66. Hengstenberg, *A Commentary on Ecclesiastes*, 246.

67. Crenshaw, *Ecclesiastes: A Commentary*, 186.

68. Gordis, *Koheleth—The Man and His World*, 342.

69. Ibid., 343.

70. Delitzsch, *Commentary on the Song of Songs and Ecclesiastes*, 405.

71. Barton, *A Critical and Exegetical Commentary on the Book of Ecclesiastes*, 188.

72. Whybray, *Ecclesiastes*, 165.

73. Crenshaw, *Ecclesiastes: A Commentary*, 186.

74. Fuller, *Proverbs-Ezekiel*, 111. Those who accept the lips or ears metaphor do so because of the dual nature of those organs. The closure of the lips would imply that little is ingested in the way of food or that little is allowed to pass out in the way of speech. The shutting off of the ears, of course, would suggest that the hearing of the older person has diminished greatly. Those who favor the lips and ears metaphor here in 12:4 tend also to argue for the eyes symbolism of verse 3 in reference to "those who look through windows grow dim." Hence they do not understand "doors" to be eyes despite what might seem to be a logical metaphoric relationship due to the dualism of the doors and the dual nature of the eyes (or of the eyelids).

75. Eaton, *Ecclesiastes: An Introduction and Commentary*, 149.

76. Fredericks states that in 12:3b and 12:4a "a chiasm is formed by two comments on the limited milling (either ceasing or its sound is decreasing) that frame the comments about the openings in the houses of the millers ('windows' and 'doors')" ("Life's Rise and Demise in Ecclesiastes 11:1–12:8," 21).

77. Whybray, *Ecclesiastes*, 165. See also Crenshaw, *Ecclesiastes: A Commentary*, 186–87.

78. Kidner, *A Time to Mourn, and a Time to Dance*, 102, n. Kidner suggests that the phrase may simply be "a note of time, like our 'up with the lark.'" Such a view again would seem to present merely a statement of fact rather than a condition of sadness related to old age. Perhaps the tragedy is to be explained by a realization that in an agricultural society everyone who works is expected to rise at the break of dawn. The elderly person who is no longer required to work and thus has the privilege of sleeping later in the morning than others finds it impossible, however, to enjoy that luxury because his sleep is disturbed by the slightest sound.

79. *Gesenius' Hebrew Grammar*, 418; and Whybray, *Ecclesiastes*, 165.

80. Fuller, *Proverbs-Ezekiel*, 112.

81. Leupold, *Exposition of Ecclesiastes*, 280.

82. Whybray, *Ecclesiastes*, 165.

83. Crenshaw, "The Shadow of Death in Qohelet," 207. Actually Crenshaw makes this statement regarding Qohelet's overall view of death as observed throughout the book of Ecclesiastes. Crenshaw's words, however, seem especially appropriate here.

84. Delitzsch, *Commentary on the Song of Songs and Ecclesiastes*, 411–12.

85. Crenshaw, *Ecclesiastes: A Commentary*, 187.

86. Delitzsch, *Commentary on the Song of Songs and Ecclesiastes*, 413; Gordis, *Koheleth—The Man and His World*, 345; and Whybray, *Ecclesiastes*, 166.

87. Hengstenberg, *A Commentary on Ecclesiastes*, 248.

88. Barton, *A Critical and Exegetical Commentary on the Book of Ecclesiastes*, 190; Gordis, *Koheleth—The Man and His World*, 345; and Whybray, *Ecclesiastes*, 166.

89. The word used here for grasshopper (חָגָב) is used only four other times in Scripture: Leviticus 11:22; Numbers 13:33; 2 Chronicles 7:13; and Isaiah 40:22. In Leviticus it is said to be an edible food, whereas in 2 Chronicles it becomes an instrument of God's plague against the people of Israel. In the remaining two passages it indicates the small stature of people compared to the Nephilim giants of the land (Num. 13:33) and to God (Isa. 40:22).

90. Fuller, *Proverbs-Ezekiel*, 112.

91. Some such as Crenshaw have suggested that the caperberry was used as an aphrodisiac, and thus the caperberry metaphor is a reference to dwindling sexual desire in old age (*Ecclesiastes: A Commentary*, 188). Delitzsch and Whybray, however, find no records from antiquity (the earliest being from the Middle Ages) that support such a usage for the caperberry (Delitzsch, *Commentary on the Song of Songs and Ecclesiastes*, 416; and Whybray, *Ecclesiastes*, 166–67).

92. Nicholas J. Tromp, *Primitive Conceptions of Death and the Netherworld in the Old Testament* (Rome: Pontifical Biblical Institute, 1969), 167.

93. Whybray, *Ecclesiastes*, 167; and Gordis, *Koheleth—The Man and His World*, 347. Youngblood provides a thorough treatment of the phrase אֶל־בֵּית עוֹלָמוֹ ("to his eternal home"). Analyzing contemporary uses from Mesopotamian, Ugaritic, and Phoenician sources on the one hand, and Egyptian sources on the other, he concludes that בֵּית עוֹלָמוֹ should be translated as "his dark house" rather than as "his eternal home" (Ronald F. Youngblood, "Qoheleth's 'Dark House' (Eccl. 12:5)," *Journal of the Evangelical Theological Society* 29 [December 1986]: 383–410).

94. Tromp, *Primitive Conceptions of Death and the Netherworld in the Old Testament*, 78.

95. Youngblood, "Qoheleth's 'Dark House' (Eccl. 12:5)," 410.

96. Gordis, *Koheleth—The Man and His World*, 347.

97. Delitzsch, *Commentary on the Song of Songs and Ecclesiastes*, 419.

98. Barton, *A Critical and Exegetical Commentary on the Book of Ecclesiastes*, 192; and Whybray, *Ecclesiastes*, 167.

99. Gordis and Crenshaw also espouse this view (Gordis, *Koheleth—The Man and His World*, 348, and Crenshaw, *Ecclesiastes: A Commentary*, 188).

100. Barton, *A Critical and Exegetical Commentary on the Book of Ecclesiastes*, 192; Eaton, *Ecclesiastes: An Introduction and Commentary*, 150; Kidner, *A Time to Mourn, and a Time to Dance*, 103; and Leupold, *Exposition of Ecclesiastes*, 283–84.

101. Leupold, *Exposition of Ecclesiastes*, 285.

102. Wright, "The Interpretation of Ecclesiastes," 147.

103. Eaton, *Ecclesiastes: An Introduction and Commentary*, 150.

104. Carl Shank, "Qoheleth's World and Life View as Seen in His Recurring Phrases," *Westminster Theological Journal* 37 (1974–75): 62.

105. Fuerst, *The Books of Ruth, Esther, Ecclesiastes, The Song of Songs, Lamentations: The Five Scrolls*, 153.

106. Whybray, *Ecclesiastes*, 168

107. Though הֶבֶל may be used in a variety of ways depending on its context, the sense of "futile" seems to fit the present context best. Furthermore it completes the introductory remarks in 1:2 and gives structure to the entire book of Ecclesiastes. For a discussion of the uses of הֶבֶל, see Theophile Meek, "Transplanting the Hebrew Bible," *Journal of Biblical Literature* 79 (1960): 331.

108. Crenshaw, "The Shadow of Death in Qoheleth," 210.

109. Goldberg, *Ecclesiastes*, 137.

110. Hengstenberg, *A Commentary on Ecclesiastes*, 257.

An Overview

The silence in Scripture regarding any literal prohibition against suicide is causing some individuals in the church to propose the idea that silence is a statement of approval. Dónal P. O'Mathúna looks at literary genre to show that the context of a narrative, like First and Second Samuel, clearly teaches a prohibition against suicide. As we evaluate the lives of those who committed suicide in the Bible, we begin to understand their inner turmoil, which resulted in a troubled relationship with the Lord—following their example is contrary to divine guidance.

Chapter Twenty-Two

BUT THE BIBLE DOESN'T SAY THEY WERE WRONG TO COMMIT SUICIDE, DOES IT?

Dónal P. O'Mathúna

CHRISTIANS MUST AT LEAST REFER TO the Bible when making decisions about the morality of suicide, assisted suicide, or euthanasia. Several accounts in the Bible describe how a number of people took their own lives. However, no explicit statement tells us whether God views these actions as right or wrong. If suicide is wrong, it seems strange that none of these accounts ends with a comment like: "and he was wrong to kill himself"; or "and God judged him for taking his own life." Nowhere does the Bible use the word "suicide," nor give a command against taking one's own life. Yet as of June 1992, almost every major branch of Judaism and Christianity officially viewed suicide, assisted suicide, and active euthanasia as immoral.[1]

The biblical accounts present people taking their own lives in a variety of situations. Abimelech, an early warrior, was hit by a millstone thrown from a tower he was attacking. Seriously injured, he persuaded his armor-bearer to run him through with his sword (Judg. 9:52–54). Samson died when he dislodged the supporting pillars of a house causing it to fall on himself and thousands of Philistines (Judg. 16:28–31). King Saul, mortally wounded after battle, threw himself on his own sword (1 Sam. 31:1–6; 1 Chron. 10:1–6).[2] Saul's armor-bearer similarly fell on his sword (1 Sam. 31:5). Ahithophel, the king's counselor, strangled himself when his counsel was rejected (2 Sam. 17:23). King Zimri burned his house upon himself after learning he had been overthrown (1 Kings 16:18). Judas Iscariot hanged himself when he realized what he had done in betraying Jesus (Matt. 27:3–5; cf. Acts 1:18). Although distinctions can be made among these deaths, we will refer to the passages collectively as the "suicide accounts." By suicide we mean an action undertaken with the primary intention of causing one's own death.[3]

The lack of explicit condemnation of suicide in the Bible has not gone unnoticed in the current debate over the morality and legality of assisted suicide and euthanasia. In November 1994, voters in Oregon approved physician-prescribed lethal doses of medications. The official voters' guide included the following supporting argument from a pastor and chaplain: "In the Bible, five people [sic] are reported to have ended their own lives (1 Sam.

31; 2 Sam. 17; 1 Kings 16; Matt. 27) and the fact of their action is simply reported with no moral judgment implied; at no point is condemnation expressed for their having done so."[4]

The pastor, mentioned in the previous chapter, who invited Jack Kevorkian to speak at his church to promote legalizing euthanasia, promotes the idea that "there are six or seven incidents in scripture where a suicide is reported, and it's treated kindly and tragically. In no way at all is the person condemned."[5] Popular magazines make similar claims.[6]

THE ARGUMENT CONDONING SUICIDE

A number of scholars have defended the view that these accounts should not be used to judge suicide negatively.[7] Some claim these accounts show that the Bible approves of suicide in certain situations. This chapter will reveal the weaknesses of this argument. We will then argue that the biblical accounts, properly interpreted, support the long-standing Christian position that suicide is morally wrong. By implication, assisted suicide and active euthanasia should also be viewed as wrong.

Those who condone suicide typically start with an extremely broad definition of suicide. Droge and Tabor claim they have "purposefully avoided" classifying the biblical suicide accounts differently, but prefer the "more neutral and descriptive term *voluntary death*"[8] (emphasis original). They define this as "taking one's life or requesting or allowing it to be taken."[9] For Clemons, "Suicide is the choice and the successful completion of the act to end one's life regardless of motive, circumstance, or method."[10] Suicide defined so broadly becomes an almost meaningless term. *They treat as one group, suicide, martyrdom, expressing a desire to die, and even the death of Jesus Christ!* Yet it is precisely the need to clearly distinguish among these ways of dying that motivates many of these discussions.

Margaret Pabst Battin has written in defense of a fundamental human right to suicide.[11] She notes that most Western prohibitions of suicide are based on Christian arguments.[12] Examining the biblical texts underlying these arguments she concludes:

> It is one of the more prevalent assumptions of Western religious culture that the Bible prohibits suicide; inspection of the biblical texts, however, shows that this is by no means clearly the case. To begin with, there is no explicit prohibition of suicide in the Bible. . . . Nor is there any passage in either the Old or New Testament that can be directly understood as an explicit prohibition of suicide; those passages that are often taken to support such a prohibition require, as we shall see, a considerable amount of interpretation and qualification.[13]

But interpretation and qualification are precisely what every text requires. Although Exodus 20:13 states, "You shall not murder," considerable debate has occurred over exactly what this means. Many qualifications have been established to determine the circumstances in which it is permissible to kill another human being. Yet these authors think an explicit rule would eliminate uncertainty about suicide. "If any of these six accounts of voluntary death contained the slightest editorial comment, say, 'and this deed was displeasing in the eyes of Yahweh,' the issue of voluntary death would have been settled among Jews and Christians long before the fourth century A.D."[14]

They assume that moral instruction requires explicit commands (or at least they view this as the best form of moral instruction). Finding none on suicide in the Bible, they question why anyone uses it to prohibit suicide. But this reflects an unfamiliarity with the ways the Bible, and in particular, the Old Testament, was written. The Old Testament records events for our instruction (1 Cor. 10:11). But it frequently does so through narratives (i.e., stories), not abstract philosophy. Not enough attention has been given "to the problem of how to extract moral principles from biblical writers who did not usually present their thoughts in abstract terms."[15]

Rather than focusing on the abstract ethics, biblical narratives show us ethics in action in people's character. Sometimes we see godly character, sometimes ungodly. Unlike Jesus, none of the Old Testament characters is perfect. "Their stories reflect all the ambiguities and complexities of human experience and the struggle to find and live out faith relationships to God in the midst of life."[16] Problems arise when readers of the Bible fail to distinguish between God's view of what is right and "descriptive sections of poor human responses to the lofty claims and challenges of the divine."[17] Just because Jews and Christians have committed suicide (recorded in the Bible or elsewhere) does not mean that Jewish or Christian teaching condones suicide.

We will argue that those who condone suicide overlook the importance of this distinction when interpreting the biblical accounts. Current philosophical approaches to ethics tend to neglect the role of character in teaching ethics and instead seek clarification of good and evil actions. Abstract ethical principles and rules are sought. Battin finds all religious arguments against suicide unconvincing because they do not lead to the type of philosophical argument she seeks.[18] These authors want ancient biblical texts to deal with ethical issues in the way many modern ethicists do. The Bible gives moral instruction in many other ways.

These authors do not find the explicit commands for which they look. They insist that the passages make no moral comment on suicide. *Yet they use these accounts to argue that the Bible condones or approves of suicide!* For example:

> It is the *way* in which these cases are reported that is significant. In all six cases the act of voluntary death itself draws no special comment. At least three of them are definitely seen in a positive light (Saul and his armor-bearer in the early source, and Samson). The other three are viewed negatively by the editors, and their downfall is said to be determined by God. But in no case is any point made about the individuals' taking their own lives or, in the case of Abimelech, demanding that his life be taken. If the act it*self* was despicable in ancient Israelite culture, the editors would not have resisted adding this to their litany of misdeeds. This point cannot be overemphasized.[19] (emphasis original)

But is this true? Could the writer have believed suicide was wrong and still have some reason to not explicitly condemn the act? John Donne, the great seventeenth-century writer, whom some claim condoned suicide, noted that Ahithophel and Saul were not excused for committing suicide, even if they were not explicitly condemned either.[20] Yet Droge and Tabor claim, based solely on the Samuel accounts, that "within Israelite society, as early as the period of the united monarchy, voluntary death, given the proper circumstances, was understood as honorable and even routine."[21] Looking at all the suicide accounts, "acts of voluntary death were reported as acceptable and, in certain circumstances, noble."[22] Clemons reveals this double-standard in forming ethical conclusions from narrative texts, this time concerning Judas.

> When we look closely at this suicide in Matthew's Gospel, it is clear that the report comes merely as a factual account. Any notion that his manner of death was condemned because it was committed by the betrayer of Jesus can only be inserted by way of eisegesis. . . . A more positive understanding of Judas sees his act of returning the thirty pieces of silver as a form of repentance and his death as an act of atonement. This exegesis has the theological impact of showing God's acceptance of a person's self-sacrifice, thus calling into question the idea of divine condemnation for any and all cases of a self-chosen death.[23]

We will not deal with the obvious theological problem with this interpretation in light of Jesus' complete atonement on the cross (Gal. 2:21; 1 Tim. 2:5–6). Our concern is that while Clemons claims that a factual account cannot be used to prohibit an act, *he uses it to approve of that same act under any and all circumstances.* Yet no explicit commendation of the act was given.

Another point frequently raised is that those who killed themselves were often buried with honor. "In fact, in the cases of Saul and his armor-bearer, Samson, and Ahithophel, an honorable burial is specifically mentioned, clearly indicating that the manner of death was not culturally proscribed."[24] However, once again they are reading ancient texts from a modern perspective. Jewish and Christian authorities have forbidden formal burial rites for those who committed suicide, but these are later laws, not found in the Bible. Droge and Tabor even admit, in a footnote, that there is no evidence of this law or practice among ancient Israelites![25] Burial of someone gives no indication of how esteemed he or she was. Many of the kings reported to have lived evil lives were buried in their ancestral graves.[26] To claim that burying the body of someone who committed suicide was anything other than common practice is reading into the text.

NARRATIVES AND ETHICS

We are confronting a common problem with the use of narratives to give moral teaching. These authors find moral teaching in the accounts, but don't describe how they developed this teaching. Their only premise seems to be that lack of an explicit prohibition should be taken as implicit approval of the act. If the words, *Do not commit suicide* are not there, suicide is not prohibited.

If this premise holds, the Bible can be read to condone many other acts that are recorded without explicit condemnation. A couple of examples from the book of Judges should suffice to show the problem. Jael killed Sisera by hammering a tent peg into his head while he slept (4:17–24). Is this then an example of what we should do to our enemies? Gideon demanded objective verification of God's will, using a sheep's fleece (6:36–40). Should we demand a similar (or identical) sign from God to discover what he wants us to do? These passages do not explicitly state if the actions were right or wrong. Yet if we hold that all Scripture is profitable for instruction (2 Tim. 3:16), we should be able to discover if we should do what these passages describe.

We need to ask *why* a passage has no explicit ethical comment. The authors who condone suicide from the biblical passages focus on the words in the text, rather than searching for the author's intention in writing the passage. Clemons at least recognizes the need to do this when he asks, "What did the inclusion of the story mean, or not mean, in the light of the author's original purpose in telling it? How does it fit in with the overall argument of the book in which it occurs?"[27]

Unfortunately, he rarely answers these questions in his own writing. When he does, it is difficult to see how he derived his conclusions, as his treatment of Abimelech shows. "What is often overlooked is that these stories were not recorded to make a point related to suicide. In the story of Abimelech, for example, the writer was primarily concerned to teach that to be killed by the hand of a woman was a shameful way to die, much worse than asking someone else to kill you."[28] But why pick this event out of the whole incident as the central message of the passage? These are the words of a man who murdered his seventy brothers, incited a rebellion, and was subsequently judged by God for his wickedness (Judg. 9:56). Why should his view be taken as authoritative teaching on the relative shamefulness of ways to die? If there are reasons for this, they are not clearly stated.

Narrative passages were never intended to be used in the ways these authors use them. When narratives are analyzed as philosophical treatises, they are found wanting. Almost every ethical conclusion will be an argument from silence, and thereby arbitrary. Battin admits, in a footnote, that she is at least aware of this problem: "That the Old Testament contains no explicit discussion of the morality of suicide is not in itself surprising; particularly before the prophetic period, the Jews did not approach ethical questions in a philosophically explicit manner."[29] Droge and Tabor similarly recognize the true nature of the suicide accounts: "This material, which lacks any theoretical or philosophical discussion, reminds one of the type of anecdotal stories in Greek and Roman literature."[30]

We need a clear and consistent methodology for interpreting narratives. This chapter will show how literary structures point to the intended meaning of a narrative. The suicide accounts, thus interpreted, reveal a perspective on suicide consistent with the rest of Scripture. Our focus will be on the narratives about Saul, as these are the most extensive. When narratives are treated as narratives, the likelihood increases immensely that the ethical conclusions will be more faithful to the intentions of the author. For those of us who hold the Bible to be the inspired Word of God, this means we are more likely to find God's perspective on these issues.

THE BIBLE AS LITERATURE

The term *narrative* is used in many different ways in current discussions of ethics.[31] We will focus on its use as a genre (or type) of literature, a synonym for story. Our concern will be how the narrative structure of a passage helps us more accurately identify the meaning intended by the author. Scholars have focused for much of this century on issues of isolating and dating passages written at different times. This focus has had unfortunate consequences. "In spite of the centrality of the narrative storytelling traditions in the OT, they have seldom been considered for their moral address. How do these stories of the biblical communities of faith impact on our efforts as the church to live life faithfully in our modern world? What does it mean that these traditions have been handed on to us as more than mere ancient stories but as scriptural canon?"[32] Also neglected was the unity of the Bible and its message, and recognition that the Bible is a work of literature. In fact, it is the most profound work of literature the world has ever received.

Leland Ryken has contributed much scholarly work on the literary nature of the Bible from an evangelical perspective. For him, viewing the Bible as literature means it is characterized by certain traits. "We know that a collection of writings is literary if its subject matter is human experience, if its genres are those we regard as literary, if it displays artistry, if it employs special resources of language, and if it makes use of literary archetypes (recurrent images, plot motifs, and character types). By all of these criteria, the Bible is a thoroughly literary book."[33]

This does not imply that the Bible is a collection of fictional stories written for our entertainment. Rather, it recognizes that, "The three main interests of biblical writers are the theological, the historical, and the literary."[34] If any one of these is neglected, the accuracy of the interpretation must be questioned. For example, if I want to understand what is meant by the phrase "The sun turned red," the type of literature in which it is found must be considered. If written in an astronomy textbook, the author most likely intended it to be taken literally. If found in a poem, it could be taken metaphorically. Recognizing the type of literature to which a passage belongs is essential to finding its correct meaning.

INTERPRETING NARRATIVES

Narrative passages are characterized by a number of elements.[35] First, there is a plot, where a series of events are related by a narrator, usually emphasizing points of conflict that lead to a conclusion. Second, we get to know a number of characters through the story, though in a limited way. Third, the story is placed in a certain setting. Biblical narratives are somewhat limited here because they describe historical events. However, the details chosen help form the atmosphere or mood and thereby contribute to the meaning intended. Fourth, the narrator presents the story from a certain perspective or point of view, which shapes how we should respond to the events and characters. *All the suicide accounts in the Bible clearly fall into the narrative category.*

When it comes to finding the meaning in a narrative (the message the narrator intends to communicate), we must pay close attention to more than just the words. As mentioned above, this is as far as the authors' condoning suicide go. However, just as important in narrative literature is the *way* the story is told. For example, if I say, "I hate Mondays," there are a number of meanings I could have intended. I may have some extremely arduous tasks to do on Mondays and may literally hate them. However, I might not mean this literally, but because I have to return to work after relaxing weekends, I just don't particularly like Mondays. On the other hand, my schedule may be wonderful on Mondays, and I actually mean that I love Mondays! The *way* in which I speak my words is very important. My tone of voice, facial expressions, etc. would help others determine what I mean.

Obviously, these ways of pointing others to my meaning will not work with written literature. However, there are other important ways that narrators give clues to the meanings they intend. In each of the literary genres certain conventions are used. These conventions are commonly recognized in poetry. The study of these patterns in narrative is called poetics. In our postmodern world some will claim that a narrative text can be given any meaning its reader desires.[36] "It is precisely in response to this danger, that a study of the poetics of Hebrew narrative can provide some controls. Since its concern is to recover, as far as possible, an ancient literary competence, poetics offers a safeguard against reading texts according to arbitrary or anachronistic criteria."[37]

Scholars have identified three elements common to most Hebrew narratives. First, the narrator tells the story as if it is a scene in a play. These are short, with an emphasis on the direct action and speech of the actors. The narrator rarely intrudes into the plot. Second, there is great economy of words.

> Because the Bible's stories are so familiar, we are prone to underestimate the considerable differences in narrative style between biblical storytelling and that of most Western literature. For example—and at the risk of oversimplifying—the Western narrative in which we are steeped is meant to be read by leaps and bounds, passage after passage. The biblical text, by contrast, is intricate and intensive, demanding slow-paced attentiveness to detail.[38]

This makes every word important. Literary devices are commonly used in biblical stories to add weight to certain words and phrases. Some of these will be discussed later, including such things as repetition of key words and word plays. Third, and of immense importance for our discussion of narratives and ethics, biblical narratives generally *show* us what they mean rather than *tell* us. "Literature enacts rather than states, shows rather than tells. Instead of giving abstract propositions about virtue or vice, for example, literature presents stories of good or evil characters in action. . . . Literary texts do not come right out and state their themes. They embody them."[39]

Modern writers on ethics tell us what they mean by concepts like mercy and faithfulness. They define their terms and concepts, tell us if they condone them or not, and explicitly explain why. The letters of the New Testament are written in this style. For example, Colossians 3 and the book of Daniel teach about godliness in very different ways.

> Literary narrative does not *tell* us about godliness as the passage from the epistle does but instead *shows* us with the example of a godly person like Daniel. . . . In a story like this godliness is not an abstraction but consists of specific people engaged in action in identifiable settings. The storyteller does not tell us Daniel was a godly person, nor does he command us to be godly. The literary approach is thus more indirect than the expository, requiring a degree of interpretation on the reader's part.[40] (emphasis original)

The Old Testament is particularly prone to use literary methods, "where instead of encountering expository essays, historical treatises, and scientific or theological explanations, we find well-told stories and beautifully constructed poems."[41] The indirect nature of this method, and the necessity for interpretation, bring certain risks. Edwin M. Good's highly acclaimed book shows how irony pervades Old Testament narratives.[42] He defines irony as a literary method for making ethical statements by juxtaposing the way things *are* to the way things *ought to be*. "[T]he ironist's method forbids his coming right out and saying, 'What you say or think is wrong; here is what is right.' The ironic criticism requires of its hearers and readers the burden of recognition, the discovery of the relation between the ironist's 'is' and his 'ought.' And to use the ironic method is to risk the failure of this recognition, the misunderstanding of the ironist's criticism."[43]

The authors who use the biblical suicide accounts to condone suicide show the reality of this risk. When the literary nature of the suicide narratives is taken into account, they reveal a strong, yet implicit, claim that suicide is not a moral option. Literature points to universal features of human experience. "Although a story or poem is filled with particular images, paradoxically these particulars capture something universal—what is true for all people in all places at all times."[44] The suicide accounts present truth that applies to us today, just as much as it did when the accounts were inspired by God.

Approaching the suicide accounts as literature does not mean that the concerns of the grammatico-historical approach to biblical interpretation can be ignored. "The literary approach to the Bible is incomplete in itself, but it is necessary."[45] The words and phrases must be properly translated, and the historical background understood. However, if the literary qualities are neglected, the correct meaning of a passage may not be discovered even if the words are correctly interpreted.

THE TRAGEDY OF SAUL

First and Second Samuel (together called "Samuel") have been described as one of the greatest literary narratives.[46] "We have in the Saul story a masterpiece of structure, dramatic order and suspense, and tragic irony."[47] A literary approach to the Bible looks for unifying themes and literary devices used to emphasize important points. For example, much of Samuel is written in prose, but it starts and ends with poetic sections (1 Sam. 2:1–10; 2 Sam. 22:1–23:7). "Thus, the books of Samuel are framed fore and aft with poetic pieces providing thematic orientation for the reading of the intervening narrative episodes. . . . This again is very much in keeping with a dominant concern of the books of Samuel: the issue of human kingship and how it should be exercised."[48]

Looking at Samuel as a whole, godly character is a central theme. The narrator sometimes makes explicit character evaluations (e.g. 1 Sam. 2:12; 25:3), but "the portrayal of character is most often achieved though a variety of implicit, or indirect, means."[49] Literary methods called narrative analogies are often used in Samuel for this purpose. "In the Bible . . . such analogies often play an especially critical role because the writers tend to avoid more explicit modes of conveying evaluations of particular characters and acts."[50]

One method of narrative analogy is when commentary on a character quality is made in a narrative or speech elsewhere in the book. Assuming unity in the biblical books, these become very important. Another method evaluates character qualities by contrasting a person with the quality to one without it. Philips Long shows in detail how this is done between Saul and his son Jonathan in 1 Samuel 13–14: "By placing Saul and Jonathan side by side in this way, the narrator creates an atmosphere in which the actions of the one will quite naturally be judged in the light of how the other acts in similar situations."[51] This technique is used quite often in Samuel, leading Long to conclude: "[T]he narrator in Samuel is a master of indirect characterization through comparison and contrast."[52]

The constant intertwining of Saul's demise and David's rise shows clearly the characteristics of a godly king. Samuel states that the king, as with all the people, must obey the Lord (1 Sam. 12:14–25). Almost immediately Saul disobeys and is rejected as king (13:8–14; cf. 10:8; 15:26, 35). The first poetic passage since Hannah's opening prayer occurs at this point, with obedience as its theme (15:22–23). God earlier rejected Eli's house because he was unwilling to rebuke his sons for their sins (3:10–18). "In the end, Saul, like Eli, is rejected for failing to give due weight (honor) to the Lord. Unlike Eli, however, Saul does not respond with 'He is the Lord, let him do what is right in his own eyes' (v. 18), but drives himself crazy (literally?) trying to maintain his grasp on a throne no longer rightfully his."[53]

The narrator teaches other important characteristics by contrasting the lives of Saul and David. Saul's obsessive grasping for control over the kingship and his life is starkly contrasted with David, the patient and faithful servant of God. Soon after David is anointed, he fights Goliath because he knows God will deliver him (1 Sam. 17:37, 46–47). David prospers in everything he does because the Lord is with him (18:14). He has given God control of his life and is willing to obey Him and wait on Him. This is most dramatically revealed when David twice has the opportunity to kill Saul (24:6; 26:9–11). He shows his willingness to allow Saul's death to come in God's time, not his (26:10). David continues to respect the life of Saul, which delays his receiving the kingship, which is rightfully his. In keeping with this, he laments Saul's death when it finally occurs (2 Sam. 1:17–27).

In contrast, as Saul seeks to establish his kingship, *his respect for life gradually diminishes*. His hunger for control leads to frequent attempts on David's life (1 Sam. 18:11; 19:10; 20:31, etc.). He orders his army not to eat and is ready to kill Jonathan for unknowingly breaking his command (14:24–46). He himself is later left with no strength for battle when he refuses to eat (28:20–25). When Jonathan defends David, Saul throws a spear at him (20:33). In anger, he kills the priests of Nob for assisting David, even though they did not know he was fleeing Saul (22:17–19). He gradually loses respect for human life and finally takes his own (31:1–7).

Along with the theme of respect for life, the narrator contrasts the relationships of David and Saul. Most importantly, David deepens his relationship with the Lord throughout his life. He prays to God for guidance before acting (e.g. 1 Sam. 23:2). Even after becoming king, he remains dependent on God (2 Sam. 7:18-29; 15:25–26; 16:10–12, etc.). We are told that David was a man after God's own heart, a man who would strive to do God's will (1 Sam. 13:14; Ps. 89:20–29; Acts 13:22).

In contrast, Saul drifts further and further away from God (1 Sam. 15:26, 35; 18:12). At one of the lowest points in the story, Saul is overcome by fear when he sees the Philistine army (28:5). He finally turns to God for guidance, but God does not answer (v. 6). Saul immediately turns to a medium for answers. He had not turned to God in repentance, and was not prepared to wait on God's answer. He just wanted information and where it came from didn't matter. The narrator uses narrative analogy to judge Saul's actions: Saul himself had been the one to remove the mediums and spiritists from Israel (v. 3). Now, completely alienated from God, he turns for guidance to those very things he himself had believed were wrong (as explicitly stated in Lev. 19:26; Deut. 18:9–14).

Saul's other relationships also suffer. "The deterioration of Saul is, in fact, partially presented in terms of the dissolution of his relations with his son and daughter brought about by his obsessive need to destroy David."[54] He is willing to kill Jonathan for unknowingly breaking an arbitrary command (1 Sam. 14:43–46). Their relationship becomes more strained as Saul pursues David, eventually forcing Jonathan to choose between them (20:30–34; 23:15–18). His relationship with his daughter Michal is similarly strained, resulting in her choosing to protect her husband David from her father (19:11–17).

In contrast, David wins the heart of Jonathan, and they become life-long friends (18:1–4; 19:1). Michal loves David, although she later comes to despise him (1 Sam. 18:28–29; 2 Sam. 6:16–23). His men show great loyalty to him, and he wins the hearts of the people (1 Sam. 18:7). He evens gains the trust and confidence of Achish, a Philistine king (27:1–7). While David certainly was not perfect, the overall pattern of his relationships, especially in 1 Samuel, stands in stark contrast to Saul's increasing isolation.

The story of Saul has been described as a great tragedy. In literary terms, the tragic hero is a prominent person with great potential who suffers greatly because of some deep character flaw. This flaw, not fate, eventually leads to a catastrophe usually resulting in the tragic hero's death. "Tragic heroes make decisions, act and live by their choices and actions in ways that make them responsible for their suffering and often their death (at times even death at their own hands)."[55]

Saul certainly fits this description. When Saul finds himself wounded on the battlefield (1 Sam. 31:1–7), his earlier decisions leave him with no one to turn to for help. David earlier rescued Saul from the Philistines by killing Goliath (chap. 17). But David cannot help now because Saul has driven him away. Saul cannot (or will not) even turn to God. *His diminished respect for life convinces him that the only answer is death: his own.* Saul's armor-bearer will not help him because of his respect for the Lord's anointed. His isolation is complete. He falls on his own sword. The tragic hero is dead.

> In embracing death Saul gives forceful acknowledgment of his final and total isolation from both men and his god. Life in the Hebraic tradition entailed the power or potential for relationships, especially relations with the deity. Death is the cessation of all relationships: in Sheol there is no effective life with Yahweh (see, e.g., Ps 88; Isa. 38:18–19). Saul is ultimately alone, cut off from his fellows and his god.[56]

His death contains tragic irony. Immediately afterward, the men of Jabesh-gilead risk their lives to properly bury Saul and his sons (1 Sam. 31:11–13; 2 Sam. 2:4–7). In spite of Saul's belief that he was small in his own eyes, he was actually highly regarded by some (1 Sam. 10:24; 15:17). David's lament shows the level of respect and love he had for Saul, in contrast to Saul's fear of him. Perhaps the greatest irony of the story is that while Saul repeatedly violated God's commandments to keep his throne from David, it was his final act that allowed David to become king.

Rather than viewing Saul's suicide as an isolated incident with no moral comment, this scene is *the tragic conclusion to a literary masterpiece soaked in moral comment.* Tragedy implies that what "is" is not what "ought" to be.[57] Saul's grasping for control put him on the battlefield alienated from God and everyone else. His story shows how he used death to deal with all his problems. Killing himself fits this pattern. To claim that Saul's suicide can be taken to commend suicide is to completely misinterpret the purpose of tragic narrative. As understandable as it may be for someone like Saul to commit suicide, it is a tragic conclusion that should never have happened.

The wrong choices of Saul contrast throughout Samuel with the righteous choices of David. In one of those explicit character statements we are told that David is more righteous than Saul (1 Sam. 24:17). *He refuses to kill unless led by God to do so.*[58] To emphasize this, Saul's suicide narrative is followed immediately by the Amalekite's story that he helped Saul commit suicide (2 Sam. 1:1–16). Enraged that he "killed the Lord's anointed," David has him executed (v. 16). No distinction is made here between assisted suicide and killing. This echoes of the general prohibition against murder: "Whoever sheds the blood of man, by man shall his blood be shed; for in the image of God has God made man" (Gen. 9:6). If so, it is a general prohibition against assisted suicide from a man whose heart was close to God's. However, it could be referring to a special case of not killing the king. If so, it condemns Saul's act of suicide since he thereby killed the Lord's anointed.

THE OTHER SUICIDE ACCOUNTS

Not everyone who notes the literary nature of Samuel agrees that Saul's suicide is thereby condemned. One commentator on Saul concludes: "Then in a final moment of grandeur he seizes control of events, comprehends his isolation, and accepts his fate. And while ironically his final request for aid is rejected (31:4b), he is able to make his life his own again in taking it."[59] However, this author admits he must appeal to classical Greek stories for parallel texts. These, and Roman suicide narratives, are commonly cited as support by those who condone suicide.[60]

But we must first evaluate interpretations in light of the biblical texts. "The validity of any interpretation will be judged by its ability to account for all the evidence and by its compatibility with the wider literary context."[61] As one commentator notes, "About Saul himself, the historians [in the Bible] have nothing to say that is good."[62] Saul's root problem is his desire for control over his life and his unwillingness to give that control to God. One of the general themes of the Bible is that Saul's problem is humanity's problem. All of us want to do what is right in our own eyes, not what is right in God's eyes (Deut. 12:8; Judg. 17:6; Prov. 21:2; Heb. 5:11–14). God is rightfully Lord of all, but we all rebel against him (1 Sam. 15:23). David is portrayed as the great example of someone who gives control of his life to God (13:14). To argue that this passage praises Saul for finally taking control of his life goes against the narrative structure of the book and the clear teaching of the rest of the Bible.

We believe a thorough literary analysis of the other suicide accounts will support this conclusion. This analysis will be developed elsewhere, but some brief comments are warranted here. The Old Testament presents a great cloud of witnesses for us to follow (Heb. 12:1), but also shows us evil actions to avoid (1 Cor. 10:6). We are frequently told whose life was characterized by obedience to God's ways and whose was characterized by evil. Five of the seven men whose suicides are recorded in the Bible are judged negatively.[63] We should be very slow to follow the example set by people whose lives are judged so negatively by Scripture.[64]

Nothing is said about the character of Saul's armor-bearer, but his death can be seen as part of the broader tragedy of Saul's life and death. "Catastrophe does not strike the tragic protagonist alone."[65] Saul's family feels the worst of these effects with the deaths of his sons (1 Sam. 31:2), and the rest of his family later (2 Sam. 4:5–8; 21:1–14). Saul's decisions also lead to the deaths of many Israelite soldiers. Having watched his king fall on his sword, it is little wonder his armor-bearer followed his example.

The last remaining suicide account is more ambiguous. "The story of Samson (Judg. 13–16) is one of the most complex stories in the Bible, despite its brevity. It is both a tragedy and a heroic folk narrative. The hero is both criticized and celebrated. As a result, most episodes are presented in an ambivalent light, depending on whether an event is viewed from the perspective of Samson as a tragic figure or a folk hero."[66] Unlike all the others in the Bible who commit suicide, Samson is presented as a hero of the faith (Heb. 11:32).

The narrative about Samson displays the characteristic traits of tragedy. Samson is a prominent person, judging Israel for twenty years (Judg. 15:20). However, his character flaws continually get him in trouble. He is a Nazirite, a man set aside for God (13:7), yet his lust for women and his explosive anger cause him to repeatedly violate his vows. Three times he kills Philistines under very ambiguous circumstances (14:10–20; 15:4–8; 15:9–17). It is difficult to know if he is to be applauded for killing Israel's enemies, or reproved for instigating violence.

Clearly, though, God remains in control of the situation. Even though Samson might not have had God's intentions in mind, God uses him to judge the Philistines. However, like every tragic hero, Samson's character flaw eventually leads to catastrophe. Blind and helpless, he stands surrounded by his enemies who boast that their god is more powerful than Yahweh (16:23–25). Samson's eyes have so far led him astray from God's ways (14:1–3, 7–8; 16:1). Now that his eyes are gone (16:21), he sees things as God does. In avenging his eyes, he also avenges God's honor (v. 28). Finally, his desires and God's are aligned, and God grants him the strength to pull the house down on his enemies and himself.

Unlike the other suicide accounts, Samson receives God's consent and cooperation in his death. Some claim Samson should not be called a suicide, but a martyr. "We know that somehow, despite massive disregard of the Nazirite vow . . . he is indeed *nazir*, separated, dedicated to God, dedicated *by* God to serve him with strength—in death"[67] (emphasis original). When his birth is foretold, his death is linked to his role in beginning Israel's deliverance from the Philistines (13:5–7). This may have been God's plan all along.

Samson may provide a biblical example of approved martyrdom. The Bible certainly teaches that sacrificially giving up our lives for the good of others can be appropriate (John 15:13; Rom. 5:7–8). However, as most commentators over the centuries have noted, it should be very clear that God calls for martyrdom. Samson receives God's approval when his strength is returned for his final act. Martyrdom is not something to be undertaken lightly. Christians are to flee or endure persecution, not embrace it unto death (Matt. 10:23; 24:15–20; 1 Cor. 4:12).[68] The gruesome Jewish suicides/martyrdoms described in the apocryphal texts are absent from the biblical canon (1 Macc. 6:43–47; 2 Macc. 10:13; 14:37–46). If the Bible condones suicide, why were these accounts omitted from the canon? This omission has not been adequately addressed by those who claim the Bible condones suicide.

Presenting Samson's story as a tragedy shows that his mistakes are not excused. "By thus linking human choice and human suffering, tragedy depicts a hero who is *responsible for* his downfall. The tragic hero always initiates his own tragedy. Usually he is also *deserving of* his tragedy, since it grew out of a flaw of character"[69] (emphasis original). He is not a shining example to be followed in every way.

The ambiguity surrounding Samson's life means we should be very reluctant to follow his example. Just as we would not condone his harlotry and violence, we should be slow to approve his "suicide," even though God worked through all these incidents to achieve his purposes. Given the clear examples throughout the Bible of men and women who thought about killing themselves and chose not to, we should follow their example.[70] At the same time, Samson is commended for his faith in God (Heb. 11:32; cf. Judg. 15:18; 16:28). As such, inclusion of Samson's story in the Bible reflects some of the ambiguity we experience in grappling with the real world.

CONCLUSION

Samuel is a fitting tribute to the universal applicability of biblical literature. People today, struggling with suicide, still deal with the same issues: those of control and relationships. Real and perceived failures in these areas frequently bring someone to consider suicide, assisted suicide, or euthanasia.[71] The Samuel narratives show that with God there is an alternative to life's ending in tragic suicide. The Bible has many accounts of potential tragedies, but most do not come to the point of disaster.

> [I]n most of these stories the tragedy is averted through the protagonist's repentance and God's forgiveness. The story of David's repentance after his sin with Bathsheba and Uriah is the great paradigm. The world of literary tragedy is usually a closed world. Once the hero has made the tragic choice, there is no escape. But the Bible is preoccupied with what is more than tragic— with the redemptive potential in human tragedy. In the stories of the Bible, there is always a way out, even after the tragic mistake has been made."[72]

Samuel shows that David's lifestyle is the right choice. However, this takes a commitment to dependence on God, not self, to direct our lives and bring the changes we desire. This dependence entails a commitment to obey God and respect all human lives, including our own. However, this way of life will also result in satisfying relationships to help us through the tough times in life.

In spite of the ambiguity with Samson, a clear line can be drawn between the suicides motivated by self-image, depression, desperation, or fear. We are left with the possibility of legitimately doing something to hasten our deaths only if motivated by the good of others, *and clearly commanded by God.* As such we can approve of those martyrs who went to their deaths rather than deny Jesus Christ. We can approve of those who sacrificially die for the good of others when no alternative exists. But we cannot approve of those who commit suicide for selfish reasons, or to escape pain or suffering, or because they see little hope in life. Admittedly this leaves some ambiguity, but this is where we must struggle with God's Word, the Holy Spirit's guidance, and the counsel of others as we seek to live and die in ways that glorify God (Rom. 13:8; Phil. 1:20).

ENDNOTES

1. Courtney S. Campbell, "Religious Ethics and Active Euthanasia in a Pluralistic Society," *Kennedy Institute of Ethics Journal* 2 (September 1992): 253–77. However, the Unitarian Universalist Association and the United Church of Christ affirm individual freedom, including the right to choose how one dies. The Pacific Northwest Council of the United Methodist Church and the Interfaith Clergy Council strongly supported Washington State's Initiative 119 to legalize physician-assisted suicide and active euthanasia. This was narrowly defeated in 1991 (Ibid., 253–54).
2. 2 Sam. 1:1–16 records a different version of Saul's death. An Amalekite tells David that he found Saul mortally wounded. Saul asked him to end his agony by killing him. Unlike his armor-bearer, the Amalekite obliged Saul, for which David executed him. Most commentators harmonize this version with the other accounts by assuming the Amalekite fabricated his story.
3. "Discussions of what constitutes suicide flourish today. Such discussions often show a lack of precision in defining the English word *suicide* and in delineating the concept usually conveyed by that word" (Darrel W. Amundsen, "Suicide and Early Christian Values," in *Medicine, Society, and Faith in the Ancient and Medieval Worlds* [Baltimore: Johns Hopkins University Press, 1996], 71). This can be traced back to Emile Durkheim's 1897 influential definition of suicide as "any death which is the *direct* or *indirect* result of a *positive* or *negative* act accomplished by the victim himself, which he knows should produce this result" (cited in Miriam Griffin, "Roman Suicide," in *Medicine and Moral Reasoning*, ed. K. W. M. Fulford, Grant R. Gillett, and Janet Martin Soskice [Cambridge: Cambridge University Press, 1994], 111). Such a broad view of suicide arose from Durkheim's rejection of the role of intention in moral reasoning. As we will see, this broad view of suicide is held by those who condone suicide.
4. Rev. Sallierae Henderson, "Measure No. 16, Argument in Favor," *Official 1994 General Election Voters' Pamphlet* (Oregon, 1994), 126.
5. Thomas Egglebeen, quoted in "Kevorkian in Church to Kick Off Push to Legalize Assisted Suicide," *Columbus Dispatch*, 31 January 1994, sec. A, 3.
6. For example, William H. A. Carr, "A Right to Die," *Saturday Evening Post* 267 (September/October 1995): 51.
7. James T. Clemons, *What Does the Bible Say About Suicide?* (Minneapolis: Fortress,

1990); Arthur J. Droge and James D. Tabor, *A Noble Death: Suicide and Martyrdom Among Christians and Jews in Antiquity* (San Francisco: HarperCollins, 1992).

8. Ibid., 58.

9. Ibid., 56. Elsewhere they defined it as "the act resulting from an individual's intentional decision to die, either by his own agency, by another's, or by contriving the circumstances in which death is the known, ineluctable result" (Ibid., 4).

10. Clemons, *What Does the Bible Say*, 13.

11. Margaret Pabst Battin, *The Least Worst Death: Essays in Bioethics on the End of Life* (New York: Oxford University Press, 1994).

12. We will focus here on Battin's use of Scripture. The theological misunderstandings and philosophical weaknesses of her argument are thoroughly described by A. A. Howsepian, "Some Reservations About Suicide," *Ethics & Medicine* 12 (1996): 34–40, and chapter 19 in this volume.

13. Battin, *The Least Worst Death*, 207.

14. Droge and Taylor, *A Noble Death*, 59. Another common argument by all these authors is that the Jewish and Christian prohibition of suicide has its origin in Augustine's writings of the fourth century rather than in the Bible. This historical argument is clearly refuted in Amundsen, "Suicide and Early Christian Values," 70-126.

15. Robert R. Wilson, "Approaches to Old Testament Ethics," in *Canon, Theology, and Old Testament Interpretation: Essays in Honor of Brevard S. Childs*, ed. Gene M. Tucker, David L. Petersen, and Robert R. Wilson (Philadelphia: Fortress, 1988), 66.

16. Bruce C. Birch, "Old Testament Narrative and Moral Address," in *Canon, Theology, and Old Testament Interpretation*, 77.

17. Walter C. Kaiser, "New Approaches to Old Testament Ethics," *Journal of the Evangelical Theological Society* 35 (September 1992): 292.

18. Battin, *The Least Worst Death*, 244–45.

19. Droge and Taylor, *A Noble Death*, 59.

20. John Donne, *Suicide: Biathanatos Transcribed and Edited for Modern Readers*, Studies in Humanities Series 1, ed. William A. Clebsch (Chico, Calif.: Scholar's Press, 1983), 90. Droge and Tabor claim that Donne was "the first to compose a formal defense of voluntary death in English" (Droge, 7). Clemons claims Donne argued "why suicide should not be universally condemned" (*What Does the Bible Say*, 31). Battin says Donne gave "a nonprohibitive interpretation" to the biblical passages about suicide (Battin, *The Least Worst Death*, 248 n. 30). Yet Donne himself believed that acts causing one's own death "should be contracted and restrained" (Donne, *Suicide*, 96) and "may be done only when the honor of God may be promoted in that way and no other" (Ibid., 88). Donne makes clear the types of "self-homicide" he approves of, something the other authors do not with their broad definitions of suicide and voluntary death.

21. Droge and Taylor, *A Noble Death*, 56.

22. Ibid., 60, cf. 113.

23. James T. Clemons, "Interpreting Biblical Texts on Suicide," *Quarterly Review: Journal of Theological Resources for Ministry* 14 (spring 1994): 24–25.

24. Droge and Taylor, *A Noble Death*, 59; see also Clemons, *What Does the Bible Say*, 19; Battin, *The Least Worst Death*, 207.

25. Droge and Taylor, *A Noble Death*, 76 n. 4.

26. Rehoboam (1 Kings 14:31), Baasha (1 Kings 16:6), Ahab (1 Kings 22:37), Ahaziah (2 Chron. 22:9), Jehu (2 Kings 10:31, 35), Joash (2 Kings 13:13), etc.
27. Clemons, *What Does the Bible Say*, 15–16.
28. Ibid., 28.
29. Battin, *The Least Worst Death*, 246 n. 6.
30. Droge and Taylor, *A Noble Death*, 57.
31. We find some of these uses problematic, but they are not the focus of this chapter. For a critical analysis of narrative methods, see Paul Nelson, *Narrative and Morality: A Theological Inquiry* (University Park, Pa.: Pennsylvania State University Press, 1987).
32. Birch, "Old Testament Narrative," 76.
33. Leland Ryken, "Bible as Literature," in *Foundations for Biblical Interpretation: A Complete Library of Tools and Resources*, ed. David S. Dockery, Kenneth A. Mathews, and Robert B. Sloan (Nashville: Broadman & Holman, 1994), 59.
34. Leland Ryken and Tremper Longman III, "Introduction," in *A Complete Literary Guide to the Bible*, ed. Leland Ryken and Tremper Longman III (Grand Rapids: Zondervan, 1993), 16.
35. Tremper Longman III, "Biblical Narrative," in *A Complete Literary Guide*, 69-79.
36. For a concise critique of these postmodern methods, see Kaiser, "New Approaches," 289–97.
37. V. Philips Long, *The Reign and Rejection of King Saul: A Case for Literary and Theological Coherence*, Society of Biblical Literature Dissertation Series 118 (Atlanta: Scholars Press, 1989), 20.
38. E. L. Greenstein, "Biblical Narratology," *Proof* 1 (1981): 202; quoted in Long, *Reign and Rejection*, 24.
39. Ryken, "Introduction," 17.
40. Ryken, "Bible as Literature," 60.
41. Tremper Longman III, "The Literature of the Old Testament," in *A Complete Literary Guide*, 95.
42. Edwin M. Good, *Irony in the Old Testament* (Philadelphia: Westminster, 1965).
43. Ibid., 31.
44. Ryken, "Bible as Literature," 60.
45. Ibid., 71.
46. Several sources are cited in V. Philips Long, "First and Second Samuel," in *A Complete Literary Guide*, 165.
47. Good, *Irony in the Old Testament*, 80.
48. Long, "First and Second Samuel," 168.
49. Ibid., 173.
50. Robert Alter, *The Art of Biblical Narrative* (New York: Basic Books, 1982), 180; cited in Long, *Reign and Rejection*, 40.
51. Long, *Reign and Rejection*, 40.
52. Long, "First and Second Samuel," 173.
53. Ibid., 179.
54. W. Lee Humphreys, "The Rise and Fall of King Saul: A Study of an Ancient Narrative Stratum in 1 Samuel," *Journal for the Study of the Old Testament* 18 (1980): 78.
55. W. Lee Humphreys, *The Tragic Vision and The Hebrew Tradition* (Philadelphia: Fortress, 1985).
56. Humphreys, "Rise and Fall," 83.
57. Good, *Irony in the Old Testament*, 30–33.

58. This contrasts with his later murder of Uriah to cover up his adultery with Bathsheba (2 Sam. 11). This sin had devastating consequences for David and his family (2 Sam. 12:10–14). However, unlike Saul, David repented of his sin once confronted by Nathan (v. 13).

59. Humphreys, "Rise and Fall," 79–80.

60. Droge and Taylor, *A Noble Death*, 17–51; and Griffin, "Roman Suicide," 106–30.

61. Long, *Reign and Rejection*, 42.

62. Wilson, "Approaches to Old Testament Ethics," 71.

63. Abimelech (Judg. 9:56–57), Saul (1 Chron. 10:13-14), Ahithophel (2 Sam. 15:31; 17:14), Zimri (1 Kings 16:19), and Judas (Matt. 26:24; John 17:12).

64. Clemons notes: "Although in some cases the person who chose suicide was condemned by the historian [in the Bible], that negative judgment was always based on how the person had lived, not how they chose to die" (*What Does the Bible Say*, 27–8). If their way of living is not a good example, surely it follows that their way of dying should not be imitated either.

65. J. Cheryl Exum and J. William Whedbee, "Isaac, Samson, and Saul: Reflections on the Comic and Tragic Visions," *Semeia* 32 (1985): 26.

66. Leland Ryken, *Words of Delight: A Literary Introduction to the Bible*, 2d ed. (Grand Rapids: Baker, 1992), 148.

67. David M. Gunn, "The Anatomy of Divine Comedy: On Reading the Bible as Comedy and Tragedy," *Semeia* 32 (1985): 121.

68. Droge and Tabor make much of the way some early Christians sought after martyrdom (*A Noble Death*, , 129–65). While this occurred, it was frequently discouraged by the early church fathers and later by Augustine (Amundsen, "Suicide and Early Christian Values," 70–126).

69. Ryken, *Words of Delight*, 146.

70. Some of the more prominent examples are Rebekah (Gen. 27:46), Rachel (Gen. 30:1), Moses (Num. 11:10–15), Elijah (1 Kings 19:4), Job (6:8–13; 10; 13:14–15), Jonah (4:3, 8), and Paul (2 Cor. 1:8–10; Phil. 1:21–26).

71. Susan D. Block and J. Andrew Billings, "Patient Requests to Hasten Death," *Archives of Internal Medicine* 154 (September 1994): 2039–47.

72. Ryken, *Words of Delight*, 156.

An Overview

Why should people afflicted with intractable suffering continue to struggle with life? Part of the answer to this question is found in the wisdom literature of Ecclesiastes and Job, especially in the advocacy of Job's friend Elihu. Well-intentioned caregivers often fall short in their interactions with patients by succumbing to the despair of the one suffering, seeking a rational explanation for suffering, or validating desires for autonomy and self-determination. In contrast, "the wise advocate" will model and encourage the biblical perspective of a passion for living while maintaining compassion for the dying.

Chapter Twenty-Three

A "WISDOM" PERSPECTIVE ON
ADVOCACY FOR THE SUICIDAL

James S. Reitman, M.D.

EVEN THOUGH A PERMANENT INJUNCTION was granted by the District Court against implementing Oregon Measure 16,[1] the recent 2d and 9th Circuit Court decisions[2] pose a serious challenge to prevailing views of the proper role of healthcare professionals faced with requests for assistance in dying:[3] Either of these decisions, if upheld, could well bear out Engelhardt's prediction that

> in a world of scarce resources and expensive technologies, it will appear only too reasonable that one should treat maximally and then freely effect death when treatments fail and pain and suffering become intolerable. . . . The use of euthanasia will appear as a responsible and appropriate individual choice.[4]

Both Engelhardt's conclusion—which also applies to assisted suicide—and the new Circuit Court precedents presuppose a libertarian or social contractarian model of decision making that holds autonomy or self-determination to be the highest value in a pluralistic secular society.[5] That this model is becoming more prevalent among physicians and medical ethicists is evident in the current debate over physician-assisted suicide.[6]

The standard of care began to evolve with the outcomes of an increasing number of court cases brought by individuals seeking to relieve suffering by terminating life support.[7] This has been especially distressing in cases of those who are severely handicapped—either from birth or because of catastrophic injury or illness—yet not terminally ill.[8] By the same token, perhaps, nowhere else has there been greater opportunity for "wise advocacy" on behalf of individuals so stricken, as illustrated in the following case:

> Larry McAfee was a single, 29 year-old avid outdoorsman and student in a mechanical engineering program at Georgia State University when a motorcycle accident in 1985 resulted in C–2 quadriplegia. He squandered his $1 million insurance policy first by extending his stay in a spinal rehabilitation facility from the average (19 weeks) to a full year, then by

demanding nurses for home health care—three times as expensive as home health aides—for another 16 months. He refused to be taken in by members of his family because he did not want to be a financial burden to them, yet he continued to demand care at public expense and was shuttled around for several more years among various public institutions. Finally, a little more than five years after his accident, he filed suit for the right to discontinue his ventilator and receive lethal drugs in the process: The lower court decision in McAfee's favor was upheld by the Georgia supreme court. Russ Fine, a disability advocate and radio talk show host, intervened (after McAfee called his show) and convinced McAfee that life could be worth living; his determined advocacy resulted in McAfee's acceptance and enrollment in a supported-employment program and independent living facility.[9]

Why do some who experience intractable suffering, like McAfee, decide to live while others follow through with their plans for suicide? Why don't more caregivers serve as advocates who, like Russ Fine, attempt to persuade the suicidal that life is worth living, rather than confirm the impression that there remains no hope for a meaningful existence?[10] While it should be obvious

> that medicine is a profession determined by the moral commitment to care for the ill . . . , the ability to sustain such care in the face of suffering and death is no easy enterprise, for the constant temptation is to try to eliminate suffering through the agency of medicine rather than let medicine be the way we care for each other in our suffering.[11]

This is precisely the challenge that confronts modern medicine in the struggle to determine just what comprises morally appropriate care for people with intractable suffering. What can wisdom contribute to the concept of advocacy for those whose suffering makes death seem preferable? Specifically, what pitfalls can wisdom help the would-be caregiver to avoid and how can it equip the caregiver to foster meaningful existence in the midst of such suffering? While these questions have been addressed previously,[12] this exposition builds on the moral framework drawn from the arguments of Job and Ecclesiastes and explores the role of Elihu in the Job narrative, as a means of further characterizing the nature and risks of credible advocacy for the suicidal.

THE "WISDOM" PERSPECTIVE

A key question facing many of those afflicted with intractable suffering is raised in Ecclesiastes from the vantage point of an observer (and in Ps. 90, from the sufferer's perspective): What is the point of continuing to struggle through life when it seems so meaningless? The first half of Ecclesiastes exposes the inevitable failure of seeking meaning from a disposition of radical self-determination,[13] so that the "wisdom" perspective already represents a clear divergence from the individualistic notions underlying the prevalent social contractarian or libertarian models. The turning point in the author's argument occurs in Ecclesiastes 7:1–14,[14] where wisdom itself emerges as the path to meaningful existence in view of the inescapable human limitations that make life seem so futile.

> Wisdom is good with an inheritance, and profitable to those who see the sun. For wisdom is a defense as money is a defense, but the excellence of knowledge is that wisdom gives life to those who have it. Consider the work of God; for who can make straight what He has made crooked? In the day of prosperity be joyful, but in the day of adversity consider: Surely God has appointed the one as well as the other, so that man can find nothing that will happen after him. (Eccl. 7:11–14 NKJV)[15]

The Job narrative offers a model exemplifying just how "wisdom gives life," when such "adversity" cannot be abated. In his repeatedly expressed desire to hasten death Job projects an image of overwhelming suffering that epitomizes a despairing sufferer's call for morally responsive care. In their ensuing dialogue with him, Job's friends completely miss his deepest existential needs and illustrate key pitfalls of advocacy that the caregiver should avoid when confronted by a sufferer in despair. Their failure then provides a contrast for the wise advocacy subsequently modeled by Elihu.[16]

THE FAILURE OF ADVOCACY BASED ON RADICAL SELF-DETERMINATION

Unmitigated suffering may have such an adverse effect on decision making that the benefits of "wise advocacy" are needed to restore wisdom to the sufferer.

> It is better to hear the rebuke of the wise than for a man to hear the song of fools. . . . Surely oppression destroys a wise man's reason, and a bribe debases the heart. The end of a thing is better than its beginning; the patient in spirit is better than the proud in spirit. Do not hasten in your spirit to be angry, for anger rests in the bosom of fools. Do not say, "Why were the former days better than these?" For you do not inquire wisely concerning this. (Eccl. 7: 5, 7; 8–10 NKJV)

The foolish, angry pride depicted here in the midst of adversity contrasts sharply with the wise disposition recommended in Eccl. 7:11–14 (above). Because "oppression destroys a wise man's reason," it is preferable for the sufferer "to hear the rebuke of the wise," which amounts to wise advocacy under these circumstances.

By contrast, when Job's three friends were confronted with his growing attitude of victimization and defiant self-determination in the midst of suffering they shrank from the task of "wise rebuke" and exemplified all the pitfalls of attempted advocacy. Risk-averse caregivers all too often succumb to the contagion of despair and (1) try to relieve suffering at all cost ("the bribe); (2) pursue rational explanations of suffering to reassure the sufferer (the "song of fools") without facing the deeper emotional or existential needs; and thereby only (3) validate the sufferer's angry, self-determined disposition ("debases the heart").[17]

DESPAIR'S CONTAGION: THE "BRIBE" OF PROMISED RELIEF

Job's initial soliloquy portrays well the despair that must characterize many requests for assisted suicide, such as Larry McAfee's court petition.

> Why is light given to those in misery, and life to the bitter of soul, to those who long for death that does not come, who search for it more than for hidden treasure, who are filled with gladness and rejoice when they reach the grave? Why is life given to a man whose way is hidden, whom God has hedged in? For sighing comes to me instead of food; my groans pour out like water. What I feared has come upon me; what I dreaded has happened to me. I have no peace, no quietness; I have no rest, but only turmoil. (Job 3:20–26 NIV)

Note how the appeal of death pervades Job's despair so that "death with dignity" may seem reasonable—even preferable—in his condition. To fully appreciate the risk of wise advocacy under such circumstances, the caregiver must understand how strong may be the temptation to relieve the suffering, even if it means hastening death.

> I . . . considered all the oppression that is done under the sun: And look! The tears of the oppressed, but they have no comforter—on the side of their oppressors there is power, but they have no comforter. Therefore I praised the dead who were already dead, more than the living who are still alive. (Eccl. 4:1–2 NKJV)

While the sufferer's desperate need is for a *comforter* (repeated twice), it is often very tempting to let that "comforter" be death.[18]

This risk of contagion by the sufferer's despair affects anyone who would dare to be a wise advocate, and it apparently overwhelmed Job's friends, who immediately tried to relieve his suffering with the false assurance that God would promptly restore him in exchange for his repentance (Job 4–5). But this only further antagonized Job.

> To him who is afflicted, kindness should be shown by his friend, even though he forsakes the fear of the Almighty. My brothers have dealt deceitfully. . . . For now you are nothing, you see terror and are afraid. Did I ever say, "Bring something to me"? Or, "Offer a bribe for me from your wealth"? Or, "Deliver me from the enemy's hand"? Or, "Redeem me from the hand of oppressors"? (Job 6:14–15, 21–23 NKJV)

Job hardly viewed their attempt to mitigate his suffering as "kindness"—

it was just a deceitful "bribe" intended only to appease his suffering. Their own "terror" at the prospect of sharing his burden of despair drove them out of desperation to employ unwarranted "cheer" to staunch his anguished expressions of despair.[19] In any case such a "bribe" cannot ultimately relieve this existential despair, for even *"If a man begets a hundred children and lives many years, . . . but his soul is not satisfied with goodness, . . . I say that a stillborn child is better than he"* (Eccl. 6:3). The prospect of restoration to health and long life is worthless if it promises no "goodness."[20]

REASON'S FAILURE: THE "SONG OF FOOLS"

In their headlong rush to relieve Job's suffering through ill-founded reassurance (Job 5:17–27; 8:5–7; 11:13–19), Job's friends add insult to injury by doggedly pursuing rational explanations for his suffering and in so doing they not only miss Job's need for comfort but actually aggravate his suffering. Ironically, Job actually recognizes his own suffering-induced need for "wise rebuke" (Eccl. 7:5) and challenges them to risk facing him as advocates who could truly mitigate the disorienting effect of his suffering.

> Teach me, and I will be quiet; show me where I have been wrong. How painful are honest words! But what do your arguments prove? Do you mean to correct what I say, and treat the words of a despairing man as wind? You would even cast lots for the fatherless and barter away your friend. (Job 6:24–27 NIV)

Job's friends failed as advocates because they held him responsible for his own restoration—he would first have to atone for the sin they believed caused his suffering (cf. Job 5:1–27; 8:5–7, 21–22; 11:13–20; 22:21–30). Job proposes instead that *they* first prove themselves true advocates by showing some compassion.

> Will your long-winded speeches never end? What ails you that you keep on arguing? I also could speak like you, if you were in my place. . . . But my mouth would encourage you; comfort from my lips would bring you relief. (Job 16:3–5 NIV)

Only by demonstrating true empathy in this way would Job's friends earn the moral standing to offer the wise advocacy he needed.[21] Instead, Job's friends continued to find ways to deflect the discomfort of his despair, and out of frustration he finally called them "worthless physicians" (Job 13:4), "miserable comforters" (Job 16:2).

The subtle but tragic fact is that caregivers are often prone—without justification—to hold the severely stricken responsible for their circumstances.[22]

> If I say, "I will forget my complaint, I will change my expression, and smile,"
> I still dread all my sufferings, for I know you will not hold me innocent.

Since I am already found guilty, why should I struggle in vain? Even if I washed myself with soap and my hands with washing soda, you would plunge me into a slime pit so that even my clothes would detest me. (Job 9:27–31 NIV)

Job clearly senses their judgmental attitude, which only reinforces his victim's mentality and fosters a demanding, self-determined response to suffering (cf. Eccl. 7:8–10, above).

RADICAL AUTONOMY'S ULTIMATE END: A "HEART DEBASED"

Job's core disposition of self-determination is revealed in a growing attitude of self-righteousness: If he could only gain an audience with God (cf. 23:3–12; chaps. 30–31) he would prove to his friends conclusively that he has been unjustly persecuted.

Keep silent and let me speak; then let come to me what may. Why do I put myself in jeopardy and take my life in my hands? Though he slay me, yet will I hope in him; I will surely defend my ways to his face. Indeed, this might turn out for my deliverance, for no godless man would dare come before him! Listen carefully to my words; let your ears take in what I say. Now that I have prepared my case, I know I will be vindicated. Can anyone bring a case against me? If so, I will be silent and die. (Job 13:13–19 NIV)

Job's oft-quoted confession of faith (*"Though he slay me . . ."*) is unmasked in context as a brazen demand for vindication, essentially pressing God for injunctive relief from his suffering, even if this demand brings on his death.[23] Like Larry McAffee's petition, Job's expressed willingness to die tested the moral responsiveness of his community.[24] But maintaining such a contentious, demanding posture while life remains only promotes overwhelming frustration and further despair.

And this also is a severe evil—just exactly as he came, so shall he go. And what profit has he who has labored for the wind? All his days he also eats in darkness, and he has much sorrow and sickness and anger. (Eccl. 5:16–17 NKJV)

Those who out of dogged self-determination refuse to acknowledge their human limitations will only remain frustrated, for in denying their need for wise advocacy they cannot benefit from the wisdom that "gives life" amid adversity.[25] The only way Job or anyone with his disposition in suffering might become receptive to such advocacy is to first be convinced that he/she can in fact control neither God nor his/her own destiny.

Whatever exists has already been named, and what man is has been known; no man can contend with one who is stronger than he. The more the words, the less the meaning, and how does that profit anyone? For who knows what is good for a man in life . . . ? Who can tell a man what will happen under the sun after he is gone? (Eccl. 6:10–12 NIV)

One wonders whether Larry McAfee would ever have sought Russ Fine's advocacy had he not first exhausted all his own resources in "contending" for continued control of his existence.

MOURNING, WISE ADVOCACY, AND HOPE
IN THE MIDST OF SUFFERING

The Role of Mourning

Ironically, the very frustration and despair that results from the self-determined pursuit of meaning in life (Eccl. 5:16–17, above) can itself vitalize a new openness to other sources of meaning in life in the sufferer who honestly faces his/her mortality.

> It is better to go to the house of mourning than to go to the house of feasting, for that is the end of all men; and the living will take it to heart. Sorrow is better than laughter, for by a sad countenance the heart is made better. The heart of the wise is in the house of mourning, but the heart of fools is in the house of mirth. It is better to hear the rebuke of the wise than for a man to hear the song of fools. For like the crackling of thorns under a pot, so is the laughter of the fool. This also is vanity. (Eccl. 7:2–6 NKJV)

Those who respond with authentic mourning to an acute awareness of the miserable "end of all men" are more disposed to wisely accept their own uncertainty and lack of control in life.[26] Thus, experiencing "sorrow" in the "house of mourning" can "make the heart better" by converting the sufferer's demand for control and certainty into a new openness to wise advocacy while life remains.[27]

In context, then, "the rebuke of the wise" implies an advocacy for the sufferer that far excels foolish attempts at vacuous cheer (the "laughter of fools") because it promotes the life-giving wisdom of genuine mourning in response to the profound disruption of suffering. Even as Job stubbornly contends with his friends and with God, he recognizes his need for an advocate who can represent him before God, whom he views as overwhelming him with intimidation in his present state of existential impotence.

> He is not a man like me that I might answer him, that we might confront each other in court. If only there were someone to arbitrate between us, to lay his hand upon us both, someone to remove God's rod from me, so that his terror would frighten me no more. (Job 9:32–34 NIV)

And although it is obvious that Job looks to this arbiter or mediator with the self-serving purpose of securing his own vindication in the eyes of his friends (cf. also 16:18–21; 19:21–29), at least his plea for advocacy prepares him for Elihu's challenge.[28]

Elihu's Credibility as an Advocate[29]

Although Elihu is not even mentioned until the second half of the book, he has obviously been present throughout the debates between Job and his three friends; he is already fully aware of the previous allegations and responses (32:1–5). Much of his credibility at this point is thus already established by his silent witness to Job's unassuaged suffering: Though provoked by their arguments, Elihu has not spoken until after he has heard all the arguments and is sensitive to the true needs behind them (32:4–9)—he knows how to "attend" the sufferer.[30]

Elihu goes on to assure Job that he cares deeply about him and is therefore credible (32:6–33:7). Having tested the words of Job's three older friends and found them wanting (32:5, 10–16), he affirms that his own counsel stems only from his passion for truth and is thus free of the terror that had plagued his other friends (32:17–22).[31] Job can confidently accept what Elihu says, because he speaks as his advocate before God with the true compassion Job had been seeking from his friends (33:6–7; cf. Job 6:14, 28; 16:4–5; 19:21–22), and he is willing to risk Job's rejection (33:31–32).

Elihu's Message of Redemption

After establishing his commitment to Job's welfare, Elihu briefly dares to challenge Job's complaint (Job 33:8–13a). But Elihu recognizes a crucial need that must be met before Job can be convinced to yield his angry, demanding disposition to the wisdom of Elihu's counsel: Job does not appreciate the extent of God's redemptive love. Therefore, in one of the most profound texts in all of Scripture (Job 33:14–30), Elihu affirms that God is unilaterally committed to restoring man—He intends to reach down to man and protect him from his own propensity toward self-destruction without first requiring that he atone for prior sins, as Job's friends had insisted.

> God does speak—now one way, now another—though man may not perceive it. . . . he may speak in their ears and terrify them with warnings, to turn man from wrongdoing and keep him from pride, to preserve his soul from the pit, his life from perishing by the sword. Or a man may be chastened on a bed of pain with constant distress in his bones. . . . His flesh wastes away to nothing, and his bones, once hidden, now stick out. His soul draws near to the pit, and his life to the messengers of death. (Job 33:14, 16–19, 21–22 NIV)

Clearly God does not intend to destroy Job or anyone racked by intractable suffering. Although God may not explain to man *why* he suffers, God is not silent or absent, as Job had inferred (cf. Job 9:1–20; 23:1–9; 30:20): He simply communicates in ways consistent with His intent to "turn man from wrongdoing and keep him from pride." He may even allow man in his suffering to "draw near to the pit" in order to persuade him of the futility of his angry self-determination and thereby "preserve his soul from the pit" of despair and death.

What then does Elihu suggest as the remedy for such self-destructive pride? Contrary to Job's contention that there is no "mediator between us" (cf. Job 9:33 NKJV), Elihu explains that God indeed sends just such a mediator, who not only reveals God's purposes for man but can accomplish them.

> If there is a messenger for him, a mediator, one among a thousand, to show man His uprightness, then He is gracious to him, and says, "Deliver him from going down to the Pit; I have found a ransom"; his flesh shall be young like a child's, he shall return to the days of his youth. (Job 33:23–25 NKJV)

Since God desires to restore the sufferer to full health, He finds a "messenger" who can communicate this redemptive purpose and then "deliver him" from his current futile estate to a life of vigor and productivity.[32]

Is it expedient, then, for a caregiver to assume this role of "messenger" for the suicidal sufferer? What about the charge of proselytizing?[33] And if the suffering then continues unabated, how can the caregiver expect this message to restore hope?

> Today's practicing physicians have accepted—often without knowing it—a far greater priestly role than any of their predecessors. In part this is attributable to the diminished impact of religion in our civilization. . . . [M]ost of the time and effort of practicing physicians is devoted to improving the life of their patients.[34]

Perhaps the greatest promise for thus "improving the life" of the sufferer who wants to hasten death is for the caregiver to emulate Elihu's example of wise advocacy—surely if the caregiver's commitment to the sufferer's welfare is similarly based on an accurate and empathic understanding of the sufferer's deepest existential needs,[35] it is worth the risk that the sufferer might reject the message of redemption.[36]

Response and Restoration

Although Russ Fine succeeded as an advocate on Larry McAfee's behalf by opening up opportunities that he might not otherwise have had, Larry had to avail himself of those opportunities, and one wonders what role mourning may have played in his change of heart after winning the "right" to assisted suicide. In Job's case Elihu left no room for ambiguity, for only when Job acknowledged his self-righteous demands and mourns the failure of angry self-determination would God then restore him to meaningful life.

> He shall pray to God, and He will delight in him, . . . for He restores to man His righteousness. Then he looks at men and says, "I have sinned, and perverted what was right, and it did not profit me." He will redeem his soul from going down to the Pit, and his life shall see the light. (Job 33:26–28 NKJV)

God's promise of present restoration to a life of purpose and vigor[37] could not be realized until he confessed that his "perversion" of God's purposes "did not profit" him.[38] Since Job's persecution complex had clouded his understanding of God's benevolence, Elihu went on to reaffirm that God's love is not *passive;* rather He proactively and repeatedly reaches out to restore suffering man.

> Behold, God works all these things, twice, in fact, three times with a man, to bring back his soul from the Pit, that he may be enlightened with the light of life. (Job 33:29–30 NKJV)

Thus, *"Anyone who is among the living has hope—even a live dog is better off than a dead lion!"* (Eccl. 9:4 NIV). If Job can be convinced of the truth of God's redemptive plan—and that he therefore has hope—he may then be more receptive to Elihu's "wise rebuke" and end up "justified" (33:31–32) as God's fruitful servant.[39]

What Is the Hope of a "Living Dog"?

It is no doubt small recompense for those with intractable suffering to be told that they have the hope of a productive life when they are utterly dependent on others for even the most basic physiological functions in life. What is it that sustains the hope for meaning when utter dependence on others remains the only apparent option? The author answers directly.

> For the living know that they will die; but the dead know nothing, and they have no more reward, for the memory of them is forgotten. Also their love, their hatred, and their envy have now perished; nevermore will they have a share in anything done under the sun. (Eccl. 9:5–6 NKJV)

As long as those who are terminally ill or severely handicapped retain the capacity for *cognition,* the "reward" of *relationship, emotional expression,* and/ or *volition,* they meet the criteria for living hope.[40] And though it may seem utterly absurd to someone whose body is totally useless to be encouraged to have hope of finding meaning in life, the example of those individuals who request assisted suicide and then change their minds testifies to the advantage of wise advocacy in transmitting such hope

If, however, the sufferer thus continues to insist that life is not worth living, the wise advocate then faces the difficult challenge of how to remain faithful.

> [W]e have had trouble considering how we should care for the dying because we have not thought enough about what kind of responsibilities the one who is dying should have. In other words the moral street here is not one way—the dying person has obligations to the living that are important for us to understand in the care of the dying.[41]

By requesting that death be hastened, the sufferer may avoid facing these responsibilities, which immediately begs this question: When death is not truly imminent for the suffering person who wants to die, how does the caregiver encourage the pursuit of responsible choices while life remains?

CONCLUSION: ACCOUNTABILITY FOR STEWARDSHIP WHILE LIFE REMAINS

The key to wise advocacy at this point lies in defeating the sufferer's overwhelming sense of victimization:[42] Elihu indicts Job for his self-justified "victim's complex" by treating him as a moral agent who is accountable for his presumption (Job 33:8–13; 34:31–37; 35:9–16), even though Job is still afflicted by suffering. Ecclesiastes establishes the basis for such accountability under just these conditions.

> For every matter there is a time and judgment, though the misery of man increases greatly. For he does not know what will happen; so who can tell him when it will occur? No one has power over the spirit to retain the spirit, and no one has power in the day of death. (Eccl. 8:6–8 NKJV)

Although there is an appropriate "time" for everything that happens, including death, we do not know when that will be, thus making suicide a presumptuous act. Moreover, since "there is judgment," one is accountable for autonomous choices, even in the midst of unabated suffering.[43] By encouraging the sufferer to acknowledge this accountability and to overcome thereby the "inertia" of victimization, wise advocacy may then enhance the appeal of the "redemptive alternative" of maximizing wise stewardship over the time and resources that remain in life.

> However many years a man may live, let him enjoy them all. But let him remember the days of darkness, for they will be many. Everything to come is meaningless. Be happy, young man, while you are young, and let your heart give you joy in the days of your youth. Follow the ways of your heart and whatever your eyes see, but know that for all these things God will bring you to judgment. So then, banish anxiety from your heart and cast off the troubles of your body, for youth and vigor are meaningless. Remember your Creator in the days of your youth, before the days of trouble come and the years approach when you will say, "I find no pleasure in them." (Eccl. 11:8–12:1 NIV)

The exhortation underscores the superiority of a model for decision making that embraces the concept of a created purpose with a personal future and promotes wise stewardship in view of that future, before the opportunity expires with the inexorable erosion of one's vitality.[44] An advocacy that can approach the sufferer with this aim in view—even in terminal illness and even for the most debilitated of His creatures ("for youth and vigor are meaningless")—sets the stage for realizing the ultimate joy and meaning of the "work of God."[45]

ENDNOTES

1. "Verbatim, 'In the United States District Court for the District of Oregon,'" *Issues in Law & Medicine* 12 (1996): 79–92; see further Jerome Wernow, "Oregon's Solution," in *Dignity and Dying: A Christian Appraisal,* ed. John F. Kilner, Arlene B. Miller, and Edmund D. Pellegrino (Grand Rapids: Eerdmans, 1996), 135–53.

2. "Nota Bene, '*Compassion in Dying v. State of Washington*'; '*Quill v. Vacco,*'" *Issues in Law & Medicine* 12 (1996): 57–67; Edward R. Grant, "Shaping Euthanasia Rights: *Compassion in Dying v. Washington* and *Quill v. Vacco*" this volume, ch. 1.

3. Courtney S. Campbell, Jan Hare, and Pam Matthews, "Conflicts of Conscience—Hospice and Assisted Suicide," *Hastings Center Report* (May-June 1995): 36–43; Joseph J. Fins, "Physician Assisted Suicide and the Right to Care," *Cancer Control* 3 (1996): 272–78; and "Constructive Alternatives," Part 4 in *Dignity and Dying,* 181–242.

4. H. Tristram Engelhardt, *The Foundations of Bioethics,* 2d ed. (New York: Oxford University Press, 1996), 352.

5. J. P. Moreland, "The Morality of Suicide: Issues and Options," *Bibliotheca Sacra* 148 (1991): 214–30, cf. esp. 223, 226–27, reprinted in this volume, chap. 11.

6. For a more extensive analysis of this debate and of the contractual model of decision making in response to requests for assisted death, see James S. Reitman, "The Debate on Assisted Suicide—Redefining Morally Appropriate Care for People with Intractable Suffering," *Issues in Law & Medicine* 11 (1995): 299–329; and James S. Reitman, "Wise Advocacy," in *Dignity and Dying,* 208–22.

7. Ezekiel J. Emanuel, "A Review of the Ethical and Legal Aspects of Terminating Medical Care," *American Journal of Medicine* 84 (1988): 291–301; Alan Meisel, "Legal Myths About Terminating Life Support," *Archives of Internal Medicine* 151 (1991): 1497–1502; and Carl H. Coleman and Tracy E. Miller, "Stemming the Tide: Assisted Suicide and the Constitution," *Journal of Law, Medicine & Ethics* 23 (1995): 389–97.

8. Stanley S. Herr, Barry A. Bostrom, and Rebecca S. Barton, "No Place to Go: Refusal of Life-Sustaining Treatment by Competent Persons with Physical Disabilities," *Issues in Law & Medicine* 8 (1992): 3–36; Carol J. Gill, "Suicide Intervention for People with Disabilities: A Lesson in Inequality," *Issues in Law & Medicine* 8 (1992): 37–53; Diane Coleman, "Withdrawing Life-Sustaining Treatment from People with Severe Disabilities Who Request It: Equal Protection Considerations," *Issues in Law & Medicine* 8 (1992): 55–79; Allen C. Snyder, "Competency to Refuse Lifesaving Treatment: Valuing the Nonlogical Aspects of a Person's Decisions," *Issues in Law & Medicine* 10 (1994): 299–320; and Tia Powell and Bruce Lowenstein, "Refusing Life-Sustaining Treatment After Catastrophic Injury: Ethical Implications," *Journal of Law, Medicine & Ethics* 24 (1996): 54–61.

9. Synopsis distilled from Gregory E. Pence, *Classic Cases in Medical Ethics,* 2d ed. (New York: McGraw-Hill, 1995), 47–50, 57–61. Two similar high-profile cases involving life-sustaining treatment of nonterminal patients are also discussed by Pence: Elizabeth Bouvia (ibid., 41–47, 60) requested discontinuation of nutrition and hydration, and Dax Cowart (ibid., 54, 61) was treated against his wishes for extensive third degree burns, insisting to this day that he should have been allowed to die. Pence rightly treats these cases as requests for assisted suicide (ibid., 50–55); they are set apart in that, after receiving extensive publicity, all three decided to live.

10. Herbert Hendin, "Selling Death and Dignity," *Hastings Center Report* 25 (May-June, 1995): 19–23.

11. Stanley Hauerwas, *Suffering Presence: Theological Reflections on Medicine, the Mentally Handicapped, and the Church* (Notre Dame, Ind.: University of Notre Dame Press, 1986), 16–17.

12. See above, note 6.

13. James S. Reitman, "The Structure and Unity of Ecclesiastes," *Bibliotheca Sacra* 154 (July-Sept., 1997): 297–319.

14. Ibid., 311–12. Compare Psalm 90:12.

15. The author has chosen those citations from either the New King James Version (NKJV) or New International Version (NIV) that reflect a better contextual understanding of the text (see James S. Reitman, "Unity of Ecclesiastes" and "There *Is* a Mediator—Finding God in the Midst of Unjust Suffering: An Exposition of the Argument of the Book of Job," [unpublished, 1994]).

16. Reitman, "There *Is* a Mediator."

17. Writing from a psychological perspective, Jay Katz affirms the caregiver's mandate to honestly engage the sufferer with a view to restoring rational decision making, while remaining alert to the often subtle pitfalls of transference, countertransference, and coercion depicted so well in Job's debates with his three friends (*The Silent World of Doctor and Patient* [New York: Free Press, 1984], 121–25, 142–50, 159–63).

18. We've all seen persons we felt might be better off dead, just because of the sheer intensity of their suffering. "The most appealing justification offered by the advocates of euthanasia and assisted suicide is that these are compassionate acts" (Edmund D. Pellegrino, "Euthanasia and Assisted Suicide," in *Dignity and Dying*, 105–19, 110).

19. "Conversation-stopping hope and reassurance are not the answer," says Katz (*Silent World*, 223), who recognizes that physicians often respond to life-threatening illness in a similar fashion.

    "Hope and reassurance need to become an echo, a creative act of reflecting back to patients . . . after they know more about [them], their illnesses and their expectations, rather than an uninformed opening move that discourages conversation. How physicians can spare patients unnecessary pain and suffering, and how they should treat or not treat patients depend ultimately on patients' individual needs and expectations, factors that only conversation can reveal." (ibid.)

    "[T]he undiscriminating expression of hope and reassurance creates doubts in patients and their families about whether doctors can be trusted" (ibid., 224).

20. In Ecclesiastes this word connotes "satisfying meaning" (Reitman, "Unity of Ecclesiastes," 301 [note 21]).

21. The word translated "comfort" in this text is literally "quivering;" the "*quivering* of my lips would bring you relief" (Reitman, "There *Is* a Mediator"). The relational and empathic capabilities of the caregiver are usually more important in end-of-life decisions than rationalistic skills, such as prognosticating survival or protecting the patient's prerogative of self-determination. See Michael T. Kovalchik, "Victor's Secret," *American Journal of Medicine* 88 (1990): 409–10; Marsha D. M. Fowler, "Suffering," in *Dignity and Dying*, 44–55; and Sally Gadow, "Aging as Death Rehearsal: The Oppressiveness of Reason," *Journal of Clinical Ethics* 7 (1996): 35–40.

22. Note the incredible ease with which questions concerning the moral status of the stricken tend to emerge—even if unspoken—in the wake of tragedy (cf. esp.

Luke 13:1–5 and John 9:1–3). This may explain much of the subtle legislative and judicial discrimination experienced by the severely disabled.

23. This of course portrays Job in a rather more unfavorable light than we may be used to viewing him, but it is just this attitude that ultimately evokes a corrective response from Elihu (34:35–37; 35:9–16) and then from God Himself (38:1–3; 40:1–2). As Larry Crabb observes,

   "Job had become convinced he had a case. No longer did he pray for relief, he was ready to demand it. The intensity of his conviction is reflected in his well-known statement, 'Though he slay me, yet will I hope in him.' This verse is often held up as an example of fervent faith, but notice the second half of the verse: 'I will surely defend my ways to his face.' . . . He goes on to say, 'Now that I have prepared my case, I know I will be vindicated. Can anyone bring charges against me? If so I will be silent and die'" (*Inside-Out* [Colorado Springs: NavPress, 1988], 141).

   "Far from humbly yielding to the decisions of a sovereign God, Job strongly asserts that he deserves better treatment than he's received. If God takes his life, Job pledges to go to his grave convinced that if the facts were known, it would be clear to everyone that he's been mistreated" (ibid.).

   In this connection the contemporary use of the term *dignity* often serves as a respectable umbrella to disguise an impatient and angry demand for control and certainty, rooted in the "ethics of autonomy."

24. "Suicide is not first a judgment about the agent," says Hauerwas, "but a reminder that we have failed to embody as a community the commitment not to abandon one another. We fear being a burden. . . . Yet it is only by recognizing that in fact we are inescapably a burden that we face the reality and opportunity of living truthfully. It is just such a commitment that medicine involves and this is why the physician's commitment to caring for the sick seems so distorted by an ethics of autonomy" ("Rational Suicide and Reasons for Living," in *Suffering Presence*, 100–13, 106–7).

25. See the expositions of Eccl. 7:5, 7 and 7:11–14 in above sections of this essay under "The Failure of Advocacy Based on Radical Self-Determination" and "The Wisdom Perspective," respectively.

26. Thus does Moses mourn our short, miserable existence (Ps. 90:3–11), imploring God to "teach us to number our days, that we may gain a heart of wisdom" (Ps. 90:12 NKJV).

27. This dynamic of "despair as a turning point to meaning" is beautifully depicted in Stanley Hauerwas, *Naming the Silences: God, Medicine, and the Problem of Suffering* (Grand Rapids: Eerdmans, 1990). The point is that the same "sorrow" or "frustration" can serve as either a *fulcrum* that reorients the sufferer to wisdom through mourning or a *millstone* that even further entrenches the sufferer in the demanding mindset of victimization. See Reitmann, "Unity of Ecclesiastes," 306–7.

28. While physician commentators readily appreciate a contemporary relevance for the ethos of Job's innocent suffering and the hypocrisy of his "caregiver" friends (see e.g., Michael M. Lederman, "AIDS and the Conundrum of Job," *American Journal of Medicine* 92 [1992]: 679–80; and H. J. Van Peenen, "Why Me? and Sic Transit . . . ," *American Journal of Medicine* 98 [1995]: 505–6), most have missed Job's need for a wise advocate like Elihu to challenge his angry sense of victimization and flawed views of God in a timely and appropriate fashion (see below). I have noted in my role as an ethics consultant that people engaged in

prolonged—even bitter—conflict over some issue are often far more receptive than anticipated to the entry of a party who dares to honestly address the authentic underlying needs.

29. Elihu's role has been poorly understood (Reitman, "There *Is* a Mediator"). There are some similarities in his speeches with the other friends, but key differences clearly set him apart, and although the author does not explicitly validate Elihu's speeches as authoritative (cf. 32:1–5), abundant internal evidence suggests that indeed they *are:* Elihu's speeches are uncontested by Job and his three friends; Elihu gives one more speech and speaks more words than any of Job's friends; Elihu's words are not rejected by God, as are those of the friends (42:7); only Elihu repeatedly claims inspiration for his words (32:8, 18; 33:3–4; 36:2–4); Elihu's wrath mirrors God's wrath in being directed toward Job's self-justification and his friends' faulty judgments (32:1–3, cf. 40:8; 42:7); God repeats nearly verbatim certain phrases or concepts mentioned by Elihu (38:2; cf. 35:16; 40:2a; cf. 33:13; 40:2b; cf. 34:37b; 40:8; cf. 35:2); and finally, God speaks "out of the whirlwind" (38:1) in fulfillment of Elihu's use of that imagery (37:9; cf. 37:2–6).

30. When people rail against life in general and God in particular (cf. above, Job 6:14; 13:13–15), we, like Job's friends, are tempted to give advice before we have established a true commitment to the other's welfare—judgment is often pronounced before deeper issues can come to light. Authentic "attending" may thus be defined as "patient, effective listening with the aim of discerning and responding to the genuine needs of another." See further, Michael and Abigail Lipson, "Psychotherapy and the Ethics of Attention," *Hastings Center Report* (Jan.–Feb., 1996): 17–22.

31. By avoiding this pitfall, Elihu emulates the ideal physician (cf. Job 6:14–23; 13:4; 16:2; and above note 19).

32. Besides serving as Job's "spokesman" or "mouth" before God (Job 33:6), Elihu also fills the role of God's "messenger" by revealing God's "upright" intentions concerning Job's destiny (Reitman, "There *Is* a Mediator"). And although this text foreshadows the Incarnation and substitutionary atonement ultimately fulfilled in Christ's life and death, the immediate promise for Job or anyone in such despair is God's offer of present deliverance from the destructive consequences of his own deafness toward God in the midst of suffering. Indeed, Christ's death is as efficacious for redeeming meaning from *present suffering* as it is for man's redemption to *eternal life*—the two are in fact directly related (cf. Rom. 8:16–25; 2 Cor. 4:7–18). The contrast couldn't be sharper between this promised "deliverance" and that touted by proponents of *assisted suicide*.

33. Edmund G. Howe, "Influencing a Patient's Religious Beliefs: Mandate or No-Man's Land," *Journal of Clinical Ethics* 6 (1995): 194–200.

34. Richard L. Landau and James M. Gustafson, "Death Is Not the Enemy," *Journal of the American Medical Association* 252 (1984): 2458. This "priestly role" undertaken by physicians "often without knowing it" is poignantly illustrated in Michael A. LaCombe, "An Innocent Tale," *American Journal of Medicine* 87 (1989): 669–70.

35. See above notes 30–31 and accompanying text.

36. For the caregiver who can accept this risk, an obvious connection to establish is the role of Christ's sacrifice in redeeming meaning out of suffering (cf. note 32), especially when the sufferer is prepared to mourn (cf. Matt. 5:4). See further, Pellegrino, "Euthanasia," 111–12, 113–16; Allen D. Verhey,

"Faithfulness in the Face of Death," in *Dignity and Dying*, 56–65, 58–63; and Russell B. Connors Jr. and Martin L. Smith, "Religious Insistence on Medical Treatment: Christian Theology and Re-Imagination," *Hastings Center Report* 26 (July-Aug. 1996): 23–30, 26–29.

37. Above note 32.
38. Published narratives of those requesting assisted suicide (cf. above note 9) suggest a similar underlying unconfessed presumption, which is all too often framed in the insidiously subversive language of autonomy and the "right to die." See also, Nigel M. de S. Cameron, "Autonomy and the Right to Die," in *Dignity and Dying*, 23–33; Moreland, chapter 11 in this volume, "Morality of Suicide;" Pellegrino, "Euthanasia," 109–10; and above note 24."
39. When Elihu says to Job, "Speak, for I desire to justify you" (Job 33:32) he invites Job to refute what he has said, while reaffirming that he is his advocate (cf. vv. 6–7) in wanting to see Job declared righteous and redeemed. Assuming that Job has no rebuttal, Elihu quickly suggests that Job would do best to listen to further wisdom. And what does Job need to know?—the perfect justice of God (chap. 34) and the total inadequacy of his own righteousness (chap. 35). If Job responds to this wisdom with authentic mourning (33:26–27), his victim's complex will be replaced with an efficacious moral agency, since God can then "restore to him His [God's] righteousness" (v. 26b) and empower him for fruitful service (36:5–11). Of interest, this was exactly what God had initially set out to prove to Satan (Job 1:8; 2:3; cf. Reitman, "There *Is* a Mediator").
40. See James Reitmann, "The Dilemma of 'Medical Faculty'—A 'Wisdom Model' for Decisionmaking," *Issues in Law & Medicine* 12 (1996): 231–64, esp. 258–61.
41. Stanley Hauerwas, "Religious Concepts of Brain Death," in *Suffering Presence*, 94. See also the more extended argument for moral agency in spite of suffering in Hauerwas' "Rational Suicide" (above note 24), esp. 106–7.
42. See above notes 23, 27–28. Philip Yancey borrows heavily from the Job narrative in interpreting his own illustrative experience as a "wise advocate" who faced this challenge (*Disappointment with God: Three Questions No One Should Ask Aloud* New York: Harper & Row, 1988, 1991).
43. This accountability is shared by the caregiver as a moral agent participating in these same choices. See Reitman, "Assisted Suicide" (see above note 6), 315–16.
44. The value of cultivating stewardship in the face of terminal illness or severe disability is nicely portrayed in the accounts of Hubert J. VanPeenen, "Net Worth," *American Journal of Medicine* 94 (1993): 438–41; Neil Abramson, "Quality of Life: Who Can Make the Judgment?" *American Journal of Medicine* 100 (1996): 365–66; and Michael A. LaCombe, "Matthew 25," *American Journal of Medicine* 89 (1990): 363–64. The question of what specific role the caregiver may play in encouraging such stewardship as a member of the sufferer's "moral community" (cf. above note) is further explored by John T. Dunlop, "Death and Dying," in *Dignity and Dying*, 34–43; and Dennis Hollinger, "Congregational Ministry," in *Dignity and Dying*, 232–42, 238–41; and Reitmann, "Assisted Suicide," 322–29; and "Medical Futility," 253–56, 261–64.
45. See Eccl. 9:1, 7. The concept of participating in the "work of God" with a view to maximizing joy in the midst of present suffering is the principal thrust and conclusion of Psalm 90.

Return, O LORD! How long? And have compassion on Your servants.
Oh, satisfy us early with your mercy, that we may rejoice and be glad

all our days! Make us glad according to the days in which You have afflicted us, the years in which we have seen evil. Let Your work appear to Your servants, and Your glory to their children. And let the beauty of the LORD our God be upon us, and establish the work of our hands for us; yes, establish the work of our hands. (13–17 NKJV)

An Overview

Could the church possibly welcome the message of Jack Kevorkian? The groundwork has already been laid. The suffering and pain connected with dying is opening the door to theological instruction designed more to soothe human desire than to direct human decision. In this look at the apostle Paul's intense desire to be with the Lord, as presented in Philippians 1:21–26, Dónal P. O'Mathúna challenges the teaching of Arthur J. Droge who is a proponent for the acceptance of suicide as a moral act.

Chapter Twenty-Four

DID PAUL CONDONE SUICIDE?

*Implications for Assisted Suicide
and Active Euthanasia*

Dónal P. O'Mathúna

THE MORALITY OF ASSISTED SUICIDE and active euthanasia is widely disputed today.[1] Jack Kevorkian has been vocal in legal and public settings, but has recently started to bring his message into the church. One pastor who invited him to speak at his church said, "The belief of many Christians that suicide is a mortal sin is a fallacy borne of politics instead of theology. It is a hoax that's been hoisted upon us by the institutionalized church. It's just not true."[2] Kevorkian himself wrote that laws against suicide and euthanasia are "taboos" arising from either superstition or "inflexible rules based on stern religious doctrines."[3] Two recent popular books (*A Noble Death* by Arthur Droge and James Tabor,[4] and *What Does the Bible Say About Suicide?* by James Clemons[5]) attempt to provide justification for this position.

The argument suggests that although the Bible describes a number of suicides, it nowhere condemns the practice. These authors note that suicide was commonly practiced and highly regarded among ancient peoples. They claim that Augustine's writings led to suicide's being viewed as one of the three unforgivable sins (the others being blasphemy and adultery). But Augustine, in their view, used Aristotle's philosophy more than Christian theology to argue against suicide.

However, many of the early church fathers spoke out against suicide. Darrel Amundsen's historical survey of this issue brings together many references written in the first three centuries of the church, known as the patristic era.[6] He concludes:

> It should be obvious to the attentive reader that a survey of the patristic literature demonstrates that it is simply wrong to suggest that Augustine formulated what then became the "Christian position" on suicide. Rather, by removing certain ambiguities, he clarified and provided a theologically cogent explanation of and justification for the position typically held by earlier and contemporary Christian sources.[7]

We will not focus here on the writings of the early Christians or Augustine. Their perspective on suicide was based on what they believed was taught by the biblical authors. While the books by Clemons and Droge and Tabor demonstrate clearly that the Bible does not teach that suicide is an unforgivable sin, they go too far in claiming that Christians should be very slow to view suicide as wrong. This is particularly the case when examining Paul's view of suicide. In another article on this issue, Droge speculates:

> What if Paul reached the position of failing health or old age, so that he could no longer carry out his divine commission? Then I think it equally possible that Paul would have committed suicide and done so with a clear conscience and with the expectation that he would pass into immortality, united with Christ.[8]

Similarly, Clemons claims that Paul "had no immediate sense of wrong-doing in contemplating his self-chosen death."[9] While he is more cautious in applying his conclusions, his argument leads in the same direction as Droge's. The implications are very clear. If suicide is not wrong for a Christian, it would be hard to argue against assisted suicide or active euthanasia.

Droge condenses his position to three main arguments. We will deal with his first and third arguments briefly. His first point is that suicide was commonly practiced and approved of in Paul's day. Many accounts of suicide in the literature of the time, including the Bible, do not condemn the practice. His third point is that "the mystery surrounding Paul's death suggests the possibility that he may have committed suicide and that knowledge of the event was suppressed in the New Testament as well as in apocryphal writings."[10] But these two arguments negate one another! Why would the early Christians hide the fact that Paul killed himself if suicide was an acceptable practice? Either it was hidden because it was not approved of, or Paul did not commit suicide.

Droge's second argument will be the focus of this paper. He sees Philippians 1:19–26 as the key New Testament passage to support his view that Paul saw nothing wrong with suicide. Was this Paul's view?

THE CONTEXT OF PHILIPPIANS

Paul wrote this letter from prison to encourage the Philippians. He points out that in spite of his apparently bad circumstances, the situation had become a great opportunity to spread the Gospel. As a result, the whole praetorian guard had heard the message of Christ (1:12–13). In addition, although some were preaching Christ for selfish reasons, the Gospel was still being proclaimed. This gave Paul great joy and confidence as he turned to reflect on his own situation and whether imprisonment would lead to his freedom or death.

Paul declares:

> For I know that through your prayers and the help given by the Spirit of Jesus Christ, what has happened to me will turn out for my deliverance. I

eagerly expect and hope that I will in no way be ashamed, but will have sufficient courage so that now as always Christ will be exalted in my body, whether by life or by death. (Phil. 1:19–20 NIV)

No matter what happens, his goal is to see Christ exalted. This resembles the confidence of Shadrach, Meshach, and Abednego as they walked into the fiery furnace, knowing that God would remain with them and be vindicated, either in their living or their dying (Dan. 3). But then we come to the controversial passage.

For to me, to live is Christ and to die is gain. If I am to go on living in the body, this will mean fruitful labor for me. Yet what shall I choose? I do not know! I am torn between the two: I desire to depart and be with Christ, which is better by far; but it is more necessary for you that I remain in the body. Convinced of this, I know that I will remain, and I will continue with all of you for your progress and joy in the faith, so that through my being with you again your joy in Christ Jesus will overflow on account of me. (Phil. 1:21–26 NIV)

Paul's situation leads him to contemplate his future. He may be released from prison and continue his ministry with the Philippians. On the other hand, he may die soon. But we are not told how he might die. The traditional interpretation is that he may be martyred if the verdict of his trial goes against him. Droge's view is that Paul is considering killing himself. "I do not know which to choose"—life or death—certainly does sound like someone contemplating suicide! Which interpretation is more accurate?

WHY IS DEATH A GAIN (1:21–23)?

Everything in Paul's life revolves around Christ and spreading Christ's message. As one commentary puts it:

Life is summed up in Christ. Life is filled up with, occupied with Christ, in the sense that everything Paul does—trusts, loves, hopes, obeys, preaches, follows, and so on—is inspired by Christ and is done for Christ. Christ and Christ alone gives inspiration, direction, meaning and purpose to existence. . . . Paul can see no reason for being except to be "for Christ" (Rom. 14:7–9).[11]

But this does not result in Paul's clinging to physical life with all his vigor. I can attest from past personal experience that committed athletes love to exercise and take care of their bodies. However, they recoil at the idea of injury or a time when they will no longer be so strong or fast. Our society tends to worship youthfulness and health, and then cannot come to grips with aging bodies and death. Medical technology has been used to help maintain our denial of death. These attitudes are linked to the current demand to legalize assisted suicide and active euthanasia.

But this is not the case for Paul. In spite of his passion for physical life, he does not recoil at the idea of death. In 2 Corinthians 5:1–10, Paul states that while we are in our physical bodies we are, by comparison, absent from the Lord. Droge claims that this passage shows how much Paul longed to die.[12] However, the Greek in verses 2–4 clearly shows that what Paul wants is to be alive at Christ's Second Coming.[13] Rather than want to die, or deliberately take his own life, Paul wants to be with Christ. Since death brings closer union with Christ, Paul tells the Philippians that it is "gain" (1:21) and "better by far" (1:23). He shows why Christians do not have to fear death (Heb. 2:15). We know that it cannot separate those who are in Christ from the love of God (Rom. 8:38). It brings a new depth to our relationship with Christ.

Some authors have proposed other reasons why Paul sees death as gain. D. W. Palmer gives many examples of ancient Greek and Roman literature, which viewed death as a legitimate way to escape the sufferings of this world. In commenting on our passage, he says, "If death is a gain, that is not because of any closer union with Christ, . . . [but] because it brings release from earthly troubles."[14] Droge agrees with Palmer, but holds that Paul saw death as a gain both because it allows escape from suffering and leads to greater union with Christ.[15] Given this interpretation, could Christians not use assisted suicide or active euthanasia to escape suffering and be with Christ?

However, as both authors clearly admit, their interpretation is an argument based on silence. Paul tells us there is gain both in living and in dying (Phil. 1:21). He qualifies what he means in the next few verses. Continued living is of gain because it will mean fruitful labor (v. 22). He will be able to help the Philippians mature in Christ (vv. 25–26). However, his only qualification for the gain from death is that he will then be with Christ (v. 23). He gives no other reason.

In spite of what other authors of his time say about the advantages of fleeing the woes of this life, Paul's writings reveal a very different attitude. He certainly had many troubles, and even refers to them in this letter (e.g. 1:17; 4:14). At one point he despaired of life, but then was thankful that he did not die (2 Cor. 1:8–10). He endured his many sufferings and persecutions (2 Tim. 3:11). He resisted the many attempts on his life by evasion (Acts 14:5–6) and possessed a tenacious will to recover from the numerous abuses he experienced (2 Cor. 11:23–27). Later in Philippians he says that his sufferings lead to fellowship in Christ's sufferings, which allows him to know Christ better (3:8, 10). Paul rejoices in the good his sufferings will accomplish in others (Col. 1:24) as they increase his dependence on Christ (2 Cor. 12:10). He does not flee from suffering but learns to be content in the midst of it, something he urges the Philippians to imitate (4:11–12). Again, his only gain from death is to be with Christ.

WHAT SHALL I CHOOSE (1:22)?

Droge's argument depends heavily on the last part of verse 22: "Yet what shall I choose? I do not know!" He comments: "This should be taken to mean what it says, that the question of life or death was a matter of Paul's *own* volition, not a fate to be imposed on him by others."[16] The danger of execution must have passed because Paul is so confident about visiting the Philippians soon (vv. 25–26). His conclusion suggests that Paul must have been contemplating whether or not to commit suicide![17]

However, this interpretation ignores the role of prisons in Paul's day. They were used only to hold prisoners while they awaited trial, sentencing, or punishment.[18] Since he was still in prison, his fate was not yet decided. While there, he was at the mercy of his captors. He was not in control of the situation at all.[19]

Further analysis of the Greek supports this. In verse 22, "I do not know" translates *gnorizo*, which is nowhere else in the New Testament translated as such. In all other passages it means "to make known" or "to reveal" (Col. 1:27; Eph. 1:9; 3:5).[20] Because of this, other translations read: "I dare not reveal my preference" or "I cannot tell what I would choose."[21]

Also, the verb translated "choose" is *haireomai*. It is in the middle voice, as opposed to the active voice. In Greek, the active voice of a verb is used when the subject does the action. The active voice of this verb "always contains an element of action and personal decision."[22] But Paul uses the middle voice here, which instead conveys the idea of preference between two alternatives.[23] The same type of word is used in 2 Corinthians 5:8, where Paul says he would prefer to be with Christ than in his physical body. In both cases he is talking about his preference, not actively choosing to pursue one option over another.

Paul is not sitting back in turmoil trying to figure out which action he will choose. The active voice of the verb would communicate this. Instead, he is caught in vice-grips, hemmed in from both sides.[24] Since he does not have control, he wonders which he prefers. But he will not reveal his preference because he is content either way. He is giving us a practical example of how he has applied Philippians 4:11–13 in his own life. He has learned to be content regardless of the circumstances. His confidence is in God's control of the situation. As one commentator put it many decades ago: "The Apostle will not venture to decide between the alternatives, and the choice must be left in his Master's hands."[25]

Job is another person in the Bible who exemplifies patience and reliance on God in the midst of suffering. Job's sufferings were similarly intense, and he openly loathed his life and wished he were dead (10:1, 18). Paul gives us an important clue that Job may have been on his mind when he was writing to the Philippians. In Philippians 1:19, the phrase "will turn out for my deliverance" is identical to the Greek Septuagint wording in Job 13:16.[26] In the two verses prior to this Job says, referring to God,

> Why do I put myself in jeopardy, and take my life in my hands? Though he slay me, yet will I hope in him. (Job 13:14–15)

In spite of his suffering and his desire to die, Job decided to put his trust in God. Paul follows this example as he contemplates his own situation. We too must learn to put things in God's hands during our illnesses and dying. Suicide and euthanasia are attempts to put our lives in our own hands.

WHY IS PAUL HARD-PRESSED (1:23)?

Deciding to rely on the Lord will not always take the turmoil and uncertainty away. In verse 23 Paul says he is still hard-pressed between the options. The Greek word used here (*synechomai*) carries the idea of external control, as in how an illness overcomes a person (Matt. 4:24; Acts 28:8).[27] Interestingly, Paul uses this word in a parallel passage when he says that "the love of Christ controls us" (2 Cor. 5:14 NASB).

The word confirms that external factors are in control of the situation rather than Paul. One of the hardest things to accept is the fact that we do not have ultimate control over our bodies or what happens to them. It often takes an illness, or our imminent death, to make this clear to us. Yet in response to this, some people pursue euthanasia as a way to regain some sense of control.

Is this what Paul does when he says, "I desire to depart" (v. 23)? This is a euphemism for dying, which Droge translates as: Paul "lusts after death."[28] Droge chooses the word "lust" to emphasize the intensity of Paul's desire to die. Ironically, the word he chooses brings out the negative connotation of the Greek word used by Paul. *Epithymia* is used of *wrongful desires* associated with natural inclinations in all but two of its thirty-eight occurrences in the New Testament.[29] When Paul speaks of praiseworthy desires, he uses the term *epipotheo* (e.g. Rom. 15:23; 2 Cor. 5:2). It seems that while Paul views one of his options as highly desirable, *it is not entirely praiseworthy*.

THE "MORE NECESSARY OPTION" (1:24)

Paul views death as "gain" and "much better," but the alternative is "more necessary" (*anagkaioteron*). This term conveys the idea of compulsion, but not due to external force.[30] It is the type of necessity that arises because of God's involvement in our lives and the world. Paul uses this word group to describe the necessity of being subject to our governments (Rom. 13:5) and the compulsion that he experienced to preach the Gospel (1 Cor. 9:16). In our passage, this word implies that Paul saw the option of his continuing to minister to the Philippians as closely linked to God's will for his life.

Droge makes much of the fact that the same word was used by Socrates in his influential discussion of suicide. According to Plato, Socrates held that people should not take their own lives unless they had received a divine *anagke* to do so.[31] This view was commonly held in Paul's day. Droge concludes that since Paul's *anagke* was for ministry in this world, he could not commit suicide. "It is not the case therefore that Paul rejects suicide *per se*, only that it is not (yet) the proper context for such an act."[32] But given different circumstances, Paul could believe it was his time to die.

Some of the possible circumstances that Droge thinks would have led Paul to commit suicide are (1) believing his missionary work was finished, (2) believing the necessity to minister was now removed, (3) becoming convinced that he had fought the good fight and finished the race, so that it was now time to depart, and (4) failing health or old age preventing him from carrying out his divine commission.[33]

These, with the relief of suffering, are exactly the same types of reasons given to support the need for euthanasia. If Paul saw these as valid reasons to take his own life, surely Christians today should support people's requests to die and even assist them in dying. Assisted suicide and active euthanasia would seem to be valid options so long as people believe it was God's will for them to die, or their suffering had become unbearable and meaningless.

But this view depends on the assumption that Paul felt it necessary to remain alive only under his current circumstances. Some believe Paul would not want this passage applied to others, regardless of their circumstances.[34] However, Dailey shows that this is not in keeping with the nature of Paul's letters. "Certainly his reflection arises from a personal, individual experience, but this reflection becomes teaching when he publicly manifests its content to the entire community by means of the particular character of an epistle."[35]

Our passage comes within a discussion of the Gospel, and is immediately followed by a call to act in a manner worthy of the Gospel (Phil. 1:27). This shows the importance and general applicability of what Paul is saying. He tells the Philippians they will experience similar conflict because they also will suffer for Christ (1:29–30). Later, he specifically tells them to have the same attitude as he does and to follow his example when dealing with suffering (3:15, 17). Thus, whatever this passage teaches, it does apply to all Christians.

PAUL IS CONVINCED (1:24–26)

Yet, from the midst of being unsure which way to turn, we find that suddenly Paul is convinced. What has he become convinced of, and why? Most obviously, Paul is convinced that God wants him to remain alive. This cannot be confidence in knowing the future. Although he says he will come to the Philippians in verse 26, in the next verse he says that he may or may not come. While convinced in verse 25 that he will not die, he again sees this as a possibility in 2:17. Paul is like the rest of us: he does not have clear insight into the future. He is convinced that God wants him to live, but he remains open to whatever may actually happen.

In the broader context, Paul is also convinced that Christ will be glorified through him. He has already seen his imprisonment turn out for good. The selfish preachers did spread the Gospel. Rather than show that Paul looked favorably on choosing one's own death, this passage shows that Paul had given complete control of his life to God. The Greek words we have examined emphasize that Paul was not in control of his circumstances. The necessity to live was determined by God, not Paul. Paul is not like today's autonomous individuals who claim the right to control their bodies, to avoid pain and aging, and yet when defied, to end their lives. Paul's life was completely under the control of God; he was Christ's bond-servant (1:1).

Knowing that God was in control, he was confident that things would work out for good for those who love God (Rom. 8:28). This means giving up the control we so desperately crave, and waiting on the Lord to act. It means relying on prayer and the guidance of the Holy Spirit, as Paul did (Phil. 1:19; 4:6). It means tough discussions within the community of believers and the willingness to accept mature counsel (Prov. 20:18). God may reveal precisely what we should do, but so often we need to trust him and accept whatever happens.

This gave Paul confidence that God would set him free to accomplish His will. It seemed clear to him that God still had much ministry for him to do on earth. In spite of his great desire to go be with the Lord, he was going to wait until he was called home (1 Cor. 6:19–20). To depart this life by one's own choice is to reject the opportunity for loving and glorifying God in our bodies. We can do this through what we say and do, or through what others do for us. It can simply be our willingness to trust God and others in our final days.[36] Rejecting suicide shows the willingness to accept God's sovereignty and grace and to depend on Him for direction.[37]

CONCLUSION

The New Testament speaks of an afterlife in which believers will have intimate fellowship with God and all pain and suffering will be wiped away (Rev. 21:1–5). Droge explains how an ancient school of philosophy viewed the afterlife as a major determinant in its view of "voluntary death," his word for suicide.

> The two schools with the strongest belief in an afterlife (the Pythagoreans and Platonists) expressed the strongest opposition to voluntary death. In contrast, the Cynics and Epicureans, who did not believe in an afterlife, were prepared to defend the right of an individual to take his own life. In fact, it appears that the Cynics were prepared to die on the slightest provocation.[38]

It is ironic that Droge then claims Paul's strong belief in the afterlife led him to "lust after death."[39] The Bible never uses the hope of the afterlife to devalue this life. It emphasizes the significance of this life and the service we can give to others.[40] Our bodies may become weak and pain ridden, but they are not to be seen as worthless or useless. They remain gifts from God through which He can be glorified (1 Cor. 6:20; Phil. 1:20), even when they suffer humiliation, loss, or pain.

Paul tells us to consider others as more important than ourselves and to look out for the interests of others (Phil. 2:3–5, 21). This was Christ's attitude and we should imitate Him. Paul endured all things for the sake of others (2 Tim. 2:10). He holds up the example of Epaphroditus, who risked his own life to serve others (Phil. 2:25–30). Even when he was sick, his focus was on the well-being of the Philippians (v. 26). We can continue to serve others even in our illnesses and in our dying. For example, we can pray for others or witness to the hope that is within us. We will always have relationships that need healing and depth.

This is the challenge that lies before us as Christians. When healthy, are we interested in serving the needs of others, especially those who are ill or dying? That will help them want to live. When ill or dying, do we continue to think about the needs of others? How we face death can be our final gift to those who survive us.[41] This is how our lives and deaths can bring glory to

God and take away the desire to hasten death. Suicide and euthanasia deny all this. As Martin states,

> If death were the answer to all hope, we would think that Paul would desire death, but this is not what we find. Rather, he considers it still an enemy (1 Cor. 15:26). He is thankful that he has escaped death (2 Cor. 1:10) and he desires to finish his ministry in this life (Phil. 1:20–24; 1 Cor. 9:23–27).[42]

Those who have a deep relationship with Christ will be better able to accept their time of death when it comes. They do not have to fear annihilation or the unknown. They will be going home to be with their Lord whom they love so much (2 Cor. 5:6–8). It is a time of release from these corruptible bodies, which groan and ache (Rom. 8:23; 2 Cor. 5:4). It takes us closer to receiving our new bodies, which will no longer experience pain, illness, or death (1 Cor. 15:42–44; Rev. 21:4). Trust in this truth should remove our fear of death (Heb. 2:15). We trust in Him for the life we live; we must trust in Him for the death we experience.

Contemplation of the afterlife should lead to a greater desire to please the Lord in this life (2 Cor. 5:9; Rom. 14:7–8). This is done by serving others and suffering with our fellow sufferers. As we do this, our relationships with Christ deepen, and we desire to be with Him even more (Phil. 3:8). As long as we live, our desire should be that others come to know and love the Lord. This should give us perseverance to endure until our ministry to others ends by divine, and not human, design.

In Philippians 1:19–26, Paul acknowledges that death can look very attractive. The desire to die can be strong. But Christians should turn aside from that temptation, as he did, and find ways to love others and glorify God.[43]

ENDNOTES

1. Assisted suicide and active euthanasia involve the administration of a lethal dose of substance with the intention of causing death. They differ in who administers the dose: in the former, it is self-administered, while in the latter it is given by another, often a physician. The withholding or withdrawing of life-sustaining medical therapy involves different ethical issues if the intention is something other than hastening death and is not the subject of this chapter.
2. Thomas Egglebeen, quoted in "Kevorkian in Church to Kick Off Push to Legalize Assisted Suicide," *Columbus Dispatch* 31 January 1994, sec. A, 3.
3. Jack Kevorkian, "The Last Fearsome Taboo: Medical Aspects of Planned Death," *Medicine and Law* 7 (1988): 1–14.
4. Arthur J. Droge and James D. Tabor, *A Noble Death: Suicide and Martyrdom Among Christians and Jews in Antiquity* (San Francisco: HarperCollins, 1992).
5. James T. Clemons, *What Does the Bible Say About Suicide?* (Minneapolis: Fortress, 1990).
6. Darrel W. Amundsen, "Suicide and Early Christian Values," in *Medicine, Society, and Faith in the Ancient and Medieval Worlds* (Baltimore: Johns Hopkins University Press, 1996), 70–126.

7. Ibid., 102.
8. Arthur J. Droge, "Did Paul Commit Suicide?" *Bible Review* 5 (December 1989): 20.
9. Clemons, *What Does the Bible Say?*, 70.
10. Droge, "Did Paul Commit Suicide?" 14.
11. Gerald F. Hawthorne, *Philippians*, Word Biblical Commentary, vol. 43 (Waco, Tex.: Word, 1983), 45.
12. Droge and Taylor, *Noble Death*, 122.
13. The verb *ependuomai* means "to put on over" (vv. 2, 4), while *enduo* means simply "to put on" (v. 3). Paul does not want to be found naked, i.e. without a physical body, as would seem to be the case for those who die before the Second Coming. He would rather be alive when Christ returns and have his physical body clothed over by his spiritual body. Gerhard Kittel, ed., *Theological Dictionary of the New Testament*, trans. and ed. Geoffrey W. Bromiley (Grand Rapids: Eerdmans, 1964), 2:319–21.
14. D. W. Palmer, "'To Die Is Gain' (Philippians 1:21)," *Novum Testamentum* 17 (1975): 218.
15. Arthur J. Droge, "*Mori Lucrum:* Paul and Ancient Theories of Suicide," *Novum Testamentum* 30 (1988): 280.
16. Droge and Taylor, *Noble Death*, 120.
17. Droge, "*Mori Lucrum*," 283.
18. Rodney R. Reeves, "To be or not to be? That is not the question: Paul's choice in Philippians 1:22," *Perspectives in Religious Studies* 19 (1992): 279.
19. Ralph P. Martin, *Philippians*, New Century Bible (Greenwood, S.C.: Attic Press, 1976), 75–80.
20. Kittel, *TDNT*, 1:718.
21. See the *New English Bible, Revised Standard Version*, GOODSPEED, KNOX, or MOFFATT; cited by Hawthorne, *Philippians*, 47.
22. Colin Brown, ed., *New International Dictionary of New Testament Theology* (Grand Rapids: Zondervan, 1986), 1:533.
23. Kittel, *TDNT*, 1:180.
24. Hawthorne, *Ephesians*, 48.
25. Maurice Jones, *The Epistle to the Philippians*, Westminster Commentaries (London: Methuen, 1918), 21.
26. Ralph P. Martin, *The Epistle of Paul to the Philippians*, rev. ed., Tyndale New Testament Commentaries (Grand Rapids: Eerdmans, 1987), 77.
27. Kittel, *TDNT*, 7:883–85.
28. Droge and Taylor, *Noble Death*, 122.
29. Brown, *NIDNT*, 1:457.
30. Kittel, *TDNT*, 1:344–47.
31. Plato *Phaedo* 62C; cited in Droge and Taylor, *Noble Death*, 22, 122.
32. Droge, "*Mori Lucrum*," 283.
33. Droge, "Did Paul Commit Suicide?" 20.
34. Most prominent among these scholars is Albert Schweitzer. See Thomas F. Dailey, "To Live or Die: Paul's Eschatological Dilemma in Philippians 1:19–26," *Interpretation* 44 (1990): 21; and Palmer, "To Die Is Gain," 204.
35. Dailey, "To Live or Die," 21.
36. Stanley Hauerwas, *Suffering Presence: Theological Reflections on Medicine, the Mentally Handicapped, and the Church* (Notre Dame, Ind.: University of Notre Dame Press, 1986), 106.

37. Karl Barth, *Church Dogmatics* (Edinburgh: T. & T. Clark, 1961), III:4:407.
38. Droge and Taylor, *Noble Death*, 43.
39. Ibid., 122.
40. Lloyd R. Bailey Sr., *Biblical Perspectives on Death* (Philadelphia: Fortress, 1979), 101.
41. Edmund D. Pellegrino, "Physician-Assisted Suicide: A Debate and Public Forum," lecture at the conference "The Christian Stake in Dignity and Dying," Center for Bioethics and Human Dignity, Deerfield, Illinois, July 13–15, 1995.
42. Ralph P. Martin, *2 Corinthians*, Word Biblical Commentary, vol. 40, (Waco, Tex.: Word, 1986), 106.
43. This is a slightly revised version of a paper published in *Ethics & Medicine*, 12:3 (1996), 55–59. Originally presented at the conference "The Christian Stake in Dignity and Dying," Center for Bioethics and Human Dignity, Deerfield, Illinois, July 13–15, 1995.

An Overview

Two distinct commands fulfill Old Testament Law and provide pertinent instruction for a biblical response to the euthanasia debate. Jesus instructs us to love God and to practice neighborly love. The example of the Good Samaritan reaches out from the pages of history to reinstruct us as to the genuine meaning of divine love and its application to modern-day concerns. The empathy or compassion for those who suffer, who are weaker, or who have a lesser quality of life must conform to the will of God, who is our Creator, not to the finite will of human beings. A Good Samaritan does not discriminate in the definition or distribution of love.

Chapter Twenty-Five

THE GOOD SAMARITAN AND
THE EUTHANASIA DEBATE

H. Wayne House

ON ONE OCCASION AN EXPERT in the law stood up to test Jesus. "Teacher," he asked, "what must I do to inherit eternal life?"

"What is written in the Law?" he replied. "How do you read it?"

He answered: "'Love the Lord your God with all your heart and with all your soul and with all your strength and with all your mind'; and 'Love your neighbor as yourself.'"

"You have answered correctly," Jesus replied. "Do this and you will live."

But he wanted to justify himself, so he asked Jesus, "And who is my neighbor?"

In reply Jesus said: "A man was going down from Jerusalem to Jericho, when he fell into the hands of robbers. They stripped him of his clothes, beat him and went away, leaving him half dead. A priest happened to be going down the same road, and when he saw the man, he passed by on the other side. So too, a Levite, when he came to the place and saw him, passed by on the other side. But a Samaritan, as he traveled, came where the man was; and when he saw him, he took pity on him. He went to him and bandaged his wounds, pouring on oil and wine. Then he put the man on his own donkey, took him to an inn and took care of him. The next day he took out two silver coins and gave them to the innkeeper. 'Look after him,' he said, 'and when I return, I will reimburse you for any extra expense you may have.'

"Which of these three do you think was a neighbor to the man who fell into the hands of robbers?"

The expert in the law replied, "The one who had mercy on him."

Jesus told him, "Go and do likewise" (Luke 10:25–37 NIV).

Few stories in the Bible have attracted the attention of the general public more than the story of the Good Samaritan. It has worked its way into our common talk, when we request of others to be "Good Samaritans," and even into the laws of some states, where one has exemption from tort liability in helping injured persons unless gross negligence is involved.[1] Even as we implore people to be Good Samaritans, we find in our experience that we and others often do not reach this lofty goal. Certainly in interpersonal relationships we fail, but these are not life and death situations generally, as is the case of the original parable given by Jesus and as are the cases of the life and death subjects of our day, such as abortion and euthanasia. In the Good Samaritan parable the Master paints a scenario in which the balance was tilted against a beaten and helpless Jewish man who had taken the dangerous trip from Jerusalem to Jericho. In similar fashion today, there are individuals who find themselves hanging between life and death, and the ethic of Jesus poses for us a similar question that Jesus posed to the lawyer in Israel almost two thousand years ago. Persons who are sick, in pain, and often dying are treated with no more sympathy today than the priest and the Levite gave to the man on the Jericho road. Yes, they may have felt something inside, a tinge of guilt, but didn't want to be bothered by this man's pain and the inconvenience he would cause them. Some wanting to promote euthanasia speak in caring, humanitarian terms but fail to make the sacrifice of the Samaritan in Jesus' story, who gave comfort, health, and even life to a dying person whom God brought to him that day. The lawyer who asked Jesus about the identity of his neighbor places each of us before the teacher who loves, gives succor and life, and bids each of us to do the same.

THE SETTING AND LITERARY NATURE OF THE PARABLE

In Luke 10:25–11:13, the evangelist Luke sets forth the characteristics of a disciple of Jesus Christ. He does so by means of three separate incidents, but all containing the motif of true discipleship. The first incident concerns the questioning by a lawyer, who is not his disciple but does not appear openly hostile to the Lord. The conversation leads to the conclusion that a disciple of Christ must follow two commandments in the law to inherit eternal life. The emphasis in this account is on the second commandment, to love one's neighbor (Luke 10:27). The second incident encourages Jesus' disciples to obey the teachings given by him (Luke 10:38–42). The third account is Christ's teaching on prayer in response to the disciples' request for instruction in how to pray (Luke 11:1–13). Thus the three accounts present instruction on one's relationship to neighbors, to Jesus, and to God, respectively.[2]

THE PROBLEM OF COHESIVENESS IN LUKE 10:25-37

Is the Good Samaritan Parable an Appendix?

The story of the lawyer's question about eternal life and the parable of the Good Samaritan is viewed by some scholars as being disjointed, reflective of a later redaction.[3] A major reason why this is seen to be the case is the relationship of this narrative to Mark 12:28–34, upon which the Lucan account is considered to be dependent. Both accounts have Jesus in a conversation with a lawyer in which the two major commandments are given. In Mark's gospel Jesus offers the summary of the law from Deuteronomy (6:5) and Leviticus (9:18), with which the lawyers agree, whereas in the Lucan narrative the lawyer cites the Old Testament passages, with Jesus confirming that obedience to these commandments brings life.

Though there are similarities between the texts, there are important reasons why Luke has probably not borrowed from Mark, though he may have been familiar with Mark's rendition. In Mark's account the lawyer asks of Christ the "first commandment of all" (12:28), while in Luke the lawyer asks the more practical question "What shall I do to inherit eternal life!" (10:25). The Marcan account begins with the Shema, "Hear, O Israel, Yahweh is our God, Yahweh is one" (12:29), but in Luke the Shema is omitted.

If Luke has not borrowed his story from Mark, is the account an independent account of the same incident, or were there two similar occurrences? Certainly it is possible that all three gospel writers developed their accounts from one basic story, but it may be better to understand the stories as reflecting different incidents. We should not suppose that the gospel writers were restricted only to single sermons of Jesus in developing their gospels. As T. W. Manson once said, "Great teachers constantly repeat themselves."[4] The gospel writers, then, may have chosen a different episode of a similar teaching for their own accounts. Marshall says,

> The sort of question raised by the lawyer was one that could arise frequently, especially since we know that it was asked in rabbinic circles; Manson makes the point that there is nothing surprising about the lawyer repeating what he already knew to be the answer of Jesus himself to the question in order to put his own counter-question regarding the scope of neighborliness.[5]

Howard Marshall concludes his discussion by arguing for the unity of the lawyer's question and the parabolic tale. He says that they "manifestly belong together in the mind of Luke; although the latter appears to follow as a kind of appendix, it is integral to the pericope and forms the climax."[6] When one reads the two accounts together, it is difficult to imagine a better contextual setting for the parable than what we observe in the text handed down to us. Even though these two pericopae form an integral whole, the story of the lawyer and Jesus, as Marshall indicates, does not simply introduce the parable but has its own significance because it poses the issue regarding how one may inherit eternal life. In answering this, it also answers the matter in a thoroughly Jewish way in citing the two commandments of loving God and one's neighbor.[7]

Luke's Emphasis on the Social Implications of the Gospel

Luke's gospel, more than any other, presents the social dimensions to the gospel. In his account of Jesus, he presents Christ's concern for weak persons, for women, and for outcasts. For example, the gospel gives special place to women. Mary, the mother of Jesus, has her story told in Luke 1:26–56, and possibly her genealogy is what is recorded in Luke 3:23–38. An elaborate account of the "sinful" woman is given in Luke 7:36–50. It is Luke who records the contrasting models of Mary and Martha, where Mary is commended for listening to His teaching rather than busying herself with cooking and cleaning (see Luke 10:38–42). Luke, as a physician, also gives special attention to the weak and infirm, often in great detail, in contrast to the rest of the evangelists.

This story also illustrates this emphasis. Through the conjunction of the two commandments found in this conjoined story, Luke is able to present the dual responsibilities that adhere to following Jesus, the commitment to God in the first commandment and concern for others in the second commandment.

The Relationship of the Lawyer's Question to Jesus' Lesson in the Parable

Though some scholars believe the story of the lawyer's question and the parable of the Good Samaritan are disjunctive, I have already argued earlier that they fit together well. By giving the parable, Jesus provides a practical expression to the lawyer's proper response to the full essence of the law found in the two commandments of loving God and then loving one's neighbor as oneself.

Let us look at the relationship of the two commandments and then determine in what sense the parable illustrates one or both of these commandments. First, are there really two commandments, or do they in reality merge into each other? In other words, are the love of God and the love for one's neighbor one and the same thing? Does love for God equate with love for one's neighbor? Moreover, is love for God the only motive for love of neighbor? Still yet, has loving one's neighbor become the same thing as loving God, so that love for one's neighbor becomes a substitute for loving God? Günther Bornkamm speaks negatively to such a proposition.

> Are the love of God and the love of our neighbor one and the same thing? Surely not. That would mean eliminating the barrier between God and man, which is in fact immovable. Whoever considers both commandments in this sense to be identical knows nothing of God's sovereign rights, and will very soon make God into a mere term and cipher, which one will soon manage to do without. In Jesus' preaching, love for God consistently takes precedence. This is made abundantly clear in the entire teaching on the reign of God, and in the call to obedience to his sovereign will. "No one can serve two masters" (Matt. 6:24)—this law cannot be repealed, not even by our duty to our neighbor.[8]

The whole idea of somehow loving our neighbor without recognizing love for God is a humanitarian dream. Just as we are unable to love God without at the same time loving our neighbors, we are also incapable of loving our neighbors without also loving God first. Love for God must have priority in our lives. This is because the union with Christ by faith is that which gives us the ability to love others.[9]

Secondly, having discussed the view that one could love God simply by loving a neighbor, the further issue remains as to whether one may, conversely, love a neighbor as a means of loving God. A person who does so responds only to the needs of others based on an attempt to please God or to receive some reward, rather than sincerely responding to the needs of one's neighbor. Bornkamm has said that "[a] love which in this sense does not really love the other person for his own sake but only for the sake of God is not real love."[10] The story of the Good Samaritan provides an opportunity to evaluate this sense of love. The Samaritan of the story gives no indication that he responds out of love for God rather than out of love for the neighbor. Speaking of the manner in which the story was told, Bornkamm remarks:

> This is told with the greatest care: he binds up his wounds, he alleviates his pain, sets the sick man on his beast, brings him to the inn, puts him into the inn-keeper's care the next day, pays the initial expenses and promises to be responsible for any further expenses incurred when he comes again. Note how simply and without sentimentality the Samaritan is described: the shrewd merchant, practical and careful with his means and money, who does nothing that is not necessary at the time. In all this there is no parade at all of "religion." What he does is aimed at the sufferer without side glances at God.[11]

Is such an approach to caring appropriate to followers of Jesus? Such may be the case in reflection on the judgment of Christ to come. Those who were rewarded for their works of mercy toward others were unaware of this service being a service to Christ, unlike those, impliedly, who would have served had they known it was service to Christ. Note the passage in Matthew 25:31–46:

> When the Son of Man comes in his glory, and all the angels with him, he will sit on his throne in heavenly glory. All the nations will be gathered before him, and he will separate the people one from another as a shepherd separates the sheep from the goats. He will put the sheep on his right and the goats on his left. Then the King will say to those on his right, "Come, you who are blessed by my Father; take your inheritance, the kingdom prepared for you since the creation of the world. For I was hungry and you gave me something to eat, I was thirsty and you gave me something to drink, I was a stranger and you invited me in, I needed clothes and you clothed me, I was sick and you looked after me, I was in prison and you came to visit me." Then the righteous will answer him, "Lord, when did we see you hungry and feed you, or thirsty and give you something to drink? When did we see you a stranger and invite you in, or needing clothes and clothe you? When did we see you sick or in prison and go to visit you?" The King will reply, "I tell you the truth, whatever you did for one of the least of these brothers of mine, you did for me." Then he will say to those on his left, "Depart from me, you who are cursed, into the eternal fire prepared for the devil and his angels. For I was hungry and you gave me nothing to eat, I was thirsty and you gave me nothing to drink, I was a stranger and you did not invite me in, I needed clothes and you did not clothe me, I was sick and in prison and you did not look after me." They also will answer, "Lord, when did we see

you hungry or thirsty or a stranger or needing clothes or sick or in prison, and did not help you?" He will reply, "I tell you the truth, whatever you did not do for one of the least of these, you did not do for me." Then they will go away to eternal punishment, but the righteous to eternal life.

In this statement of judgment, those who were rewarded were responding to those in need without regard to reception of rewards or as another way to love God. The cursed, on the other hand, used their ignorance of Christ's presence in these "neighbors" as a basis for their actions. Certainly, they reasoned, they would have loved their neighbor if in doing so it would have been as a way to meet Christ himself. The lesson, then, is that love for a neighbor cannot be an indirect love as a way to meet Christ; we must love people because of who they are.[12]

If the meaning of the two commandments is not blending the love of God into the love of our neighbor, or the love of our neighbor does not fuse with the love for God, then what is the meaning of the double commandment of love? Bornkamm says,

> Clearly the inseparable unity into which Jesus brings them has its reason and meaning not in the similarity of those towards whom this love is directed, but in the nature of this love itself. It is in Jesus' own words the renunciation of self-love, the willingness for and the act of surrender there where you actually are, or, which is the same, where your neighbor is, who is waiting for you. In this way and no other God's call comes to us, and in this way the love of God and the love of our neighbor become one. Surrender to God now no longer means a retreat of the soul into a paradise of spirituality and the dissolution of selfhood in adoration and meditation, but a waiting and preparedness for the call of God, who calls to us in the person of our neighbor. *In this sense the love of our neighbor is the test of our love of God.* [emphasis added].[13]

In this regard, we come to understand the meaning of love and the nature of a neighbor in the parable and the question and answer that gave rise to the parable. First, love must be more than mere humanitarianism, a general concern for persons. Such general concerns translate into meaningful action not much different from the value, following our mother's advice, of eating everything on our plates since people in other parts of the world are starving. Obviously our eating or not has no meaningful impact on whether people in other parts of the globe starve or not. Likewise, general statements of sympathy have no impact on the needs of others. In James' epistle we find the tour de force to such sophistry: "Suppose a brother or sister is without clothes and daily food. If one of you says to him, 'Go, I wish you well; keep warm and well fed,' but does nothing about his physical needs, what good is it? In the same way, faith by itself, if it is not accompanied by action, is dead" (2:15–17 NIV).

Fyodor Dostoyevsky, in *The Brothers Karamazov*, provides a helpful illustration of the difference between loving in general and loving in particular: a "lady of little faith" who proclaimed pretentiously that she had such love for humanity that she frequently dreamed of surrendering everything for mankind. Father Zossima commended her dreams reservedly and then said, "Sometime, unawares, you may do a good deed in reality."[14] Whereas the priest and Levite might have "talked a good game," to speak in the vernacular, the Good Samaritan put into practice his love. Loving in particular stands in stark contrast with loving mankind in general.

> "The more I love humanity in general, the less I love man in particular. In my dream," he said, "I have often come to making enthusiastic schemes for the service of humanity, and perhaps I might actually have faced crucifixion if it had been suddenly necessary; and yet I am incapable of living in the same room with any one for two days together, as I know by experience. As soon as any one is near me, his personality disturbs my self-complacency and restricts my freedom. In twenty-four hours I begin to hate the best of men: one because he's too long over his dinner, another because he has a cold and keeps on blowing his nose. I become hostile to people the moment they come close to me. But it always happened that the more I detest men individually, the more ardent becomes my love for humanity. . . ." I could never understand how one can love one's neighbors. It's just one's neighbors, to my mind, that one can't love, though one might love those at a distance. . . . For any one to love a man, he must be hidden, for as soon as he shows his face, love is gone. . . . Beggars, especially genteel beggars, ought never to show themselves, but to ask for charity through the newspaper. One can love one's neighbors in the abstract, or even at a distance, but at close quarters it's almost impossible.[15]

Ramsey comments about this love for men in general that it is "merely a bifocal 'self-regarding concern for others,' a selfish sociability, while love for neighbor *for his own sake* insists upon a single-minded orientation of a man's primary intention toward *this* individual neighbor with all his concrete needs."[16] Such concreteness is conspicuous in the portrayals of Christ. His illustrations of love are always concrete; in the words of White,

> [T]he cup of water where water was not always plentiful; visiting the sick, clothing the naked, feeding the under-nourished, befriending the ill-deserving prisoner; forgiving the offender, doing good, giving, lending without expectation of return; returning good for evil, prayers for cursing, gentleness for all ill-treatment. The ministry of Jesus is the enduring object-lesson in Christian love—His time, His sympathy, His unwearying service, ever at the command of the outcast, the helpless, the repulsive, the unvalued, the sinful, the blind and lame and leprous; His friendship toward sinners; His unfailing courtesy, His adaptation of His teaching to the comprehension of His hearers; His patience with the disciples; His resolute refusal to meet His enemies with their own weapons; His unembittered, undefeated good will in severest

rejection and extreme torture; His ability to love to the uttermost and to the end. And we are to love one another as *He* has loved us.[17]

The command to love with its accompanying surrender and sacrifice of self is clear, but the question still looms as to the recognition of the neighbor. This is the very question that the lawyer poses to Jesus. The Old Testament commandment of love for God was at the heart of the Jewish faith, requiring an undivided loyalty to Him. The second commandment (elided in Luke, unlike Matthew and Mark, to be in unity with the first commandment), bound the believing Hebrew to love not only the fellow Hebrew but the strangers among them: "When an alien lives with you in your land, do not mistreat him. The alien living with you must be treated as one of your native-born. Love him as yourself, for you were aliens in Egypt. I am the LORD your God" (Lev. 19:33–34 NIV). Carl F. H. Henry says, "Strangers were to be loved as though they were covenant-members, but they were prohibited from sharing in the covenant until they obeyed its demands."[18] In fact, the Septuagint (LXX) used ὁ πλησίον σου, meaning "anyone around you."[19] Marshall comments concerning this usage,

> The Jews interpreted this in terms of members of the same people and religious community, fellow-Jews (cf. Matt. 5:43–48). There was a tendency on the part of the Pharisees to exclude the ordinary people from the definition, and Qumran community excluded those whom they termed "the sons of darkness." . . . In Leviticus 19:34 (cf. Deut. 10:19) the same obligation of love is extended to the *ger*, the resident alien, but Jewish usage excluded Samaritans and foreigners from this category. . . . The Greek term admitted of a wider meaning, but in the present context the Jewish usage is decisive; this is how the lawyer could be expected to understand the phrase.[20]

The Jewish leaders of Jesus' time went beyond this attitude. They distinguished between neighbor and enemy. A rabbinical saying ruled that heretics, informers, and renegades "should be pushed [into the ditch] and not pulled out,"[21] and a widespread saying in Israel exempted one's enemies from one's duty to love others: "You shall love your fellow-countryman; but you need not love your enemy."[22] Even Philo said, "The Jew must first show love to his fellow Israelite: he stands at the center; round him are proselytes and resident aliens; then follow enemies, slaves, beasts, and plants in ever-widening circles until at last we arrive at the love of all creation."[23] Jesus' teaching regarding love for enemies (Matt. 5:43–48) is a "rebuke," says Henry, "to this degeneration of the spirit of revealed ethics into a political morality comparable to that of the Gentiles."[24]

Unlike those around him, Jesus demanded a love toward strangers and even those considered enemies. This Christian love (ἀγαπή, equivalent to the Hebrew אהב) does not choose who is a stranger, enemy, or friend. None of these are loved because they add to or subtract from us; they are loved because they are human beings in the *imago Dei*. Ramsey elucidates:

Never is it said that "neighbor" includes "enemy" among those who ought to be loved because they are human beings, but rather that love for another *for his own sake*, neighborly love in the Christian sense, discovers the neighbor in every man it meets and as such has never yet met a friend or an enemy. Christian love does not mean discovering the essentially human underneath differences; it means detecting the neighbor underneath friendliness or hostility or any other qualities in which the agent takes special interest.[25]

The words of Jesus, in which he chides them for merely loving friends, ring clear in light of disinterested love:[26]

You have heard that it was said, "Love your neighbor and hate your enemy." But I tell you: Love your enemies and pray for those who persecute you, that you may be sons of your Father in heaven. He causes his sun to rise on the evil and the good, and sends rain on the righteous and the unrighteous. If you love those who love you, what reward will you get? Are not even the tax collectors doing that? And if you greet only your brothers, what are you doing more than others? Do not even pagans do that? Be perfect, therefore, as your heavenly Father is perfect. (Matt. 5:43–48; see also Luke 6:27, 32, 35)

Ramsey amplifies this teaching of Jesus when he says that a Christian "does not love his enemy for being his enemy any more than he loves his friend merely for being his friend: in either case he loves his neighbor, in spite of his hostility or, what may be just as much a hindrance, *in spite* of his friendship. Love for enemy simply provides a crucial test for the presence or absence of regard for the neighbor for his own sake."[27]

Ramsey, continuing, enlightens this emphasis:

Properly understood in the same sense, loving one's enemy is no more difficult than loving one's friend or the man next door with Christian love. Instances in which an enemy is excepted from neighbor-love and hated on account of his hostility are really no more unusual than excepting a friend from neighbor-love and loving him merely on account of his friendliness. In the case of a friendly neighbor it is possible in loving him to love only his friendliness toward us in return. Then he is not loved for his own sake. He is loved for the sake of his friendliness, for the sake of the benefits to be gained from reciprocal friendship. Thus, very often, love for a friend shows up as "enlightened selfishness," which is a very good thing, indeed, in comparison with crude selfishness, but still quite different from Christian love for neighbor.[28]

Who, then, is my neighbor? This is the burning question that the lawyer poses to Jesus, thinking that he has escaped the Teacher's grasp. Kierkegaard poignantly observes that the teaching of Jesus leaves no doubt of who the neighbor is, either for the lawyer of the story or for all of us. It is now forever impossible to be mistaken about the neighbor's identity: "You can never confuse him with another man, for all men are the neighbor. If you confuse another man with your neighbor, then in the last analysis there is no mistake, for the other man is also your neighbor."[29] The ultimate Christian teaching, then, is found in the admonition of the writer of Hebrews that the Christian is to do "good unto all men" (Heb. 13:16 KJV).

HOW SHOULD WE APPROACH THE
INTERPRETATION OF THE PARABLE?

The Allegorical Method

Especially due to the influence of Clement of Alexandria and his pupil Origen, for centuries the parables were treated by much of the church as allegories in which each term stood as a cryptogram for an idea. A person was required to decode the parable term by term. Probably the most famous example of this approach is Augustine's interpretation of the parable of the Good Samaritan:

> *A certain man went down from Jerusalem to Jericho;* Adam himself is meant;
>   *Jerusalem* is the heavenly city of peace, from whose blessedness Adam fell;
>   *Jericho* means the moon, and signifies our mortality, because it is born, waxes, wanes, and dies.
>   *Thieves* are the devil and his angels.
>   *Who stripped him,* namely, of his immortality;
>   *and beat him,* by persuading him to sin;
>   *and left him half-dead,* because insofar as man can understand and know God, he lives, but insofar as he is wasted and oppressed by sin, he is dead; he is therefore called *half-dead.*
>   The *priest* and *Levite* who saw him and passed by signify the priesthood and ministry of the Old Testament, which could profit nothing for salvation.
>   *Samaritan* means Guardian, and therefore the Lord Himself is signified by this name.
>   The *binding of the wounds* is the restraint of sin.
>   *Oil* is the comfort of good hope;
>   *Wine* the exhortation to work with fervent spirit.
>   The *beast* is the flesh in which He deigned to come to us.
>   The being *set upon the beast* is belief in the incarnation of Christ.
>   The *inn* is the church, where travelers returning to their heavenly country are refreshed after pilgrimage.
>   The *morrow* is after the resurrection of the Lord.
>   The *two pence* are either the precepts of love, or the promise of this life and of that which is to come.
>   The *innkeeper* is the Apostle (Paul). The supererogatory payment is either his counsel of celibacy, or the fact that he worked with his own hands lest he should be a burden to any of the weaker brethren when the Gospel was new, though it was lawful for him "to live by the Gospel."[30]

The Typical Method

The approach of Augustine is easily dismissed by the modern mind not easily affected by allegorical thought, but the temptation to consider the parable of the Good Samaritan as a type of Christ and redemption is not so easily dismissed. Rather than taking the parable at face value, it is attractive to see in the parable the person of Jesus and the redemption he brought to the world. John Martin exemplifies this approach when he speaks of two levels of meaning in the parable. The first level is the "plain teaching that a person, like the Samaritan, should help others in need."[31] Martin continues regarding the second level:

> However, in the context of the rejection of Jesus, it should also be noted in this parable that the Jewish religious leaders rejected the man who fell among the robbers. A Samaritan, an outcast, was the only one who helped the man. Jesus was like the Samaritan. He was the outcast One, who was willing to seek and to save people who were perishing. He was directly opposed to the religious establishment. The theme is reminiscent of Jesus' words to the Pharisees (7:44–50). The theme of Jesus' going to those who needed Him became more and more evident.[32]

The typical approach, though not totally abandoning the plain meaning of the passage, still commits the error of placing into the text something not immediately evident in the teaching itself or even implied by Jesus. Using this technique leaves one with the question, "Why not see other possible types of Jesus in the parable or even other types for other persons and events in the parable?" For example, why would Jesus not be a type of the beaten and robbed man? He was taken advantage of by religious leaders, finally even put to death.

The Literal Method

The most natural way to interpret the parable is literally. This is not meant to disparage the figurative nature of parables but to recognize that parables are given to teach, at most, a few truths, but those truths should relate to the contextual setting of the parable and the theological development of the gospel writer. Here the issue relates to the specific question of the lawyer, "Who is my neighbor?" so the emphasis of the parable should be to elucidate that point.

THE INTERPRETATION OF LUKE 10:25–37

Good Questions with Bad Motives—Luke 10:25

What must I do to inherit eternal life? In Luke 10:25–37, the gospel writer presents Jesus before a crowd of listeners hanging on his every word. From this crowd comes a lawyer, an expert in the laws of Israel and Moses. The man addresses Jesus as Teacher, someone who had the position of authority in presenting the revelation of God to His people of Israel. As a Teacher of

Israel, a rabbi, the man from Galilee had awesome responsibility to set forth what the lawgiver Moses and the subsequent prophets had revealed about God's will for His people.

The lawyer could have asked Jesus many questions, questions that many other lawyers and religious leaders had asked Jesus before to find fault. Many of their questions related to transient and temporary issues, often matters of secondary importance. On one occasion the Pharisees questioned Him and His disciples as to why they did not properly honor the Sabbath (Luke 6:1–11). Whereas in the records of Matthew 12:1–8 and Luke 6:1–5 the purpose of the account's inclusion was to emphasize the lordship of Christ over the Sabbath—after all, as the Creator of all things, Jesus created the Sabbath—in Mark, Jesus used the question to teach that people were more important than the observance of religious rituals. In fact, He says that God actually created these activities for the benefit of humans: "And He said to them, 'The Sabbath was made for man, and not man for the Sabbath.'"[33] At another time He was asked to arbitrate regarding a theological debate between the Sadducees and the Pharisees on the resurrection. Certainly the issue of resurrection was important, but the manner of the discussion moved from intelligent theological concerns to absurd logic.[34]

Here, however, we have a lawyer asking the pivotal question for all humanity, "What shall I do to inherit eternal life?" This question was asked by others of Jesus,[35] but only here does Christ take this eternal question and seemingly tie it to temporal matters. One's vertical relationship to God is the most important matter that a human must confront.[36] Though this expert in the law posed the question of participation in God's future kingdom, the text indicates that he did not do so sincerely; he asked the question to *test* Jesus. It is not clear how this question may be compared with others asked by lawyers and religious leaders who sought to position Jesus in conflict with either Rome, the people, or religious leaders, or with a tricky theological issue that the rabbis had been debating for years. This question, as already noted, was the right question to ask, and it was properly addressed to the one Person who could answer it, the Giver of Life Himself.

Whatever the reason for the particular question, the matter of motives is central to the asking of the question. Here this legal scholar from the outset was not really interested in the answer Jesus gave. When Jesus responded to his answer in verse 28, the lawyer who sought to put the Lord on the witness stand found himself uneasy with the implications of the answer. He sought to justify himself.

Jesus' answer to this lawyer indicates that he considered a way of life as important but does not require the concept of salvation by works. Marshall says, "Just as in John 6:28f. the 'work' required is faith, so here it is love, an inner disposition, not an outward qualification."[37] Moreover, one need understand the request to be for blessings in the future kingdom of God rather than justification per se. The perspective of inheritance speaks of obtaining this blessing.

We have our questions too! The problem of how to find eternal life is one that each of us must face, but there are other questions too that must be addressed in this life. There were many other major questions that a sincere seeker could have asked Jesus. Establishing a vertical relationship with God is primary and logically correct for a true disciple of the Lord, but it is the wrong place to stop. Jesus took the young lawyer to the next level of discussion, namely, the horizontal dimensions of life. There is an old adage that we are not to be so heavenly minded that we are of no earthly good. God wants people to challenge Him to the hard questions of life. He does not turn aside the inquirer or even the doubter. Too many people are willing to go through life and never really penetrate the superficial, to seek the satisfying answers of the deeper knowledge of the world around us. The "enquirer's theological knowledge is of no avail if his life is not governed by love to God and his 'friend.'"[38]

What are our motives? There are many difficult questions on life and death about which we wonder. How do we balance the life of the unborn child against the concerns of a pregnant woman? When do we cease providing treatment for a terminally ill or comatose patient? These are matters with which we have deep feelings. Foremost, however, in our research and activities must be proper motive. This is a major concern. Are our actions honorable and ethical? Do they come from the desire to be honest with facts, to look outside our own selfish desires? Are they within the framework of treating other persons as being in the image of God and worthy in themselves of our concern? Too often our motives are suspect.

Good Answers with Inadequate Application—Luke 10:26–28

A theologically correct answer is offered. The lawyer in this story knew the law. Whether he had heard Jesus speak these words or whether he had drawn the proper conclusions from his study of Deuteronomy 6:5[39] and Leviticus 19:18[40] is unknown. We need to note here that Jesus' concern is the written words of God in the Old Testament rather than the oral traditions of the rabbis. The rabbis, when confronted by similar ideas, drove the students to the commentaries on the Scripture, whereas Jesus sent them to the revelation of God. The rabbis sought to deal with all the commandments without placing any one above the other, whereas Jesus views these commandments to be the completion and fullness of the law:

> Jesus stands entirely outside the evolution of Jewish legalism for the reason that he taught not simply the superiority of love for God and for the neighbor over any other commandment; what is more, he taught that these commands were infinitely superior to all the rest. . . . Man's obligation arose out of these two commandments alone, there could be no conflict with other parts of Torah, this was for him the *whole* law of God.[41]

When confronted with the issue posed by the lawyer, he posed a retort that forced a solution to life in the attitude of love required by the author of love.

Sometimes we fail to do what is right because we do not have our theology straight: This is ignorance. The lawyer provided the correct answer to the quizzing of Jesus. He had no excuse for his lack of proper understanding of the demands of God expressed in the law. Had he considered the ramifications of God's commandments, he would not have needed the further lesson provided in the parable of the Good Samaritan.

The failure of most modern medicine and law in the matter of ethics is that there is no real basis for ethics. If there are right and wrong, good and evil, the knowledge of these absolutes resides outside humanity, and they stand as objective realities whether a person recognizes or honors them. On the other hand, if truth and ethics are relative and reside only within the subjective opinion of each person, then there can never be a final answer to our concerns of abortion, euthanasia, or other medical or social ethics matters. If there are no absolutes, then all ethics are defined in the subjective opinions of each of us; and if rules are established, it is merely a matter of transient contemporary consensus or force, which changes with the power structure.

Our greatest ally to gain the high moral ground in this or any other ethical debate is to refuse to let the flag of absolute reality be lowered, despite ridicule or pressure of other sorts. Eventually the foolishness of religionless ethics and morals will be unable to stand against this epistemological bulwark.

Sometimes we fail to do what is right in spite of having good theology: This is slothfulness, if not rebellion. The lawyer really had the proper answer and ethical response in his grasp. His theology was good, but he chose to avoid the implications of his doctrine. When finally he was forced to admit the Samaritan's righteous acts toward the wounded Jewish man, in contrast to the Jewish religious leaders, he still could not bring himself to say "the Samaritan" but instead "he who showed mercy" (Luke 10:37 NIV).

Improper Responses to God's Direction

The lawyer sought to alleviate his guilt. The text says that on receiving the response by Jesus on how to live—a response demanding action on his part—the lawyer sought to "justify himself."

> The lawyer is depicted as wishing to justify his earlier question and regain the initiative after the command which he has just received. He looks rather foolish having asked a question to which he himself has been forced to give the answer; Jesus has said in effect, 'You have no need to ask me the question about eternal life; as a lawyer you know the answer. All you have to do is practice what you preach.' So he professes inability to practice the law until its meaning has been clarified.[42]

Confronted with the obvious responsibility to contexualize his theology, to move beyond orthodoxy to orthopraxy, the lawyer feigned ignorance. He would be more than willing to practice the law he claimed to honor if only he could figure out who his neighbor was.

What are our attempts? Most of us have become aware of the issues relating to life and death, but the ultimate question is not what we know or believe but what we are doing in real terms to rescue people who are being unjustly treated by the legal, medical, and popular cultures. Those who do not fit the current image of worthiness—i.e., inadequate quality of life—are simply relegated to a status less than full persons. We must never let ourselves think or act in these terms. Even those of us who are pro-life may err in this area of equity and dignity for all persons, judging persons because of their utility rather than simply because they are in the image of God.

God's Teaching on Fulfilling the Second Table of the Law: Love Your Neighbor as Yourself

Christ poses a politically incorrect example. Jesus poses the story of the Jewish man robbed and left for dead. First the priest comes by and second the Levite. Popular stories of the time would include a third person of a triad, and the crowds would expect an Israelite layman, setting forth an anticlerical point.[43] Jesus' mention of a Samaritan would have been totally unexpected and no doubt caused inner conflict for the Jewish listener. In the Greek text there is a clear grammatical contrast between the priest, the Levite, and the Samaritan since "Samaritan" occurs in the emphatic position of the sentence (Luke 10:33). As much as the Israelites would have been willing for Christ to poke fun or bring into disrepute the self-righteous temple leaders, making a Samaritan the hero of a story was unacceptable or politically incorrect. Christ, however, was not attempting to win laurels from the people or the lawyer but to cause them to confront the truth and the implications of that truth for their daily living.

Hesitation in stating the truth in an agnostic society is unworthy of one who seeks to be a follower of the great Teacher.

Helping people when they make bad decisions. The wounded man in the parable was traveling from Jerusalem to Jericho. There was a drop of thirty-three hundred feet in elevation over the course of only seventeen miles, and this road was well known for treacherous bandits. In view of this the Roman army patrolled the road. One could say that the man brought his calamity on himself. The road was not well traveled, and a person might have to wait a considerable time for help to come by.[44]

The sometimes failure of religiously motivated people. The fact that the first two persons who came across this unfortunate man on the road were religious leaders is no accident. These are the persons who one would expect would be the first to come to the aid of the weak and injured. Sad to say, as many have experienced in their attempts to publicize ethical concerns in society, the clergy often are the greatest obstacles encountered. For some reason many in the clergy mistakenly believe that social issues are inferior to the loftier goals they seek to preach. This dichotomy of secular and sacred, the eternal and now, smacks of a gnostic element in the church who believe that God is unconcerned with the current problems of life. It is little more than the "be warm, be filled" response condemned in the New Testament.

Some believe that concerning ourselves with so-called worldly problems distracts us from spiritual issues or causes us to lose an anticipation of the Lord's return. Yet we observe in the life of Jesus the incarnation of God in its fullness. God has made himself near to us and given us an example of love to follow, the person of Jesus. Believers are called to sacrifice and service, not to large congregations and successful programs.

The church must be willing to fly in the face of the culture to uphold the needy and rejected if she would follow her Lord. And this attitude does not depend on considerations of race, creed, religion, or particular beliefs.

Doing good requires sacrifice. The Good Samaritan stopped to help the Jewish man on the road. The text says his immediate response was compassion (Luke 10:33). Pride causes the potential helper to turn aside from the work of God.

The Samaritan did not hesitate in using up his wealth and possessions to come to the aid of the wounded man. Whereas the religious leaders saw their spiritual duties to take priority over helping the man in need, the Samaritan surrendered what he had for the benefit of a person he had never met. He probably tore his headdress for a bandage, poured oil to mollify the wounds, and used wine for disinfectant. He put the man on his donkey and took him to an inn. The Samaritan gave two denarii to the innkeeper for the room and board of the injured Jew. The costs of a day's board would be about one-twelfth of a denarius, so we may see that he did not leave the man stranded. He also promised to provide more money if necessary when he made his return trip (Luke 10:35).

One sees in this story a person who went far beyond talk to the performance of deeds.

Christ Frames the Question Correctly: Who Will Be a Neighbor?

The all-important "I will." Christ's question to the lawyer at the end of his parable turned the question of the lawyer on its head. The lawyer said that if he could only recognize his neighbor, he would be willing to fulfill the law of God (Luke 10:29). Jesus never addresses this question. Note Jesus does not ask at the end, "Which of these three, do you think, knew best who his neighbor was?" Instead he asked who proved to be a neighbor (Luke 10:36). One does not need to define who is a neighbor. One needs to be a neighbor.

Ramsey sets forth the sense of the meaning of the parable.

> This parable tells us something about neighbor-love, nothing about the neighbor. What the parable does is to demand that the questioner revise entirely his point of view, reformulating the question first asked so as to require neighborliness of himself rather than anything of his neighbor. A shift is made from defining the qualities of the man who rightfully ought to be loved to the specific demand that the questioner himself become a neighbor. The parable actually shows the nature and meaning of Christian love which alone of all ethical standpoints discovers the neighbor because it alone begins with neighborly love and not with discriminating between worthy and unworthy people according to the qualities they possess. Perhaps

it would be better to forgo using the expression "love for neighbor," which puts the emphasis on who the neighbor is, and use instead "neighbor-love" or "neighborly love," expressions which have the advantage of stressing what love ought to be.[45]

The importance of openness. The Jewish lawyer had difficulty in transcending racial barriers in responding to Jesus' call for a response. Jesus, on the other hand, called for the irrelevancy of racial considerations, demonstrating that the giving and receiving of mercy transcends national and racial barriers.

Christ's Short But Unequivocal Command: Go and Do the Same as the Good Samaritan

The command of Jesus is clear and unequivocal: "Go and do likewise" (Luke 10:37 NIV). The problem of the lawyer, and usually of us, is not whether we know what to do but whether we are willing to do what we know.

QUESTIONS AND IMPLICATIONS ON THE MATTER OF EUTHANASIA

I believe that there are several crucial questions for each of us to answer in this debate, and there are a number of principles and implications that one may derive from the parable. A careful examination of the discussion between Christ and the lawyer and the parable of the Good Samaritan answers many of these questions.

Questions for Christians to Consider on Euthanasia

Does anyone have the moral right to participate in active euthanasia? From the discussion of the lawyer and Jesus in Luke 10:25 we can draw some implications to answer this question. To participate in active euthanasia is failure to love God and to love neighbor. Love of God is not merely an affirmation that He exists but a commitment to obey His commands, live in fellowship with Him, and recognize His uniqueness as our Creator and Savior. Active euthanasia is failing to recognize the uniqueness of God as the giver of life and presuming the right to end life. How can we truly love God and yet desire to usurp His authority and right as the giver of life?

Should an individual, for humanitarian reasons, be able to end suffering by any means necessary? At first glance one of the strongest arguments for the "right" of euthanasia is a call to humanitarianism in the face of unending pain. Although participation in the alleviation of pain is essential to the parable (here the Samaritan does not end the suffering but assists the sufferer through the pain back to health), the context is given of loving God and loving our neighbor. Therefore humanitarianism not founded in loving God and loving neighbor can only be founded in egoistic or utilitarian principles. Social, medical, and legal matters should not be divorced from a theological base if they are to have any reasonable legitimacy or moral force. The utilitarian arguments of our day provide little capacity to support and defend the weak persons among us. The attempt to do this has left the discussion of life and

death issues in a sea of nebulousness and relativity. In regard to the matter of
ending life, the primary issue must be the fact that all humans have been
created in the image of God. It is the fact of being equally created in the
image of God that motivates the Samaritan to action.

*Are there not, in fact, some people who have no quality of life, and therefore ending
their lives would be acts of mercy?* This question arises from the false assumption
that man's ability substantiates his right and responsibility to life. The idea of
the quality of life is foreign to the parable of the Good Samaritan. In fact there
is no mention of age, social standing, intellect, or race of the man who is beaten
by the robbers. The beaten man's quality of life is not a factor in the mind of
the Samaritan. The only determining factor for the Samaritan is that a human
life, equal to his own, is at stake. If the Samaritan's pity had been motivated by
humanitarian mercy based on utilitarian principles, then he would have needed
to ascertain the wounded man's usefulness in society versus the risk involved
in helping this man or the need to help more useful people with his finances.
If the euthanasia debate is decided along utilitarian lines, the question of
euthanasia will become one of a person's social usefulness. The atrocities for
all minorities under this system will be far removed from the original question
of mercy for those "lacking quality of life."

Implications for the Euthanasia Debate

There are several implications that arise from the teaching of Jesus in Luke
10:25–37.

*We must never separate ultimate theological questions from practical realities of
everyday life.* The lawyer was concerned with the future blessings of God,
which was certainly appropriate, but Jesus sought to drive him to an awareness
of his current responsibilities in this life. Theological questions, then, need
practical applications.

*When dealing with the helpless, the Samaritan is seen as the morally superior
person.* Though the priest and Levite had the public position of moral duty,
it is the despised among the people who stood forth with moral action.
Dietrich Bonhoeffer is correct when he argues that the strong man is the
one who is ready to risk his life for a lesser man, and the sound man for the
sick.[46] He continues that the "idea of destroying a life which has lost its social
usefulness is one which springs from weakness, not from strength."[47]

Humans can always find excuses for failure to do the will of God. Had the
Samaritan left the wounded man on the road, as did the priest and the Levite,
he would never have served as such an example for us of the love of God. He
could have argued that the man was probably dead and after all he was in a
hurry. He could have said that it was too expensive to take care of the person.
He could have rationalized as a Samaritan that Jews were his enemies and
the person was not worthy of his help. He could have said that his chances of
life were meager and that he should simply let him die rather than seek to
prolong his life. He could have declared that it was an act of mercy to allow
him to die rather than prolong his agony. He could have absolved himself in
spite of the clear teaching of Jesus.

Our prejudices can get in the way of our doing the work of God. Issues of race, sex, disability, incapacity, position in society are illegitimate walls that separate us from fulfilling our duties to one another. When we fail to see each person as being our neighbor simply because of some perceived deficiency, we err in not seeing the image of God that person shares in common with us. Helmut Thielicke said that it is not only this act of creation that gives each person worth, but that Christ has bought each person with a price and bestowed on him or her an "alien dignity."[48] This dignity asserts itself at the very point that a person's value is questioned, where "his functional value is no longer listed on society's stock market and he is perhaps declared to be 'unfit to live.'"[49]

We cannot wait on our religious or legal leaders to lead the way in this battle nor to forge the weapons. The Samaritan was not the example of the parable because of brilliance, leadership qualities, prestige, or influence. He was the hero because he had compassion and responded without hesitation to the situation that God placed before him with the resources that God gave him. He was not trying to save the world; he tried to save the particular person to whom God called him. On the other hand, we don't want to minimize the value of a moral or religious leader who is willing to place others above himself.

A good example of such a leader is Clemens Count von Galen, bishop of Münster, during the horrors of the Third Reich. Quoting at length from the account in *The Nazi Doctors: Medical Killing and the Psychology of Genocide* by Robert Jay Lifton:

> The most ringing Catholic protest against "euthanasia" was the famous sermon of Clemens Count von Galen, then bishop of Münster. It was given on 3 August 1941, just four Sundays after the highly significant pastoral letter of German bishops had been read from every Catholic pulpit in the country; the letter reaffirmed "obligations of conscience" at opposing the taking of "innocent" life, "even if it were to cost us our [own] lives." The first part of Galen's sermon explored the Biblical theme of how "Jesus, the Son of God, wept," how even God wept "because of stupidity, injustice . . . and because of the disaster which came about as a result." Then, after declaring, "It is a terrible, unjust and catastrophic thing when man opposes his will to the will of God," Galen quoted the pastoral letter of 6 July and made clear that the "catastrophic thing" he had in mind was the killing of innocent mental patients and "a doctrine which authorizes the violent death of invalids and elderly people."
>
> He further declared that he himself had "filed formal charges" with police and legal authorities in Münster over deportations from a nearby institution. He went on in words that every farmer and laborer could understand.
>
> "It is said of these patients: They are like an old machine which no longer runs, like an old horse which is hopelessly paralyzed, like a cow which no longer gives milk.
>
> What do we do with a machine of this kind? We put it in the junkyard.

What do we do with a paralyzed horse? No, I do not wish to push the comparison to the end. . . . We are not talking here about a machine, a horse, nor a cow. . . . No, we are talking about men and women, our compatriots, our brothers and sisters. Poor unproductive people if you wish, but does this mean that they have lost their right to live?"[50]

He continues his denunciation of the Nazi regime, speaking of divine justice on those who blaspheme the faith by persecuting clergy and "sending innocent people to their death."[51]

He asked that such people (who could only be the Nazi authorities) be ostracized and left to their divine retribution.

"We wish to withdraw ourselves and our faithful from their influence, so that we may not be contaminated by their thinking and their ungodly behavior, so that we may not participate and share with them in the punishment which a just God should and will pronounce upon all those who . . . do not wish what God wishes!"[52]

Knowing theology is not the same as doing theology. Certainly we must know what is right to do and the reasons for the rightness of our beliefs, but we must make efforts that go beyond belief. A faith that has no works is a dead faith (James 2:17).

The way that Jesus dealt with the lawyer and the people listening to the parable indicates that we need to frame the questions rather than letting other people define them. Often, those who seek to restrain the rise and tragedy of sin and its effects are like the little boy sticking his finger in the dike, futilely trying to keep the onrush of the sea from bursting in on him and his friends. Because of this, the challengers, like the sea, are able to find any number of places to charge in. We must be diligent, then, to set the debate, to establish the agenda, to herald the call to responsibility, and to define what the real issues are in the fight for life. We must take the offensive whenever we can.

Christians, especially, possess great opportunities and have the ability to live the teachings of Christ in front of others. We have been called to an active seeking out of opportunities to sacrifice ourselves for others. There will be no better opportunity than the care of elderly and dying persons. It is not enough to fight against euthanasia; we must also be involved in the providing of care for our "dying neighbors." If we do not actually move to caring for people, we will be similar to the priest and the Levite in the parable.

There are responsibilities on our part to provide pain management. A person should see his or her role as one of comforting, including the limiting or eliminating of pain. The Samaritan was willing and able to go to extreme measures to bring comfort to the wounded man. We should be equally willing to bring comfort that still respects the dignity of being created in the image of God.

The Samaritan was also willing to provide the necessary financial provision to bring comfort to the wounded man. In the near future in this country, economics will play an important role in the discussion of euthanasia. Will believers be willing to provide financial resources when individuals have lost their "usefulness to society?" The desire of some to eliminate the "unproductive elements" of society will provide new and vivid opportunities for believers to prove who is a neighbor.

ENDNOTES

1. See Paul B. Rasor, *A Law Teacher Looks at the Good Samaritan Story*, 31 Washburn L. J. 71 (1991); Robert A. Mason, Note, Good Samaritan Laws—Legal Disarray: An Update, 38 MERCER L. REV. 1439 (1987).

2. I. Howard Marshall, *The Gospel of Luke* 439 (1978).

3. See E. Klostermann, *Das Lukasevangelium Handkommentar Zum NT* 118 (1929); J. Schmid, *Das Evangelium Nach Lukas, Regensburger NT* 190 (1960); E. Earle Ellis, *The Gospel of Luke* 158 (1974); Marshall says, however, that this view does not explain some important factors:

    "First, there are a number of contacts between Mt. and Lk. . . . which strongly suggest that Matthew knew a recension of the story also familiar to Luke. Second, these and some other features are hard to explain as being due to Lucan redaction of Mk.; cf. especially the phrase πῶςἀυγιυυώσκεις and the wording of the second commandment. These two factors make it likely that Luke was following an independent version of the story which was also known to Matthew. . . . It is possible that this version was in Q . . . but we cannot be certain (Marshall, *supra* note 6, at 441).

4. T. W. Manson, *The Sayings of Jesus*, 259–61 (1949).

5. Marshall, *supra* note 6, at 441.

6. Id. at 440.

7. Id.

8. Günther Bornkamm, *Jesus of Nazareth* 110 (Irene McLuskey et al., trans., Harper & Row 1960) (1956).

9. Robert L. Short, *The Parables of Peanuts*, 219 (1968).

10. Bornkamm, *supra* note 18, at 110.

11. Id.

12. "A Christian man lives not in himself but in Christ and his neighbor. Otherwise he is not a Christian. He lives in Christ through faith, in his neighbor through love; by faith he is caught up beyond himself into God, by love he sinks down beneath himself into his neighbor" (Paul Ramsey, *Basic Christian Ethics*, 101 [1954] [quoting Martin Luther, *Treatise on Christian Liberty, in Works II*, 342] [n.d.]).

13. Bornkamm, *supra* note 18, at 111.

14. Ramsey, *supra* note 23, at 95 (quoting Fyodor Dostoyevsky, *The Brothers Karamazov* 56 [Modern Library Giant, n.d.]).

15. Id. at 95 (citing Dostoyevsky, *supra* note 25, at 245–46).

16. Id. at 95.

17. R. E. O. White, *Biblical Ethics*, 83 (1979).

18. Carl F. H. Henry, *Christian Personal Ethics*, 226 (1957).

19. Id. at 226; see also Marshall, *supra* note 6, at 444.

20. Marshall, *supra* note 6, at 444.

21. Joachim Jeremias, *The Parables of Jesus*, 202-203, trans. S. H. Hooke (Charles Scribner's Sons, 1963) (quoting b. 'A. Z. 26a [Bar.]).

22. Id. at 203; see also Matthew 5:43.

23. Henry, su*pra* note 31, at 227 (quoting Philo, De Virtut).
24. Henry, *supra* note 31, at 227.
25. Ramsey, *supra* note 22, at 94.
26. In Thornton Wilder's Julius Caesar we find the opposite, the desire for disinterested hate: "Would it not be a wonderful discovery to find that I am hated to the death by a man whose hatred is disinterested? It is rare enough to find a disinterested love; so far among those that hate me I have uncovered nothing beyond the promptings of envy, of self advancing ambition, or of self-consoling destructiveness. It is many years since I have felt directed toward me a disinterested hatred. Day by day I scan my enemies looking with eager hope for the man who hates me 'for myself' or even 'for Rome'" (Ramsey, *supra* note 22, at 96 [quoting Thornton Wilder, *The Ides of March*, 113, 218 (1948)]).
27. Ramsey, *supra* note 22, at 99.
28. Id. at 96.
29. Kierkegaard, su*pra* note 39.
30. C. H. Dodd, *The Parables of the Kingdom 1–2* (Charles Scribner's Sons, 2d ed. 1961) (quoting St. Augustine, *Quaestiones Evangeloirum II*, 19).
31. John Martin, *Luke*, in The Bible Knowledge Commentary, 233 (John F. Walvoord & Roy B. Zuck eds., 1983).
32. Id. at 234.
33. Mark 2:27 (NIV); the statement by Jesus in Mark 2:27 had a similar parallel in Jewish sayings but with an entirely different meaning. Paul Ramsey comments, "The verbally parallel statement which may be cited from a number of rabbis, 'The Sabbath is given for you and not you for the Sabbath,' had, coming from their mouths, an absolutely different meaning. It meant: the Sabbath is given *for you to keep*, in order that you and your servants and domestic animals may have rest" (Ramsey, *supra* note 22, at 63).
34. Matthew 22:23–33; Mark 12:18–27; Luke 20:27–40.
35. Matthew 19:16–22; Luke 18:18–23; see John 3:1–15.
36. Rabbi Eliezer (ca. A.D. 90) was asked by his students, "Rabbi, teach us the ways of life so that by them we may attain to the life of the future world" (Marshall, *supra* note 6, at 442 [quoting b Ber. 28b; SB 1, 808]).
37. Marshall, *supra* note 6, at 442.
38. Jeremias, *supra* note 33, at 202.
39. See *supra* note 8.
40. See *supra* note 9.
41. Ramsey, *supra* note 22, at 65.
42. Marshall, *supra* note 6, at 447.
43. Jeremias, *supra* note 33, at 204 (quoting B. T. D. Smith, *The Parables of the Synoptic Gospels*, 180 [1937]).
44. The Greek text uses the word *sugkuria*, which means "coincidence" or "chance."
45. Ramsey, *supra* note 22, at 93.
46. Dietrich Bonhoeffer, *Ethics* (1955).
47. Id.
48. Helmut Thielicke, 3 *Theological Ethics: Sex*, 231 (Eerdmans, 1979) (1975).
49. Id.
50. Robert Jay Lifton, Th*e Nazi Doctors: Medical Killing and the Psychology of Genocide*, 93–94 (1986).
51. Id. at 94.
52. Id.

PART 5

PASTORAL AND PERSONAL REFLECTIONS

An Overview

The lives of people who commit suicide are complex, and their mental and emotional pain is substantial. Through a candid look into the life of a struggling evangelist and famous painter, Vincent van Gogh, we become aware of the process that leaves a person helpless, isolated, and eventually hopeless. Then a wife, who suffered the loss of her husband to suicide, openly discusses her thoughts and emotions in a letter she wrote to her husband after his death. Regrettably, the tears that lead to suicide become the tears of those who are left behind.

Chapter Twenty-Six

SUICIDE'S COMPANION
A Trail of Tears

Gary P. Stewart

SUICIDE IS A PERMANENT, INTENTIONAL AND SELFISH action taken against one's self in order to eliminate what for the moment appears to be unrelenting and unaltering pain. It is a tragic culmination of a process in which unresolved events converge, leaving a person lonely, depressed, and thoroughly hopeless.[1] The popular notion that "suicide is a permanent solution to a temporary problem" sounds plausible but fails to grasp the intensity and complex circumstances that surround and lead to the hopelessness that provokes suicidal consideration. Though suicide is permanent, the reasons that provoke suicide are generally, if not always, long term. One unresolved problem seldom leads to suicide unless that one problem remains unresolved for an extended period of time, e.g., extensive paralysis. For the vast majority of suicides, there is an undercurrent of unresolved issues that continue to mount until they become a river of despair and unending pressure from which there seems no escape. Rather than live in a state of perpetual drowning, people choose to escape the raging river through the use of suicide.

The more an individual fails to resolve life's challenges, the greater risk he or she takes of developing psychological handicaps connected with depression and substance abuse. For this reason, studies from 1958 to the present have revealed that psychiatric illness is present in over 90 percent of those who commit suicide.[2] Though some people *may* have genetic disorders that affect their ability to handle difficult situations, I believe the vast majority of suicides are the result of normal people's not being able to resolve difficult events that mount throughout their lives. Speaking of his father, Ross Lockridge Jr. (author of the controversial novel *Raintree County*), Larry Lockridge affirms that it was "one thing after another, in a *relentless sequence of events* that wore my father down. He was a vulnerable person *caught in a web of events* he couldn't negotiate" (emphasis added).[3] Jesus' desire to give us rest from our burdens (Matt. 11:28) and Paul's admonition to carry one another's burdens (Gal. 6:1–2) gives evidence to the destructive force that *continued* physical, mental, emotional, and spiritual burdens bring to a person. Relief is necessary to survival!

Suicide is the hinge on which the trail of tears for one's earthly life closes and the trail of tears in the lives of others is thrown wide open. What is difficult, painful, and hopeless to the one who commits suicide becomes the difficulty, confusion, and pain of those who must pick up the pieces of an unwanted and unchosen new life. This chapter will look at both sides of the door that hinges on one's irreversible decision to commit suicide. First we will examine the life of the famous painter, Vincent van Gogh, to uncover the trials that led to his suicide at the age of thirty-seven. Then we will look on the back side of suicide through the tear-stained eyes of a woman whose husband chose suicide over life. His story is told by her own hand through a letter she wrote to him, after his death, as a response to his suicide note. The letter chronicles the trail of tears that she and her three children have experienced because of the death the man they loved chose to escape his own trail of tears.

VINCENT VAN GOGH

His Personal Life

Vincent van Gogh was born in the Netherlands in 1853 to a minister who lived life from a legalistic perspective, always concerned about evil and materialism and the effects they could have on corrupting his family. He was opposed to any literature or ideas outside of the Bible itself:

> Pastor van Gogh's dealing with his children apparently emphasized human sin and the enormity of the world's evil, and this likely played its role in determining Vincent's attraction for the narrow path. If this deep suspicion of the world were accompanied by the affirmation that the van Gogh elders were "pure gold" and so deserved perfection from their children, one might well expect a heavy burden of guilt and anxiety on Vincent and Theo.[4]

Vincent's father was constantly reminding his son that his interest in reading Michelet and Victor Hugo would corrupt his mind the same way it did a great uncle who was infected with French ideas and became an alcoholic. Vincent wanted to please his father but his interest in books (which included the Bible to a great extent), art, and nature left him and his father disconnected. Though he tried to abandon his reading to please his father, even be more like his father by becoming an evangelistic preacher, he eventually became disenchanted with a dispassionate faith that focused on the evils of the world, and he began to pursue a life that would bring love and meaning to himself; he renewed his interest in the literature of his time and in art. His disassociation with his father left Vincent hurting and sometimes angry; it was a problem that found no resolve. "Upon his father's death, Vincent renounced his part in the inheritance, sent his father's most precious possession, a Bible, to Theo (his younger brother), and moved out of the parsonage forever."[5]

Vincent also had to deal with the reality of being unpleasant to the eye. His appearance and mannerisms were viewed by many as awkward. Vincent had an ugly exterior and often looked forlorn beyond his years. A schoolmate of Vincent later described him as "an ugly red-headed boy who liked to go by himself on many long walks across the fields. . . ."[6] Noticing the pitiful glances of those who knew him and from whom he wanted so much but could receive so little, he removed himself to solitude. But his desire to find love and to provide love never left him. Vincent believed that the "best way to know God is to love many things. Love a friend, a wife, something—whatever you like—you will be on your way to knowing more about Him." At least two times, possibly three, he opened up his heart to the hope of loving a wife only to experience heartache and rejection. Vincent also felt deeply for the pain and suffering of the poor working class, so much so that he often deprived himself of sleep and food, possibly to identify with them or to exemplify their plight to a detached clergy of which he had become a part and with which he had grown weary and frustrated. Ken Gire describes the turmoil that filled the soul of a man screaming for love while being heard by none but his brother, Theo:

> To feel so deeply, to want to communicate those feelings so passionately, and yet to have people stand off at a distance, shake their heads, and walk away. Eventually his physical, spiritual, mental, and emotional states all deteriorated. Darkness was everywhere.[7]

It is also plausible that Vincent struggled from the realities of being a replacement child. His parents had lost a child a year prior to his birth whose name just also happened to be Vincent. Scholars vary on their understanding of the extent of the impact being a substitute child may have had on Vincent; some believe that the impact was great, while others, like Edwards, believe that there is not enough evidence in his personal letters to suggest that he was adversely affected.[8] However, it is hard to reject the fact that there is a notion of replacement in the minds of his parents, seeing they used the same name, Vincent. Could it be that Vincent was unable to fulfill the expectations his parents had transferred from the first Vincent to the second? Was this another aspect of Vincent's life for which he was unable to find resolve? Quite likely there was some negative psychological effect that Vincent was unable to overcome. This fact may help to explain his awkwardness, distant countenance, and, quite possibly, his compassion for the less fortunate. Dr. David Allen discusses the impact of childhood hurt.

> Sadly, a child's worth is very fragile, and so often when children are hurt their world falls apart. The child looks for support. If that support is not available or accessible, the child buries the hurt deep inside. As this process continues, these hurts, embodying many feelings and psychic energy, are repressed within the inner real self. Then the child develops a defensive, false self to cope with the world.[9]

Vincent's trail of tears was saturated with rejection, loneliness, and disappointment that permeated his personal life; however, his disappointment went beyond his personal life to his professional life as well.[10] For him, life was a series of unresolved events that continued to mount until isolation in nature and art became his last attempt to inform the world of his identity and longings.

His Professional Life

Van Gogh's search for meaningfulness took him through a career as a clerk at an art establishment, with the clergy, and finally as an artist. He seemed to be doing well as a clerk. As time passed, he gradually put his interests in art and reading aside (he had sadly come to accept the erroneous belief that his love for art, nature, and literature were not consistent with a sound theology) and devoted much of his time to reading the Scripture. He even informed his brother Theo of his intent to destroy his books, and suggested Theo do the same. His desire to fulfill his father's dream of having another van Gogh in the ministry was compelling; even his father's narrow approach to study had tremendous influence. (His natural love for nature and art would remain in constant conflict with his father's, as well as the clergy's narrow understanding of ministry, until 1880, when Vincent focused all his attention on art.)

In 1876, after being dismissed from the art establishment because of his seclusive lifestyle, Vincent began assisting a Methodist preacher in Isleworth, England. His preaching and visitation with the local people gave Vincent the confidence that he had found his way in life; he was so full of energy and commitment that some, including his own sister-in-law, viewed his efforts as fanatical. Even his father was not pleased with this simple ministry to the poor; the itinerant ministry of a Methodist preacher didn't compare with the prestige and stability afforded a minister of the Dutch Reformed Church. His family convinced him to return home where he began to study for entry examinations for the university under the watchful eye of his well-known uncle, who was a pastor in the Reformed Church.

Becoming frustrated with academics and believing that he would not pass the entry exams, Vincent rejected family counsel and gave up studying for the university and in 1878 entered a missionary training school in Brussels. He was given a six month probationary appointment as an evangelist to a poor mining district called Borinage. Unwilling to submit to the authority of his supervisors, he was dismissed from his job in 1879. By this time, Vincent had returned to reading other literature and doing sketches. His empathy for the poor shaped the direction of his art. He wanted to paint things as they really were and through his painting, speak to the world about his concerns and sorrows. He spent the remaining ten years of his life pursuing art (he was especially enchanted with the simplicity of nature as depicted through Japanese art—he seems to have been influenced by the Zen-Buddhist teaching that promotes spiritual oneness by intertwining oneself with nature), misunderstood by his father, passionate for the suffering of the poor, in debt, and discouraged. Eventually, he admitted himself to an asylum in 1889.

Vincent van Gogh's trail of tears ended with a pistol shot to his side that took two days to take his life. Too many unresolved events left him alone looking to nature for meaning. A man who so badly needed love sought to find it in an environment that would not provide it. Nature is given for our enjoyment, but not as our sustainer. His father's faith taught him only of the horror of sin and its power to destroy. It failed to teach Vincent of the love and forgiveness that he had read about in Scripture, yet never saw in practice among the clergy he wanted to please. Believers who fail to surround themselves with friends who love them or believers who are unable to find support and love in the local church, often find themselves carrying burdens from which they find no relief. Any believer, or congregation, who forgets his or her first love is unable to care for themselves or others who may need them. Solomon informed us years ago that "two are better than one because they have a good return for their labor. For if either of them falls, the one will lift up his companion. But woe to the one who falls when there is not another to lift him up" (Eccl. 4:9–10 NASB).

Believers must place their ultimate priority on knowing and loving Jesus Christ above every other endeavor. Everything, whether it be literature, art, nature, career, friends, or family must remain secondary to one's faith, for only through the eyes of the Savior do we understand these things for what they really are and receive the rewards they bring. Vincent made the mistake of seeing himself through his own eyes and through the eyes of others, rather than through the eyes of the God who loved him for what he was physically and could be morally and spiritually in Christ. The tissue for his tears was always near in the hand of his Savior.

> Through the years of rejection, loneliness, and depression, Vincent's mental state deteriorated. So did the state of his spiritual life. The erosion of faith is chronicled in the letters he wrote over the ten years that spanned his life as an artist. The Scripture quotations, references to God, and reflections of his faith, gradually grew fewer and farther between. At the same time, the anguish and despair grew greater and darker and more turbulent.[11]

It is not surprising to learn that his last words reflected the inner turmoil of a life whose unresolved disappointments created an ocean in which he could do nothing more than drown: *"La tristesse durea."* "The sadness will never go away."

A SURVIVOR'S RESPONSE TO SUICIDE

The following letter was written by Rachel in hopes that those who read it would know the tremendous pain and loss that she and her children have had to endure, but even more, to challenge people not to allow their personal struggles to lead them to the selfish conclusion that suicide will cause their own problems and the problems they have created for their loved ones to disappear. Not only do the problems not go away, they intensify and become more in number. We resolve difficult issues by working through them with a counselor and those we love. Suicide is not a method for resolve; it is an impetus for another trail of tears and a victory for the Destroyer.

Dear Mark,

How could someone I know so well deceive me? Your note said, "I'm sorry, I am not well, I'm no good." This is what you left for a legacy for your loving wife of thirty-three years and three beautiful children who respected, adored, and loved you, a big brother who called you his best friend, and so many others I couldn't begin to count, who were impressed by your work ethic, sense of humor, sincerity, and respected you as a solid Christian man. All the good you did in your life is now *shadowed* by the way you ended your life.

Just in case you want to know what your death has caused your family, let me give you a brief rundown. None of us understand what happened to the faith you had in the Lord. Why did you give up on yourself and Him? Why did you leave us here to try to make sense out of our lives together? As your wife, I want you to know that I feel you threw away my love, devotion, and dedication. You just threw me away after giving you everything I had to give. You left me to deal with all your problems as well as leaving me to grieve the loss of the most important man in my life. I have no sense of belonging, no encourager, no best friend, no lover, no helper, no sweetheart to go on adventures with. I have no one. You have left me empty, with no desire to do anything but mourn and grieve. I have literally lost all the hair on my head due to the trauma and shock. I have been constantly sick because the stress has torn down my immune system. I have horrible nightmares and flashbacks of your body lying in a pool of blood, and I can't sleep much of the time. I don't cook and have no desire to eat. You have broken my heart and my spirit with this terrible act of selfishness.

I want you to know that our first born was married almost a year ago, and it was so painful to sit in that first row without you. It was so horrible watching your son give his sister away because you chose not to be there. The most important day in a young woman's life and our beautiful daughter had to endure the pain of not having you there to hold her hand and give her hugs and encouragement. You missed out on the joy of knowing your son-in-law and his family. God blessed us richly by bringing them into our lives. I know you would have loved them had you stayed. Your only son has been so brave, been a wonderful helper and encourager, and has given up his career as a basketball coach just to be closer to our family. You had so much love and compassion for each of your children. WHY did you do this to them? They are such beautiful people and they surely didn't deserve this heartache. Our youngest daughter just graduated from college with a double-major, was a starter for three years in a Division 1 soccer team and managed to do it all with the honor of magna cum laude. I was so proud of her to have done so well with all the horror she has had to face in her young life. It was so lonely watching her walk across the stage; I needed you to be proud with me and to share this wonderful time in her life. But no, you took the selfish way out. I was angry and I wanted to scream at the top of my lungs, "WHY did you do this to your family?"

It was only seventeen years ago that WE faced my father's suicide together. We cried, grieved, and mourned; both of us couldn't understand it. Now, you have done it too. I still can't believe it. You were the one that kept asking: "WHY did he do this to us?" Did you think it was okay because he did it? I am a woman who has lost the two most important men in her life to suicide, first my father and now my husband. I feel sometimes that it must be me. Didn't I love you enough? What did I do wrong? But God has let me know that I was your encourager, your helper, your lover, your best friend, and I know that I tried everything to save you. Remember the night I was holding you and I said, "Mark, don't ever leave me," and your response was "I Won't." It was only two short weeks later that you left anyway. You gave us no warning. You hid your plan so well. You seemed so much better and we were all so encouraged. I am still shocked by your deceit. It has just blown me away. I trusted you so much that when you told me something, I took it at face value. I shouldn't have trusted you this time. You were always concerned for my safety and care, and yet you knew that I would be the one to shoulder the burden of finding your body. It doesn't make sense.

You were a wonderful husband to me, so loving and patient. We laughed so much because you were so funny. You had a different way of looking at things that never ceased to amaze me. Whenever I was blue, you could cheer me up in a minute. You made me feel so special all the time. I couldn't wait to get home to you because you were so interesting and always, always had those stories of your most unique customers of the day. You told me everyday how nice I looked and how much you loved me. Now, I'm not special to anyone and I have a hard time laughing and nothing seems interesting. You were a great dad and parent partner. You never missed a game or event our children were in. You were a devoted and proud father and that always made me so happy. Didn't you know I and the children would suffer this tremendous pain and emptiness? Yes, you did, because you went through it with Dad's death. There are no excuses for you, Mark. None. This was the most selfish act, and it is hard for me to grasp because you were always the most unselfish person I knew. You were so generous to your children and to me. What made you do such a horrible thing?

I would have lived anywhere or done anything for you. I will never understand why you thought you were a failure when you had so much success. You had very high expectations of yourself and, more importantly, unrealistic expectations. Why did you put wealth and success so high on the ladder when you knew that living a life for Christ is all that counts? We can't take anything from this earth with us. Why did you feel like you were no good when you accomplished so many good things? You were a great teacher, a loving father, a superb husband, an expert craftsman, a compassionate friend, and a wonderfully decent man. You were such a terrific buddy; I could tell you anything and you knew where I was coming from. We could sit in the movie theater and hold hands and feel the love flow between us. I loved our trips to the mountains to see the turning leaves. Remember how we used to guess what each other was hungry for? I would make you write it down on a piece of paper and invariably you would be right on. You knew me like a book and you made my life so rich in love and compassion that my heart was overflowing most of the time. People used to ask me why I was smiling all the time, and I would tell them I had a wonderful husband, three great kids, and God in my life. Why shouldn't I smile? I don't smile as much now. Remember how we always called each other "boyfriend" and "girlfriend" and we made special dates? Remember all the little "Love is . . ." messages we would send each other? Remember how we had to call each other at least once a day and if we didn't, we knew one of us was slightly miffed? That didn't happen often, but we weren't perfect! It was an awesome experience to be your wife and I thank God daily for that. Remember how I would always tell you that God's light was glowing around you the night we met. It truly was. We were only sixteen years old, and I knew at that moment that we would be husband and wife one day. God filled me with love for you, and you have been the only man in my life to truly know me, and I felt great comfort and safety in that. You knew I wasn't perfect but you loved me anyway. You knew I had weaknesses and strengths and you always dwelled on my strengths. I thank you for the confidence you have given me. God definitely matched us up as a team, and boy we were a solid team. We had more adventures and business dealings than most couples will ever experience. We had the ability to compliment each other's strengths and to help each other with our weaknesses. It was truly an awesome relationship. I'm so sorry you got sick, Mark. I'm sorry I couldn't help you more. I tried so hard. I know that God's Word comforted you and that you looked forward to our Bible study and devotions each night. I know the Devil was attacking you and somehow he got in your mind; he really got you in a headlock didn't he? You believed the lies about yourself that he was filling your mind with. You know the Devil pounces on us when we are at our weakest. Those were all lies, Mark. You were a good person. Our lives would have been much more enriched with your presence had you decided to fight the battle with the Devil and believe that you would again be healthy.

I am angry at you for not having faith in the Lord and not trusting Him to get us through whatever it was you were afraid of. I'm angry because you lied when both Pastor John and the psychiatrist asked you if you had considered suicide. Your response, "I have thought of it but I would never do that to my family," made me trust in you. I was certain that you wouldn't do it. You lied and deceived all of us. I have forgiven you, Mark. I know that you had a very tough childhood and maybe things were never resolved there. I don't know. I know that having an alcoholic father and a very unstable home life was not a great experience for you. You have talked many times about how you felt unloved, and you told me that was why you strived to be a loving parent. I know you were ashamed of your brother because he had swindled your parent's farm out from under them and became an alcoholic. I know you were sickened by the fact that your mother always defended him even after he stole everything from them. I know that it troubled you that your nephews were becoming alcoholics just like their father. I don't know if all of this baggage, plus the changes that were taking place in your career, caused you to become so depressed that it consumed you. I just don't know. I can only speculate, and that doesn't help. It doesn't bring you back to me. I only wish you could've verbalized to me what brought it all to the surface. You said many times you couldn't understand why this was happening to you.

I know you are at peace now with the Lord and He is comforting and loving you. You were a faithful servant and a man of God, and I know God has a special place for you in His mansion. I will one day join you; however, none of this takes the horrible loneliness and huge emptiness away each and every day that I have to spend without you. I don't know what God has planned for me, but I feel His Spirit in me, giving me strength to go on. I just don't have the same spark and spunk I had when you were here to share my life with me. We were so strong together and I always felt like we could conquer the world as long as we were together. I know there will never be another man like you, Mark. You were a great person and I thank God every day that I was privileged to be your wife. So until we meet again at Jesus' feet I know I must do all things through Christ who strengthens me.

I will end this letter by saying: "You were the love of my life as well as the greatest disappointment in my life."

Your grieving wife,
Rachel[12]

Could Rachel have done anything to delay or divert her husband's decision to commit suicide? It is difficult to say. People who decide to kill themselves are not always transparent, and when we are aware of their intentions, often their difficulties are deeply emotional, so emotional that sound reason cannot be considered. What we must never do is blame ourselves for the suicide of a loved one. Even though we may have made mistakes or failed to see what someone else considered an obvious sign, the decision to die (or end his or her pain) is in the mind of the person who has reached the point that life is not worth living. Suicide survivors need not add unnecessary pain to what is already one of the most difficult, if not the most difficult, experience of their lives. No matter how difficult or how unbearable life becomes, suicide is never the answer. It is a selfish act that considers the concerns of only one person. Though some victims think they are doing what is right for those around them, I have yet to see a family or friend benefit from the loss of a loved one to suicide.

CONCLUSION

Christ came that we might have abundant life; Satan is here to bring death. Christ died so that we might live; Satan works to destroy all that is good. God is the Father of truth; Satan, the father of lies. We may experience affliction of every kind, but we are never beaten; we may become confused, but we won't despair; people may abuse us, reject us, even attempt to destroy us, but we do not lose hope. Though the world may want us dead, our pursuit of life is a reflection of the hope for eternity that is found in a genuine faith in the Son of God (John 10:10; 2 Cor. 4:8–10, paraphrased). Though some attempt to connect honor to suicide, this idea must be rejected for it throws into the face of God the idea that Christ's death for a dying world is insufficient; that we, in our arrogance, have the right to decide what we do with the life God has loaned us to use for the welfare of others and His glory. Life is a loan that is paid back through faithful service, not a commodity that we can trade or a gift that we can do with as we please. Death is the last enemy, not a peaceful choice of a new generation. All things work together for good to those who love God, not to those who undermine His will. The trail of tears that lead to suicide and the trail of tears that are left in its wake are clear evidences that suicide is not the desire of God. Depression is a warning sign that asks us to evaluate the direction of our lives and make the necessary moral and spiritual changes that are consistent with God's plan. If we fail to heed the signs, depression intensifies and disappointments accumulate until hopelessness becomes the driver of a life out of control. Almost nothing good ever comes from a life that crashes; in fact, the only good that can come from tragedy (especially suicide) is the good that God accomplishes through His gracious work in the survivors who look to Him. Be an ambassador for Christ: each day, reach out to someone and try to accomplish at least one thing that will count for eternity. Love of God, others, and self overcomes the potential disasters that are connected with selfish living.[13]

ENDNOTES

1. Suicide is "permanent" in the material sense. From the immaterial perspective, it is an untimely transition from this life to the next. Cf. Thomas E. Joiner Jr. and M. David Rudd, "Disentangling the Interrelations Between Hopelessness, Loneliness, and Suicidal Ideation," *Suicide and Life-Threatening Behavior,* 26, no. 1 (spring 1996), 19–26.
2. George E. Murphy, "39 Years of Suicide Research: A Personal View," *Suicide and Life-Threatening Behavior,* 25, no. 4 (winter 1995), 450–55.
3. Larry Lockridge, "Least Likely Suicide: The Search for My Father, Ross Lockridge, Jr., Author of Raintree County," *Suicide and Life-Threatening Behavior,* 25, no. 4 (winter 1995): 435.
4. Cliff Edwards, *Van Gogh and God: A Creative Spiritual Quest* (Chicago: Loyola University Press, 1989), 29. Though this book gives an excellent view of the life and struggles of Vincent van Gogh, it attempts to downplay the theological confusion that permeated his experience by describing a "spiritual quest" toward an ecumenical openness that merges Christianity with Zen-Buddhism. It comes from a postmodern philosophic perspective that sees van Gogh's quest as wonderful and far superior to a spiritual journey that is limited by the narrowness of Christianity as van Gogh leaves the truth of Scripture to the illusive truth that can be found through oneness with nature. Because of this approach, Edwards gives some spiritual honor to van Gogh's suicide by suggesting that there "was a rightness and consistency to his shooting himself in a harvested field" (chapter 5, "The Oriental Connection," 116).

5. Ibid., 8. To understand more of Vincent's frustration with the cold and hard-hearted Christian leadership of his time and the struggle he had with his father, see pages 43–47.

6. Ibid., 3.

7. Ken Gire, *Windows of the Soul* (Grand Rapids: Zondervan, 1996), 91.

8. Edwards, *Van Gogh and God*, 18.

9. See David Allen, *In Search of the Heart: The Road to Spiritual Discovery* (Nashville: Thomas Nelson, 1993), 23–47, for his personal story of childhood pain, which included his being named David after a brother who had died from pneumonia.

10. In a response to a letter from Theo, Vincent reveals the degree of his and his brother's self-renunciation: "A phrase in your letter struck me: 'I wish I was far away from everything; I am the cause of all, and bring only sorrow to everybody; I alone have brought all this misery on myself and others.' These words struck me because that same feeling, exactly the same, neither more nor less, is also on my conscience" (Letter 98).

11. Gire, *Windows of the Soul*, 90.

12. Manuscript letter presented to the author, June 1996. The names have been changed to protect the privacy of the writer.

13. For an excellent book on making the choice to live, see Joni Eareckson Tada, *When Is It Right to Die? Suicide, Euthanasia, Suffering, Mercy* (Grand Rapids: Zondervan, 1992).

An Overview

Adolescent suicide is a growing problem in our society. Pastors who are called upon to minister in the aftermath of a suicide face a unique challenge. How they respond and the sensitivity they provide is a crucial element of personal, parish, and community healing. The decision of whether to normalize or pathologize the act is a critical decision. We must balance compassion and empathy with hope and guidance. The problems of adolescents are very real, but so is the hope offered to them by God, through us, His messengers.

Chapter Twenty-Seven

PASTORAL REFLECTIONS ON ADOLESCENT SUICIDE

Jeffrey A. Watson

INTRODUCTION

AT THE SOUND OF THE EXPLOSION, the eyelids of the neighbors snapped to attention. Starting toward the drape of darkness on the bedroom's back wall, the neighbor couple thought in unison: "A shotgun? This time of night? Our backyard?" Within minutes, the county police found the quivering neighbor boy, alive, but with his face severely traumatized from the gunshot.[1]

"Dad, are you and Mom really happy?" he had ventured earlier that night. Dad's unconvincing answer had triggered another cycle of worry for the son, worries about how many logs this thirteen-year-old had supposedly piled on the fire of his family's unhappiness. What began that night with a melancholy note and daddy's gun, ended with the neighbor's 911-panic call and a medevac chopper. Life-saving surgery and months of rehab would hold him temporarily on this side of heaven's gate. But before his birthday cake would host sixteen candles, his troubles would push him in the path of a sixteen wheeler. Handsome and bright, confused and cowardly, the fatal choice would eventually rush him through reluctant portals, leaving a grieving family's lives changed forever.

LIVES TERMINATED IN MIDSENTENCE

If the death of a child feels for parents like a period placed at midsentence,[2] then the suicide of a teen stands in the same spot like a broken exclamation mark, twisting in the shape of a question mark. "Why?" The gift of life, once given, has been hurled back toward its Maker. The message of a life, now severed, leaves family and friends to ponder what it meant and what it might have been.

According to the Centers for Disease Control, the lives of forty thousand American adolescents (ages 10–24) are cast back toward their Maker every year through accidents, homicides, and suicides.[3] Each of these deaths, preventable by definition, leaves its unique legacy of survivor guilt. Though *accidental death* for adolescents has been decreasing for a decade, *intentional death* continues its disastrous climb. Most tragically, ten to fourteen year olds are catching "the hand grenade from hell"[4] 75 percent more often than they were ten years ago.[5]

FUNERALS, COUNSELING, AND TALK:
HOW MANY AND HOW MUCH?

How should clergy frame and respond to such fatal acts? Should funeral sermons, counseling sessions, and pastoral conversations *normalize* or *pathologize* teen suicide?[6] Both options have strengths, though each can also be detrimental if used as an absolute model. Each incident should be evaluated and the circumstances and unique pastoral concerns considered before deciding where on the continuum to place the response. For the pastor whose parishioner succumbed to the sixteen wheeler, the choice seemed clear: normalizing the suicide would risk copy-cat behavior. Idealizing this handsome, bright boy, might invite the hundreds of teen mourners at the funeral into a sickening preoccupation with their own deaths. News reports and crowded wakes might create the mirage of instant popularity. Another teen, diving toward death's door, might try to join the deceased friend, announcing "You're not alone!"

Defying the Devil who yearns "to steal and kill and destroy" (John 10:10a), this boy's pastor would instead seek to build a retaining wall. By weaving a pathological thread into the fabric of every communication, he would frame the deed as "disturbed . . . mentally ill . . . irrational." By distancing himself from the fatal choice, and by not condoning the act, he would deny permission to other mourners who might be tempted to follow suit. By refusing to empathize with the deceased teen's newfound notoriety, the pastor would stubbornly refuse to idealize any existential leap.

"EXCEPT WHAT IS COMMON TO MAN"

But would it be wrong for a pastor to empathize with adolescent suicide's primary victim, the teen himself or herself? If not, how much is too much? In a second case, a pastor would not be permitted to engage in theoretical discussion only, but would be pushed to personally answer that question. Still numb, he would begin to mentally replay the conversation of his own shocking call: "Reverend, your daughter has disappeared . . . her car has been found near the playground pond . . . the police suspect foul-play." After several days of searching the area, investigators eventually sent an emergency-response diving team into the water. There, voluntarily weighted down, the body of an otherwise strong swimmer was found, quietly resting, eyes open.

Horror-struck and grieving, the clergy-dad helped construct the psychological autopsy on his daughter: her tender heart, wounded by a broken romance and made toxic by a probable eating disorder, was now stilled at the age of twenty. Not only did this dad resist pathologizing his daughter, he chose to rally to the ex-boyfriend, nurture her girlfriends, and pronounce her suicide not wrong and "not even a sin."

Unfortunately, understanding that 80 percent of Americans report that they've thought about taking their own life at least once,[7] the father rationalized and normalized excessively the self-destructive option. After all, he stated, Christ had been tempted that way, "tempted in every way, just as we are" (Heb. 4:15). In looking for comfort, this saddened shepherd reasoned that we are all vulnerable to similar impulses (1 Kings 19:4; James 5:17), capable of making tragic choices when pressured by what feels like overwhelming stress.

CONCLUSION

Suicidologists have expressed concern and debated the deadly influence of certain rock musicians on young minds through suicidal lyrics, suicidal gestures on stage, and suicidal acts in real life.[8] But today's youth have not only the poisoned well of prosuicidal music, they have a tidal wave of suicide coming directly at them. When Nobel laureates and millionaire supermodels orchestrate their final curtain calls,[9] can dozens of impressionable adolescents be far behind? When role models such as presidential attorneys and Navy admirals use a trigger to flee troubles,[10] how long can America's on-looking youth resist their own escapist devices? When America's most talked-about physician is a "suicide doctor" and a national best-seller is a suicide "how to" manual,[11] can the reckless rush of thousands of teens be far behind?[12]

The challenge of providing pastoral care and education regarding suicide is enormous. Whether suicidal musings should be viewed as normal or pathological, we know they are here to stay. Broadly reported among us and deeply recognized within us, these beginnings of that deadly spiral have touched nearly everyone—at least for a moment. We must speak words of passion and compassion. As Christians, we must voice our passion for life and the biblical understanding of it as a gift from God. We must also speak and listen with compassion to those who believe there is no hope. Without caricaturing the deed as unpardonable nor romanticizing the deed as courageous, we must beg the God of hope to fill us (Rom. 15:13), offer to us like a fragrant bouquet of hope through the Word (Rom. 15:4; 2 Cor. 2:15), that none should perish (2 Peter 3:9).

For adolescents who have yet to experience the fullness and richness of life, may God grant them the desire for a long and fruitful life. May He use us to assist them in their struggles and to encourage them to live fully the life God gives them. May they understand that He is their protector, comforter, and guide. They are too precious to us, and to Him, to lose.

ENDNOTES

1. The cases presented in this chapter are real; however, biographical details have been changed to protect the privacy of those involved.
2. E. Grollman, *Talking About Death: A Dialogue Between Parent and Child* (Boston: Beacon, 1970).
3. Centers for Disease Control and Prevention, *Mortality Trends, Causes of Death, and Related Risk Behaviors Among U.S. Adolescents* (Atlanta: Centers for Disease Control and Prevention, 1993). CDD Publication No. 099-4412.
4. G. Laurie, *The Final Cry* (Eugene, Oreg.: Harvest House, 1987).
5. Centers for Disease Control and Prevention, *Mortality Trends, Causes of Death, and Related Risk Behaviors Among U.S. Adolescents*.

6. For a comparison of the psychiatric and sociological models for explaining suicide, see J. Watson, *Courage to Care: Helping the Aging, Grieving, and Dying* (Grand Rapids: Baker, 1992).

7. J. Watson, *Looking Beyond: A Christian View of Suffering and Death* (Wheaton, Ill.: Victor Books, 1986).

8. Judas Priest, Prince, and Kurt Cobain, respectively.

9. Ernest Hemingway and Margeaux Hemingway, respectively.

10. Vince Foster and Jeremy "Mike" Boorda, respectively.

11. Jack Kevorkian, M.D. and Derek Humphry, *Final Exit: The Practicalities of Self-Deliverance and Assisted Suicide for the Dying* (Eugene, Oreg.: The Hemlock Society, 1991), respectively.

12. For an excellent summary of issues and guidelines involved in dealing with adolescent suicide, see Moses Laufer, ed., *The Suicidal Adolescent* (Madison, Conn.: Brunner/Mazel, 1995), especially 3–21.

An Overview

The ministry of the local church is foremost to equip the people of God with the tools necessary to survive the false and antitheistic philosophies of the world that, if left thriving and unchallenged in the believer, debilitate personal and spiritual growth, and subsequently, a Christian witness to the world. For those who don't appropriate the message of Christ to their lives, don't find fellowship and participation in the local church necessary, or who have been associated with a church that fails to represent the forgiveness, unity, and love available in Christ, experiences of loss, disappointment, humiliation, and depression find little to no permanent resolve. In this condition, even a believer can find suicide the least of two evils: death, or continuous failure and emotional pain.

Chapter Twenty-Eight

PASTORAL REFLECTIONS ON SUICIDE AND THE LOCAL CHURCH
Humanity Against Itself

Fred C. Chay

IT WAS TWO A.M.—AN EARLY, DREARY HOUR—when the call came. Most people who reach me on the Suicide Prevention Line are filled with frightful feelings. They have a sense of isolation from people, and they often have created a layer of insulation between themselves and God. I answered the phone. She was depressed, disillusioned, and desperate. A Christian and a medical resident involved in our ministry, she had tried to suck life's marrow. Unfortunately, life had lost its meaning after a series of tragic events. Hope was gone. I listened and shared. I never knew what happened after she hung up. Unfortunately, I can make an educated guess. When hope is gone, life is on the edge. She felt that life had given up on her. So she gave up her life.

In the afternoon mail came a letter from a friend, a member of the family. "I fell again today. I can't take another day. I don't want to live through another night. I really can't wait. I will do it tonight. A few pills, then sleep, never to awaken. Blackness, nothing—so long forever, Fred. Be of good cheer. EJ"

Try as we may, it is hard to conceive of the world in concord. Each day the evidence points to conflict. It is no wonder that modern man turns to magic, mystery, morality, and even medicine to make sense of the brief span of time we call life. The Christian may turn to the sovereign God of the Bible. But for those who cannot conceive of God, or who think they have killed Him, Nietzsche's prophecy is frightfully accurate: "When the world discovers that God is dead then there will be universal madness." An honest look at the world today might seem to confirm Nietzsche's prediction, if it is a look without benefit of the light of Holy Scriptures that reveals our Savior. Nietzsche is dead and Jesus is alive. Nevertheless, we often feel the madness of life, experience the malady and melancholy of existence, and find ourselves asking, "Why, Lord? How long O Lord? I wish I had never been born."

CRISIS SITUATION
Long before T. S. Elliot claimed that "man cannot bear much reality," the preacher Qoheleth revealed, "With much knowledge there is much pain."

Both prophetic voices, one of the ancient Near East, the other of the modern West, echo through time, each having put his finger on the perennial problem: Life is difficult and precarious. In either an ancient or modern world, and especially in a postmodern culture, society is filled with people who experience fear, fatigue, and failure. Christians are not immune. It is all too evident that Christians of all stripes and theological colors have chosen to end their life in despair, choosing the final exit.

CRITICAL SYMPTOMS / CULTURAL SOURCES

The problem of persistent, physical pain is often cited as an acceptable reason for suicide, in light of the principle of personal autonomy. It would seem, however, that for the Christian this principle should be overruled by the sovereignty of God. The God of the Bible is too kind to be cruel and too wise to ever make a mistake. On a practical level, the advances of pain management in medicine provide the physician the tools needed to be both compassionate and competent without aiding in killing. Apart from the problem of persistent physical pain, the symptoms that lead to suicide are manifested in the sociological and psychological matrices. As always, these areas find their antecedents and answers in the theological context.

The first critical symptom sourced in our culture is the *absence of identity*. For a recent generation, it was the standard rite of passage for the college student or young adult to "go and find himself." This progress sometimes included archeological digging into the past to pronounce blame on parents, police, or political parties. It often routinely involved a temporary geographical relocation via Volkswagen bus or bug, perhaps to the ski slopes for an extended time of thinking, skiing, and meditation—and then a little more skiing and socializing. In time, the search for identity of the self was finished. The return home, to school, or to a new job resulted in the advance toward adulthood. However, the discovery was often made later that the crisis of identity was not resolved, only postponed or confused. Here we see the cultural source of the identity problem—confusion. It has been said, "When you cannot find repose in yourself, do not seek for it in another." However, that is exactly what the sacred and secular realms of our society instruct us to do. This has been observed and explained by David Reisman in his seminal work, *The Lonely Crowd*. Reisman declares that people are "other directed" as opposed to "self directed." The observation was widened by social analyst Putny Snell in his exegesis and explanation of American culture in *The Self Adjusted American*. His penetrating analysis reveals that the average American, especially one involved in religion, often seeks for "indirect self-acceptance." When we engage in this adventure of folly, we will never find peace of mind. The truth is, that you can never have enough of what you don't really need. It is imperative that a person's sense of identity be created accurately, based on reality so that a person experiences genuine self-acceptability.

The second critical symptom is the *abundance of shame*. Notice the cause-and-effect relationship. When our sense of identity is not accurate or acceptable, the result is a sense of shame. Shame is created out of the seeds of comparison, which lead to competition. Was this not the case with Cain as recorded in Genesis? In his jealousy Cain compared himself and thus competed with his brother Able to the point of killing him. It was Alfred Adler who rediscovered what the Bible has always taught: "When we compare ourselves with one another, we are without understanding." When we compare we become confused. Having lost self-confidence and a sense of self-acceptance, we begin to compete with others. If we are unsuccessful in our competition in the cultural matrix, we can begin to capitulate ourselves to the culture, which is an indirect self-killing of the person.

The popularity of the "Self-Esteem Movement" from the late 1960s until today bears testimony to the importance of our inner view. Pastors, psychologists, and sociologists know all too well that self-hate often leads to death of the self and results in suicide. This is clearly not death with dignity.

The third critical symptom sourced in culture is built upon the previous two. It is the symptom of *aberrant validation*. When cultural confusion causes a lack of clear identity that is acceptable and accurately constructed on reality, shame is experienced. Individuals will then automatically look for those with whom they can compare themselves and compete. This leads to a validation system that is naturally competitive and corrupt, as well as carnal. The cultural source is corrupt in that it is tied only to regional norms seen as cultural values that change with the times and seasons. This is even more exacerbated in a postmodern society that has no notion of *truth that is true*, only that which is true for "me," even if it is not true for "you." The postmodern self is left to ponder the tension of meaning versus meaninglessness. Built upon the Kantian division of "objective fact and subjective value," it leads to the contemplation of the difference between existence and essence and one's relation to them. Having traveled the pathways of stoicism, existentialism, or pantheism, one finds all roads lead to the same destination—formal or functional deification of the self for the survival of the self. This comes about from—and continues to lead to—a life of confusion and competition, and corruption of self and others.

Absence of identity causes confusion. Abundance of shame creates competition. Aberrant validation of the self results in the inevitable internal corruption of the self. This triad is the internal thinking that produces the external manifestation and symptoms leading to suicide. These critical symptoms are forged from a cultural climate. This relationship was seen by Karl Marx who stated, "Environment determines expression." The environment we live in, with its toxic beliefs, leads to disastrous behavior. In the midst of all of this, we must ask, "Does Jesus Christ and His church provide a means to correct the confusion of identity, curb our competition with others, and counteract the corruption of ourselves in our culture?"

CHRISTIAN SOLUTION

The church of the Savior and the Savior Himself are uniquely able and available to counteract the psychological and sociological symptoms that invade Christians living in a postmodern culture. Jesus Christ provides a threefold antidote to the alienation and anxiety felt by those of us living and serving in a lost and dying world.

The first antidote that Christ provides is *acceptance*. This is not the warmth of the welcome wagon nor the keys to the city. It is the power of propitiation. The wrath of God has been averted, covered, and canceled for the Christian. The apostle John reminds us,

> My little children, I am writing these things to you that you may not sin. And if anyone sins, we have an Advocate with the Father, Jesus Christ the righteous; and He Himself is the *propitiation* for our sins; and not for ours only, but also for those of the whole world. . . . In this is love, not that we loved God, but that He loved us and sent His Son to be the *propitiation* for our sins. (1 John 2:1–2; 4:10 NASB)

Paul makes the definitive declaration in Romans 3:23–26 (NASB):

> . . . for all have sinned and fall short of the glory of God, being justified as a gift by His grace through the redemption which is in Christ Jesus; whom God displayed publicly as a *propitiation* in His blood through faith. This was to demonstrate His righteousness, because in the forbearance of God He passed over the sins previously committed; for the demonstration, I say, of His righteousness at the present time, that He might be just and the justifier of the one who has faith in Jesus.

The power of the Resurrection is seen in the propitiation of the sinners to be called the children of God. Jesus did not come to earth out of curiosity or out of personal need. The Father sent Him on an errand of mercy. As theologian Charles Hodge declared, "Fallen men, ignorant, guilty, polluted and helpless, need a savior who is a prophet to instruct us; a priest to atone and make intercession for us and a king to rule over and protect us."

We have what we need, and we are who we are—saints, holy and beloved. The apostle Paul attempts to capture the essence of our newly found acceptance. He reminds the Ephesians (chapter 1) that they, and we, partake of the triune God's personal and powerful care in that we are chosen and elected by the Father, reconciled and justified by the Savior's own blood, and sealed for all time by the ministry of the Holy Spirit. The past, present, and future work of the triune God in the life of the Christian should result in the believer's joining in a resounding chorus with the apostle Paul "to the praise of His glory" (Eph. 1:14).

We live in a day when "acceptance" has been reduced to tolerance. Yet Jesus Christ offers us the ultimate acceptance at humanity's deepest level of need. For He has not tolerated our sin and rebellion; but rather He has paid for it and offers us a new and vibrant way for life. When the Christian understands that true acceptance is seen in his new position in Christ, there is no need for pretense with others. The Lord Jesus knows all about us and still loves us. There is no more shame and no need to compete with others for we all receive the gift of eternal life based on the same gracious offer: "For by grace you have been saved through faith; and that is not of yourselves, it is the gift of God; not as a result of works, so that no one may boast" (Eph. 2:8–9 NASB).

The second antidote is *access* to the body of Christ. The new identity that one has with Christ by conversion also incorporates one into the church, the body of Christ. The apostle Paul explains that "we were all baptized into one body" (1 Cor. 12:13). Our new acceptance by Christ allows for a new access and association. This theological reality carries with it sociological and psychological consequences that should remove the sense of isolation or insulation from self or others. The church must maintain its corporate consciousness even in a society that is increasingly directed by a commitment to individualism and autonomy. It is incumbent upon the local church to maintain the unity of the Spirit in the bond of peace. This means that the right mechanisms must be in place to help assimilate people as they enter into the local church. The small group movement certainly can contribute to the need that people have to belong. Parachurch groups can also aid the local church. The church is, at its core, a family. In every family there are those who are big brothers or sisters. Also, some siblings, by nature and constitution, are stronger than other siblings. It is incumbent upon each family member to minister to one another and build one another up as we love, serve, and forgive one another for the common good of the family. The essence of the church is the model of reciprocal living as explained by the "one another" (e.g., 1 John 1:7) passages in the Bible, as well as a biblical theology of spiritual gifts.

The third antidote is the *attitude of love*. Building upon the acceptance of Christ and the access to the church, the basis of the intergenerational and interpersonal relationships in the body is seen and experienced in the attitude of love. Jesus said, "The world will know that you are my disciples if you have love for one another." The fact of our new identity in Christ and the incorporation into the body of Christ, which provide fellowship, become felt by the infusion of love.

When I was in high school, our principle reported the suicide of one of our classmates to the student body. The explanation was that he simply did not feel accepted or sense that he belonged. That young man had no friends. This should never be the case in the body of Christ. A spirit of belonging and being befriended is a basic byproduct in the church. If it is not, then something is wrong in the church, regardless of external appearances of success. In the age of the "church growth industry" and paradigm shifts, we must make sure that we do not exchange effectiveness for efficiency or substance for style. The blending of managerial skills and psychological principles can have a place in the church. However, as Peter Berger has warned, "He who dines with the devil better be sure to use a very long spoon." One of the potentially dangerous byproducts of the fast-paced culture in which the church exists is becoming so concerned about programs and procedures that we forget the purpose and, as a result, harm people. It is a sad irony that many who are calling for transparency and vulnerability are simply using it as a means to market themselves and manipulate others. Once, when I took over a ministry position, I went to meet one of the "powerful people." It seemed to me that he was very angry with me for no apparent reason since I had only met him one time. (I trusted it was not his first impression of me that elicited such a response.) As we unraveled the emotional issues, it became all too clear that he was angry at the person I replaced. The reason was that after my predecessor left, this man felt betrayed because all communication was broken off. His response was classic. "I'm mad because I thought we were friends. I guess I was only a donor." This man felt "worked, and used." Feigned friendship is hurtful to all parties. At its root it is sinful and produces fruit that is harmful. There is the danger in this age of peacocks, prima donnas, and predatorial self-promotion that we forget that ministry to people needs to be genuine and authentic, not simply a parasitic way of working the crowd. Conversely, when people truly care and share the love of Christ, then there is evidence of resurrection power. When people experience this, then there is reason for hope. Hope replaces despair, discouragement, and depression, alleviating the potential of suicide.

CONCLUSION

It was Camus who said, "There has been one truly serious philosophic problem, and that is suicide." We have a theological answer that is practical and powerful. The church of Jesus Christ provides for us our access and identity in Christ. It provides the association and incorporation in the local body of Christ. It also provides the operational attitude of love, infused in the members of the family of God.

The sardonic Dane, Hamlet, cried out and postulated the perennial existential proposition, "To be or not to be, that is the question." Let the Christian's answer to this proposition be a resounding, *"To be,"* as we find dignity, not despair, in life together in the body of Christ.

An Overview

To lose one's father to suicide creates feelings of loss and mental files of lessons that last a lifetime. Charles Ballard opens his heart to share with us the lasting impact his father's suicide has had in his personal and professional life. Through this difficult labor of love, he outlines sound advice for others who find themselves in the position of healer to someone who has become the unwilling victim of a suicide and to those who find themselves trapped in an emotional turmoil that makes life appear unlivable.

Chapter Twenty-Nine

PASTORAL REFLECTIONS ON THE SUICIDE OF A FAMILY MEMBER

Charles Ballard

THE CALL CAME IN THE EVENING while I was visiting with some friends at their home in Dallas. A friend from my dorm at Dallas Theological Seminary somehow tracked me down to tell me that I was supposed to call my brother Jerry at my mother's house back home in Austin. I knew it was serious when my sister-in-law answered the phone and immediately handed it to my brother with the words, "Jerry, its Chuck." The words "Daddy is dead" were bad enough, but when I asked, "How?" and received the answer, "He shot himself," there was a sense of overwhelming emotion that I had never experienced before or since.

It has been over nineteen years since my father took his life in the backyard of the home in which I grew up. The difficulty I have had in writing this chapter is testimony to the depth of personal pain and loss that the suicide of a personal family member can create. You would think that after nineteen years had passed, with much time given to processing the whole event, I would be "on top" of the pain, but even as I typed the preceding words I had to stop because of my tears. Believe me, anyone who loses a family member through suicide doesn't just "get over it."

As I think about the impact of my father's death, I realize that my life has been affected both personally and professionally, or maybe better that the personal impact in my life has carried over as well into my professional life as a pastor. Though I still often miss my father, I can say that I am truly thankful for what I have learned through the whole experience.

PERSONAL IMPACT OF SUICIDE

Personally, I have come to have a deeper appreciation for people who struggle with the sense of loss that comes with the death of a family member, whether by suicide or by any other means. It really does help to identify with others if you have "been there" at least in some similar way. But I have also seen how God has used this as a means to identify with others who have experienced other types of losses (e.g., divorce, financial failure, illness), particularly losses that seem to produce an initial reaction of "It's not fair!" When losses are imposed upon us by others or through circumstances that are not a direct result of our own actions, the struggle seems to be much deeper. I think I am able to be a little more in touch with others' losses because of my own loss.

My sense of seeing God as my heavenly Father has also deepened as a result. Though I had been a Christian for over four years at the time of my father's death, I related to Him more as God than as a personal Father. After my dad's suicide, I was driven deeper into relationship with my heavenly Father. The reality of my intimacy with God has grown over the years since my father's death.

LASTING IMPACT

I still experience occasional grief and a sense of loss. Even with the assurance of my relationship with an all powerful, all knowing, perfectly loving heavenly Father, I have missed my earthly father. Sometimes I've felt like I've wanted somebody with "skin on" to talk to as a father. I remember a number of years ago being at my father's grave site with my brother John. We talked about Dad's parenting, good and bad, all the things he had done for and to us (good and bad!). We both ended up acknowledging that at times we were still mad that he hadn't been there for us when we felt we needed him. Sometimes it would have helped greatly to have had him around.

THEOLOGICAL REFLECTION

The greatest theological help to me in experiencing the suicide of my father was the sovereignty of God. Romans 9 was the central passage that enabled me to keep some sense of perspective on my dad's death and the consequences that grew out of it. Verses 19–21 were particularly helpful to me as I meditated on the fact that God is God and I am the creation of God, not one to question Him. I can't accuse Him of "ruling unjustly" or "improperly" as the sovereign God of all creation. In His sovereignty He allowed my earthly father to take his own life. That did not mean He was unloving to me as my heavenly Father. Though I have some questions I would like to have answered some day, I know that neither I nor my family have been mistreated by God in any way.

Consequently, Romans 8:28 has become a true comfort to me personally and a vehicle to encourage others going through difficult times in their life. Some of the "good" that God has created from my loss is: (1) greater empathy and effectiveness with others who have experienced loss or tragedy. I have been able to identify more compassionately with others, not just in cases of death, but also in divorce, sexual abuse, unjust treatment by others, financial setbacks, and physical suffering; (2) personal challenge in my own life regarding my role as a father and how effective I am being as a model of love to my children. I never want them to feel the pain or live with the memory of a father who would not or could not be available to them.

ASSISTANCE TO VICTIMS OF SUICIDE

As I remember the day of my dad's suicide and particularly the first week or two afterward, I realize that the personal presence of a minister means more than the right words or accurate theology during the initial loss and adjustment. Two instances of this stand out in my own experience. The first was a visit from the pastor of the church I attended when I came home to Austin. This was a large church, and the pastor was extremely busy as a result. I vividly remember his coming to my house and our standing around together in the front yard. We didn't talk about much. He didn't try to give me unsolicited advice to make me "feel" better. He was just there, letting me know that he cared for me and that he knew I was hurting. The second example of caring through presence was on my return to Dallas. It was the Fourth of July weekend, and the family of the girl I was dating at the time picked me up at the airport and took me out to a local lake with some of their friends. They didn't worry about finding out how I was doing or seek to give me any answers to questions they assumed I must be asking. *They just allowed me to be with them.* Their presence is what ministered to me the most.

I want to emphasize that theology is essential to dealing with suicide, particularly in helping to protect against bitterness and anger against God, others, or even self. However, the *initial need* is not proper doctrine but people who care for those who have lost their loved one. Whether you are a pastor or not, don't worry about having "just the right words at just the right time." Your presence will probably mean more than any words you say.

Another issue pastors may find helpful to keep in mind is that many family members do not just struggle with their loss and grief but also with a sense of shame that accompanies the suicide. Though it was their family member who took his or her life, the family will often struggle with personal shame, as if the suicide was something for which they were responsible. Experiencing the consequences of a family member's decision to take his or her life is enough in and of itself. The burden of shame does not need to be added.

Family members need to be reminded, at the appropriate time, that individuals make a choice to take their own lives. They decided to kill themselves. One of the hurdles I had to overcome was the feeling that I was somehow responsible. So often family members seek to assume responsibility, to blame themselves. The "if only's" can kill you with guilt. They can hold you emotionally hostage for years. "If only I had been there, I could have stopped this from happening." "If only I had listened or been more sensitive." "If only I wouldn't have argued with him or denied him what he wanted." "If only I had recognized how badly she was struggling and gotten her help." Those counseling with the family members must be alert to this kind of thinking.

The family also needs assurance that it is okay to take plenty of time to work through their loss. Often individuals will deny their loss by attempting to appear strong and to "get this thing behind them as soon as possible." In reality, victims of suicide never thoroughly get past the death of their loved one; rather, they find ways to live with it. They learn to handle their grief so that it doesn't keep them from moving on with their lives. The healthy response they need to come to is, "I feel I have been able to control the grief over my loss" not, "I should feel better by now." Time does help to heal. If an individual is unable to process or work with their grief so that they can function more productively in life, a pastor or family member should assist the victim by encouraging that he or she seek additional professional help.

ASSISTANCE TO THE SUICIDAL

In counseling a suicidal individual, I do not initially focus on the consequences that his decision will have in the lives of others, which is the first course of counsel in an effort to *logically* reason with the individual as to why he should not take his or her life. It must be realized that the individual is not thinking logically but emotionally at first. Though logical or practical reasoning can certainly contribute to an individual's thinking process, the emotional issues need to be approached firstly so that the logical outcome or consequence of the suicide (negative impact on others) can be understood and handled more completely.

I believe it is important to first identify with the individual's mental and emotional pain that is contributing to the suicidal thinking, i.e., to try to identify what it is in the individual's life that is driving him or her to consider suicide. Rather than expressing condemnation, try to understand why he or she is so inclined. If I can identify with the individual's pain in a noncondemning and compassionate way, I am more likely to create a common ground to help him or her understand the seriousness of the course of action he or she is contemplating. My experience has been that the suicidal individual is looking for someone to listen compassionately and empathetically, someone who understands what he or she is going through. If this common ground can be established, then there is much greater hope of sharing other truth that may encourage him or her further.

If there is any sense of the individual's having a specific suicide plan (means, place, time), immediate intervention must be taken to preserve his or her life. One additional note here—every pastor or Christian counselor should know the respective state laws that deal with reporting an individual with suicidal tendencies. Some states may legally require notification of authorities in certain circumstances in spite of counselor/client confidentiality.

CONCLUSION

As a pastor and one who has been through the loss of a family member to suicide, I know there are no simple formulas guaranteed to help in every case. But from one who has been there, I offer some additional suggestions to help when working with someone who has lost a family member.

1. *Be honest.* Denying the reality of what has happened does nothing for the one who has lost a family member, and it lessens your ability to effectively minister to them. Respond honestly and compassionately with the facts of the incident as they become known. Never guess or provide palliative possibilities for a suicide.
2. *Be present.* Your presence will usually minister more than any words you can say, especially during your initial visit to the family. Being with

a family after a suicide is disconcerting and you may experience feeling a little out of place, but you have a critical role to play. Be patient with a quiet and sensitive spirit, and God will show you your role and help you to meet the needs of the survivors.

3. *Listen carefully.* Do your best to listen not only to the words the grieving family shares but also to the emotions behind the words. Identifying the emotions will keep you aware of the inner thoughts that regularly invade and confuse the minds of victims of suicide. This skill will pay great dividends toward clarifying your thoughts on how to best minister to the family, particularly when planning the funeral.

4. *Love unconditionally.* Love needs to be unconditional because humanity's finiteness or imperfection constantly puts it to the test. To experience the extent of God's love for humanity, those who suffer from the collateral damage of a suicide must see it portrayed in the life of their pastor who is God's professional representative and their friends who are His children. Unconditional love and acceptance will go far in granting peace to a heart torn by inner turmoil.

5. *Don't blame.* Blaming accentuates shame. The family will struggle enough with this as it is. Don't add to their load and be careful to protect them from others who tend to stereotype and cast blame on families of suicide. Casting the first stone only adds to the pain and delays healing.

6. *Be patient.* Time does help to heal, but it is not the only means of healing. Allow individuals the time to process and hopefully grow through their experience. There is no established timetable for recovery that should be imposed on someone under the pressure of processing the suicide of a loved one.

The challenge associated with suicide is not that a family member has died, but that he or she has chosen to die. The decision was made without regard for the feelings, sense of loss, and probable damage to others. And in the event that the individual did consider their family or friends, somehow they inaccurately believed that their immediate departure would be a benefit. Nothing is easy in dealing with this kind of mental and emotional challenge, but the caring, sensitive pastor or counselor can be a vehicle of God's grace and peace to the grieving family.

An Overview

Suicide creates victims who unexpectedly and unwillingly find themselves forced into the role of being survivors. Though the troubles of life end for the person who commits suicide, an avalanche of anguish is left behind for a victimized community who must pick up the pieces. It is for this community that Gary Weeden has worked to provide the grace of God in the midst of chaos and confusion. Gary discusses three doors of opportunity that present themselves in grief and suicide care through which a caregiver can pass to present the grace of God.

Chapter Thirty

BRINGING THE GRACE OF GOD
TO VICTIMS OF SUICIDE

Gary P. Weeden

MY PHONE RANG ONE SATURDAY afternoon as I was preparing for a trip to Topeka, Kansas, to attend a conference at the Menninger Clinic on "Responding to Suicide." Ironically, the sober voice on the phone informed me that one of our sailors had committed suicide earlier that morning and they needed my grief intervention skills. This was not my first occasion to respond to a suicide, and the same feeling of heaviness greeted me that had in the past. What was going to be my plan of action for grief intervention, what was I going to hear, and who did I need to visit? These and other questions immediately occupied my thoughts, as they always do when I have to respond to the aftermath of a suicide. Just a few weeks after this experience, I was informed that another life had been cut short. The car of one of our sailors had been found abandoned on the side of a rural Michigan road, where he left it before entering the woods to end his life with a gun. The optimism with which he spoke of his future the day before the suicide left his peers confused, numb, and shocked.

The suicides that I have encountered are portraits of individuals resolved to conquer their troubles; the irreversible irony is that they eventually were conquered by the very things haunting them. This harsh reality is seen in the story of a young husband who went home from work during lunch. An argument erupted and in the heat of the marital conflict he pulled a gun and shot himself as his wife watched. A few short hours later, in the intensive care unit, his struggle with life ended. I tried to imagine what his wife and kids witnessed and wondered how I was going to walk them through the next few weeks. Though wanting to have a relationship, he was unable, for whatever reason, to communicate his thoughts, needs, and desires effectively. Though he desired companionship, his inability to maintain the kind of relationship he desired became his undoing. Clearly, he was attempting to communicate a message. A suicide attempt that intends to convey a message is described as a pattern of thinking "in which the individual does not desire to end his life as much as to change the way other people act toward them. The message may be hostile and angry. The suicide attempt may have been meant to embarrass and hurt someone."[1] Dr. Karl Menninger offers a triad model for motives, which includes to kill, to escape, to inflict injury. Whatever the motive, suicide is that permanent threshold through which one walks but never returns. Dr. Menninger's experience suggests that suicide does more to us than create a loss of another person—it produces other victims.[2] The only thing that remains is the heavy burden that has been imposed upon this unwilling community of victims.

Among all the suicide situations in which I've been involved, one case in particular sticks with me. I was awakened early to be informed that a young man had ended his life by jumping from the seventeenth floor of his apartment building. A note was found leaning against an empty bottle, which gave police a hint to some of his internal conflict. Later that evening I met with his father and brother who had flown in from the West Coast. Shocked and full of disbelief, the father pulled me aside and asked, "Where do I go from here? Please tell me, where do I go from here?"

From the time I receive that first suicide call, to grappling with families as they attempt to put their lives back together, to ultimately bringing God's perspective to the situation, I have often asked myself the same question: "Where do I go from here?" Solomon reminds me that there is "a time to embrace and a time to refrain, a time to search and a time to give up, a time to be silent and a time to speak."[3] To stand in the gap for those dealing with the loss of a loved one to suicide is to stand in the precarious position of encountering a grief unequaled; you search for answers that you may never find and discover that the impact of this mode of death carries a tremendous community burden.

Webster defines "community," as *(1) a body of individuals organized esp. as a unit, (2) any group sharing interest or pursuits.* Community may be the campus on which you study or teach, the church at which you worship, the marketplace you patronize, or the neighborhood you call home. With suicide, I have come to expect certain behaviors from the immediate community of family and friends, to hear similar emotions, questions, and concerns. But equally as important, I have recognized that pastoral care extends beyond the immediate family. I need to consider the marketplace the victim shared, the church where the person worshiped, and the neighborhood in which he or she lived.

My initial understanding of the impact of suicide on a community came from a personal experience I encountered upon entering seminary. It was the beginning of the summer semester. I knew something had happened because conversations on campus didn't center around the usual finer points of theology, the challenge of Hebrew exegesis, or the leading of God in one's life. Joy had turned to mourning as students painfully discussed the loss of a beloved professor who had recently committed suicide.

His final words were penned on a note and taped to the front door of his home. These words could only give us a glimpse into some of the pain he wrestled with that last week: "Dear Pastor R____: My poor brain is hard to figure out. It is not sending me the right messages one wants to hear. You know that deep depression has been my unwanted lot for a long time. It may be a Satanic attack, but it has seemingly not been possible for me to shake. . . ." The president was immediately called out of class to discuss the issue with school officials. He capsulized the incident with these emotional thoughts, which so often express the feelings of confusion we experience when confronted with suicide: "My heart cried out to God: 'Lord, how do I put all of this together? How will I explain it to the stunned faculty, staff, and student body?'"

His response reminds us of the theological, mental, and emotional complexities connected to suicide and the many questions it creates with which we must wrestle. Even though I was removed from this man's life, his teaching, and his struggles, I was not immune from the impact that his death had on the community I now shared. As I tried to reconstruct and understand the events that shaped this professor's hopeless view of life, it became certain that from this point onward I would look at my life differently. I witnessed a campus looking for an answer to the question, "How would God be glorified through this?" It was at this juncture in my life that I recognized the collateral damage and far-reaching impact of suicide. As I evaluate my experience with suicide and postsuicide intervention, I have discovered that suicide exposes some basic worldview questions that open three separate doors for God's grace to enter into a community. I quickly realized that what I thought or believed about suicide was *not* very important in postsuicide care; the most important role for me was the administration of God's grace to the situation. My focus turned to helping the surviving victims of suicide explore the ramifications of this death, and understand suicide in terms of eternity and the availability of God's grace.

VULNERABILITY FACTOR OF SUICIDE

The first door to gaining insight into God's grace can be opened through one's encounter with death. Death often provides a significant moment when one is forced to stop and appraise the reality of his own mortality. Dr. J. I. Packer states, "Death has been called 'the new obscenity,' the nasty thing which no polite person nowadays will talk about in public. But death, even when unmentionable, remains inescapable. The one sure fact of life is that one day, with or without warning, quietly or painfully, it is going to stop. How am I going to cope with death when my turn comes?"[4] It serves more than any other event to underscore the finality of life, help a person rethink his or her own basic worldview, and amend one's lifestyle. As D. L. Moody once stated, "If I can get a man to think seriously about death for five minutes, I can get him saved."[5] Funerals and memorial services are important because they give pastors the opportunity to inject the grace and love of God into an incredibly mortal moment. The great equalizer of all humanity (death) needs to be challenged by its Conqueror if hope is to be grasped by its victims.

The issues on the brevity of life and the way we live tend to be more punctuated because suicide brings to the surface many unique questions about life and one's own vulnerability. The fact that suicide never seems to be left to the back pages of the news broadens its collateral effect. For example, on

May 16, 1996, news from the Washington Navy Yard sent a shock wave around the navy. Admiral Boorda, Chief of Naval Operations, shot himself outside his home. As the information tremor traveled out beyond the family and friends around Washington D.C., the worldwide community was forced to face questions of vulnerability. "What was so terribly wrong or so overwhelming that he would end his own life?" or "What is wrong with the system that it would drive him to this or even allow it?" or "Am I also susceptible to the same pressures that confronted him?" These questions could be related to any community. Memorial services were held worldwide to remember a leader who was called the "sailors' admiral." However, what many needed to come to grips with was not only the admiral's unexpected absence but the unbelievable manner in which his life disappeared. A chaplain, who led one of the services, injected this perspective when he stated, "Surely he would agree if he were here with us now that we must not accept the way his life ended."[6] To call his loss a "warrior's death," as the media did,[7] gave false credibility to what in reality was a personal escape from responsibility. The broader community was looking for direction in the midst of their vulnerability. They didn't need to have suicide justified; they needed to understand the responsibilities associated with honor, the proper reaction to accountability, and the grace that God can bring to a tragic situation. Vulnerable people need to hear the truth spoken in love.

In an article entitled "A Political Suicide" (*Time*, 13 May 1996), the tragic suicide of one of the Coast Guard's top officers was examined. Although it painted a picture of hidden agendas, the real portrait involved a family and a community torn by confusion and profound grief, facing a long recovery and many unanswered questions. As I talked with and observed some of this officer's close friends, it became apparent that his death had a paralyzing and lasting effect; recovery would be arduous. Two and a half years after the tragedy, there are those who still have the need to talk about it, and some have significantly altered their lives as a result.

The shock of suicide often makes people vulnerable as they seek for answers to a tragedy, they neither wanted nor expected. The door that their vulnerability opens to caregivers is brief. We must pass through it gently, honestly, and with compassion. It is through us who love and serve God that victims of suicide see the grace of God.

THE STORY BEHIND THE SCENE

Learning about the events that precede a suicide provides another door through which God's grace can pass. I have presided over numerous funerals from infants to the elderly who died as a result of war, accident, or illness. The causes leading up to these deaths were most often conclusive, involving perhaps some anticipatory grief. However, the factors that lead one to hopelessness and eventually to suicide are not so definitive. Although the grief associated with nonsuicidal deaths can be inexorable, the suddenness, shock, and unanswered questions associated with suicide seem to amplify the loss. Though we understand that people die from many causes, we are unprepared and confused by a person's unwillingness to live. Therefore, suicide becomes a focal point for questions that will hopefully uncover someone or something to blame. What the *story behind the scene* uncovers are the common struggles that the survivors share with the suicide victim. Perhaps that is what makes suicide so discomforting. What confronted those who took their lives often strikes too close to home. All of us hope for peace, loving relationships, and success in what we do, but there are personal and societal expectations that encourage us to hide any shortcoming. The reasons why some people, who have the same dreams as us, are not able to balance their expectations with reality are not always clear or known. To ascertain a person's struggles and make them known helps survivors understand the complexities and confusion that led the suicide victim to despair. Following a suicide, when others need and want to talk, it's important to provide a safe opportunity for friends and family to share their concerns without fear of criticism. For caregivers, this is initially a time of listening, of gathering data, and identifying needs. Caregivers run the risk of not being heard or being misunderstood if they share their personal insights and knowledge about suicide or the investigation too early.

When listening, I learn about the others who were a part of the suicide victim's life, the events of the last days, the regrets people sense when they believe they missed signs that might have prevented the incident, and numerous other essential clues that I need to help the family move on in their grief. Many of the survivors with whom I have worked developed overwhelming personal problems that led to a deep sense of hopelessness. The personal and relational problems of the suicide victim sometimes become the impetus for personal and relational problems in survivors. In his discussion of the destructive nature of unresolved problems, Dr. David Allen advises that "any problem . . . occupying our waking and sleeping moments, which causes us to withdraw from our faith and to isolate ourselves from our supporting community, has in essence, been elevated to god-like status in our life. . . . When a problem is elevated to god status, it becomes so massive that it is not resolvable and it eventually destroys us."[8] Dr. Aaron Beck, through his study on the severity of depression, "became convinced that hopelessness, one component of the depressed state, was most critical in suicidal people. Their hopelessness is not rational in most cases and results from distorted patterns of thinking."[9]

It is in this time of emotional pain, confusion, and hopelessness that pastors and caregivers must be the best of listeners so that they can understand the depth of the loss, *and then* compassionately speak to the family and extended community about the hope and grace of God in Christ. Mother Teresa said, "The biggest disease today is not leprosy or tuberculosis, but rather the feeling of being unwanted, uncared for, and deserted by everybody."[10] Chaplain Peter Ross-Gotta of the Menninger Clinic, explains it this way: "One might believe with all one's heart that there is hope for a person, but simply telling someone to have hope is probably the least effective way to communicate hopefulness. Hope is much more than a word. It is more than an idea. For hope to become an operative experience in another person's life, that person needs to experience it in another."[11] It is through the understanding ministry of the caregiver that the hope of God is seen. Be visible first and heard appropriately.

The information gathered through good listening gives the caregiver the ability and opportunity to be the supportive spokesperson for the immediate family to an interested, bewildered, or hurting community. Adina Wrobleski says to the family: "It may not seem so at the time, but if your pastor or rabbi discusses suicide at the funeral service, they are doing you a favor. He is telling a large group of people the awful fact that is so hard to repeat over and over."[12] Because a funeral is God's time to speak about the incident, it is critical that pastors have the facts or the story behind the scenes well in hand as they bring the message of the Scriptures to bear on the issue.

A GRIEF UNEQUALED

A third door through which God's grace can be extended is the personal suffering or the "grief unequaled" that families must journey through following a suicide. My experience has led me to believe that suicide prolongs the grief process because of the unanswered questions it leaves. "Death rarely allows for elegant departures and tidy farewells. It comes between people randomly. Someone is left with the anguish of having been left unilaterally and unfairly. The leaving is not so bad when there is an agreed understanding beforehand, when there is time and space for a good good-bye. It's when there was no good-bye, or worse, a bad good-bye, that death becomes hateful, leaving one with a feeling of incompletion and irresolution."[13] Apart from possibly the death of a young child, there is nothing that compares with the grief and shock of suicide. The disbelief that someone they loved and thought they knew would end his or her life haunts survivors of suicide. Why didn't she reach out for help? Didn't he know I loved and needed him? Why didn't I see the signals? Who or what's to blame? How do I face the unfinished business? Time is the enemy that threatens to tear the heart apart and the friend that eventually provides enough answers to heal it. Though most people learn to deal with the grief, it never completely goes away.

Grief is often proportionate to one's investment in a person or thing. The greater the attachment the greater the grief. Grief can be expressed through shock and denial, with concurrent anger and guilt. "Grief is like a raging river, and shock is like ice on that river that enables one to walk on it—to do the things we have to do. But the ice is thin in places and we fall through, and have to climb out again, and go on."[14] Many of those left behind also have difficulty directing their focus off the mode of death. Denial is often seen in those left behind, who deal with their own anger and guilt. Following the funeral of one young man, the father pulled me aside and urged me to influence the final outcome of the death report. "We all need to understand that he didn't commit suicide!" "A very persistent denial that death has been by suicide is not uncommon in instances where there is not a note or physical evidence which is irrefutable."[15]

In addition to denial, anger often intensifies. Anger flows down two streams—away from oneself or toward oneself, hoping to find someone or something on which to place blame. When anger is directed outward on others, an organization, or God, I let it take its course without immediately arguing its validity. In time, understanding will prove or disprove the merit in this expression. When anger is directed inward, feelings of guilt for having missed possible signals eats away at the individual's conscience. "Guilt is an expected aspect in grief of those bereaved through suicide, for suicide is an aggressive and hostile act towards those left behind, often culminating an earlier stormy relationship."[16] The overriding concern in this case is how long one camps in anger and guilt.

As acceptance and understanding develop, the grief fades, shock subsides, denial and anger diminish, and life goes on, but always with something, someone missing. Life is a series of losses that shape and mold us or crush and destroy us. The Christian caregiver's understanding, attitude, and grief care can apply the grace of God to the emotional, mental, physical, and hopefully, the spiritual struggles left in the wake of suicide.

CONCLUSION

In all these situations the most difficult thing to face was the community left behind. I recall one particular funeral in which four young children walked cautiously to the open casket to see their father. As they stopped and stared, they began to look at each other as if to say, "Where do we go next?" A community that has experienced suicide expresses this same sense of loss or lack of direction. When I approach postsuicide care now, it is to discover an open door through which I, as God's representative, can enter to offer the grace of God. It is only in its aftermath that God can meet the victims of suicide. Christian caregivers must stand at these doors ready to reflect the grace of God to people whose hearts are torn open (vulnerable), who are a part of a story that needs to be understood (listening), and whose emotional pain (grief unequaled) needs the soothing touch of God's compassionate Word. "But God, who is rich in mercy, because of His great love with which He loved us, even when we were dead in trespasses, made us alive together with Christ (by grace you have been saved), and raised us up together, and made us sit together in the heavenly places in Christ Jesus, that in the ages to come *He might show the exceeding riches of His grace in His kindness* [emphasis added] toward us in Christ Jesus."[17] To those who have been recipients of God's grace and kindness, there exists a responsibility to provide the same.

ENDNOTES

1. Jeffrey T. Mitchell and H. L. P. Resnick, *Emergency Response to Crisis* (Ellicott City, Md.: Chevron Publishing, 1981), 147.
2. Ronald Maris, et al., eds. *Assessment and Prediction of Suicide* (New York: Guildford Press, 1992), 483.
3. Ecclesiastes 3:6–7 (NIV).

4. James Packer, *I Want to Be a Christian* (Wheaton, Ill.: Tyndale, 1977), 62, quoted in Colin Chapman, *The Case for Christianity*, (Grand Rapids: Eerdmans, 1981), 28.
5. Dwight L. Moody in *Pentecostal Testimony*, February 86, 17, rpt. in *Inspiring Quotations*, comp. Albert M. Wells Jr. (Nashville: Thomas Nelson, 1988), 55.
6. "Around the World, Struggling with the Unacceptable," *Navy Times*, 3 June 1996, 4.
7. Peter J. Boyer, "Admiral Boorda's War," in *The New Yorker*, 16 September 1996, 86.
8. David Allen, M.D., *Shattering the God's Within* (Chicago: Moody Press, 1994), 16.
9. David Lester, *Questions and Answers About Suicide* (Philadelphia: The Charles Press, 1989), 38.
10. Malcolm Muggeridge, *Something Beautiful for God* (San Francisco: Collins Fontana, 1972), 73–74, quoted in Colin Chapman, *The Case for Christianity*, 22.
11. Becquer Benalcazar, M.D., et al., *Suicide Awareness & Prevention: A Resource Manual for Military Chaplains* (Topeka: Menninger Division of Continuing Education), 54.
12. Adina Wrobleski, *Suicide: Survivors* (Minneapolis: Afterwords, 1994), 113–14.
13. Alla Bozarth-Campbell, *Life is Goodbye, Life is Hello* (Minneapolis: CompCare Publishers, 1986), 111.
14. Wrobleski, *Suicide*, 51.
15. David K. Switzer, *Pastoral Care Emergencies* (Mahwah, N.J.: Paulist Press, 1989), 141.
16. Bertha G. Simos, *A Time to Grieve* (New York: Family Service Association of America, 1979), 116.
17. Ephesians 2:4–7 (NKJV).

An Overview

Many who serve as pastors and counselors are literally thrown into life and death situations. Some of these situations involve people who are in the process of ending their lives. Timothy Tatum, a retired United States Army chaplain, delineates seven rules of intervention that he learned while working with people trapped in depression and hopelessness. These rules provide realistic insight into the intangible world of suicide intervention.

Chapter Thirty-One

PASTORAL REFLECTIONS ON SUICIDE INTERVENTION

Timothy C. Tatum

STANDING OUTSIDE MY KITCHEN door on a bright Saturday morning was a young, Army-enlisted woman. Debbie had been seeing me for counseling, and I wasn't making much progress in getting her past her feelings of family rejection. Saturday was the only day as an army chaplain that I had to spend with my family, and I wasn't looking forward to another session with her. But I didn't have the heart to tell her to come see me in my office on Monday. Over the next few minutes she shared that she had stopped to say good-bye, thanks, she was leaving this world. A little prying revealed that she was fed up with her family and her life and, as a result, had recently taken a hand full of sleeping pills.

I was no expert on suicide intervention, but I knew enough to take her comments seriously. She might be bluffing to get attention, but I couldn't take that chance. I informed her in my most commanding voice that she must go with me to the military hospital to have her stomach pumped. She informed me that nothing of the sort was going to happen and told me to get out of her way so that she could leave. A major verbal standoff developed until she saw a knife on the kitchen counter. Seizing the opportunity to tilt the conversation in her favor, she started toward me with the knife. Thank the Lord for our protective wives. Having overheard most of the conversation, my wife ran into the kitchen, jumped on Debbie from behind, wrestled her to the floor, and gave her a tongue lashing that the three of us will never forget. Debbie, still in shock from my wife's actions, quickly agreed to go to the hospital. It turned out that she had ingested enough pills to kill her but the medical intervention had saved her from any permanent harm.

Starting with Debbie, I began to learn some practical rules for practicing suicide intervention. (1) *Suicidal individuals will appear at your door whether or not you are prepared to deal with them.* Over the years that followed Debbie's case, I had numerous people show up at my office, in my home, and in the workplace threatening to take their own lives. Pastors, chaplains, and Christian counselors are often sought out by these individuals because they want someone who loves and cares and can bring a word of hope. We must be prepared to deal with them because we may be their last stop.

Debbie's case also taught me the second rule. (2) *Stand firm, take control, but remember that you may be in a dangerous situation.* Individuals intent on taking their own life may not like you standing in their way. My experience has been, however, that most respond to a firm word of instruction that must be followed. Death is not an option here. They must go to the hospital for medical intervention or observation, or be placed under the care of friends who will not leave them alone until the crisis has passed. Like me, you may find yourself praying for extra wisdom when the individual is holding a knife or a gun. Facing this kind of situation on several other occasions, I found that a firm voice, exercised with patience, followed by words of assurance, usually worked in disarming the individual.

Roger, like Debbie, had enlisted in the Army and was going through Advanced Individual Training. Life had become overwhelming. His future looked dismal and he had sunk into a deep depression. I first met Roger when I received a call from the duty officer. He had Roger on the phone threatening to commit suicide and didn't know what to tell him. He managed to link our phones together. After much coaxing, I learned that Roger had already taken a variety of pills. His speech was beginning to slur. I finally convinced him to tell me where he was located. It turned out to be a pay phone on the other side of the installation. By the time I arrived he was too weak to resist my efforts to get him to the hospital. Fortunately it was not too late. I left him in the hands of the hospital psychiatrist. The next day, while still in the hospital, Roger tried again. Two days later he tried a third time.

Roger's case taught me another rule. (3) *A crisis averted is not a crisis solved.* Even though I managed to get Roger to the hospital in sufficient time to save his life, the crisis wasn't over. I later found out that Roger would not respond to the psychiatrist. He only wanted to see the chaplain who brought him in. I thought I was through the immediate crisis and was happy to be out of the picture. But Roger was still in crisis, and his picture included me. I worked along with the psychiatrist in bringing Roger's world back into focus. The words of hope that Roger discovered in God's Word made the difference. Roger never knew that there was a Savior that loved him enough to die for him in order that Roger might really live. It was a life-changing discovery.

This case added a fourth rule. (4) *A case transferred may be a case that comes back.* I would strongly urge all Christian counselors who do not have extensive training in the treatment of suicidal cases to refer these cases to a professional. It is easy to get in over your head. Having said that, I would not minimize the ability of a well-trained pastoral counselor to help someone in this situation. Several times I have had secular psychiatrists and psychologists refer cases to me because they had thrown up their hands in despair and thought some pastoral counseling might help. The Lord may be using you to save a life for Him. I have been amazed on several occasions as I witnessed the power of the Lord and His Word in turning around a suicidal person who was in total despair.

Years of counseling with Helga added a new rule to my list. Helga was born in Germany several years prior to World War II. She was sexually abused by her father on numerous occasions prior to and during the early days of the war. Her mother showed her little regard. When the allied bombing grew intense in their area of Germany, her mother left to live with a relative, leaving Helga alone with her father. After an evening of drinking with his friends from the German military, Helga's father made another sexual advance. This time she rose up in anger and broke an earthen jar over his head. This so infuriated her father that he sent her to a women's concentration camp in Slovakia.

When the Russian advance drew near the camp, the guards sent the women home in pairs, with only their feet for transportation. Helga and her traveling companion witnessed a farmer's wife being raped by Russian soldiers. The poor woman had befriended the two girls and given them shelter for the night. Later in their travels, Helga and her friend were beaten by several Italian soldiers and brutally raped. Battered, bruised, bloody, and covered with lice, Helga found the house where her mother was living, only to be told that she could not come in. Her mother put her in the chicken coop for the night and told her to return to her father. Knowing she could not return home and having lost all hope, she made her first attempt to kill herself. An American soldier found her in time and nursed her back to health.

As unbelievable as the story is to this point, it gets worse. Helga became this soldier's girlfriend. Several months later he returned to the states leaving Helga pregnant. He neglected to tell Helga, until just before he left, that he was married. He also didn't tell her that he had given her syphilis. Since Helga did not know she had contacted this disease, she never sought medical attention. Her daughter, born with the disease, only lived two months. The local German clergyman refused to bury the child unless Helga could pay the costs associated with the burial. Fortunately another American soldier heard of her plight and helped pay for the expenses. Helga, her soldier benefactor, and her landlady, were the only ones at the funeral. Later she married an Army sergeant who brought her to the states. She entered this country a young wife with deep emotional and spiritual wounds that would not heal.

I first met Helga after her husband had retired from the army. The untreated wounds were driving her into periods of deep depression and anger. Late at night she would vent this anger on the duty chaplain at the local military installation. Sometimes she ended these calls with a statement that she was going to kill herself. I was always ready for a new challenge, so I decided that with the Lord's help I would take on this case. I felt certain that if I exercised patience and the love of Christ I could successfully intervene and the crisis would pass in a few weeks or months. Ten years later I was still explaining to Helga, usually in the middle of the night, that God was not finished with her yet and it was not part of His plan for her to take her life. We were making some progress; the suicide attempts and threats were not coming as often, but it was slow going. Helga taught me a new rule. (5) *Be prepared for the long run.* Successful intervention may be a onetime thing. In other cases, like Helga's, where the wounds are deep and numerous, successful intervention could mean the investment of years.

My mother taught me rule number six. (6) *Your best efforts may fail.* I still remember sitting at my mother's desk addressing announcements for my graduation from high school. Just thirty feet away, my mother pulled the trigger on a .22 revolver, ending her life. It took me years of thought, prayer, and reflection to come to terms with this tragic event. Her children loved her. Her husband loved her and was faithful to her. My father had intervened as best he could when she threatened suicide on previous occasions. Professionals counseled her at length. She was even on her knees beside her bed in prayer the evening before she died, in spite of the fact that she had severe back pain. But all of this did not save her.

If you have not experienced this already, you will encounter suicidal people that will successfully end their lives in spite of your best efforts. What do you do after you have followed all the rules; you've invested your time, your talents, and your prayers; you love them unconditionally; and, nothing seems to work? It is during these times that you grieve; you grieve for the person and you grieve for your lost efforts. It is also a time as Christian counselors that we lean on a Savior who cares and on Christian brothers and sisters who will come alongside. By God's grace we move on hoping that the next case may be different.

Fortunately, I have learned one last rule. (7) *Successful intervention pays dividends for eternity.* Remember our young enlisted woman, Debbie? I am happy to report that she gave her life, and all she had, to the Lord. Debbie later developed health problems that led to several serious surgeries. In the midst of all this the Lord honored her prayers by giving her a son. During her last surgery she received several blood transfusions. One was tainted with the AIDS virus. For the last seven years Debbie has been courageously fighting the various stages of that disease. During that time she has not been idle. She has been sharing her story and her testimony with various youth groups. Only the Lord knows how many lives she has touched. The Lord may be welcoming her home soon, but it will only be after her work here on earth is done. It will not be a life cut short by a handful of pills.

Helga began to discover that a personal Savior can heal even the deepest of wounds. She began to search the Bible for answers to some of the problems that had plagued her all her life. With each passing day she leaned more and more on the Lord for wisdom and understanding. It was only a few years ago that she lost her husband to lung cancer. God's grace got her through that difficult time. She hasn't entertained the thought of suicide for several years. Very recently she gave in to my request to write her life's story. Hopefully, we will all see it someday in print. In the last chapter of her rough manuscript she writes,

> There is little doubt in my mind that the times we live in are demanding and stressful. It seems to me that survival will greatly depend upon people's ability to find inner strength and peace. We have huge billboards in our town stating, "Hate and Rage are four letter words, but so are Love and Hope!" Such a simple message, yet words which could indeed assist us in finding

the help we need to rid ourselves of all the feelings which serve us in living unhappy and dissatisfied lives. One can hardly live a life such as mine without marveling at how much suffering one person can endure. In writing about my experiences, there were times when I wondered how one person could have endured the pain and the feelings of hopelessness. Yet the answer is rather simple. Somehow God had never deserted me nor forgotten me. Even in my darkest hour and my moments of total rejection of Him, He stood by my side. The many times I have pleaded with Him to allow me to die, He refused to fulfill my wish. I do not know why but I have learned to accept that He has a plan for me. May I have the grace to accept His plan and live or die knowing that I have been granted one very great discovery.

I lost contact with Roger. He was given a general discharge from the army and sent home. I was never able to contact him after his departure. I can only pray that a Christian counselor took on Roger's case, a counselor willing to stay in there for the long run.

Successful intervention pays dividends for eternity. We serve a great God who can reach the unreachable. It is very humbling to know that He has chosen to work through us to reach those who are hurting the most. Intervening with someone about to commit suicide can be a frightening, stressful experience. The Lord knows how fast my heart has raced at times like this. Most of us would be very happy if the Lord chose someone else for the task. Like it or not, we may be the ones with a knock on our doors. It is then that we will find that His grace is sufficient, even for the counselor.

An Overview

Many of us who have gone through the agonizing process of helping a loved one "die with dignity" have felt the tension between sustaining life and knowing when and how to let go. This inevitable enemy of life coupled with the medical advances of the past few decades has forced us to seek God's direction in this delicate and controversial matter. Joni Eareckson Tada provides four biblically based decision making principles upon which her family relied to make the last moments with their dad as meaningful and humane as possible.

Chapter Thirty-Two

DECISION MAKING AND DAD

by Joni Eareckson Tada

MY FATHER SHOULD HAVE BEEN RAISED as a cowboy on the open plains. Actually, he almost was. Born in 1900, he led a rough-rider life, trading with Indians in the northwest and scaling the highest peaks of the Rockies. I loved following in his footsteps, riding fast horses, hiking high mountains, and camping under the moon and stars. Dad was my hero.

When I was little, he took me and my sisters to see a movie about Eskimos called "The Young Savages." I was troubled by a scene in which an elderly Eskimo was left to die on an ice floe. We talked about it on the way home, and although I can't remember my father's words, I knew that Daddy would probably have chosen the same path.

I forgot about that movie until decades later when my father became physically and mentally debilitated by a series of strokes, which left him virtually bedridden. It was the long-feared nightmare that we, while growing up, always pushed from our minds. Our ninety-year-old dad was but a shadow of his former self, and it crushed our hearts to think that Daddy was probably going to die soon.

The family house in Maryland was sold. Mother moved her and Dad to Florida where he resided in a cheery little nursing home. Mom walked from my uncle's house to the nursing home every morning to care for her husband's needs and then returned at night after he was put to bed. My sisters and I often visited, stretching our visits to help my mom with Daddy.

Then, in a span of less than two weeks, everything changed. My father began to quickly fail. He was rushed to the hospital. An IV was inserted. The tube was later removed when his body bloated and lungs filled. He was sent back to the nursing home. We agonized and conferred with doctors. After much prayer and painful discussion, we made a decision: no feeding tube. It was clear Daddy was dying, and knowing my father, he would not want his death prolonged. My sisters and mom tenderly cared for Daddy around the clock during his last days, camping on couch pillows by his bedside and giving him what little water he could take.

Within days, I received a telephone call from my sister, Jay. Daddy had passed away.

SUSTAINING LIFE OR PROLONGING DEATH?

Who would have dreamed the day would come when the family of a dying loved one would have to study a medical dictionary to discern exactly what "dying" was. We all wish dying was as easy to read as Job 1:21: "Naked I came from my mother's womb, and naked I will depart. The LORD gave and the LORD has taken away . . ."

Within the last decades, medical technology has given us high-tech helps, which not only sustain life but sometimes prolong death. Kidney machines, pacemakers, chemotherapy, respirators, spinal shunts, and even medication to manage either pain or depression—all these things can in one case sustain life, and in another, prolong death.

I have talked to terminally ill persons who feel trapped in a web of tubes and machines as they face one surgery after another. The jargon in right-to-die or right-to-life brochures is of little use to them. They could care less that an aid-in-dying initiative on some state ballot is politically delicate or socially objectionable. They want to be allowed to die.

On the other hand, I have talked to people who are disabled by spinal cord injury or multiple sclerosis. They are not dying, but they want the right to be killed because they despise with a passion their wheelchairs or hospital beds. People with debilitating conditions hopefully would never qualify for physician-assisted suicide even if it were legal. But they, too, feel trapped by technology.

And what about those with more severe handicapping conditions? Fifty thousand people a year survive brain injury—some of them left in comas or persistent vegetative states. Their families grieve as they watch their loved one lie flat and face up on the bottom rung of society's qualifty-of-life scale. And when you are on the bottom rung, society shrugs its shoulders and asks: "Why not pull the plug? He's better dead than disabled." Even from those who come out of comas, remain disabled, and are barely able to communicate, you will often hear them hoarsely whisper, "I don't want to live like this anymore." The hard, cold reality of severe suffering seems beyond debate.

It should be simple—God gives life, God takes life away, and there's a line between the two. But where? Is the severely brain-injured man, who can barely communicate, in the same boat as the man whose brain is half destroyed by cancer? Why would we sustain the life of one and quit dragging on the death of another?

Has modern technology presented God with problems to which even He has no answer? If God provides man with the talent to advance and invent on behalf of life, He must also provide the wisdom to make decisions regarding the issues these advances create. And the question begging wisdom is this: *What is the distinction between providing a person with all the life to which he's entitled as opposed to artificially prolonging his death?*

Most of us wish that someone else would do the moral choosing for us, minimize the gray areas, or simply make the differences evident. But wisdom is not found by polling the majority, going by our gut feelings, or listening to our conscience.

THE SOURCE FOR DECISION MAKING

The Bible is full of God's wisdom. And from it, we can derive wisdom—that is, the power of judging the soundest course of action based on knowledge and experience. In plain language, in order to gain wisdom, we need to

1. get well acquainted with Scripture,
2. understand how Scriptures apply to the situation, and;
3. put the two together in a process of personal decision making.

First, getting acquainted with Scripture begins with the definite "dos and don'ts." "Thou shalt not murder" and "Choose life" are pretty straightforward. However, when there are no scriptural commands, you are forced to look closer. The Bible is a big book and it takes a little research to decipher between the "don't dos" and "maybe dos." To understand what is morally right in a situation, Scripture insists that we use *it*, not the circumstances, to examine complex life and death problems. Every situation has to be viewed under the magnifying glass of God's Word.

When my family needed to decide about Dad's situation, it was helpful to be able to reach for a verse from the shelf of theological insight and use it in the hospital ward where our decisions had to be made. James 1:5 was our guide: "If . . . any of you does not know how to meet any particular problem he has only to ask God . . . and he may be quite sure that the necessary wisdom will be given him. But he must ask in sincere faith without any secret doubts" (PHILLIPS).

Right there, God supplies almost half the answer for our need. He promises He will give *necessary* wisdom to a *particular* problem—that is, wisdom tailored to the problem at hand. Every situation is different, every person is unique. So when it comes to the "pull the plug" question, don't waste your time looking for a tidy list of rules—one-two-three. My family couldn't superimpose on Dad the experience of other families in that nursing home. In the same way, you can't take our decision and overlay it like a template on your family's situation.

PRINCIPLES FOR DECISION MAKING

Some decisions are easy. "Thou shalt not murder" is an obvious "don't." Life is the most fundamental and irreplaceable condition of the human experience, and no thinking person with biblical scruples would dare inject a lethal drug into the veins of a person who possesses full vitality.

But what about a person in the final death throes? Is "Thou shalt not murder" violated if one refuses to pump him up with treatments and machines? The Christian Medical and Dental Society states that dying begins when a person rapidly and irreversibly deteriorates, a person for whom death is imminent, a person who is beyond reasonable hope of recovery . . . such people have a right to not have death postponed.[1]

Yes, there is a point when it is futile and even burdensome to go into a full-court press against death using every last bit of high-tech heroic treatment available. Dr. C. Everett Koop, former Surgeon General, advises, "If someone is dying and there is no doubt about that, and you believe as I do that there is a difference between giving a person all the life to which he is entitled as opposed to prolonging the act of dying, then you might come to a time when you say this person can take certain amounts of fluid by mouth and we are not going to continue this intravenous solution because he is on the way out."[2] This is what "death with dignity" is suppose to be all about.

But stop here. Are we free to thoughtlessly pull the plug, even if it is clear our loved one is rapidly deteriorating? It may look easy to unhook life support, but Scripture demands that we examine our judgments through the lens of God's Word. So look closely at each of these criteria from Scripture before you unplug a respirator or say "no" to a feeding tube.

Scripture underscores that life is precious. From the moment God formed man and breathed into his nostrils the breath of life, God sanctified life—it is precious because God made humankind in His image. The traces of this intention are found in creation (Gen. 2:4–7), in a commandment (Ex. 20:13), in an empty tomb (John 11:23–26), and in a vision (Rev. 21:1–8). The point? Scripture reveals a God who intends life and forbids trespass against it. So before you say "no" to life support for your loved one, make certain he is imminently dying.

Scripture underscores that suffering people should have every access to the means of God's grace. Whether through the Scriptures or fellowship and support with Christians, James 5:14–16 reminds us that the church plays an indispensable role in the treatment of a dying or debilitated person. In the case of a dying person who is a nonbeliever, treatment should leave the broadest possible opportunity for evangelism—if we believe that a dying person will soon either see the face of God or the gates of hell, then we'd want to provide the widest window of opportunity for the Spirit to work. That might mean no prescribed isolation, mind-numbing drugs, or nontreatment that might cloud the dying person's response to the Gospel.

Scripture underscores that love for God and love for others is paramount. Matthew 22:37–39 reminds us , "Love the Lord your God with all your heart. . . . Love your neighbor as yourself." The biblical ethic, then, is to do no harm to your neighbor, but pursue good on his behalf. For some terminally ill persons close to death, "the loving thing" may mean foregoing burdensome, painful treatment or expensive surgeries. For other terminally ill persons, "the loving thing" may mean opting for an affordable and comfortable treatment that significantly sustains life in a beneficial way. Love for God and for the person must be the underlying motive.

Which brings us to the next principle. *God demands that we examine our motives.* Scripture demands nothing less than a righteous heart (Matt. 5:8) and condemns lip service or hypocrisy (Isa. 29:13; Matt. 23). Some people may secretly want a loved one to die to relieve suffering of the family, for economic considerations, or perhaps even out of convenience to the caregivers or society. If family members insist that IV's and tubes be withheld or withdrawn because "Dad's best years are being wasted taking care of Mother," or, "they left that nest-egg for us, not for paying hospital bills," then they are not pursuing good on the behalf of the dying person. Faith and love must always guide one's actions if his/her conscience is not to be violated. These guidelines have a powerful bearing on whether or not we are free to pull the plug.

But don't be overwhelmed and throw your hands up in despair. Your process of making personal decisions is as close as your doctor, family, and clergy. Historically, life-and-death decisions have always been made this way—"safety is found in the abundance of counselors" (Prov. 11:14 KJV). Wisdom is gathered from a physician who knows the facts, a patient who has expressed his or her wishes, a family who is looking out for their loved one first and foremost, and from a pastor who can give compassionate and biblically sound guidance.

QUESTIONS FOR DECISION MAKING

My family's personal process of making a decision regarding my father's care involved several final questions. The first and most important question: Were we *certain* Dad had begun to actually die? Then, was he, in fact, unable to process food—even through a tube? Were our motives pure? Our conscience clear? Did we thoroughly seek the counsel of our doctor and clergy? Were we convinced of God's will in this situation? And most importantly, were we sure of Dad's salvation in Jesus Christ?

Yes. Yes, to all those questions. And basic decency was lived out poignantly as Kathy, Jay, and my mother moistened Dad's lips with ice chips, helped him sip juice when he was able and even clear broth when possible.

By the way, had my father not been a Christian, I seriously doubt we would have pumped up his dying body with life supports. Rather, we would have enlisted extra prayer support and provided, in a sensitive way, the broadest opportunity to help him find final rest in Christ.

THE BIBLE SPEAKS OUT ON DEATH . . . SORT OF

Wouldn't it be easy if the Bible spelled out everything in black and white? "Dos and don'ts" clearly defined? But what Scripture lacks in absolute definitions, it makes up for in absolute decrees. There is a kind of medical dictionary exactness to a verse like Job 14:5, "Man's days are determined; you have decreed the number of his months and have set limits he cannot exceed." Perhaps we ought not to grumble about rapidly advancing medical technology. We are living in such a time as this in order that our powers of judgment might be sharpened, our capacity for compassion might be stretched, and our dependence on God might be continued or renewed. As we sit at the bedside of a dying loved one, perhaps it would be good to pray, *Lord, death will one day be the last enemy to be destroyed. In the meantime, help me to sustain every ounce of life You give. And give me the wisdom to know the difference.*

ENDNOTES

1. "Euthanasia," *Ethical Statement*, Christian Medical and Dental Society, 3 May 1990.
2. C. Everett Koop, "The Surgeon General on Euthanasia," *Presbyterian Journal* (25 September 1985): 8.

An Overview

Many of us experience the loss of friends to suicide during our youth. In his very personal essay, Stan Kellner reflects upon his own loss of a teenage friend, the questions that still remain unanswered, and the lessons he takes with him.

Chapter Thirty-Three

PERSONAL REFLECTIONS ON THE DEATH OF A TEENAGE FRIEND

Stan R. Kellner

IT SEEMS LIKE JUST YESTERDAY. I had just come home from working at Brigham's, an ice-cream store well-known in the New England area where I worked part-time after high school several days a week. I walked in the door and sat down on the living room couch. Just as I was settling in, my parents approached me. Something wasn't right. Had I done something wrong? Maybe I got in too late from work? Quickly I realized that the uneasiness I felt was not related to anything I had done.

The words ring in my ears like it was yesterday, even though it has been well over three decades. "Terry is dead! He committed suicide by hanging himself in his bedroom closet!" Even now, as I write these words, I get a cold chill and an ache in my heart. I couldn't believe what I was hearing. My best friend, my only friend was dead!

A thousand thoughts and questions rushed through my mind. Why would he do this? I was angry! How could he leave his best friend like this? Had I done something to motivate this senseless act? How was I, a fourteen-year-old, to deal with this painful loss and tragedy?

You must realize the gravity of the situation. We had moved within a year after my bar mitzvah from the city in which I was born and raised. I grew up in a Conservative Jewish home north of Boston. We moved to a new city, and I was in junior high school. You remember the awkwardness of junior high, don't you? Your clothes didn't fit, your hair didn't comb the right way, and your complexion became a perpetual obsession.

I remember my first day in junior high. I was the new kid on the block. I walked up to this rather large structure, wondering who I was going to meet and if I was going to fit in. One of the first people I met was Terry. At first, I was hesitant. He seemed okay, but was almost too outgoing. In fact, if he wasn't careful, he would turn people off. He was rambunctious and, at times, a bit overbearing. However, he was one of the few people who even paid attention to me. We quickly became friends.

Terry was from a Jewish background like mine, but, at the time, neither of us were going to Temple regularly. We each had completed our bar mitzvah. We had become "sons of the commandments." We were supposed to feel like men after this ceremony, but we still had a lot of growing up to do. Eventually, we both became thoroughly disinterested in Temple attendance. Terry was liked pretty well by our classmates, but sometimes I think people were actually patronizing him rather than genuinely relating to him. Even I had a hard time really getting to know him. We hung around together a lot after school, and I regularly joined him and his family for dinner. As a fourteen year old, I wasn't able to identify the warning signals that spelled trouble for Terry. Like many teens, Terry's mom had divorced and then remarried. I could see that he had absolutely no relationship with his stepdad, and I was aware that Terry also had no relationship with his biological dad. Back then I did not comprehend the level of dysfunction in Terry's family. I remember that his older sister was a developing drug addict. He also had a stepbrother who was less than energetic. He was certainly not making a *mensch* of himself. (*Mensch* is a Yiddish word that describes someone who has made something of himself.)

Terry and I were like many other teens—passing through puberty, teasing girls, and trying to cope with our changing bodies. But, suicide! Who would have ever thought of it? During our time together as best buddies, *I do not remember any time that Terry ever let on to me that he was unhappy enough to end his own life*. At times, he seemed troubled and had the usual frustrations, but if he was facing deep struggles, I never noticed, and he never mentioned them. Then the unforgettable day came when I was told by my parents that Terry had taken his own life. I was devastated. I didn't know how to deal with the situation. I wrestled with guilt: "Could it have been my fault? Could I have done something, anything differently?" I could not figure out what Terry had been facing that would bring about this type of reaction. Regrettably, I do not remember mourning for him, at least not immediately. I did not know how to respond to the news that my best friend, my only friend, had committed suicide.

I wish I could say that my Jewish upbringing prepared me for this moment in my life. But, unfortunately, that was not the case. Although I grew up in a conservative Jewish home, we did not really talk about death. My grandfather died when I was ten, but I'm not clear how I grieved for him. But Terry's loss was different. This was my best friend who was only fourteen years old, not a seventy-eight-year-old man who had lived a full life. Terry took his own life, my grandfather did not.

In our synagogue worship, we regularly repeated the mourner's kaddish (a remembrance prayer for the dead). But I don't remember being taught how to deal with death itself. Biblical Judaism teaches about life after death. However, in what would be more accurately termed Rabbinical Judaism, we were not instructed in our upbringing about life after death. Even now, my family believes that when we die our body goes back to the ground and we are, in effect, "recycled." Therefore, when Terry died, *I had absolutely no sense of hope*, as I would now as a believer in Jesus as my Messiah. In fact, it was not until I became a follower of Jesus as Messiah, eight years after the suicide, that I could begin to deal with my grief about Terry. Until then, the best I could hope for was a future Messianic or golden age where all mankind would be at peace. But personally, this brought little comfort to me as I thought about Terry.

Why should such a young life be wasted? Why did Terry do what he did? I will never know the answer to these questions. But I know a God who is all-wise and all-knowing. He understands the beginning from the end. As an adult looking back on this experience, I come away with a few lessons:

1. *I want to understand better the warning signals of someone considering suicide.* In my ministry over the years, I've dealt with suicidal individuals and have become more aware of those signals: discussing suicide, even joking about it; bitterness and resentment or any unusual change in behavior; thoughts that suicide may be the best answer; or giving personal possessions away.

2. *I must trust in an all-knowing God.* Even though my Jewish upbringing did not prepare me for the event of my best friend's committing suicide, I realize now, as a believer in Jesus, that I have the complete picture and can more effectively deal with these issues. Trusting in Jesus does not bring dismay and destruction to our lives; it brings understanding, direction, and a hope that takes us through life's personal struggles to growth and contentment.

3. *Suicide is not the answer.* Terry was a good kid. He had tremendous potential. It is now over three decades later, and I still stop and ponder over the impact that was never made because of a life that was snuffed out at such a young age. God wants to use you in a very special way. You are unique, one of a kind, and the Lord has a very special way in which He wants to bring glory to Himself through your life. Tenaciously pursue, know, and learn to trust Him, and He will shine His light in and through you.

4. *You are somebody's friend!* Talk with your friends about your fears and concerns, and let them share themselves with you so that you might experience the specialness of God's love through human friendship. Don't let the opportunity slip away, as in Terry's case! I'll never know what type of friendship Terry and I might have had. He is a loss that can never be replaced. I miss him even today. Thank God that, in Jesus, survivors can experience an abundant life.

An Overview

From time to time a person comes into our life who has a profound influence on the way we live. The attention given to our issues, the patience extended toward our shortcomings, and the meaning his or her example has provided us creates a relationship so full of respect that their future actions carry tremendous impact, especially those actions that are inconsistent with what we have previously experienced. Like it or not, some people become heroes to others, and this potential carries great responsibility. John Hannah describes the loss of one such person and the impact his uncharacteristic choice of suicide has had on the remainder of his life; he also shares three resolutions to which he has committed his life that govern the way he interacts with those to whom he becomes a mentor.

Chapter Thirty-Four

CONFIDENCE BETRAYED

Personal Reflections on the
Suicide of a Friend and Mentor

John D. Hannah

AN UNEXPECTED EVENT

IN AN AUDITORIUM OF AN URBAN university campus, a considerable entourage of colleagues, friends, and former students met on a particular early afternoon some few years ago. We had assembled to say our good-byes to a professor, who, for reasons beyond understanding, took his own life; it was a suicide. The fatal blow was not administered by a tranquilizing chemical but with a torn skull ripped apart by a handgun. An accomplished professional in his fifties, facing the prospect of the ravages of an irreversible disease, had found the unrelenting pain unbearable and ended his life in a solitary apartment with no one to comfort or dissuade him. There were the usual testimonies that you might expect in an academic community, the rehearsal of his professional career, which seemed impressive. He was a fine intellectual, a caring teacher, a good colleague, tenured, a writer. The solemn ceremony ended in a rather ironic manner, a strange touch to a confusing time for me. Since the deceased wrote his doctoral dissertation on Charles Ives, a turn-of-the-century Connecticut insurance agent who was reduced by the necessity of earning a living for his family to being an amateur song writer (the arts could not fund professionalism at the time), what must have been conceived as an appropriate selection from his works was chosen. It was "The Unanswered Question." With the audience hushed and the lights dim, we listened to Ives. The song was noisy; there was some strange, nontraditional arrangement of notes; and it concluded with no resolution leaving the piece seemingly unfinished (it anticipated the advent of twelve-tonal music, jazz, in the 1920s). It ended with a sense of the uncompleted, the unfulfilled. In a way, the piece seems apropos after all. The senselessness of such a wonderful man taking his life left me with a feeling of emptiness.

AN UNEXPECTED AFFECTION

To gain some idea of the personal sense of loss and hurt I experienced, let me tell you the background to the event I just related. Having completed a doctoral program and secured a teaching post where I felt quite happy and fulfilled, I decided to return to the other side of the lectern. What followed was the attainment of another graduate degree, which I hoped would qualify me to enter a doctoral program in the field of philosophy. Though my family was young and I continued to teach full-time, I entered a nearby university. In the years that followed I met and had several classes with one particular professor in the humanities program. Though he had a reputation for being difficult and exacting as a teacher, and even more so as a director of dissertation projects, I enjoyed him. I was delighted that the topic for my dissertation was one that he was willing to direct. The "horror stories" of his attachment to details all proved true in my experience of attempting to write for him. Though possessing a doctorate already (the degree, however, was in another field), I really struggled. Revision followed other revisions, and the project was elongated over three years before it was completed. In all the fears and anguish that only those who attempt to write a dissertation know, I realized that the man was a crafter of words, and he expected a work that was scientifically correct but artistically balanced and accurate. This was a rather new concept to me at the time, which added to my frustration.

Through the struggle with its wide-range of emotions (elation, depression, joy, despair, accomplishment, self-doubt), something that I had not expected in doctoral studies began to happen. My professor became a friend; he became so much a part of the project that the critic turned into the helper. He took my poor ability at literary expression and worked on my dissertation page after page, making it into a work that both of us could be proud to have written; he taught me how to write! Somehow the guy who seemed so demanding and distant had become my biggest advocate. I cannot express in words the depth of my personal appreciation for all the work that he did. He truly became a mentor, a model of a compassionate and demanding teacher who took his profession as a serious calling. I worked hard after a while, not merely to write a paper but to please a man that had become my ideal as a teacher. I wanted to be like him, deeply caring for students, carefully and constructively reading their papers, striving to make them better people through my discipline. He became a hero in a world where there seems to be few authentic ones.

Well, the long-anticipated day arrived; the paper was finished at the level of his demands (I lost count of the number of revisions the paper had undergone!). The examining committee was favorably impressed, and I was awarded my second doctorate. With anticipation I awaited my graduation; this professor-friend, my doctor-father was to place the hood over my head signifying the program's completion, my earned acceptance into the guild of scholar-teachers. With my name called, I stood on the platform before hundreds of people to receive a parchment from the director of graduate studies and then hand my professor my academic hood, which he would wrap over my shoulders. As I handed him the green, yellow, and blue garment, I looked into his eyes to say thank you. It was truly a great moment. He expressed words that I did not deserve to hear. I quickly joined my appreciative wife and children; he returned to his office. I never saw him again. A chapter closed in my life; he was gone and I did not say good-bye! I expected to return to the university in some near-distant time to say hello and thank him for all that he had done for me and meant to me. Somehow in the rush of "important things to do" I did not get around to it. When the news of his death came, it was too late.

AN UNEXPECTED EFFECT

As I now reflect on this sad moment in my life, the suicide of my doctor-father, various thoughts continue to cross my mind. I find myself both angry and hurt. I continue to be upset with him for not realizing that he had a vitally important role in another human being's life; with the privilege of being a mentor comes a responsibility. He must not have realized that we need heroes. I cannot call him anymore to ask the exhaustive list of technical questions about thesis form that emerged because I was too unfamiliar or lazy to consult the *Chicago Manual of Style*, 14th edition for myself. Kindly and gently he had answered my questions citing page and paragraph from memory when I could find it for myself. He could have easily rebuked me, but he always gently replied to my inquiries. Nor can I call him in my frustration to ask if there was any real hope that I would ever graduate, only to hear him express amazement that I would have any doubts; he was genuinely hurt that I would have any misgivings. What can I say about a person who knew my carefully hidden weaknesses and strove to remedy them? I wanted to express my thankfulness for his contribution to me personally and professionally; I did not; and, now, I cannot.

I feel anger and emptiness in my inner being because he must not have known how significant his life really was to me. Suicide is the ultimate assertion of the futility and worthlessness of one's life, yet his life was neither of those. In taking his own life, he seemed to assert that my affection and appreciation of and for him was ill-advised. I do not believe that, but I can't visit with him and say, "You're wrong, your life had meaning, you touched me deeply." He must not have understood his obligation; heroes have duties!

Ultimately, however, I believe that anger and hurt are flipsides of the same "coin." Anger is hurt expressed; the sense of hurt and loss is expressed in the form of anger; they are occasioned by a sense of robbery! Both are manifestations of love frustrated. I feel a sense of rejection because he worked so hard to help me and I, in return, labored arduously for him. Though I know that there were many other factors that must have pushed him to the brink of despair, I find it hard to imagine what those factors must have been. There is simply a special relationship between a student and a teacher when a teacher lifts up his pupil the way he did me. Suicide does immeasurable damage to the living and the dead. The living find themselves in a vacuum of silence; I cannot speak and he cannot reply. The dead have surrendered to foolishness and futility. Time is medicinal; it heals wounds. With it a thin scab covers old wounds and we find it easier to manage. However, as we reflect on the loss, the scab is lifted off, and the sad memories cause us to bleed again.

I am impressed that the Lord has given us a wonderful coping mechanism to handle such things; it is the amazing ability to forget negative things while retaining the memory of good things more readily, permanently, and consistently.

There is, yet, another side to this sad and disappointing event in my earthly journey. You see, I am a Christian; I find it hard to view life with a despairing attitude. Christ has brought profound contentment to me; the reality of forgiveness has caused me to see the world about me with vigor and hope; and I possess a peace in trouble, hope in life, and expectancy of freedom from the body as I experience it now in the presence of the One who loved me and gave Himself for me. I earnestly sought to tell my mentor of Christ. However, though he had an accurate knowledge of Christianity, having been raised in a conservative, evangelical setting, he felt no affinity, need, or desire for the Lord Jesus Christ. His loss, therefore, grieves me even more deeply because I will never see him again. I lost more than a mentor; he lost his only hope.

The Bible is full of hope; suicide seems, therefore, bizarre and pathetic. It is the ultimate statement of despair. My friend made no claim to an interest in Christ, yet he was made in God's holy image, however effaced it may have become. Life is so precious and important that no one has a right to threaten it or take it away. That is only a divine prerogative because He alone gave life and is the Sovereign over it.

A NECESSARY RESOLVE

"The Unanswered Question" ended the ceremony, and the participants and attendees filed out of the auditorium with the respect and solemnity that one would expect. Life has to go on; rehearsing the disappointment has its justifiable limits. So now it is time to go on with life and not allow one senseless, unnecessary act be the cause of others. I will always remember my doctor-father and believe that what he did was wrong. It hurt him; it deprived our culture of his valuable contribution; it cast into momentary question all the good and right things that he had taught. From this sad tale, I have made three resolutions for my own life: (1) I will always appreciate the impact (that he demonstrated to me) that a caring teacher can have upon students. He singularly touched my life, and I am grateful. (2) I am resolved to strive to be the kind of teacher for my students that he modeled as my teacher. I am determined to not only give lectures, keep appointments, and attend committee assignments, but I will care for the emotional and physical well-being of my students, carefully reading their work. I will strive to improve them both personally and professionally. I want to be a hero to students, someone whom they can look up to and draw strength from as they reflect upon their education. (3) I will live for my students, no matter how difficult it may become, until death is imposed upon me so that I can continue to be a role model, to not only enter the race of life and run in it, but to finish well also. I have a moral obligation to my students that my mentor somehow lost sight of along the way. May God give me the grace to serve Him until He calls me to a better place.

On June 26, 1997, the United States Supreme Court handed down its decisions regarding two cases, *Washington v. Glucksberg, No. 96-110*, and *Vacco v. Quill, No. 95-1858*, both of which address the constitutionality of physician-assisted suicide.[1] The unanimous decision in both cases found that bans on assisting suicide enacted by the states of Washington and New York do not violate the 14th Amendment.

In the case of *Washington v. Glucksberg* the Supreme Court reversed a Ninth Circuit ruling that declared Washington's ban on assisted suicide unconstitutional. The Supreme Court framed the issue in terms of whether or not the "due process" clause of the 14th Amendment protects a "right to commit suicide which itself includes a right to assistance in doing so." In deciding due process issues, according to Chief Justice Rehnquist, the Court begins by observing that the "due process clause specially protects those fundamental rights and liberties which are, objectively, 'deeply rooted in this nation's history and tradition,' and 'implicit in the concept of ordered liberty,' such that 'neither liberty nor justice would exist if they were sacrifice.'" Accordingly, the Court reviewed seven hundred years of Anglo-American common law to determine if such a "right to commit suicide" had ever received any support. The Court found that Anglo-American common law tradition has generally punished or otherwise disapproved of both suicide and assisting suicide.

The next step the Court takes in deciding due process issues is to examine whether or not the right asserted to exist is protected by substantive due process. In examination of this issue, the Court requires the respondents to make a careful description of the asserted fundamental liberty interest. The Court found that the respondents' descriptions of the asserted right, i.e., a right to "determin[e] the time and manner of one's death," the "right to die," a "liberty to choose how to die," a right to "control of one's final days," "the right to choose a humane, dignified death," and "the liberty to shape death," were so vague that the Court would have been irresponsible to recognize such a right.

In the second case, that of *Vacco v. Quill*, the Supreme Court reversed a Second Circuit ruling which held that New York's differential treatment of competent, terminally ill patients (i.e., allowing competent terminally ill patients to refuse life-sustaining treatment but not receive life-ending medications) violates the equal protection clause of the 14th Amendment. The Supreme Court held that it did not and disagreed with the Second Circuit that refusing life-saving treatment is fundamentally similar to assisted suicide. In regard to this issue, the Court claimed that two actions that end in the same result may be distinguished by the intent and purpose of the actor. According to Chief Justice Rehnquist, the distinction between letting a patient die and making that patient die is important, logical, rational, and well established. "The distinction comports with fundamental legal principles of causation and intent. . . . [W]hen a patient refuses life sustaining medical treatment, he dies from an underlying fatal disease or pathology; but if a patient ingests lethal medication prescribed by a physician, he is killed by that medication."

Both cases essentially closed in the same way. The Court ruled that the constitutional requirement that a given state's assisted-suicide ban be rationally related to legitimate government interests was unquestionably met in both cases. These interests include prohibiting intentional killing and preserving human life; preventing a serious public health problem of suicide, especially among the young, the elderly, and those suffering from untreated pain or from depression or other mental disorders; protecting the medical profession's integrity and ethics and maintaining physicians' role as their patients' healers; protecting the poor, the elderly, disabled persons, the terminally ill, and persons in other vulnerable groups from indifference, prejudice, and psychological and financial pressure to end their lives, thereby avoiding a possible slide towards voluntary and perhaps even involuntary euthanasia.

While the opinions were unanimous, there were in both cases concurring opinions that reflected varying views about assisted suicide in certain circumstances that suggested that the decisions were a tentative first step rather than a definitive final ruling on the issue. In his opinion in *Washington v. Glucksberg*, Chief Justice Rehnquist concluded by stating that "throughout the nation, Americans are engaged in an earnest and profound debate about the morality, legality, and practicality of physician-assisted suicide. Our holding permits this debate to continue, as it should in a democratic society." As this debate continues, Christians must remain clear about the issues and help inform others by providing a reasoned reply from a biblical perspective. A Christian response is essential.

ENDNOTES

1. Adapted from a Center for Bioethics and Human Dignity Internet news service release, "U.S. Supreme Court and Assisted Suicide," July 2, 1997.